How To Respond In Class With F

Web Browser:

Access your instructor's unique Poll Everywhere web page from any device connected to the internet. Example: PollEv.com/username

Once on the page, click the option you prefer.

This page will "follow" your instructor and display the current question. If you see a piece of pie, wait for the instructor to activate a poll.

Note:

If your instructor needs to know who you are for grading or attendance, make sure to log in first.

Web Browser (alternate):

Access PollEv.com from any device connected to the internet. Once on the page, enter the CODE for your choice and click submit. Example: 458456

Note:

If your instructor needs to know who you are for grading or attendance, make sure to log in first.

Text Message:

Use your mobile phone's text message (SMS) feature. No internet or smartphone required! Standard text messaging rates apply.

Text the CODE for your choice to 37607. Example: 458456

Note:

If your instructor needs to know who you are for grading or attendance, make sure you've certified your mobile number.

How To Respond In Class With Poll Everywhere

Twitter:

Use Twitter to respond. Works with Wi-Fi or mobile devices with access to Twitter via their data plan. Requires instructor activation of Twitter option first.

Navigate to www.twitter.com or one of Twitter's apps in your mobile device. Tweet the CODE for your choice to the Twitter handle indicated (@poll pictured).

Note:

Remember to certify your Twitter account before responding if required by your instructor.

Need A Hand?

Check out our FAQ at www.polleverywhere.com/faq
Or send an email to questions@polleverywhere.com

Let Us Know What you Think!

   www.facebook.com/polleverywhere

   www.twitter.com/polleverywhere

HUMAN COMMUNICATION

Principles and Contexts

Thirteenth Edition

STEWART L. TUBBS

Eastern Michigan University

COMM1000 | University of Connecticut Storrs

 Learning Solutions

Boston Burr Ridge, IL Dubuque, IA New York San Francisco St. Louis
Bangkok Bogotá Caracas Lisbon London Madrid
Mexico City Milan New Delhi Seoul Singapore Sydney Taipei Toronto

Human Communication: Principles and Contexts

1 2 3 4 5 6 7 8 9 0   QMF QMF   14 13 12

ISBN-13: 978-0-07-783294-0
ISBN-10: 0-07-783294-9

Learning Solutions Consultant: Jessica Runnals
Learning Solutions Representative: Nicole Schmitt
Project Manager: Melissa Reinhardt
Printer/Binder: Quad Graphics Menomonee Falls

CONTENTS

PREFACE

This thirteenth edition of *Human Communication* continues a long and engaging journey in which I have traced many new developments in this fascinating and extremely relevant field. This book is designed to give students a broad-based and up-to-date exploration of the entire discipline. As always, I am committed to presenting students with a comprehensive theoretical base and an understanding of how modern communication has evolved and continues to grow, resulting in changes that affect numerous aspects of their everyday lives.

Once again I have focused on the traditional concerns of this discipline while expanding upon specific areas of interest for today's curriculum. Along with my traditional approach of fusing current and classical communication theories, concepts, and skills, I have also significantly expanded the coverage of media and technology and its effects on communication; conflict as it relates to business communication; trust and interpersonal communication, specifically as they relate to marriage; and the complexities of intercultural communication and ethics.

As a result of this focus, I have tried to create a text that has immediacy and relevance for students and instructors, one that reflects my long-term goal of understandability while introducing rich concepts and theories without oversimplification and using language that is clear, vivid, and precise.

NEW TO THIS EDITION

In this edition, Practical Tips boxes have been included to increase the book's practical applications, and new information has been added to each chapter:

- Chapter 2 includes a new discussion of James Pennebaker's research about the different communication styles of men and women in human relationships.

- In Chapter 4 a new Practical Tips box examines the visual and vocal cues to watch for when a person is lying.
- In Chapter 5 a new Listening Test gives readers the chance to evaluate their own communication styles to determine whether they are technical or feeling listeners.
- In Chapter 6 a new discussion on negotiation explores how the incidental communication that occurs before the formal phases of negotiation can impact the outcome of a deal.
- Chapter 7 examines how Americans perceive ethics and honesty standards of 20 professions.
- Chapter 8 has an entirely new section on trust and a significantly shortened section on family communication.
- Chapter 9 discusses six steps for improving interpersonal skills, especially within a marriage.
- Chapter 11 explores what employers find to be most valuable in job candidates and what types of skills you should convey in an interview in order to land the job.
- Chapter 12 examines the impact of size on the effectiveness of a group in business and recent research on the "rule of seven."
- Chapter 13 includes two new Practical Tips boxes on public speaking: one details ten steps in preparing a speech, and another provides a checklist of all the important items to consider when preparing and presenting an "A" speech.
- A new Issues in Communication box in Chapter 15 examines how the Internet and social media are affecting our brains, our psyches, and our relationships.
- Chapter 15 includes new information on flash mobs and information about security risks on smart phones and the ways that organizations use technology to track our purchases.

RESOURCES

Human Communication continues to incorporate a variety of teaching and study aids throughout the text that I hope will benefit both students and instructors. Each chapter has a list of *Key Terms,* a *Summary,* a set of *Review Questions, Exercises,* and an annotated list of *Suggested Readings* of both popular and scholarly works.

The chapter pedagogies are supported by the text's free Online Learning Center (OLC) Web site, *www.mhhe.com/tubbshc13e,* which provides further study aids with updated *PowerPoint* presentations, *Learning Objectives, Glossary,* and Web links. The updated *Instructor's Manual* and revised *Test Bank* are also available on the Web site.

ACKNOWLEDGMENTS

First, I would like to express my deep gratitude to Darrell H. Cooper who provided the funding for the Darrell H. Cooper Endowed Chair in Leadership. This support has allowed me to focus on all of my scholarly writing over the recent years. For their valuable reviews and critique of the twelfth edition, I wish to thank the following reviewers: Martha Antolik, Wright State University; James A. Danowoski, University of Illinois at Chicago; Kyle Tusing, University of Arizona; Alice E. Veksler, University of Connecticut; Patty Wharton-Michael, University of Pittsburgh at Johnstown; Karen Osgood, Santa Barbara City College; Travice Baldwin Obas, Georgia Highlands College; Danna Prather, Suffolk County Community College; Jeff Farrar, University of Connecticut; Andrea Pearman, Tidewater Community College; Thomas J. Knutson, California State University, Sacramento.

I wish to express my thanks to my editors at McGraw-Hill: Nicole Bridge; Susan Gouijnstook, Katie Stevens, sponsoring editor, for her commitment and support; Lisa Pinto, managing editor, for overseeing the project; and Joyce Watters, Project Manager, for guiding this book through the various stages of production. Special thanks to Phillip Butcher for his editorial guidance and contribution to the online aspects of this revision, and Kate Petrella.

Finally, I would also like to thank Sylvia Moss for her brilliant work as co-author of the first eleven editions.

Stewart Tubbs

ABOUT THE AUTHOR

Stewart L. Tubbs is the Darrell H. Cooper Professor of Leadership in the College of Business at Eastern Michigan University and former Dean of the College of Business. He received his doctorate in Communication and Organizational Behavior from the University of Kansas. His master's degree in Communication and his bachelor's degree in Science are from Bowling Green State University. He has been named an Outstanding Teacher eleven times, has consulted extensively for *Fortune 500* companies, and is former Chairman of the Organizational Communication division of the Academy of Management. He is also an inductee in the Lakewood, Ohio Distinguished Alumni Hall of Fame.

Dr. Tubbs is the author of *A Systems Approach to Small Group Interaction* and *Keys to Leadership: 101 Tips for Success,* and coauthor with Sylvia Moss of *Interpersonal Communication;* with John Baird of *The Open Person;* and with Robert Carter of *Shared Experiences in Human Communication.* He is listed in *American Men and Women of Science, Contemporary Authors, Directory of American Scholars,* the *International Who's Who in Education,* and *Outstanding Young Men of America.*

PART ONE

Principles

The Process of Human Communication

Chapter Objectives

After reading this chapter, you should be able to:

1. Define the term "communication."
2. Explain the term "input" as it is used in the communication model.
3. List four types of messages and give an example of each.
4. Distinguish between technical and semantic interference and give an example of each.
5. Describe the impact of feedback on behavior.
6. Identify seven different contexts of communication and explain how each is distinctive.
7. Define effective communication in terms of five possible outcomes of human communication.

On August 23, 2011, at 1:51 p.m. a 5.8 magnitude earthquake occurred in Virginia that caused cracks in the Washington Monument. It took 40 seconds for the first shock waves to reach New York. However, tweets started reaching New York before the shock waves were actually felt! Such is the state of human communication in the twenty-first century (Hotz, 2011, p. C1).

Fast forward to today. Stop for a moment and think about what you would like to happen in your life. In other words, what would constitute your happiness and well-being? The Gallup organization has been asking that question since 1930 in over 150 countries. They have found that well-being has five components: (1) career, (2) social, (3) financial, (4) physical, and (5) community (Rath and Harter, 2010). As you might guess, these five are all interrelated. As it turns out, social well-being is at the heart of your career, financial, community, and even your physical well-being. In this book, we will be looking at ways that can help you strengthen your social well-being by improving your communication competencies. In this second decade of the twenty-first century, the ancient rhetorical traditions of the communication discipline are being applied in some of the most new and challenging ways. The wisdom and principles dating back to the days of Aristotle in Greece, Cicero in Rome, and up to modern times are being fused with applications such as Skype, YouTube, Facebook, podcasts, text messaging, smart phones, and webinars. Human communication has never been more exciting!

Human communication is the most important skill that you can learn! A study of 975 business managers published in the *Harvard Business Review* showed that many people are so overloaded today that they have reached a "conversational dead zone," which wreaks havoc on communication at home (Schellenberger, 2007). However, some couples have avoided this by talking on the phone during the day; others schedule time after the children are in bed to "debrief." This example illustrates both the importance of communication and some promising methods for overcoming communication challenges.

In another case, premier schools such as Harvard, Michigan, MIT, Dartmouth, University of Pennsylvania, and Stanford have beefed up their emphasis on communication skills—including interpersonal communication, listening, interviewing, leading meetings, managing conflict, public speaking, and organizational communication—to better equip their graduates for the real world of work (Dvorak, 2007; Korn, 2011, p. B9). Warren Bennis, professor at the University of Southern California and former president of the University of Cincinnati, states that, "It isn't just nice—these interpersonal skills. It's about stuff that's necessary to lead a complex organization" (Middleton and Light, 2011, p. B8; Dvorak, 2007, p. B3).

At home and at work, effective communication skills can make you or break you. This book is dedicated to helping you improve your communication skills in all the various contexts of your life.

Following is perhaps the most telling example that we can offer about how to be a successful communicator. A woman was given the opportunity to meet two of the most famous men in England, William Gladstone and Benjamin Disraeli. Afterward she was asked her impressions. She said that after meeting Gladstone she was convinced that she had been talking to the most important person in England.

However, after meeting Disraeli, she said that she was convinced that she was the most important person in England.

Psychiatrist Mark Goulston (2010) puts it this way, "The way to truly win friends and influence people is to be more interested in listening to them than you are in impressing them" (Goulston, 2010, p. 57). I have also found that once you start taking an interest in the other person, they almost always have something in common with you that makes the conversation interesting for you too. The communicated message is therefore not just about the speaker's intention, but about how the message is received. Throughout this book, we will be offering many examples and concepts as well as practical guidelines designed to help you improve your communication.

For many years it has been thought that the speech function was unique to modern Homo sapiens. However, recent evidence indicates that the first creatures to use spoken communication were Neanderthals—more ancient Homo sapiens dating back 60,000 years. Garrett (1989) reports: "Now an international research team has found what it believes is the Neanderthal version of a bone that is a key to modern human speech. . . . Baruch Arensburg of Tel Aviv University and his team unearthed the hyoid bone while digging in Israel's Kebara cave. . . . The hyoid is a U-shaped bone that supports the tongue and its muscles" (p. 560).

Begley and Gleizes (1989) report this additional evidence:

> Early Orators: Although Neanderthal's brain was bigger than ours, ever since his discovery "he was considered dull-witted and inarticulate," says neuroanatomist Terrence Deacon of Harvard University. Now that prejudice is yielding. Fossil brain casts show a well-developed language area, says Dean Falk of the State University of New York at Albany. His speech was only slightly inferior: using skull fossils to infer the position of the voice box in early humans, . . . [researchers concluded that] Neanderthals had a more restricted vocal range than we do. They had nasal voices, but could probably pronounce every consonant and vowel sound except "oo" and "ee," adds Deacon. "They were articulate, intelligent humans we would be able to understand and interact with," he says. (p. 71)

In 2003, 50 million people in the United States and Canada all lost power. The blackout was initially caused by sagging electric lines in a grove of trees, but the cascading impact of the blackout was largely blamed on a breakdown in communications between Ohio energy supplier FirstEnergy and neighboring systems. Computer systems and networks are vulnerable, but communication between individuals working with these systems was critical and could have prevented the blackout from becoming so widespread ("Lessons from a Blackout," 2004, p. A18). As a result, cell phone networks became overloaded by people trying to communicate with one another across the nation. Without power, there were no e-mails, no instant messages, no televisions, and no fax machines. People sat on their porches, met their neighbors for the first time, had picnics, and had a moment's rest from electronic communications, estimated to total over 2,000 messages a day (Carr, 2011).

In addition to all of these personal messages, mass-delivered consumer messages have become overpowering. Companies now advertise during movie previews and video games. Computer pop-up advertisements have increased, as have spam messages. It is becoming more and more difficult to filter out the noise to concentrate on the messages that we want to receive. Nicknamed *information pollution,* information overload can actually steal away our time while increasing stress and decreasing the time we spend with our families and friends. Carr (2011) has shown research that all this information pollution has increased depression and decreased our ability to think and read for more than a few seconds at a time. Other symptoms of information overload that emerged included exhaustion, trouble sleeping, and memory problems (Carr, 2011).

Keep in mind that all of the messages that make up information pollution do not even include all the interpersonal communication events we experience. It is no wonder that we need to learn more about human communication!

For over 60,000 years men and women have been communicating. Yet we still feel the need, perhaps more than ever, to find ways to improve these skills.

Even though you will be learning new ideas and even techniques about how to communicate more effectively, keep in mind that you must be genuine and authentic in your communication behaviors. Do not ever try to be someone you are not. Huszczo (2009) makes the case that you can best make a difference by being true to who you really are.

THE IMPORTANCE OF HUMAN COMMUNICATION

According to numerous research studies, for your entire life you have spent about 75 percent of each day engaged in communication. Therefore, you may be wondering why you need to study communication at all. There is a good reason: Quantity is no guarantee of quality. Given the number of divorces, unhappy workers, and ruptured parent-to-offspring relationships, quantity and frequency of communication are clearly no measure of how effectively people communicate with each other.

In another example of the importance of communication, Microsoft researchers are investigating ways that we can save messages for delivery to our descendants in later decades, centuries, or even longer. Labeled "immortal computing," this project would allow us to offer insights to our grandchildren and future generations, thus capturing the lessons we have spent our lifetimes learning. It will even be able to capture visual images, much like electronic photo albums (Bishop, 2007).

Communication is also closely associated with one's *definition of self.* Rosenberg (1979) relates the story of the "wild boy of Aveyron," who was raised by wolves. He developed no identity as a human being until he began to interact with humans. Individuals gain a sense of self-identity by being paid attention to and getting feedback from others. Also, a sense of identity and worth develops from comparing ourselves with others.

What do you think companies like Costco, Best Buy, Toyota, and JetBlue have in common? According to a scientific study of several hundred major companies, these companies have CEOs (chief executive officers) who exhibit extraordinarily effective communication skills. In fact, these companies with highly effective communicators at the top show an average financial return of 758 percent over ten years versus an average for Standard & Poor's top 500 companies of 128 percent. Even in recent bad years, the S&P companies averaged −13 percent while the exceptional companies in this study showed a financial return of 205 percent.

What do these CEOs do? They are described as inspiring respect, loyalty, and even affection rather than fear from employees. They are farsighted, tolerant, humane, and practical. The authors of this study write that corporate boards of directors are increasingly looking for leaders who can demonstrate superb communication skills in dealing with employees or other stakeholders (like customers, suppliers, and stockholders) while delivering consistent results. Experts agree that leadership is more important than strategy. The same strategy can be executed by two different leaders with dramatically different results (Sisodia, Sheth, and Wolfe, 2007).

On-the-job communication is constantly cited as one of the most important skills in "getting ahead." Whetten and Cameron (2010) identified 402 individuals rated as highly effective managers in their own organizations in such fields as business, health care, education, and government. They interviewed the individuals to determine what attributes were associated with their effectiveness. The table below shows the top ten list of most frequently cited skills of effective managers.

These research findings have been confirmed by a ten-year study conducted by researchers at Carnegie Mellon University, which identified the most important skills that distinguished average job performers from outstanding job performers (Kelley, 1998). They found that interpersonal communication, relationship building, leadership, teamwork, networking, and persuasion were some of the most important skills for career success.

In this book, we shall explore each of these aspects of human communication—all the way from the first impressions we form of one another to how human relationships are maintained and sometimes terminated.

Most Frequently Cited Skills of Effective Managers

1. Oral communication (including listening)
2. Managing time and stress
3. Managing individual decisions
4. Recognizing, defining, and solving problems
5. Motivating and influencing others
6. Delegating
7. Setting goals and articulating a vision
8. Self-awareness
9. Team building
10. Managing conflict

What are some of the complications that have arisen as a result of the increased communication through such media as telephones, cell phones, fax messages, and e-mail? How do you resolve some of the difficulties? Audrey Glassman (1998; see also, Turkle, *Alone Together,* New York: Basic Books, 2011) raised some of the following issues:

Telephones

1. How do you feel when you are on a call and someone takes another call on "call waiting"?

2. How do you feel when someone puts you on a speaker phone and your side of the conversation is more or less public?

3. What do you do if you are on a conference call and you cannot clearly hear one or more parties on the other end because of a bad connection or other interference?

Cellular Phones

4. Have you ever had any unusual experiences in which a person is talking on a cell phone while driving?

5. Can you think of any situations in which it is appropriate to receive cell phone calls when you are in a movie theater?

6. What are some examples of locations that you feel may be inappropriate for cell phone usage?

Fax Messages

7. When is it appropriate to send your résumé by fax if you are applying for a job?

8. Should you send confidential messages by fax? Are there any exceptions?

E-mail Messages

9. How many pages long should your messages usually be?

10. Have you ever had your message forwarded to someone you didn't expect? What should you do to anticipate this?

11. Have you ever sent a message when you were angry? Have you learned anything from this?

12. Have you ever exchanged messages with someone who has copied in another party to exercise authority or make a point? How did this make you feel?

13. What emotions do e-mails in all uppercase letters send to the recipient? What about a message scribed in all lowercase letters?

WHAT IS HUMAN COMMUNICATION?

What do you think of when the word "communication" is used? Students answering this question may mention anything from the use of electric circuits to prayer. Communication is a subject so frequently discussed that the term itself has become too meaningful—that is, it has too many different meanings for people. Agreeing on a working definition is the first step toward improving our understanding of this complex phenomenon.

Communication has been broadly defined as "the sharing of experience," and to some extent all living organisms can be said to share experience. What makes human communication unique is our superior ability to create and to use symbols; this ability enables humans to share experiences indirectly and vicariously. A symbol can be defined as something used for or regarded as representing something else. Briefly, then, human communication is the process of creating a meaning between two or more people. I will expand this partial definition in discussing communication outcomes later in this chapter under "What Is Effective Communication?"

A MODEL OF HUMAN COMMUNICATION

Since human communication is an intangible, ever-changing process, many people find it helpful to use a tangible model to describe that process. Actually, a motion picture would be a better form for modeling communication. As you read this book, think of the model that follows as one frame of a motion picture—a momentary pause in an ongoing process. The model is not an end in itself; it is only a means to help explain the ways in which the various component parts interact.

Figure 1.1 is a model of the most basic human communication event; it involves only two people. Initially, we shall call them Communicator 1 (the sender/receiver) and Communicator 2 (the receiver/sender). In actuality, both are sources of communication, and each originates and receives messages simultaneously. In addition, both

Figure 1.1 *The Tubbs Communication Model*

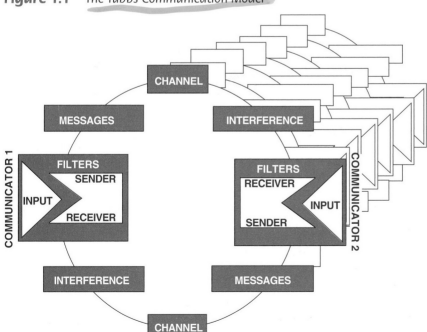

parties are simultaneously being influenced by each other in the transaction. Communicator 1 may originate the first message, and Communicator 2 may be the first person to perceive the transmitted stimuli, but most of our daily communication activities are spontaneous and relatively unstructured, so that these are overlapping roles.

Thus, as represented in the present model, a great many transactions can be initiated from either the right or the left side. For example, when you got up this morning, did you speak to someone first, or were you spoken to first? You probably don't even remember because who spoke first was a matter of chance. In an important sense, it is arbitrary to call yourself either a sender or a receiver: You are both. Even while you are speaking, you are simultaneously observing the other person's behavior and reacting to it. This is also true of the other person as he or she interacts with you.

The transactional view also emphasizes that you change as a result of the communication event. Have you ever been drawn into an argument so intense that the more you told the other person how angry you were, the angrier you became? The reverse is also possible. If a man tells a woman how much he cares for her and goes out of his way to do something thoughtful for her, what is the result? Typically, he increases his feeling of closeness to her, even though she may not respond well to his gesture. The research on self-persuasion shows that when you give a persuasive presentation to others, you are often the person who is most persuaded by it. Alcoholics Anonymous has worked with this principle for many years. The people who get up at meetings and try to persuade others to stay sober are also doing a lot to keep themselves persuaded. The transactional viewpoint, then, emphasizes the simultaneous and mutually influential nature of the communication event. The participants become interdependent, and their communication can be analyzed only in terms of the unique context of the event.

As you read more about our model, keep in mind the transactional viewpoint with its emphasis on the extent to which the two or more people involved create a relationship as part of their communicating.

Communicator 1: *Sender/Receiver*

Let's take a closer look at Communicator 1, who is trying to transmit a message—a process that requires sending a message from Communicator 1's nervous system to that of Communicator 2, with the intention of creating a meaning similar to that in the sender's mind. Keep in mind that both people are simultaneously sending and receiving all the time. What characteristics of this person would be important in the communication process? Obviously, mental capacities are of central importance. Inside the human brain are millions of nerve cells that function together to store and utilize knowledge, attitudes, and emotions. We want to know what makes Communicator 1 distinct from any other. Like those of any other human being, Communicator 1's senses are continually bombarded by a wealth of stimuli from both inside and outside the body. All that he or she knows and experiences—whether of the physical or the social world—comes initially through the senses. Borrowing from computer terminology, we call these raw data input—*all the stimuli, both past and present, that give us our information about the world.*

All of this affects the message Communicator 1 will send.

From the accounts of explorers, castaways, and prisoners of war, we can learn what it is like to experience a long period of isolation, but even in these extreme situations there has been some sensory stimulation. The effect of radically decreased input—in solitary confinement, for example—is more difficult to imagine. You can get some notion of how dependent you are on a steady flow of stimuli by supposing that your senses were shut off one by one. Imagine what it would be like without them for a day or just an hour or even 15 minutes.

Messages

Looking again at the model in Figure 1.1, we can think of the messages that Communicator 1 transmits as being conveyed. These **messages** may be verbal or nonverbal, and they may be intentional or unintentional. Thus, four types of messages are possible: (1) intentional verbal, (2) unintentional verbal, (3) intentional nonverbal, and (4) unintentional nonverbal. As we examine these categories individually, keep in mind that most messages contain two or more types of stimuli and that they often overlap.

Verbal Messages   A **verbal message** is *any type of spoken communication that uses one or more words*. Most of the communicative stimuli we are conscious of fall within the category of *intentional verbal messages;* these are *the conscious attempts we make to communicate with others through speech*. Undoubtedly, the most unique aspect of human communication is the use of verbal symbols. It is somewhat of a miracle that we can look at ink marks on a piece of paper or listen to sounds carried on air waves and be able to create images in each other's brains. In fact, the process works so well that we often are surprised when problems occur.

For example, a friend once commented to her mother (who came to this country from Europe) that she had just received a new VISA card. Her mother responded by saying, "Oh really, I didn't know you were planning a trip." To the mother, the term "visa" referred to a permit used to travel to foreign countries. In fact, this "visa" was a credit card. This example illustrates the common principle that words themselves do not contain any meaning. Haney (1992) calls this the "Container Fallacy." In other words, it is a fallacy to believe that meanings are carried or contained by words. If it is possible to have misunderstandings using words that refer to such tangible objects as credit cards, imagine how difficult it is to be able to communicate to another person what we mean by such abstract terms as "truth," "justice," and "fair." Many labor contracts state that if a dispute arises, it must be resolved "within a reasonable period of time." Imagine how much confusion could potentially occur trying to agree on the meaning of "reasonable."

Unintentional verbal messages are *the things we say without meaning to.* Freud argued that all the apparently unintentional stimuli we transmit—both verbal and nonverbal—are unconsciously motivated. We cannot discuss the merits of this argument here, but we can cite an amusing example of a slip of the tongue described by one of Freud's colleagues: "While writing a prescription for a woman who was especially weighed down by the financial burden of the treatment, I was interested to hear her say suddenly: 'Please do not give me *big bills,* because I cannot swallow them.' Of course, she meant to say *pills"* (Freud, 1938, p. 82).

Everyone makes slips occasionally. In 2004 in New Orleans, a member of Mayor C. Ray Nagin's office slipped when describing the success of the year's Carnival celebration. The mayor's spokesperson wrote, "Early economic indicators reveal that this year's Carnival celebration was slightly better than average when it comes to the number of *revealers* and the economic impact" (italics added). Clearly, the spokesperson meant to say "revelers" ("Staffer of New Orleans Mayor. . . ," p. 1)!

Sometimes it's only when we get feedback from others (laughter, for instance) that we become aware we have transmitted such messages. Even in mass communication, which generally involves a great deal of planning and control, such unintentional messages make their appearance. Obviously, those people who represent the mass media are expected to be skilled communicators.

Nonverbal Messages   Nonverbal messages cannot be described as easily as verbal messages, probably because the category is so broad. They include all the nonverbal aspects of our behavior: facial expression, posture, tone of voice, hand movements, manner of dress, and so on. In short, *they are all the messages we transmit without words or over and above the words we use.* Each school year, controversy arises in high schools regarding the dress code, especially for women. The so-called Shakira (or Fergie) look, with low hip-hugging pants and bare midriff, is usually not allowed. More recently, teenagers have resurrected the '80s fashions, which included colorful jelly bracelets. However, in 2011, wearing a certain colored bracelet represented certain specific sexual activity in which that person had participated. Some high school students stopped wearing them because of the impression they might be giving.

Let us first consider *intentional nonverbal messages, the nonverbal messages we want to transmit.* Sometimes we rely exclusively on nonverbal messages to reinforce verbal messages. For example, you can greet someone by smiling and nodding your head, or you can say "Hello" and also smile or wave. At times we deliberately use nonverbal messages to cancel out a polite verbal response and indicate our true feelings: The verbal message may be positive, but the tone and facial expression indicate that we mean something negative.

Much of what we are as a person "communicates" itself every time we behave. Much of this behavior is unintentional. Some writers on the subject go so far as to assert that what we communicate in this way is what we are. *Unintentional nonverbal messages* are *all those nonverbal aspects of our behavior transmitted without our control.* For example, your author once told a student speaker to relax. "I am relaxed," the student replied in a tight voice, trembling, and speaking over the rattling of a paper he was holding. A problem frequently raised in management classes is that store managers unintentionally communicate anger or impatience to their customers.

Ralph Waldo Emerson phrased it well when he remarked to a speaker, "What you are speaks so loudly that I cannot hear what you say." As your communication skills improve, you may find that the number of unintentional messages you transmit will decrease significantly.

Channels

If you are talking on a cell phone, the channel that transmits the communicative stimuli are the air waves via phone towers. The *channels* of face-to-face communication are the sensory organs. Although all five senses may receive the stimuli, you rely almost exclusively on three: hearing, sight, and touch. For example, you listen to someone state an argument, or you exchange knowing glances with a friend, or you put your hand on someone's shoulder. In addition to the sensory organs, the channels of organizational communication include text messages, Twitter, company e-mail messages, newsletters, bulletin boards, printed memoranda, media advertising, and annual reports. In mass communication, the primary channels would be newspapers, films, radio, television, Facebook, Twitter, and the Internet.

In the less formal contexts of communication, we rarely think about communication channels. Usually, a person becomes aware of them only when one or more are cut off or when some sort of interference is present. For example, imagine how you have felt when your e-mail stops working or when your cable television goes down. In another example, we all become very aware of communication channels when there is static on our cell phone, making it impossible to hear another person. The presence of communication channels becomes readily apparent in the absence of these resources. These instances reveal channels to the communicators and are often a single channel experience using either hearing, sight, or touch.

Videoconferencing and Skype calls present some interesting problems with face-to-face communication. Not only are sight and hearing critical, but delays, static or choppy video, or sound problems may affect the communicators' abilities to react to facial cues. In other words, face-to-face communication is a multichannel experience, including hearing, sight, and touch in many cases. Simultaneously, we receive and make use of information from a number of different channels. In general, the more channels being used, the greater the number of communicative stimuli transmitted.

Each communication channel serves its specific purpose, but each possesses merits and limitations. Not all messages belong equally on all channels. In professional as well as in other types of communication "knowing which medium is best suited to your particular communication needs is the key to ensuring that your message is received and understood" (Carr, 2011). For example, the Web is best suited for quick information retrieval, as the Web's strength lies in the ease of information search, not ease of comprehension.

> The Web's use of hyperlinks is the reason for its lower comprehension. Links focus the mind on navigating, squeezing out the mental energy left for comprehending. Click one and you may be taken to the definition of a highlighted word; click another and you may be taken to a picture; click yet another and a video commentary begins, or an e-mail page opens inviting your comments to the site host. Thinking about where to go next is the dominant mental activity, not understanding the content. (Carr, 2011)

Consider an example of just how effective this communication channel can be: Consumer behavior research shows that a word-of-mouth recommendation is

13 times more powerful than print or television advertising when it comes to buying a product for the first time (Sultan et al., 1990).

A recent study of effectiveness of different media in organizational communication found that employees considered the information about their job most satisfactory when it was received from rich communication channels such as face-to-face meetings with their bosses, phone conversations, and departmental meetings. In contrast, employees were more satisfied with information about the company when it was delivered via lean communication media, such as the quarterly meetings, the employee newsletter, or written memos and notices (Byrne and LeMay, 2006).

Having originated as personal online diaries where people kept accounts of their personal lives, blogs are increasingly attracting the attention of businesses that view them as a useful communication channel for receiving customer feedback or early warning systems for product or service problems (Carr, 2006). Dell, Microsoft, and Apple are currently running such corporate blogs. In addition, Dell is reaching out to bloggers to reinforce the company's corporate strategy of selling directly to buyers; Microsoft, to promote its new products (Xbox); and Wal-Mart, to improve its battered image (Barbaro, 2006). Along with the definition, the rules for blogging behavior are also changing:

> Anything that goes up on the Internet is immediately available to a worldwide audience of billions—and it becomes a permanent part of the public record. Independent bloggers may not have to think before they post, but corporate bloggers do. (Carr, 2006)

Interference

After initiating a message, the sender almost always assumes that it has been received. The sender is puzzled or annoyed if he or she is misinterpreted or gets no response, as shown in recent Cingular/AT&T commercials on TV. The sender may even have taken special pains to make the message very clear. "Isn't that enough?" the sender asks. In effect, he or she wants to know what went wrong between the transmission and reception of the message.

The communication scholar would answer, **interference** or **noise**—that is, *anything that distorts the information transmitted to the receiver or distracts him or her from receiving it*. In communication theory, "interference" and "noise" are synonymous terms. "Interference" is probably a more appropriate word, but because "noise" was the term first used in studies of telecommunication, you should be familiar with it too. One recent example is fashionable clothing. High school dress codes now prohibit clothing that is considered a distraction. This includes plunging necklines, low-riding jeans paired with midriff-baring T-shirts, and tops with spaghetti straps. This interference is also present in the workplace. Many companies have dress codes to prevent distraction due to inappropriate attire. Presenters and interview candidates should also pay close attention to their attire to make sure that they are not distracting from their intended message.

Remember that there are many kinds of noise, not just sound. A smoke-filled, overheated room; a student who has made abundant use of a very strong perfume or aftershave; and a lecturer dressed in weird clothing can all become sources of interference.

We can distinguish between two kinds of interference: technical interference and semantic interference. **Technical interference** refers to *the factors that cause the receiver to perceive distortion in the intended information or stimuli.* And the sender may create the distortion: A person who has a speech impediment or who mumbles a great deal may have difficulty making words clear to someone else. At a party, one person may not be able to hear the response of another because the stereo is blaring or because other people standing nearby are speaking so loudly. In this case, the interference is simply the transmission of the sounds of other people in conversation.

Semantic interference occurs when *the receiver does not attribute the same meaning to the signal that the sender does.* For example, a city official and a social worker got into a heated argument over the causes of crime. The city official argued that the causes were primarily "economic," and the social worker maintained, quite predictably, that they were largely "social." Only after considerable discussion did the two begin to realize that although they had been using different terms, essentially they were referring to the same phenomenon. Bear in mind, however, that no two people will attribute exactly the same meaning to any word and that it is also possible to attribute different meanings to nonverbal messages.

As we have seen, interference can exist in the context of the communication, in the channel, in the communicator who sends the message, or in the one who receives it. Some interference will always be present in human communication.

Communicator 2: Receiver/Sender

Traditionally, emphasis has been given to the communicator as message sender, but equally important to any viable model of human communication is an analysis of the communicator as receiver. For most communication, visual perception will be an essential aspect of message reception. Another critical aspect of message reception is *listening*.

Listening

Consider this ancient Chinese saying, "From listening comes wisdom, from speaking repentance." Listening and hearing are far from synonymous. When Communicator 2 (the receiver/sender) listens, four different yet interrelated processes will occur: attention, hearing, understanding, and remembering.

Thus far we have discussed the transmission and reception of a single message. At this point, however, our model departs from several current models that create the illusion that all human communication has a definite starting point with a sender and a termination point with a receiver. When Communicator 2 in Figure 1.1 has received a message, we have come only halfway through the continuous and ongoing process that is communication. For each receiver of a message is also a sender of messages—hence, the term "receiver/sender." Moreover, that person's uniqueness as a human being ensures that his or her attempts to communicate will be very different from those of the other person in the model. For example, Communicator 2's cultural input may be quite unlike that of Communicator 1. His or her filters, both physiological and psychological, will be different. The stimuli he or she transmits will be different. Even the selection of channels and sources of difficulty, or interference, may differ.

The present model includes these differences as inherent parts of the communication process. Although the left half of the model lists the same elements as the right half—input, filters, messages, channels, interference—and these elements are defined in the same way, they are always different in content from those in the right half.

Feedback

The transmission and reception of a single message are only part of our model. Face-to-face communication in particular is characterized by its interdependent participants and the explicit and immediate feedback between them. Even in organizational and mass communication, where the sender/receiver may represent a social organization, the receiver/sender is still able to supply feedback. It may take any number of forms, from a union slowdown in response to the visit of a time-study analyst to an angry letter to the editor of a major newspaper.

A common definition of **feedback** is *the return to you of behavior you have generated.* When we examine feedback solely in interpersonal terms, we can be more specific and say that feedback reinforces some behaviors and extinguishes others. For example, one story has it that a psychology instructor who had been teaching the principles of instrumental learning was actually conditioned by his own class. The students decided to give him reinforcement by taking lots of notes, looking attentive, and asking questions whenever he moved to his right. Whenever he moved to his left, they tried to extinguish this behavior by not taking notes, being inattentive, and not asking questions. He was just about teaching from the right front corner of the room when he realized what was happening.

Knapp and Hall (2011) also observed,

> Many times we talk about our relationships with people as if we had no relation or connection to them—as if our behavior had nothing to do with what the other did. In actuality, however, we have a lot more to do with our partner's responses than we may wish to acknowledge. (p. 11)*

In our personal and professional lives, this interdependence must be recognized in order to ensure effective communication in the workplace. *Emotional intelligence*, a term coined by author Daniel Goleman, includes self-awareness, which allows individuals to understand their own behavior and communications and the effect that these behaviors and communications have on others. Other aspects of emotional intelligence include ability to empathize and ability to control emotions (Valentis, 2004, p. 1). These are especially critical in communication. Individuals

---

* See also Stewart, 2012, p. 135.

with high emotional intelligence recognize their interdependence and are more effective partners or leaders. As a result, companies are hiring executive coaches to teach emotional intelligence to their leaders.

Thus, feedback is an essential characteristic of relationships as well as an important source of information about yourself. (If you would like to know more about yourself, check out the Keirsey Temperament Sorter at *www.keirsey.com*.)

Time

Once Communicator 2 responds to Communicator 1, their interaction can be represented by a circle. But as their exchange progresses in time, the relationship between them is more accurately described by several circles. In fact, all but the briefest exchanges entail several communication cycles. Thus, time itself becomes the final element in our model.

Figure 1.1 conveys the presence of time by representing communication in a form somewhat like a spiral, or uncoiled spring. Some writers prefer to symbolize time as a helix; the only difference between these forms is that the spiral is usually regarded as two-dimensional whereas the helix is thought of as three-dimensional. We shall treat them as identical.

The spiral also illustrates that participants in the communication process can never return to the point at which they started. The relationship must undergo change as a result of each interaction.

Throughout this text, we shall point out the effects of time on communication. Implicit in this emphasis is our belief that time is one of the most relevant variables in the study of human communication. If it does nothing else, the spiral or transactional model should remind us that communication is not static and that it thus requires methods of analysis different from those applied to a fixed entity.

The model identifies some of the major elements that exist in all human communication. We have discussed such communication only in its simplest form. As we add more communicators, change the kind or amount of interference, or vary the messages transmitted, our subject increases in complexity. We shall see this especially when we turn to the study of **communication contexts**. As you read on, you may want to look at other models, some of which are mentioned in the books listed at the end of this chapter. You may even want to try your hand at developing a model of your own. In either case remember that each communication event you will study has something unique about it, and no model can be used as a blueprint of the communication process.

COMMUNICATION CONTEXTS

Human communication occurs in several kinds of situations. Seven different contexts seem to be widely agreed upon in the communication literature: (1) interpersonal, (2) intercultural, (3) interviewing, (4) small group, (5) public communication, (6) organizational communication, and (7) mass communication. Keep in mind that while each of these contexts has some unique characteristics, all of them share *the process of creating a meaning between two* or more people. And all of these contexts sometimes involve intercultural communication, another variable we will examine.

Interpersonal Communication

Interpersonal communication is the basic unit of communication. Although it may occur among three or more individuals in some special circumstances, our communication model depicts this context as occurring between two people. Some scholars believe that the most important defining element in interpersonal communication is the level of closeness or intimacy between the parties. That is felt to be more important than the number of individuals participating. However, we believe that interpersonal communication also includes most of the informal, everyday exchanges that we engage in from the time we get up until the time we go to bed. While a lot of very informal and superficial communication may occur between two people (i.e., a dyad), this is also the context that includes the most intimate relationships we ever experience.

In Mitch Albom's best-selling book *Tuesdays with Morrie*, he tells the true story of his last conversations with his former teacher, Morrie Schwartz, who was dying of ALS (Lou Gehrig's disease). He writes,

> "I don't know why you came back to me. But I want to say this . . . "
> He paused and his voice choked.
> "If I could have had another son, I would have liked it to be you."
> I dropped my eyes, kneading the dying flesh of his feet between my fingers. For a moment I felt afraid, as if accepting his words would somehow betray my own father. But when I looked up, I saw Morrie smiling through tears and I knew there was no betrayal in a moment like this. All I was afraid of was saying goodbye. (Albom, 1997, p. 168)

This passage illustrates the deep love that can develop through interpersonal communication.

Intercultural Communication

Another category we shall be exploring is *intercultural communication*—that is, *communication between members of different cultures (whether defined in terms of racial, ethnic, or socioeconomic differences, or a combination of these differences)*. **Culture** is *a way of life developed and shared by a group of people and passed down from generation to generation*. Gudykunst and Kim (2002) offer the following example of intercultural communication:

> Consider a visit to North America by strangers from a culture with a communication rule requiring that direct eye contact always be avoided. . . . If the strangers do not look them in the eye when talking, the North Americans will assume that the strangers either have something to hide or are not telling the truth. (p. 35)

Similarly, Chin, Gu, and Tubbs (2001) write, ". . . being outgoing, as it is normally understood in the U.S., may be perceived as being rude in other cultures, thereby provoking rather than preventing social isolation" (p. 21).

The significance of intercultural communication will only increase as companies strive toward global operations. Along with globalization of the market comes globalization of knowledge, which today is perceived as a vital tool in maintaining a company's core competencies. Companies that have implemented knowledge management programs have been increasingly confronted by the fact that cultural barriers today are major obstacles to the success of any such program (Kaweevisultrakul and Chan, 2007).

This dimension of experience cuts across all communication contexts: It may occur in two-person communication, interviews, small groups, or any of the other categories we examine in Part Two. Thus intercultural communication will be discussed not only in Chapter 10 but also in many other chapters of this text—for example, in relation to person perception, human attraction, and verbal and nonverbal communication. In a society such as our own, with its rich mix of cultures, intercultural communication will be especially relevant.

Interviewing

An *interview* is often defined as *a communication transaction that emphasizes questions and answers* (Camp, Vielhaber, and Simonetti, 2001). Whether it is talking to a physician to help diagnose an illness, to a prospective employer for a job, to a professor for help in a course, to a market researcher to identify strengths in a product, or to a prosecuting attorney from the witness stand, interviewing is often targeted toward accomplishing a specific purpose. Since interviewing is such a stylized form of communication, specific techniques can be used to best accomplish the interviewer's purpose. These techniques, along with specific types of interview questions, and so on, can be observed on such television programs as *60 Minutes, 20/20,* and *Meet the Press.* I encourage you to watch one of these shows to see how skillfully the moderators use interview questions.

Small-Group Communication

Small-group communication is defined as *"the process by which three or more members of a group exchange verbal and nonverbal messages in an attempt to influence one another"* (Tubbs, 2012, p. 5). Since this context involves three or more people, the degree of intimacy, participation, and satisfaction tends to be lower than in two-person communication. Small-group communication occurs in churches, in social situations, in organizations, and in therapeutic settings, to name a few examples. Group dynamics is a well-researched field of study and tends to focus on small groups that engage in problem solving and decision making. Small-group communication, therefore, tends to focus on the ways to improve the work that can be accomplished in groups. Work teams are but one example of small groups dedicated to improving organizational performance (see Liker and Franz, 2011).

Public Communication

Often referred to as "public speaking," this is a distinct context in a number of ways. First, it occurs in public rather than private places—that is, in auditoriums, classrooms, ballrooms, and so on. Second, public communication is relatively formal as opposed to informal, unstructured communications. Usually, the event is planned in advance. Some people are designated to perform certain functions (such as introducing the speaker). In a commencement exercise, for example, there may be several speakers, as well as a prayer and a ceremony in which degrees are awarded. And third, there are relatively clear-cut behavioral norms (Reynolds, 2008). For example, questions are usually addressed to the speaker after the speech is completed. Thus, *public communication* usually requires that the speaker do significantly more preparation, and he or she should expect a more formalized setting than in two-person or small-group communication.

Organizational Communication

Organizational communication is defined as *"the flow of messages within a network of interdependent relationships"* (Harris and Nelson, 2008, p. 6). This definition fits not only businesses but also hospitals, churches, government agencies, military organizations, and academic institutions. Here we are concerned not only with the effectiveness of the individual communication but also with the role of communication in contributing to or detracting from the effective functioning of the total organization.

A study of U.S. hospitals conducted by the *Wall Street Journal* found that communication problems occurring when a patient is handed over to a new nurse or doctor during a shift change are the "single largest source of medical error" ("*Wall Street Journal* Examines. . . ," 2006). According to the *Journal,* hospitals generally have hand-off arrangements that "vary from unit to unit or even nurse to nurse," resulting in errors that range from giving a patient the wrong medication to reviving a patient who has a "do not resuscitate" order.

To address the problem, the Joint Commission on Accreditation of Healthcare Organizations has begun requiring hospitals to develop formal procedures addressing hand-off communications. For example, when St. Joseph Medical Center in Chicago implemented a communication model called SBAR (Situation, Background, Assessment, and Recommendation)—which originally was used to quickly brief nuclear submariners during a change in command—the rate of adverse events dropped to 39.6 from 89.9 per 1,000 patient days in the first year ("*Wall Street Journal* Examines. . . ," 2006).

The nature of organizations is radically changing, and the complexity of organizational communication increases as companies enter the global market. The same study also found that most companies competing internationally (60 percent of surveyed companies had global operations)—even those with a high degree of communication effectiveness—often fall short when it comes to global communication mainly because what companies regard as communicating is often merely translating (Finney, 2006).

The use of an intranet greatly increases the role communication can play in an organization. Because of the number of assignments at distant locations, Banco do

Brasil, a large financial services company in South America, has used an intranet to successfully improve the quality of intradepartment communication, as well as communication with clients (Correia and Menezes De Faria, 2004, p. 32).

Although modern communication channels increase the efficiency of communication among a company's employees, they also bring a greater risk of release of sensitive information, intentional or unintentional (Vandermeer, 2006). E-mail, being the preferred communications venue for employees today, presents the greatest risk. According to a recently completed audit of e-mail traffic of several *Fortune 500* companies, approximately 2 to 5 percent of all corporate e-mail messages contain data or information that is legally protected or considered proprietary to the business from which it originates (Vandermeer, 2006).

Mass Communication

This last context involves *communication that is mediated*. That is, the source of a message communicates through some print or electronic medium. And mediated encounters differ from personal encounters (Dominick, 2009). In addition, the message is intended for masses of individuals rather than for only a small number of individuals. Of the seven contexts of human communication discussed in this book, *mass communication* is the most formal—and the most expensive. Television advertisements during the Super Bowl each year cost millions of dollars per minute!

Osama bin Laden was killed on May 1, 2011. After official confirmation, the news spread throughout the entire world by the following morning. In addition, the opportunities for feedback in mass communication are somewhat limited, especially when compared with interpersonal or small-group communication. The audience is relatively large, heterogeneous, and anonymous to the source. However, with the advent of Facebook, Twitter, and numerous blogs, the feedback loop has become shorter and shorter in time. Finally, communication experience is characterized as public, rapid, and fleeting.

Bernard Goldberg states in his book *Bias* (2002) that in his many years as a television correspondent for CBS News, he noticed a systematic liberal bias in the coverage, not only in his network, but also at ABC and NBC. He carefully documents numerous specific examples of this bias starting with the coverage of "conservative millionaire" Steve Forbes as a presidential candidate in 2000. If you are interested in this topic, you also would enjoy the opposing point of view expressed in the book by James Carvill and Paul Begala entitled *Buck Up, Suck Up . . . and Come Back When You Foul Up* (2002). Both of these are really great treatments of some of the issues regarding mass communication.

COMMUNICATION TECHNOLOGIES

We are all becoming increasingly familiar with what was once considered complex communication technology. For example, laptop computers have become a daily tool for many. Students walking across campus are often talking or texting on their smart phones. Fax machines are so popular that many restaurants like McDonald's use them to take orders.

The most powerful technological wonder that has revolutionized human communication is the Internet. Although this has had positive effects, there have been some downsides too. One major study at Carnegie Mellon University (Harmon, 1998*) found that people who spend even a few hours a week online experience higher levels of depression and loneliness than people who use the computer less. The researchers concluded that Internet use itself appeared to cause a decline in psychological well-being. The study was funded by high-tech companies such as Hewlett-Packard, AT&T Research, Intel, Apple Computer, and the National Science Foundation, and the findings were exactly the opposite of what researchers were expecting to find. The researchers also concluded that the study "raises some troubling questions about the nature of 'virtual' communication and the disembodied relationships that are often formed in the vacuum of cyberspace" (p. A4).

Another study looked into so-called Internet addiction (Lorek, 1998; Carr, 2011). How would you answer the following questions, using: 1, not at all; 2, rarely; 3, occasionally; 4, often; and 5, always?

Do you stay online longer than you intended?   3

Do you prefer the excitement of the Internet to the intimacy of your partner?   1

Do you check your e-mail before something else that you need to do?

Do you lose sleep at night due to late-night log-ons?   1

Do you choose to spend more time online than going out with others?   3

If you scored 5–9, you have average online use. If you scored 10–17, this would indicate some tendency toward Internet problems. If you scored 18–25, this would indicate a stronger tendency toward Internet problems. This is according to Kimberly Young at the University of Pittsburgh, who is cofounder of the Center for Online Addiction.

Few areas have been affected by computer-based communication technologies more profoundly than the areas of learning and education. Today's learning groups often interact solely by means of technology; the participants may be colleagues, friends, or even strangers (Imamoglu, 2007). The benefits of today's distant learning, or e-learning, include

- Video-Conference Classrooms that eliminate the boundaries of place-dependent, face-to-face classrooms so that two or more distinct social networks can be joined together.
- Group Discussion Spaces that provide a site for a working group, such as a project team, consulting team, or student learning team.
- Online Communities—Internet-based forums that anybody can join to discuss themes of common interest. (Imamoglu, 2007)

---

*See Chapter 15 for more on the social effects of Internet use.

With all this high-tech communication potential, human communication is at once more possible and perhaps less human. Regardless of your sentiments regarding these innovations, there is no question that they are having a profound and permanent impact on human communication.

Communication Ethics

This edition includes a chapter on ethics in communication. It seems that hardly a day goes by without some controversy being reported, whether it's deciding whether to clone human beings, or corporations abusing the environment, or Stanford University being accused of misusing overhead expense accounts from research grants.

Ethical questions also arise about how information is communicated to mass audiences, especially through television. For example, during the 2004 Super Bowl, Janet Jackson revealed her breast during the half-time show. The Super Bowl audience is traditionally a family audience. The FCC has attempted to regulate the material allowed on network television, but there are often discrepancies between programs allowed on network television and cable stations.

Advertisements on television and magazines also present what may be considered unethical behavior. Ads tout harmful products such as cigarettes and promote unrealistic body images to young audiences. The chapter on communication ethics should provide you with some helpful insights and guidelines on how to avoid difficulties in all of these areas.

WHAT IS EFFECTIVE COMMUNICATION?

Have you ever wondered what they teach in an "information literacy" class? Or what exactly a vendor who "offers printing solutions" does? These and other examples are the reason that communication expert Gerard Braud says that he finds himself asking the question "What does that mean?" more and more often. "In an age of information overload, audiences don't have time to decipher techno-speak, double-speak, acronyms, and *make it up so I sound smarter than you*–speak" (Braud, 2007, italics in original). "While preparing someone for an interview or writing notes for the spokesperson and organization, I have to ask 'What does that mean?' no less than three times before I can get to what the person is really trying to say" (Braud, 2007).

A charity needed help with its messaging. In a role-playing media training interview, one executive said, "Our clients have barriers to employment." My first "What does that mean?" came because I wanted an explanation of the word clients. I was told it meant the people who come to the charity for help. My second "What does that mean?" came as I asked about "barriers to employment." The executive's response was that some individuals are unable to obtain employment because of barriers related to their social, economic, and/or physical conditions. In my third attempt at clarification, I asked if it was because they were poor, divorced, uneducated, living without a car, raising children as single parents, or living with a physical or mental disability. The answer was yes, all of the above. The organization's new clarified key message is: "Our goal is to help people find jobs, whether it's people with physical limitations, single mothers, people with no transportation, or a variety of other issues that keep them from getting and keeping a good-paying job." (Braud, 2007)

The following few simple rules, Braud says, are essential for effective communication:

Rule No. 1: Make it clear.

Rule No. 2: Say what you mean.

Rule No. 3: Avoid acronyms and abbreviations.

Rule No. 4: Get to the lowest common denominator.

Earlier in this chapter we said that we would be concerned not only with human speech communication but also with the concept of effective communication. But what are the criteria that make for effective communication? Students sometimes say that communication is effective when a person gets his or her point across. This is but one measure of effectiveness. More generally, communication is effective *when the stimulus as it was initiated and intended by the sender, or source, corresponds closely to the stimulus as it is perceived and responded to by the receiver.*

If we let *S* stand for the person who is the sender or source of the message and *R* for the receiver of the message, then communication is whole and complete when the response *S* intends and the response *R* provides are identical:

$$\frac{R}{S} = \frac{receiver's\ meaning}{sender's\ meaning} = 1$$

We rarely reach 1—that is, perfect sharing of meaning. As a matter of fact, we never reach 1. We approximate it. And the greater the correspondence between our intention and the response we receive, the more effective we have been in communicating. At times, of course, we hit the zero mark: There is absolutely no correspondence between the response we want to produce and the one we receive. The drowning man who signals wildly for help to one of his friends on a sailboat only to have her wave back is not accomplishing his communication objective, to say the least.

The example of the drowning man is extreme. By now you may be wondering just how important effective communication is on a day-to-day basis. A long-term study of Massachusetts Institute of Technology (MIT) graduates who were interviewed several times over a 15-year period has revealed that even for those very talented, technically competent graduates of a prestigious school, effectiveness in communication was one of the most important skills in achieving a successful and fulfilling life, if not the *most* important. On the basis of his research, the author of this study stresses the increasing importance of interpersonal competence as a skill critical "not only for dealing with self and family development, but for career advancement as well" (Schein, 1978, p. 77. See also Martin Seligman, *Flourish,* New York: Free Press, 2011).

But how do we measure our own effectiveness? We can't judge our effectiveness if our intentions are not clear; we must know what we are trying to do. What makes that first definition of effectiveness inadequate ("when a person gets his or her point across") is that in communicating, we may try to bring about one or more of several possible outcomes. We shall consider five of them here: understanding, pleasure, attitude influence, improved relationships, and action.

Understanding

Understanding refers primarily to *accurate reception of the content of the intended stimulus*. In this sense, a communicator is said to be effective if the receiver has an accurate understanding of the message the communicator has tried to convey. (Of course, the communicator sometimes conveys messages unintentionally that are also quite clearly understood.)

The primary failures in interpersonal communication are failures to achieve content accuracy. For example, the service manager of an oil company had a call one winter morning from a woman who complained that her oil burner was not working. "How high is your thermostat set?" he asked. "Just a moment," the woman replied. After several minutes she returned to the phone. "At 5 feet 3½ inches," she said, "same as it's always been." This confusion is typical of a failure to achieve understanding. Most misunderstandings of this kind are relatively easy to remedy through clarifying feedback and restatement.

As we add more people to a communication context, it becomes more difficult to determine how accurately messages are being received. This is one of the reasons that group discussions sometimes turn into free-for-alls. Comments begin to have little relation to one another, and even a group with an agenda to follow may not advance toward the resolution of any of its problems. Situations such as these call for more clarifying, summarizing, and directing of group comments.

With respect to public communication, much has been written about how to improve understanding when speaking to inform—with "understanding" often being referred to as "information gain." What the public speaker must remember is that the feedback he or she receives is often quite limited; the speaker should therefore make a concerted effort to be as objective and precise as possible in explaining his or her subject. The use of supporting materials—examples, analogies, and the like—helps clarify an explanation of almost any subject.

Within an organizational setting, accurate understanding is one of the most basic desired outcomes. It is not possible, for example, for an organization to function efficiently unless employees understand what they are expected to do at their jobs. This may involve understanding not only verbal directives from immediate superiors but also information disseminated through interoffice memos, employee handbooks, and other restatements of company policies on the intranet.

In mass communication, the dissemination of information is also a primary objective on many occasions. (Newscasts, podcasts, documentaries, and videotape programs immediately come to mind.) Presumably, those who work in the mass media have developed their communications skill to a high degree so that they are able to organize, present, and interpret information in a way that promotes understanding. For example, in a single hour a television special can present a program on depression: its symptoms, causes, and possible treatment. Because feedback is somewhat limited in this setting, however, it is difficult to assess the level of information gain within the audience.

Pleasure

Not all communication has as its goal the transmission of a specific message. In fact, the goal of the transactional analysis school of thought is simply to communicate with others in a way that ensures a sense of mutual well-being. This is sometimes referred to as a *phatic communication,* or maintaining human contact. Many of our brief exchanges with others—"Hi"; "How are you today?"; "How's it going?" have this purpose. Casual dates and cocktail parties are more structured occasions on which we come together to enjoy the company and conversation of others. The degree to which we find communication pleasurable is closely related to our feelings about those with whom we are interacting. The most recent research available on cell phone usage shows that the average U.S. teenager uses his or her cell phone 500 minutes a month, but 800 or 900 minutes per month is not unusual (LeDuc, 2001). Also, according to a study by Context, the cell phone has become such a primary mode of communication for teenagers that they may even unintentionally avoid contact with friends who don't have cell phones (Batista, 2003).

The purpose of public communication can also be pleasure; the after-dinner speech and the speech intended to entertain fall into this category. Much of the informal communication within an organization takes place during lunch hours, coffee breaks, company picnics, and management dinners. And certainly in movies, situation comedies, and televised sports events, we see entertainment provided on a grand scale.

Attitude Influence

Understanding and agreement are by no means synonymous outcomes. When you understand someone's message, you may find that you disagree with him or her even more strongly than you did before.

Products created in response to the latest diet trend, the "low-carb diet," are advertised everywhere. Now you can buy almost anything in a new low-carb version, even beverages. Coca-Cola has launched Coke Zero, a low-carb version of Coke, to market to those who have jumped on the low-carb bandwagon (Dominick, 2009). As more products are developed and the diet hype continues, consumers are influenced to purchase and consume certain types of foods. On one hand, a consumer may feel the pressures of choosing low-carb foods because of all the advertising and focus on the diet. On the other hand, the feelings of those who do not agree with the diet may grow even deeper when the hype is all around them.

Influencing attitudes is a basic part of daily living. In many situations, we are interested in influencing a person's attitude as well as in having him or her understand what we are saying. The process of changing and reformulating attitudes, or *attitude influence,* goes on throughout our lives. In two-person situations, attitude influence is often referred to as "social influence." In the counseling interview, it might be called "gentle persuasion." Attitude influence is no less important in the small-group or the organizational setting. For example, consensus among group members is an objective of many problem-solving discussions. And industries often try, especially through the mass media, to influence public attitudes toward big business by presenting themselves in a flattering light. (For example, Exxon/Mobil commercials about ecology suggest that the fuel industry is greatly concerned about the pollution problems caused by industrial waste.) When applied to public and mass communication contexts, the process of attitude influence is usually referred to as "persuasion." Studies of mass communication are particularly concerned with the persuasive impact of the message on various opinion leaders within the larger mass audience.

In determining how successful your attempts to communicate have been, remember that you may fail to change a person's attitude but still get that person to understand your point of view. In other words, a failure to change someone's point of view should not necessarily be written off as a failure to increase understanding.

Improved Relationships

It is commonly believed that if a person can select the right words, prepare his or her message ahead of time, and state it precisely, perfect communication will be ensured. But total effectiveness requires a positive and trusting psychological climate. When a human relationship is clouded by mistrust, numerous opportunities arise for distorting or discrediting even the most skillfully constructed messages. Voters may well be suspicious of their mayor's promise that if reelected, he will fulfill all the campaign promises he failed to keep during his first term in office. A young man will probably discount a young woman's assurances that she is very interested in him after she breaks a date for the third or fourth time. A professor may begin to doubt the excuses of a student who is holding court at the student union an hour after the student was too sick to take the midterm.

We mentioned that the primary failures in communication occur when the content of the message is not accurately understood. By contrast, secondary failures are disturbances in human relationships that result from misunderstandings. They stem from the frustration, anger, or confusion (sometimes all three) caused by the initial failure to understand. Because such failures tend to polarize the communicators involved, they are difficult to resolve. By acknowledging that the initial misunderstandings are a common occurrence in daily communication, we may be able to tolerate them better and avoid or at least minimize their damaging effect on interpersonal relationships (see Stewart, 2012).

Still another kind of understanding can have a profound effect on human relationships: understanding another person's motivations. At times each of us communicates not to convey information or to change someone's attitude but simply to be "understood" in this second sense. Throughout this text, we shall discuss various facets of human relationships: motivation; social choice; confirmation, self-disclosure, trust; group cohesiveness; and source credibility in public and mass communication. We hope to show that all these concepts are bound together by a common theme: The better the relationship between people, the more likely it is that other outcomes of effective communication in the fullest sense will occur.

Action

Some would argue that all communication is useless unless it brings about a desired action. Yet all the outcomes discussed thus far—understanding, pleasure, attitude influence, improved relationships—are important at different times and in different places. There are instances, however, when action is an essential determinant of the success of a communicative act. In the sales interview, an automobile salesman who wants you to think more favorably of his car than his competitor's also wants you to act by buying a car; his primary objective is not attitude change. A math tutor is far from satisfied if the student she is coaching says he understands how to do a set of problems but fails to demonstrate that understanding on his next exam. And we might question the effectiveness of a finance committee that reaches consensus on how to balance a budget yet fails to act on its decision.

Eliciting action on the part of another person is probably the communication outcome most difficult to produce. In the first place, it seems easier to get someone to understand your message than it is to get the person to agree with it. Furthermore, it seems easier to get that person to agree—that he or she should exercise regularly, for example—than to get the person to act on it. (We realize that some behaviors are induced through coercion, social pressure, or role prescriptions and do not necessarily require prior attitude change. Voluntary actions, however, usually follow rather than precede attitude changes.) If you are trying to promote action on the part of the receiver, you increase your chances of getting the desired response if you can (1) facilitate understanding of your request, (2) secure agreement that the request is legitimate, and (3) maintain a comfortable relationship with the receiver. The desired action does not follow automatically, but it is more likely to follow if these intermediate objectives have first been accomplished.

The difficulties of eliciting action on the part of the receiver are further compounded in organizational and mass communication settings. The plant manager's abrasive memo on absenteeism, for example, may trigger more absenteeism, or the sick calls may taper off and some form of sabotage may appear in the products turned out on the assembly line. Certainly, the mass media are often concerned with promoting audience action—whether it be promoting a particular brand of detergent, getting mothers to immunize their children against rubella, or changing audience voting patterns. Yet researchers have questioned the effectiveness of mass communication in changing behavior. It has been found, for example, that political campaigns conducted through the mass media have little direct influence on changes in voting behavior. One interesting new development intended to improve action as a result of communication is that the Federal Communications Commission has directed cell phone companies to start issuing phones that determine their locations through transmission towers or by global positioning satellites. In some cases, the accuracy must be within 150 feet. This is so that emergency crews can respond more quickly to urgent phone calls. However, it also raises the question of privacy, since all calls can be traced to the sending location. You may want to discuss the pros and cons of this in your class (Kanaley, 2001).

In short, the five possible outcomes of effective human communication are understanding, pleasure, attitude influence, improved relationships, and action.

At different points in this book, I will give special attention to each of them. For example, the concepts of attitude similarity, status, social influence and consensus, and persuasion all have some bearing on attitude influence. Similarly, the concepts of trust, cohesiveness, and source credibility are all relevant to improved human relationships.

The five outcomes I have discussed are neither exhaustive nor mutually exclusive. Thus, a look at the relationship aspects of communication in Chapter 8 will illustrate that defensive behaviors distort understanding, that the so-called disconfirming responses are not pleasurable. In the chapters that follow, I will show some of the many ways in which communication outcomes are interdependent and to demonstrate that this is true for many different communication contexts, or settings.

Summary

In this book, I view human communication as the process of creating a meaning between two or more people. Today, many communication scholars emphasize the transactional nature of the communication process so that one person's communication can be defined only in relation to some other or others.

In this chapter, I presented a model to help us conceptualize the relationships between the elements of human communication. Like all human beings, both communicators in our model originate and perceive messages. Both depend on the steady flow of physical, social, and cultural input, and both select from the total input through their perceptual filters and sets.

I then discussed the components of a message in terms of the types of stimuli transmitted: verbal and nonverbal, intentional and unintentional. We learned that, though all five senses are potential channels for receiving stimuli, face-to-face communication relies primarily on hearing, sight, and touch and is usually a multichannel experience. The channels of organizational communication would extend to newsletters, memos, e-mails, and the like, whereas those of mass communication would include newspapers, films, radio, the Internet, and television. Anything that distorts the information transmitted through the various channels or that distracts the receiver from getting it would be considered interference.

We saw that all the elements in Communicator 1's half of our communication cycle—input, filters, verbal and nonverbal messages, channels, and interference—are different for Communicator 2 because of his or her uniqueness as a human being. Emphasis was given to the receiver as listener. We examined the importance of feedback, and we examined the effect of time, represented in the model by a spiral, as a crucial variable in all studies of communication.

Much of the time people spend communicating involves interpersonal communication. But in studying human communication, we are also concerned with contexts in which a great many parties are involved, feedback is limited, and messages are transmitted through such media as newspaper, radio, and television. We are interested therefore in the principles of human communication as they apply not only to the two-person setting and the interview but also to small-group, public, organizational, and mass communication. We are also interested in communication behaviors that are ethical.

After a brief discussion of each of the communication contexts, I turned to an examination of what constitutes effective communication. It was established that communication is effective to the degree that the message as it is intended by the sender corresponds with the message as it is perceived and responded to by the receiver. We learned that effectiveness is closely linked with intention and that in communicating, we usually want to bring about one or more of several possible outcomes. Five of the major outcomes—understanding, pleasure, attitude influence, improved relationships, and action—were considered here, with emphasis on their application to the various communication contexts. Another area of interest is intercultural communication, which cuts across all the contexts we shall be discussing.

Key Terms

Communication
Communication
  context
Culture

Feedback
Input
Interference
Messages

Noise
Nonverbal message
Semantic interference

Technical
  interference
Verbal message

Review Questions

1. Provide your own personal definition of "communication." How is it similar to, or different from, the definitions given in this text?

2. What is input, and how does it influence a person's communication?

3. Name the four types of messages. Give a specific example of each from your own experience.

4. Explain the difference between technical and semantic interference and give an example of each.

5. Discuss the influence of various kinds of feedback.

6. List seven different communication contexts. Explain the distinctive characteristics of each.

7. What is effective communication? Think of arguments for and against the types of communication effectiveness that have been described in this chapter. Are there some that the text has not included? Are there some it has discussed that you think should not be included? What do you think is the most important outcome of face-to-face communication?

Exercises

1. Start a personal log on the computer in which you record your daily reaction to perhaps ten members of your class. Only some will impress you (favorably or unfavorably) at first. Note details of their behavior. Describe your own responses as candidly as possible.

2. a. Draw and label a model of human communication. If possible, include components that can be appropriately labeled as Communicator 1 (sender/receiver), Communicator 2 (receiver/sender), input, filters, messages, channels, interference, and time.

   b. Examine the model carefully and formulate five statements that describe how two or more components of the model may influence

communication effectiveness as defined in this chapter.

3. Write a short paper in which you analyze the strengths and weaknesses of the communication model in this chapter. Compare and contrast it with some other models, which may be found in the books in the suggested readings.

4. Divide the class members into groups of five or six; then have each group member discuss a personal problem in communication. Have each group select its "best" example of a communication problem as well as a spokesperson to present the example to the entire class. Then analyze each example in terms of the communication model given in this chapter.

5. Observe several communication events and keep a record of their outcomes. Which outcomes occurred most frequently? Under what conditions did these outcomes seem to occur? How can you explain these results?

6. Write a one-page case study of a communication failure that you have experienced or observed. Then write an analysis of its causes, and suggest a way to resolve it.

7. Think of two people you know, one an excellent communicator, the other quite ineffective. Write a highly specific description of each; then write a comparison of the two in which you contrast and evaluate their communication styles. On the basis of this analysis, set yourself three specific objectives for improving your own communication behaviors.

8. Check out the Internet for sources of information regarding communication.

Suggested Readings

Acuff, Frank L. *How to Negotiate Anything with Anyone Anywhere around the World*, 2nd ed. New York: American Management Association, 1997.

This excellent book helps explain how to apply communication principles in 41 countries. It is a very valuable resource.

Daly, John. *Advocacy: Championing Ideas and Influencing Others*. New Haven: Yale University Press, 2011.

This book specifically focuses on how to make your communication efforts more influential and successful. A great read.

Carr, Nicholas. *The Shallows: What the Internet Is Doing to Our Brains*. New York: W. W. Norton, 2011.

Gladwell, Malcolm. *BLINK*. Boston: Little, Brown and Company, 2004.

This best-selling book offers numerous principles and examples of communication in society.

Goldberg, Bernard. *Bias: A CBS Insider Exposes How the Media Distort the News*. Washington, D.C.: Regnery Publishing, 2002.

This best-selling book details a carefully researched account of the liberal bias in television news.

Hartman, Laura P., and Joe Desjardins. *Business Ethics: Decision-Making for Personal Integrity & Social Responsibility*. New York: McGraw-Hill, 2008.

This is an excellent book with many examples of thorny ethical decisions for readers to make.

Lucas, Stephen. *The Art of Public Speaking*. New York: McGraw-Hill, 2008.

This excellent book demonstrates the ways that public speaking can be adapted to today's much more global society.

Rath, Tom, and Jim Harter. *Wellbeing: The Five Essential Elements*. New York: The Gallup Press, 2010.

Tapscott, Don. *Grown Up Digital: How the Net Generation Is Changing Your World*. New York: McGraw-Hill, 2009.

An excellent source of information about how the Internet is and will be used as a growing communication alternative at work, at play, and as a learning tool.

 # For Supplementary Information

Log onto the Online Learning Center at *www.mhhe.com/tubbshc13e.*

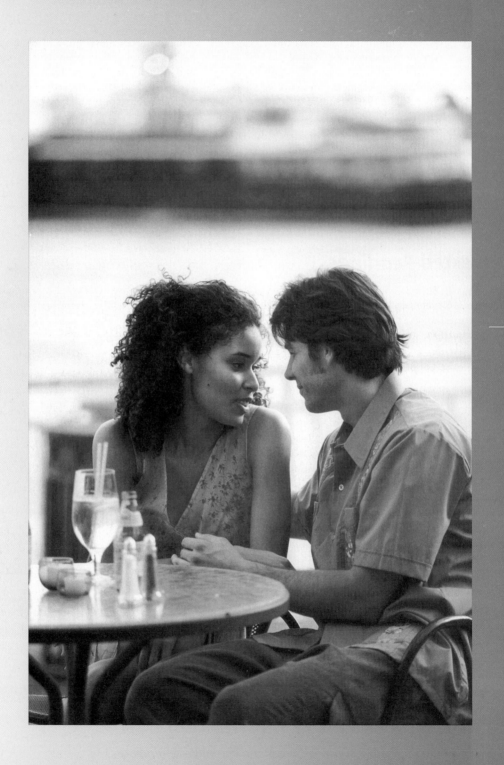

Person Perception

Chapter Objectives

After reading this chapter, you should be able to:

1. Explain the difference between a perceptual filter and a psychological set and discuss the selective nature of all perception.
2. Describe how person perception differs from object perception and explain the implications of such differences for communication.
3. Discuss the development of self-concept as well as its relationship to gender.
4. Explain some of the variables that influence self-esteem and state current research findings about self-esteem, shyness and Internet use, and the Pygmalion effect.
5. Describe the concepts of private personality theory, central traits, primacy, and empathy.
6. Discuss several variables, including perceived traits, physical attractiveness, expressiveness, and charisma that influence our impressions of others.
7. Distinguish between personal generalizations and stereotypes, and discuss the effects of stereotyping.
8. Discuss how work, student, gender-linked, and marital roles influence person perception.
9. Describe several variables including interpersonal sensitivity involved in forming accurate perceptions of others, and identify three ways to improve person perception and communication effectiveness.

In the spring of 2012 the shooting death of a black Sanford, Florida teen named Trayvon Martin by George Zimmerman, a white Hispanic man, in a perceived assault, touched off a national debate about racial relations. Florida has a so-called "Stand your ground" law, which permits citizens to defend themselves when they feel that their life is threatened. As a result, George Zimmerman, the man who shot Trayvon Martin, was allowed to remain free. This shooting sparked a great deal of discussion and debate about racial relations and their impact on incidents such as this. Even President Obama personalized the discussion by saying that if he had a son, the young man would look like Trayvon.

The national dialogue resulting from this tragic incident can potentially lead to some important and valuable lessons for the future. For example, if you would like to learn more about how you perceive other people who are different from yourself, you can go to *projectimplicit.net* to take one of their free tests that measure perceptions between people who are from different groups such as black–white, Christian–Muslim, thin–obese, and others. These perception tests have been developed by researchers at Harvard University along with other top universities and appear to be of high quality. Once we know how we perceive others who are different, we can potentially learn avenues for improving our tolerance toward others who are different from us.

When it comes to first impressions, how much time does it take after seeing a person's face before you make up your mind? One new study asked people to make judgments of unfamiliar faces (Willis and Todorov, 2006) and found that you can form such a judgment within a tenth of a second. "In fact, for all judgments—attractiveness, likeability, trustworthiness, competence, and aggressiveness—increased exposure time [to viewing a face] did not significantly increase the correlations" (p. 592). Most scholars agree that impressions based on facial appearance tend to be fast and intuitive.

On the other hand, with increased time, research finds, your confidence about your judgments also increases and impressions about the traits of others become more differentiated. People become more individualized. For example, the effects of facial attractiveness seem to decrease over time.

In this chapter we examine many of the variables that affect our initial perceptions of others. For example, we will consider what we judge to be physically attractive in others as well as other traits we regard as central in forming such judgments. Our impressions of others form the basis for countless decisions throughout our lives—not only about romantic relationships, but also about choosing a roommate, a friend, a business partner, an advisor, or a doctor. In the following pages, we will consider the initial process by which all such impressions of other human beings are formed but, equally important, we will also examine how we look at ourselves.

PERCEIVING PEOPLE AND OBJECTS: A COMPARISON

Our total awareness of the world comes to us through our senses. Thus, all our perceptions—whether they be of drawings, household objects, or other people— have a common basis. Yet, as we've seen countless times, two people often disagree sharply in their judgments about a third. Have you ever been "fixed up" with some-one described to you as just your type, only to be thoroughly disappointed from the very beginning of the evening? You might have even asked yourself whether the person who arranged the date perceived you or the other party with any accuracy. The reasons for such varying perceptions should become apparent as we consider similarities between interpersonal perception and perception in general.

Two Kinds of Filters

Your capacity to register sensory stimuli is limited. You cannot take in everything. Nor do you always want to. You choose certain aspects of your environment over others. What you are aware of at any time is determined in part by what you as a re-ceiver select out of the total input. David Eagleman, a neuroscientist and director of the Laboratory for Perception and Action at Baylor College of Medicine, says that most people can hear their name being spoken in another conversation that they didn't think they were listening to (Eagleman, 2011). *The ability to process certain of the stimuli available to us while filtering out others* is called **selective attention**.

The American philosopher and psychologist William James explained the pro-cess of selection at work here in terms of interest: "Millions of items of the outward order are present to my senses which never properly enter into my experience. Why? Because they have no *interest* for me. *My experience is what I agree to attend to.* Only those items which I *notice* shape my mind—without selective interest, experi-ence is an utter chaos" (James, 1950, p. 402).

Each of us, then, perceives only part of the available stimuli while filtering out other stimuli. There are two kinds of filters through which all input or sensation will pass: physiological and psychological.

Perceptual Filters and Psychological Sets

Among the inherent structures of our sense organs are our **perceptual filters,** *physi-ological limitations that are built into human beings* and cannot be reversed. Such limitations on our capacity to perceive exist whether we are experiencing an object or a person. And they vary considerably from one individual to another so that we differ in the degree to which our various senses are accurate.

To the human communicator one extremely troublesome perceptual filter is the limit on one's ability to hear. Sometimes we think we hear a person say one thing when actually he or she said another. We then act on the basis of what we think that person said. Or we may act without hearing what a person said at all. Many com-munication difficulties are rooted in this kind of misunderstanding.

A psychological set is a second type of filter that influences our perceptions. Our **psychological sets**—that is, *our expectancies or predispositions to respond*—have a profound effect on our perception of objects. Similarly, psychological sets affect our perception of other people. Suppose you were asked to interpret the scene in Figure 2.1. How would you answer? Is the young woman sitting with her lap-top annoyed with the man beside her? Is she waiting for someone else? Or is she

Figure 2.1
Perceiving People

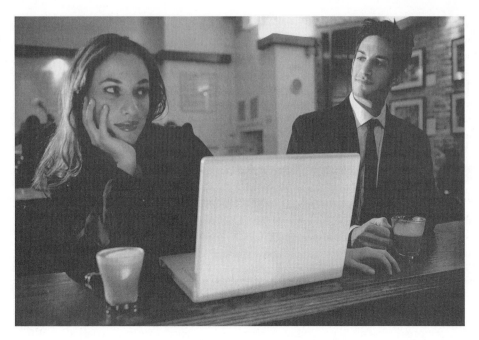

attracted to him? And why is he looking toward her? Has he just said something sarcastic—or flattering? Is he flirting? Do the two know each other well? An almost infinite number of interpretations can be evoked by an ambiguous photograph such as this one. Each of us has a story for this scene; with a little prodding, each of us could elaborate on it.

If you've been involved in a recent romantic relationship, you might be more inclined to perceive these people in a more positive way because you've come to expect and anticipate caring behavior. On the other hand, the two might be having a difficult time or they might be strangers with little connection to each other. Whatever your interpretation, it reveals much about your own expectations and past experiences. As you read on, you will see that past experience is a strong influence on what you select from all the available stimuli, and often you are judging another person, at least initially, by the group or context in which he or she is first seen. This will certainly be apparent when we discuss stereotyping.

As two people communicate, each formulates ideas that become the content of the communication event. How accurately a message is received depends on the other person's perceptual filters and sets. Remember that psychological and physiological characteristics will influence which stimuli are selected and how they are perceived.

Selective Perception, Organization, and Interpretation

Today we don't believe, as early philosophers did, that the human mind is a blank tablet on which impressions are imprinted. We know that perception is not a passive state in which stimuli are received and automatically registered. Quite the opposite. Perception is an active process: Each of you *selectively* perceives, organizes, and interprets what you experience.

In general, you perceive stimuli that are intense, repetitious, or in the process of changing. Nonetheless, each person actively chooses what to attend to depending on personal interests, motivations, desires, and expectations. Entranced by a young woman's appearance, a man sitting next to her at a party may notice what great legs she has and pay little attention to what she's saying. Someone else in the group may be more interested in her remarks about working in the personnel department of a large company because he is looking for a job.

In addition to the selective perception of stimuli, you tend to organize stimuli selectively—that is, you order the stimuli with which you are presented into a "whole," a complete, sensible picture. Psychological tests with ambiguous scenes such as the one in Figure 2.1 are based on this notion.

People organize stimuli according to different schema and expectations: They attribute cause and effect uniquely. Your author once had a graduate student who was very critical of everyone else's presentations during class, saying often that they were "amateurish." Other students thought that perhaps this was because the student was such a good presenter. However, when the day came for the student to present, he was absent and later e-mailed the professor saying that he was "too terrified" to speak. He ended up dropping the course.

After stimuli are selectively perceived and selectively organized, they are selectively interpreted—that is, the stimuli are assigned meanings unique to the perceiver. Personal interpretations are based on the perceiver's past experiences, assumptions about human behavior, knowledge of the other's circumstances, present moods/wants/desires, and expectations.

Person perception then is a special form of perception. As we go on to examine how impressions of others are formed, we will also give some attention to how members of other cultures tend to be perceived.

FORMING IMPRESSIONS

Our concern with the process of forming impressions involves the discussion of many variables, but it begins with you, the perceiver, and how you view yourself.

Looking at Yourself

If asked to describe yourself, what information would you give—a physical description, your age, gender, membership in an ethnic group? Perhaps you would define yourself by certain traits or by what you do. You might say you are a student, that you are outgoing and interested in politics, or that you are athletic and somewhat shy. For some, self-description is an uncomfortable process. For example, one college application asks prospective students to describe themselves by using ten adjectives. One reason college applications can be so difficult to fill out is that they often require statements about self-concept.

Self-Concept

Your **self-concept,** *your relatively stable impressions of yourself,* includes not only your perception of your physical characteristics but also your judgments about what you "have been, are, and aspire to be" (Pearson et al., 1995). Self-concept develops partly out of the feedback you receive from the people around you. In fact, some early theorists believe that there is a **"looking glass self"** that develops out of our relations and interactions with others. In other words, you evaluate yourself primarily on the basis of how you *think* others perceive and evaluate you. You combine all these reflected perceptions, ways in which you think others see you, and they make up your self-concept.

Such a view gives great weight to your experiences as a child. If, for example, Maria's parents, relatives, and school friends all come to think of her as "the good student," she may learn to regard herself in the same way and strive even harder to do well in classes. Academic performance may become an essential aspect of the way she thinks of herself. Conversely, if Jermaine is viewed by his parents, relatives, and neighbors as "the black sheep," he may come to see himself in this light.

Self-concept not only grows out of your social interactions but also changes with your age as well as your situation—for example, you might see yourself very differently when at home than you do when you are away at college (Hinde et al., 2001, p. 190). Self-concept can vary so much with context that some suggest viewing the self "not as a unitary structure, but as multiple." It's been proposed also that different people who know us know different aspects of the self. "And the self must be seen as an active agent, providing expectancies and directing attention to whatever is of significance to the individual" (pp. 190–191). So a good part of how you think about yourself may have to do with how you judge yourself in relation to others.

Self-Concept and Gender

The way you see yourself in terms of what your culture regards as masculine or feminine traits is an important part of your self-concept, an aspect of gender as distinct from sex. *Sex* refers to *your biological and physiological characteristics, what makes you male or female.* **Gender,** a broader, more complex concept, *is in part shaped by culture and includes your "biological sex (male or female), psychological characteristics (femininity, masculinity, androgyny), attitudes about the sexes, and sexual orientation"* (Ivy and Backlund, 2004, pp. 32–34, 75).

Your attitudes toward gender affect both how you look at yourself and how you look at others. For example, one recent study found that people who have sexist attitudes also used gender as a basic category in perceiving others and that this contributed to gender stereotyping (Harper and Schoeman, 2003).

Much has been written about women valuing social relationships more than men do. In a study in which young adults were asked to write 20 sentences about themselves, young men used twice as many statements that were based on their membership in groups as women did. These included such sentences as "I am a Northwestern student" and "I am a member of Pi Kappa Alpha." Young women, on the other hand, were almost twice as likely as men to describe themselves in terms of their close relationships—for example, "I am Amanda's best friend" and "I am Pam's sister." This does not mean that one gender showed more interdependence than the other. Social bonds were of importance to both men and women, but they were expressed differently. When stressed, women tended to turn more to their close relationships, men to their social groups. Many studies confirm these findings (Gardner and Gabriel, 2004). "Belonging is an essential component of the human experience" (p. 186).

When men and women from 12 countries were asked to describe themselves in terms of masculinity or femininity, "men in all countries described themselves as more masculine than women." But when asked to describe their ideal self, both men and women "wished to be 'more masculine' than they thought they were." This recent cross-cultural study also found greater similarity between the self-concepts of men and women in more developed countries and where women had worked outside their homes and had attended college (Best and Thomas, 2004, p. 303).

In general, many scholars now believe that we can best view the ways in which men and women are similar and different as a continuum, not a dichotomy (Beall, Eagly, and Sternberg, 2004, p. 4).

Self-Esteem

One of the chief measures of self-concept is **self-esteem,** *your feelings of self-worth.* Your self-esteem might be linked with your physical appearance, intelligence, work, any number of qualities, traits, and affiliations, but self-esteem may be entirely subjective. The research on self-esteem is becoming increasingly complex (Seligman, 2011).

Martin Seligman at the University of Pennsylvania has devoted his entire career to the study of what makes people happy. In his book entitled *Flourish,* he examines the factors (including self-esteem) that lead to a long-term feeling of happiness and well-being. He teaches the ABC model for dealing with life's difficulties.

A stands for the adversity that you may experience. For example, you get a grade on an assignment that is lower than you wanted.

B stands for your beliefs about that event. For example, this grade means you are not smart or that you are a "loser." A better alternative is to believe that if you tried harder, or found a better way to study, or started studying earlier, you could probably do better next time.

C stands for the emotional consequences of your beliefs. If you believe you are a loser, you are more likely to give up (which becomes self-defeating). On the other hand, if you believe that you probably didn't do your very best, you are more likely to do better the next time (Seligman, 2011, pp. 167–170).

This approach has proven to have a significant impact on people's performance and on their subsequent self-esteem.

Some theorists believe that at times we try to protect our self-esteem in areas where social comparisons are made—for example, if you don't do as well as your brother or sister who excels in academic work, you may find friends whose grades are not as high. There is, they suggest, a *frog pond effect*. According to this theory,

> being a "big frog in a small pond," or a success in a relatively unsuccessful group, is preferred over situations in which the performance of an individual's group may outshine the individual's own successes. (Gardner and Gabriel, 2004, p. 183)

Other research indicates that mind-set (of which self-esteem is a part) is not only a predictor of success, but is also what employers want most when they are looking to hire (Reed and Stoltz, 2011). Ironically, there may be no direct relationship between your actual traits, achievement, or competence and your feelings of self-worth (Sternberg and Kolligian, 1990). For example, a study of 1,000 women who achieved considerable success in their careers finds that many described themselves as "shy," "sensitive," and "self-critical" (Rimm, 1999, p. 8). Other research on exceptionally bright students shows that academic excellence does not necessarily make for high self-esteem. Similarly, Shawn Achor (2010), who is a Harvard professor, found that many Harvard students were so used to being at the top of their high school class that they became quite distressed and even depressed once they got to college. It is a statistical reality that in every college and university, and in every organization, half of the people there will be below average. So, even very highly accomplished people may feel low self-esteem because of this reality.

Feedback

Feedback often has a direct effect on level of self-esteem. When people are asked to predict their own performance on a test—whether it be of social, intellectual, or physical competence—and are later given feedback on how well they scored, they revise their predictions for the next experimental task in the direction of that feedback. This is true regardless of whether the feedback is accurate.

Numerous studies of speech communication feedback suggest that this commonsense hunch is correct: When you get positive feedback, you gain in self-confidence. Negative feedback can make you flustered and cause disruptions in your delivery, whether this is indicated by the loudness of your voice, rate of speech fluency, nervousness, stage fright, eye contact, or body movement.

Research on how we *perceive* our own abilities supports the view that our relationships with others make up the foundation out of which we develop a sense of self and competence. Some researchers believe that earlier theories about self-concept are still useful as a base for further studies on how the self develops in social contexts (Hinde et al., 2001).

There seem to be some gender differences with respect to feedback. Because women tend to give more importance to how others evaluate them, research has found, "women were more likely to consider . . . feedback accurate and to take it seriously (unrelated to any differences in self-confidence)—in other words, feedback

We take for granted our sense of self. If you have been raised in a Western culture, you probably tend to see yourself as independent of others—you make choices, decide for yourself, and feel relatively autonomous. Yet theorists are finding that there may be great cultural variation in self-concept—that is, in how the self is conceived. Western culture tends to promote *an independent self* that values self-direction, personal self-esteem and achievement, and freedom in relationships. Other cultures, including those from East Asia, seem to promote *an interdependent self* that places highest value on connection, collective self-esteem, group achievements, and being part of the in-group (Ting-Toomey, 1999, p. 29).

Thus Japanese students are more responsive to situations and self-criticism than students from the United States are (Kanagawa et al., 2001). For example, to someone Japanese describing yourself as kind or attractive might not be appropriate because that judgment should be made by the person you are with (p. 101). While American culture encourages developing "an independent view of the self—to be unique, to express the self, and to realize [your] own thoughts, feelings, and capacities," Kanagawa finds the Japanese emphasize their similarity to others and how they fit into different social situations (p. 99).

Like Japanese culture, Chinese culture seems to foster an interdependent self. The emphasis in Confucianism is on relatedness to others—often in a hierarchical relationship. In Chinese, for example, there is no word for brother. Instead, there is one word for older brother and a different word for younger brother.

"For the Chinese," writes Stella Ting-Toomey, "the 'self' is both a center of relationships and a dynamic process of development within a network of relationships. In Chinese culture, to be aware of one's relations with others is an integral part of *zuo ren,* or 'conducting oneself properly' in getting along with others. . . . Chinese can never separate themselves from obligations to others and Chinese sense of self-worth is closely tied with kinship and social networks" (Ting-Toomey, 1999, p. 78).

What has shaped your own self-concept? Do you think of yourself as more independent or more connected with others?

---

had more information value for women than for men" (Deaux and LaFrance, 1998, p. 810). For example, the effect of negative stereotyping by employers would seem to influence a woman's evaluation of herself more than it would a man's self-evaluation.

Self-Fulfilling Prophecies

For artists, writers, and scientists, early rejection has usually been "the rule rather than the exception"—the careers of architect Frank Lloyd Wright, dancer Martha Graham, sculptor Louise Nevelson, and novelist James Joyce offer just a few examples. After studying people who have a sense of their own competence, two psychologists observe:

> The power of efficacy [competence] beliefs to affect the life paths of men and
> women . . . is clearly revealed in studies of career and choice development. . . .

Those who have a strong sense of personal efficacy consider a wide range of career options, show greater interest in them, prepare themselves better for different careers, and have greater staying power in their chosen pursuits. (Bussey and Bandura, 2004, p. 100)

Our expectations also have an influence on our impressions of other people. People who expect to be accepted by others and who perceive others as friendly are often outgoing and congenial; and their behavior accounts in good measure for their popularity and the positive way in which others respond. On the other hand, people who expect to be rejected often are (Adelmann, 1988). Perceiving others as hostile or unfriendly, they often act defensive or superior; this behavior may very well set in motion the rejection they fear. And a person who thinks his relationship with someone is casual rather than exclusive may therefore spend little time with the other person so that indeed the relationship never deepens (Honeycutt and Cantrill, 2001, p. 166).

According to a study by the University of Toronto, researchers suggest that expecting to be treated with prejudice may also be part of a self-fulfilling prophecy. The study used a series of computer-animated male and female faces with expressions ranging from rejection to acceptance. The participants had to distinguish the point at which the expressions changed within the series. The female participants who told the researchers that men stereotyped them and/or treated them with prejudice saw rejection and contempt on the animated men's faces more readily and for a longer period of time than they did on the women's faces. This study suggests that the participants' sensitivity to being **stereotyped** distorted their perception of reality (Joshi, 2008). More recent research cited by Eagleman (2011) confirms this self-fulfilling prophecy. In many cases, prejudice is perceived even when it is not there. Because of their psychological set, these people help to confirm their own expectations so that a favorable self-concept may lead to success, an unfavorable self-concept to failure. This phenomenon is called a **self-fulfilling prophecy**.

A Greek myth tells the story of Pygmalion, a young sculptor who created an exquisite ivory statue of a beautiful woman and fell in love with it. Pygmalion prayed to Aphrodite, the goddess of love, that the statue might come to life, and the ivory figure became flesh and moved on her pedestal. Pygmalion named her Galatea, and the two were married in the presence of Aphrodite.

In a much-discussed experiment, Rosenthal and others studied what came to be known as the *Pygmalion effect, a self-fulfilling prophecy in which "one person's expectation for another person's behavior can quite unwittingly become a more accurate prediction for its having been made"* (Rosenthal and Jacobson, 1992, p. vii, emphasis added). Essentially, Rosenthal's study found that when, at the beginning of the school year, elementary school teachers were given information that led them to believe certain pupils ranked higher than others in intellectual competence (supposedly measured by IQ tests), those "special" children showed dramatic intellectual growth and ranked far above the "ordinary" children. A striking example of self-fulfilling prophecy, the Pygmalion effect has been observed in educational, medical, and many other contexts.

More recent research finds that the inaccurate beliefs of mothers about the alcohol use of their children had distinct effects on their children's later use of alcohol. Over time unfavorable beliefs of mothers were shown to have a cumulative negative effect, increasing alcohol use by children who were "consistently exposed to unfavorable versus favorable beliefs year after year" and contributing to a self-fulfilling prophecy (Madon et al., 2006, p. 911). Another recent study finds that in close relationships romantic partners who view things in an optimistic light (expecting positive outcomes) tended to be more satisfied in their relationships (Srivastava et al., 2006)—another instance of the long-lasting effects of self-fulfilling prophecy.

Looking at Others

In many situations, we find ourselves making several judgments about others—and all at once. For example, you go to a party and meet several new people. You immediately tend to like some and dislike others based strictly on first impressions.

Most of us form impressions of others quite easily; yet we find it difficult to explain the process. In fact, many feel that they make their judgments intuitively.

In one study of how people form impressions of others in cyberspace, Jacobson (1999) looked at online expectations and offline experiences in text-based virtual communities called MOOs. One woman explained how she perceived the difference:

> On MOO everything can seem larger than life—it can be quite a surprise to realize the people are ordinary. People here can seem more witty and amusing and clever and sexy than the people one knows irl [in real life]. People project a persona here sometimes, and when you meet them they are shyer or whatever. A friend of mine said he was disappointed when he first started meeting people from the MOO. He had the impression they were demi-gods. (p. 12)

"Impression" is a word we use about our personal judgments. We speak of being "under the impression," or of someone making a "lasting impression," a "false impression," or a "good impression." We know that our initial impressions also influence election outcomes. For example, a study of the 2000, 2002, and 2004 congressional elections (Todorov et al., 2005) finds that inferences about the competence of various candidates that were based exclusively on their facial appearance successfully predicted the election outcomes. These inferences were made with only a one-second exposure to candidates' faces. And it turns out that competence was the trait that subjects considered most important for all candidates.

Our legal system certainly reflects the degree to which we rely on snap judgments. Before a trial begins, prospective jurors are screened by the defense and the prosecution. In addition to raising specific objections to certain candidates for the jury, both the defense and the prosecuting attorneys are allowed to reject a certain number of would-be jurors without stating their reasons. Attorneys often make their decisions rapidly, though they are complex ones and are probably based on several considerations. They will probably take into account their perception of the potential juror and the client and the impression they feel that the client will make upon that juror. And, of course, the attorney for one side might be more than willing to accept a juror whom opposing counsel finds objectionable.

Attorneys usually seem to be rather skilled perceivers, accustomed to formulating judgments about others very quickly. But think of the members of the jury. They will be meeting and evaluating many people for the first time and presumably doing this entirely on their own. In a short time each juror will probably have formed an impression of most if not all of those involved in the case—including the witnesses, the defense attorney, the prosecuting attorney, and even the judge.

Research on person perception in legal settings confirms that a juror's perception of an attorney's credibility and of the defendant's guilt will be influenced not only by the attorney's opening statements but by various nonverbal cues in delivering those statements. According to a recent article on msnbc.com, people who wear square-patterned clothing are perceived to be more masculine. And people who wear oval patterns or softer shapes such as paisley are perceived to be more feminine (Hopkins, 2008). We also know that a juror's early impressions of a defendant can be influenced by the defendant's race. Now some studies (Sargent and Bradfield, 2004) suggest that in subtle ways a defendant's race can affect how jurors process the information within the defendant's testimony. Much more research is needed on this subject.

Because a juror's final judgment about the person on trial can have dramatic consequences, it is important to consider how he or she forms initial impressions and whether those impressions will have any effect on later perceptions. Our own evaluations of people also have important if less dramatic consequences, so we might all benefit from looking more closely at how an impression of another person is formed.

The First Impression

One of the major uses of evaluating personality is to explain and predict behavior on the basis of very limited information. How do we put this information together and come up with a first impression? Actually, each of us seems to hold a **private theory of personality** (sometimes known as "implicit personality theory"). Essentially, the term refers to *how we select and organize information about other people on the basis of what behaviors we think go together.*

Suppose you are given the following list of words describing a man you have never met and are then asked to write a personality sketch of him:

energetic	ironical
assured	inquisitive
talkative	persuasive
cold	

In a classic experiment, Solomon Asch (1946) used this list to learn more about how impressions of others are formed. He read the list to a group of students and asked them to write a full impression of the person described by these adjectives. There were two important findings.

Unity   Asch's first finding was unity. All the students were able to organize the scanty information they received and create a consistent, unified impression, though there was a great deal of variation in their personality sketches, and they all went beyond the terms of the original description. Here is a sample:

> Possibly he does not have any deep feeling. He would tend to be an opportunist. Likely to succeed in things he intends to do. He has perhaps married a wife who would help him in his purpose. He tends to be skeptical. (Asch, 1946, p. 261)

Central Traits   Second, Asch found that certain traits are more *central,* more influential than others in forming impressions of personality. When one of the adjectives on the list was replaced by its opposite, the personality descriptions were radically different. Whether a person is warm or cold was more important than whether he is blunt or polite.

For a long time, theorists believed that impressions of others were interpreted on the basis of the *halo effect,* the tendency to extend a favorable or unfavorable impression of one trait to other traits. Thus, you might think of Kate as honest and polite, just because you consider her intelligent. The opposite of the halo effect is the "horns effect." For example, if you feel Justin is cheap, you might attribute several other undesirable traits to him. This explanation sounds reasonable, but we now know that the halo effect is too simple a concept to account completely for the way we interpret our perceptions.

Indirectly, experiments tell us that certain traits carry weight and are clearly more decisive in our judgments than others. Somehow we manage to make all the information we have about a person—all those distinct verbal and nonverbal cues—fit together (Asch and Zukier, 1984; Bruner, 1986). If they don't seem consistent, we build in an explanation.

People seem more reliable, more knowable, when we can predict some aspects of their behavior. Perhaps that explains our need to perceive another human being as a "personality"—to see that personality quickly; to see it vividly, with certain dominant or central traits; and, most important, to see it as a unity.

The Primacy Effect

Time is one of the most significant variables in our communication model. Thus, it seems natural to ask what effect the first impression you form will have on your later perceptions of another person. Ideally, as you learn more about someone, you continually revise or refine your impressions in the light of new information. But is this in fact so? Does a first impression enhance or interfere with later knowledge, or does it have no effect at all?

Earlier research on attraction found that first impressions tend to have long-term consequences. People in long-term romantic relationships often make judgments soon after getting acquainted and feel that their impressions are confirmed during

Simon Baron-Cohen, professor of psychology and psychiatry at Cambridge University and head of its Autism Research Centre, proposes a controversial theory about an essential difference between the male and the female brain. On the basis of research, he theorizes that the male brain is "predominantly hardwired for understanding and building systems," whereas the female brain is "predominantly hardwired for empathy" (2003, p. 1).

He is not saying that males, because of their capacity for systemizing, are more intelligent. Nor that all women are more empathic than men. There are many exceptions. Not only that: These qualities—empathizing and systemizing—are present in both sexes and differ among individuals. There are women in whom systemizing rather than empathic abilities will be dominant, men in whom empathic abilities will be dominant. In effect, what he is describing are two predominant qualities of the human brain.

Whether or not his theory proves valid, his characterization of empathy is of great interest to those who study person perception. Empathy, he maintains, has two components: "understanding the other's feelings and the ability to take their perspective" is a cognitive ability; being able to make "appropriate emotional response[s] to another person's emotional state" is an ability involving feelings (p. 26).

Empathy is fundamental to communication—an ongoing process that ensures genuine exchange between people and involves an awareness of how the other is thinking and feeling, sensitivity to subtle changes in the other person's mood, as well as an ability to respond spontaneously and adapt conversation when needed. Hence, says Baron-Cohen, it is "a defining feature of human relationships" (p. 23).

Imagine yourself being asked whether you strongly agree, slightly agree, slightly disagree, or strongly disagree with statements such as the following:

"I am quick to spot when someone in a group is feeling awkward or uncomfortable."

"If I see a stranger in a group, I think that it is up to them to make an effort to join in."

"Friends usually talk to me about their problems as they say that I am very understanding."

"If anyone asked me if I liked their haircut, I would reply truthfully, even if I didn't like it." (pp. 201–207)

Because the measurement of empathy is central to his work on autism—a condition characterized by a deficiency in this dimension—Baron-Cohen has developed a test that measures a person's empathic abilities. The questions above and many others, 60 in all, are from that test. How would you rate your own empathic abilities? To determine your Empathy Quotient or EQ, see the complete test in Baron-Cohen (2003, pp. 201–207).

the first few weeks. A newer study strongly supports these findings that first impressions can be "strong and lasting" and that we may know something about how a relationship will develop as early as within the first few weeks or even days of meeting the other person (Sunnafrank and Ramirez, 2004, p. 377).

Among early studies of impression formation, those of Luchins have been very influential. In one of Luchins's experiments, subjects read two paragraphs describing a young man named Jim. One paragraph described actions of Jim that were pre-dominantly introverted; the other described actions that were predominantly ex-troverted. All subjects read the same paragraphs; only their order varied. Luchins found that a **primacy effect** did exist—that *the first information we receive about a person is the most decisive in forming our impression* (Luchins, 1957). So first meetings—especially the very first minutes of those meetings—are important.

Primacy has a clear-cut effect on communication. If you look once more at the model in Figure 1.1 (page 9), you can see that each communicator should be receiving input and feedback. The primacy effect blocks both. It is, in our terms, a source of technical interference, and this time the interference is within the communicator. If Sandra, after spending five minutes with her roommate's brother Bill, is sure that he is overbearing and phony, she is not going to be very interested in getting any feedback about her impression of him. Most of you have been in Bill's place at least once. It's as though you suddenly had become invisible. No matter what you said or did, the other person no longer seemed to respond; you couldn't change that first impression of you.

We all know how often first impressions can be mistaken ones, and we also know how often decisions depend on first impressions. Imagine that you are being interviewed for your first job after graduation. You look very nervous and were ten minutes late for the interview. Then you make an obvious grammatical mistake in speaking. What is likely to be the outcome?

It's disturbing to think that first impressions can have such dramatic effects on judgment. But Luchins found that if people were warned not to make snap judg-ments, the primacy effect was reversed or eliminated completely. Several other stud-ies confirm that the primacy effect is not inevitable (Fletcher et al., 2004).

Physical Attractiveness

In some ideal world we will all be beautiful. Until that time, however, it seems likely that those of us who are physically attractive will have a slight edge—at least initially—on those of us who are not (Maner et al., 2003). Among scholars there is general agreement: Physically attractive people are considered by others to be more sociable, more popular, more sexual, more successful, and more persuasive. Frequently they are thought to be happier and to have more appealing personalities (Berscheid and Reis, 1998). Two scholars sum up research findings on the social benefits of physical attractiveness over the lifespan:

"In infancy, more attractive babies are preferred by their own parents."

"More attractive people are more likely to marry and, among those who do marry, those who are more attractive marry sooner . . . ."

"More attractive adults also have more occupational success."

"Physically attractive defendants are less likely to be convicted and, if convicted, they receive more lenient sentences than those convicted of equally serious crimes." (Adapted from Zebrowitz and Rhodes, 2002, pp. 61–62)

Additionally, tall men make more money. It is estimated that each inch of height (presumably above the average) corresponds to $6,000 of annual salary in America (Brooks, 2011).

Classic research on facial attractiveness shows that even infants as young as two to three months old prefer attractive faces. People of many cultures seem to agree on which faces are perceived as attractive, which also suggests that this response may be universal (Zebrowitz and Rhodes, 2002, p. 263). But two important research questions remain: How much do individual cultures value attractiveness? And how does a person's behavior modify our perception of his or her attractiveness? (Dion, 2002).

Standards of beauty may be universal. It turns out that standards of female beauty are quite similar around the world. Eagleman (2011) reports on a study conducted in 37 countries which found that men prefer women with a waist to hip ratio of between .67 and .80. As it turns out, the average *Playboy* centerfold, not coincidentally, has a .7 ratio, although the average weight has been steadily dropping since 1953. Women in this range are also judged to be more healthy and intelligent (Eagleman, 2011, p. 91).

We take many of our images of beauty from the mass media, yet consider the following statistics:

- The average American woman is 5′ 4″ tall and weighs 140 pounds.
- 80 percent of American women are dissatisfied with their appearance.
- The average American model is 5′ 11″ tall and weighs 117 pounds.
- Most fashion models are thinner than 98 percent of American women. *(www.edap.org)*

Many studies of body images that appear in women's magazines confirm what most of us already know: Ads do not represent a diversity of body types. Instead they promote the stereotype of a "thin ideal," which has become a social and cultural norm associated not only with beauty but also with success (Gustafson et al., 2001).

Aside from liking physically attractive people because they are good to look at, we sometimes like them because we feel that by being seen with them, we will enhance our own image. The college man who consistently dates beautiful women is very likely to improve his own image among both his male friends and his prospective female acquaintances. The woman who dates handsome men is also increasing her own self-esteem. One article described arrangements in which a man or woman seeks "arm candy," a good-looking escort for an evening out—someone who will make others envious.

Attractiveness may also be linked with perceptions of power and status. A recent study of how physical and vocal attractiveness affects our perception of political candidates had subjects rate hypothetical candidates for competency, trustworthiness, qualification (competence), and leadership ability (Surawski and Ossoff, 2006). Researchers found a stronger halo effect for political candidates who were physically attractive than for candidates whose voices were attractive. When candidates were physically attractive but had an unattractive voice, they received lower ratings. We will discuss both physical and vocal attractiveness in more detail in Chapter 4 on nonverbal communication.

In academic life, physical attractiveness can affect student evaluations of teaching. When college students were asked to evaluate their college professors, those professors perceived as attractive were given more favorable evaluations (Riniolo et al., 2006). This was not an isolated finding. Evaluations for both female and male professors were higher for those perceived as attractive, but other studies report that physical attractiveness in male professors has a greater influence.

Despite the association of beauty with talent, however, career success for women is not furthered by their good looks. Studies point to a bias against good-looking women in managerial and executive positions (Zebrowitz, 1997). Attractive women who run for public office, unlike their male counterparts, also seem to be at a disadvantage. The so-called beauty backlash applies only to women. Both Sarah Palin and Michele Bachmann are generally perceived as attractive, yet have been savaged by the media. Both have been featured on the cover of *Newsweek* magazine in controversial photos that appear to diminish or ridicule them. The August 10, 2011, *Newsweek* cover photo of Michele Bachmann labels her as "The Queen of Rage." Both liberals and conservatives complained about this blatant attack (Lombarde, 2011).

The influence of physical beauty seems to be most powerful early in a relationship; as we acquire more and more information about a person, the effects of physical appearance diminish considerably.

Expressiveness and Charisma

Today there is a growing body of research about expressiveness and charisma. According to recent findings, **expressiveness,** *a dimension of nonverbal communication that influences our first impressions, has been linked with animation, dynamism, expansiveness, and intensity of both nonverbal and verbal behaviors* (DePaulo and Friedman, 1998; Guerrero and Floyd, 2006). On the basis of their work, Boone and Buck (2003) confirm that the influence of emotional expressiveness—their research was on nonverbal expressiveness—on a first impression is immediate and that often we believe emotionally expressive people are more trustworthy. In addition, this often functions as a signal for cooperative behavior. Expressive people are also thought to be higher in self-esteem as well as more extroverted and less inhibited (pp. 171–177).

Charisma has been defined as *"personal magnetism that enables an individual to attract and influence people"* (*Random House Webster's*, 2000) and as *a divinely conferred power or talent* (*Shorter OED*, 2002). The origin of the word itself is Greek and means "divine gift." Sometimes charisma is associated with what is "attractive and influential"—notice the word "influential." It implies the power to move people. Actors are sometimes referred to as having charisma. Many religious and political leaders have also been considered charismatic. One fascinating study analyzed the facial features of three charismatic presidents: Kennedy, Reagan, and Clinton (Keating, 2002).

We can say that while charisma and expressiveness may sometimes be linked, charisma is a more rare and elusive quality. Who would you describe as charismatic?

Social Roles

Among the several social roles that influence how we perceive others and are ourselves perceived by others are work roles, student roles, sex-linked roles, and marital roles.

Work Roles

A classic example of how our work roles may alter perception is Zimbardo's so-called prison experiment (1971) in which students randomly assigned to be "guards" and others designated "prisoners" quickly came to see and respond to each other in stereotypical guard-prisoner fashion: The guards became cruel and unjust, the prisoners rebellious. Although planned to last for two weeks, the experiment was stopped after only six days. Students no longer thought like students, but like guards and prisoners. They truly lived their parts.

Later research on Hispanics and whites (Jones, 1991) supports the view that perceived differences in social status (as defined by work roles) influence ethnic stereotypes and that "occupational status . . . is often used to make rather confident judgments of personal attributes." According to this study, "occupational title appears to be a more central trait than ethnicity in determining American students' perceptions of people" (p. 475).

Student Roles

As for student roles, research on perceptions in the classroom finds that teachers perceive the model student as a communicator—"well-behaved, patient, controlled, and polite. He or she waits before speaking, listens intently and politely, sits quietly while others talk, and contributes clear and germane comments" (Trenholm and Rose, 1981, p. 24). Teachers describe the model student as one who willingly does all assignments, "never criticizes the teacher or gives way to frustration, and accepts and even welcomes criticism" (p. 24). According to these findings, compliance rather than inquiring behavior would be rewarded. What a contrast with the way most students feel about unquestioning compliance.

Another aspect of student–teacher roles is the perception of power in the classroom. Although teachers and students generally agree on power bases, some important differences exist. Both groups see most power as stemming from the teacher's ability to give rewards (e.g., high grades, approval), ability to make the student identify with the teacher, and perceived expertise. Again students, as you might expect, have a less positive view of the teacher's use of power (McCroskey and Richmond, 1983).

Gender-Linked Roles

That gender-linked roles also influence perceptions is confirmed by many research summaries. The consensus is that women are perceived as more supportive than men, laughing more often, intruding less on others, and being more deferential. Men, on the other hand, are considered more dominant and more achievement- and task-oriented. These descriptions reflect the more stereotypical views that women place a higher value on establishing and maintaining relationships while men tend to perceive the world more as a place to "win" or "achieve" (Rosenthal and DePaulo, 1979; LaFrance and Mayo, 1979; Pearson et al., 1995).

Some argue that a person whose self-concept is highly sex-typed may strive to behave consistently with various internalized standards for that role and to suppress behavior seen as inappropriate. They cite Bem's suggestion "that an androgynous self-concept might allow individuals to engage freely in both masculine and feminine behaviors and allow greater human potentiation" (Veenendall and Braito, 1987, p. 32).

Marital Roles

Perceptions of marital roles have undergone considerable change in the last decades, particularly with the great number of married women who have joined the workforce (Cherlin, 1998). A study attempting to predict marital and career success among dual-working couples (Hiller and Philliber, 1982) identifies four major marital types: These are based on how the husband and wife perceive themselves.

In a *traditional marriage relationship,* the husband sees himself as masculine and the wife sees herself as feminine. For example, although both work outside the home, the husband is perceived as bringing home the proverbial bacon whereas the wife has sole responsibility for all the housework. Housework is her province, and he won't help with any of it.

In a *reluctant wife marriage relationship,* the wife views herself as feminine and her husband sees himself as androgynous (having both masculine and feminine characteristics). If the wife in this relationship does not perceive herself as furnishing most of the emotional support, she may perceive her husband as "too feminine." And if her husband helps with the housework, sharing these tasks because she is so busy as a result of her successful career, she may feel guilty—both because she neglects "her duties" at home and because her professional skills seem "unfeminine."

On the other hand, in a *reluctant husband marriage relationship,* the husband sees himself as masculine and his wife sees herself as androgynous: He may feel threatened by her broad range of activities if he defines her role more narrowly. Suppose, for example, that she wants to split all the housework whereas he believes that if she hasn't the time for all the domestic concerns, she should spend less time at the office.

In the *androgynous marriage relationship,* the fourth type, both spouses see themselves as androgynous: Both engage in so-called masculine and feminine behaviors, making adaptation easier. He may even do most of the cooking; she may do most of the cleaning and laundry. Problems may still arise based on social expectations of appropriate or "proper" husband/wife roles.

It might be interesting to try classifying the marriages of those you know—relatives, friends, neighbors—and see whether you can discover any pattern related to age, work, and psychological makeup of the spouses involved. Or ask yourself which type of marriage you have or expect to have. (For a further discussion of marital roles, see Chapter 9.)

We've looked at several factors influencing our impressions of others. In addition to their physical attractiveness, expressiveness, and social roles, our own self-perceptions, our notions of personality, and the stereotypes we hold and our own generalizations also come into play. So we turn in the final section of this chapter to questions concerning the accuracy of these impressions.

SOME VARIABLES INVOLVED IN ACCURATE PERCEPTION

Granted the selective quality of human perception, we must ask what are the other variables that will affect the accuracy of our perceptions. Early studies suggest that at least three generalizations can be made:

1. Some people are easier to judge than others—perhaps because they are more open about themselves.
2. Certain traits are easier to judge than others—e.g., it is much easier to identify people who are not shy than it is to pick out people who consider themselves shy (Zimbardo, 1990).
3. People are better at judging those who resemble themselves.

The desire to improve one's accuracy in judging others seems to be virtually universal. Following are several of the important variables that researchers have examined.

Context   Some communication scholars believe that the ability to judge other people may be quite specific to context. For example, students were asked to view a person bargaining, first in a very cooperative situation and later in a very competitive one. Group influence was so strong that when their perception of the bargainer did not correspond to the perceptions of other group members, subjects denied what they had seen with their own eyes. In fact, they came to believe the opposite of what they had seen. Majority or group opinion is just one instance in which context—the third element of perception—exerts its subtle influence.

Interpersonal Sensitivity   Research on accurate person perception increasingly refers to the concept of **interpersonal sensitivity**, sometimes defined as *"success in decoding nonverbal communication"* or *"the accurate recall of another person's nonverbal behavior"* (Noller, 2006, p. 404; Hall et al., 2006, p. 141; italics added).

A good deal of recent research confirms that women are more accurate than men in their recall and decoding of nonverbal cues. For example, at least nine studies show that women have an advantage over men in recalling the physical appearance of others (Mast and Hall, 2006). And in judging the meaning of nonverbal cues, women have higher accuracy than men when it comes to personality traits, intelligence, facial expressions, and vocal expressions of emotion; on the other hand, women are no more accurate than men when it comes to judging cues for deception or dominance (Hall, 2006). We will look at findings on gender differences again and some possible explanations in Chapter 4.

Perceiver Self-Confidence

For a long time, psychologists have tried to establish whether some people are indeed better judges than others. Certainly, we all know people who feel their perceptions to be extremely accurate. But is there a relationship between self-confidence and accuracy? Does self-confidence about our ability to judge others make a difference in how we see them?

In terms of our communication model, we might say that a person who forms impressions of others solely on the basis of personal expectations avoids the task of person perception. Researchers have found no correlation between confidence in our perceptions of others and the accuracy of those perceptions.

Other Perceiver Traits

Despite the fact that accurate person perception varies from one situation to another, theorists generally agree that certain characteristics are associated with sound perceptions of others.

First, *intelligence* is a prime factor. Second, *the ability to draw inferences about people from their behavior* seems related to accurate perception. Third, people who score low on tests of authoritarianism tend to be better judges of others. They are *less rigid* in their *expectations*, judging more from what they know about the person and assuming less that he or she is like themselves. And fourth, those with *a high degree of objectivity* about themselves tend to have insight into the behavior of others. Openness and awareness of our own shortcomings seem to play a part in this process.

In "The Good Judge Revisited," a study of the accuracy of personality judgments, Christiansen and others examined a range of individual differences in judgment that they argue can be explained by "a combination of cognitive and personality factors" (2005, p. 144). They studied accuracy in employment interviews and found the best predictor of accuracy was "dispositional intelligence (knowledge of how personality is related to behavior)" (p. 123):

> More accurate judges are higher in cognitive ability and openness to experience, which appears to affect accuracy by way of general knowledge of how personality relates to behavior. Overall, judgments of people known fairly well will be most accurate when this knowledge is possessed by individuals who are more conscientious and more agreeable. (p. 144)

The importance of openness has been confirmed in a number of other communication contexts.

A survey of *empathic accuracy and inference*, how good we are at reading the thoughts and feelings of other people, finds that intelligence, cognitive complexity, positive adjustment, and interpersonal trust as well as social sensitivity—in combination—all play a part (Davis and Kraus, 1997, p. 163). And though women are generally regarded as being more intuitive and more empathic, Graham and Ickes say that although the stereotype of "women's intuition" might have a "proverbial kernel of truth, gender differences in empathic skills and dispositions appear to be small rather than large and specific rather than general in their scope" (1997, pp. 139–140). For more on empathy, see page 50.

How can this information be applied to improving our effectiveness as communicators? We certainly cannot improve our intelligence directly—and the ability to draw valid inferences about people from their behavior probably depends in part on intelligence. Nor can we simply tell ourselves to be less rigid or authoritarian. Research demonstrates that attitudes are rarely changed so easily. One thing we can do is become conscious of, and less defensive about, our own limitations. And the more sensitive we become to cues outside ourselves, the more we listen instead of projecting our own feelings onto others, the more accurate we are likely to be in our evaluations of others.

IMPROVING PERCEPTION AND COMMUNICATION

Failures in communication frequently occur because people have inaccurate perceptions of each other. If a man is told that a woman he knows only casually is snobbish and standoffish, he is not very likely to ask her out. If you feel that a particular instructor is stubborn and somewhat hostile, you probably won't consider questioning her about your low grade on the last exam. But how do you know you are right? In many ways, your perceptions of others can determine not only the kind of communication that takes place but whether you attempt to communicate at all.

It would seem then an easy matter to facilitate communication by simply improving the accuracy of our perceptions. Yet the three elements of perception—perceiver, object, and context—are so interwoven that one cannot be analyzed apart from the others. One of the most important things the perceiver can do is take into account the need to make perceptual adjustments as any of these three components varies.

Among the primary elements in accurate person perception is an awareness that your own perceptions may be inaccurate. Improved perception and communication can occur only if you are willing to acknowledge that your perceptions are subjective.

Another requirement is empathy. **Empathy** involves *experiencing the other's perception—that is, seeing and feeling things as the other does.* We've already seen in the research on behavior attribution how people tend to view their own behavior as response to a given situation and to interpret the same behavior in another person as an expression of stable traits or needs. For example, you lose your temper and explain you've had a hectic and frustrating day, but when one of your co-workers loses his temper, you say he has "a short fuse."

Ideally, we work toward developing the kind of sensitivity or responsiveness to others that actually extends perception. Many scholars believe empathy is the key to effective listening and therefore to communication. In Chapter 5, the role of empathy in listening and in resolving conflicts should become clear: Perceiving something the way the other person perceives it—taking the other's perspective—provides insights and paves the way for effective relationships.

It would be utopian to say that more accurate person perception always makes for more effective communication. Nevertheless, communication in both long-term and short-term relationships is often enhanced when the participants perceive each other accurately. The same principles apply to marital and dating relationships and to many less intense interpersonal encounters including job interviews.

We have tried to suggest that interpersonal sensitivity is important to both long- and short-term encounters. In the chapters that follow, we shall also see that although early impressions depend to a great extent on the perceiver's preconceptions and stereotypes and on the other person's physical appearance, as contact with a person continues, the content of his or her messages (both verbal and nonverbal) plays a greater role in modifying our perceptions of that person.

Summary

In this chapter, we looked at person perception as an active process in which communicators selectively perceive, organize, and interpret what they experience. We began by considering the physiological and psychological filters that affect all our perceptions. After suggesting some parallels between object and person perception, we looked first at how we form our perceptions about ourselves. Thus, we examined some of the many variables that influence self-concept including gender and self-esteem and looked at recent research findings about shyness and trait attribution. We then focused on how our impressions of other human beings are formed. We spoke of how we tend to view our own behaviors as opposed to those of others. We discussed trait centrality and associations of traits, primacy, empathy, and the effects of physical attractiveness, expressiveness, and charisma. Personal generalizations and stereotypes and the influence of work, student, gender-linked, and marital roles were also discussed.

We saw that our impressions, while formed with relative ease, are not necessarily accurate. Some characteristics of perceivers were mentioned, including interpersonal sensitivity, but judging ability itself was seen as sometimes specific to context. In concluding, we discussed inaccurate perception as a source of communication failures and how improved perception enhances communication. Empathy was seen to be one of the crucial elements in this process.

Key Terms

Charisma	Looking glass self	Psychological sets	Self-fulfilling prophecy
Empathy	Perceptual filters	Selective attention	Stereotype
Expressiveness	Primacy effect	Self-concept	
Gender	Private theory of	Self-esteem	
Interpersonal	personality		
sensitivity			

Review Questions

1. Distinguish between a perceptual filter and a psychological set.

2. Discuss two ways in which person perception is different from object perception. What are the implications of these differences for communication?

3. Discuss the formation of self-concept, including recent findings about self-concept and gender.

4. Explain recent findings about the attribution of humanness.

5. Discuss two important influences on self-esteem as well as recent research findings.

6. Describe some of the new research findings about shyness, including shyness and Internet use.

7. What is the Pygmalion effect? Discuss some of the research on it.

8. Identify the single most significant implication of behavior attribution research for the study of person perception.

9. Explain the concept of central traits and its significance for person perception.

10. What is the primacy effect? How might it influence communication?

11. Give a brief summary of the major research findings on physical attractiveness and its influence on first impressions.

12. Explain how expressiveness and charisma affect person perception.

13. How do personal generalizations and stereotypes differ?

14. List four statements about stereotypes that are supported by recent research.

15. Describe the influence of work, gender-linked, student, and marital roles on how we perceive and are ourselves perceived by others.

16. What three generalizations can you make from the research studies cited here about how various traits of the perceived affect the accuracy of person perception?

17. What is interpersonal sensitivity?

18. Discuss four perceiver characteristics associated with accurate perception of others.

19. What are two ways in which person perception and communication effectiveness can be improved?

20. Explain the concept of empathy and its significance for accurate person perception.

Exercises

1. Write a description of yourself in which you use ten adjectives. Then ask a person in your class to describe you in the same way and compare the results. You might try this again with a close friend.

2. Write down some of the perceptions you have of your classmates. Then refer to your earlier comments in the personal log on the computer that you began in Chapter 1, exercise 1. Have you changed or confirmed some of your original impressions?

3. Reread your descriptions (in Chapter 1, exercise 1) of people who really impressed you at first. Write a list of words describing each person. Then try to identify the specific verbal and nonverbal behaviors that led you to draw

up each list. Now that you know each of these people better, what additional experiences have shaped your perception of each of them?

4. Write a paragraph describing someone you think is an effective communicator. List all attributes that seem to contribute to this effectiveness. Now think of a poor communicator. What characteristics seem to cause the ineffectiveness?

5. What characteristics do you possess that affect how you perceive these two people?

6. Have the class split up into groups of five. Your instructor will give you copies of the "Preliminary Scale of Interpersonal Perceptions." Fill out these forms, giving your perceptions of each of the other members in your group.

Do not put your own name on the forms. When everyone has filled out all the forms, exchange them so that each person has a rating from every other group member. Then look at the ratings you received from the rest of the group. You might want to discuss these with others in the group to gain additional feedback.

7. Interview a person who does a lot of interviewing. Discuss communication and person perception with that person. Have the interviewer elaborate on how he or she perceives interviewees and selects cues in assessing them.

Suggested Readings

Baron-Cohen, Simon. *The Essential Difference: The Truth About the Male and Female Brain.* New York: Basic Books, 2004.

This fascinating and controversial book developed out of the author's work on autism. Can we really describe brains as predominantly male or female? What would be the advantages or disadvantages of each?

Cole, Jonathan. *About Face.* Cambridge, MA: Bradford Books, 1999.

A study of the human face, its expressiveness, and what happens to people who lose their capacity to make facial expressions. The author presents research on the importance of the face in the development of communication and emotion.

Eagleman, David. *Incognito: The Secret Lives of the Brain.* New York: Pantheon Books, 2011.

This fascinating book examines in great depth all aspects of human perception.

Gladwell, Malcolm. *Blink: The Power of Thinking Without Thinking.* New York: Back Bay Books, 2007.

An informative and entertaining book about the way people make snap judgments. Several of the leading researchers on the subject are discussed.

Goleman, Daniel. *Social Intelligence: The New Science of Human Relationships.* New York: Bantam Books, 2006.

On the basis of new findings in neuroscience and biology the author discusses the development of "social intelligence" in human beings, including a built-in bias for empathy and altruistic behavior.

Ickes, William, ed. *Empathic Accuracy.* New York and London: Guilford, 1997.

An excellent collection of essays on many aspects of empathic accuracy. See, especially, Chapter 5 on the limits of women's intuition and Chapter 6 on the relationship between personality and empathic accuracy.

Paul, Annie Murphy. *The Cult of Personality.* New York: Free Press, 2004.

The author examines the uses and misuses of personality tests not only by psychologists but by the corporate world in its hiring practices. Specialized reading on the methods and biases of personality testing, this book is controversial, intriguing, and well written.

Zebrowitz, Leslie A. *Reading Faces: Window to the Soul?* Boulder, CO: Westview Press, 1997.

A fascinating discussion of research and theory about self-fulfilling prophecies as well as responses to baby-faced people and physical attractiveness in general.

 ## For Supplementary Information

Log onto the Online Learning Center at *www.mhhe.com/tubbshc13e.*

3

The Verbal Message

Chapter Objectives

After reading this chapter, you should be able to:

1. Explain what is intended by the statement "The word is not the thing" and distinguish between denotation and connotation.
2. Differentiate between private and shared meanings and explain the concepts of overlapping codes and codeswitching.
3. Discuss two theories about how message encoding skills develop.
4. Summarize the Sapir-Whorf hypothesis and describe two ways in which language and thought are related.
5. Specify five problem areas in our use of language and give an example of each.
6. Explain how one's cultural frame of reference influences communication and give examples from two different cultures.
7. Discuss the effects of sexist language on communication, how male and female language usage differs, and several language forms perceived by others as powerful.
8. Explain the concept of metacommunication and give an example.

Have you ever noticed how much you use the word "I" in conversations, e-mail messages, texts, and so on? It turns out that this use of the personal pronoun is a predictor of your power and leadership in a group (Pennebaker, 2011). We will have more to say about that later in this chapter. According to askoxford.com (the experts at Oxford dictionaries), there are over a quarter of a million words in the English language. No one knows for sure the exact number because of the complexity of the language. It's no wonder that we have trouble finding the right words to express our feelings—there are so many words to choose from. Well, prepare for even more confusion! Merriam-Webster Inc. added more than 100 new entries to its 2008 edition of the Collegiate Dictionary. As Merriam-Webster adds new words every year, just imagine the words and phrases we'll have to choose from in another 20 years (Carlic, 2008).

In the fall of 2011, Vice President Joe Biden created a firestorm of controversy when he said that rape would increase if the Republicans in the United States Senate did not vote for President Obama's jobs bill. In another 2011 controversy, Herman Cain, Republican candidate for president, said that poor people had themselves to blame for not being ambitious enough to go out and find a job. In both cases, these two men had to back down from their statements after they realized the reaction to their words.

A few years earlier, the famous comedian Michael Richards, known as Kramer from the sitcom *Seinfeld,* had a racial rant at the Laugh Factory in Los Angeles. In response to an African American audience member's heckling, Richards started using the "n word" repeatedly and made many other racial comments. A few months earlier, actor and director Mel Gibson had a similar incident: When he was pulled over by the police, he began yelling anti-Semitic comments, saying that, "The Jews are responsible for all the wars in history" (Hamilton, 2006). In each instance, these outbursts have permanently tainted society's perception of these celebrities. In communication terms, the saying "You can't unring a bell" applies to all three events. In other words, no amount of apology can ever reverse the damage.

In the spring of 2004, the Federal Communications Commission (FCC) ruled that Bono was indecent and profane for describing one of the 2003 Golden Globe movie award winners as "f——brilliant." At about the same time, Howard Stern was slapped with three indecency fines for his radio broadcasts, two against Infinity Broadcasting and one against Clear Channel Communications. To avoid a repeat incident at the Golden Globes broadcast in 2005, NBC instituted a 10-second delay, and ABC did the same with its telecast of the Academy Awards show (Salant, 2004).

In the wake of these types of issues, eight U.S. senators and movie stars along with Rabbi Chaim Feld, head of Aish Hatorah, an international Orthodox Jewish educational organization, launched a media campaign to stop the harmful use of words in our society. Their organization is called Words Can Heal (see *www .wordscanheal.org*). Some of the spokespeople have included stars Tom Cruise and Goldie Hawn and politicians Rudolph Giuliani, John McCain, and Bob Dole. This is one of the most public pronouncements demonstrating people's awareness of the positive and negative power of words (Reuters, "Gossip," 2001, p. 5A).

As we examine verbal messages in this chapter, we will take up four major concerns. The first is the relationship between words and meaning. Thus, we will be talking about the symbolic nature of language, the descriptive and associative aspects of words (denotation and connotation), as well as private and shared meanings.

A second section takes up the complex process of formulating verbal messages and how we all learn to do this. As we examine the third issue, how language and thought are related, you will learn about a highly influential theory on the subject, the Sapir-Whorf hypothesis, and then look at several ways in which language use—abstraction, for example—affects your thinking.

In the fourth section, you will also learn about the influence of language usage on feelings and behavior. You will be looking at sexist language, gender differences in the use of language, and the linguistic forms considered most powerful or effective.

Let's turn first to a consideration of the nature of language.

WORDS AND MEANING

We saw in Chapter 1 that the communication process involves sending messages from one person's nervous system to another's with the intention of creating a meaning similar to the one in the sender's mind. The verbal message does this through words, the basic elements of language, and words, of course, are verbal symbols.

Symbols and Referents

In Chapter 1, we defined a symbol as *something used for or regarded as representing something else*. Thus, the image of a lion can serve as a symbol of courage, a red-and-white striped pole as a symbol of a barber shop. Symbols can be defined as representations of an event, action, object, person, or place. Symbols can take many forms, including words. In English, the word "sun" is the verbal symbol used to designate the star that is the central body of our solar system; the French use another symbol, "soleil"; the Turkish call it "gunes"; and the Germans call it "sonne." All four symbols represent the same star.

Consider the term "compact disk." "CD" is the name given to a round magnetic recording medium or storage device. The term is arbitrary. It was assigned to the recording device so that we could communicate about it without pointing each time we referred to it. "CD" might have been called "record" or "blank" or even "urg." So initially, no real association exists between a word we agree to call something and its referent, *the object for which it stands*. Clearly, the word is not the thing. A word is merely a verbal symbol of the object it represents. Such words as "text message," "blogosphere," "podcast," "Skype," and "webinar" are but a few of those that have entered our language as a result of the new communication technologies.

For the most part when a company changes its name it is usually to increase sales—except for when AT&T and Cingular merged in 2005. AT&T and their owners, SBC, spent over $4 million to increase brand awareness of Cingular and made it the most popular carrier among the younger generation by using *American Idol* as one of its liaisons. In spite of this successful and expensive campaign, the company elected to replace "Cingular" with "AT&T" after the merger (Hood, 2006).

Once we agree on a system of verbal symbols, we can use language to communicate. Of course, if all the words we used referred only to objects, our communication problems would be eased considerably. We could establish what referents we were speaking about with somewhat less difficulty. But words also refer to events, properties of things, actions, relationships, concepts, and so on.

The relationship between meaning and referent becomes especially clear when we encounter words in a foreign language. If we see **МИР**, the Russian word for "peace" and "world," for the first time, we have no way of determining what concepts that word represents simply by looking at the word itself. Even with new words in our own language, we have to learn what concepts they represent. Notice how we carefully avoided saying, "what the words mean." Meanings are not inherent in words. Words in and of themselves are meaningful only after we have associated them with some referents. It is human beings who assign meanings to words.

Denotation and Connotation

In discussing meaning, some students of language make the traditional distinction between "denotation" and "connotation." We have said that words are meaningful only after we have associated them with some referents. When we speak of **denotation, we refer to** *the primary associations a word has for most members of a given linguistic community.* When we speak of **connotation,** we refer to *other, secondary associations a word has for one or more members of that community.* Sometimes the connotations a word has are the same for nearly everyone; sometimes they relate solely to one individual's experience or, more often, to the experience of a particular subgroup.

The connotations of words have many uses and focus on the personal meanings that words have in our minds. For example, poets use the connotations of words in order to utilize words in a variety of symbolic ways, allowing readers to create a new referent for a word that they may never have identified before (Chandler, 2002, p. 19). However, the connotations of words are often the occasion of misunderstanding in other contexts.

Are you interested in using Barf Detergent to clean your clothes? You might be interested if you live in Iran. Barf Detergent and dozens of other unintentionally offensive products are scattered throughout the world. The product name may be acceptable in one country, but have a totally different and/or offensive meaning in another country. Barf, or "برف," means "snow" in Farsi. An apt name for a detergent.

Another example is a German-made MP3 player named for its sleek black finish, Trekstor iBeat Blaxx. The name was supposed to mimic the very popular iPod; however, due to lack of research, it wound up sounding like a violent assault on racial minorities.

These and many other examples can be found by looking at Benjamin Mako Hill/List of unintentionally offensive product names from Wikipedia, the free encyclopedia (Ruben, 2007).

Culture has a large impact on the connotation of words. For example, the word "red" in Russian, "krasnyj," is a positive term and is a root of the word for "beautiful," which is "prekransyj." In English, the word "red" has connotations such as "blood" (Ministry of Education, 1996) or "stop" as on a stop sign.

Did you know that after ten years of falling sales, the prune industry decided to officially change the name of that fruit to "dried plums"? The California Prune Board spent over $10 million to market its new brand image. The term "dried plums" tested much more positively by 90 percent of those surveyed. Similarly, kiwi fruit used to be known as Chinese gooseberries, but the name was changed for better marketing and sales (Condor, 2001, p. 5H).

In the new age of technology and the high use of the Internet, the Urban Dictionary helps us decode the new slang that is being spoken across the United States. This useful resource can be found on the Internet and in its printed form. The Urban Dictionary (2007) is a guide for pop culture (*www.urbandictionary.com*); some of its newer and most popular entries are the following:

Babysit: To pay little or no attention to your alcoholic beverage, letting it sit idle, while you pretend to nurse it.

Betty: Hot chick.

Biff: To fall hard.

Brokeback: Used to describe anything of questionable masculinity; originated from the 2005 motion picture *Brokeback Mountain.*

Five: Akin to the words "cool" and "awesome."

Gore Effect: The phenomenon that leads to unseasonably cold temperatures, driving rain, hail, or snow whenever Al Gore visits an area to discuss global warming—hence, the Gore Effect.

Hater: A person that simply cannot be happy for another person's success, so rather than be happy, they make a point of exposing a flaw in that person.

Heisman: A rejection given to a member of the opposite sex, a job, or anything no longer wanted; named after the Heisman trophy, which depicts a football player giving a stiff-arm block to a tackle.

January joiner: Someone who joins the gym in January as part of a New Year's resolution and by February is back to being a couch potato. Example: "I can't get a treadmill until February because the January joiners are all using them."

Punked: A way to describe someone ripping you off, tricking you, or teasing you. It is also known for the TV show *Punk'd.*

Did you also know that SPAM means a spiced lunch meat product made of pork shoulders and ham that is sold by Hormel Foods Corporation? To many young people spam means junk (unwanted) e-mail. Hormel Foods went to court to ensure that when you use the word in uppercase letters—SPAM—it refers to their product and when you use spam in lowercase letters it refers to junk e-mail. According to one source, "The slang meaning of 'spam' is said to have been inspired by a skit by British comedy troupe Monty Python in which a group of Vikings mutter 'spam, spam, spam,' with an ever increasing volume, drowning out normal conversation" (*www.spam.com*).

When scientists recently retracted Pluto's status as a planet, a new form of the word "pluto" emerged: as a verb. The meaning of "to pluto" is "to demote or devalue someone or something" (*www.cnn.com*). One might say, for example, that "She was plutoed like the trash." A similar noun-to-verb transformation occurred with "google," which was originally a proper noun. "Plutoed" was the American Dialect Society's 2006 Word of the Year.

Negative-Positive Connotation

Because words can elicit such powerful emotional reactions, they are often said to have negative or positive connotations for people. Today, many people prefer to be called "senior citizens" rather than "elderly." And though parents may take equal pleasure in hearing their children referred to as "brilliant" or "gifted," those with "retarded" children are sensitive to the many negative connotations of the word.

In the second decade of the twenty-first century, politicians formerly called "liberals" have begun referring to themselves as "progressives." A very large amount of money is paid to political consultants who test every word to see how it resonates with potential voters. Luntz (2011) developed a list of phrases that have tested the most positively through extensive research. They are:

1. You deserve/You have the right to …
2. Life-changing impact
3. Breakthrough
4. A forensic approach
5. Re-engineered
6. American ingenuity
7. Consumer-driven technology
8. Patent protected
9. The new normal
10. Wow (Luntz, 2011, p. 94)

Luntz's earlier book, entitled *Words That Work*, have even more great advice for speakers at every level, from high school students to presidential candidates (Luntz, 2007).

In the past it was perfectly acceptable to have very gender-specific language. For example, the mail<u>man</u> delivered mail to the house<u>wife</u> while she patiently waited for her husband to come home from his job as chair<u>man</u> of the board. Now there are so many new ways to make people and professions gender neutral. Stereotypes about people and professions are not so cut and dried. Now men can be homemakers and flight attendants, and women can be mail carriers or police officers. But the big question is, should we be teaching or introducing our young and teen learners to gender-free language? The answer is yes. In the long term this information will allow students to communicate more clearly and set the scene for those young adults who will go on to work in international business where biased words may alienate them from their peers or even find them being accused of discrimination (McGready, 2008).

In research on word connotations, subjects were exposed to various words on a screen, and their galvanic skin responses were measured. Although nonsignificant differences occurred between responses to "good" words (e.g., "beauty," "love," "kiss," and "friend") and "aversive" words (e.g., "cancer," "hate," "liar," and "death"), some words caused significant reactions in both men and women. These were called "personal" words and included the subject's first name, last name, father's first name, mother's first name, major in school, year in school, and school name. Subjects were more physiologically aroused by the personal words than by either the good or the aversive words (Crane et al., 1970). (For a discussion titled "What Makes Bad Language Bad?" see Davis, 1989.)

Girl talk is a phrase we use to describe when girls or women are talking with one another. But do men have boy talk? According to a study done using prime-time television programs, researchers found that men and women do use different language to talk to one another. They found that swearing and profanity occurred most often in man-to-man interactions followed by woman-to-man interactions. Men seemed to tone down the cursing in front of women and the women seemed to save their cursing for men (Sapolsky and Kaye, 2008).

The Semantic Differential

Some of the most influential research on the measurement of meaning has been conducted by Osgood and his associates (1957), who developed an instrument called the *Semantic Differential*. With the Semantic Differential, a researcher *can test a person's reactions to any concept or term*—sex, hard rock, mother, political correctness, apartheid, ego, cigarettes, gay, lesbian, queer, Madonna, capital punishment—and then compare them with those of other people.

One social movement has changed its name several times to utilize research on what words or verbal symbols have a more positive connotation. Today, this movement refers to itself as *LGBTQ*. This term tests better than the words lesbian, bisexual, queer, and so on. The term "gay" used to be "homosexual," but that term has also been modified to be more socially acceptable. Words matter!

The Semantic Differential test itself is a seven-interval scale with limits defined by sets of bipolar adjectives. "The words used to anchor the scales," explains Griffin (1991), "are concerned with feelings (connotation) rather than a description (denotation)" (p. 32). Figure 3.1, for example, is a Semantic Differential for the word "commitment." The subject rates the concept by checking the interval between each

Figure 3.1   *Example of a Semantic Differential Scale*

Commitment

Sharp	____ : ____ : ____ : ____ : ____ : ____ : ____	Dull
Courageous	____ : ____ : ____ : ____ : ____ : ____ : ____	Cowardly
Dirty	____ : ____ : ____ : ____ : ____ : ____ : ____	Clean
Hot	____ : ____ : ____ : ____ : ____ : ____ : ____	Cold
Good	____ : ____ : ____ : ____ : ____ : ____ : ____	Bad
Fair	____ : ____ : ____ : ____ : ____ : ____ : ____	Unfair
Powerful	____ : ____ : ____ : ____ : ____ : ____ : ____	Weak
Deceitful	____ : ____ : ____ : ____ : ____ : ____ : ____	Honest
Fast	____ : ____ : ____ : ____ : ____ : ____ : ____	Slow
Cruel	____ : ____ : ____ : ____ : ____ : ____ : ____	Kind
Active	____ : ____ : ____ : ____ : ____ : ____ : ____	Passive

pair of adjectives that best describes it. The researcher then draws a line connecting each point made by the subject, thus creating a profile of the subject's concept of commitment.

Statistical analysis of the work of Osgood and his associates suggests that our judgments have three major dimensions: evaluation, potency, and activity. Thus, we say that commitment is good or bad and cruel or kind (evaluation), that it is powerful or weak and hot or cold (potency), and fast or slow and active or passive (activity). One result of this type of testing has resulted in one social movement to drop the terms *gay, lesbian,* and *queer* and to use the new acronym *LGBTQ* (lesbian, gay, bisexual, transsexual/transgender, and queer) instead. It turns out that this new label has a more neutral connotation that helps promote tolerance for nonheterosexual preferences (Wikipedia, 2011).

Private and Shared Meanings

In psychology and semantics, much research is based on the distinction between denotation and connotation. The Semantic Differential, for example, is said to

3.1 ISSUES IN COMMUNICATION
A Word about Semantics

When do words make a difference? When you give someone your "word," what does that imply? Have you ever seen communication difficulties arise over the use and assumed meaning ascribed to certain words?

When Chevrolet introduced the Nova into Spanish-speaking countries, it had disappointing sales. *No va* means "it does not go" in Spanish. How could this have been avoided?

When AT&T lays off 40,000 employees, it is called "downsizing" or "restructuring." What do you think it would be called if 40,000 people were permanently put out of work by an act of nature?

Some authors (Tubbs, 2012) have referred to different types of words as "purr" words versus "snarl" words. Imagine a work situation in which someone has just submitted a report and you want to give the person some feedback that you think it has some good aspects, but it could be improved. Try creating two scenarios in which you give the feedback using "snarl" words and another using "purr" words.

measure "connotative meaning." But when we examine it closely, the distinction between denotation and connotation seems to break down. All people who speak English are members of the same linguistic community; yet within that community certain groups exist for whom even the primary associations, or denotations, of a given word are different.

Take the case of the Americans and the British. In England you take a "lift," not an "elevator"; if you ask for the "second floor," you get the "third." You take the "underground," not the "subway." You "queue up"; you don't "stand in line." You go to a "chemist's," not a "pharmacy." The list seems virtually endless.

Private Meaning

We can all use language idiosyncratically, assigning meanings to words without agreement and, in effect, creating our own private language. We can decide, for example, to call trees "reds" or "cows" or "haves." Schizophrenic speech is often private in this way, but schizophrenics are unaware that they sometimes use language in a way that is not shared by others: They use the words they have recreated and expect to be understood. When one young patient was admitted to a hospital, she continually referred to her father, a lawyer by profession, as "the chauffeur." Everyone with whom she spoke found this reference bizarre. Only in treatment was it learned that when she called her father a "chauffeur," she meant that he was completely under her mother's domination. In his book *Philosophical Investigations,* philosopher Ludwig Wittgenstein defined private language as follows: "The words of this language are to refer to what can be known only to the speaker; to his immediate, private, sensations. So another cannot understand the language" (Candlish, 2004).

Shared Meaning

Presumably, if we assign private meanings to words, we are aware that we can use them to communicate with someone only if we let that person know what the referents of these words are. **Shared meaning** requires *some correspondence between the message as perceived by the sender and the receiver.* Two friends, a husband and wife, an entire family, or a group of physicists may decide to use language in a way that makes little sense to others. Among themselves, however, they can communicate with no difficulty.

Shared meaning is essential in building culture within organizations. Organizations have their own terminology, industry vocabulary, acronyms, and definitions within the environment. It is easy to spot an outsider to an organization while a group is within the throes of conversation using shared language. This sharing creates a sense of belonging to the organizational culture. Can you think back on your own experience on the first day of a job and how it felt to suddenly be immersed in a new culture with shared meanings that you did not yet understand? How did you feel once you understood these meanings?

The ever-growing popularity of text messaging has led to the formation of a new "language" for the individuals who use cell phones for more than the average phone call. Most of those who fit into this group are teenagers and young adults across the globe; they have created an abbreviated version of their existing languages to type faster. Following are some examples of English language text-messaging shorthand, according to *www.netlingo.com* (2007):

CUL8R—see you later

BRB—be right back

2BZ4UQT—too busy for you cutie

@TEOTD—at the end of the day

LOL—laughing out loud

P911—parent alert

TNX—thanks

The same phenomenon occurs among members of many other kinds of groups. Actors understand each other when they talk about scenes being "blocked." Physical therapists refer in their work to "trigger points" and "jelling pain." An extensive vocabulary describes the various moves possible on a skateboard, such as "ollies," "bonelesses," "720s," "thread the needles," and "slob airs." For the subgroup that uses this language, the meaning of "bonelesses" and "thread the needles" is always clear.

One writer described the insider language of those who approve screenplays for major motion pictures such as producers, directors, and lead actors. He wrote that when people use the following terms they really mean something else: "Wonderful means change it. Fantastic means change it. Terrific means change it. Thank you means you're fired" (Applebome, 1998, p. E1).

Group members have no difficulty understanding one another when they use language in this way because they share a code. Communication difficulties emerge only when they expect meaning to be shared by those outside the group. This is a recurring expectation, especially in a country such as the United States, where so many different ethnic groups coexist.

Overlapping Codes and Codeswitching

In intercultural communication, the sender and the receiver often have overlapping codes, "*codes which provide an area of commonality but which also contain areas of unshared codification*" (Martin and Nakayama, 2008, p. 140, emphasis added). Even if the code they use at home is very different, members of minority groups are usually compelled to learn and make some use of the language of the majority because in education, business, and politics this language dominates.

Restricted codes of communication seem to be common among intimate dyads. A study of young lovers (Bell et al., 1987) found the number of personal idioms they used—that is, "words, phrases, or nonverbal signs they had created that had meaning unique to their relationship" (p. 47)—to be highly correlated with love, commitment, and closeness. This proved to be true for both premarital and marital relationships. The couples studied had private idioms, which they used only when they were alone, and public idioms, which they could use when others were present: The private idioms were usually sexual references or euphemisms and sexual invitations (e.g., "Let's go home and watch TV"), whereas the public idioms were often nicknames, confrontations, teasing insults, and requests.

Shifts in codes occur in many different communication contexts. An analysis of such American television interviewers as Piers Morgan, Oprah Winfrey, and Ellen DeGeneres shows that a pattern of frequent codeswitching within a single conversation can be used by a speaker for the purpose of negotiating power. *Codeswitching* is referred to here as *shifting to different styles* (casual, quasi-literary, and so on) *and introducing shifts in vocabulary or syntax*. Codeswitching is used in many contexts. For example, salespeople must be able to codeswitch both in developing customer relationships and in negotiations. They must mirror the communication style of the customer in many cases to develop the relationship and be able to shift into a mode of negotiation when necessary. Additionally, there are many contexts in which codeswitching establishes or reinforces intimacy. Novelist Amy Tan (1991), author of *The Joy Luck Club,* writes of speaking to an audience about her life and work when suddenly her talk sounded "wrong." Her language was formal and literary, but her mother, who was born in China, was in the audience and had never heard her speaking this formally. Tan goes on to describe how later, when taking a walk with her mother, she once more became aware of the English she was using:

> We were talking about the price of new and used furniture and I heard myself saying this: "Not waste money that way." My husband was with us as well,

and he didn't notice any switch in my English. And then I realized why. It's because over the twenty years we've been together I've often used the same kind of English with him, and sometimes he even uses it with me. It has become our language of intimacy, a different sort of English that relates to family talk, the language I grew up with. (p. 197)

The several "Englishes" used by Tan will also be familiar to other children of bilingual families.

LANGUAGE AND THOUGHT

In discussing message encoding, we've seen that language and thought are often said to be interrelated. But the nature of their relationship is far from clear. Is language a precondition of human thought? Is thinking simply inner speech? There are no easy answers. Students of communication have been particularly concerned with the question: Does language shape our ideas, or is it merely an instrument of thought?

The Sapir-Whorf Hypothesis

One version of the view that our thought is shaped by the language we speak is the Sapir-Whorf hypothesis that *the world is perceived differently by members of different communities and that this perception is transmitted and sustained by language.* Benjamin Lee Whorf (1956), whose work was shaped by that of the great linguist Edwin Sapir, regards language as the primary vehicle of culture. In short, the language we speak influences our experience of the world, while the evolution of language also reflects changes in the predominant modes of expression.

Whorf supports this theory with findings from studies of Native American languages. In English, he points out, we tend to classify words as nouns or verbs; in Hopi the words tend to be classified by duration. For example, in Hopi "lightning," "flame," "wave," and "spark" are verbs, not nouns; they are classified as events of brief duration. In Nootka, which is spoken by the inhabitants of Vancouver Island, categories such as things and events do not exist; thus it is said that "A house occurs" or "It houses."

The Sapir-Whorf hypothesis is based on two types of determinism, which define how our language determines how we view the environment. "Strong" determinism is the belief that language has the power to determine our thoughts; "weak" determinism is the belief that our way of viewing the world and our thoughts are influenced by language but not controlled by it. The latter type of determinism is the most important line of thought among current cognitive psychologists. Alison Motluk (2002), a writer for the British magazine *New Scientist,* wrote an article titled "You Are What You Speak." She noted differences in language construction and how individuals see the world. She cites the following example: When describing 11 pens lying on a table, a person from Russia would have to consider the gender of the pens in the answer, a Japanese person has to look at the shape of the pens, and an English speaker just has to count the pens. She questioned if these linguistic differences actually change how we think about the world ("Sapir-Whorf Hypothesis Redux," 2002/2003, pp. 456–457). In spite of opposing lines of thought, the current consensus is that language does have some influence on our thoughts but does not determine them.

As stated before, Whorf's hypothesis that language can determine the nature and content of thought is useful in explaining this peculiar evidence. A linguist from Columbia University did a study on the Piraha tribe and discovered that they use a three-word number system ("one-two-many"). This addresses the classic Whorfian question about whether language can determine thought. Results of numerical tasks with varying cognitive demands show that numerical cognition is clearly affected by the lack of a counting system in the language (Gordon, 2004).

The specific mechanism for increasing success is self-talk, which refers to the messages we communicate to ourselves. When an event occurs, such as our boss criticizing us on a task, we can use positive or negative self-talk. This results in either a positive or a negative feeling or behavior. To quote one source: "The difference between a really good day and a really awful day is not in what happened but in what you tell yourself about that day" (Stewart, 2008, p. 260).

Language does two important things. First, it serves as an aid to memory. It makes memory more efficient by allowing us to code events as verbal categories. Researchers have shown, for example, that we find it easier to recognize colors of low codability again if we named them for ourselves the first time we saw them (Brown and Lenneberg, 1954). It is now believed that an adult's memory is primarily verbal. And second, language also enables us to abstract indefinitely from our experience, which is especially important in communicating about abstract relationships (something animals are unable to do).

Language Problems

Ideally, language is a valuable instrument of thought; yet we know that language can sometimes interfere with our ability to think critically. Although Whorf was best known for his writings on linguistics, he was trained as an engineer. When he became an accident investigator, he began to realize that a certain percentage of accidents occurred as a result of what might be called "careless thinking." For example, people would be very careful around barrels labeled "gasoline" but would smoke unconcernedly around barrels labeled "empty gasoline barrel," though the fumes in the empty barrels were more likely to ignite than the actual gasoline (Whorf, 1956, p. 135). Imprecise use of language can interfere with our thought processes in many ways. We shall examine several that have a direct influence on our communication.

Abstract Language

When people use *abstract* language, they frequently cause communication difficulties that have to do with the *vagueness of words*. As concepts become more vague, or abstract, it gets harder and harder to decode the intended meaning. S. I. Hayakawa has written several books on semantics, and in one he included the so-called abstraction ladder we see in Figure 3.2.

Figure 3.2 *Abstraction Ladder*

Start Reading from the bottom *UP*

8. "wealth"

7. "asset"

6. "farm assets"

5. "livestock"

4. "cow"

3. "Bessie"

2.

8. The word "wealth" is at an extremely high level of abstraction, omitting *almost* all reference to the characteristics of Bessie.

7. When Bessie is referred to as an "asset," still more of her characteristics are left out.

6. When Bessie is included among "farm assets," reference is made only to what she has in common with all other salable items on the farm.

5. When Bessie is referred to as "livestock," only those characteristics she has in common with pigs, chickens, goats, etc., are referred to.

4. The word "cow" stands for the characteristics we have abstracted as common to cow_1, cow_2, cow_3 . . . cow_n. Characteristics peculiar to specific cows are left out.

3. The word "Bessie" (cow_1) is the *name* we give to the object of perception of level 2. The name is not the object; it merely *stands for* the object and omits reference to many of the characteristics of the object.

2. The cow we perceive is not the word, but the object of experience, that which our nervous system abstracts (selects) from the totality that constitutes the process-cow. Many of the characteristics of the process-cow are left out.

1. The cow known to science ultimately consists of atoms, electrons, etc., according to present-day scientific inference. Characteristics (represented by circles) are infinite at this level and ever-changing. This is the *process level.*

Source: From Hayakawa. Language in Thought and Action, 4E. © 1978 Heinle/Arts & Sciences, a part of Cengage Learning, Inc. Reproduced by permission. www.cengage.com/permissions.

In general, the more abstract the term, the greater our chances of misunderstanding. Consider this exchange between father and teenage son:

Father: Have a good time, and don't stay out late.

Son: Thanks, I will. Don't worry. I'll be home early.

The next day they may get into a disagreement because they were not thinking the same thing when they used the words "early" and "late." Perhaps the son purposely did not clarify what the father meant by "late" because he didn't want to be held to a strict time limit. And the father may have been vague intentionally so that his son would have a chance to exercise judgment and learn to become more adult. On the other hand, if the son came home at 4:00 A.M., both father and son would probably agree that he had indeed stayed out "late."

The following may help you understand the abstract meaning of "love":

Take *love* as an example. You have heard and used that word since you were three or four years old. Does it mean to you now what it meant to you when you were five? when you were ten? when you were fourteen(!)? I am sure you will share my certainty that the word changes meaning when we marry, when we divorce, when we have children, when we look back at lost parents or spouses or children. The word stays the same, but the meaning keeps changing. (Friedlander, 2007)

Often, in an attempt to avoid ambiguity, we use very precise wording to clarify meaning. Legal contracts are such an example. But no amount of care is sufficient to avoid all ambiguity of interpretation. We need only look at the differences in how Supreme Court justices have interpreted the Constitution, or at the different ways in which the Bible has been interpreted, to see the inherent ambiguity in our use of language. Keep in mind the abstraction ladder, however, for some terms are considerably more abstract, and therefore more subject to misinterpretation, than others.

Inferences

An *inference* is *a conclusion or judgment derived from evidence or assumptions.* Every day you make dozens of inferences. When you sit down, you infer that the chair will support your weight. When you go through a green light, you infer that the traffic moving at right angles to you will stop at the red light. When you drive down a one-way street, you infer that all the traffic will be going in one direction. You may have good reason to expect these inferences to be correct, but there is also some uncalculated probability that events will not always go as you expect. Drivers who have been involved in traffic accidents frequently say that the accident occurred because they inferred that the other party would act in a certain way when in fact he or she did not. Every year we read of people who were accidentally shot with guns they inferred were not loaded.

As students of communication, we are concerned with the inferences implicit in verbal messages. If you say, "It is sunny outside today," your statement can be easily verified. It is a factual statement based on an observed and verifiable event. If you say, "It is sunny outside; therefore, it is sunny 50 miles from here," you draw a conclusion based on more than what you have observed. You have made a statement based in part on an inference.

Consider a more complex situation. Sheila Waring has broken off a substantial part of one of her front teeth. Her dentist takes an x-ray, covers the tooth with a temporary, and gives her an appointment for the following week; she may, he mentions, need root canal work. The next week Sheila returns, and as she walks into the office, the dentist says, "I'm sorry, Sheila. You do need root canal work. This calls for a heroic effort." Hearing this, Sheila is terrified and during the next hour sits in the chair awaiting the awful pain that never comes. "There. Finished—" says the dentist, "I've taken out the nerve." "But I didn't feel it at all. I thought you said I would have to be heroic about it." "No. I said '*a* heroic effort,'" answers the dentist. "I didn't say *your* effort."

We make inferences in every imaginable context, and it is neither possible nor desirable to avoid them entirely. Nevertheless, to use language more precisely and to be more discerning when we hear others speak, we should learn to distinguish between factual and inferential statements. "You spend a great deal of time with my roommate" is a statement of fact. It involves a low level of uncertainty, it is made as a result of direct observation, and it can be verified. Add to it "I'm sure he won't mind if you borrow his coat," and you have an inferential statement that may well jeopardize a friendship. In becoming more conscious of inference making, we can at least learn to calculate the risks involved.

To compound the problem, our language is structured so that no distinction is made between facts and inferences. It is the verb "to be" that creates the difficulty: No grammatical distinction is made between a fact verified through sense data (e.g., "She is wearing a red coat") and a statement that cannot be verified through sense data and is merely an inference (e.g., "She is thinking about her upcoming date this weekend").

Dichotomies

Dichotomies, or *polar words,* are frequently responsible for another type of language problem. Some semanticists classify English as a "two-valued" rather than a "multivalued" language. By this they mean that English has an excess of polar words and a relative scarcity of words to describe the wide middle ground between these opposites. Obviously, every person, entity, or event can be described in terms of a whole array of adjectives ranging from very favorable to very unfavorable. (Recall the Semantic Differential, discussed earlier in this chapter, which uses a seven-interval scale.) Yet we tend to say that a student is a "success" or a "failure," that a child is "good" or "bad," that a woman is "attractive" or "unattractive." Try, for example, to think of some words to describe the spots marked on the continua in the scale of dichotomies in Figure 3.3. As you search for words, you begin to see that there are a lot of distinctions for which we lack single words. The continua also illustrate how our language suggests that certain categories of experience are mutually exclusive, when in truth they are not.

Figure 3.3

SCALE OF DICHOTOMIES

Success	___	___	X	___	___	___	___	Failure
Brilliant	___	___	___	X	___	___	___	Stupid
Handsome	___	___	X	___	___	___	___	Ugly
Winner	___	___	___	X	___	___	___	Loser
Honest	___	___	___	X	___	___	___	Dishonest
Black	___	X	___	___	___	___	___	White

Source: From the *Journal of Applied Behavioral Science*, 6, "The Fifth Achievement," by Blake and Mouton, p. 418. Reprinted by permission of Sage Publishers.

Consider the first set of terms, "success" and "failure." Every human being undoubtedly meets with some success and some failure during the course of a lifetime. An insurance broker unemployed for many months and unable to find work may also be a supportive and much-loved father and husband. Yet our language suggests that he be classified as either a success or a failure. Similar difficulties crop up if we are asked to apply such adjectives as "brilliant" and "stupid" or "winner" and "loser" to other people. Is the math major with a straight-A average brilliant or stupid if she can't learn to drive a car or ride a bike? If the author of a recent best seller is divorced for the third time, is he a winner or a loser?

When polar terms are used in a misleading way, they suggest false dichotomies, reducing experience in a way that it need not be reduced. Differences are emphasized and similarities are overlooked, and in the process a great deal of information is lost. This is certainly true in our country at election time.

One way to avoid making false dichotomies, as Haney (1992, p. 374) has pointed out, is to make use of the questions "How much?" and "To what extent?":

How much of a success am I?

How much of a change is this from his former stand on gun control?

To what extent is he honest?

To what extent is her plan practical?

With the aid of such questions, perhaps we can keep in mind that we have many options that we need not cast our messages in black-and-white terms, and that we need not accept these either-or distinctions when they are made by others.

Euphemisms

Through *euphemisms* we *substitute mild, vague, or less emotionally charged terms for more blunt ones*—"campaign of disinformation" for "smear campaign," "security review procedure" for "censorship," "discomfort" for "pain," "memory garden" for "cemetery," "powder room" for "bathroom," "attack" for "rape." "Portly," "stout," and "heavyset" are ways to avoid saying "fat." Southwest Airlines employees refer to fat customers with the euphemism "COS" (customers of size). These customers may be charged extra for taking up more than a single normal-sized seat. It is easier to speak in code like this to avoid offending those people being referred to. Of course, these euphemisms lack the specificity of "fat" as well as the affect (emotion) attached to the word. If we hear that a woman was "attacked," we don't know if she was verbally assaulted or raped. Often the problem created by using euphemisms is that the intent may be conveyed but not the degree to which the intent is felt. So-called empty words are euphemisms because they are pleasant sounding yet indirect enough to avoid being blunt: "nice," "wonderful," and "pleasant" appear to be all-purpose euphemisms. They make for dull conversations. And on many occasions, euphemistic language is used to misrepresent what is being said. In the economically hard times of the twenty-first century, many cities and states have had to cut back services and lay off employees. This is euphemistically referred to as "service level insolvency," which means that a very nice community building cannot be opened for use for lack of funds to staff it (Lewis, 2011, p. 198). In Vallejo, California, all traffic lights are permanently set to blink, since there are no longer any police officers to write tickets. Similarly, since there are no longer meter maids, you do not have to worry about getting a parking ticket (Lewis, 2011, p. 199). In another example, one high school counselor revealed several phrases he used in writing student recommendations for college applications: describing a student with serious emotional problems as "having peaks and valleys"; saying a student "likes to take risks" when referring to a drug problem; characterizing an arrogant student as "pushing against the limits" (see www.generalsemantics.org, 2009).

Equivocal Language

Misunderstandings often occur because people assume that a word, a phrase, or even a sentence is unequivocal—that is, it has only one meaning. Hayakawa refers to this as "the 'one word, one meaning' fallacy" (1978). But much of the language we use is *equivocal*; it has *two or more possible interpretations.*

We've seen the problems created by disagreements over the referents of such words as "peace," "truth," and "freedom." Misunderstandings are also quite common when the words and phrases in question sound far more concrete. If your date says, "Let's get a drink after the show," the drink may refer to an alcoholic beverage, continuing the evening in a club, or a desire to stay together for simple conversation.

There seem to be two sources of confusion about words or phrases. First, people may assume that because they are using the same word, they agree, when in fact each interprets the word differently. In a comical incident, a woman asks a pharmacist for a refill of her prescription for "the pill." "Please hurry," she adds, "I've got someone waiting in the car." Much humor is based on such double meanings. In daily communication, this type of confusion may not be so funny:

Husband: You know, the travel literature on Switzerland that I borrowed is still in the house. Since we're not going, I'd better return it to that fellow in my office. Could you get it together for me so I can take it in tomorrow?

Wife: I don't know where it is.

Husband: What kind of answer is that? If it's too much trouble, forget it.

Wife: What do you mean, "What kind of answer is that?" How can I do anything with it if I can't find it?

Husband: There's nothing to do. All I asked you to do was find it. You don't have to give me a smart answer.

Wife: But you said "get it together." I thought you meant put it in some sort of order.

Husband: I meant "find it." Don't you know what "get it together" means?

Wife: Well, I didn't know it meant that.

Husband: If you didn't know, why didn't you ask me?

Wife: Because I thought I knew. I speak English, too, you know.

For a time this misunderstanding created a lot of ill feeling. Both husband and wife were insulted—the husband because he felt his wife had refused to do something relatively simple for him, and the wife because she felt her husband had insulted her intelligence.

A second type of misunderstanding occurs when two people assume that they disagree because they are using different words when actually they may agree on the concept or entity represented by those words. That is, they use different terms that have the same referent. For example, a school psychologist and a guidance counselor were discussing a student who was failing several of her classes though she was of above-average intelligence. A disagreement developed when the counselor insisted that the girl definitely needed "help." "She certainly does not," countered the psychologist. "She needs psychological intervention." "That's what I'm saying," said the counselor. "She should be getting psychological counseling." "Well, then we agree," answered the psychologist. "When you said 'help,' I thought you were talking about tutoring." The psychologist and counselor were able to resolve their apparent differences because they did stop and redefine their terms.

The point is that any message derives a great part of its meaning from the context in which it is transmitted. Our knowledge of the speaker and the speaker's use of language, our own associations with the words he or she chooses, our previous relationship, and the messages we have already exchanged should all play a part in how we interpret what is said.

Culture as Our Frame of Reference

Although all our behaviors have possible meaning for a receiver, language is by far our most explicit form of communication. In using it, we usually desire to facilitate thought, not to obscure it. Language is potentially the most precise vehicle we have for human communication. Even if we grant the infinite richness of language and the precision it is capable of expressing, however, a look at intercultural communication makes clear that often people are divided, not because of a failure to understand grammar or vocabulary, but because of a failure to understand rhetoric or point of view.

Kenneth Kaunda, the former president of Zambia, insists that Westerners and Africans have very different ways of seeing things, solving problems, and thinking in general. He characterizes the Westerner as having a "problem-solving mind." Once a Westerner perceives a problem, he or she feels compelled to solve it. Unable to live with contradictory ideas, the Westerner excludes all solutions that have no logical basis. Supernatural and nonrational phenomena are regarded as superstition. The African, on the other hand, allows himself or herself to experience all phenomena, nonrational as well as rational. The African has a "situation-experiencing mind." Kaunda believes that "the African can hold contradictory ideas in fruitful tension within his mind without any sense of incongruity, and he will act on the basis of the one which seems most appropriate to the particular situation" (Legum, 1976, pp. 63–64).

In ancient India, according to Kirkwood (1989) and other students of Indian rhetoric, truthfulness was considered the prime standard for speech. Emphasis was placed not only on the value of truthful speech to listeners but on the profound effects for the speaker as well. The practice of speaking truthfully was regarded as spiritually liberating, and the performance itself—the act of speaking the truth— brought with it self-knowledge as well as freedom, thus transforming the speaker. Such ideas date back to the tenth century B.C. and are an enduring aspect of India's culture.

On the other hand, a study of Chinese and Japanese attitudes toward speech communication in public settings offers several reasons for the lack of argumentation and debate in the Far East. According to Becker (1991), social history contributed to an aversion to public debate. For example, in the Chinese and Japanese traditions, "taking opposite sides of an argument necessarily meant becoming a personal rival and antagonist of the one who held the other side. The more important concomitant of this idea was that if one did not wish to become a lifelong opponent of someone else, he would not venture an opinion contrary to the other person's opinions in public. Even the legal system was set up in such a way that it avoided direct confrontations" (p. 236).

In addition, various linguistic features of Chinese and Japanese (e.g., Chinese lacks plurals and tenses) as well as great differences between Western and Eastern philosophy and religion all presented powerful barriers to the widespread use of debate and argumentation for considering new proposals or strategies for implementing social and political change (Becker, 1991, p. 242). Becker emphasizes that the Westerner's ideal speech situation requiring "equality of participants, freedom from social coercion, suspension of privilege, and free expression of feeling … [would be] both impractical and even theoretically inconceivable to traditionally educated Chinese and Japanese" (p. 242).

In looking at different **cultural frames of reference,** we seem to have come full circle, recalling elements of the Sapir-Whorf hypothesis. To some degree, linguistic traditions help shape our thought processes, but for members of different cultures, these traditions can be a barrier.

We've considered several language-related problems that interfere with your ability to think and communicate clearly. Of course, there are numerous others. But just being aware of the *possibility* that language can be a source of misunderstanding should enable you to be more perceptive about verbal messages.

WORDS IN ACTION

In this final section of our chapter, we will examine some ways in which words influence human actions, both directly and indirectly. In ancient times, people of many diverse cultures believed that words had magical powers. For example, in ancient Egypt a man received two names: his true name, which he concealed, and his good name, by which he was known publicly. Even today many primitive societies regard words as magical. Members of some cultures go to great lengths to conceal their personal names. They avoid saying the names of their gods. The names of their dead are never uttered. Presumably, we moderns are far more sophisticated. Yet we have our own verbal taboos. And the euphemisms we've just talked about are part of our everyday vocabulary. Thus, we often hear not that someone "died" but that he or she "passed away." And a sudden drop in the stock market is often termed a "correction."

Recently, the use of the term "mother" has come into some controversy. According to one source, "In Massachusetts and many other states, only the woman who gives birth is presumed to be the mother and can have her name on the original birth certificate. The law does not address women becoming mothers by having embryos implanted in a surrogate. . . . More than a month after they were born, a baby boy and his twin sister still have no birth certificates. The paperwork is being held up in a dispute over the legal definition of the term mother" (Lavoie, 2001, p. A7).

Writers on public communication traditionally refer to the effective use of language as "eloquence." In public speaking, eloquence describes a more dramatic, stirring use of language—often for the purpose of inspiring or persuading others. One thinks of the famous speech of Dr. Martin Luther King, Jr., "I Have a Dream," through which thousands were inspired to work for equal rights:

> I have a dream that one day, even the state of Mississippi, a state sweltering with the heat of injustice, sweltering with the heat of oppression, will be transformed into an oasis of freedom and justice....
>
> With this faith we will be able to hew out of the mountain of despair a stone of hope. With this faith we will be able to transform the jangling discords of our nation into a beautiful symphony of brotherhood.

With these words, Dr. King was able to move people's feelings more powerfully than he could have with more commonplace language. On January 20, 2009, President Barack Obama spoke the following eloquent words in his inaugural address:

> Forty-four Americans have now taken the presidential oath. The words have been spoken during rising tides of prosperity and the still waters of peace. Yet, every so often the oath is taken amidst gathering clouds and raging storms. At these moments, America has carried on not simply because of the skill or vision of those in high office, but because we the people have remained faithful to the ideals of our forebears, and true to our founding documents.

Sometimes our decisions are based in part on how a thing is labeled. For example, certain words clearly have greater prestige than others. A "classic car" is better than an old one. "Vintage clothing" is more appealing than old secondhand clothing. The same desk commands different prices when it is called "used," "secondhand," or "antique." "Doctor" is another powerful word. In many situations, for example, it is undeniable that "Dr." Bradley will get more attention than "Ms." Bradley or "Mr." Bradley.

Sexist Language

For years many students of language, a good many feminists among them, have argued that our language is sexist, that it reflects a bias affecting how women are perceived and treated by others and sometimes how they regard themselves. For example, words associated with the descriptions of males often have positive connotations—"confident," "forceful," "strong," and the like—whereas females are more often described as "fickle," "frivolous," "timid," and so forth (Heilbrun, 1976).

In studies at three different universities, Pearson and her associates (1991) found that when students were asked to list all the terms for men and women, the list of words for women was longer and generally much less favorable than the one for men. (See Table 3.1.) It's the group in power, these writers point out, that "typically does the naming or labeling. In our culture men tend to name people, places, and things."

Some words in the English language indicate a lower status for females. An example that illustrates this is how the language makes a distinction between "Mrs." and "Miss," which shows that a woman is either married or single, respectively. Conversely, males have only "Mr.," which gives no indication of marital status (Lei, 2006).

The following are some examples from Lei (2006) of occupational nouns and job titles ending in "-man" that make the presence of women unclear in such professions and positions as well as some alternative terms:

policeman—police officer

businessman—business executive

Table 3.1	**Terms for Women and Men**				
Women				**Men**	
Chick	Wife	Honey		Gent	Boy
Girl	Old maid	Madam		Man	Stud
Old lady	Bitch	Whore		Guy	Hunk
Piece	Lady	Dog		Male	Bastard
Female	Broad	Cow		Husband	
Prostitute	Woman	Old biddy			

Source: From *Gender and Communication*, by Judy Cornelia Pearson. Copyright © 1985. Reprinted by permission of the author.

chairman—chair, chairperson

clergyman—member of the clergy

weatherman—meteorologist

Women tend to be referred to by euphemisms far more frequently than men are. And although men are not often called "gentlemen" or "boys," "ladies" and "girls" are terms still frequently heard by women as forms of address. Women use them too—hence such comments as "I'm going out for lunch with the girls."

A more subtle but extremely influential form of sexist language is the high frequency of familiar—or overly familiar—terms applied to women, terms that reflect lower social status. Although men are more frequently addressed formally ("Sir," "Mister," and so on), it is quite common for women to be called by their first names, or even to hear themselves called "honey," "hon," "baby," "sweetie," "dear," or the like—and sometimes by people they've never met before (Pearson et al., 1991, p. 100).

The implication that men are the more important members of the human race can be changed in many ways. For example, "manhood" may be replaced by the term "adulthood," "firemen" by "firefighters," and so on. The use of such words as "chairperson," "businessperson," and "he/she"—for all their attendant awkwardness—attempts to address this problem.

The insistence of many groups on such changes is legitimate because, as we have tried to indicate, words shape perceptions and self-concepts. Linguistic changes evolve slowly, but they are taking place.

Male and Female Language Use

Are there true differences between the ways males and females use language? Most research supports the stereotypic view that in contrast to males, females are more submissive, affected by social pressure, and responsive to the needs of others. It has been found that, although women seem to respond more to the remarks of other people, work harder at maintaining conversations, and give more "positive minimal responses," men generally initiate as well as receive more interaction. Men

Figure 3.4

Source: DILBERT: © Scott Adams/Dist. by United Feature Syndicate, Inc.

also interrupt others more and ignore the remarks of others more frequently than women do. Such differences are often explained in terms of the greater social power men enjoy in most communication contexts (Haslett, 1987, p. 216).

Language differences that give rise to these perceptions have been described in this way: Females use more words, intensifiers, questions (including tag questions, such as "That's great, isn't it?"), and affect words (i.e., words implying emotion) than males use (Berryman and Wilcox, 1980). Male speech, on the other hand, shows more instances of incorrect grammar, obscenities, and slang (Liska et al., 1981). Apparently both males and females expect males to use more verbally aggressive strategies and females to use strategies that are more social and less verbally aggressive (Burgoon et al., 1983).

The *Dilbert* joke (Figure 3.4) helps illustrate the difference in male and female language usage. In the joke, the male's only focus is the work aspect of Yvonne, whereas the woman is focused more on the personal aspects.

In *You Just Don't Understand,* a popular book that became a national bestseller, sociolinguist Deborah Tannen (1990) proposes that communication difficulties between men and women often originate in gender differences in conversational style.

She makes the distinction between "report talk" and "rapport talk." Tannen argues that most men use conversation primarily as a language of **report**, that is, "as *a means to preserve independence and negotiate and maintain status in a hierarchical social order*" (1990, p. 77). This conversational style emphasizes demonstrating knowledge and skill and in general having the right information. "From childhood," writes Tannen, "men learn to use talking as a way to get and keep attention" (p. 77). Thus in the world of many men, "conversations are negotiations in which people try to achieve the upper hand if they can, and protect themselves from others' attempts to push them down and push them around" (p. 24).

To most women conversation is, for the most part, "a language of *rapport,*" with which they have learned since childhood to *establish connections and negotiate relationships, often for greater closeness.* What women emphasize in their talk are their similarities with other people and their comparable experiences ("I'm just like that," "The same thing happened to me ..."). Women also have interests in achievement or status goals, says Tannen (1990), but they tend to go after them "in the guise of connection." Similarly,

> Men are also concerned with achieving involvement and avoiding isolation, but they are not focused on these goals, and they tend to pursue them in the guise of opposition. (p. 25)

According to Tannen, it's these differences in style that account for so many misunderstandings. She gives a striking example:

> Though both women and men complain of being interrupted by each other, the behaviors they are complaining about are different.
> In many of the comments I heard from people I interviewed, men felt interrupted by women who overlapped with words of agreement and support and anticipation of how their sentences and thoughts would end. If a woman supported a man's story by elaborating on a point different from the one he had intended, he felt his right to tell his own story had been violated. (p. 210)

Feminist critic Deborah Cameron identifies two current approaches to the language styles of men and women. She contrasts *theories of difference,* such as Tannen's, with *theories of dominance.* In theories of dominance, "Women's style is seen as the outcome of power struggles and negotiations ... played out under the surface of conversation" (Cameron, 1990, p. 25). This, for example, is how a theory of dominance would interpret research findings about questions:

> Women ask more questions than men . . . not because insecurity is part of [their] psychology and therefore of [their] speech style . . . but because men in a dominant position often refuse to take responsibility for the smooth conduct of interpersonal relations. . . . Asking them a question is thus an effective strategy for forcing them to acknowledge and contribute to the talk. It can be argued that features like question-asking are not deferential at all. . . . (p. 25)

Theories such as these are a source of spirited debate and will be most valuable if they generate further research in language studies.

Powerful and Powerless Language

As we speak, many of us use tag questions—for example, "Let's go to the movies, okay?"—in making simple statements. We also use hedges—"kinda" and "I think"—or disclaimers such as "I probably shouldn't say this" and "I'm not really sure." In examining seven message types of differing **power,** Bradac and Mulac (1984) found that the language forms just described as well as hesitations such as "uh" and "well" are perceived by other people as forms of powerless and ineffective speech; on the other hand, speech free of such usage is considered both powerful and effective.

Another study explored the relationship between language style and gender stereotypes (Quina et al., 1987). Researchers found that individuals using a so-called feminine style of speech characterized by politeness, exaggeration, hedging, and illogical sequence—one that was generally nonassertive—were perceived as having greater warmth but less competence than those having a "masculine" style. The authors remind us that "a polite, warm linguistic style is not consistent with the popular image of American corporate success or achievement" (p. 118). Nonetheless, qualities associated with a feminine style included sensitivity, friendliness, and sincerity.

In general, communicators who use a powerful style are considered more competent and attractive. Legal situations are different, however; plaintiffs and defendants using a more powerful style are also considered more blameworthy, perhaps because they seem "in control" of themselves. Less powerful speakers are more often seen as victims (Bradac et al., 1981).

Extensive research conducted by James Pennebaker at the University of Texas (2011) has confirmed the findings mentioned above. As you might expect, when women get together, they talk about other people, whereas men talk about cars, sports, other objects and things. Pennebaker (2011) writes that, "Human relationships are not rocket science—they are far more complicated" (pp. 42–43). He also finds that women view men's speaking styles as blunt and uncaring, while men view women's as indirect and obscure (p. 45).

Also, people who are higher in social status, like leaders, use the personal pronoun "I" much less than people lower in status. In addition, when people are assigned a leadership role, they stop using "I" as much.

Metacommunication

In addition to trying to use a more powerful language, there's another very important way to increase the effectiveness of verbal messages. With practice, you can use language to change your relationship to others through **metacommunication**—that is, *communication about communication*. This is a concept closely linked to the relationship level of human encounters. For example, if you say to your mother, "Tell him to mind his own damned business," and she replies, "I wish you wouldn't swear so much. You do it more and more, and I don't like it," she is responding not to the content of your remark but to your method of getting your point across. The topic of her communication is communication itself.

Any comment directed at the way in which a person communicates is an example of metacommunication. For years the procedure in public-speaking classes has been for students to give practice speeches and then have the instructor and class members give their reactions to the speaker and the speech. Such comments as "I thought you had excellent examples," "You could have brought out your central idea more explicitly," and "Try to be a little more enthusiastic" are all instances of metacommunicating.

Writing about families, Galvin and Brommel (1991) observe:

> Metacommunication occurs when people communicate about their
> communication, when they give verbal and nonverbal instructions about how
> their messages should be understood. Such remarks as "I was only kidding,"
> "This is important," or "Talking about this makes me uncomfortable" are signals
> to another on how to interpret certain comments, as are facial expressions,
> gestures, or vocal tones. (p. 18)

Both humans and other animals give nonverbal instructions about how their
messages should be understood. For example, dogs change their posture when sig-
nifying that they want to play to make sure that the recipient understands the intention of their message. Monkeys use actual facial expressions when communicating
to express intentions as well (Wain, 2004).

Metacommunication is not always explicit, even when it is verbal. Sometimes
conversations that begin at the content level become forms of metacommunication.
We can best illustrate with an anecdote. Ahmet and Sunita, dressed for a night on
the town, have just stepped out of a cab. As they stand at the corner waiting for the
light to change, they rapidly become involved in a heated argument:

Sunita: Next time try to pick me up earlier so we can be on time.

Ahmet: It's only a party. Next time tell me beforehand if you think it's so
important to be there at eight sharp. And don't sound so annoyed.

Sunita: But you're always late.

Ahmet: I'm not always late. Don't generalize like that.

Sunita: Well, you're late a lot of the time. Why do you always put me down when
I say something about you?

Ahmet: I don't "always" put you down. There you go again, generalizing.

Although they may well remember it simply as a quarrel about lateness, Ahmet
and Sunita are arguing about how they communicate with each other. He tells her not to
sound so annoyed, he informs her that she makes too many generalizations, she coun-
ters that he puts her down, and so on. In effect, they are arguing about their relationship.

As we will see in Chapter 6, when there are serious conflicts about relationships rather than content, metacommunication is often especially difficult (Sillars
and Weisberg, 1987). Two people may lack the skill to use metacommunication,
and the source of the conflict may be "diffuse and selectively perceived. Attempts to
communicate are therefore frustrated by a failure to agree on the definition of the
conflict and by an ability to metacommunicate" (p. 151).

In a more supportive situation, the use of metacommunication might help people become aware of ways in which their communication practices are ineffective. For
example, one teenage girl finally confided to her mother that she was embarrassed
when the mother tried to sound "hip" in front of the daughter's teenage friends. It is

sometimes awkward to provide such feedback. When given in a kind rather than a hostile way, however, it can be a valuable impetus to self-improvement.

Summary

Our analysis of verbal communication began with a consideration of the concept of meaning. In discussing the symbolic nature of language, we saw that symbols and referents are associated with each other only by convention and that it is human beings who assign meanings to words. We reviewed the traditional distinction between denotation and connotation and suggested that it might be more useful to distinguish between private and shared meanings. In this connection, we discussed overlapping linguistic codes and codeswitching.

Our next concern was the relationship between thought and language, and after examining the Sapir-Whorf hypothesis, we considered several language problems created through abstracting, inferences, dichotomies, euphemisms, and equivocal meanings. We went on to observe that when people of different cultures communicate, they may be separated not so much by grammar or vocabulary as by frame of reference.

To study words in action, we examined sexist language, differences between males and females in their use of language (these seem to be context-bound), and the language forms perceived by others as powerful or powerless. In closing, we saw that metacommunication (communication *about* communication) is potentially a means of improving one's relationships.

Key Terms

Connotation	Denotation	Report	Sexist language
Cultural frame of reference	Metacommunication	Sapir-Whorf hypothesis	Shared meaning
	Power		

Review Questions

1. What is intended by the statement "The word is not the thing"?

2. What is the difference between denotation and connotation?

3. What is the Semantic Differential? Give an example of a differential.

4. Explain the difference between private and shared meanings.

5. What are the concepts of overlapping codes and codeswitching?

6. What is the Sapir-Whorf hypothesis?

7. Discuss two ways in which language affects thought.

8. Describe the concept of abstracting and give examples.

9. Describe at least four problem areas in our use of language. Give an example of each.

10. Discuss the use of sexist language and give two examples.

11. What are some of the differences between how males and females use language?

12. Specify the difference between the ways males and females use language on the job.

13. Identify powerful and powerless language and explain its relationship to communication style.

14. What is metacommunication? Give an example.

Exercises

1. a. Construct a Semantic Differential consisting of ten bipolar adjectives. Assess the potential marketability of a fictitious product name by asking several classmates to react to two or more names using the Semantic Differential. The sample scale below shows two names for a perfume.

Bouquet		Summer Nights	
Good X _ _ _ _ _ _ Bad		Good _ _ _ _ _ X _ Bad	
Sharp _ X _ _ _ _ _ Dull		Sharp _ _ _ _ _ _ X Dull	
Active _ _ _ X _ _ _ Passive		Active _ _ _ X _ _ _ Passive	
Pretty _ _ X _ _ _ _ Ugly		Pretty _ _ _ X _ _ _ Ugly	

   b. How do the responses on the Semantic Differential reflect the difference between denotation and connotation; between private and shared meaning?

2. Construct a two-column list with proper names in one column and stereotypical occupations associated with those names in the second. Mix up the order of names and occupations in each column. Present the lists to several people and ask them to match the names and occupations. A sample list appears follows:

Miss Flora	Ballet dancer
Spencer Turnbull	Teacher
Harry Hogan	Car thief
Speedy	Banker
Dominique Dubois	Hairdresser
Ken Sharp	Wrestling coach

   a. To what extent do people agree in their responses? How do the results relate to the statement "The word is not the thing"?
   b. How do the results relate to the three factors that affect stereotype perceptions (see Chapter 2)?
   c. What implications do these results suggest about the relationship between language, stereotyping, and communication effectiveness?

3. Interview two people who are ostensibly very different—a local politician and an artist, for example. Ask each of them to make a list of adjectives describing (a) himself or herself and (b) a member of the other group. Compare the lists to see how differently each group member perceives himself or herself from the way he or she is perceived by the other person. Notice how the perceptual differences are manifested in the words chosen for the descriptions.

4. Prepare an oral persuasive message in two forms. Use the most tactful language possible in one and the most inflammatory terms you can think of in the other. Give the messages to two groups and try to assess their reactions on an attitude scale. Which message is more effective? If the audiences are similar and your messages alike except for word choice (and assuming the nonverbal cues are similar), any difference in your results should be due to the difference in the language you use.

5. In a chance conversation, deliberately assume that individual words have only one meaning and try to interpret them in a way that the other person does not intend. What are the results?

6. Prepare a short presentation in two forms. In the first, use words that are high on the ladder of abstraction (i.e., vague); in the second, use much more concrete, highly specific words. Discuss class reactions to these different presentations.

Suggested Readings

Bate, Barbara, and Anita Taylor, eds. *Women Communicating.* Norwood, NJ: Ablex, 1988.

An important collection of studies on women's talk.

Donnellon, Anne. *Team Talk: The Power of Language in Team Dynamics.* Cambridge: Harvard Business School Press, 1996.

This excellent book analyzes teams from the standpoint of their members' language. It offers an excellent framework for analyzing and improving teams.

Ivy, Diana, and Phil Backlund. *Gender Speak,* 3rd ed. New York: McGraw-Hill, 2004.

This book is one of the best in the field of gender communication. It is a "must read" for those interested in this topic.

Luntz, Frank. *Win.* New York: Hyperion, 2011. Also, Frank Luntz. *Words That Work.* New York: Hyperion, 2007.

Both books describe the results of extensive public opinion research testing of key words or phrases that get positive responses from a strong majority of listeners. Both are very useful as handbooks for speakers.

Pennebaker, James. *The Secret Life of Pronouns.* New York: Bloomsbury Press, 2011.

This book reveals some fascinating research on people who use the word "I" more often than most, and the effect it has on their overall effectiveness as communicators.

www.slanguage.com

A Web site that monitors current and changing slang words and expressions. It focuses on the slang terms used by younger generations. It beautifully illustrates the ever-changing nature of language.

Tannen, Deborah. *The Argument Culture: Moving from Debate to Dialogue.* New York: Random House, 1998.

This outstanding author relates the use of language to improving communication in conflict situations. The book includes information on communication between genders, communication across cultures, and the role of technology.

 # For Supplementary Information

Log onto the Online Learning Center at *www.mhhe.com/tubbshc13e.*

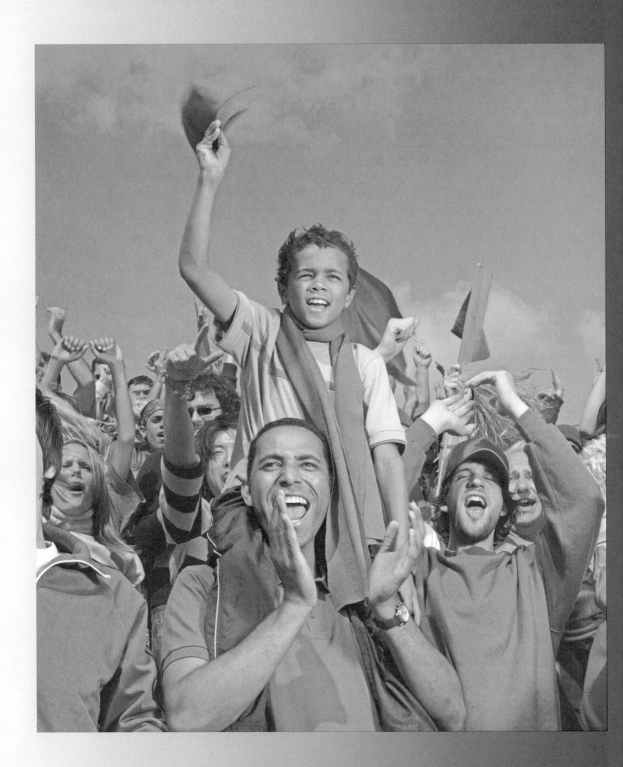

The Nonverbal Message

Chapter Objectives

After reading this chapter, you should be able to:

1. Describe four categories of communication, distinguishing between verbal and nonverbal as well as vocal and nonvocal, and give an example of each.
2. Discuss the kinds of information conveyed by nonverbal and verbal messages and three ways in which they are related.
3. Identify several of the nonverbal cues associated with power and dominance.
4. Discuss the concepts of personal space and interpersonal distance.
5. Explain how we communicate through our use of time and how timing can interfere with intercultural communication.
6. Identify the major visual cues given by facial expression and head and body movements and discuss the kinds of messages they convey.
7. Describe how one's choice of physical objects, including clothing, communicates messages to others.
8. Explain the concept of paralinguistics and identify four kinds of vocal cues, giving an example of each. Discuss some gender differences in vocal cues.
9. Discuss deception cues and recent research findings on accuracy in reliably judging deception and the mutual influence of deceivers and detectors.

PANTS-WEARING CONTROVERSY

In the past few years, a major controversy has arisen over young men wearing their baggy pants too low. Although this situation occurs all over the country, the police department of Flint, Michigan, began arresting young men who wore their pants low enough to expose "skivvies, boxer shorts or bare bottoms." Police Chief David Dicks said, "Some people call it a fad, but I believe it's a national nuisance. It is indecent and thus it is indecent exposure, which has been on the books for years." The crime is a misdemeanor and is punishable by 93 days to a year in jail and/or fines up to $500. The law is interpreted specifically as, "Pants pulled down completely below the buttocks with underwear showing is disorderly conduct; saggy pants with skin of the buttocks showing is indecent exposure, and saggy pants, not completely below the buttocks, with underwear exposed results in a warning" (Schmitt, 2008, p. 1A).

"If I pay for my pants, I should be able to wear them how I want to," said 16-year-old Montez Phifer. "Everyone thinks it's gangster, but it's a fashion. Nothing more."

Senita Abrams, 18, and Tia Cotton, 17, both of Flint, expressed their admiration for males who wear saggy pants. "I think it's cute when boys sag," Abrams said.

Sanek Nichols, 32, said, "The sagging is out of control. It went from being a style to a disruption" (Schmitt, 2008, p. 9A).

The American Civil Liberties Union (ACLU) offered to support any plaintiff who needed legal representation over such cases. Greg Gibbs, a lawyer and chair of the Flint ACLU chapter, said the crackdown is a "vast waste of [police and taxpayer] resources." Meanwhile, Flint is often called one of the most violent cities in America (Schmitt, 2008, p. 9A).

Michigan ACLU executive director Kary Moss said that race could become an issue if the chief aggressively enforces the law disproportionately to African Americans. However, police chief David Dicks, who is black, said, "This is not a black issue. Many people from different ethnic backgrounds and races are doing this."

Discussion questions:

1. What do you think about this controversy?
2. How does this illustrate the ways that nonverbal behavior sends messages?
3. What steps could be taken to have a useful discussion about this issue?
4. What other underlying issues may be impacting this controversy?

The Actor was the 2012 winner of the Golden Globe Award for best picture. What makes this award so unusual is that this is a silent film about an actor during the era of silent films, who has a very hard time adjusting when films change over to "talkies." Since there are also very few subtitles explaining the silent dialogue, the movie is almost entirely nonverbal. Producer Harvey Weinstein wrote that of all the movies in his career, this was the most difficult to "sell" to his financiers, since most successful modern movies have over-the-top special effects or explosions, or car chase scenes. It was also in black and white, which is also nearly unheard of in modern movies. The film relies solely on the excellent story line and outstanding nonverbal acting (Weinstein, 2012, p. 84).

Figure 4.1

Source: From "The 'Reading the Mind in the Eyes' Test," *The Essential Difference: The Truth About the Male and Female Brain.* Copyright © 2003 Simon Baron-Cohen. Reprinted by permission of Basic Books, a member of Perseus Books Group.

The photographs in Figure 4.1 are from "The 'Reading the Mind in the Eyes' Test." Before you read any further, for each photograph select one of the four surrounding words that best describes what the person in the photograph is thinking or feeling (see page 95 for the answers). Later in this chapter you'll learn something about your accuracy in judging facial expressions on the basis of eyes.

In this chapter we look at the broad spectrum of nonverbal communication behaviors. We begin by considering the relative weight people give to verbal and nonverbal messages. Thus, we will look at how nonverbal messages are interpreted, what types of information we receive through them, and how they interact with verbal messages.

INTERPRETING NONVERBAL MESSAGES

During the training of astronauts, NASA told all the male astronauts that when they placed their hands on their hips, they should always have their thumbs pointing backwards to convey masculinity. It was taught that to have your hands on your hips with the thumbs facing frontward would look feminine and would not be consistent with the image they wanted the astronauts to convey.

The literal definition of nonverbal communication, communication without words, is something of an oversimplification, because written words are considered "verbal" although they lack the element of sound. Stewart and D'Angelo (1980) propose that if we distinguish verbal from nonverbal and vocal from nonvocal, we have four types of communication. *Verbal/vocal communication* refers to *communication through the spoken word*. For example, Mira and her father discuss the

According to Jan Hargrave, in a 30-minute encounter with someone, over 800 different nonverbal messages are exchanged. These messages may give some important first impressions about you. There are three steps to increase your nonverbal competency. First, you must have an awareness of the other person, and be able to identify the major nonverbal messages the person is sending. Second, have an awareness of yourself. Understanding and controlling your movements and expressions can make or break an encounter. Third, you must manage yourself and others. Once you have an understanding of signals being sent by you and others, you will be able to detect nonverbal signals early in the encounter, respond faster and more accurately, and combine your nonverbal with verbal skills to intensify yourself (Hargrave, 2008, pp. 17–18).

new car Mira wants to buy and her plans for getting together the money. In *verbal/ nonvocal communication, words are involved but no speaking takes place.* If she writes a letter to her father about the car, her communication is verbal but nonvocal. Or suppose that Mira asks her father for a loan for the car, and he simply groans. Such *groans, or vocalizations, constitute a form of* **nonverbal/vocal communication.** A fourth kind of communication, **nonverbal/nonvocal communication,** *involves only gestures and appearance*—imagine Mira's father looking angry or pleased. Seen in these terms, **nonverbal communication** *conveys nonlinguistic messages.*

Such messages take any number of forms. You raise your hand to vote yes at a committee meeting, hail a cab, exchange signals with someone on your basketball team. You sit on the edge of your seat in a dull class and keep twisting a lock of your hair. You touch the arm of a friend to reassure him. You buy a red sports car because you think it's more your kind of car than a brown sedan. In this chapter, we will be looking at nonverbal messages of all kinds, and one of the first issues we will explore is the division often made between meanings conveyed by nonverbal and verbal communication.

The Verbal/Nonverbal Split in Meaning

Nonverbal communication—indeed the entire communication process—must be viewed as a whole that is greater than the sum of its parts. Outside the laboratory we do not depend on isolated **cues,** or *hints.* In face-to-face communication, all cues, both verbal and nonverbal, are available to us. Even in communicating online, we have access to some, though limited, nonverbal cues. As much as 65 percent of all social meaning in face-to-face communication is conveyed through nonverbal cues.

There are many times when we give greater credence to nonverbal cues. These include when we judge interpersonal style; when we respond to questions requiring interpretation; when we evaluate a person's genuine emotions, ideas, and attitudes from "inconsistent expressions"; and when we judge credibility and leadership qualities (Burgoon et al., 1996, p. 137). According to one study, nonverbal responsiveness in students significantly increases both teacher liking and compliance in granting student requests (Mottet et al., 2004).

As we've seen in Chapter 2, nonverbal cues also have greater influence when it comes to forming first impressions. And we give greater weight to nonverbal over verbal cues when they are contradictory. When it comes to deceptive behavior, nonverbal as well as verbal, it seems to be easier to tell the difference between liars and truth-tellers when we judge by all those behaviors—including, it turns out, how much they move. According to recent studies, both children and adults make fewer movements when they are lying (Vrij et al., 2004; Vrij, 2006).

Communication scholars agree that in most messages we get information from several nonverbal channels at once:

> Consistent multichanneled messages communicate sincerity, honesty, and believability because each channel provides additional weight to the overall message. Also, it is hard to lie in ten channels, whereas verbal lies are relatively easy to achieve. . . . However, this same multichanneled system has the capacity to send simultaneously contradictory messages such as approach and avoidance, ecstasy and guilt, joy and sorrow, or love and hate. (Andersen, 1999, p. 22)

Nonverbal Information

We learn most about the meaning of nonverbal messages by studying them in relation to verbal messages. Essentially, a nonverbal message functions in one of three ways: It replaces, reinforces, or contradicts a verbal message.

A nonverbal message that substitutes for a verbal one is often easy to interpret. Our culture provides us with gestures and expressions that are the equivalents of certain brief verbal messages: "Yes," "No," "Hello," "Good-bye," "I don't know," and so on. Likes and dislikes can also be expressed without words—for example, by smiling, clapping, smirking, or frowning.

When a nonverbal message reinforces a verbal message, meaning is conveyed quickly and easily, and with increased comprehension. Sometimes a single cue such as a hand movement or a long pause gives special emphasis to one part of a message so that we are able to discern what the speaker feels is most important.

Nonverbal cues predominate by sheer number. In general, if as receivers we are caught between two discrepant messages, we are more inclined to believe the nonverbal message. Nonverbal cues, we assume, give information about our intentions and emotional responses. Thus, in business many people still prefer face-to-face communication—whether it be meeting for lunch or in the formal setting of an office—to a fax, e-mail, letter, or telephone call when solving problems or negotiating critical decisions. In negotiation, much is learned from watching the other person's facial expression and gestures so that you can adapt your own responses. (The use of Skype teleconferencing, which provides a wealth of nonverbal cues, is also on the increase.)

Another reason the nonverbal message seems to have greater impact is the popular belief that body movements, facial expressions, vocal qualities, and so on cannot be simulated by the average person. Even children are quick to sense gestures or expressions that are not spontaneous.

Answers to Figure 4.1: (1) uneasy, (2) decisive, (3) flirtatious, and (4) concerned.

ISSUES IN COMMUNICATION

Herr von Osten purchased a horse in Berlin around 1900. The horse was trained to do tricks that brought fame and fortune to Herr von Osten. He became very famous and was soon dubbed "Clever Hans." He could answer mathematical questions by tapping his front hoof. So, if he were asked, "How much is two plus two?" he would tap his hoof four times. And so it went until some scientists administered several tests to determine if this was trickery. Hans passed most of the tests, until the scientists found one that he could not pass. When Hans was not able to see the audience, he could not answer the questions correctly. It turns out that Hans noticed the audience, and when he counted up to the correct answer, the audience members would stand upright and relax. He had learned that when this happened, he would be rewarded and the task was accomplished. So, this classic story was one in which body language or nonverbal communication was the key to Clever Hans's success (Knapp and Hall, 2010, pp. 4–5). This realization in part has ultimately led to the "double-blind" procedure for conducting human experiments. The experimenters, who know what they are trying to test for, never come in direct contact with the human subjects. Those experimenters who do come in contact with the subjects do not know what the experiment is trying to find. Thus, both groups of experimenters have some degree of blindness to the study. This is to prevent them from inadvertently giving off body language cues that could influence the study's outcome.

Nonverbal channels convey primarily relational messages, messages about the feeling/emotional level of our communication, rather than the thoughts (best communicated by verbal communication); also, nonverbal messages are ambiguous for the most part, except perhaps for certain gestures. Ambiguous facial expressions and gestures have sometimes been the cause of subway violence and street fights.

We all have some sensitivity to nonverbal cues, or we would not be able to communicate with the ease we do. Still, we know there are differences among people in how skilled they are in interpreting what they perceive. Through tests such as the popular Profile of Nonverbal Sensitivity Test—the PONS—researchers have confirmed that some people do have greater sensitivities to nonverbal cues. "Success in decoding nonverbal communication" is important not only in forming our initial impressions of others but also in maintaining our close relationships (Noller, 2006; Guerrero and Floyd, 2006).

As we discussed in Chapter 2, there are gender differences not only in interpersonal sensitivity but also in the ability to recall the physical appearance of others (Hall et al., 2006; Mast and Hall, 2006). Women seem to have the advantage in both cases. To explain this some scholars have proposed that, for women, social status and appearance are more closely linked and that women themselves are often judged on the basis of appearance so that possibly they are more aware of appearance and more competitive about it (J. Hall, 2006).

Most of our problems in interpreting meaning arise when we receive a nonverbal message that contradicts a verbal message. Suppose, for example, that a supervisor always cautions her employees not to postpone discussing problem areas in their work. "Don't wait till it's too late to remedy the situation. I want you to come and tell me when you run into problems," she repeats. Yet as one of the assistant managers enters her office, she looks up annoyed and gives him an icy stare. Then, as the employee starts to back out of her office, the supervisor says, "Well, don't stand there looking so frightened. Tell me what's on your mind."

Birdwhistell (1970) uses the term **kinesic slips** for mixed messages—*contradictory verbal and nonverbal messages.* Imagine this conversation between a couple who have just had a bitter quarrel. She asks, "Honey, are you still angry?" "No," he replies, "it's all right." "But you sound as though you're still angry," she insists. "I'm telling you I'm not angry!" he answers. His words give one message, his voice and frowning face another. He may not even be aware of the second. Which message is she likely to believe?

Verbal/Nonverbal Interaction

For purposes of analysis we speak of verbal and nonverbal messages as distinct, yet in daily life we are rarely able to separate their effects. For example, what we say is qualified, modified, by how we say it—tone of voice, facial expression, eye contact, and so on—as well as by the almost instantaneous verbal and nonverbal responses of others. And this interaction is ongoing.

The statement is often made that we cannot *not* communicate, that everything we do—or refrain from doing—communicates something. The playwright George Bernard Shaw once wrote, "Silence is the most perfect expression of scorn." But that is just one state of feeling that can be conveyed by silence. Being motionless and silent can convey confusion, awe, resistance, doubt, withholding, agreement, boredom, rejection—a seemingly infinite variety of responses.

In the remainder of this chapter, we shall see how through their nonverbal messages people give us many cues—spatial, temporal, visual, and vocal—about their emotions, their intentions, their personalities, and even their social status.

SPATIAL AND TEMPORAL CUES

Only when we interact with people of other cultures do we begin to realize that some of our most cherished ideas about what is appropriate conduct are norms, or rules, whether stated or unstated, about behavior; that is, they are relative, not absolute, values. Indirectly, our culture teaches us to communicate in many ways—through our voices, our gestures, and even our style of dressing. Yet each of us interprets and expresses these conventions somewhat differently.

Culture has an even more subtle and pervasive influence on nonverbal communication, however. Each culture continually provides its members with input about how the world is structured. Slowly we develop preconceptions about the world. It is the cues derived from these preconceptions that we take most for granted and that imperceptibly set the limits for our style of communication. Our cues about space and time are among those most significantly influenced by culture and sometimes the source of difficulties in intercultural communication.

Guerrero and Floyd (2006) distinguish between power, "having the ability and potential to influence others as well as to resist the persuasive attempt of others," and interpersonal dominance, "communication strategies that people use successfully to gain or express power" (p. 160).

Their extensive survey of research finds that nonverbal cues of power and dominance are numerous and often interrelated. For example, people who are powerful have greater control of personal space and also establish dominance visually. In meetings, they tend to position themselves centrally, whether seated at a table or standing in a room. They look at people more directly when they are speaking than when they are listening. When speaking, they can express power by choosing to stand when others are seated, thus reinforcing their height. Often, they speak more than others in conversation, also interrupting and changing topics of conversation more frequently.

These and other dominant behaviors often associated with strong social skills include direct gaze; expressiveness, both in touch and voice;

frequent eye contact when conversing; open arms and open body positioning; a strong and relatively loud voice; smiling and generally pleasant facial expressions (pp. 133–161).

One of the most interesting aspects of this research summary concerns nonverbal cues that convey poise and self-confidence:

> [People] judged as dominant typically appear poised, relaxed, and composed. . . . Poise and relaxation are communicated nonverbally through a set of behaviors that include asymmetrical leg and arm positions, sideways leaning, arm openness, open body position, expressive gestures, less swiveling, and less random leg and foot movement. . . . Greater facial pleasantness, smiling, eye contact, and proximity can also send messages of poise, relaxation, and composure. . . . (2006, p. 152)

Do you think of yourself as powerful? dominant? How would you rate your own nonverbal behavior in terms of poise and self-confidence?

Space

Personal Space

Personal space centers on the body and can be thought of as *a person's portable territory, which each individual carries along wherever he or she may go.* Robert Sommer, a psychologist at the University of California–Davis, refers to it as *"an area with invisible boundaries surrounding a person's body into which intruders may not come"* (1969, p. 26; italics added).

In research in libraries and parks, Sommer took on the role of intruder, systematically violating the personal space of others and observing the resulting tensions and anxieties. Much research on personal space focuses on the relationship between spatial arrangements (architectural elements, interior design, seating, and so on) and human feelings and interaction. For instance, in the study halls of college libraries, students tend to protect privacy by sitting as far away from each other as possible. One way of communicating this need is by occupying a corner position. Or students sprawl out, resting their legs on a nearby chair. If they get up from the table, they may "reserve" the place by spreading out books and papers or leaving clothing draped over the chair. How far you go in defending your personal space will depend, of course, on both your personality and your communication style. If you sit too close to me in the library, I may get up and move. But reverse our roles and you may glare at me and even spread out your notebooks and papers so that they take up a good part of the table.

Other research finds that personality variables such as need for affiliation influence the size of one's personal space (Rosenfeld, 1965). In his study of prison inmates who had committed violent crimes, Kinzel (1969) observed that these men had a personal space, or "body buffer zone," twice as large as that of nonviolent prisoners. Recently, it's even been suggested that "air rage" is related to a perceived invasion of personal space.

Another familiar aspect of personal space is the greater feeling of confidence when we are within our own surroundings:

> To allow yourself to be summoned voluntarily to someone else's home turf is a show of weakness. Inexperienced diplomats and politicians learn this only after having made too many concessions to adversaries or having lost the respect of allies. The recognized territorial advantage is the reason for insisting on a neutral locale for summit meetings and other serious talks. (Burgoon et al., 1996, p. 307)

Interpersonal Distance

Millions of people communicate nonverbally every day through use of text messaging and online applications like instant messaging, e-mail, blogs, chat rooms, forums, Web sites, and even gaming. With so much interaction between people through use of the Internet, a recent Stanford University study has taken a new approach to studying nonverbal communication in human behavior. Their main source for studying these behaviors is through an MMORPG, which is known as a massively multiplayer online role playing game.

The researchers state two main reasons for comparing the virtual world to the physical world. They are to "determine the positive and negative affects that online environments have on users in a media effects tradition, and to validate online games as a platform to study physical social interaction, both on the micro and macro level." The research platform would be a unique way to study social sciences and clinical therapy. In order for it to work, they must prove that social norms that apply to our world also apply to the virtual world. In an MMORPG, players can create their own unique avatar (a character representing themselves) and move about a huge virtual world through their mouse and keyboard. In these worlds players communicate through typing and can also make their character communicate through dancing, laughing, flirting, and other life-like movements. The MMORPG they are using is called "Second Life." Results from their studies have shown that interpersonal distance and eye gaze are credible findings that transfer from the physical world to the virtual world. They also find that the amount of social norms that apply to the virtual world depend on how real the users perceive the virtual world to be. With results shown positive, this will indeed be a research platform as technology and online gaming advance.

Students of nonverbal communication are indebted to the anthropologist Edward Hall for his cross-cultural studies of space as well as time. Hall has given the name **proxemics** to *the study of how human beings communicate through their use of space*. If you were to enter a restaurant with only one customer in it, chances are that you would not sit down right next to him or her. Hall explains that though this behavior seems natural to a North American, an Arab might have a very different notion of appropriate distance between strangers. By contrast, if you visited a new doctor and she sat down in the chair next to you rather than behind her desk, her closeness might communicate warmth and a lack of formality far beyond the norm.

Social scientists make use of the Scale of Social Distance, an instrument that uses the term "distance" figuratively, to indicate degree of liking or preference. Hall (1959) goes a step further and speaks of four measurable distances between people: intimate, personal, social, and public. Each distance is differentiated by a close and a far phase within which different behaviors occur (Figure 4.2). There is nothing arbitrary about these distances, as he explains:

> It is in the nature of animals, including man, to exhibit behavior which we call territoriality. In so doing, they use the senses to distinguish between one space or distance and another. The specific distance chosen depends on the transaction, the relationship of the interacting individuals, how they feel, and what they are doing. (p. 128)

Here we look briefly at the four distances and Hall's findings about what they mean to most North Americans.

Intimate Distance   At *intimate distance, 18 inches or less*, the presence of another person "is unmistakable and may at times be overwhelming because of the greatly stepped-up sensory inputs" (Hall, 1959, p. 116). In its close phase (6 inches or less) intimate distance lends itself primarily to nonverbal communication. This distance is usually reserved for very close friends and family. Subjects discussed are usually top secret. The far phase (6 to 18 inches) is often used for discussing confidential matters, with the voice usually kept to a whisper. Such close proximity is considered improper for public places, though dormitories seem to be exceptions to the rule. In general, Americans try hard to avoid close contact with people they do not know on buses and other public vehicles.

Personal Distance   *Personal distance,* from *1.5 to 4 feet*, can be thought of as "a small protective sphere or bubble that an organism maintains between itself and others" (Hall, 1959, p. 119). Topics discussed would still be personal. The close phase (1.5 to 2.5 feet) is still a distance reserved for very close relationships; the far phase (2.5 to 4 feet) is a comfortable distance for conversing with friends.

Figure 4.2 Interpersonal Distance Zones

Intimate Distance 0–18 in.		Close phase	Far phase
	Voice:	Soft whisper	Audible whisper
	Message:	Top secret	Very confidential
Personal Distance 1.5–4 ft.			
	Voice:	Soft	Slightly lowered
	Message:	Personal subject matter	Personal subject matter
Social Distance 4–12 ft.			
	Voice:	Full	Full with slight overloudness
	Message:	Nonpersonal information	Public information for others to hear
Public Distance 12–25 ft. or more			
	Voice:	Loud, talking to a group	Loudest
	Message:	Public information for others to hear	Hailing, departures

Source: From *The Silent Language* by Edward T. Hall, Copyright © 1959, 1981 by Edward T. Hall. Used by permission of Doubleday, a division of Random House, Inc.

Social Distance   *Social distance,* ranging from *4 to 12 feet,* is a psychological distance, "one at which the animal apparently begins to feel anxious when he exceeds its limits. We can think of it as a hidden band that contains the group." The close phase (4 to 7 feet) is suitable for conversations at social gatherings and business discussions. The far phase (7 to 12 feet) is appropriate for meetings in a business office. People who are in the room but outside the 7-foot boundary can be ignored without being offended. Those who violate the 7-foot boundary tend to be surprised if we do not acknowledge their presence, unless we are very busy. Humans have extended social distance by means of the telephone, radio, television, fax, computer (e-mail), and teleconferencing.

Public Distance   *Public distance, 12 feet or more of space,* is the largest of the zones and it exists only in human relationships. In fact, the public relationships and manners of Americans and Europeans are considerably different from those of other cultures. At the close phase (12 to 25 feet), a more formal style of language and a louder voice are required. At the far phase (25 feet or more), further accommodations to distance are usually made: Experienced public speakers exaggerate body movements, gestures, enunciation, and volume while reducing their rate of speech. Figure 4.2 is a brief summary of how message content and vocal shift vary with distance between communicators.

High- and Low-Contact Cultures   Within a culture as diverse as the United States, various co-cultures may develop their own proxemic norms. (A **co-culture** is *a group having sufficient distinctive traits to distinguish it from other members of the same dominant culture.*) In research on intercultural communication, the distinction is often made between high-contact and low-contact cultures. Members of **high-contact cultures** *touch each other more often, sit or stand closer to each other, make more eye contact, and speak louder.* Members of **low-contact cultures** *touch each other less often, maintain more interpersonal distance, and are more indirect in facing each other and in their eye contact. They also tend to use a lower, softer tone of voice.* French, Italian, Latin American, Russian, Arab, and African cultures are some high-contact cultures; German, Danish, and East Asian cultures include those seen as low-contact cultures (Figure 4.3). Moderate-contact cultures include the United States, New Zealand, Australia, and Canada (Ting-Toomey, 1999, p. 129).

Though there is a tendency to generalize about distance norms within Europe, it seems that people from northern European cultures—Sweden and Scotland, for example—require greater interpersonal distance than people from Mediterranean countries such as Italy and Greece.

Researchers are not saying that we calculate these differences while communicating. On the contrary, our sense of what distance is natural for a given interaction is so deeply ingrained in us by our culture that we automatically make spatial adjustments and interpret spatial cues. Latin Americans, Arabs, and the French, for example, stand so close to each other that if they exercise their own distance norms while conversing with a North American, they may arouse hostile or sexual feelings. If you want, test this concept the next time you converse with someone. See how close you can get before the other party starts backing away.

Orientation   Your **orientation**—that is, *the angle of your body as you interact with another person,* may also reflect the nature of the relationship between the two of you. For example, some studies of British and North American seating patterns have shown that a 90-degree-angle orientation facilitates conversation, face-to-face orientations tend toward competitive behaviors, and side-by-side orientations are more often viewed as showing cooperation (Hargie et al., 1987, p. 27). In Figure 4.4 we see several preferences in orientation for sitting at a table. Notice how situation often determines choice of orientation.

According to psychiatrist Albert Scheflen, you use certain frames, or positions, to define your space when you interact with others. For example, in the *side-by-side*

Figure 4.3   *Selected High- and Low-Contact Cultures*

Low-Contact Cultures		High-Contact Cultures	
Myanmar	Taiwan	Mediterranean region,	Northern Africa
(formerly Burma)	Thailand	including:	Eastern Europe
China	Vietnam	France	(including Russia)
Hong Kong	Norway	Greece	Indonesia
Japan	Sweden	Israel	Middle East
South Korea	Finland	Italy	Latin America
Philippines	Germany	Portugal	(including Mexico)
		Spain	South America

Source: Reprinted by permission of Waveland Press, Inc. from Peter A. Andersen, *Nonverbal Communication: Forms and Functions*, 2nd ed. (Long Grove, IL: Waveland Press, Inc., 2008). All rights reserved.

frame you are sometimes closer to the other person (shoulder to shoulder), but you have no eye contact. In the *vis-à-vis frame,* you face the other person, modulate the distance between you, and maintain eye contact. It is striking, one consultant on nonverbal communication points out, that the side-by-side frame is preferred by men, the vis-à-vis frame by women (Nelson, 2004, pp. 164–165).

Research on doctor-patient communication confirms the importance of how doctors orient themselves toward their patients:

> One of the most well-documented interrelationships is between gaze and body orientation. . . . Although different segments of the body (e.g., the head, torso, and legs) can be oriented in different directions . . . , there remains a socially understood body-segment hierarchy in terms of [a person's] levels of attention and engagement. Specifically, though gaze orientation communicates . . . [a person's focus] of attention, relative to upper-body segments (e.g., the head), lower body segments (e.g., the legs) more strongly communicate . . . dominant orientation. (Robinson, 2006, p. 452)

This applies, of course, to many forms of interpersonal communication.

Figure 4.4   *Seating Preferences at a Rectangular Table*

Type of interaction	Position of participants	Suggested situations
Conversation		• Counseling interview • Employer interviewing an employee • Some progressive job interviews
Cooperation		• Friends meeting in a pub • Teacher helping a pupil in his work • Staff cooperating on the same project
Competition		• Some job interviews • Principal interviewing pupil • Playing games such as chess, poker, etc.
Coaction		• Strangers in a public eating place • Unfamiliar students working at same library table • Strangers sharing a seat on the train

Source: Adapted from *Social Skills in Interpersonal Communication* by Hargie et al., 1987. Reprinted by permission of Taylor and Francis.

Time

A study of 36 cities across the United States finds many differences in the pace or tempo of life: Researchers used four measures—the walking speed of pedestrians, work speed, concern with clock time (e.g., whether people wore watches), and talking speed. The fastest city was—no, not New York—but Boston, with New York ranking third. "The fastest overall times were in the northeast, followed by the midwest, the south and then the west" (Levine, 1997, pp. 146–151).

When we study *how human beings communicate through their use of time*, we are concerned with **chronemics**. At what time in the evening is it too late to call someone? How many days or weeks in advance can a first date be arranged? How quickly do you expect a friend to reply to an e-mail from you? In each case, timing leads to certain expectations that influence the face-to-face communication that subsequently occurs. Being very late for a job interview can have a disastrous effect, not just a dramatic one. Much of the ensuing verbal communication may be spent explaining away the nonverbal message that has already been conveyed.

Conceptions of what is "early" or "late" vary from culture to culture. Americans tend to be "busy" people. They tend to like schedules and agendas. They value doing things "on time." So it is sometimes jarring to see themselves as others do. For example, *In the Time of the Butterflies,* a novel by Julia Alvarez, is set in the Dominican Republic. A woman from the United States phones to set up an appointment to meet Dedé:

"So if I'm coming from Santiago I drive on past Salcedo?" the woman asks.

"*Exactamente.* And then where you see a great big anacahuita tree, you turn left."

"A . . . great . . . big . . . tree . . . ," the woman repeats. She is writing all this down!

"I turn left. What's the name of the street?"

"It's just the road by the anacahuita tree. We don't name them," Dedé says, driven to doodling to contain her impatience . . .

The voice laughs, embarrassed. "Of course. You must think I'm so outside of things." *Tan afuera de la cosa.*

Dedé bites her lip. "Not at all," she lies. "I'll see you this afternoon then."

"About what time?" the voice wants to know.

Oh yes. The gringos need a time. But there isn't a clock time for this kind of just-right moment. "Any time after three or three-thirty, four-ish."

"Dominican time, eh?" The woman laughs.

"*Exactamente!*" Finally, the woman is getting the hang of how things are done here. (1994, p. 4)

Martin and Nakayama (2008) distinguish between monochronic and polychronic conceptions of time (Table 4.1). **Monochronic** time is time thought of as *linear and segmented.* In cultures with monochronic time, people perceive time as "almost tangible," speaking of it as if it were money (time gets "saved," "spent," "wasted," "lost"). People like to do one thing at a time, and their preference is for precise scheduling. Making appointments and deadlines is highly valued. In cultures with a **polychronic** conception of time, on the other hand, *many things are going on at once.* Nor is there great surprise when delays or interruptions occur. Indeed, they seem to be expected, and people take them in stride.

The new technologies seem to be influencing how people handle their use of time, even in monochronic cultures. Have you ever talked to someone on the phone only to hear him using his computer as he spoke with you? A recent cartoon showed a woman sitting alone and speaking on her cell phone. "Are you multitasking me?" she asks the person she is talking to. Some cognitive scientists caution that there are limits to how many activities we should be involved in at a given time and that doing several things at once sometimes interferes with the ability to concentrate and results in mistakes. According to one expert, "Disruptions and interruptions are a bad deal from the standpoint of our ability to process information" (Lohr, 2007, p. 1).

Table 4.1   *Some Differences between Monochronic and Polychronic People*

Monochronic People	Polychronic People
Do one thing at a time	Do many things at once
Concentrate on the job	Are highly distractible and subject to interruptions
Take time commitments (deadlines, schedules) seriously	Consider time commitments an objective to be achieved if possible
Are low-context and need information	Are high-context and already have information
Are committed to the job	Are committed to people and human relationships
Adhere religiously to plans	Change plans often and easily
Are concerned about not disturbing others; follow rules of privacy and consideration	Are more concerned with those who are closely related (family, friends, close business associates) than with privacy
Show great respect for private property	Borrow and lend things often and easily
Emphasize promptness	Base promptness on the relationship
Are accustomed to short-term relationships	Have strong tendencies to build lifelong relationships

Source: From *Understanding Cultural Differences* by Edward T. Hall and Mildred R. Hall, Intercultural Press. Copyright © 1990 Edward T. Hall Associates. Published by Intercultural Press, Inc.

It has been said that for the American businessperson discussion is simply "a means to an end: the deal." Moreover, it's a sign of good faith to agree on major issues, assuming that details will be worked out later on. But like the Latin American, the Greek businessperson engages in what may seem to others as prolonged discussion and an excessive preoccupation with details. For the Greek, these concerns usually signify goodwill (Martin and Nakayama, 2008).

Do you think of yourself as monochronic or polychronic? Some of the differences between monochronic people and polychronic people are listed in Table 4.1. Hall believes that these approaches to time are learned. And if his distinction is a valid one, the culture your family is from probably influenced your own use of time.

VISUAL CUES

The second category of nonverbal cues we will discuss is extremely broad, ranging from facial expressions and body movements to the clothing we wear and the objects we display.

In *The Story of Clever Hans,* as discussed in the chapter earlier, people who came to see Hans perform would have been shocked to learn that they were, by their body movements, transmitting the correct answers visually. Yet they were probably leaning forward eagerly to take in every aspect of the spectacle before them, for we all know how much we gain by seeing a performer, a lecturer, or any person we are speaking to. In fact, members of discussion groups interact more frequently when seated facing each other rather than side by side. In other words, the greater our visibility, the greater our potential for communicating. And, as we saw in Chapter 1, the greater the number of channels the sender uses, the more information is received.

Visual cues add to the information transmitted through other channels and at times stand alone. Specific motions of the head, for example, give the equivalents of certain brief verbal messages such as yes and no, and these movements may vary from culture to culture. Even head orientation, the direction in which we turn our heads, communicates something. Mehrabian (1967) found that a person who gives more head orientation while speaking conveys more positive feeling.

The British actress Helen Mirren won an Academy Award in 2007 for her performance as Queen Elizabeth in *The Queen*. Asked during an interview how she had prepared for this commanding role, she spoke, among other things, of posture; she said she projected authority in part by the way she stood, the way she carried herself. In playing Elizabeth, she said she learned to carry herself as the police do, with her arms at her sides, never folded, since folding one's arms conveys being submissive. Mirren has played a London police inspector, the present queen of England, and Elizabeth the First—all roles that demanded the projection of great power.

A pioneering figure in research on nonverbal communication, Ray Birdwhistell (1952) introduced the term **kinesics** to refer to *the study of body movements in communication*. "Body movements" is used in a broad sense and refers also to movements of the head and face. Birdwhistell has estimated that over 700,000 possible physical signs can be transmitted via body movement. The first group of visual cues we will look at has to do with facial expression.

Facial Expression

One example of the popular interest in nonverbal communication is the 2012 Fox television show named *Lie To Me*, about Dr. Cal Lightman, an expert in reading nonverbal behavior. The show centers around this expert's ability to tell when people are lying to enable the police to solve criminal cases.

The human face is so mobile that it can effortlessly register boredom, surprise, affection, and disapproval one after another in a few seconds. *We constantly read expressions from people's faces*. In fact, *facial cues* are the single most important source of nonverbal communication. Comments such as "If looks could kill" and "It was all over her face" bear witness to the significance we give to facial expression.

We make use of information about the face in many ways:

1. To identify a person's social category memberships
2. To discern others' personality traits

3. To detect the direction of their attention
4. To gauge the sincerity of their verbal behavior
5. To understand [their] thoughts and minds
(Bodenhausen and Macrae, 2006, p. 511)

During the last 25 years there has been an upswing in research on the human face, and it's being led by researchers in neuroscience. Nonetheless, a review of past and current research emphasizes that contributions from many disciplines are needed to add to this growing fund of knowledge (Zebrowitz, 2006). What's particularly interesting is that there seems to be what some refer to as "a kernel of truth" about the judgments we make about character or personality based on facial traits (Penton-Voak et al., 2006). For example, one study looked at teaching fellows at Harvard University. The researchers found that students rating video clips of teachers lasting as short as ten seconds had a remarkably high correlation with actual teacher-effectiveness evaluations made by students of those same teachers after an entire semester. Similar results have been found of those interviewing for a job. Very brief video clips yielded results that had very high correlations with the actual outcomes of the job interviews (Gladwell, 2009, p. 381).

We like a face or we don't; we think it's animated or relatively inert. These are general impressions. But what do we see that makes us judge someone to be sad or happy or frightened or angry? Isolating which facial cues specify particular emotions is more difficult than simply judging a face.

Ekman and Friesen (1971) asked members of a preliterate New Guinea culture to judge emotions from the facial expressions of Westerners. The subjects had had virtually no exposure to Western culture. Yet they made the same identifications that Westerners made, with one exception: They were not able to differentiate between fear and surprise. The researchers concluded that, at least in some respects, expressive facial behavior is constant across cultures. They acknowledged that cultural differences exist but argued that the differences are reflected "in the circumstances which elicit an emotion, in the action consequences of an emotion and in the display rules which govern the management of facial behavior in particular social settings" (p. 129).

According to anthropologist Melvin Konner (1987), smiling seems to be a human social display that is universal. For example, Eibl-Eibesfeldt's films from many remote parts of the world show smiling as a "consistent feature of greeting, often in combination with raising of the eyebrows" (p. 42). How our smiles are interpreted, however, will depend on many variables including physical attractiveness (Forgas, 1987). We know, for example, that in Japan a smiling face is often interpreted as more "feminine" than is a serious face (Kawamura and Kageyama, 2006, p. 210).

Research on more than 30 different cultures suggests that there is a high level of agreement in judging emotions from photographs of people's facial expressions. Matsumoto (2006) and many other scholars maintain that there is convincing evidence for the universality of facial expressions of emotion. The six universal expressions he identifies are disgust, fear, happiness, sadness, surprise, and anger. They can also be found in animals.

Nonetheless, there seem to be cultural differences in the expression of emotion. Through *cultural display rules,* rules that we learn in early childhood, we manage and adapt how we express emotion. Matsumoto and colleagues, who created the DRAI (the Display Rule Assessment Inventory), have also found that *control* over the expression of various emotions varies from one culture to another. For example, among Russians, Americans, and Japanese, "Americans and Russians both expressed anger and contempt more than Japanese, Americans expressed fear and distrust more than Russians, and Americans expressed happiness more than did Russians and Japanese" (2006, pp. 226–227).

There is also a growing body of research about emotional contagion (Andersen and Guerrero, 1998) and how perceiving an emotional expression—a smile, for example—might cause us to mimic that expression and thereby experience that state of feeling. The implication is that we "catch" another person's emotions, through feedback from either the face or the body (Doherty, 1997). Generally, our accuracy in identifying emotions seems to increase with the number of cues we receive.

We mimic others—that is, we tend to repeat their gestures, their mannerisms, and the way they move—but most of the time we are not doing this consciously. Your author observed a woman who always visited the local library and sat in a chair scowling. He decided to smile at this woman and discovered that each time he did, the woman's face relaxed and she smiled broadly. Several researchers believe that this *chameleon effect,* as nonconscious mimicry is sometimes called, actually promotes our relationships with other people and results in increased liking and affiliation. They argue that this two-way relationship is evidence that "mimicry has played an important role in evolution" (Lakin et al., 2003, p. 145).

In a recent experiment on cross-cultural understanding of facial expressions, Elfenbein observed that accuracy in judging emotion on this basis is "a core component of emotional intelligence" (2006, p. 21). Her study of improving accuracy through feedback is particularly interesting because she found greater improvement of accuracy skills when subjects were judging cultural groups more distant from their own familial backgrounds. She suggests that perhaps this occurs because the feedback had "greater novel information" (p. 21). Her work would seem to contradict Matsumoto's findings about familiarity, but her conclusions are only concerned with the influence of feedback. Further research is needed, although Elfenbein's study offers more evidence that accuracy in our judgments about emotions can be improved. For a detailed look at how the face works, go to *www.artnatomia.net/uk/index.html.*

Oculesics

"In the right context, even a glance held a fraction longer than normal may be perceived as an act of intimacy. The glance penetrates the private psychological space of the other, and also reveals one's own" (Bates, 2001, p. 113). Prolonged eye contact, of course, can also be seen as aggressive. The many rules implicit in our culture about looking at others are a tacit admission that eye contact is perhaps the single most important facial cue we use in communicating. *The study of the role of eye behaviors such as eye contact, eye movements, and pupil dilation in communicating* is called **oculesics.**

At present most of the research on eye behaviors has to do with eye contact. One study estimates that in group communication we spend 30 to 60 percent of our time in eye contact with others (10 to 30 percent of the looks last only about a second). Four unstated rules about eye contact are:

1. A looker may invite interaction by staring at another person who is on the other side of a room. The target's studied return of the gaze is generally interpreted as acceptance of the invitation, whereas averting the eyes is a rejection of the looker's request.

2. There is more mutual eye contact between friends than others, and a looker's frank gaze is widely interpreted as positive regard.

3. Persons who seek eye contact while speaking are regarded not only as exceptionally well-disposed by their target, but also as more believable and earnest.

4. If the usual short, intermittent gazes during conversation are replaced by gazes of longer duration, the target interprets this as meaning that the task is less important than the personal relation between the two persons. (Argyle, 1985)

The second rule is corroborated by other researchers: Frequent eye contact does seem to be a sign of affection or interest. For example, flirting will often begin "with a quick upward glance, followed by averting the gaze and then another bout of eye contact, and a friendly smile" (Bates, 2001, p. 113). "Eye contact," writes Andersen, "does more than signal availability: it is an invitation to communicate" (1999, p. 191). A recent review of research on nonverbal communication and interaction between physicians and their patients reports one study in which "physicians' eye contact while patients spoke was positively associated with physicians' psychodiagnostic abilities" (Robinson, 2006, p. 441). And in the absence of such gaze orientation on the part of the doctor, patients were less likely to disclose information about themselves.

Even in public communication, frequency of eye contact affects the message sender. When an audience gives negative feedback (including poor eye contact), a speaker tends to lose fluency and to do poorly in presenting his or her message. In turn, audiences prefer a speaker who gives good eye contact. Researchers report that the best nonverbal predictor of perceived social support and coping is eye contact.

Why is eye contact so rewarding to others? Perhaps it is because the eyes are considered such a valuable source of information. There are several popular beliefs about what can be learned from watching someone's eyes. For example, two people who exchange knowing glances at a party seem able to communicate without words. Being able to look another person in the eye traditionally implies that you are being truthful and that your intentions are not to be questioned. Conversely, the person who averts his or her eyes is thought to be hiding something. In the Mediterranean, belief in the power of eyes is seen, for example, in the eye painted on Greek boats and the glass eyeball worn as a charm (sometimes on a key chain or bracelet) that is thought to protect the wearer against the curse of "the evil eye." (See Chapter 10 on the intercultural aspects of eye contact and cultures in which avoiding eye contact is a sign of respect.)

Body Movements

If during a party you were asked to record and classify all the body movements of two people in conversation during a five-minute period, you would probably find this an impossible task. Nothing short of a film captures the rapid, often subtle changes of the body.

Take flirting, for example. What are the nonverbal behaviors that signal flirting? The classic work of Scheflen (1965) grew out of his filming and analysis of patterns of "quasi-courtship" that he noticed between males and females during psychotherapy as well as at conferences and business meetings. After studying films, he was able to classify typical behaviors. Some were simply movements to establish greater rapport and closeness between participants; others were signs of nonverbal flirting. For example, how we position our arms and legs transmits cues about who we include and exclude, as in Figure 4.5: (a) "We're not open to others" and (b) "I'm with you—not him" (Knapp and Hall, 2005, p. 429).

Signs of *courtship readiness* included *preening* by playing with the hair, pulling at stockings, adjusting the tie, and so on.

Positioning was another source of cues about interpersonal attraction. For example, two people might face each other and lean forward eagerly. Sometimes they sat with the upper half of their torsos turned in an open position so that a third person might enter the conversation but with their legs forming a circle and thus excluding the intruder.

Actions of appeal included flirtatious glances and head cocking. Women signaled sexual invitation by crossing the legs, exposing the thigh, exhibiting the palm of the hand, and protruding the breast.

To find out how people choose a mate, Steven Gangestad, an evolutionary psychologist, has studied the universality of flirting behaviors: In all cultures there seems

Figure 4.5 *Positional Cues*

a　　　　　　　　　　　　　　　　　　　　b

Source: From KNAPP. Nonverbal Communication in Human Interaction, 5E. © 2002 Wadsworth, a part of Cengage Learning, Inc. Reproduced by permission. www.cengage.com/permissions

to be a set of gestures we use to express sexual interest. Some researchers including David Givens, an anthropologist, and Timothy Perper, a social psychologist, have studied flirting in cocktail lounges and bars: It seems that "if all went well, a couple would invariably progress from touching themselves to touching each other" (Rodgers, 1999, p. 39). One study (Simpson et al., 1993) found that, though the sets of nonverbal behaviors were different for men and women, there was a clear-cut pattern. Men who were flirting smiled and laughed more often, showed more flirtatious glances, and looked downward less frequently than men who were not flirting. In flirting women, body movements seemed to be more pronounced; women tended to cant their heads during conversation and to lean forward; of course, by leaning forward you maximize other cues from your face and head. Although earlier researchers have connected head canting with communicating submissiveness, this seems not to be the case here. Women who canted their heads were actually rated not only as more engaging but slightly more dominant (p. 456). Future research may explain these discrepancies.

In a totally different context, a study by Maddux, Mullen, and Galinsky (2008) suggests that mirroring your opponent's body movements during negotiations could produce better outcomes. Participants were either instructed to subtly mirror their partner (for example, leaning back in your chair if the other person does), or were not asked to mirror their partner. In the "mirroring" condition, the two parties reached agreement 67 percent of the time. However, in the "nonmirroring" condition only 12.5 percent of the participants reached agreement. So, body movements can play an important role in communication effectiveness.

Hand Gestures

Anthropologists distinguish humankind from other animals by their use of language and their superior manual dexterity. Flexible hands enable human beings to use tools and to draw on a wide range of gestures in communicating. As a mode of nonverbal communication, *hand gestures rank second in importance only to facial cues.*

The palm of the hand conveys some of the "least-noticed, but most powerful, body signals," according to Pease and Pease (2006, p. 36). They identify three *major palm-command gestures:*

Palm-Up: The upward facing palm is nonthreatening, a sometimes submissive gesture. "If you want someone to talk, you can use the Palm-Up as a 'handover' gesture to let them know you expect them to talk and that you're ready to listen." A throwback, perhaps, to earlier times when the open palm was an indication that the person was not carrying any weapons.

Palm-Down: In contrast, the palm that is facing downward conveys authority immediately, so that when you use this gesture "the other person will sense that you've given them an order . . . and may begin to feel antagonistic toward you, depending on your relationship with him in a work environment" (pp. 36–37).

Palm-Closed-Finger-Pointed: A closed palm and pointed finger is, according to this research, "one of the most annoying gestures anyone can use while speaking, particularly when it beats time to the speaker's words." It is considered an insult in some cultures (p. 38). Apparently, this gesture elicits the least positive response from listeners and the least recall of what the speaker has said.

Sometimes pointing is solely nonverbal, and pointing at others is often considered an offensive gesture. The author recalls an incident in a crowded restaurant in which someone at his table proceeded to collect all the empty plates, put them on top of his own, and then point at a busy waiter and point down at the pile of plates, gesturing for the waiter to take them away immediately. The atmosphere became decidedly frosty. The pointing gesture not only offended the waiter but also the other guests at the table.

It is not only broad, expansive gestures that communicate mood. Less animated people often communicate inadvertently by means of their hands. The rather reserved husband of a lawyer we know repeatedly drums his fingers on a table or chair whenever his wife speaks about her practice. This behavior is the only sign of his impatience with her deep involvement in her profession.

Even those who were born blind gesture with their hands when they speak. Although our hand gestures can convey nonverbal messages on their own, when we gesture with our hands we actually enhance our ability to think (Goldin-Meadow, 2003). When children are prevented from gesturing—for example, using their hands when explaining a mathematical method that had been taught to them—they remember less of what they'd been taught (Watts, 2006, p. 1384). And when people are lying, there is an increase in the number of their metaphoric hand gestures (those that are pictorial and represent abstract ideas—for example, drawing a shape with one's hands, such as a fist to indicate strength). The number of pointing gestures also decreases (Caso et al., 2006).

Hand gestures sometimes substitute for verbal communication. Deaf mutes use a system of hand signals so comprehensive that it literally replaces spoken language. The signals themselves are arbitrary. Many of our hand movements are culturally determined. Hand gestures may be used differently even within a single location. In New York there are at least 100 ways of greeting someone by shaking hands. Between 2003 and 2004 Michael Britton and his crew filmed many kinds of New York handshakes for a one-hour documentary called "Gimme Five: History of a Hundred Handshakes" (Moynihan, 2004, B1). Imagine—an entire hour of handshakes.

The same gestures can convey different things to members of different cultures, and, over time, gestures change even within the same culture. To an American, for example, making a circle with one's thumb and forefinger and extending the other fingers means "okay," but to a Brazilian it is an obscene sign of contempt.

Desmond Morris and his colleagues in England (1979) have identified what they call twenty key gestures used in Europe. They are shown in Figure 4.6. Some of these, such as the nose thumb (no. 3), the forearm jerk (no. 7), the ring (no. 9), and the palm-back V-sign (no. 20), are quite familiar to us. Others, however, such as the cheek screw (no. 5), the horizontal horn-sign (no. 11), the chin flick (no. 14), and the fig (no. 12) are almost completely unknown in the United States. They found that different meanings were assigned in different countries. The fig, for example,

Figure 4.6   *Key Gestures*

Source: From *Gestures* by Desmond Morris, P. Collett, P. Marsh, and M. O'Shaughnessy, 1979. Reprinted by permission of Desmond Morris.

is interpreted in many different ways including as sexual comment, sexual insult, or protection. Similarly, the nose tap (no. 19) has several interpretations—among them, complicity, be alert, you are being nosey, I'm alert, he is clever, and awareness that a threat is present.

Haptics

Touch is one of our most important means of communicating nonverbally. **Haptics,** *the study of how we use touch to communicate,* has been receiving increasing attention among communication scholars.

We know that touch is essential for psychological and physical development in children and emotional well-being in adults. In our culture, being able to touch other human beings seems to be linked with high self-esteem and sociability. And our experience of intimacy, connectedness with others, and satisfaction in relationships is intensified by being touched (Prager, 2000). In the play *Dinner with Friends* by Donald Margulies, one of the characters describes when he finally decided to divorce his wife: He notices that during an entire week she has never touched him once.

In addition to conveying nurturance and caring, touch is also used to signify a professional relationship (being touched by a barber, for example); a social relationship (handshakes); friendship (for example, touching the upper arm); intimacy (hugs, for instance); and sexual arousal (for example, certain types of kisses). In each instance, touch is a bonding gesture (Heslin and Alper, 1983).

Touching is thought by scholars to vary with gender and culture. A recent study attempted to test the widely held theory that "touching behavior is an expression of dominance" by examining whether in traditional male-dominated cultures men will touch more than women will (Dibiase and Gunnoe, 2004, p. 49). The study also looked at whether men will touch more with their hands. Those who participated were young men and women from Italy, the United States, and the Czech Republic. Results showed that women did more nonhand than hand touching. The most significant differences between men and women were in the Czech Republic, which, like Italy, is a high-contact culture. In the Czech Republic, where the society is more stratified by gender, there were more gender differences in hand touching. And Italians, who belong to a high-contact culture, "touched significantly more than Czechs, who touched more than Americans" (p. 59).

We also use touch to persuade or influence other people; in fact, touching increases self-disclosure and compliant behavior. The influence of touching on compliance has been demonstrated in several fascinating studies. For example, subjects touched lightly on the arm were more likely to sign a petition than those who were not touched (Willis and Hamm, 1980). Besides the need for touch to establish and develop our relationships with others, some touch appears to have unambiguous symbolic content or meaning. Further, the codes of interpersonal touch encompass a great range of meanings, so we use touch to convey many different things, some far more ambiguous than others.

Research (Jones, 1999; Jones and Yarbrough, 1985) identifies seven types of touches:

Positive affect touches include touches of support, appreciation, inclusion, affection, physical attraction, and sexual interest.

Playful touches show playful affection or playful aggression.

Control touches gain compliance or attention or emphasize a response.

Ritualistic touches are more formal touches that signal greeting or departure.

*Hybrid touche*s are those of greeting or departure that express affection.

Task-related touches might accompany a task (e.g., helping someone put on a coat) or be used along with a comment ("I like your coat," said while touching the coat).

Accidental touches are perceived as unintentional (e.g., brushing past someone on the street). (Adapted from Jones, 1999, pp. 196–200)

The University of Arizona did a study about the interpretations of touch between men and women, particularly concerning their age and marital status. Their study consisted of 305 adults, both married and unmarried, ranging in ages from 18 to 69. In general, interactions such as sitting on one's lap, intertwining each other's legs, or kissing were interpreted by women as playful and warm whereas men interpret them as signs of sexual desire. Their research goes further to discover that men under the age of 30 as well as unmarried men of any age had more favorable reactions to intimate touch than did women. The same is true if the situation is reversed as well. Women over the age of 30 and married women react more positively toward intimate touch than did men. The study shows that the effects of touch to men and women do not rely solely on being young and single, so the question is why does marriage change the way men and women interpret it? (Hanzal, Segrin, and Dorros, 2008).

Touch is involving; it is an approach form of behavior. On the other hand, **touch avoidance** is *"a negative attitude toward touch that also affects [your] proxemic behavior and other types of nonverbal communication"* (Andersen, 1999, p. 173). Touch avoidance is not about how much you touch others but your feelings and attitude about touching and being touched; it can be thought of as reflecting your general level of intimacy. Touch avoidance is also a good predictor of how much interpersonal distance we maintain, particularly when the other person is female (Anderson and Sull, 1985).

In discussing proxemics, we examined the distinction between high- and low-contact cultures. Edward Hall (1959) identifies the United States and Northern European cultures as low-contact cultures, but one study of patterns of touch (McDaniel and Andersen, 1998) finds a broad range of touching behaviors in members of most cultures. The exception is to be seen in Asian countries, especially in Northeast Asia. Like many others, the authors cite Confucianism as a possible influence on the "East Asian reluctance toward interpersonal touch" (p. 70). Other variables affect patterns of touching—among them the degree of familiarity between people, their status, and, of course, the communication context itself.

Physical Appearance and the Use of Objects

It is said that when Albert Einstein was asked by his wife to change his clothes to meet the German ambassador, Einstein replied: "They want to see me. Here I am. If they want to see my clothes, open my closet and show them my suits."

There are not many people who show such complete disregard for appearance. **Objectics,** *the study of how we select and make use of physical objects in our nonverbal communication,* is concerned with every kind of physical object—from the clothing you wear to the furniture you choose to the car you drive. For example, whether you intend to or not, you often project a personal style through how you dress. Clothes may not make the person, but dress, general physical appearance, and grooming are often the basis of first and relatively long-lasting impressions.

Martha Stewart, a high-visibility defendant, seemed unaware that the French handbag she wore at her trial, an exclusive model that cost upward of $6,000, would create an uproar. It was widely commented on by reporters, and there was also some question as to whether the cost of the bag had been discussed among the jurors. Because her trial concerned whether she lied about selling a stock illegally to protect an investment, wearing the handbag in the courtroom was probably an unfortunate choice, conveying a degree of affluence that did not serve her case well.

Even whether you wear glasses can affect the way you are perceived by others. It's well known that among architects the *style* of glasses they wear is always noted. Although glasses are often associated with intelligence and deliberately used to convey it (see Stephen Colbert's parody of newscasters on "The Colbert Report"), glasses are sometimes interpreted as conveying sincerity. Consider this description of a character in Eileen Chang's story "Red Rose, White Rose":

> Zhenbao wasn't tall, but he was vigorous and quick. He . . . wore black-rimmed glasses, with something peculiarly untouched in his facial expression. His posture was excellent and he didn't joke around—unless, that is, it was appropriate to joke. He seemed frank and open, a man you could take in at a glance—and if you couldn't quite pinpoint the sincerity in his eyes those eyeglasses were proof enough. (2007, p. 256)

For those in the public eye, even a change in hairstyle can reinforce an impression. For example, after Angelina Jolie made unflattering statements about one of her children in a widely publicized video interview, her appearance at the 2007 Golden Globes drew this criticism: "And while she looked ultra-glamorous at the premiere of her latest film, 'The Good Shepherd,' the perfectly upswept hair and self-contained demeanor of her recent appearances have also made her seem plastic" (James, 2007, E7).

Uniforms tell us a great deal about rank and status. In several studies, people received greater help or compliance with their requests (e.g., signing a petition) when they were formally or neatly dressed than they did when their dress was casual or careless (Kleinke, 1986, pp. 77–78).

How formally you dress can be another sensitive indicator. Most people tend to comply with office dress codes, which until recently were extremely casual. There seems to be a return to more formal dress not only for job interviews but in the workplace as well, at least for meetings with bosses and clients. "Credibility," says one young lawyer, "is a suit" (Parnes, 2001, p. G1). (For more on dress as well as other nonverbal cues during job interviews, see Chapter 11.)

The clothing you wear often communicates your compliance or noncompliance with traditional values. And being overdressed for a social function can suggest a lack of sophistication. Interestingly, it's people with higher status who usually have the option of dressing up or down (Andersen, 1999).

Even your choice of color can may be interpreted as communicating something about you. For example, the novelist Sandra Cisneros created an uproar in a historic district of San Antonio when she painted her house purple. At times, your choice of accessories or equipment suggests a desire to communicate status or power—for example, through a Rolex watch, a state-of-the-art laptop, or a BlackBerry. In fact, high-end cell phones have been compared to cars: "Phones, like cars, are fashion items: people generally replace them long before they actually wear out. Both are social technologies that bring people together and act as symbols of independence for teenagers" ("Phones Are the New Cars," 2006, p. 16).

Objects can also come to have symbolic value. Following the terrorist attacks on New York and Washington, many people displayed American flags on their cars, and we heard of one Sikh who started wearing a turban that was red, white, and blue. Similarly, a small pink triangle on an envelope conveys support for gay rights, and wearing a red ribbon may draw attention to AIDS awareness. A nose ring may signal something about the wearer's unconventionality. In general, cosmetics, jewelry, and tattoos or decals—seen even on high-fashion models—often evoke strong responses from others.

And, of course, choices vary from one culture to another. The manager of Porsche in China, a country of many new millionaires, explained that the Chinese are not interested in sports cars and that the luxury car of choice there is a 911 convertible rather than a coupe, "the opposite of Germany and the States," because "in a convertible, people can see you" (Smith, 2004, p. 14). And while Rolls-Royces in most other parts of the world are owner-driven, in Asia they are chauffeur-driven because owners want to be seen being driven.

We have discussed a great many visual cues individually, but remember that as a communicator you are also taking in and interpreting cues about space and time as well as vocal cues, which we will look at in some detail.

VOCAL CUES

When they are online, many people also add nonverbal cues to their text-based messages (Walther, 2006). When they want to create an impression or express feelings, or convey variations in tone or volume, they use capital and lowercase letters differently, typing errors, exclamation points, and other punctuation marks and emoticons (sometimes called smileys) along with their verbal messages.

Early in this chapter, we described communication that was verbal/vocal—that is, both verbal and vocal. One difference between the verbal and the vocal message is the difference between what is said and how it is said.

Take the sentence "I hate you." Imagine these words being said to show anger or in a much different way to sound seductive. The simple sentence "I'm glad to meet you" can sound cold and insincere despite its verbal message. Or suppose you go to a friend's apartment and she opens the door and says, "Oh, it's you." The vocal cues, perhaps in combination with several visual cues, tell you whether she is really pleased to see you, indifferent, or even disappointed. Of course, if she simply groans when she opens the door, this is an example of nonverbal/vocal communication.

The study of vocal phenomena, **paralinguistics** or *paralanguage, refers to something beyond or in addition to language itself.* Paralanguage has two components: *voice qualities,* such as *pitch, range, resonance, lip control, and articulation control;* and *vocalizations,* or *noises without linguistic structure, such as crying, laughing, and grunting* (Trager, 1958). So using paralinguistic cues online such as those mentioned above is another attempt to go beyond communicating simply by verbal means.

Several distinct emotions can be accurately identified solely on the basis of vocal cues, but the more similar the emotions—admiration and affection, for example—the greater our difficulty in identifying them. For example, when Kevin Costner spoke at Whitney Houston's funeral on February 18, 2012, his voice broke several times, showing the deep affection and respect he had for her as his co-star in the movie *The Bodyguard.* You can watch his very touching 17-minute speech on YouTube.

Much research on vocal characteristics and emotions parallels the studies of facial expressions. Mehrabian (1968) found that people are easily able to judge the degree of liking communicated vocally. One team of researchers identified four categories of emotion: positive feeling, dislike, sadness, and apprehension or fear. The results confirm that "voice sounds alone, independent of semantic components of vocal messages, carry important clues to the emotional state of a speaker" (Knapp and Hall, 2005, p. 410). People can detect aggressiveness from a tape recording of a speaker's message, though not from a written transcript, and we can judge intensity of emotion from vocal characteristics. We cannot assume, though, that vocal cues are similar across cultures.

A common problem in interpreting vocal cues is misunderstanding sarcasm. This is especially true for children and people with poor listening and/or intellectual skills.

Vocal cues are sometimes the basis for our inferences about personality traits. If people increase the loudness, pitch, timbre, and rate of their speech, we think of them as more active and dynamic. If they use more intonation, higher speech rates, more volume, and greater fluency in their speech, we find them more persuasive (Knapp and Hall, 2005, p. 410). In computer-mediated communication, even limited paralinguistic cues can influence how people form impressions of others; this is true, for example, in online communities (Jacobson, 1999).

It's interesting that judgments about status can be made quite rapidly (for example, after listening to a sample of a person's speech for only 10 or 15 seconds). Apparently, we can make such inferences with a high degree of accuracy.

Despite wide agreement about certain relationships between voice qualities and personality traits, no conclusive evidence supports such inferences. They seem to derive from vocal stereotypes. Even if our beliefs have no basis in fact, however, they have striking effects on our response to others; we act on what we believe to be true. Thus, when the talkies appeared, several stars of the silent films were ruined because the public expected their voices to sound consistent with their screen personalities. The passionate lover with the high-pitched voice was too great a disappointment.

Volume

One precondition of effective verbal communication is adequate *volume.* If your voice is so low that you can barely be heard, people rapidly become too tired or too embarrassed to ask you to repeat your last remark. In this case, it is you, the message sender, who becomes a source of interference for the receiver. In organizational communication, vocal intensity can reinforce or enhance a person's power base and convey a sense of confidence. For example, an employee who speaks loudly is more likely to enhance the perception of his or her expertise. And higher volume also seems to be one of the cues associated with perceived dominance (Tusing and Dillard, 2000).

Most people link volume to certain personality traits; thus it is commonly thought that an aggressive person speaks in a louder voice than one who is reserved and shy. Volume, however, is not necessarily a function of personality. Our models in childhood also influence our volume level.

Feedback from the receiver is the best check on volume. If you are not getting through or if you're coming on too strong, adjust your voice accordingly.

Rate and Fluency

Your **rate of speech** is the *number of words you utter within a specified time.* The unit most often used is one minute, and the average speaking rate is about 125 to 150 words per minute.

Speech rates are highly stable for individuals. For this reason, a faster rate (as well as shorter comments and more frequent pauses) seems to be linked to fear or anger and a slower rate to grief or depression (Barnlund, 1968, p. 529). Some people are able to control their rate of speaking despite their emotions, but the strain of maintaining this control is often expressed in other vocal or facial cues. There is no optimum speaking rate. Like many other vocal qualities, rate of speech is more effective when adapted to the verbal content of the message and to the specific receiver.

The **fluency,** or *continuity,* of our speech is closely related to rate, and pauses, of course, affect fluency. The person who pauses continually, whose speech is full of vocalizations such as "um," "er," and "ah," may destroy his or her effectiveness as a communicator. Pauses that are frequent, long, and vocalized, and that come in the middle of an idea, are usually unsettling and undermine the sender's purpose. When used for emphasis and variation, pauses often enhance the verbal message—particularly if they are infrequent, short, and silent, and are used at the end of an idea.

When Caroline Kennedy was seeking the senate seat vacated by Hillary Clinton in 2009, she began giving a number of speeches at press conferences. One of the major reasons people criticized her was because of her excessive use of "you know" and "um" during her speeches. Fred Dicker of the *New York Post* wrote, "She seemed less like a candidate than like an idea of one; eloquent but vague, largely undefined and seemingly determined to remain that way" (News Wire Service, December 30, 2008, p. A2). Kennedy later withdrew from consideration.

Pitch

Pitch is *the frequency level (high or low) of the voice.* Your pitch range is determined by the size and shape of the vocal bands within your larynx, or voice box. Optimum pitch, the level most comfortable for you, is usually one-third above the lowest pitch you are capable of producing. Most untrained speakers use a pitch somewhat higher than their optimum pitch, but it has been found that lower pitches are most pleasant to listen to.

Although women's voices tend to be more high-pitched than men's, the difference may not simply be a question of biology:

> When women's and men's voices are compared to the respective size of their vocal tracts, women talk as if they are physically smaller than they actually are. Their voices are pitched to the upper range, the decibel level is reduced, and vowel resonances are thinned. These paralinguistic elements are not the effect of biology but of socialization and learning—the imperative [for women] to be soft-spoken. (Nelson, 2004, p. 209)

Pitch is an important element in people's judgments about a speaker. A voice with unvaried pitch is monotonous and usually disliked; in fact, a monotone seems to be as unpopular as a poker face. People sometimes derive information about emotions from changes in pitch. Pitch can even influence our judgments about a doctor's professional competence and social attractiveness.

Apparently, pitch level does influence your attitude toward the communicator and the content of the message. Exaggerated pitch changes are even more unpopular than the monotone. A naturally expressive voice has a variety of pitch levels that are spontaneous and unforced changes.

Quality

Think of a violin, a viola, and a cello. Each is a stringed instrument but each has a different size and shape. The same note played on each of these instruments will therefore have a different *resonance—a distinctive quality of sound.* Similarly, each of you has a distinctive voice quality because the resonance of your voice—which to a great extent determines its quality—is a function of the size and shape of your body as well as of your vocal cords.

There seems to be wide agreement in responses to vocal qualities. Judges could reliably distinguish voices described as shrill or harsh from those considered pleasant, or "resonant." In our culture, several voice qualities considered particularly unpleasant are hypernasality (talking through the nose), denasality (which sounds as though the speaker has a constant head cold), hoarseness, and harshness (or stridency). Voices considered attractive and influential are "more resonant and calm, less monotonous, lower-pitched (especially for males), less regionally accented, less nasal, less shrill, and more relaxed" (Andersen, 1999, p. 71).

Having an attractive voice is a distinct advantage, and apparently we operate from a "what sounds beautiful is good" hypothesis. People with voices that are clear, warm, expressive, and robust are more likely to be seen as powerful, dominant, assertive, and socially skilled. This is especially the case when you use voice mail and answering machines, which rely so heavily on vocal cues. One study of messages left on business answering machines found that when people left taped excuses for not taking their phone calls, a person whose voice was attractive was seen—no matter what the excuse was—as "more competent, likeable, and dominant" (Semic, 1999, p. 153). So know how you sound and sharpen those vocal skills.

Through practice and training, almost all of us can improve our vocal quality. One of the best media available for studying communication style is the videotape recorder, though even videotape loses some nuances of vocal inflection, eye contact, postural cues, and the like. The audiotape recorder is another valuable aid.

Summing up research findings on vocal cues, Knapp and Hall (2005) point out:

> You should be quick to challenge the cliché that vocal cues only concern how something is said; frequently they are what is said. What is said might be an attitude ("I like you" or "I'm superior to you"); it might be an emotion; it might be the coordination and management of the conversation; or it might be the presentation of some aspect of your personality, background, or physical features. (p. 410)

For discussion purposes, we have isolated three categories of nonverbal cues. But as we pointed out early on, people interpret messages on the basis of multiple nonverbal and verbal cues. This is certainly the case with deception.

DECEPTION

One of the defining characteristics of successful salespeople, politicians, and poker players is their ability to appear truthful when their truthfulness is challenged. Even daily life seems to require this ability, because diary studies suggest that everyone admits to lying a few times daily.

—Frank and Ekman (2004, p. 486)

It seems that in judging whether people are deceiving us or telling the truth, we're not that accurate. According to one source, "the accuracy rate for detecting deception is only about 55 percent to 60 percent, with people less likely to be accurate when a person is lying compared to telling the truth. This percentage does not improve with close relationships." On the other hand, researchers find that we tend to be far more accurate in judging when people are telling the truth (Guerrero and Floyd, 2006, pp. 197, 181).

So just because we know a person well—a friend or romantic partner or sibling—doesn't mean that we will be able to detect when he or she is not telling the truth. Our confidence that we know the other person very well may lead us astray.

As you might guess, when the stakes are high, people who are lying tend to give more nonverbal cues that might indicate deception. For example, there might be less foot and leg movement, less arm and hand movement, an increased rate of speech, and more pauses (Vrij, 2006).

According to Aldert Vrij, many of us are looking at the wrong nonverbal cues. First, we often mistakenly believe that people who are lying will increase their movements, and also that they tend to avoid looking at the other person. But in fact it seems that "liars tend to *decrease* rather than increase their movements . . . " (2006, p. 352). Some of our ideas about deceptive behavior are acquired from the media. And there may be a "confirmation bias" so that we select data that reinforce our own beliefs. Then, too, since we rarely get feedback on whether we were right about someone we think was deceiving us, we have no way to determine how accurate our judgments have been (p. 352).

Guerrero and Floyd's recent review of reliable nonverbal indicators of deception (2006) discusses facial, vocal, and kinesic behaviors. Counter to what many of us believe, direct gaze, maintaining eye contact, and smiling do not seem to be completely reliable cues concerning truthtelling. Some researchers—notably Ekman and his colleagues, whose work is known worldwide—have distinguished between "felt" and "false" smiles. Unlike felt or genuine smiles (sometimes referred to as "Duchenne smiles"), which involve not only muscles around the mouth but the eyes, smiles that are false seem to involve only the muscles around the mouth.

As for nonverbal cues involving the eyes, it is not, as many of us believe, maintaining briefer or less frequent eye contact that is a reliable predictor of truthfulness. Two other cues from the eyes that involve less control—blinking and the dilation of the pupils—seem to be more reliable. Apparently, when we are under stress—and this includes when we are behaving deceptively—we blink more often than we do when we are relaxed, including when we tell the truth. And when we are deceptive, as when we are generally aroused or emotional, our pupils dilate. Blinking is difficult to control, and dilation of the pupils is completely automatic behavior.

Vocal cues that seem to be important indicators of deception include more frequent errors in speaking, longer pauses and more pauses filled with sounds such as "ah" and "um," markedly higher pitch, and greater "vocal stress."

Table 4.2 *Nonverbal Behaviors Reliably Associated with Deception*		
Facial Behaviors	*Vocalic Behaviors*	*Kinesic Behaviors*
Smiling: Deceivers use more fake smiles than truthtellers; no difference in overall amount of smiling	Pitch: Deceivers have higher pitch than truthtellers	Deceivers engage in fewer hand/finger movements, fewer foot/leg movements, and fewer illustrator gestures than do truthtellers
Eye behaviors: Deceivers blink more and have more pupil dilation; no difference with respect to eye contact	Vocal stress: Vocal stress and nervousness are elevated during deception	
	Speech errors: Deceivers commit more speech errors than do truthtellers	

Source: From *Nonverbal Communication in Close Relationships* by Laura Guerrero and Kory Floyd (Lawrence Erlbaum, 2006), p. 181.

The third category outlined by Guerrero and Floyd, kinesic behaviors, involves "movement-oriented nonverbal behaviors, including gestures, head movements, postural shifts, and foot and leg movements" (2006, p. 179). Although you might expect people to move more when they are lying rather than when they are telling the truth, research suggests that deception cues involve fewer movements of the hands, fingers, legs, and feet. For a summary of all these cues, see Table 4.2.

The kinds of **leakage,** or *signals of deception,* that take place depend on whether the lie is spontaneous or rehearsed and whether we are concealing something emotional or factual. Deception cues are most likely to be given when the deceiver wants to hide a feeling experienced at that moment or feels strongly about the information being hidden. They also tend to occur when a person feels anxious, or guilty, or needs to think carefully while speaking.

One study found that deceivers delivering a prepared lie respond more quickly than truth tellers mainly because less thinking is necessary (Greene et al., 1985). When they are unprepared, however, deceivers generally take longer than both prepared deceivers and truth tellers. Those telling the truth generally maintain more eye contact than deceivers. Deceivers also show less body movement, probably in an attempt to avoid leakage cues. At the same time, they laugh and smile more often, presumably trying to keep their faces from displaying other expressions that may turn out to be leakage cues. It's especially interesting that these people continue to behave "deceptively" even when telling the truth. They probably fear that they will lose control if the situation in which they need to lie should recur (Greene et al., 1985). We must note here the great potential for intercultural misunderstandings when cultural conventions of little gesturing and infrequent eye contact may be interpreted as deception.

Voice stress analysis, which detects very minute changes in a person's voice that are then displayed on a computer screen, is not a new technology—it has been available for almost 15 years, but its use is growing. Those who market it claim that

PRACTICAL TIPS

4.4

Visual Clusters

Grooming gestures
Hand-wringing
Inward-curled feet
Stiff upper body, inappropriate stillness
Pursed lips or biting of the lips
Slumped or self-protective posture
Moving objects in front of them
Postinterview relief expression
Excessive sweating, breathing, finger-tapping
Shift in blink rate
Shrugs, clenched fists, winks
Fake smile
Closed eyes

Vocal Clusters

Qualifying statements, "As far as I know . . . " "To tell the truth . . . "

Repeating your question verbatim
Nonspontaneous response time
Apologetic tone of voice
Dodging the question ("I already told so and so that.")
Inappropriate detail
Short, clipped answers
Religious references ("I swear on the Bible.")
Objections to irrelevant specifics ("No—I had the chicken, not the steak.")
Whining about the interview itself ("How much longer will this take?")
Uncooperative or dismissive attitude
More emphasis on persuading you than the facts

Source: Adapted from Pamela Meyer. *Liespotting: Proven Techniques to Detect Deception.* New York: St. Martin's Griffin, 2010, pp. 127–128.

voice changes can be interpreted as registering subtle emotional changes including stress (Heingartner, 2004).

Most deception studies have used college students as subjects. Over the last 25 years of research, Ekman and Sullivan observe, "people have not been very accurate in judging when someone is lying" (1991, p. 913). One study of professional lie catchers looked at members of the U.S. Secret Service, federal polygraphers, judges, police, psychiatrists, a diverse group of working adults, and college students. Most groups did no better than college students. Secret Service people were the only ones who had greater than chance accuracy in detecting liars. Recent research has revealed the following nonverbal cues when people are lying: (1) the voice takes on a higher pitch, (2) long pauses before speaking, (3) speaking at a slower rate, with more errors and hesitations ("ums" and "ahs"), and (4) the voice taking on a strained or tense quality (Meyer, 2010, p. 103).

The study of deception has much to teach us not only about individual nonverbal cues but also about the interaction of verbal and nonverbal behavior. Even though analysis often requires that we speak of verbal and nonverbal messages as if they could be separated, in practice this is nearly impossible. Face-to-face communication is a total experience. No matter what a person is trying to say, you can see his or her face, body movement, clothing, and so on, and you are responding, whether you are aware of it or not, to all these cues.

Summary

Nonverbal communication is going on all the time. In discussing the interpretation of nonverbal messages, we saw that a significant percentage of all social meaning is conveyed through nonverbal stimuli. We also saw that nonverbal channels convey primarily relational messages—messages about the emotional level of our communication—and that a nonverbal message can replace, reinforce, or contradict a verbal message. Yet verbal and nonverbal responses qualify each other in so many ways that they are not totally separable.

Three broad categories of nonverbal cues were examined. First we discussed space and time, cues that have a subtle but pervasive influence on communication style and are, to a great degree, determined by one's culture. We saw that assumptions about nonverbal cues may create misunderstandings in intercultural communication. Visual cues from facial expressions, eye contact, body movements (particularly hand gestures), touching, physical appearance, and the use of objects were analyzed. We found that these cues give us information about human emotions and intentions; they are also the basis for some of our judgments about personality and social status. Vocal cues are another source of information, and we discussed volume, rate and fluency, pitch, and quality, as well as gender differences.

In closing, we looked at an area of nonverbal behavior that cuts across all the individual nonverbal cues, the study of deception. We examined some conditions under which signals of deception are most likely to occur as well as new research findings about accuracy in decoding deception cues and the mutual influence of deceivers and detectors.

Key Terms

Chronemics
Co-culture
Cues
Fluency
Haptics
High-contact culture
Interpersonal distance
Kinesic slips
Kinesics
Leakage
Low-contact culture
Monochronic
Nonverbal communication
Objectics
Oculesics
Orientation
Paralinguistics
Personal space
Pitch
Polychronic
Proxemics
Rate of speech
Touch avoidance

Review Questions

1. Specify four categories of communication associated with verbal and vocal communication.

2. What is the relative weight we assign to verbal and nonverbal messages? What type of information does each convey?

3. What are three ways in which nonverbal messages relate to verbal messages?

4. What is a mixed message or kinesic slip? How does it relate to both verbal and nonverbal communication?

5. Specify five or more nonverbal cues associated with power and dominance.

6. What is personal space? Give an example.

7. Specify four kinds of interpersonal distance. Give an example of each kind.

8. What are some differences between high-contact and low-contact cultures?

9. What is chronemics? Give an example of how timing might interfere with intercultural communication.

10. Explain the difference between monochronic and polychronic time, giving an example of each.

11. What is kinesics?

12. What are four unstated rules in our culture about eye contact?

13. Describe three categories of nonverbal courtship behavior. Give an example of each type.

14. What is the relationship between head and body movements in communicating emotion?

15. What are the three major palm-command gestures and what do they convey?

16. What is haptics?

17. Describe how touch might influence bonding, dominance, compliance, and self-disclosure.

18. What is touch avoidance? Give an example from your own experience.

19. Describe how one's choice of physical objects can communicate messages to others.

20. What is paralinguistics? Give some examples of paralinguistic cues.

21. What four categories of emotion are consistently identified by paralinguistic cues? Give some examples of gender differences in vocal cues.

22. Discuss several of the nonverbal behaviors reliably associated with deception.

23. Identify the conditions under which signals of deception are most likely to occur.

24. Describe the possibilities for mutual influence between detectors and deceivers and discuss recent research findings about accuracy in decoding deception cues.

Exercises

1. Form several two-person teams consisting of one male and one female. Have each team select a place where several people are likely to pass by. Have both members take turns asking strangers the time of day or some other standard question. While speaking, slowly violate the stranger's proxemic norms until you are very close to him or her. The other member of the team should observe and record the stranger's reactions. When all the teams have collected data, discuss these questions in light of the data collected:

   a. In what ways did the strangers demonstrate nonverbal/vocal and nonverbal/nonvocal communication?

   b. How did the strangers respond to the questioner as he or she began to violate proxemic norms?

   c. Did male and female strangers respond differently to proxemic norm violation depending on whether a male or female did the violating?

2. Repeat the exercise just described, but this time have one questioner dress very neatly and the other look sloppy and unkempt. Discuss the differences in the strangers' reaction to the questioner.

3. Go to center-for-nonverbal-studies.org/6101 .html and access *The Nonverbal Dictionary*. Read all the entries on facial expressions including the "blank face" and "zygomatic smile." Find three unposed examples of both in current online sources, magazines, or newspapers and identify each by context.

4. Make a list of the various paralinguistic and vocal cues discussed in this chapter. Tape-record a series of short messages presented by a male and a female that illustrate the various types of paralinguistic and vocal cues. Construct a Semantic Differential similar to the one suggested in exercise 1a in Chapter 3. Then ask a number of people to listen to the recorded messages and rate the speakers using the Semantic Differential. How did the various paralinguistic and vocal cues affect the listeners' perceptions of the speaker? Relate the results to the concepts discussed in Chapter 2 on person perception.

5. The next time you get angry with someone, try to observe your own nonverbal behavior. Most people look and sound like their parents or other members of their family. Facial expressions, posture, gestures, and vocal cues are often similar among family members. Do you notice similarities and differences? Can you account for these similarities and differences?

6. Select three shopping sites on the Web and find three magazine ads that advertise (a) clothing, (b) furniture, or (c) cars. Analyze and compare what the advertisers suggest would be the nonverbal messages—for example, status, intelligence, power, physical attractiveness—the consumer would be able to convey by purchasing and using these items.

Suggested Readings

Andersen, Peter A. *Nonverbal Communication: Forms and Functions.* Mountain View, CA: Mayfield, 1999.

This is an excellent survey of nonverbal communication, organized in an original and very useful way. Chapter 4 on cultural cues, Chapter 5 on gender differences, and Chapter 6 on nonverbal communication in intimate relationships are of special interest.

Bates, Brian, with John Cleese. *The Human Face.* London: BBC, 2001.

A popular book, written in connection with the BBC presentation of a documentary on the face. It's informative and easy to read; it has a host of wonderful illustrations and photographs. Try getting hold of the BBC video of the same title.

Ekman, Paul. *Emotions Revealed: Recognizing Faces and Feelings to Improve Communication and Emotional Life.* New York: Times Books, 2003.

An expert in the study of human expressions looks at how we experience and interpret emotions and explains how to develop better communication skills by learning more about basic emotions. The Appendix has a test for reading faces.

Hall, Edward T. *The Dance of Life: The Other Dimension of Time.* Gloucester, MA: Peter Smith, 1996.

The author views time as culture and explores how, both consciously and unconsciously, time is formulated, patterned, and used in diverse cultures.

Hall, Stephen S. *Size Matters: How Height Affects the Health, Happiness, and Success of Boys—and the Men They Become.* Boston: Houghton Mifflin, 2006.

This book examines the psychological and social effects of height on males from childhood on. Not all will agree about the advantages of height, but the studies, anecdotes, and arguments are interesting.

Knapp, Mark L., and Judy A. Hall. *Nonverbal Communication in Human Interaction,* 7th ed. Boston: Wadsworth, Cengage Learning, 2010. Belmont, CA: Wadsworth, 2005.

An excellent resource for the student of nonverbal communication. The approach is research-based and comprehensive. Chapter 4 covers the effects of the environment—including architectural design, color, and structure—on communication.

Martin, Judith N., and Thomas K. Nakayama. *Intercultural Communication in Contexts,* 4th ed. New York: McGraw-Hill, 2007.

The authors of this intercultural text present their subject from three different perspectives. Chapter 7 is devoted to nonverbal codes and cultural space.

Meyer, Pamela. *Liespotting.* New York: St. Martin's Griffin, 2010.

This very readable book shows how to detect the nonverbal cues of liars.

Nelson, Audrey, with Susan K. Golant. *You Don't Say: Navigating Nonverbal Communication between the Sexes.* New York: Penguin Group, 2004.

A popular book about misunderstandings between men and women because of gender differences in nonverbal communication. It has many engaging examples and a great deal of practical advice.

Pease, Alan, and Barbara Pease. *The Definitive Book of Body Language.* New York: Bantam Books, 2006.

The revision of a popular book on interpreting body language. The authors include many simple and instructive illustrations and some amusing photographs.

The Artist.

This outstanding award-winning silent film is based almost exclusively on nonverbal behaviors.

 For Supplementary Information

Log onto the Online Learning Center at *www.mhhe.com/tubbshc13e.*

6

Conflict and Negotiation

Chapter Objectives

After reading this chapter, you should be able to:

1. Define conflict and discuss the important elements in the definition.
2. Define and discuss the four levels of conflict.
3. Discuss and explain the Kilmann-Thomas conflict resolution model.
4. Define negotiation.
5. Identify and use the six-step process in negotiations.
6. Identify and discuss five assumptions of successful negotiation.
7. Define principled negotiation and discuss four basic rules of thumb.
8. Identify and discuss five techniques of principled negotiation.

CONFLICT

If two people are honestly talking, they cannot be hitting each other.
—Dzwonkowski (1998)

Many times communicating with others is enjoyable and fun. However, conflict sometimes arises and then communicating is not fun at all. It can be agonizing. It can keep you awake at night. It can tie your stomach in knots. It can lead to violence and death. In recent years Americans have had intense conflict of ideas about how best to improve our country. Because of unemployment, housing foreclosures, and other such problems, federal, state, and local leaders have had to discuss budget cuts, which results in a great deal of further protests and conflict over who should bear the brunt of these cuts. Pulitzer Prize–winning author Thomas Friedman and his co-author Michael Mandelbaum (2011) document some of these problems along with best-selling author Michael Lewis (2011). You may have discussed these very issues within your family and with your friends. We are all affected. In every case, these are dramatic reminders of the need for each of us to develop our negotiation and conflict management skills.

This chapter is about communicating in conflict situations and negotiating your way through to possible resolution.

On a lighter note, a friend of mine recalls that her three-year-old son, seeing his parents in a heated argument, stepped in between them, held his arms straight out, and said, "Now just a minute, you two." Many of us go out of our way to avoid conflict and might characterize ideal relationships as free of argument. However, by the time we become adults, we've usually been at least a witness to a great many conflicts both minor and intense. Few young people reach adulthood without experiencing some conflict with their parents, siblings, or peers.

Experts tend to regard conflict as a natural part of human relationships, one that is not necessarily destructive, although, as we'll see in the chapter on intercultural communication, in some cultures it is traditional for conflict to go unexpressed.

Conflict is defined as *"an expressed struggle between at least two interdependent parties who perceive incompatible goals, scarce resources, and interference from others in achieving their goals"* (Wilmot and Hocker, 2005, p. 9). Let's briefly examine each of the important elements in the definition.

Expressed Struggle An interpersonal communication approach to this topic focuses on the communication exchanges that compose the conflict. In other words, there must be communication messages exchanged in order for the conflict to be expressed.

Interdependence If we don't have some need for the other person to cooperate, then there is no conflict. It is only when we are interdependent that the conflict exists. For example, you agree to play tennis with another person. If either of you doesn't show up, neither can play. The two of you are interdependent.

ISSUES IN COMMUNICATION

Principled Negotiation

Fisher, Ury, and Patton (1991) have suggested an approach referred to as "principled negotiation." They contend that negotiation and conflict resolution can be more successful if you follow their guidelines. What do you think are the advantages and disadvantages of each of these guidelines?

Separate people from the problem. This means that you should try not to get angry with the other party. Try to remain neutral toward the person, even if he or she is arguing a point of view that you feel is very distasteful.

Focus on interests, not positions. Look for common interests and avoid sticking to a certain fixed position, like how much you want to get if you are selling a car.

Invent various options for mutual gain. Look for a variety of possible solutions, not just *x* versus *y* as your only possible solutions.

Use objective criteria to determine outcomes. See if you can find information that both parties agree is accurate as guidelines for finding a solution.

Perceived Incompatible Goals Two or more people may have a conflict that is based solely on perception (see Chapter 2). They may actually agree, but think they don't. Or they may in fact have goals that are in conflict. You may like to stay home and your spouse may want to eat out. Or, two parties may be in love with the same person. In the story of Camelot, King Arthur and Sir Lancelot both love Queen Guinevere. What really complicates things is that Arthur also considers Lancelot his closest friend. Try to imagine how psychologically painful that would be. In the present context, we would say that they have incompatible goals.

Perceived Scarce Resources Again, the problem may solely be in the perception. Or, there may simply not be enough to go around. If there truly are insufficient resources, it can often create conflict. As one clergyman has said, "Lack of money is the root of all evil." Stephen Covey, in his famous book *The 7 Habits of Highly Effective People* (1990), writes eloquently about the perception part of this type of conflict. He feels that there are two types of attitudes, (1) a scarcity mentality and (2) an abundance mentality. Those with the scarcity mentality feel that if you gain, they must lose. They feel jealous or threatened if you get positive recognition or success. He writes, "The abundance mentality, on the other hand, flows out of a deep inner sense of personal worth and security. It is the paradigm that there is plenty out there and enough to spare for everybody" (p. 220). The scarcity mentality's analogy is that if one person gets a bigger piece of a pie, then others get less. The abundance mentality says that all can get more if you work together to create a bigger pie. Wiseman (2010) puts it similarly, in that she calls these two styles the "diminisher assumption" versus the "multiplier assumption." The first style is threatened by the success of others, but the second sees the benefits of a win-win. See also *www.multipliersbook.com*.

Perceived Interference   If we would like something and another person keeps us from getting it, then interference has occurred. Let's say that you would like to get a promotion and your boss won't do it. How would you feel toward her or him?

Levels of Conflict

Intrapersonal Conflict   One way of classifying types of conflict is by level (Lewicki et al., 2010). The first level of conflict takes place within the individual. This is called **intrapersonal conflict.** Sources of internal conflict can include ideas, attitudes, emotions, values, or personality drives that are in conflict with each other. Certainly, you have found yourself torn between, for example, wanting to go out with friends versus staying in and studying! (See also Hames, 2012.) This is an example of intrapersonal conflict. Since intrapersonal conflict is felt inwardly but not yet expressed, it would not be included in Wilmot and Hocker's definition of conflict. However, some would argue that the more an individual is internally conflicted, the more likely he or she is to become involved in conflicts with others. So there is a possible connection between intrapersonal conflict and interpersonal conflict.

In the preceding example, if a person has a hard time deciding between the need for affiliation (going out with friends) and the need for achievement (staying in to study), this could lead the person to "snap" at the person who is inviting him or her to go out. Another similar example is the difficulty of saying no to things people ask us to do. Part of us wants to be liked, but part of us doesn't want to do certain tasks that others ask of us.

Interpersonal Conflict   A second major level of conflict occurs between individuals. This is called **interpersonal conflict.** This can occur between friends, roommates, fraternity or sorority members, family members, co-workers, lovers, or total strangers (as in cases of "road rage"). Witness the popularity of television and radio programs that frequently show people involved in conflict. The *Jerry Springer Show* was the source of much controversy a few years back because it showed outlandish displays of conflict. Often television and radio shows will have people who represent both sides of a controversy, first in order to show both sides of an issue, but more importantly, because conflict is interesting and improves their viewer and listener ratings. Examples are numerous—*Survivor, Lost,* other so-called "reality TV shows," *The View,* Maury Povich, Dr. Laura Schlessinger, Rush Limbaugh, Al Sharpton, Howard Stern, and many others.

In interpersonal conflicts the parties usually communicate directly with one another. Most of the principles of conflict and conflict resolution relate to interpersonal conflict, since this is the basic unit of interpersonal communication and interpersonal relations.

Interpersonal conflict is the most common type of conflict occurring in the workplace. Its causes may be numerous, but they chiefly stem from unfulfilled or ignored human needs. Common human needs found in the workplace include acceptance, acknowledgment, affirmation, appreciation, autonomy, belonging, clarity, collaboration, completion, compassion, consideration, cooperation, fun, freedom, help, honesty, humor, inspiration, order, participation, planning, power, reassurance, respect, structure, support, to contribute, to share, tolerance, trust, understanding, and variety (Jannetta, 2006).

Intragroup Conflict   A third major level of conflict is within a small group. It can take place within a family, between team members, on a committee, or in any small group of individuals. Individual differences can affect how small groups interact during conflict situations. Researchers (Goleman, 2001) have identified four categories of emotional competencies needed for effective emotional self-management as well as for effectively relating to others in a group: self-awareness, self-management, social awareness, and relationship management (cited in Hede, 2007).

The first, self-awareness, is seen as the ability to monitor one's own emotions, to accurately self-assess, and to be self-confident (Goleman, 2001, cited in Hames, 2012).

> If an individual has low inner-awareness . . . it will actively seek an emotional trigger to . . . unleash itself onto the group in relationship conflict. (Hames, 2012)

The second set of competencies in the Goleman (2001) model is self-management. It involves such skills as emotional self-control, adaptability, conscientiousness, trustworthiness, achievement, drive, and initiative. The key skill here is the ability to control one's own emotional reactivity. This involves being able to

- Identify one's own habitual emotional triggers.
- Detect the physical warning signs of an "emotional hijacking" (e.g., increased heart rate, rush of blood, surge of adrenaline). (Baumeister and Tierney, 2011)
- Avoid identification with the reactive thoughts that accompany an acute emotional response.
- Implement effective protocols for defusing one's own emotional reactivity, thereby avoiding any behavioral outburst. (Hames, 2012)

The third set of emotional competencies proposed by Goleman (2001) is social awareness consisting of empathy, service orientation, and organizational awareness. In relation to shadow group management, empathy plays a crucial role. As Goleman has pointed out:

> An emotionally intelligent team . . . has the collective equivalent of empathy, the basis of all relationship skills. (Goleman, 2010, p. 182)

If group members have a high level of empathy, they understand each other's sensitivities and can read each other's emotional state. This enables them to anticipate a negative emotional reaction in another group member and to avoid behaviors that could trigger an outburst (Hames, 2012).

The fourth and final set of emotional competencies in the Goleman (2001) model is relationship management. This includes the following skills: developing others, influence, communication, conflict management, visionary leadership, catalyzing change, building bonds, teamwork, and collaboration (Hames, 2012).

Having analyzed a number of conflict situations according to Goleman's model, Hede formulated several viable conflict management hypotheses:

- Individuals who have high inner-awareness are less likely to experience negative emotionality in groups.
- Individuals are most likely to experience relationship conflict with the group member they perceive as the most opposite to themselves.
- Escalation of task into relationship conflict is more likely to occur in groups that use the same terminology for "debates" and "fights." (Hames, 2012)

If you would like to test your Emotional Intelligence Quotient (EQ), click on *www.myskillsprofile.com*.

Intergroup Conflict   This final level of conflict occurs between groups. This could involve feuding families, labor and management, rival street gangs, some groups and the U.S. government, and even warring nations. Communication at this level of conflict is often through representatives. When conflict gets to this level, it is often very complicated since it involves more people and may even involve centuries of history. Of course, conflicts may also occur at more than one of these levels simultaneously.

Some scholars would add another conflict type to this classification: conflicts between large ethnic systems or civilizations. Such approach derives from the works of the great fourteenth-century Arab historian Ibn Khaldoun and was further developed in the twentieth century by Arnold Toynbee (1889–1975) in his principal work *A Study of History*. In recent years, this view was espoused most notably by two scholars: Lev Nikolayevich Gumilev (1912–1992) in Russia and Samuel Huntington (b. 1927) in the United States.

For both Gumilev and Huntington, the key notion governing intercultural (intercivilizational) relationships is a subconscious sense of sympathy or antipathy shared by the members of an ethnic group, which serves to determine the distinction between "one's own" and "strangers" (Goudakov, 2006). This stands in contrast with the more common approach among many historians and political scientists who speak of political will as the force behind intercivilizational cultural exchanges.

These issues have come much closer to home in recent years with the huge debt in the so-called PIIGS countries of Portugal, Ireland and Italy, Greece, and Spain. Germany resents having to bail out these other countries because of their reckless and irresponsible spending (Lewis, 2011).

Stages of Conflict

Every conflict is believed to occur in stages, and each stage is characterized by different communication patterns. Brahm (2003) summarized the six phases of conflict: latent conflict, emergence, escalation, de-escalation, resolution, and reconciliation.

Latent Conflict and Emergence

The initial phase is represented by a lack of overt conflict where only latent, or potential, conflict exists. Latent conflict is the existence of opposing goals. If some event triggers the latent conflict, then the conflict may emerge and become overt. These triggers can take many forms. First, an unfortunate comment or verbal interchange is the most common trigger. Second, if one party does not hear the other party accurately, a comment may be taken as negative when it was not intended to be. (Chapter 5 discussed the importance of effective listening; listening is critical in the prevention of emergent conflict.)

Third, differences in semantics can be blamed for conflict emergence. Words must not be used that have negative connotations to the other party. For example, the concept of "reasonable spending" may mean entirely different things to a husband and a wife. Fourth, body language can speak volumes. If someone says something with a sneer on his or her face, for example, the perception of the verbal message will be combined with the negative facial expression. Negative comments, ineffective listening, semantic differences, and inconsistent body language can all act as triggers resulting in the emergence of a latent conflict (Akin, 2003).

Escalation and Resolution

The emergent conflict may then, and often does, escalate to a higher level of intensity. A conflict generally escalates until both parties have reached a "stalemate" where neither party feels that they can "win" the argument. A stalemate generally causes the parties to decide to de-escalate or negotiate to reach conflict resolution. Negotiation will be discussed later on in this chapter.

A resolved conflict may still leave behind damaged relationships and hurt feelings. Reconciliation must occur as the final phase of conflict to ensure that the residual negativity released by the conflict has abated and both parties can move forward productively (Brahm, 2003).

Of course, conflict does not always follow these general phases in a prescribed order and can return to escalation after resolution, or can skip escalation altogether. There is no set prescription for conflict, but only a model that can assist in understanding and improving our chances for conflict management. Conflict resolution is the goal of all episodes of conflict as you will see in the next section.

Conflict Resolution

One of the best models for conceptualizing conflict resolution has been offered by Kilmann and Thomas (1975). Their two-dimensional model is illustrated in Figure 6.1. The model suggests that individuals may have a preferred style for resolving conflicts. However, as we develop a broader range of style flexibility, our skill in dealing with a broad range of conflict situations is enhanced. We shouldn't limit ourselves to using only one style. The model offers five basic styles of conflict resolution: (1) avoidance, (2) competition, (3) compromise, (4) accommodation, and (5) collaboration. Let us look a bit at each of these styles.

Figure 6.1   *The Kilmann-Thomas Conflict Model*

Source: This two-dimensional model of conflict handling behavior is adapted from "The Kilmann-Thomas Conflict Model" by Kenneth Thomas. Reprinted by permission of Grid International, Inc.

Avoidance

Winston Churchill once remarked that he and his wife had decided at the beginning of their marriage that, if they were going to remain married, they should never have breakfast together.

The first choice in trying to resolve conflict is whether to deal with it at all. The easiest way is just to avoid it. Some of us may have grown up in a home in which the prevailing advice when it came to conflict was "The less said the better." Avoidance behaviors include a wide spectrum of evasive strategies intended to head off a confrontation. In simple **denial,** unelaborated statements are made denying that there is a conflict ("Who's fighting? I'm not angry at all!"). **Underresponsiveness** is a *"failure to acknowledge or deny the presence of a conflict following a statement or inquiry about the conflict by a partner"* (Sillars, 1986) ("I still don't think you've fixed the car. What if it stalls again on the highway?" "You'll manage"). In addition to **shifting** and **avoiding topics,** other tactics you probably recognize include semantic focus, abstractness, joking, ambivalence, and pessimism.

Semantic focus is an especially interesting dodge. The *person trying to avoid conflict focuses on what is being said, then makes statements about what the words mean or how to characterize the ongoing conflict and this discussion of words.* So terminology or "semantics" replaces the original conflict issue. Often, as I suggested in Chapter 2 and in the discussion of confirmation, the issue is about relationships, not about content. Pessimistic remarks tend to downplay or undermine a discussion of causes of conflict ("Let's not rehash everything. We've been through this over and over").

Postponement, although it is sometimes a strategy for avoidance, can work well, but only if both parties will work out a discussion time that is not too far in the future (Wilmot and Hocker, 2005). Planning to have a discussion two weeks after the incident that sparked the disagreement is unlikely to be very beneficial.

The advantage of the **avoidance** approach is that you avoid saying things that sometimes may escalate the conflict. All of us have probably said things in the heat of the moment that we later wished we could take back. The disadvantage of this style is that the conflicts never get resolved and the tension tends to mount as the conflict festers. Another disadvantage is that as the conflicts go unresolved the anger may increase within one or more parties so that, when there is a discussion, the angry feelings explode.

Unfortunately, avoidance seems to work only in the short run. Eventually, the conflicts need to be addressed in order to be resolved.

Competition

In the **competition** style of conflict, *one party tries to use aggression or power to beat the other party.* The conflict is seen as a "battleground." People sometimes get caught up in the excitement of the fight. Competition may also be exhibited in an assertive way rather than an aggressive way. The difference is whether you are injuring the other party while trying to accomplish your goals. Competition may take the form of threats, criticisms, confrontational remarks, or extreme language choices.

Sillars's schema includes several competitive tactics. These include faulting (direct personal criticism, such as "You look like a mess"), hostile questioning ("How can you stand to live like that?"), hostile joking ("If your friends jumped off a cliff, would you jump too?"), presumptive attribution, avoiding responsibility, and prescription.

Presumptive attribution refers to *making statements that attribute to the other person feelings, thoughts, or motives that he or she does not acknowledge.* Examples: "You're just saying that because you know it makes me angry." "You'd like to see me make a fool out of myself." "So you think I can't stand up to my boss."

One of the most competitive and forceful of the strategies is **prescription,** which can take many forms. The confrontational person makes requests or demands, threatens, or argues for a given behavior change in the other person that presumably would resolve the conflict. Examples: "Get the job done by tomorrow or I'm not paying." "Clean up your room or you're grounded for the weekend." "If you leave this apartment, don't come back." Threats are among the most frequent responses people use during conflict, and there are times when they can generate change, but only if the person being threatened believes, and cares, that the threat will be carried out. For example, the "tough love" program for working with juvenile delinquents is based on this premise.

The advantages of competition are that it can stimulate creativity and energize people to a very high degree. Witness the enthusiasm at many sporting events. Among the disadvantages of competition is that it usually runs the risk of harming the relationship between the parties involved. Winning takes a higher priority than building the relationship. Competition may also drive the other party "underground" if he or she is not in a position to respond openly. The best example of this is the sabotage that employees resort to when they feel abused by their bosses. Perhaps the greatest disadvantage is violence. All you have to do is look at the news each day to witness the many cases in which conflict escalates into violence.

Compromise

Many times, in order to resolve a conflict, both parties have to give in a bit so as to reach a compromise solution. Note the definition of "negotiation" later in this chapter as finding mutually acceptable tradeoffs. The key here is that the tradeoffs must be mutually agreeable. Sometimes compromises are just poor solutions in which nobody really gets what he or she wants. The classic example comes from the Bible: Wise King Solomon is asked to settle a dispute between two women who both claim to be a baby's mother. He says that in order to satisfy them both he will cut the baby in half and give each woman one-half. The baby's birth mother offers to give the baby to the other woman to save the child's life. King Solomon gives the baby to the birth mother instead, because only the birth mother would rather give up the child than see it harmed. In many modern-day legal cases, lawyers refer to a judge's decision as "cutting the baby in half." This simply means that if one party is suing the other for $1 million damages, the judge will settle on $500,000. This is a typical example of a compromise solution.

One advantage of compromise is that it does often lead to resolution of the conflict. It can also be used as an alternative when other styles such as competition have failed. A disadvantage is that it can be used as the easy way out. It may also be that $500,000 is still much too much for the party to pay in damages. Compromise may also be used instead of more creative solutions that might be better and even more satisfying to both parties. Compromise does not involve a strong drive for the relationship and for the substantive goals, but rather a half-hearted attempt to meet both.

Compromise happens every day—even in apparently silly situations. Recently, in Canton Township, Michigan, a controversy occurred over a Big Boy restaurant's icon, a fiberglass 6-foot-tall statue of the Big Boy. A Canton ordinance prohibits businesses from having more than one monument-size sign on their property. The issue was taken to court, where the judge recommended the statue be considered a piece of art instead of a sign. After the prosecution realized this wasn't worth all the trouble, they compromised and changed the ordinance to make the Big Boy statue legal ("Canton Township . . . ," 2004).

I once heard about a faculty committee that could not decide whether to adopt textbook A or textbook B. They compromised on textbook C, a book that no committee members really felt excited about. This is an example of the downside to compromise as a conflict-resolving style.

Accommodation

In this style, the *person suppresses his or her substantive needs and emphasizes harmony with the other party* ("Go ahead and do it your way. I don't want to fight about this"). This approach is also called **appeasement** or smoothing over the conflict. Again, this appears to be a short-term strategy. All of us have human needs, as we shall discuss in the section on negotiation. If we chronically suppress these needs in order to please another person, sooner or later the unmet needs will rise to the surface.

However, this style has the advantage in the short run of demonstrating to the other person our willingness to put the relationship above our own selfish needs. We are reminded of this in the story "The Gift of the Magi," by O. Henry, in which a man sells his watch to buy jeweled combs for his wife's hair, while she sells her hair to buy a chain for his gold watch. Each person is thinking first of the other. It would seem that this style would work best in the family or among very close friends. One rule of thumb is to decide if the relationship is more important than winning the point. If your feelings for the other person are really strong, it may be best to just let go of the issue.

Collaboration

Collaboration requires the highest level of commitment to the relationship of any of the conflict-resolving styles. It involves a high degree of concern for achieving the goals of both parties, as well as a high degree of concern for the relationship between the parties. This is often very difficult to accomplish. The discussions continue until both parties are satisfied. In the best cases, the relationship can be strengthened in the process.

Sillars (1986) provides a summary of the following collaborative tactics. *Description* is just that, not blaming or making evaluations of the other. It involves simply describing (not "You never want to go out," but rather "I'm feeling depressed because we don't go out as much as I would like").

Qualification *involves limiting the subject at issue* ("Let's not get into why we don't have enough money. Can we figure out how we can manage what we have right now to make it less stressful for both of us?"). By disclosing your own thoughts and feelings and soliciting disclosures from the other person, you are trying to establish a supportive climate in which conflict may be resolved ("When you talk about dating other people, I get anxious. Are you trying to say that you want to stop seeing me?"). Negative inquiries also help to elicit disclosures and greater openness from the other person ("Honey, if there's some way in which I've hurt your feelings, I'd really like to know about it").

Two important ways in which we can be confirming and still move toward resolution are by showing empathy or support ("It's rough right now. We seem to be at each other's throats all the time, and I suppose you're feeling as down about it as I am") and by emphasizing commonalities ("Well, we may not agree on how to cut the budget, but can't we come up with something to save our department from being eliminated?"). Other behaviors that may facilitate conflict resolution are accepting responsibility ("We've both been at fault. I know I was getting more and more hostile, and I just had to get it off my chest") and initiating problem solving ("What would be best for the kids? Let's try to work this out").

The advantage is that collaboration can lead to some of the most effective conflict resolutions achievable. The disadvantage is that many times only one party is willing to utilize this style. Unless both parties are willing to use this style, it is not very likely to work. It also takes a lot of time, energy, and skill. But the results are often worth it. Recent research on career success and success in getting hired for a job shows that being resilient and managing conflict well are major predictors of success (Reed and Stoltz, 2011).

However, all in all, this style appears to have the most promise for effective conflict resolution. Keep in mind that none of us uses any one style in the textbook sense. In real life we often see a mixture of different styles. The Kilmann-Thomas model, an excellent way of conceptualizing the process, offers an idealized way of attempting to improve our conflict-resolving skills.

> *Who desires peace, should prepare for war.*
>
> —**Vegetius (De Re Militari)**

Some conflicts may not follow the Kilmann-Thomas model. Consider the following situations (Bester and Warneryd, 2006):

1. Two countries negotiate about the division of fishing waters located between them. If negotiations break down, they go to war.

6.2 **PRACTICAL TIPS**   *Conflict Management Skills*

- Pick your battles. Don't argue over everything.
- Develop a reputation as someone who admits when you are wrong.
- Provide an alternative for ideas you oppose. Don't knock down the ideas of others without having something else to suggest.
- Let the other person speak first. This will encourage the other person to listen better. You will also gain insight into what it takes to satisfy him or her.

- Base your statements on facts. Avoid exaggeration.
- Don't lose your temper.
- Avoid sarcasm, disbelief, and caustic humor.
- Develop a win-win mentality. Aim to meet both your needs and the other person's. Avoid simply trying to defend your position. Never try to win by destroying the other person. (Adapted from Boles and Moeller, 2012).

2. A buyer and a seller of a good try to renegotiate the terms of a trading contract. If they fail to reach an agreement, they go to court.

3. Two political parties try to form a coalition. If their negotiations are unsuccessful, they enter the elections on uncoordinated policy platforms.

These examples represent bargaining in the absence of well-defined property rights (Bester and Warneryd, 2006).

NEGOTIATION

When Jeffrey Katzenberg was CEO of Disney Studios, he described his style of negotiating in the following way:

> I operated like a mercenary soldier . . . If someone poked me in the chest, I would hit them with a baseball bat. And if they hit me with a bat, I would blast them with a bazooka. And I would escalate this until I reached nuclear-bomb time. This was the way I was taught . . . It's a hostile and predatory way to live life. The truth is, if you asked me to look back and say, because I behaved that way, that's why I was successful, I would now say: No. If I had been more conciliatory, I would have been more successful. (In Cloke and Goldsmith, 2005, p. 45)

Negotiation is another set of methods for resolving conflicts between and among people. We define negotiation as "a communication process of resolving conflicts through mutually acceptable concessions." This chapter is intended to take some of the angst out of your negotiations.

Fairness

During the presidential campaign of 2012, the Democrats and Republicans argued over who should pay their "fair share" of the tax burden. Democrats frequently said that the "rich" should pay their fair share and pitted Wall Street against "Main Street." They stated that the disparity between the super-rich and the middle class has simply gotten bigger over the past ten years. The Republicans, on the other hand, stated that those earning in the top 10 percent currently pay 75 percent of the federal taxes, and that was already more than a fair share. The problem is not too few taxes, but too much wasted federal government spending.

Inherent in all social exchanges are both elements of cooperation and competition. The outcome of such exchanges is often affected by whether the exchange partners perceive each other's behavior as fair. Sociological research defines fairness primarily as justice judgment, but it has also been suggested that such perception is directly linked to the nature of exchange in which the parties are involved—reciprocal or negotiated (Molm et al., 2006). "The more competitive and conflictual the actors perceive their relationship, the more likely they are to perceive the inequalities as unjust and their partners as unfair" (Molm et al., 2006). It follows, therefore, that parties in negotiated

One of the easiest ways to envision a negotiation is to think in terms of the "Wish, Want, Walk" method.

Wish

Your Wish is your goal, your dream result, often referred to in negotiation as your aspiration level.

Want

Your Want is the point where you think the negotiation will realistically end up, based on external marketplace forces. This is where the vast majority of deals end up. It is often the result of mutual concessions and compromises. For example, in labor negotiations, even though labor unions start out asking for 6–10 percent per year wage increases, and management starts out asking for

wage concessions, it is often the case that they end up agreeing to about 3 percent per year increases.

Walk

Your Walk is the point at which you will walk away from an agreement because it is simply not worth it. It is the point at which you lose money or pride or status. It is the point beyond which you feel you will have lost too much to accept the agreement. For example, your employer may offer you a promotion, but ask along with it that you move to a place far away from your extended family, friends, and loved ones, and with too many hours dedicated to work-related travel. The promotion may just not seem worth the sacrifice.

Adapted from Michael Donaldson. *Fearless Negotiating*. New York: McGraw-Hill, 2007.

exchanges are more likely to perceive their partner's behavior as more unfair than in reciprocal exchanges. In other words, reciprocal exchanges are perceived as more fair than negotiated exchanges because they are perceived as less conflictual and competitive (Molm et al.). It is useful to keep this in mind when planning a negotiation process.

Six-Step Model

Many times negotiations seem to be a mystery. However, there are ways of organizing the negotiation process that help to simplify and demystify it.

Walker and Harris (1995) have identified the following six predictable steps in the negotiation process: (1) analyzing the negotiation situation, (2) planning for the upcoming negotiation, (3) organizing, (4) gaining and maintaining control, (5) closing the negotiations, and (6) continuous improvements. Let's look at each of these steps a bit more closely.

Step 1: Analyzing the Negotiation Situation

In this step, you can begin to establish what your objectives are or what you hope to accomplish from the negotiation. For example, if you want to sell your used car, what price do you need to feel that you have been successful?

You need to determine what your "bottom line" is, but you also need to determine an acceptable range of alternatives just to give yourself some bargaining room. You should also think about what the other person's needs are. What attributes or benefits can you sell about your car that will help meet this person's needs? What is there about the environment that will affect the negotiation? For example, if you have a convertible and it is summer, the physical environment will be more favorable to the sale than if it is the dead of winter. A good economic environment will help your sale, as compared to when the economy is weak. How many others are competing for your buyer? Is it a buyer's market or a seller's market? All of these are questions that you will want to consider in your analysis.

Sometimes you may have a best alternative to a negotiated agreement (BATNA). This is your best way of satisfying your interests without the other's agreement (Boles and Moeller, 2012). In this case, you don't need the other person's cooperation, and the two of you are not interdependent. For example, it is better to keep your used car than to sell it for too little money.

Step 2: Planning for the Upcoming Negotiations

Henry Kissinger negotiated many diplomatic agreements and has been quoted as saying that 50 percent of negotiation time is spent in planning prior to the actual negotiation. The inexperienced negotiator tends to underestimate the need for careful preparation.

As one research notes, negotiations are often "complex, ill-structured, and evolving tasks, which require sophisticated decision support" (Lim and Yang, 2007). Moreover, human negotiations are often susceptible to various "stumbling blocks," such as cognitive biases as well as emotional complications (Lim and Yang). These stumbling blocks, combined with the increasing complexity of negotiated issues, have led to

---

Stealth Negotiation

Babitsky and Mangravati (2011) remind us that before the negotiation ever begins, there is a lot of incidental communication that occurs. This offers an opportunity to gather important information that can be used later in the more "formal" phases of the negotiation. For example, you can ask, "How did you hear about us?" This can potentially yield good information about your reputation and who they heard from about you. Second, you can ask, "How have things been going?" or "How's business?" Sometimes they may reveal that they are in a weak financial position and really need to bargain. Third, you can ask, "What is your time frame for wrapping up this negotiation?" Or if you are buying a house, you can ask, "When do you plan to move?" If they reveal their deadline, this is one of the most important bits of information you can get. As people near their deadline, they usually give in more quickly. In fact, this is known as the 80/20 rule. Eighty percent of the concessions on both sides usually happen in the last 20 percent of the time left before the deadline.

development of the notion of Negotiation Support Systems (NSS). The purpose of NSS is "to assist negotiating parties in reaching mutually satisfactory decisions by supporting information analysis and communication protocols" (Lim and Yang). NSS may be especially helpful during the planning stage of negotiations as in many cases planning is the key element. For example, one challenge faced by business negotiations (e.g., buyer-seller, labor-management, international business merger) is to jointly identify and set ranges on critical issues to be negotiated prior to the actual negotiation (Lim and Yang).

Most negotiations revolve around three basic components: (1) money, (2) people, and (3) timing. As you plan the negotiation, you should consider what goals you have for each of these three key components.

Another important consideration is what communication strategies and tactics you will plan to use. What kind of psychological climate would you like to establish in the negotiation? Are you trying to gain a win-win outcome or a win-lose outcome? A lose-lose outcome is also possible.

In a formal negotiation you can begin to work out the structure of the negotiation with such items as: Where will it take place? What will be the agenda (what points will be discussed)? Who will be involved? When will the sessions occur? Who will take minutes or notes of the agreements reached? How many sessions will there be? All these are items that may need to be negotiated. During the Vietnam War era, it took 18 months for the two sides to agree on the shape of the negotiating table and who the participants would be in the negotiations! A key thing to remember is that everything is potentially negotiable.

Step 3: Organizing

The first thing to do in this phase is to determine who will be the most effective people for your negotiation team. In a business setting, the sales and purchasing people may be supported by legal, financial, or other technical experts. In common life situations, you may be negotiating alone or you may bring a significant other. Often two heads are better than one.

The second thing is to develop your game plan, which means determining your objectives for the negotiation. If you are buying a home, some of your objectives should include (1) an affordable purchase price, (2) occupancy date when you need it, (3) a good mortgage rate, (4) negotiating what is included in the purchase price, and perhaps, (5) an inspection paid for by the seller.

Third, you should determine ahead of time your opening offer, then what your next offer might be, and finally what is the highest you can afford to offer.

Fourth, you should conduct a mock negotiation to practice how you will react to issues brought up by the other party.

Finally, expect surprises. Negotiation is by its very nature highly unpredictable.

Step 4: Gaining and Maintaining Control

Sometimes negotiations can get out of control. Emotions tend to escalate, voices are raised, positions become polarized, and agreement becomes less and less likely to occur. One way to gain some control is to create the draft agenda. Then you can ask for the reaction to it, and you may make adjustments. If you leave the agenda to the other party, he or she will often gain control of not only the agenda but other items as well. A typical agenda will include the following items:

Date	List of topics
Attendees	Order of the topics
Time	Length of time for each topic
Location	Beginning and ending times
Ground rules for the sessions	

A good exercise would be for you to practice by creating an agenda for an upcoming negotiation to develop your familiarity with this process.

Step 5: Closing the Negotiations

The information on brainstorming covered in Chapter 12 will also be valuable in negotiations. Many times agreements can be achieved if people are creative enough to invent options that are not immediately obvious. We may be limited primarily by our own lack of creativity. Once, your author was negotiating with a moving van company over the price of a cross-country move. In order to save money in the cost of the move, the following items, among many others, were brainstormed:

- Packing some household items instead of having the movers do it.
- Packing boxes of bed linens.
- Shipping boxes of books instead of having them hauled in the moving van.
- Having a garage sale to cut down on the amount to be moved.
- Getting used boxes instead of buying new ones from the mover.
- Changing the type of insurance to reduce costs.

However, the two parties still remained about $500 apart. So the moving company representative came up with the idea of a customer endorsement and awarded me a $500 discount if I would write a letter as a satisfied customer, which the company could then use in their advertising. This became an ingenious way to accomplish a very satisfying agreement for both parties.

Step 6: Continuous Improvements

This is perhaps the least often practiced step. Once the negotiation is over, there is real value in going back over the process and analyzing ways to improve. You can go back over each of the previous steps and look for things that could be done differently. For example, Were your objectives met? How well did your outcomes match your "bottom line"? Was your planning sufficient? Did your organization plan work? How would you do it next time? Were you able to gain and maintain control? If not, what did you learn that you could do more effectively next time? How well were you able to close the negotiation? It has been said that the mark of a really good negotiation is that both parties would come to the same agreement again if they had it to do over. Keep in mind that people can negotiate for many years and still learn more about it. Negotiation is a highly complex set of communication skills, as we shall see in the next section.

Negotiation Strategy and Tactics

A survey by the J. D. Power company (1992) found that 68 percent of car buyers dreaded negotiating with the auto salesperson for a new car, whereas 32 percent said that they enjoyed it. In our culture we are not used to negotiating. We pretty much pay whatever price is shown on a product. However, as we saw in the moving van example, there is often some room to negotiate.

Negotiation Styles and Outcomes

Personal traits of negotiators often affect negotiation outcomes. It is therefore of practical value to understand various negotiating behaviors.

Cheung and colleagues (2006) identified five negotiating styles: integrating, obliging, compromising, dominating, and avoiding. They are characterized as follows:

Integrating

- I collaborate with the other to come up with a decision acceptable to us.
- I try to bring all concerns out in the open so that the issues can be resolved in the best possible way.
- I exchange accurate information with the other so that we can solve the problem together.
- I try to work with the other to find solutions to a problem that will satisfy our expectations.

Practical Tips

Research from over 100 negotiations shows how you can increase your negotiation effectiveness by following some of the following tips:

1. Research areas for common ground with the other side (TOS).
2. Establish a settlement range rather than one specific price. (For example, $500–600 for an item rather than $550).
3. Ask many questions to obtain as much information from TOS as you can.
4. Avoid attacks on TOS.
5. Be careful to avoid words that irritate TOS. (Boles and Moeller, 2012, p. 6)

- I try to investigate an issue with the other to find a solution that will be acceptable to everyone involved.
- I try to work with the other for a proper understanding of a problem.

Obliging

- I try to satisfy the expectations of the other.
- I usually try to accommodate the wishes of the other.
- I generally try to satisfy the needs of the other.
- I give in to the wishes of the other.
- I often go along with the suggestions of the other.
- I usually allow concession to the other.
- I attempt to avoid being "put on the spot" and try to keep my conflict with the other to myself.

Dominating

- I use my authority to make a decision in my favor.
- I use my influence to get my ideas accepted.
- I sometimes use my power to win a competitive situation.
- I am generally firm in pursuing my side of the issue.
- I use my expertise to make a decision in my favor.

Compromising

- I try to find a middle course to resolve an impasse.
- I negotiate with the other so that compromise can be reached.
- I try to integrate my ideas with the other to come up with a decision jointly.
- I use "give and take" so that a compromise can be reached.
- I try to avoid unpleasant exchanges with the other.

Avoiding

- I try to stay away from disagreement with the other.
- I avoid an encounter with the other.
- I try to keep my disagreements with the other to myself to avoid hard feelings.

These distinctions are more than merely theoretical. In their study of negotiating styles and dispute resolution outcomes in the highly conflict-saturated Hong Kong construction industry, Cheung and colleagues (2006) found that the use of obliging, dominating, and avoiding styles was less influential in achieving functional negotiation outcomes. Integrating style was found to be useful in achieving the functional negotiation outcomes while the use of compromising style was practical in resolving disputes.

Assumptions

Before actually entering into a negotiation, we should first check our assumptions. The following are a few assumptions often recommended by experienced negotiators.

Both Parties Have Some Needs to Be Met   If you are selling a car, then the buyer obviously has some need for transportation. He or she also has financial needs, time constraints, psychological needs, and so on. The more we are able to recognize the other party's needs, the more likely we are to be successful in negotiating.

Both Parties Should Avoid a Win-Lose Philosophy   Sometimes it may seem that the negotiation is a one-shot experience. This may lead us to conclude that we don't have to worry about the ethics involved. However, many times we cross paths with the same people again, so our long-term reputations are very important. People have long memories. If we mistreat them, they are likely to want to return the favor at some future date. This is especially true in ongoing relationships—in families, with friends, and at work, experienced negotiators work hard to have the other party feel good about the negotiation's outcome.

Many Issues Are (Potentially) Negotiable   When we see a formal contract such as a printed form, the power of authority leads us to feel that we do not have the discretion to change any of the terms in that contract. This may be a false assumption (Babitsky and Mangravati, 2011). Your author was once trying to hire a very prestigious man. His attorney presented me with a formal employment agreement on behalf of this man. The terms of employment were very extreme. It seemed he was asking for a lot more than I would ever be able to provide in the way of salary, benefits, travel budget, clerical support, and so on. When I actually sat down to negotiate in person with the man, he said the document was only intended to get the discussion started. He ended up agreeing to work for a grand total of $1 per year (since he was wealthy enough to work without need for pay). He did, however, have psychological needs that were met by his affiliation with our organization.

Think about a top-performing basketball player such as Rasheed Wallace. The Detroit Pistons were eager to sign Wallace after he helped the Pistons win the national title in 2004. At one point, the Pistons were just waiting for a "yea" or a "nay" from Wallace. "And the 'nay' is just to bump it up (meaning salary) a little more" (Lage, 2004). After negotiation, Rasheed signed a deal worth $57 million over 5 years.

Physicians have confirmed to me that even the definition of who is dead and who is alive has been negotiated. A few years ago the definition of death was renegotiated between the American Bar Association and the American Medical Association. In order to harvest organs from a donor, there has to be an agreed-upon definition of when the donor is legally dead. Prior to the redefinition, a person was dead when his or her heart stopped beating. With the new definition, a person is dead when he or she is "brain dead," even if the heart continues to beat. This seemingly extreme example shows that even the distinction between dead and alive is negotiable.

One of the most flexible or negotiable issues is a deadline. For example, someone may ask you to complete a task by a certain deadline. You might want to try negotiating that deadline as you begin to gain more experience as a negotiator. You may have already negotiated with a professor for an extension on a deadline for an assignment. Some expert attorneys advise that we can even ask, "What is your time frame for wrapping up this negotiation?" to determine their deadline (Babitsky and Mangravati, 2011, p. 19). To be sure, you will encounter some situations in which there may be no room to negotiate. That is why we hedge when we say that many issues are (potentially) negotiable.

To Be Successful, You Must Consider the Other Person's Needs As with all forms of communication, you must analyze your audience in order to tailor your communication strategies and tactics to the particular situation. You would certainly behave differently in trying to ask one of your parents for something as opposed to asking a friend. Always keep in mind that in order to negotiate successfully, you must keep the other person's needs in mind.

Meanings and Standards Are Not Always the Same In Chapter 3, we saw that there is a great deal of potential for misunderstanding based on the use of language. In negotiating, it is very important to keep in mind that there is great potential to assume that we are using meanings the same way, when in fact we are not. For example, in many labor contracts it is written that things will be done within a "reasonable period of time." You can imagine how this is open to many different interpretations. On the other hand, so-called weasel words (called this because they enable you to weasel your way out of a firm commitment) are sometimes used on purpose, to allow both parties flexibility.

Different people interpret language in different ways. For example, in real estate contracts, it is typical to include language that states the draperies, wall coverings, carpeting, and other items that are affixed by screws, nails, glue, and so on will be included in the property. However, your author once bought a house and discovered upon taking occupancy that the mailbox had been taken off its post, all the light bulbs had been taken out of their sockets, and a number of other items had been removed as well.

This example may appear trivial, but it points to a fundamental cognitive problem of conflict management: "Whatever happens in negotiations will be interpreted and framed by stakeholders based on their different belief-value systems and world views" (Hoffmann, 2005). An example of this discrepancy occurred in 2000, during the Camp David summit between Israeli Prime Minister Barak and Palestinian Chairman Arafat. The issue of sovereignty over Jerusalem's holy places was discussed—namely, the problem of what for Israel is the "Temple Mount" and for Palestinians "Haram al-Sharif." Among formulations offered as framework for an agreement for the division of Israeli and Palestinian sovereignty was the following: "Israeli sovereignty over the Western Wall and the space sacred to Judaism of which it is a part" or "the Western Wall and the holy of holies of which it is the part" (cited in Hoffmann, 2005). One of Barak's advisors clarified that while historically "holy of holies" referred to the "four square meters that the High Priest would enter on Yom Kippur," Barak used it to refer to the territory that included Haram al-Sharif (Hoffmann). Such interpretation, however, directly contradicted the Palestinian idea of sovereignty of the Haram. Since Arafat could not know how "the sacred places of Judaism" or the "holy of holies" would be interpreted by his counterparts, agreement on the issue was not reached.

Principled Negotiation

Roger Fisher and his colleagues at Harvard University have devised a method for bringing a higher level of professionalism to negotiation. Fisher, Ury, and Patton (1991) write persuasively that negotiators typically see negotiations as either soft or hard. They reject this view and suggest that a third approach is the better way. This is **principled negotiation,** or deciding an issue based on its merits rather than by taking positions and trying to get the other party to come to our position. As we shall see, principled negotiation has four primary rules of thumb: (1) separate people from the problem; (2) focus on interests, not positions; (3) invent various options for mutual gain; and (4) use objective criteria.

Separate People from the Problem   As I mentioned earlier, people have psychological needs as well as substantive needs in a negotiation. Most negotiation takes place in the context of an ongoing relationship. In some cases, the relationship is far more important than any one specific negotiation. In negotiations, often tempers flare and the disagreement over issues tends to erode or even destroy the relationship. The lesson here is that we can be more effective if we treat each other with respect than if we get sarcastic, insult each other, or call each other names. Fisher, Ury, and Patton (1991) put it this way: "[Be] hard on the problem, [but] soft on the people" (p. 54). If the other party behaves emotionally, it is usually best not to escalate the conflict by reacting in kind. The following is an excerpt from an actual conversation that occurred in the presence of the author.

> *Nahal:* Would you enter the accounts payable a different way next time? I think this new method would streamline the process.

6.4 **ISSUES IN COMMUNICATION**

Negotiation Tips

Herb Cohen is one of the country's foremost negotiation experts. Here are a few tips from his book *Negotiate This!* (2003):

- Detach yourself emotionally.
- Set high goals.
- Remember, "no" does not mean never.
- Generally, begin in an amiable fashion.
- Keep the ultimate decision maker out of the nitty-gritty dealmaking.
- Display respect.

- Start with mutual interests.
- Try to acquire information about the other party's beliefs, motives, values, and needs.
- View yourself as a problem solver.
- Attempt to see the problem through their eyes.
- When we care too much the adrenaline starts flowing, causing us to become doped up and dumbed down.
- Strive for an attitude of caring, but not t-h-a-t much.

Heather: Why is it that you can't do things our way? You're not even from this country!

Nahal: Well, I wouldn't talk! You can't even keep a husband! How many times have you been divorced?

What do you think is the likelihood of these two people ever reaching agreement on the accounting system (or much of anything) after that exchange?

Focus on Interests, Not Positions   Your author was in a negotiation recently in which there were three people on one side and five people on the other. In the opening remarks, the speaker on the one side stated that the discussion was to center on three alternatives (positions). Much arguing followed and a lot of time was wasted until someone suggested that we start over and look at what we all could agree was in our mutual best interests. Then a lot of ideas were suggested, and resolution came about rather quickly.

The second approach in this example focused on mutual interests rather than on the three specific positions. Most negotiators focus on positions because they may not be aware of the alternative approach. If you try to decide where to meet, you may say, "My place or yours?" This is a very common way to decide things. However, it is not always the best way when parties have a hard time agreeing. Perhaps a better alternative would be to ask, "Where would you feel comfortable meeting?" One natural outcome of positional bargaining is that once you have stated your position, it makes you look and feel foolish if you have to "back down." This causes you to "lose face" or feel embarrassed. Thus, it is better to take the focusing-on-interests approach rather than the focusing-on-positions approach in the first place.

Fisher, Ury, and Patton (1991) offer the following example. At one point, the Egyptian-Israeli peace negotiations reached an impasse because the Egyptians wanted the Sinai Peninsula returned to them, whereas Israel insisted on keeping the territory. Both sides were focusing on positions.

When they looked at interests instead of positions, they found that Israel's interests were in security. The Israelis did not want Egyptian tanks near their border, ready to strike. Egypt's interests were focused on national sovereignty. The Sinai had been part of Egypt since the time of the Pharaohs. The two parties eventually agreed to a plan that returned the Sinai to Egypt, but made it a demilitarized zone (with no tanks or guns), so that both parties could satisfy their interests (Fisher, Ury, and Patton, 1991, pp. 41–42).

Focusing on interests usually involves each side's asking questions instead of making statements. The more information that is shared, the easier it is to determine what the other party is seeking. Keep in mind that the motivation behind many actions is rooted in such basic interests as:

- Security
- Economic well-being
- A sense of belonging
- Recognition
- Control over one's life

If you keep these in mind, you improve your chances of negotiating effectively. Also keep in mind that the more complex the negotiation, the harder it is to use positional bargaining. There may simply be too many issues. Your author was once on a management team that negotiated with labor union representatives on a contract worth over $300 million. There were a total of 1,013 articles in the union contract and each one had to be negotiated. As you can imagine, it would be pretty hard to formulate positions on that many issues.

Invent Various Options for Mutual Gain   As we shall see in Chapter 12, problem solving and decision making can be complex processes. One of the most common mistakes is to jump immediately to the solution phase without carefully looking at the definition of the problem, the symptoms of the problem, the root causes of those symptoms, and the criteria for an effective solution. Only after we take those steps can we begin to effectively brainstorm multiple potential solutions to be compared to our criteria. The same is true in negotiation situations.

Use Objective Criteria   Imagine that you are trying to negotiate with your boss for a pay increase. How would you go about proving your case? One way is to compare what you are doing with others who are doing the same thing with the same number of years' experience. What if you are trying to sell a house? How do you decide what to ask for it? The typical method in real estate is to get three other examples of "comparable" property in comparable locations and look at their value. When you plan to buy or sell a used car, you can use the *Kelley Blue Book,* which lists the values of all makes and models of cars of each model year. In the labor contract negotiations mentioned above, both management and the union used national studies that showed what the pay rate was for comparable employees. Both sides also showed agreements from other comparable institutions that had recently completed their contract negotiations. The union showed other organizations that had given large percentage increases, while management showed settlements that had given smaller percentage increases. These are all examples of using objective criteria on which to base your discussion.

Using objective criteria tends to make a negotiation efficient, especially if both parties can agree on the criteria at the beginning of the negotiation. The alternative is to argue different perceptions, which often gets us nowhere. One party thinks workers are underpaid; the other thinks the opposite. In a divorce settlement, a way of using this method would be for the two parties to decide on rights for visiting the children, before deciding which parent gets custody. No methods are foolproof, but principled negotiation methods tend to offer an alternative to the traditional cut-throat methods often encountered.

The following are a few principled negotiation techniques that are very helpful:

"Correct me if I'm wrong." One party may say, "You have mentioned that this program would have to operate at a loss. Correct me if I'm wrong, but hasn't this program made a profit for the organization?" This conveys the message that you think the facts are different from the ones that have been stated, but leaves open the possibility that you may not have all the facts.

"We appreciate what you have done." This shows that you are recognizing the other party's efforts. It acknowledges the need in all of us to have our efforts, patience, consideration, creativity, and so on appreciated.

"Let me check to see if my facts are correct." It helps to say something like, "According to my notes, we have agreed on the following four items. Would you agree with these as I have stated them?" Negotiations can often become complicated. This technique gives both parties the opportunity to review and to make sure that misunderstandings have not occurred.

"Let me see if I understand what you are saying." One party may say, "As I understand it, you are saying that if I loan you my tennis racket this Saturday, you will let me borrow five CDs for our party." Again, this restatement gives both parties the opportunity to double-check to see whether they have misunderstood one another.

"Here is where I have trouble following your reasoning." Another way to say this is "Help me understand your reasoning on this point." This is a nonthreatening way to ask the other person to explain his or her thinking a different way. You can also ask, "Can you explain that a different way? I am not following your line of reasoning." The goal is to clarify the understanding without antagonizing the other party.

We have found these five principled negotiation techniques to be invaluable over many years of negotiations. We recommend that you try them to see if they work as well for you. Remember that principled negotiation is only effective if you use effective communication techniques. Sam Horn, author and speaker, takes a close look at effective communication techniques in conflict and negotiation. She defines the martial arts of communication as "Tongue Fu®" (Horn, 2004). The goal of Sam Horn's organization is "to create a diplomatic group dynamic in which everyone has an incentive to get along." If people get along, then they can effectively negotiate to reach commonality in their goals. Effective communication is critical in this pursuit (Horn, 2004).

Horn (2004) illustrates some of the Tongue Fu practices that can lead to more effective conflict resolution and conflict diffusion. For example, Horn recommends asking questions to get to the root of the problem instead of responding to the verbal attacks of an opposing party. She suggests using hand gestures to pause a heated discussion, such as using the "time out" symbol instead of verbally jumping into the conflict.

Horn stresses the use of empathy and listening and warns against the use of the word "but." Imagine that you are in a negotiation and the opposing party says something like, "I agree with your plans on addressing the issue *but* I still think that you could have worked more effectively with the team." You automatically only hear the part of the sentence that occurs after the "but."

You can read these steps in detail along with information about her earlier book, *Tongue Fu! How to Deflect, Disarm, and Defuse Any Verbal Conflict* on her Web site at *www.SamHorn.com.*

If you practice effective communication when you find yourself in a conflict situation, you can facilitate the negotiation and resolution processes to the benefit of both parties. Effective communication is essential in making progress toward mutually beneficial solutions.

Summary

In this chapter, we have focused on communication situations that involve conflict and negotiation. There is potential for conflict in virtually every arena of human communication. It is a normal and predictable part of the communication process. Therefore, the better equipped we are to manage conflict, the more likely we are to improve this aspect of our communication skills.

We discussed the definition of conflict and several different levels of conflict. We also discussed the Kilmann-Thomas model of conflict resolution, as well as several tactics and techniques for resolving conflicts. In the negotiation section, we defined negotiation and examined a six-step model of the negotiation process. We then described negotiation strategy, including some important assumptions and several negotiating styles that often affect outcomes. Five techniques for conducting "principled negotiation" were also discussed.

Key Terms

Appeasement
Avoidance
Avoiding topics
Competition
Conflict

Denial
Intergroup conflict
Interpersonal conflict
Intragroup conflict
Intrapersonal conflict

Postponement
Prescription
Presumptive attribution
Principled negotiation
Qualification

Semantic focus
Shifting
Underresponsiveness

Review Questions

1. Define and discuss the definition of "conflict" given in this chapter.

2. Discuss the important elements in this definition.

3. Define and discuss the four levels of conflict discussed in this chapter.

4. Discuss and explain the Kilmann-Thomas model of conflict resolution. Discuss each of the major parts of the model.

5. Define negotiation.

6. Identify and discuss the six-step process in negotiations.

7. Identify and discuss five assumptions of successful negotiation.

8. Define principled negotiation and discuss four primary rules of thumb.

9. Identify and discuss five techniques of principled negotiation.

10. Write an essay discussing the most important ideas that you feel you have learned from this chapter. How can you put these to use?

Exercise

1. Use the Kilmann-Thomas conflict model to identify your preferred style. In small groups, discuss the advantages and disadvantages of each style.

Suggested Readings

Acuff, Frank. *How to Negotiate with Anyone Anywhere around the World.* New York: AMACOM, 1997.

This excellent book covers negotiations with people from different cultures.

Babitsky, Steven, and James Mangravati. *Never Lose Again: Become a Top Negotiator by Asking the Right Questions.* New York: Thomas Dunne Books, 2011.

This excellent and unique negotiation book describes the best fifty questions a negotiator can ask and explains how to use them.

Boles, Terry, and Lon Moeller. *The Road to Success: Learning How to Become an Effective Negotiator.* Dubuque, Iowa: Kendall Hunt, 2012.

This introduction to negotiation is a good source for the beginning student in the field.

Cloke, Kenneth, and Joan Goldsmith. *Resolving Conflicts at Work,* 2nd ed. San Francisco: Jossey-Bass, 2005.

This book offers eight strategies for resolving conflicts on the job.

Cohen, Herb. *Negotiate This!* New York: Warner Books, 2003.

Once again Herb Cohen has written a very readable book filled with practical advice for any negotiator.

Coltri, Laurie. *Conflict Diagnosis and Alternative Dispute Resolution.* Upper Saddle River, NJ: Pearson/Prentice-Hall, 2004.

This book is for the very advanced student. It is excellent in that its approach is unique and well grounded in legal issues.

Donaldson, Michael. *Fearless Negotiating.* New York: McGraw-Hill, 2007.

This very good book introduces the "wish, want, walk" method of negotiating.

Fisher, Roger. *Getting Past No,* 2nd ed. New York: Bantam Books, 2006.

An excellent follow-up to Fisher's original book.

Fisher, Roger, William Ury, and Bruce Patton. *Getting to Yes: Negotiating Agreement without Giving In,* 2nd ed. New York: Penguin, 1991.

A groundbreaking book on "principled negotiation."

Hames, David. *Negotiation: Closing Deals, Settling Disputes and Making Team Decisions.* Thousand Oaks, CA: Sage Publications, 2012.

This comprehensive text is an outstanding source for the student of negotiation.

Karrass, Chester. *Give and Take,* 2nd ed. New York: William Morrow, 1995.

A worthwhile list of many negotiation strategies and tactics. This is the most exhaustive list available.

Lewicki, Roy, David Saunders, and Bruce Barry. *Essentials of Negotiation,* 5th ed. New York: McGraw-Hill, 2010.

This excellent book is a comprehensive look at negotiation principles and practices.

Reardon, Kathleen. *Becoming a Skilled Negotiator.* New York: John Wiley & Sons, 2005.

This book takes a more quantitative approach and is somewhat more advanced.

Walker, Michael A., and George L. Harris. *Negotiation: Six Steps to Success.* Upper Saddle River, NJ: Bantam Books, 1995.

A comprehensive explanation of the six-step model for structuring the negotiation process discussed in this chapter.

Whetten, David, and Kim Cameron. *Developing Management Skills,* 8th ed. New York: McGraw-Hill, 2011.

This book has a chapter on managing conflict that is worth reading.

Wilmot, William, and Joyce L. Hocker. *Interpersonal Conflict,* 7th ed. New York: McGraw-Hill, 2007.

A theoretical book with an excellent coverage of the topics.

 # For Supplementary Information

Log onto the Online Learning Center at *www.mhhe.com/tubbshc13e.*

7

Ethics and Communication

Chapter Objectives

After reading this chapter, you should be able to:

1. Define ethics and identify three of the most common principles people use in making ethical decisions.
2. Discuss Aristotle's concept of the golden mean and give two examples of it.
3. Compare and contrast the ethical views of Kant and the utilitarians.
4. Discuss the concept of the veil of ignorance and its relationship to a theory of justice.
5. Identify the excuses people give in defending lies and discuss three ethical issues concerned with lying. Give examples from at least three communication contexts.
6. Discuss three forms of intentional misrepresentation.
7. Define plagiarism and explain the difference between plagiarism and paraphrasing.
8. Discuss three issues concerning the disclosure of information. Give four examples of contexts in which they might occur.
9. Discuss the ethical issues that grow out of the use of the new technologies.
10. Explain the difference between whistleblowing and leaking information. Discuss the ethical issues raised by each and the concept of moral courage.

The Golden Rule of Influence is, Live a life of undivided integrity.

—**Widener** (2008, p. 102)

ETHICS AT PENN STATE

Penn State University has for many years had one of the most admirable records in intercollegiate football when it comes to balancing athletics and academics. Joe Paterno, the head coach for many years, had primarily been credited for this high-quality program. However, in 2011, arguably the biggest scandal in the history of NCAA football erupted. Former assistant coach Jerry Sandusky was accused by numerous young men of having sexually abused them. On December 6, 2011, Sandusky was charged with 21 felony counts of sexual abuse and 8 more counts of indecent assault, all occurring between 1995 and 2009. Paterno was notified years ago of at least one such incident and reported it to his immediate supervisor, Tim Curley, the athletic director at the time, who subsequently reported the incident to his boss, Vice President Gary Schultz. Sandusky was relieved of his duties, but was still allowed access to the university facilities including the men's shower room, where some of the incidents occurred (Miller, 2001, p. A3). Coach Paterno was fired in his 46th year, as was Penn State's president, Graham Spanier, for their part in this scandal. After the firing, 2,000 students flocked to Paterno's house to show their support for the beloved coach, who was the best known individual at the university (Shad, 2011).

Although Paterno did what he was supposed to do, by reporting the one incident to his superior, ethical questions have been raised that he did not do more, and that he had a relatively uncooperative approach to disciplining those who broke the rules, and even the law. A former school official said that Paterno insisted that his players get special treatment when they got into trouble, which was quite often. Vicky Triponey, who resigned in 2007 as standards and conduct officer, frequently clashed with Paterno according to e-mails sent at the time (Gay, 2011, p. D6). She alleged that Paterno told his players that "they could not cooperate with judicial affairs or they would be kicked off the team." Triponey went on to say, "This would be so much easier if you would tell your players to just tell the truth. He was livid and the message to me was, 'I can't do that. They have to play for me and I can't ask them to rat on each other'" (Schrader, 2011, p. 3B). Other sources say that Triponey was a control freak who resigned over her repeated clashes with Paterno. In addition, she apparently faced "structural" barriers within the university. According to Rosa Eberly, a Penn State professor of communication, "She was a woman who was attempting to be just in the face of a patriarchy" (Albergotti and Bachman, 2001, p. A3). Students also complained about her cutting the student radio station's budget and her changes to student government, which gave more control to administrators and less to students (Albergotti and Bachman, 2011, p. A3).

Everyone agrees that, in addition to the 21 sexual abuse victims, Penn State has been seriously damaged. What is not so clear are the ethical questions surrounding Coach Paterno's behavior, and that of his boss, the athletic director, and his boss, the vice president, and his boss, the president. Do these firings seem appropriate to their actions, or lack thereof? What do you think?

Figure 7.1

Please tell me how you would rate the honesty and ethical standards of people in these different fields – very high, high, average, low or very low? How about – [RANDOM ORDER]?

	% Very high/ High	% Average	% Very low/ Low
Nurses	84	15	1
Pharmacists	73	23	4
Medical doctors	70	23	6
High school teachers	62	29	8
Police officers	54	35	11
Clergy	52	36	9
Funeral directors	44	43	9
Accountants	43	49	7
Building contractors	26	58	15
Journalists	26	46	27
Bankers	25	48	26
Real estate agents	20	57	22
Lawyers	19	43	37
Business executives	18	48	32
Labor union leaders	18	37	41
Stockbrokers	12	46	40
Advertising practitioners	11	52	34
Telemarketers	8	38	53
Car salespeople	7	44	47
Lobbyists	7	27	62
Members of Congress	7	27	64

Gallup, November 28 to December 1, 2011

GALLUP

Source: *http://www.gallup.com/poll/151460/record-rate-honesty-ethics-members-congress-low.aspx.*

The study of communication has always reflected an interest in ethics. Confucius wrote on ethics in the sixth century B.C., and in the fourth century B.C. Aristotle discussed the importance of appeals to *ethos,* personal qualities such as honesty and credibility, in communication. This chapter considers some of the thorny issues related to ethics in communication, or "communicating with integrity." Figure 7.1 shows the relative perceived ethics of various professions from the end of 2011.

Trust in members of Congress is at an all-time low of 7 percent. So, the study of ethics is as relevant today as it has ever been.

Ethics has been defined as *the study of the general nature of morals and of the specific moral choices to be made by a person.* Notice the word "choices." Ethics involves communication choices so that, by examining and becoming more aware of our own values, we become more responsible for the consequences of our actions.

Yet our moral choices and subsequent actions often lead to conflict when people feel we are trying to impose our own ethical values on them. How to reconcile the claims of personal freedom with those of moral responsibility has been debated over the centuries. The communications scholar Nick Couldry writes:

> By *ethics,* I mean neither a specific moral code . . . nor an agreed list of specific, narrowly circumscribed "virtues" . . . but rather an open-ended process of reflecting on how we need to act so that we can live well, both individually and collectively. (2006, p. 102)

Giving thought beforehand to the basis of our ethical choices enables us to think through rather than rationalize our decisions:

> If ethical principles are to be a guide to future behavior rather than a rationalization of acts already performed, it's important for us to stake out our moral turf before we are thrust into a specific situation. . . . The motivation to act ethically can be self-imposed, socially mandated, or divinely inspired. But regardless of the impetus, we need to have a way to determine the difference between right and wrong, good and bad, virtue and vice. (Griffin, 2006)

Many theories have been proposed about the basis for our ethical choices. *Moral Minds,* a recent book by Harvard professor Marc Hauser, brings together the findings of several disciplines including neuroscience, linguistics, and evolutionary biology. He argues that human beings have evolved a moral instinct, "a capacity that naturally grows within each child, designed to generate rapid judgments about what is morally right or wrong based on an unconscious grammar of action" (2006, p. xviii).

In other words, the moral instinct itself is universal, and human beings build moral systems that are specific to the culture they grow up in. Once our own moral limits are fixed, Hauser explains,

> we may be as perplexed by another community's moral system as we are by their language. Appreciating the fact that we share a universal moral grammar, and that at birth we could have acquired any of the world's moral systems, should provide us with a sense of comfort, a sense that perhaps we can understand each other. (p. 426)

In this chapter we begin by looking at some of the major ethical principles proposed by Western thinkers and then examine several issues that arise in many different communication contexts including the many challenging problems that have emerged with the use of the new technologies.

PRINCIPLES

The Golden Mean

Aristotle is thought of by many scholars as the founder of the communication discipline. A Greek biologist—and a tutor to Alexander the Great—he believed that ethics had to do with inner character rather than just overt behaviors.

Perhaps no concept in philosophy has been more widely cited than Aristotle's **golden mean.** According to Aristotle, *morality is to be found in moderation.* Aristotle views moral virtues as choices or modes of choice. He considers each virtue as the mean, *the middle path between two extremes—excess and deficiency.* We can see this most clearly with the virtue of temperance, the mean between eating and drinking too little or too much. Similarly, courage would be the mean between the extremes of fear (deficiency) and overconfidence (excess). Truthfulness would be the mean between false modesty and boastfulness; justice would be the mean between distributing too few goods (or punishments) and too many (Aristotle, 1947, pp. 333–337).

Some have interpreted Aristotle as saying that good is that which is desirable for its own sake—in other words, it is an end in itself. Since Aristotle was a biologist, he might have been interested in modern studies showing that people who report having committed fewer acts they consider immoral also report significantly lower levels of stress; other studies find that those who volunteer to help others actually live longer (Schuller, 1991, p. 97).

Though Aristotle is emphasizing what is within the range of human possibility, it is important not to misinterpret the principle of the golden mean. To advocate moderation is not to say that all behaviors are acceptable: "There is no mean for adultery, murder, theft. . . . Not every action nor every passion admits of a mean" (1947, p. 341). Similarly, Aristotle condemns lying; saying that "truth is noble and full of praise."

The aim of ethics for Aristotle is the happiness of the individual; the aim of politics involves the welfare of the entire community. Although Aristotle believed personal ethics to be subordinate to politics, this did not create a conflict of loyalties:

> This principle does not entail that the individual must sacrifice his interests to those of the community, except under unusual conditions such as war, because he assumed that the needs of both normally coincide. (Abelson, 1967, p. 85)

Our own interests, Aristotle would say, are usually in harmony with those of our society.

The Categorical Imperative

Suppose that every time you made a decision about ethics and acted on it, your decision became a universal law. This is the guiding principle proposed by the eighteenth-century German philosopher Immanuel Kant:

> Act only according to that maxim by which you can at the same time will that it should become a universal law. (1959, p. 39)

Kant's principle is known as the **categorical imperative**—that is, *a command or obligation to act (an "imperative") that is absolute ("categorical")—one with no exceptions or conditions.*

A categorical imperative makes certain behaviors unacceptable under any circumstances. For example, to Kant telling the truth is a sacred duty. There are no circumstances under which it would be acceptable for us to lie because, says Kant, we always harm someone by telling a lie: If we don't harm a particular person, still we do harm to humankind by undermining the nature of law. Take an extreme case—one that Kant himself considered: Would you tell a lie to prevent a murder? Kant argues that telling a lie even to prevent a murder would not be justified.

For Kant morality is measured by our intentions to obey universal laws of morality rather than by the consequences or outcomes of our actions—even if they will spare another's feelings or protect that person's welfare.

Many consider Kant's most significant contribution to ethical theory to be his requirement of "universal obedience to a rule of action":

> It expresses more precisely and unambiguously the "golden rule" to be found in all the great religions, and it has been incorporated, in one form or another, in most modern systems of ethical theory. (Abelson, 1967, p. 95)

We find an emphasis on universals similar to that of Kant in many religious systems and writings, including the Ten Commandments of the Old Testament and Saint Augustine's prohibition that all lies are sins:

> To use speech, then, for the purpose of deception, and not for its appointed end, is a sin. Nor are we to suppose that there is any lie that is not a sin, because it is sometimes possible, by telling a lie, to do service to another. (Augustine, 1961)

People traveling to China have noticed that Chinese ethics are based less on formal rules or laws and are more situational. Social relations and trust are more important than paper contracts. For example, Microsoft could not get the Chinese government to enforce its intellectual property laws for years, until the company developed a relationship with top Chinese officials and convinced them that Microsoft wanted to help develop China's economy and educational system (Zakaria, 2008, p. 113).

Utilitarianism

In sharp contrast to Kant, British philosophers Jeremy Bentham and John Stuart Mill place primary value not on our moral intentions but on *the outcomes or consequences of our actions.*

Bentham proposed a "hedonistic calculus," in which the amount of pleasure an action creates is weighed against the amount of pain it causes. Mill refers to the foundation of utilitarianism as the Greatest Happiness Principle:

> Actions are right in proportion as they tend to promote happiness, wrong [insofar] as they tend to produce the reverse of happiness. (Mill, 1968, p. 249)

Happiness is the greatest good, and for Mill "happiness" refers to "pleasure and the absence of pain," unhappiness to pain and the lack of pleasure. Mill extends the notion of happiness to include not simply pleasure but quality, so that pleasure is defined more broadly and includes intellectual pleasure and other values.

Mill's later formulation of **utilitarianism** in the nineteenth century is the best known:

> Seek the greatest happiness for the greatest number.

Utilitarianism grew out of concern for political and social reforms—hence its emphasis on what will benefit the greatest number of people—and was responsible for English legislative reforms during the nineteenth century. According to this view, the claims and welfare of individuals or smaller groups have to be subordinated to the claims of the greatest number of people.

Utilitarianism has more recently been criticized on the grounds that it is not always practical in analyzing moral choices. For example, suppose insurance companies decided to deny coverage to people who were known to have a genetic tendency to get a disease (like diabetes or colon cancer), but who had not yet contracted the disease. Utilitarian philosophers would argue that this is in the interests of the greater society by keeping insurance costs down. However, those who were denied the insurance based on what might or might not happen in the future would certainly feel that this was a poor moral choice on the part of the insurance companies (Beauchamp, Bowie, and Arnold, 2009, p. 23).

Justice and the Veil of Ignorance

The contemporary American philosopher John Rawls argues for a principle of justice rather than utility. In *A Theory of Justice* (1971), a book on political and social philosophy, he suggests a fair procedure by which we can agree on common ethical principles: To free ourselves of bias and self-interest because of our social position, education, and so on—what are sometimes called "accidents of birth"—Rawls proposes that we should all be placed behind a **veil of ignorance:**

> First of all, no one knows his place in society, his class position or social status; nor does he know his fortune in the distribution of natural assets and abilities, his intelligence and strength, and the like. Nor, again, does anyone know his conception of the good, the particulars of his rational plan of life, or even the special features of the psychology such as his aversion to risk or liability to optimism or pessimism. More than this, I assume that the parties do not know the particular circumstances of their own society. (p. 137)

Because we do not know our situations in society or our natural assets, argues Rawls, "no one is in a position to tailor principles to his advantage" (p. 139). We don't know which principles would be in our own interest. This also eliminates the possibility of groups banding together to form a coalition, for they do not know how to favor themselves. Once all these factors are corrected for, we make an ethical decision in which there will be unanimity of choice—fairness: No single person, group, or generation will be favored. (Rawls believes the "notion of the veil of ignorance is . . . implicit in Kant's ethics" [p. 140].)

Rawls proposes then that a principle of justice or fairness must include protection of those whose position in the society is weakest—whether due to age, illness, status, or income—and that what is moral is what is fair for all.

Rushworth Kidder, who founded the Institute for Global Ethics, identifies three of the most common principles people use in ethical decision making (2005):

> *Ends-based principles* are exemplified by those we saw in discussing utilitarianism. The focus here is to reach "good outcomes and results rather than on the motives or rules that guided us in our choices" (p. 93).

> *Rule-based principles,* such as the categorical imperative, stress the unchanging, universal codes of behavior. The focus is on duty and obligation.

> *Care-based principles* ask, "What would we want others to do to us?" Kidder links care-based principles with compassion. The Golden Rule is a prime example: "This principle of reciprocity or reversibility calls on us to imagine that we are in another's shoes, about to be impacted by the very actions we're contemplating" (p. 93). Hauser writes that we find the Golden Rule "in one form or another in all cultures, through either explicit religious doctrine or implicit social norms" (Hauser, 2006, p. 410).

After observing thousands of people in seminars at the Institute for Global Ethics, Kidder has concluded that "most people have more than one principle to which they appeal as the basis for moral choice" (2005, p. 92).

Ethical principles from many other cultures and other times could, of course, be represented here. Our hope is that those we have looked at will serve as a springboard for discussion and reflection as you consider some of the issues involved in making ethical choices about communication.

ISSUES

There are many reasons why someone may feel compelled to lie or stretch the truth on a résumé; however, it is obvious that the consequences are often overlooked. The frequency at which this occurs is truly alarming.

Marilee Jones, the former dean of admissions at the Massachusetts Institute of Technology, made headlines in the *New York Times* when she resigned after 28 years. Jones confessed to lying on her résumé and misrepresenting educational credentials. Although she admits the information was inaccurate when she first applied to M.I.T., Jones issued an apology and said she "did not have the courage to correct [her] resume" (Lewin, 2007).

CRUISE SHIPS AND DISPOSAL OF WASTE AT SEA*

Cruise ships are floating hotels. They provide every imaginable comfort for their guests. However, unlike hotels, they are not connected to municipal water and sewer systems. Human waste from toilets is stored in large tanks that are emptied when the ships return to port. However, so-called gray water from showers, baths, and sinks creates too much volume to be stored in tanks and is disposed of at sea. This also includes water from laundering sheets and towels, dishwater, and water from garbage disposals.

Cruise line executives say that the water volume is too large to be stored in tanks onboard. If tanks large enough to carry the waste water were built onboard, it would reduce passenger quarters by 15–20 percent and would force cruise lines to raise prices by 15–20 percent. Island officials complain that the contaminants in the water upset the ecological balance in the ocean.

What do you think you would do to address these issues?

*Based on a case in LaRue Hosmer. *The Ethics of Management,* 6th ed. New York: McGraw-Hill, 2008, pp. 21–22.

According to a survey conducted by CareerBuilder.com (Haefner, 2008), the following were the most commonly falsified pieces of information on résumés:

38%	Job Responsibilities
18%	Skill Set
12%	Employment Start and End Dates
10%	Academic Degree
7%	Previous Employment
5%	Job Title

Forbes.com lists the following as the top résumé lies:

Lying about getting a degree. Sure, you had every intention of finishing up that wildlife biology degree. That doesn't mean you can claim you got it. Dave Edmondson, the former CEO of RadioShack, learned this lesson the hard way when it was found that his college degrees were bogus.

Playing the dates. So you graduated from college in 1955. Don't fake it. Be proud. Presumably, you've gained some wisdom of the world by now. (And by the way, your age will be abundantly apparent if you're lucky enough to get the interview, unless you have an excellent plastic surgeon.)

Exaggerating numbers. Want to claim you made your previous employer a million dollars last year? That will look impressive. But remember that your new boss will expect you to deliver the same for him.

Increasing previous salary. What's the harm in innocently exaggerating your salary to get the best offer you can from your new employer? Just hope the company you want to work for doesn't request a recent pay stub, because then you'll have a whole lot of explaining to do.

Inflating titles. You would have been promoted to vice president of sales at your prior job if the company had truly realized your value as an employee, right? So why not just anoint yourself with the title you deserved? Wrong.

Lying about technical abilities. Your résumé says you're proficient in Photoshop. But on the first day of the job, you can't figure out the software. What now? It's probably best to avoid this situation.

Claiming language fluency. Sure, you took French when you were a freshman in high school. But don't forget that a claim on your résumé that you speak the language could be tested by your interviewer. If it happens, you'd better hope that everything you learned comes back to you *tout de suite.*

Providing a fake address. You haven't lived in your hometown since you left for college 20 years ago. Why not use Grandma's address when applying for a job there? A good reason might be the ease of using the White Pages these days.

Padding grade point averages. That 3.8 grade point average and magna cum laude honors speak volumes about your intelligence and diligence. Too bad a call to the school could reveal that your claim doesn't jibe with your C-student status.

Lying and Misrepresentation

> Truth exists as a human need in two ways: First, in the sense that human beings do not wish to lose their relation to tangible reality. . . . Second, human beings feel that communication between them is worthy of respect only if the criterion of truth is given its proper place. Otherwise, communication between human beings is felt to be disrespect. Thus, we can speak of truth as a threefold need of human beings: in relation to reality, to oneself, and to other people. (Mieth, 1997, p. 90)

Perhaps one of the most obvious breaches of ethics is lying. Distorting the truth is so common that over the last decade people have become increasingly disenchanted with politics. At times loss of credibility has also led to the public's disenchantment with the mass media. In his memoir *A Million Little Pieces,* James Frey described spending three months in jail and recounted his addiction and recovery. Highly acclaimed, the book sold over 3 million copies, was praised in literary circles, and singled out as an Oprah Book Club selection. Then it was discovered that much in the book had been invented by the author. Oprah Winfrey made a public apology for at first having defended Frey. He appeared on her television show, during which she questioned him, "getting him to admit that he'd inflated his story partly out of a need to look macho and partly because he (correctly) suspected it would sell better" (Freedman, 2006, p. 53):

> Writers do not write only for themselves. The events that Frey inflated or invented—jail time, the suicide of a friend, the severity of his stay in a rehab

clinic—went right to the core of his story of debasement and redemption. If he never bottomed out the way he described it and if his recovery was not one long, sadistic humiliation, then he is conning readers, passing off snake oil as an antibiotic.

Fiction isn't the spackle you use to fill in the cracks of your research. Fiction and nonfiction make fundamentally different compacts with a reader and are held to fundamentally different standards. . . . In return for the allegiance to factuality, nonfiction can present what may seem implausible and tell a reader, *But that's what really happened.* (p. 53)

Notice the use of the word "compacts"—a compact is an agreement between two parties. Anyone who writes a memoir has made an implicit agreement with the reader that what he or she writes will be true.

Similarly, we expect a newspaper account to be true. Consider the case of Jayson Blair, a well-regarded journalist who had worked at the *New York Times* for five years, advancing from an intern to a national reporter. Then, in 2002, his work at the newspaper came into question. One incident involved a reporter who noticed that one of her stories appeared as part of a story by Blair, but without her byline.

On May 11, 2003, a four-page article about Blair appeared in the *Times:*

The reporter, Jayson Blair, 27, misled readers and *Times* colleagues with dispatches that purported to be from Maryland, Texas and other states, when often he was far away, in New York. He fabricated comments. He concocted scenes. He lifted material from other newspapers and wire services. He selected details from photographs to create the impression he had been somewhere or seen someone, when he had not.

And he used these techniques to write falsely about emotionally charged moments in recent history, from the deadly sniper attacks in suburban Washington to the anguish of families grieving for loved ones killed in Iraq. (Barry et al., 2003, A1)

In one instance Blair reported in a front-page article that he had talked to six wounded marines in a Bethesda naval hospital, but he had never been there and some of the marines were not even in the hospital on the dates he mentioned (Hassan, 2003).

The *Times* itself called Blair's actions "a profound betrayal of trust and a low point in the 152-year history of the newspaper" (Barry et al., 2003, p. A1). Among journalists there was much concern about how Blair's deception could have gone undetected for so long and revived discussion about the issue of plagiarism.

Of course, plagiarism occurs in many different communication contexts (see Wiener [2007], for example). Here **plagiarism** is broadly defined as *using or presenting as your own the ideas, images, or words of another source—for example, from books or online information—without acknowledgment or permission.* It need not involve the use of a written text; it might be an idea for a screenplay, a passage of music, song lyrics, or an image created by an artist. Legal scholar Richard Posner writes that "concealment is at the heart of plagiarism. . . . It is not a mere failure to acknowledge copying" (2007, p. 17). **Paraphrasing,** on the other hand, is *using your own words to express or restate someone else's words or ideas,* and appropriately acknowledging all your sources is a legitimate way to do academic work (Fox, 2004).

When it comes to plagiarism and misrepresentation, academic life is not exempt. For example, how would you feel about one of your professors giving higher grades to student athletes even though they were undeserved? What about someone who received a research grant and did not use any of the money received on the project for which it was intended? Many dramatic instances of fraud and misrepresentation with wide repercussions for the public and for academic life involve misconduct in scientific research. Consider the case of Dr. Hwang Woo-suk of South Korea, who falsely claimed that he had cloned a human embryo in his laboratory and produced stem cell lines from it. In 2004 he was proclaimed a national hero. By 2006 he was disgraced and had admitted to charges of altering his data as well as to the misuse of state funds.

Another recent case is that of Eric Poehlman, a faculty member of the University of Vermont, who falsified data on clinical research: The studies of aging, menopause, and obesity that he supervised in his lab were used in support of other medical experiments. "He presented fraudulent data in lectures and in published papers, and he used this data to obtain millions of dollars in federal grants from the National Institutes of Health" (Interlandi, 2006, p. 98). He was brought to trial in 2005 because a young research assistant at his lab, who had looked up to him as a mentor, began questioning and cross-checking Poehlman's data.

> More frequent, according to a study published in *Nature* in June 2005, are smaller lapses in ethical judgment, like failing to present data that contradicts your previous research or inappropriately assigning author credit. (Interlandi, 2006, p. 101)

Though at times they seem remote, ethical questions occur in many other academic contexts—for example, in graduate study. After the oral defense of her thesis, a doctoral candidate in psychology was told by an eminent psychologist on her dissertation committee that he wanted her to add his name to her forthcoming research. In actuality, he was a guest reader and had nothing to do with her work. She refused. Some graduate students have also seen their research papers used, without credit, in the publications of their supervising professors.

Cheating and academic fraud have many unforeseen consequences. This is certainly true of teachers who pad grades or even alter student answers on tests. In *Freakonomics,* economist Steven Levitt and his coauthor discuss the case of a grade-school teacher who cheats by changing the answers of her grade-school students on a high-stakes test so that their grades will be higher and they will be promoted. Incentives for the teacher might include praise and professional advancement. She might even rationalize that she was helping her students to succeed, but as the authors point out, "these students (and their parents) would be in for a terrible shock once they reached the seventh grade" (2006, p. 30). The very students who most need to be identified as weaker so that they get appropriate help and placement are thus promoted to the next grade, where the possibility of failing only increases.

On a personal level, what is your feeling about cheating and plagiarism in school? If a good many classmates do it, does this make it all right? Results of research conducted nationwide by the Center for Academic Integrity and released in 2005 show that cheating and plagiarism are on the upswing:

> On most [college] campuses, 70% of students admit to some cheating. Close to one-quarter of the participating students admitted to serious test cheating in the past year and half admitted to one or more instances of serious cheating on written assignments.

The figures for high-school students are also high:

> Studies of 18,000 students at 61 schools, conducted in the last four years [show] over 70% of respondents at public and parochial schools admitted to one or more instances of serious test cheating and of plagiarism using the Internet. 60% admitted to some form of plagiarism. Slightly less than half of the respondents from private schools admitted similar behaviors. About half of all students admitted they had engaged in some level of plagiarism using the Internet. (*www.academicintegrity.org*)

At schools that had honor codes, there was a significantly lower incidence of both cheating on tests (33 to 50 percent) and on assignments (25 to 33 percent). As it turns out, cheating is somewhat sensitive even to physiological factors. In one series of studies, it was found that people who get even twenty minutes a night less sleep tend to cheat more than those who get a full night's sleep (Barnes et al., 2011).

In her study of lying, philosopher Sissela Bok defines a **lie** as *"any intentionally deceptive message that is stated"* (1999, p. 13; italics added). Thus, she emphasizes a person's intention to deceive or mislead through verbal communication. Paul Ekman, whose research on deception in nonverbal communication we looked at in Chapter 4, also links lying with the liar's intention either to conceal by "leaving out true information" or to falsify, "presenting false information as if it were true" (1985, p. 41). Chris Matthews, the moderator of MSNBC's *Hardball* program, wrote a recent best-seller about President John F. Kennedy. Matthews is a lifelong admirer of JFK's. However, he writes that the first time Kennedy ran for office, he forgot to file the necessary papers and only realized it after the deadline. The campaign workers "opened up the proper office and filed the papers. . . . This is a loyalist's account of an after-hours escapade that had to have been blatantly illegal. But what's remarkable is that Jack himself went into the municipal building that night and did what had to be done, putting those petitions in the right pile as if they'd been there by the deadline" (Matthews, 2011, p. 82). And Kennedy is one of our most admired former presidents. What sort of message does this send to rank-and-file Americans?

There is less agreement on how to regard ambiguous or equivocal communication. We've already spoken of euphemisms and unintentionally equivocal language in Chapter 3. Bavelas and her colleagues (1990) define "equivocation" as "avoidance," "communication that is not straightforward: it appears ambiguous, contradictory, tangential, obscure, or even evasive" (p. 28). They argue that the person who equivocates "is not the cause of equivocation. Rather [equivocation] is the result of the individual's communicative situation" (p. 54). In our discussion, the assumption will be that we can and do make choices about ethical and unethical behaviors.

Movies such as *The Lives of Others, The Croupier, Closer, Glengarry Glen Ross,* and *House of Games* deal with issues of trust, lying, and deception. In *Glengarry Glen Ross,* several real estate salesmen try to hustle and swindle customers into buying large land deals. At one point in the film, a customer is having second thoughts and wants his large check back. The salesman played by Al Pacino says that it has not been cashed by the home office yet, and the customer has nothing to worry about, whereupon another salesman comes into the office and says that he has in fact sent the check in. Later Pacino's character virtually explodes over the incident, telling the other salesman that he is never supposed to open his mouth in front of a customer until he knows what the customer has already been told. In other words, any lie is all right as long as it gets the sale.

Although these films portray an absolute low in personal and business ethics, situations in which we encounter lying are not always so sharply drawn. People have even cited moral reasons for lying. Thus, a perennial question in ethics is whether there are circumstances in which telling a lie is acceptable.

One of the most common reasons that people lie is to protect their reputation. They may be "concerned with what other people think." The *Journal of the European Economics Association* published an article by Cesar Martinelli and Susan W. Parker titled "Deception and Misreporting in a Social Program." They captured interesting insight into the theory of lying to protect one's reputation. Using data from *Oportunidades,* a Mexican welfare program, they researched the records of "household goods that people say they have when applying for the program." Once the application is accepted, they "record the household goods that were actually found."

The following are underreported items that applicants felt might exclude them from getting benefits: car, truck, video recorder, satellite TV, gas boiler, phone, washing machine. These findings were not uncommon as "you might expect people to lie to gain the advantage of a welfare benefit."

What was more surprising were household items that were overreported; applicants claimed they had these items but did not: toilet, tap water, gas stove, concrete floor, refrigerator. "Four out of 10 applicants without a toilet said they had one. Why?" Martinelli and Parker say the explanation is "plain and simple . . . embarrassment." This was the most alarming example of protecting one's reputation (*New York Times,* 2008).

Let's consider a lie that is told to avoid harm by protecting someone else's feelings. In discussing the many behaviors and strategies people use to maintain close relationships, Knapp and Vangelisti (2000) include lying:

> For most couples, the real issue is whether a lie will have a damaging effect on the relationship and whether the motivation for lying is well intended or not. (p. 264)

They then propose three questions in thinking about a lie:

1. Will this lie help both of us? If the lie is solely for the benefit of one partner, it is more likely to be viewed negatively and incur more relationship damage . . .

2. Is the lie consistent with the rules of fairness in the relationship?

3. Does your partner (the lied to) believe you have his or her best interests at heart—both generally and in this specific situation? (p. 264)

Imagine yourself as the person lied to in this relationship and consider your own views. Would you want to know if someone you loved was unfaithful to you, or would you prefer to be spared the pain (Knapp, 2006)? A related issue here is whether a lie such as this, which seems to protect, actually does. Granted, it avoids conflict, one of the reasons people frequently give for lying; but what does it protect—the relationship itself, the person lied to, the liar? Is it in your best interest to remain in the same relationship to the other person, or might you be better off finding out "the worst," trying to hammer out the difficulties, and having the option of ending the relationship?

Consider a more structured two-person relationship. Suppose you are a doctor who discovers that your elderly patient is suffering from a terminal illness and has only a few months to live. Your patient is terrified of even the slightest illness. Do you tell him the truth about his condition?

We know that Kant's categorical imperative would prohibit lying under any circumstances. Aristotle's golden mean might suggest some middle ground between assuring the patient he is fine and telling him everything about his condition, including the amount of time he has to live. On the other hand, a utilitarian might argue that the patient would be happiest not knowing—happiness here being defined as pleasure, or the absence of pain. We also know that it's on such grounds that the family of a patient often asks a doctor not to tell the truth: A utilitarian might think of this decision as producing the greatest happiness for the greatest number. A principle of justice is more difficult to apply, unless we agree on what constitutes "protection." If everyone must be treated equally, the doctor's decision will be the same for all patients.

In a recent article on medical ethics, several doctors affirmed their obligation to tell the truth, unless patients had made clear that if they were dying they did not want to be told. Patients, it was suggested, should state early on the level of information they are comfortable with. This position is a subject of ongoing debate even among doctors.

Issues about lying arise in virtually every communication context. For example, would you lie about having been fired from your last job? Or during a job interview suppose you say you have far more computer experience than you do because you think that will ensure getting hired. If you then go home and learn what you need before you get the job, would you say this is a "white lie," one that is not meant to harm anyone? Many people seem to have a repertoire of lies they identify as harmless—for example, statements that flatter others or statements made to protect people's feelings. "What a perfect gift!" "Mr. Thomas is out for the day."

"I have to work late tonight." "I'd love to stay, but I have so much work to do this evening." Do you think white lies are harmless?

Suppose you have just graduated from college and will be going to graduate school in September. You need to earn money over the summer and find a job listing that seems to fit your qualifications perfectly. At the interview you find there is only one hitch. The interviewer makes clear that this is a permanent job and wants a commitment from you of at least a year. There are very few summer jobs. What do you do?

Although you might argue that saying you will stay for the year is a harmless lie, from the employer's point of view it is not. You may do your work well over the summer, but the employer has lost an investment of time and training. It's also a lie that works against you; you certainly can't list this job on your résumé. As Bok points out, many lies described as harmless are not and telling white lies may later necessitate more frequent lies—sometimes lies that are more serious. "And even those lies which would generally be accepted as harmless are not needed whenever their goals can be achieved through completely honest means" (1999, p. 72).

In public and mass communication, lying is sometimes defended for the sake of producing benefits, even for the sake of truth. The ethical dimension of public communication raises many questions, especially about communication from government sources, where so much depends upon public trust. There have been times when governmental decisions about deception were later justified as being in the interest of national security.

Let's consider arguments in mass communication about lying for the sake of some greater truth. For example, suppose a reporter is writing about the welfare system, and, to gain access to inside information, she misrepresents herself: Under an assumed name, she applies for welfare by posing as a homeless person. Suppose also that her intention is to write an article that will not only sell newspapers but may institute possible reforms. Is her lying justified—and if so, on what grounds?

We might return again to the ethical principles looked at earlier. It seems difficult here to follow the golden mean. Given the extremes of identifying oneself as a reporter or posing as a welfare applicant, perhaps a middle path could be taken if the reporter requested interviews with administrators (noting too if they declined to give information) and also interviewed many applicants to the system.

Kant's universal rule suggests that our reporter's deception is just plain wrong; regardless of her motive, the means cannot justify the end. In contrast, utilitarians might argue that the negative consequence of lying (the harm it might cause to the few deceived) would be far outweighed by the number of others who would benefit so that the ends justify the means. (The assumption here, of course, is that we can be sure of the consequences of our actions.) A theory of justice requiring fairness for all might argue against unfairness to those being lied to.

Issues about the media's obligation to its audience are well framed in the following questions:

> Does the press have a legitimate advocacy function, or does it best serve democratic life as an intermediary, a conduit of information and varying

opinions? In a similar vein, should the press mirror events or provide a map that leads its audience to a destination? The kind of responsibility for justice that a particular medium is seen to possess often depends on how we answer these intermediate questions about the press's proper role and function. (Christians et al., 1998)

The new technologies have compounded ethical problems, creating an enormous potential for deception. For example, throughout school you've probably seen students cheat on exams, exchange work on assignments, or hand in papers they didn't write themselves. Students can copy someone's work through fax or e-mail, download material from the Internet, and hand it in without crediting the source; they can even download an entire paper. Web sites with digital libraries of term papers on every subject—sometimes at no charge to the user—and other term-paper sources are widely available.

Ironically, the same technology that makes forms of cheating so widespread is also being used to check this form of plagiarism. Through *www.turnitin.com, www.mydropbox.com,* and other sites teachers can—and increasingly are—able to discover plagiarism by comparing student work "against millions of websites, a database of previous submissions and papers offered by the so called term-paper mills" (Hafner, 2001, G6). Students who make use of such papers not only misrepresent themselves by handing in such work; they also undermine the original work of fellow students and affect grading for the entire class.

How do the new technologies affect personal relationships? We know that today many relationships are established over computer networks through chat rooms and forums, and that people meet for the first time and develop relationships online, some of which later become face-to-face relationships. We develop our identities as members of online communities and form impressions of others who are online. (For how people represent themselves in online dating, see Chapter 9.)

Consider the case of a young neuropsychologist who uses a wheelchair after being in a car accident that had disfigured her and killed her boyfriend. Although she had also lost her ability to speak, Joan began making online friends through CompuServe, where her upbeat attitude and emotional strength made her a source of support for many other disabled people. Over a period of two years, Joan formed many friendships and even became involved in some online romances. Then came an extraordinary discovery:

> Joan was revealed as being not disabled at all. More to the point, Joan, in fact, was not a woman. She was really a man we'll call Alex—a prominent New York psychiatrist in his early fifties engaged in a bizarre, all-consuming experiment to see what it felt like to be female, and to experience the intimacy of female friendship. (Cited in Lea and Spears, 1995, p. 199)

Misrepresenting one's identity—even gender—is not that uncommon in online communication, though the outcome and repercussions are usually not so dramatic. Yet this kind of manipulative interpersonal deception is part of what some communication scholars describe as "the darker side of relationships" (p. 224).

For complex issues involving freedom of speech and allegations of bias on the college campus, see Box 7.1 on academic freedom.

Secrets, Disclosures, and Privacy

Issues about disclosures and secrecy naturally dovetail with those about lying. Many philosophers and theologians have debated the ethics of lying. But what about the ethics of disclosing information known to us—particularly the secrets of other people? What are your obligations? Do you have to protect others? Do you always have to make known what you know? And how should you protect yourself when your welfare seems to depend upon exposing others?

Take a case in which disclosing what you know about someone's behavior will probably result in disciplinary action. Vijaya and her three roommates are first-year college students. They live in a two-bedroom suite that has its own bathroom. Vijaya and Lisa share a bedroom, and so do their suite-mates, Karen and Deborah. In this dormitory students are allowed to sign in guests who can then sleep overnight. The problem begins when Lisa starts signing in guests who stay several days at a time, take drugs in the room, and camp out in the bathroom. The other three roommates become very ill at ease. They never know who might turn up in the suite or exactly what will happen. More significant—they don't know what is the right thing to do about it.

If you were one of these three students, what would you do? Consider some of your alternatives. You start by ignoring the parade of visitors, but suppose it only gets worse, and you find you can't study in the room or even feel comfortable when you go to sleep. Do you decide on a moderate course of action and make a firm request that Lisa tell her friends to leave? If that fails, what are some of your options—calling your parents, talking to the dean, going to the residential assistant (RA) in your dorm? For these students, the next step seemed to be going to the RA, the resident for their floor in the large dormitory. Even then, they felt a conflict—Lisa's behavior was endangering their welfare, yet appealing to a higher authority felt like turning someone in, "ratting" on her.

Here's an instance in which a conflict can arise not about whether to lie but whether to tell the truth. In a sense, this is an issue about loyalties—about getting a fellow student in trouble even though you feel that what she is doing is wrong. (This is what makes the honor system so difficult to enforce.) By disclosing information about someone else, you know that you will affect her welfare. Her parents might find out. She might be expelled. Perhaps Vijaya also fears that she may be harmed when Lisa's friends learn what has happened.

Issues concerning disclosure of information occur in many different communication contexts. For example, imagine yourself as a reporter for the school newspaper. As part of your job, you interview a university official, and she gives you some controversial information on the promise that you will not reveal her as the source: Grades of several athletes have been altered to raise their academic averages. Later a heated debate is stirred up by your article, and the dean of students demands to know the source

At Columbia University a dispute between students and faculty over the Middle East and Asian Language and Cultures (MEALAC) department has touched off a fierce debate about bias and academic freedom—that is, *"liberty to teach, pursue, and discuss knowledge without restriction or interference, as by school or public officials"* (*American Heritage Dictionary,* 2004). In *Columbia Unbecoming,* a low-budget 40-minute film, several Columbia students allege that three pro-Palestinian professors in the MEALAC department have intimidated them in the classroom because of their pro-Israel sentiments. The film also critiques the political writings of the three and their alleged intimidating behavior toward students outside of class (Kleinfield, 2005). One criticism of the film has been that it fails to distinguish between what goes on in the classroom and outside it.

Since the film was shown in spring of 2004, the controversy has only escalated—dividing faculty members as well as students. The three MEALAC professors "accused of being intimidating and anti-Semitic" have received hate mail and death threats, and the president of Columbia has appointed a panel to investigate (Kleinfield, 2005).

But this is by no means an isolated controversy. In a time of much political division and intercultural conflict, the concept of academic freedom is being tested and debated at many colleges and universities. How far does that freedom extend and what of First Amendment rights to protect free speech and freedom of expression? At Columbia, Professor Patricia Williams suggests that if there is to be "any hope of reconciliation," the focus should be questions such as these:

- What are the limits of academic freedom for professors?
- Must all courses be "fair and balanced"—that is, neutral and impartial?
- To what extent should students have the ability to influence course content? (adapted from Williams, 2005, p. 9)

What is your opinion and what has been your experience in the classroom?

---

of your information. Of course, the dean also controls the budget for your paper, and though he does not threaten to take money away, there is always that possibility. What would you do? What are your loyalties to the newspaper, the source, and the dean?

Even more difficult situations present themselves within families. Put yourself in the place of Derek, a college junior so concerned with his older sister's drinking problem that he struggles with whether to tell his parents, who have already asked him if something is wrong. Would they be able to help? Would his sister ever trust him again? And what would be the effect on their close relationship?

And we face far more dramatic tests of our loyalties. Consider the many reported planned attacks on schools after the Columbine High School massacre in Littleton, Colorado. In almost 75 percent of school shootings since 1974, the person or people who planned the attack had told someone else about it in advance, and usually the person told was a fellow student ("See Evil," March 19, 2001). In a California college and at high schools in Kansas, Colorado, and New York, authorities were tipped off by students who learned about peers who were stockpiling weapons and planning massacres. Here the consequences of a failure to disclose far outweighed any sense of concern about loyalty to a peer group. In such volatile situations, the decision was loyalty to the greater student body.

In mass communication troubling questions concerning disclosure and the right to privacy have been raised by a growing number of memoirs and biographies. "The fact is," writes one columnist, "we are not sure where we want to draw the line when it comes to knowing about other people's lives" (Franklin, 1998, p. 12). We have an appetite for information about people's private lives, especially public figures. The reclusive fiction writer J. D. Salinger, author of *Catcher in the Rye,* is the subject of a 1998 memoir by Joyce Maynard, who had a brief affair with him when she was 18 and he was in his forties.

The right to privacy, so often discussed as an ethical issue, becomes particularly complex in connection with all the mass media—not merely with books. Journalists are repeatedly faced with the need to balance concerns about what is often called "the public's right to know" against concerns about an individual's right to privacy. Is it, for example, the public's right to know that a person is a homosexual? Is it the public's right to know the name of a rape victim in a much-publicized trial?

For example, privacy became an issue in a court case against Kobe Bryant, a basketball star who was accused of raping a young woman in 2003. After her name and other private information about her was published in several newspapers, she refused to appear in court and the case never came to trial. But after she had filed a civil suit in her own name seeking financial compensation, she was named by another newspaper even though an advocacy organization had asked that her privacy be protected (Simpson, 2004).

Questions about the public's right to know are especially common in political reporting, and there has been an increasing demand for full disclosure of all kinds of personal information about public figures—from their love lives to their medical history. In "'The President Is Fine' and Other Historical Lies," presidential historian Richard Norton Smith (2001) explains that traditionally "journalists have covered up White House illnesses as much as they have covered them." The public never knew, for example, that John F. Kennedy had Addison's disease or how seriously President Reagan had been shot in an assassination attempt by John Hinckley.

Things have certainly changed. For example, today it is expected that presidential candidates will release all necessary information about their health. In spring of 2007, presidential hopeful John Edwards and his wife announced his intention to continue his campaign after disclosing a recent recurrence of his wife's breast cancer, which her doctor said was now treatable but not curable. Public opinion ran the gamut from high praise to criticism of his decision.

Regarding invasion of privacy issues, Christians and others (1998) point out that

> . . . the law that conscientiously seeks to protect individual privacy excludes public officials. [Chief Justice] Brandeis . . . while condemning intrusion in personal matters, . . . insisted on the exposure of all secrets bearing on public concern. In general, the courts have upheld that political personalities cease to be purely private persons. (p. 109)

Since the press has tremendous latitude in deciding what is newsworthy and has sometimes catered to tastes for gossip and sensationalism, these writers advocate "additional determinants . . . to distinguish gossip and voyeurism from information necessary to the democratic decision-making process" (p. 169).

Ethical questions concerning privacy are reversed somewhat in connection with the new technologies. Because we often give out personal information on the Internet—for example, when trying to get information or buying something online— there is increasing concern over the scams that lead to identity theft. And did you know that many Web sites place cookies on your computer? **Cookies** are *small files that a Web site can use to track a visitor's preferences*—data you reveal when you are making a purchase or just surfing the Net; the sites you access can gather information you type in about yourself and store it. This is usually done without online notification. If you are concerned about privacy, you should be aware that cookies are quite difficult to remove from your computer (Schwartz, 2001).

More questions about the protection of our privacy are raised by electronic surveillance. For example, should the government have the right to monitor your e-mail? What about your activities while you are online? According to The Pew Internet & American Life Project, a year after 9/11 people were "evenly divided" on the issue (Rainie, Fox, and Madden, 2004). What about surveillance of employees on the job, an increasingly common practice? Employees sometimes abuse their access to computers at work. They may be researching their interests on company time, job hunting, playing games, writing personal e-mails, or even watching pornography. Given such abuses of company time, however, do you think that there should be monitoring of employees' online habits—and if so, should they be told?

Former Detroit mayor Kwame Kilpatrick resigned in 2008 after pleading guilty to two felony charges and accepting a plea bargain. The downward spiral of events began with "a whistle-blower lawsuit that cost the city $8.4 million." Kilpatrick and Christine Beatty, a former top aide, testified in a case over the firing of two police

MEDICAL ETHICS*

One medical device company paid doctors as much as $50,000 per day as consultants to help design their medical devices. Those doctors were also prescribing these same devices to their patients. These doctors were specialists in performing intricate back surgeries and, as a result, they were valuable resources for the company's research and development efforts.

One employee filed a class-action lawsuit against the company alleging that the company had paid surgeons millions of dollars to ensure that they would use the company's medical devices in their surgeries and that this amounted to bribery.

Discuss the ethical issues in this case. What do you think of the employee's whistleblowing behavior? What do you think of the company's practices?

---

* Based on a case in Peter Stanwick and Sarah Stanwick, *Understanding Business Ethics.* Upper Saddle River, NJ: Pearson/Prentice-Hall, 2009, pp. 101–102.

ISSUES IN COMMUNICATION

Ethics in Shopping

Which of the following would you say is more ethical?*

1. File false insurance claim
2. Return goods to wrong retailer
3. Do not return extra change
4. Return used goods for refund
5. Claim better price elsewhere

*Your instructor has the answers.

Source: Larry Neale and Sam Fullerton, "The International Search for Ethical Norms," *The Journal of Services Marketing*, Vol. 24, 2010, pp. 476–486.

officers in which they claimed the officers were "engaged in an unauthorized investigation." The investigation was ultimately what led to uncovering an extramarital affair in which Kilpatrick and Beatty had lied under oath. When text messages were discovered contradicting their statements, they were charged with perjury, misconduct, and obstruction of justice. Kilpatrick faces 120 days of jail time, $1 million in restitution, probation, and restriction from running for public office for five years (NPR, 2008). See Box 7.2 for a case of ethics and shopping. In 2011 Kilpatrick was repaying approximately $100 a month (of his $1 million debt) to the City of Detroit, while at the same time living in a mansion in a suburb of Dallas.

Whistleblowing

As members of groups, we enact certain roles and adopt specific behavioral norms. Many of these are implicit, unstated, but nonetheless they are expectations about our behavior as a group member. Each professional organization also has its principles and standards of behavior that all members promise to uphold. In **whistleblowing**, *a member of a group makes a charge about the violation of ethical standards or norms within that group itself.* A journalist publishes a story about how another journalist has misled a criminal into giving self-incriminating information. A doctor on the staff of a large hospital accuses the chief surgeon of malpractice.

Issues of privacy and whistleblowing overlap in the case of Russell Tice, a former intelligence agent at the National Security Agency (NSA), a high-level government secret agency. Tice admitted to being one of the sources for a *New York Times* article in December 2005 concerning how the NSA had been eavesdropping electronically—without a warrant—on thousands of U.S. citizens. In 2006 he testified before Congress that he felt domestic spying was a violation of the Fourth Amendment and that the use of electronic surveillance in the future might have ramifications for millions of citizens ("NSA Whistleblower . . . ," 2006). Tice was fired in 2005 and is now a member of the National Security Whistleblower Coalition.

Bok identifies three elements that make whistleblowing particularly charged: dissent, breach of loyalty, and accusation (1989, pp. 214–215). First, it is a form of *dissent* because "it makes public a disagreement with an authority or majority view" but also has "the narrower aim of casting light on negligence or abuse, of alerting the public to a risk and of assigning responsibility for that risk." Second, the message itself is viewed "as a *breach of loyalty* because it comes from within. The whistleblower, although he is neither coach nor referee, blows the whistle on his own team." The third element, *accusation*, "singles out specific groups or persons as responsible"—and furthermore, the accusation is about "a present or an imminent threat" (pp. 214–215).

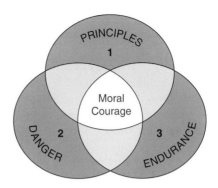

Figure 7.2

The Three Elements of Moral Courage

Source: From *Moral Courage* by Rushworth M. Kidder, Figs. 2 (p. 51) and 7 (p. 73). Copyright © 2005 by Rushworth M. Kidder. Reprinted by permission of HarperCollins Publishers.

As in many other forms of ethical decision making, in whistleblowing the stakes can be extremely high, requiring great courage. Kidder considers the concept of **moral courage,** what he defines as "the courage to be moral," and describes it in terms of "adhering to the five core moral values of honesty, respect, fairness, responsibility, and compassion" (2005, p. 10).

For him, morally courageous action involves three interrelated elements: "a commitment to moral *principles,* an awareness of the *danger* involved in supporting those principles, and a willing *endurance* of that danger" (p. 7). Think of the three as intersecting, as we see in Figure 7.2.

"The point," he writes, "at which the circle of our deepest values, or principles, intersects with the twin circles of danger and endurance is the point at which we find moral courage most clearly in evidence" (p. 10).

Whistleblowing is an act that often requires great moral courage. Jensen (1997) emphasizes that it is an intentional public act and that its objective is "to enlist support from a large outside audience" with the aim of informing and arousing that audience (pp. 74–75). In addition, whistleblowers "usually act alone, they tend to be subordinate to those whom they are accusing, and to be well-informed." This last point is extremely important: "They possess something others do not possess—valuable inside information—which makes them potentially powerful communicators" (p. 76).

In recent years, whistleblowing has become extremely common in many types of organizations—even in government. On May 21, 2002, Coleen Rowley, a special agent and Minneapolis chief division counsel of the FBI, wrote a letter to FBI director Robert Mueller. In it she described how, in the weeks before the attacks of September 11, the FBI's Washington supervisors had dismissed repeated requests by Minneapolis agents for greater authority to broaden their investigation of Zacharias Moussaoui, who had been identified as a terrorist threat after a call about his flight training. (He was later indicted as a conspirator in the 9/11 attacks.) Here is the opening of her letter:

Dear Director Mueller:

I feel at this point that I have to put my concerns in writing concerning the important topic of the FBI's response to evidence of terrorist activity in the United States prior to September 11th. The issues are fundamental ones of INTEGRITY and go the heart of the FBI's law enforcement mission and mandate. . . .

To get to the point, I have deep concerns that a delicate and subtle shading/skewing of facts by you and others at the highest levels of FBI management has occurred and is occurring. The term "cover up" would be too strong a characterization which is why I am attempting to carefully . . . choose my words here. . . .

I feel that certain facts, including the following, have, up to now, been omitted, downplayed, glossed over and/or mis-characterizd in an effort to avoid or minimize personal and/or institutional embarrassment on the part of the FBI and/or perhaps even for improper political reasons. . . .

Rowley's letter, which was 13 pages long, goes on to describe her concerns in detail and closes this way:

. . . I hope my continued employment with the FBI is not somehow placed in jeopardy. I have never written to an FBI Director in my life before on any topic. Although I hope it is not necessary, I would therefore wish to take advantage of the federal "Whistleblower Protection" provisions by so characterizing my remarks.

Sincerely,
Coleen Rowley
Special Agent and Minneapolis Chief Division Counsel
(Coleen Rowley, cited in *time.com/time/covers*)

Rowley's letter is striking not only in its content but also in her acknowledgment that whistleblowing involves great risk for the person who initiates it. By the end of the year she had testified before Congress and her letter had been leaked and widely published in major newspapers. In a 2002 issue of *Time* magazine, she was one of three women who appeared on the cover; the other two—Sherron Watkins and Cynthia Cooper—were business executives. Named "People of the Year," all three were whistleblowers (Lacayo and Ripley, 2002).

Sherron Watkins, an Enron vice president, sent an anonymous memo to Kenneth Lay, CEO of Enron, then the premier energy company in the country. Her memo was long and detailed and discussed the company's alarming business practices. She later met with Lay, but her concerns were ignored. When Enron was investigated, Watkins's testimony was crucial.

The second executive singled out by *Time,* Cynthia Cooper, was a vice president of internal auditing at WorldCom. She uncovered bookkeeping practices that inflated company earnings by $3.9 billion. After she presented her discoveries to WorldCom's controller as well as to its CFO, they told her to postpone her audit. But Cooper continued and contacted the audit committee of the chairman of the board. "Two weeks later WorldCom announced it would restate earnings by $3.9 billion—the largest restatement ever" (Colvin, 2002, p. 56).

Writing about corporate whistleblowing, Geoffrey Colvin of *Fortune* suggests that it may be no accident that at Enron and WorldCom the whistleblowers were women:

When a business needs shaking up, the best candidate is often an "insider outsider"—someone who has long experience with the company (an insider) but who works away from headquarters or in a noncore division (an outsider); more generally, it's someone who knows where the bodies are buried yet isn't tied deeply to the established powers. (Colvin, 2002, p. 56)

Whistleblowing requires great courage regardless of gender, and the consequences of whistleblowing have often been severe. People have been ostracized by colleagues, lost their jobs, been threatened, and been put at risk in many ways. For example, Jeffrey Wigand, a biochemist with the tobacco company Brown & Williamson, came forward to object to company practices including knowingly manipulating the nicotine levels of tobacco products to intensify the impact. He lost his job, was sued by the company for appearing on a television program about his accusations (he had signed a confidentiality agreement), and is now a high school teacher. Wigand's story is dramatized in the film *The Insider.*

More recently, Peter Rost, a former vice president of Pfizer, the largest drug company in the world, became one of a number of outspoken critics of the pharmaceutical industry and their efforts to withhold information that would affect their profits. He has not only spoken out for off-label marketing but also filed a whistleblower lawsuit against Pfizer alleging that Pharmacia, acquired by Pfizer in 2003, had tried to market Genotropin, a growth hormone, for inappropriate uses. The government did not join the suit, and Pfizer subsequently fired Rost. He went on to gain attention from the media when he advocated reimporting lower-cost prescription drugs from other countries. Rost has appeared on *60 Minutes* and continues to write and lecture on the pharmaceutical industry (Rost, 2006). Numerous other whistleblowers have taken on the drug companies. Other lawsuits include those in which sometimes-fatal side effects of drugs were concealed or drugs were kept off the market because they affected profits from drugs still under patent.

Whistleblowing occurs not only in business organizations and government, but also in many other kinds of groups. Law enforcement officers have reported cases of police brutality, doctors who work for HMOs have blown the whistle on health insurance companies, and as we've seen, there have been controversial cases involving misconduct in scientific research. Here issues of whistleblowing can be further complicated by the status, reputation, and credibility of the people involved (Glazer, 1997). A recent article on professional ethics in a British medical journal was titled "Whistleblowing or Professional Assassination?"

Although motives remain a question in whistleblowing cases—a whistleblower may be awarded a significant sum from monies reclaimed by the government—the consequences of whistleblowing are well documented. A recent column asks "Whistleblowing Workers: Becoming an Endangered Species?" and cites research by Spherion Workplace (*www.spherion.com*):

Although 34% of the respondents said they have seen unethical activities at the workplace, only 47% said they are likely to blow the whistle for such activities. ("Whistleblowing Workers . . . ," 2006, p. 9)

For many the costs of whistleblowing are simply too high—from being ostracized by friends and co-workers to losing one's job and even being sued. In sum, "whistleblowers are viewed by many in their group as traitors and by many of the public as heroes" (Jensen, 1997, p. 77).

Leaks

Another way of making information public is through a **leak**—*previously unknown information is made known to others, but its source,* unlike that of whistleblowing, *remains anonymous,* at least to the general public. For example, information might be leaked to the press by someone who may be a familiar source but whose identity is concealed. Of course, leaking information protects the source and often evades the responsibility of confirming the truth about the information that is given.

According to *Fortune* magazine, by 2007 there were an estimated 70 million blogs in the so-called blogosphere. Blogs can leak information anonymously at a stunning rate of speed, much faster than the mainstream media. Many blogs openly reflect a point of view (also called bias). When information such as this is leaked, the damage that can potentially be caused is irreparable. One YouTube video got over 9 million hits. Compare this to a successful cable television program that has 800,000 viewers. You get the picture (Bennis, Goleman, O'Toole, and Biederman, 2008, pp.14–17).

Leaks often have serious ramifications for people's personal lives. For example, a violation of confidentiality about your medical records can affect your employment. In formal contexts, the repercussions of leaks may be immediate and widespread. A leak to the news media about the ineffective leadership of a large corporation's president may not only damage reputations but may also have disastrous effects on the company's stock, thus affecting thousands of shareholders as well as employees. Similarly, a leak about the imminent merger of a company can be a manipulation that artificially drives up stock values. Now the anonymity or possible concealment of sources on the Internet makes it another potentially dangerous channel for the communication of leaked information. And if you use search engines fairly often, you will probably run into shadow pages. The source of a **shadow page** is anonymous; it is *a Web page "established to attack the reputation of a person, corporation, or another site"* (Wood and Smith, 2001, p. 67).

Leaks often destroy professional reputations, as in the case of Dr. Wen Ho Lee. Part of the headline for a *Washington Post* story in 2006 reads "News Organizations Pay to Keep Sources Secret."

> Wen Ho Lee, the U.S. nuclear scientist once identified in news reports as the target of a spying operation [a charge that was later withdrawn], will receive more than $1.6 million from the federal government and five media organizations, including *Washington Post,* to settle allegations that government leaks violated his privacy. (Farhi, 2006)

Notice the statement in the story's opening paragraph: *Washington Post* discloses that it was one of the five media organizations involved.

When leaks to the media concern government information, sources are often accused of being motivated by partisanship, which is almost impossible to verify.

In recent years, we have been inundated by leaks about politics and government. The timing of leaks is often manipulated to head off the response to unfavorable news or scandal, as when the government leaks the news to the press so that it is published at the end of the work week. Friday is notorious as the day to leak bad news because the assumption is that people will be preoccupied with personal affairs over the weekend.

Leaks have plagued the presidencies of political figures as different as Richard Nixon, Ronald Reagan, Bill Clinton, and, most recently, George W. Bush. One of the longest controversies during the Bush administration was over who leaked information to the press about the identity of Valerie Plame as a CIA undercover agent.

In early July of 2003, Joseph Wilson, a former ambassador, wrote an op-ed piece in the *New York Times* titled "What I Didn't Find in Africa." In it he alleged that President George W. Bush's claim that Iraq had tried to buy uranium from Niger—for the purpose of building weapons of mass destruction—was untrue. The basis of Wilson's criticism was that earlier the CIA had sent him on a mission to Niger to investigate whether Iraq had tried to purchase uranium; Wilson had found no evidence of such a purpose and concluded that it was highly unlikely. His report (then classified) was available well before President Bush in his 2003 State of the Union address referred to Iraqi attempts to purchase the uranium. "Mr. Wilson concluded that the administration later manipulated intelligence about whether Iraq had sought to buy uranium from Niger" (Liptak, 2004, p. 18).

On July 14, 2003, eight days after the Wilson article was published, Robert Novak, a syndicated columnist with the *Chicago Sun-Times,* published a story in which he said that, according to two senior administration officials, Valerie Plame, Wilson's wife, was an undercover CIA agent and that she had worked in Niger. (Novak's column is published in over 300 papers, so its circulation is wide.)

Wilson then accused the administration of leaking information about his wife to the press and blowing her cover. It's a felony to disclose the identity of a covert intelligence agent; it can put the agent's life in danger, and, of course, also has a direct effect on the agent's career.

A special prosecutor was appointed by the Justice Department to investigate who had leaked the information. Apparently, it had been leaked to at least six reporters. In 2004 the six reporters were subpoenaed to testify: Robert Novak, Tim Russert of NBC, Matthew Cooper of *Time,* Walter Pincus and Glenn Kessler of The *Washington Post,* and Judith Miller of The *New York Times.* It is customary for reporters to resist attempts to reveal the identity of confidential sources and while we know that four reporters testified (Liptak, 2004), Judith Miller refused. Although she had written no story about Plame or Wilson, she went to jail for 85 days until her source of information, Richard Armitage, U.S. deputy secretary of state, freed her of their confidentiality agreement. Columnist Richard Novak finally acknowledged that Armitage was his source and that Karl Rove, chief of staff to President Bush, had confirmed Plame's identity as an undercover agent to Novak (Carr, 2007).

As a result of the investigation, in 2007 Vice President Cheney's former chief of staff, I. Lewis Libby, was found guilty not of leaking Plame's identity to the press, but of perjury and obstruction of justice concerning the leak—lying to FBI agents and during the grand jury investigation.

The freedom of the press and the right to protect its confidential sources is an issue of utmost concern for journalists but also an issue of great complexity. In 2004, FAIR (Fairness & Accuracy in Reporting), a national media watch group, argued that several reporters had violated Valerie Plame's privacy and that they should not protect the identity of officials who outed her:

> Protecting the identities of confidential sources is a journalistic right that should be recognized by the courts, but only when it protects genuine whistle-blowers, not when it shields government wrongdoing. . . .
> The ability to protect confidential sources who reveal government wrongdoing is an important journalistic protection that deserves judicial respect. ("Media Advisory . . . ," 2004)

Although most of us may not be in a position to "leak" information in the strict sense of the term, gossip and rumor are common communication behaviors that raise ethical questions. (The subject of rumors will be discussed in more detail in Chapter 14.)

In comparing whistleblowing and information leaks, Bok (1989) weighs the consequences of each:

> In fairness to those criticized, openly accepted responsibility for blowing the whistle should . . . be preferred to the secret denunciation or the leaked rumor—the more so, the more derogatory and accusatory the information. What is openly stated can be more easily checked, its source's motives challenged, and the underlying information examined. Those under attack may otherwise be hard put to it to defend themselves against nameless adversaries. Often they do not even know they are threatened until it is too late to respond. (p. 215)

As you think about the ethical issues we have been discussing, keep in mind that intercultural communication often increases their complexity. For example, we sometimes have no knowledge about another culture's ethical values. Rhetorical frames of reference may be very different: What is regarded as a lie in one culture may be understood by members of another as an exaggeration for the sake of politeness. And as we will see in Chapter 10, norms about disclosures and privacy also vary considerably. What is a harmless disclosure in one culture may constitute a betrayal in another.

With the emergence of new communication technologies and the growing number of clashes between people of different cultures, the need for an ethical base that is morally inclusive becomes an issue that affects us all. In writing about media ethics, two scholars propose a basic principle that underpins all systematic ethics: the sacredness of human life.

> Its universal scope enables us to avoid the divisiveness of appeals to individual interests, cultural practices, and national prerogatives. . . .
> A commitment to universals does not eliminate all differences in what we think and believe. . . . The only question is whether our values affirm the human good or not. (Christians and Nordenstreng, 2004, pp. 21, 24)

From this universal—the sacredness of human life—they derive three related ethical principles: respect for human dignity, truthtelling, and nonviolence. These "master norms" are based on an earlier study of ethical norms in 13 countries across five continents (Christians and Traber, 1997). We will look at these principles in more detail when we discuss intercultural communication in Chapter 10.

Summary

In this chapter, we explored ethical decision making in communication. To establish a baseline for discussion, we considered some representative ethical principles that have been proposed by Western thinkers. We examined Aristotle's concept of the golden mean, a middle path between two extremes. In Kant's categorical imperative, we saw human actions judged as ethical by their intent rather than their outcomes. In the utilitarian view, on the other hand, greatest value was placed on the outcomes or consequences of our actions, with moral choice being governed by the greatest good for the greatest number of people. And in Rawls's theory of justice the guiding principle was fairness for everyone in society, including the most vulnerable. We also looked at three of the most common principles people use in ethical decision making.

We then turned to several fundamental issues in ethics. We discussed lying and misrepresentation as well as the reasons often given to defend lying—for example, lying to avoid harm or to protect another person. Next, we examined questions about the ethics of secrecy, disclosures, and rights of privacy, in public, academic, and personal life. We examined as well the ethical questions raised by the increasing use of computer-mediated communication. Finally, we looked at the complex issues of whistleblowing, in which a group member makes an accusation about the violation of ethical standards within the group itself, and of leaking information, in which the source of information remains anonymous. We also considered the concept of moral courage.

As we have tried to show, difficult ethical questions surface not just in organizational, public, mass, and computer-mediated communication but also in the most informal and intimate contexts. Ethics are not lofty principles for other people; we are all involved in making moral choices—often on a daily basis.

Key Terms

Categorical imperative	Leak	Plagiarism	Whistleblowing
Cookies	Lie	Shadow page	
Ethics	Moral courage	Utilitarianism	
Golden mean	Paraphrasing	Veil of ignorance	

Review Questions

1. Give your definition of "ethics."

2. What is Aristotle's concept of the golden mean, and what is its implication for ethical choices? Give two examples.

3. Explain Kant's principle of the categorical imperative.

4. Discuss the basic ethical principle of the utilitarians.

5. Compare and contrast the views of Kant and the utilitarians on making decisions about ethics.

6. What is the concept of the veil of ignorance, and how does it relate to Rawls's theory of justice?

7. Identify three of the most common principles people use in making ethical decisions.

8. What are the four principles people often appeal to in defending lies?

9. Identify three ethical issues concerned with lying or misrepresentation and include examples from at least three communication contexts in your discussion.

10. Give your own definition of plagiarism and explain the difference between plagiarizing and paraphrasing.

11. What are some of the ethical issues that have developed out of increasing use of the Internet and other new technologies?

12. Summarize three ethical issues related to the disclosure of information. Describe four contexts in which they might arise.

13. Discuss the concept of moral courage.

14. Identify three elements that are present in whistleblowing and give two examples of it.

15. What is the difference between whistleblowing and leaking information?

16. What ethical issues are raised by whistleblowing and leaks?

Exercises

1. Describe three different situations, involving (a) your friend, (b) your parents, and (c) your employer, in which you had to make a difficult decision about ethics. In each case, discuss the basis and motives for your decision; then evaluate whether your decisions were consistent from an ethical standpoint. If not, why not?

2. At a small party, your friend reads aloud a very personal letter, identifies who wrote it, and then asks the entire group what they think of it. No one at the party knows the letter writer. Discuss the ethics of this behavior and of possible responses from people at the party.

3. Identify a controversial news story with international implications that involves an ethical issue discussed in this chapter. Compare and contrast coverage of the incident by two major U.S. newspapers, a tabloid, two television stations, a weekly newsmagazine, and two Web sites for news: for example, *www.cnn.com* and *www.guardian.co.uk*. Compare how the different media present the issues. In each case, how is the information presented? What kind of language is used to describe the people involved? Is the treatment objective or partisan? Which media seem most impartial?

Suggested Readings

Bennett, Lance W. *News: The Politics of Illusion,* 7th ed. New York: Pearson/Longman, 2006.

A recent update of this classic on the relationship between the news media and politics. The author looks at information biases in the news, freedom of the press, and the subtle relationship between government and the media. News sources, leaks, censorship, and a host of other ethical issues are examined.

Bok, Sissela. *Mayhem: Violence as Public Entertainment.* Reading, MA: Addison-Wesley, 1998.

In her examination of media violence and its long-term effects, the author, a contemporary philosopher, discusses issues of free speech and censorship. This is a timely book that suggests innovative ways of resolving a pressing moral dilemma.

——. *Lying: Moral Choice in Public and Private Life,* 2nd ed. New York: Vintage, 1999.

The author analyzes lying in terms of ethical theory and illuminates her discussion with examples from many different contexts. This book has become a classic.

Christians, Clifford G., Mark Fackler, Kim B. Rotzoll, and Kathy Brittain McKee. *Media Ethics: Cases and Moral Reasoning,* 7th ed. Reading, MA: Allyn & Bacon, 2004.

An excellent and comprehensive treatment of media ethics, with detailed case studies on each of the issues discussed.

Ibsen, Henrik. *An Enemy of the People.* In Henrik Ibsen, *Selected Plays,* New York: Modern Library, Random House, n.d.

A complex and provocative play about the effects of whistleblowing, written by a great Norwegian playwright of the nineteenth century.

The Insider.

This film examines the costs of whistleblowing and how an issue with ramifications for large corporations affects the ethics of the mass media.

Johnson, Craig. *Meeting the Ethical Challenges of Leadership,* 4th ed. Los Angeles: Sage, 2012.

Kidder, Rushworth M. *Moral Courage.* New York: HarperCollins, 2005.

This book examines what it means to stand up for your values—its costs, risks, potential hardships, and rewards. It combines practical analysis with

many excellent examples of how ethical dilemmas are approached and resolved.

Levitt, Steven D., and Stephen J. Dubner. *SuperFreakonomics.* New York: HarperCollins, 2009.

An engaging and unconventional book in which a maverick economist explores how people pursue what they want—including by cheating. Not one dull chapter here.

The Lives of Others

An award-winning German film about the effects of the Stasi, the German secret police, and how the network of spying intimidated and sometimes recruited civilians.

Posner, Richard A. *The Little Book of Plagiarism.* New York: Pantheon, 2007.

A very brief, thought-provoking book by a legal scholar on current issues about plagiarism.

The Smartest Guys in the Room.

This documentary delves into the scandal at Enron Corporation.

Wiener, Jon. *Historians in Trouble: Plagiarism, Fraud, and Politics in the Ivory Tower.* New York: New Press, 2007.

A specialized but intriguing study of selected cases in which historians were accused of plagiarism. The author, an investigative journalist and a professor of history, examines how academic politics and media coverage contributed to which historians were condemned and which escaped censure.

 # For Supplementary Information

Log onto the Online Learning Center at *www.mhhe.com/tubbshc13e.*

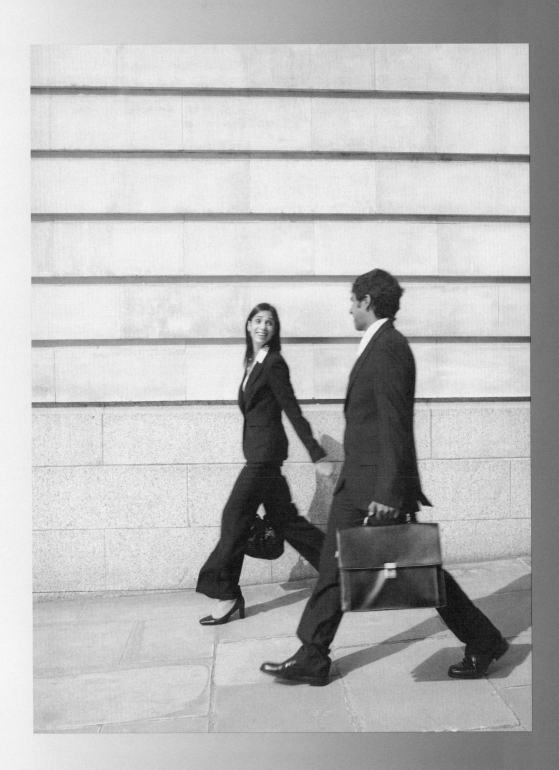

8

Relationships in Process

Chapter Objectives

After reading this chapter, you should be able to:

1. Discuss the influence of proximity on attraction.
2. Describe the relationship between similarity and attraction and identify three variables that qualify predictions about similarity and attraction.
3. Discuss recent research on online dating, and singles and their relationships.
4. Differentiate between the setting and the climate of a relationship and discuss two critical measures of climate.
5. Discuss the concepts of time and trust as defining characteristics of relationships.
6. Outline both the building and the declining stages of a close interpersonal relationship as described by Knapp. Compare this theory with Duck's view of the four phases of relationship dissolution.
7. Discuss various strategies that have been proposed for maintaining relationships.
8. Discuss the defining characteristics of family, the risks of divorce, and the distinctive nature of family communication.

In *Blink,* his book about how we make decisions that seem instantaneous, Malcolm Gladwell takes a look at speed-dating:

> Speed-dating has become enormously popular around the world over the last few years, and it's not hard to understand why. It's the distillation of dating to a single snap judgment. Everyone who sat down at one of those tables was trying to answer a very simple question: Do I want to see this person again? And to answer that we don't need an entire evening. Velma, for instance, . . . said that she picked none of the men and that she made up her mind about each of them right away. "They lost me at hello," she said, rolling her eyes. (2005, p. 65)

What Velma describes are first impressions (see Chapter 2). And yet, Gladwell writes, we're not at all insightful about explaining our choices. Psychologist Sheena Iyengar and economist Raymond Fisman, both at Columbia University, are jointly researching speed-dating decisions and tell Gladwell that

> what they find when they compare what speed-daters say they want with what they are actually attracted to in the moment is that those things don't match. For example, if Mary said at the start of the evening that she wanted someone intelligent and sincere, that in no way means she'll be attracted only to intelligent and sincere men. It's just as likely that John, whom she likes more than anyone else, could turn out to be attractive and funny but not particularly sincere or smart at all. (pp. 65–66)

In this chapter we look in depth at the complex processes that underlie and create human relationships and those that maintain or undermine the stability of those relationships, sometimes resulting in their decline or deterioration. This chapter is about friends, it's about lovers, and it's also about families.

In recent years, the study of close interpersonal relationships—both theory and research—has become an area of tremendous interest and activity for communication scholars (Guerrero and Floyd, 2006; Canary and Dainton, 2003; Hendrick and Hendrick, 2000). We begin by looking at the major variables of human attraction and several of the characteristics that define all our relationships.

BASES OF HUMAN ATTRACTION

Shauna can have lunch with you in the school cafeteria, but Stephanie can't. You'd love to go to the movies with Michael, but not with Dennis. You express your preferences when choosing friends, school leaders, roommates, dates—and eventually a marriage partner.

Even when forced to communicate with people you yourself have not chosen—classmates, the people you work with, and so on—you prefer some people to others. As we examine the major bases of *human attraction,* or *liking,* we shall be looking at many kinds of relationships. The principles discussed here have a bearing on marriage, friendship, family, small-group, and work relationships, for all of these can be seen within a single framework. You should be thinking, then, of the entire web of human relationships as you read about attraction.

Proximity

The most obvious determinant of attraction is **proximity,** or *geographic closeness.* Other things being equal, the more closely two people are located geographically, the more likely they are to be attracted to one another. The effects of proximity are seen in a number of ways. If you are not within a reasonable distance of another person, your chances of meeting and becoming friends are quite slim. How many of your friends live more than 3,000 miles away from you? Probably very few. In support of the notion that proximity fosters attraction, researchers have found that you are far more likely to marry a person who is geographically close to your home or school than someone living or studying far away.

Once you get to know people, proximity also affects whether your relationships will continue. A great number of friendships and courtships are damaged by the effects of physical separation. Perhaps the old saying "Out of sight, out of mind" has some validity simply because of the effort it takes to sustain relationships across many miles. Relationships that do continue despite this obstacle are maintained by the intensity of the rewards derived from them.

Much smaller distances also influence attraction, as seen in a classic study of residents in housing projects: Neighbors chose to socialize most with neighbors from the apartment next door and least with those at the opposite end of the floor.

Why should a few feet make any difference in how friendships are formed, and why, in general, should proximity tend to foster attraction? One theory is that *if we know we are going to be in very close proximity to someone*—living next door or working side by side over a long period of time—*we tend to minimize or even overlook that person's less desirable traits.* It has also been proposed that proximity tends to intensify liking *because opportunities for communication clearly increase as a function of proximity.* In one study of couples who applied for marriage licenses, the researchers found that "54 percent of the couples lived within sixteen blocks of each other when they started going out, and 37 percent lived within five blocks of each other" (Brooks, 2011, p. 11). For example, in a large company, people who work on the same floor are more likely to share coffee breaks and gossip, go out to lunch together, or even meet after work. And the more two people see of each other, the more likely they are to spend leisure time together, exchange confidences, and offer support in difficult times.

Other experiments (Zajonc, 1968) suggest that familiarity in and of itself may increase liking. According to Berscheid and Reis (1998), the early research demonstrates that it is "interaction, not distance per se, that is important" and they cite recent advances in telecommuting (see Chapter 15) to bear out this conclusion.

But when people in proximity are of equal status and start off without negative attitudes toward one another, we cannot predict which people will become friends. Given physical proximity, we still favor some people and reject others. In short, proximity is often a precondition of liking, but there are other bases for attraction.

A recent review of research summarizes several other variables associated with liking in general, and, more specifically, with romantic love:

Reciprocal liking: discovering that the other likes the self
Desirability of the other: kindness, intelligence, humor, good looks, social
   status, etc.
Similarity, especially of attitudes, personality, and demographic characteristics
Exposure and social appropriateness, support and encouragement from one's
   social network . . . (Aron et al., 2006, adapted from p. 602; emphasis added)

When it comes to falling in love, reciprocal liking and desirability seem to have the most influence.

Similarity

Despite the romantic notion that opposites attract, there is little evidence that this is so. And a look at online dating sites such as *match.com* and *personals.aol.com* and the personals columns of many newspapers and magazines will show you how important *similarity* is perceived to be: Most people want to meet others who share many of their interests, whether it be in sports, music, or travel, and they often seek someone of the same religion, race, and social background.

In a study of mate selection, Buss (1985) found substantial evidence for assortive mating—that is, mating based on similarities. For example, husbands and wives are usually similar in age, education, ethnic background, race, religion, and socioeconomic status (p. 47). These six variables show the strongest correlations. As for psychological characteristics, the greatest similarities are in attitudes, opinions, and worldviews. Other strongly correlated characteristics include verbal abilities and degree of quarrelsomeness, ingenuousness, and extroversion (p. 49). Romantic couples also tend to have comparable levels of physical attractiveness.

These researchers suggest that this evolution in values is in part a response to cultural changes. Internet dating and the threat of AIDS have changed patterns of mating. Women's many gains in the workplace have increased their economic power and financial security. And we are immersed in a visual culture that, through television and film, as well as Internet images, places extraordinary value on physical appearance.

The force of similarity as a basis for attraction is seen not just in selection of mates, but in all types of human relationships and thus in many forms of communication. Observation, research, and theory all bear out the statement that we like people who appear to be similar to us. Over a hundred years ago Disraeli remarked, "An agreeable person is a person who agrees with me." In other words, "We tend to like people who have the same beliefs and attitudes we have, and when we like people we want them to have the same attitudes we have" (Heider, 1983). In addition, personality, style of dressing, socioeconomic level, religion, age, status, and so forth will affect our feelings toward others. We tend to attract and be attracted to people who are like us, and conversely, we tend to dislike and be disliked by those who differ from us.

If this is the case, then given adequate knowledge of people's attitudes, interests, values, and backgrounds, it should be possible to predict which members of a group will become friends. A classic study in how college friendships are formed (Newcomb, 1961) confirms this prediction. On a long-term basis, those who remained friends after college had shown many similarities when they first met.

Here and elsewhere when we describe the link between similarity and attraction, we are speaking of *perceived* similarity. As we emphasized in Chapters 1 and 2, human perception is a selective process and not always an accurate one; often we are influenced by how we expect people to look or think or behave. For example, we expect our friends to agree with us on a wide range of topics, and we probably exaggerate the extent of this agreement. No doubt we also tend to overemphasize our differences with those we dislike.

Situations

We qualified our statement about the effect of proximity on attraction with the phrase "other things being equal," and we must temper statements about similarity and attraction in the same way. For things rarely are equal. As we saw in Chapter 2, variations in the behaviors and personal characteristics of others—physical attractiveness, for example—influence liking.

Several situations also qualify what can reasonably be predicted about your attraction to others.

Perceived Reciprocity of Liking

First, your attraction to others can depend on **perceived reciprocity of liking**—*whether you feel that the people you like also like you.* Your liking for a person is intensified by your feeling that he or she likes you too. When you like someone and your feeling is not reciprocated, you tend to lose interest in that person. Many studies report that reciprocity is "one of the most important predictors of attraction"; a recent one by Lehr and Geher on short- versus long-term dating contexts finds that reciprocity rather than attitude similarity is particularly important in predicting long-term relationships (2006, p. 434).

Finding out that another person likes you is rewarding because it increases your own self-esteem. Suppose, for example, that you are asked to serve on a prestigious committee by one of its members. Once you are on the committee, new elections are held, and the person who endorsed you is nominated for chairman. It is very likely, especially if the committee members are people you don't know, that you will want to vote for the person who picked you—not so much because you owe a favor as because you feel you like that person.

The explanation for such reciprocity is twofold: First, people who like you increase your sense of self-worth; and, second, their "liking" behavior is a compliment, and you return the compliment with reciprocal liking.

Changes in Self-Esteem

A second situation that may influence your choice of people is *a change in your level of self-esteem*. Consider this example. Carlos and Elsa have dated for almost six months when suddenly she drops him. Because he feels that he is not good enough for her, Carlos finds his self-esteem at an all-time low. Then along comes Kim. Carlos has never considered her as attractive or intelligent as Elsa, but she seems to be interested in him. Carlos strikes up a romance on the rebound.

The rebound phenomenon illustrates what can happen to attraction as a result of a change in the level of one's self-esteem. Studies suggest that when self-esteem has recently been lowered, our need for affiliation increases, and we become more accepting of affection from others. It's then that people we might have considered unappealing may seem more desirable as companions.

Building Self-Esteem   "Your sense of self-esteem relates to the value you place on your identity. It is the perception of your own worth." Experts have identified many behavior patterns that help encourage a high sense of self-esteem. "A positive feedback loop is formed as the better you feel about yourself, the more you engage in these behaviors and the more you engage in these behaviors, the better you feel about yourself" (Dhillon, 2008).

- **Reality Orientation**—Develop a strong desire to see reality as it is, free from pessimism or overoptimism. Be willing to see yourself as you truly are. Resolve cognitive distortions.
- **Acceptance**—Accept yourself as you are and accept others as they are.
- **Autonomy**—Take full responsibility for your life. Live in a way that makes sense to you instead of unconsciously conforming to the expectation of others.
- **Principle-centered**—Hold your principles and sense of integrity in the highest regard. It is better to stay true to your principles and meet with disapproval than have the approval of others at the cost of your integrity.
- **Connection**—Develop a feeling of commonality with others. Learn to see yourself in other people and resist the urge to judge (Dhillon, 2008).

Anxiety

Anxiety affects your need to interact or affiliate with others. In a classic experiment, Schachter (1959) found that high-anxiety conditions (painful electric shock) produce a much more intense desire for affiliation than low-anxiety conditions. And though "misery loves company," it isn't just any company: Anxious subjects prefer to be with others who are anxious too (pp. 17–19).

Anxiety-producing situations can increase your need to be with others and also change your criteria for choosing companions. Imagine yourself stuck in a fogged-in airport for most of a day or waiting for hours in a hospital to visit a loved one in the intensive-care ward. Apparently, the need to be comforted when sharing unpleasant experiences supersedes other needs for associating with people. Boot camps have long operated on this principle. People who share relatively unpleasant experiences often become more cohesive as a group.

Isolation

Isolation from the rewards of others also influences your choice of receivers. Although brief isolation can sometimes be peaceful and pleasant, prolonged isolation is almost always unpleasant. Hence, in prisons, one of the severest forms of punishment is solitary confinement.

In general, social isolation tends to be less pleasant than interaction with others. Some researchers have found that as we are deprived of the rewards possible from human interaction, we become more receptive to those rewards. Thus, as we are deprived of social reinforcement, our strong need to interact with other human beings tends to override our standards for acceptable friends.

Some theorists believe that in addition to the many variables we have been discussing, some differences between people can also be a basis for attraction—particularly if the people involved have needs that are complementary—but little evidence supports this theory of complementary needs.

Online Dating

35 percent of U.S. adults have fantasized about a co-worker.

6 percent of U.S. adults have dated a relative of a co-worker.

16 percent of U.S. men and 5 percent of U.S. women say they've been rejected by a co-worker.

5 percent of U.S. adults said they've had romantic relations with a co-worker that made work uncomfortable.

7 percent of U.S. men and 11 percent of U.S. women have dated a boss or superior.

9 percent of U.S. adults said they've had romantic relations with a co-worker that resulted in office gossip.

16 percent of U.S. men and 7 percent of U.S. women reported having sex in the office.

A survey by the Pew Internet & American Life Project (Madden and Lenhart, 2006) increases our knowledge not only about online dating but also about unmarried Americans in general. For example,

Most Internet users who are married or in committed relationships met each other offline. Only 16% of single Americans, or 7% of all adults, say they are hunting for a partner. (p. 6)

The survey makes clear that not all single Americans are actively seeking a romantic partner, and this is the case even among young adults.

Table 8.1 *Singles and Their Relationships*			
	All Single Americans	Single Men	Single Women
In committed relationships	26%	30%	23%
Not in committed relationship and not looking for partner	55	42	65
Not in committed relationship but looking for partner	16	23	9
Don't know/Refused	3	5	3

Source: Pew Internet & American Life Project Online Dating Survey, September–December 2005 (retrieved July 16, 2007 from *www.pewinternet.org/pdfs/PIP_Online_Dating.pdf*). Margin of error is ±3% for all singles, ±5% for single men, and ±4% for single women.

When surveyed, relationship-seeking singles described how many dates they had been on in the past three months:

> 36% said they had been on no dates in the previous three months. 13% had been on one date. 22% had been on 2–4 dates. 25% had been on 5 or more dates. (Madden and Lenhart, 2006, p. 7)

Table 8.1 summarizes additional findings from this survey. For more about online dating, see Chapters 2, 9, and 15.

DEFINING CHARACTERISTICS OF RELATIONSHIPS

The authors of a study of platonic friendships among young adults (Kaplan and Keys, 1997) challenge the truth of Billy Crystal's line in the movie *When Harry Met Sally*—"No man can be friends with a woman [because] he always wants to have sex with her." According to the results of this study, "while sexual attraction is present in many cross-sex friendships and presents a challenge for a sizable minority of . . . friends, there is much more to these relationships than just sexuality." Supportiveness, trust and understanding, sharing of information, and several other factors clearly play a part. In the pages that follow, I shall be discussing three of the basic perspectives from which many kinds of relationships, however different they seem, may be described.

Context

The **context** of every relationship has two aspects: the setting and the social-psychological environment in which communication takes place and relationships develop.

Setting, or *physical environment,* has an important connection with the principle of similarity: We form relationships with people with whom we share a certain setting, probably because that shared setting is indicative of similarities. Work relationships, relationships with neighbors, relationships with those who participate in the same sport or are members of the same religion; each takes place within a given physical environment, and we are unlikely to have a relationship outside that setting. For example, your supervisor at the office is unlikely to visit you at home.

Although setting may be significant for some relations, **communication climate,** or *social-psychological context,* is important for all of them. Among the most critical measures of climate are confirmation and supportiveness.

Confirmation and Disconfirmation

In studying human communication, we distinguish between message *content* and the *relationship* between communicators. It seems obvious that every message has content, whether the information is correct or incorrect, valid or invalid, or even indeterminable. But every message also defines how it is to be interpreted and, consequently, something about the relationship between the people involved.

Suppose a man is driving and his six children, who are in the back of the station wagon, are arguing among one another. He might say, "Please stop it or I'm going to pull over"—a parental request that is serious but not intimidating. Or "Stop it right now"—a command that conveys parental power. Or, as Al Roker's father used to say in that situation, "DON'T MAKE ME STOP THIS CAR!"—a command that by its very tone is an immediate unspecified threat.

Even the most casual, seemingly neutral message—for example, the statement "It's up to you"—exists on the relationship level: "Every courtesy term between persons, every inflection of voice denoting respect or contempt, condescension or dependency, is a statement about the relationship between the two persons" (Ruesch and Bateson, 1968, p. 213). Thus, as we communicate, we expect more than a simple exchange of verbal and nonverbal information. Each person conveys messages that tell how he or she perceives the other and their relationship, and each expects to receive similar responses.

Perhaps the most satisfying interpersonal response we can hope to receive is total **confirmation,** or as Sieburg and Larson define it, "*any behavior that causes another person to value himself more*" (1971, p. 1; italics added). We can also think of this as any behavior that strengthens or reinforces the other person's self-esteem. The theologian Buber writes: "In human society, at all its levels, persons confirm one another in a practical way, to some extent or other, in their personal qualities and capacities, and a society may be termed human in the measure to which its members confirm one another" (1957, p. 101).

We can illustrate this through a series of brief exchanges between husband and wife. Suppose Kathy comes home after work and says to her husband, "Brian— guess what? I was promoted to divisional manager today. Isn't that great?" "That's wonderful, Kathy," replies Brian. "You've been working so hard. You really deserve this." Here Brian responds to Kathy and agrees with the content of her statement, thus confirming her very existence as a person. Yet what if he says, "Well, it sounds like a pressure job to me. I hope this isn't going to interfere with our life at home." Brian responds, but rejects the central content of Kathy's statement (that the promotion is a positive thing) and by implication Kathy herself. His statement acknowledges that she received a promotion but is disconfirming as to its value (for both of them). A third response is possible. Suppose Brian ignores Kathy's statement altogether and asks, "What's for dinner tonight?" This remark probably would have the same impact as complete silence. Both are totally disconfirming behaviors, behaviors that cause people to value themselves less; they reject both the speaker and what the speaker has to say (Sieburg and Larson, 1971).

Psychotherapeutic literature tells us that **disconfirmation** is *one of the most damaging interpersonal responses:* "While rejection amounts to the message 'you are wrong,' disconfirmation *says in effect 'you do not exist'*" (Watzlawick et al., 1967, p. 86). Consider the following experience. Martine, whose parents are Haitian, was born in Brooklyn and grew up in South Miami. She and her boyfriend are sitting at a dinner table in a New York restaurant with his parents, who are from Texas. She and her boyfriend announce that they plan on moving to Texas:

> My boyfriend's mother, under the influence of too much Chianti, would not be stopped. She and her husband began a conversation that went like this. As if I wasn't there:
>
> *Mother:* So I just want to tell you that we really like Martine. We think she's just wonderful.
>
> *Father:* Sue!
>
> *Mother:* She's smart.
>
> *Father:* Sue, shut up!
>
> *Mother:* I am just trying to say that we like her but . . .
>
> *Father:* Sue. Please.
>
> *Mother:* Texas is not New York.
>
> *Father:* I'm sorry, Martine. She's had too much to drink.
>
> *Mother:* No. Martine. Like I said, we think you're great. What do your parents think about all this?
>
> I ran to the bathroom to cry. (Bury, 2001, p. 103)

The practical question becomes: What kinds of responses are most confirming or disconfirming? We find part of the answer in the Sieburg and Larson (1971) study. Members of the International Communication Association were asked to describe the behaviors of the persons with whom they most enjoyed and least enjoyed communicating. As we look at the results of this survey, two distinct response styles emerge. They are summarized in Figure 8.1, which gives selective examples of confirming and disconfirming responses.

These behaviors are by no means exhaustive, but they highlight the differences between a confirming response style, which generally acknowledges, supports, and accepts other human beings, and a disconfirming response style, which denies and undermines their personal sense of worth.

Figure 8.1   *Confirmation and Disconfirmation: Some Ways of Responding*

Confirming Responses	Disconfirming Responses
Direct acknowledgment "Yes. I see where you're coming from."	Tangential response ["Do you know what I mean?"] –"Yes, I'm thinking of going to the movies."
Expressing positive feeling "That's a very good idea."	Impersonal response "Well, that's one way of thinking about it."
Clarifying response "Could you explain? I'm not sure I understand."	Impervious (disregarding) response "Have you seen my computer case?"
Agreement "You're absolutely right."	Irrelevant response ["I'm afraid I might lose my job."] –"I wonder if he's going to ask me out?"
Supportive response "I'm sure you'll make a good decision."	Incongruous response (mixed message) "Of course, it's your decision. It's up to you." (frown and exasperated tone of voice)

Confirmation/disconfirmation is a major dimension of human relationships with potential for influencing a range of communication outcomes. For example, perceived confirming behavior contributes to greater rapport between college roommates (Hawken et al., 1991, p. 306).

Yet to expect all your responses to others to be totally confirming would be unrealistic. There are times when you want to or must reject the communication of others, at least at the content level. Even in taking issue with others, however, keep in mind the importance of maintaining a confirming response style. Supportiveness is another important measure of climate.

Supportiveness and Defensiveness

A study (Schimel et al., 2001) finds that being accepted for who you are reduces your defensiveness. But it's not being liked for your accomplishments and achievements that makes you less defensive; it's the sense that you are liked for your intrinsic or

Table 8.2 *Supportive and Defensive Communication Climates*		
Defensive Climate	Problem Created	Supportive Climate
Evaluation	Feeling judged increases our defensiveness.	Description
Control	We resist someone trying to control us.	Problem orientation
Strategy	If we perceive a strategy or underlying motive, we become defensive.	Spontaneity
Neutrality	If the speaker appears to lack concern for us, we become defensive.	Empathy
Superiority	A person who acts superior arouses our defensive feelings.	Equality
Certainty	Those who are "know-it-alls" arouse our defensiveness.	Provisionalism

Source: From "Defensive Communications" by Jack R. Gibb, *Journal of Communication*, 11 (3), 1961, pp. 141–148. Reprinted by permission of the International Communication Association.

true self. We can be supportive in all our interpersonal relationships if we know more about several of the responses that reduce or arouse **defensiveness**—that is, *behaviors used to protect ourselves from what we perceive to be a threat.*

In his classic work on interpersonal trust, Gibb (1961) contrasted two atmospheres that could be established through communication. He called them **supportive** and **defensive climates,** and he described them in terms of six sets of behaviors listed in Table 8.2.

Evaluative, or judgmental, behavior arouses defensiveness, but so does complete neutrality. We can reconcile this apparent contradiction if we recall that complete neutrality is disconfirming: It communicates a lack of concern, an indifference to the other person. Gibb points out that attempts to reassure a troubled person by saying that he is overanxious or should not feel bad may be interpreted as a lack of acceptance. It can be highly supportive, however, to show empathy with the person's emotions without trying to change him—for example, "I understand how concerned you are" rather than "Relax, there's nothing to worry about." Pearce and Newton (1963), who consider it "the basic mode of significant communication between adults," refer to **empathy** as *"perception and communication by resonance, by identification, by experiencing in ourselves some reflection of the emotional tone that is being experienced by the other person"* (p. 52, italics added). (See the discussion of empathic listening in Chapter 5.)

Statements that reflect an effort to control rather than solve a problem also arouse defensive responses. For example, compare the effect of "If you come home late again, you're grounded" to "Is there anything you can do differently so that you get home on time?" And compare statements that convey certainty—e.g., "You're making a big mistake by renting that apartment"—with those that reflect a provisional attitude—e.g., "Perhaps you should look a little more before you settle for an apartment that expensive." The first implies that the other person is foolish, the second simply suggests an alternative without telling her what to do.

From his survey Gibb concluded that when trust increases, efficiency and accuracy in communication also increase. To this, we might add that while a supportive climate is important even in short-term relationships, in more permanent relationships (e.g., in marriage or on the job) it has even greater possibilities for influencing all five communication outcomes. As we suggested in Chapter 1, the better the relationship between people, the more likely it is that the other outcomes of effective communication will also occur.

In addition to climate, time is another dimension that helps to characterize relationships.

Time

Time is required for all the qualities of a relationship to develop and evolve (Chelune et al., 1984). In general, our knowledge of another person is usually acquired slowly; interdependence, trust, and commitment also develop over time.

Time also affects the *intensity* of human relationships. For example, if you take a cross-country car trip with a friend, your relationship can become much closer than it would if you just met for an hour or two once a week. In terms of our model, it is as though one were pulling the ends of the spring in Figure 1.1 (Chapter 1, page 9) farther and farther apart. In other words, a human relationship is not constant; its intensity is affected by the amount of time that passes between encounters.

Communication style tends to change with the passage of time. When two people first meet, they usually try to be as explicit as possible. Even if the two share several interests, one does not assume knowledge of what the other is thinking or trying to say. This kind of insight develops only after long acquaintance. Sometimes two people get to know each other so well that each anticipates what the other is trying to say—they even finish each other's sentences, so to speak.

Although time spent is a way of characterizing relationships, it is meaningful only when integrated with such dimensions as the *quality* of the time and the *desire to spend it.* Desire to spend time and the amount of time two people spend do not always mesh. For example, you may find yourself in a relationship where you and the other person want to be together almost constantly, yet circumstances make it impossible. On the other hand, a man and woman who have been married for many years may spend most of their free time with each other yet have little desire to do so. Or the wife may feel she always wants to spend her weekends with her husband, and the husband may have less desire to be with her; perhaps he'd rather go sailing some weekends even though she doesn't like sailing. Spending more time together is not always the solution. Many counselors and therapists advise that the quality of the time two people spend together—and the degree to which they express their mutual regard—can be more significant than the amount of time spent.

Currently, there is great interest in the long-term effects of living together. A study by Stafford and colleagues (2004) looked at married couples, couples who lived together and then married, and couples who simply lived together, tracking them over time in terms of their personal well-being and satisfaction with the relationship. Though the researchers report no significant differences, they did find that couples who lived together for many years but did not marry had more conflict and were more at risk of separating.

Trust

On April 10, 2010 Poland's president Lech Kaczynski and 96 other top Polish officials were killed in a plane crash in Smolensk in western Russia. They were coming to commemorate the massacre of Polish military officers by the Russians in World War II. The massacre had been denied for decades by officials in the former Soviet Union. The crash occurred in the thick fog, and despite strong warnings from the air traffic controllers not to land. Cockpit recordings confirmed that Gen. Andrzej Blasik was in the cockpit with the door open. Although we may never know, there was speculation, according to the *Wall Street Journal* (Sobczyk, 2010) and the *New York Times* (Barry, Kulish, and Piotrowski, 2010), that the Polish president ordered the pilot to land because he did not trust the Russians who had told the pilot to divert the landing to another airport.

In another case closer to home, the United Auto Workers elected Bob King as their new president. According to the *Detroit Free Press* (Walsh, 2010), one of the key issues facing King is to reduce 2,000-page labor agreements, which limit flexibility and retard productivity by spelling out every possible work issue in great detail, and to replace the agreements with briefer, more broad-based work rules. Tom Walsh writes, "Trust and shared goals must replace adversarial relations. No other viable options remain" (Walsh, 2010, p. A1).

The common denominator in these two cases is that the lack of trust often leads to undesirable consequences. So what do we mean by trust? One excellent definition is "a psychological state of individuals involving confident, positive expectations about the actions of another" (deJong and Elfring, 2010, p. 535).

More than forty years ago, I conducted an experimental study for my doctoral dissertation in which subjects observed either cooperative or competitive behaviors of an individual in a "prisoner's dilemma game" type of situation. Then they wrote down the degree to which (on a 5-point scale) they would trust or not trust that individual. We conducted the experiment sixty times to verify the findings. So, what do you think we found?

We found that cooperative behaviors tended to induce cooperative (trusting) responses, and competitive behaviors tended to induce competitive (distrusting) responses (Tubbs, 1971). However, there was one complicating factor, and that was the majority opinion of three other observers in the experiment. When observers heard the other three people say that they thought the individual was behaving the *opposite* of the way she had actually behaved, then the trust was lost. In other words, she had actually acted in a cooperative, trusting way, but the others in the group (who were part of the experiment) said that she had acted in a competitive, distrusting way. So, even consistently trust-inducing behaviors can be ineffective if a majority of others tell us that our perceptions were wrong (Tubbs, 1971). No wonder trust is such a fragile phenomenon.

That study had all the limitations of any experimental study conducted in a laboratory setting. However, deJong and Elfring recently published the results of a study of 879 tax consultants working in 92 actual work teams. Their study confirmed the main findings of my study that cooperation leads to trust and co-operation, and that competition and distrust breed more distrust and poor team performance. Moreover, they studied teams over time and found that the longer the teams worked together, the more pronounced the findings were.

More recently, Hurley (2012) has studied trust in a very comprehensive way and found that there are a number of situational factors that have an impact on our decision to trust another person. One is called *benevolent concern*. This refers to a person's perceived willingness to do something to help us, without expecting anything in return. Our parents and other loved ones often do this as a natural way of relating. Another factor is *capability*. We trust those who seem to have the ability to do what we expect of them. Airline pilots would be one example. Our tax accountant or attorney would be two others. *Integrity* is a third important factor that affects our trust of an-other. People who do what they say they will do build our trust. Ironically, these three factors are virtually the same as those Aristotle identified in 324 B.C. He called them "competence" and "character." In the 2012 presidential contest, Texas governor Rick Perry had a few embarrassing slip-ups in the debates, which rightly or wrongly called into question his competence. Former Speaker of the House of Representatives Newt Gingrich had his character called into question because of his extramarital affairs, and because of the ethics investigations against him when he was Speaker of the House.

In a business context, Lyman (2012) has found that companies whose leaders rate high on trust are roughly three times as profitable as those whose leaders don't rate so highly.

Lying and Deception

It might not surprise you to learn that people are often willing to lie to someone they consider a very attractive date. In one *Seinfeld* episode, the character George Costanza tries to impress a young woman by pretending to be a successful architect when actually he's not an architect and he's unemployed.

But what are the effects of lying between people who have already established a close relationship, presumably one based on trust? Whatever the lie, some would say, it was meant to protect the other person, to spare feelings. Communication scholar Mark Knapp's overview of lying and deception in close relationships (2006) finds that counter to what we might expect, partners may lie to each other more often than they do to other people. Sometimes the motive for such lying may simply be to maintain the existing bond. Much lying is done to maintain harmony or to protect the other's feelings and self-esteem. For example, despite voicing harsh criti-cism to her husband, a spouse may lie about having had the negative feelings: "Of course I love you. I was just kidding." But that may well have been her feeling at that moment. So total honesty is sometimes more ideal than real.

Knapp (2006) explores the consequences of what he calls "undiscovered lies." Reassuring someone of your love, even though you don't feel it at the time, is at times considered an altruistic lie. Many people openly acknowledge that they some-times lie about their feelings. But lying to someone you're close to can make you feel angry, guilty, embarrassed.

"Sometimes lies are not uncovered, but suspicion has been aroused to such an extent that trust in one's partner is negatively affected" (Knapp, 2006, p. 527). Sus-picions of *sexual infidelity* take questions of trust to an extreme. Fidelity in marriage is closely linked with issues of trust as well as intimacy. In marriage, sexual fidelity is a fundamental norm. According to a survey of marriage therapists, extramarital sex is among the most common problems for which couples enter therapy.

A study (Previti and Amato, 2004) examined whether extramarital sex is a cause or consequence of poor marital quality. Researchers found that among cou-ples who had not been unfaithful "a high level of proneness to divorce (thinking that the marriage is in trouble, thinking about divorce, and talking about divorce with one's spouse or others) predicts that at least one spouse" is more likely to be unfaith-ful (p. 227). If infidelity does take place, it increases the likelihood of unhappiness in marriage as well as the probability of divorce. Infidelity can be seen, then, as both cause and consequence of the breakdown of the relationship.

Knapp reminds us that "self-deception clearly plays an important role in close relationships" (p. 521)—and there may be no more serious self-deception than one that involves infidelity. Sometimes we deny what seems clear to other people:

> *Little by little things were happening that didn't make sense, but I can remember making excuses for them myself . . . . I didn't want to believe there was anything to find out . . . . I didn't confide in anyone, too, because I was afraid of what they would tell me. I wanted to believe everything was going to be fine and I wasn't deceived . . . . But as much as I wanted to be a detective and find him out, I didn't want to either. Because the truth—I was afraid more of the truth than living in the lie kind of.* (cited in Knapp, 2006, p. 522; italics in original)

Infidelity need not destroy a close relationship. For example, Dr. Keith Ablow (2006) has found that if a couple can learn why one of the spouses has been unfaith-ful, they may have an opportunity for change and the rebuilding of trust. Mitch, one of Ablow's patients, sought counseling after discovering that while on vacation with her girlfriends, his wife had met and been intimate with an old college sweetheart. Mitch was devastated and had initiated a divorce despite the fact that he still loved his wife and the couple had three children.

"There's a critical moment at hand," Dr. Ablow told Mitch, "and it could be the beginning of the best part of your marriage" (p. F5). He urged questioning and frank discussion between husband and wife about what had led to her actions and what changes—on both sides—needed to be made in the marriage.

In other kinds of relationships, people sometimes perceive *deception* either as a "normal" or necessary communication alternative. Research by Lippard (1988) with adolescents and young adults identified five primary motives for deception: resources, affiliation, self-protection, avoiding conflict, and protecting others.

One of the most interesting findings is a correlation between power, fre-quency of interaction, and deception. For example, those most often deceived were the subjects' parents—in other words, those who had the most control over their lives. This finding reinforces earlier research that deception "is frequently a power-balancing strategy" (p. 99). Note that almost 22 percent of all the deceptive actions involved loyalty to friends. And here women were reported to be more likely than men to lie in order to protect another person's feelings, a finding that supports stereotypical perceptions concerning women's behavior.

The subjects in this study were all young, of an age at which the shaping and preservation of one's self-identity seems to be a central task. Thus, further research must be done before it can be established that at other life stages—middle age, for example—the frequency of deception behaviors changes. Lippard (1988) shrewdly points out that "the easy resort to deception as a manipulative strategy does not truly change the power balance; rather, it reinforces the role relationship which creates the imbalance" (p. 102).

THEORIES OF RELATIONSHIP DEVELOPMENT

Potentially, every new person you meet may become that one lifelong friend in a relationship you treasure or the romantic partner with whom you want to spend your whole life. Although the odds are against it with most acquaintances, there is always that possibility.

Many scholars from communication and other disciplines have examined what they see as the linear development of personal relationships—viewing them as a sequence of stages or phases, each described by a particular set of behaviors. We will consider this approach by looking at the work of Mark Knapp.

A Theory on the Life Cycle of Relationships

Mark Knapp has written an extensive analysis of the stages of building, experiencing, and ending relationships and of the kind of communication that characterizes each stage. He sees these stages as building to a peak and sometimes declining—in his terms, "coming together" and "coming apart" (Knapp and Vangelisti, 2000). The outline that follows pertains to relationships geared toward intimacy and permanence. This theory assumes that the projected stages may be sequential, that one often follows the other, but that sometimes relationships move more rapidly, skipping stages to move either forward (toward greater intimacy) or backward (toward dissolving).

Knapp proposes a staircase model, seen in Figure 8.2. Imagine yourself on the left side of the staircase (coming together). You are at the bottom (initiating) and as you develop a closer relationship with someone, you move up the steps (stages). The central staircase depicts states of possible equilibrium, or stabilizing, at each of the relationship stages.

Communication plays a different role at each stage in a relationship. During the early stages, it is aimed at learning about the other person so that decisions concerning the relationship can be made—whether to form a relationship, what subjects are open for discussion, how close or intimate the relationship should be. After this phase, communication is used to maintain, develop, and enhance the relationship

Figure 8.2 A Staircase Model of Human Relationships

Source: From *Interpersonal Communication and Human Relationships,* 4th ed., by Mark L. Knapp and Anita L. Vangelisti. Published by Allyn & Bacon, Boston, MA. Copyright © 2000 by Pearson Education. Reprinted by permission of the publisher.

as well as to negotiate differences that will increase the satisfaction derived from it. During the final stages, communication helps the partners terminate their relationship by providing a means of saving face, resolving feelings, and parting (ideally, on a positive basis).

Coming Together → "Stage 1"

Knapp proposes ten stages in all: the first 5—"coming together"—describe the slow growth of interpersonal relationships.

Initiating refers to the very first attempts you make at conversation with a new person. In Chapter 1, we referred to this as phatic communication: "Hi," "How's it going?" "Think it will rain today?" During this scanning process, communication is generally more cautious and conventional: You are trying to establish contact and express interest. Much of what we said about perception and first impressions in Chapter 2 relates to this stage of communication. Of course, these days the initiating phase may be taking place on the Internet.

Experimenting is the phase in which you try sample conversational topics in an attempt to gain some knowledge of the other person. Usually two people will ask a lot of questions and exchange a lot of small talk: "What's your major?" "What kind of music do you like?" "Where are you from?" Experimenting is a safe way of learning about similarities and differences. In this stage you're continually looking for ways of building on some area of common interest. Any commitments at this stage are generally very limited and the relationship is usually casual and relaxed: "Like it or not, most of our relationships probably don't progress very far beyond this stage" (Knapp and Vangelisti, 2000).

Intensifying marks the beginning of intimacy, sharing personal information, and the beginning of greater informality. This stage is marked by many changes in communication behaviors, both verbal and nonverbal, that take place when acquaintances become close friends. Physical closeness, hand holding, and greater eye contact are just a few of the various indicators that a relationship is intensifying. A greater degree of openness about yourself ("My parents are divorced"; "I'm not a very good student") is another. (We will have a great deal to say about self-disclosure in Chapter 9.) During the day you may be e-mailing each other at work, even if you are going to meet in the evening.

Integrating takes place when two people begin to consider themselves a couple. Often this attitude is mirrored in the way others begin to treat them. At this time, they actively cultivate all the interests, attitudes, and qualities that seem to make them unique as a couple. They may also do this in a symbolic way, identifying a song as "our song," or even exchanging rings. As the two begin to value more and more of the same things, they intensify some aspects of their personalities and minimize others.

Bonding is a more formal or ritualistic stage. It may take the form of engagement or marriage, but even "going steady" is a form of bonding. Through bonding, the couple gain social or institutional support for their relationship and agree to accept a set of rules, or norms, governing their relationship. But bonding itself may change this relationship because it is now "more difficult to break out of . . . . The contract becomes, either explicitly or implicitly, a frequent topic of conversation" (Knapp and Vangelisti, 2000).

Coming Apart → ˒Stage 2˓

Relationships may stabilize at any of the building stages preceding bonding, the most intimate stage, but even relationships that reach the closest phase may begin to deteriorate. For Knapp, the termination of a relationship is not simply the reverse of what has been referred to as "coming together." People just don't "drift apart" or "separate"; only when both want to terminate the relationship is the process one of reversal, marked by decreasing contact, intimacy, and so on.

The other five stages, seen on the right side of the staircase model, describe the increasing deterioration that can occur in relationships that have been at the bonding stage—or in some cases, never achieved it.

Differentiating occurs when two people decide that perhaps their relationship may be too confining. This can be early on in a relationship. For example, a couple can pull back once a relationship intensifies and quickly begin to focus on their differences rather than their similarities. Or a couple who were at the bonding stage may decide they want to "do their own thing," "have a little breathing room"; in other words, they begin to emphasize their individuality. The most obvious change in communication is the increase in the number of fights.

Circumscribing refers to a stage in which couples begin to reduce the frequency and intimacy of their communication. Certain hot topics like money and sex tend to be avoided, since they are too likely to produce more quarreling. Greater formality returns, as if the two people didn't know each other very well. "Is it okay with you if I go for a walk now?" "I don't care. Do whatever you want to."

Stagnating reflects the increasing deterioration of a relationship that the participants are trying to hold together. It might be for religious or financial reasons, or for the sake of children involved, or because of other factors no longer having to do with attraction to the other person. Verbal and nonverbal messages become more and more like those conveyed between strangers. The relationship itself is no longer discussed.

Avoiding is a coping tactic to minimize the pain of experiencing a totally deteriorated relationship. Physical separation often takes place. Of course, this is easier if two people live apart, but we all know couples who live in the same house yet lead completely separate lives. Avoiding often takes place between neighbors or co-workers after a major argument. The participants still must remain physically close, but they manage to keep contact to a minimum.

Terminating is the final stage in any relationship. Knapp, who applies his theory to the briefest of encounters as well as to long-standing relationships, proposes that termination may occur after only a brief conversation or after a lifetime of intimacy. Generally, the longer and more meaningful the relationship, the more painful and drawn out its termination. Messages of distance and dissociation are often exchanged at this time, and usually these summarize and clarify what is happening between the two people—for example, "I don't ever want to see you again!" or "I'll always respect you, but I don't love you anymore" (Knapp and Vangelisti, 2000). Movement down the staircase can also skip several steps, going for example from a bonding stage to a sudden rather than gradual termination—as when one person suddenly breaks off the relationship because he's found out that his partner was unfaithful.

Knapp's stage theory applies to same-sex as well as male–female relationships. And certainly some of the phases described are familiar to us all, but the lingering question is how well these categories account for the real discontinuities and jumps we find between stages and the degree to which we can generalize this theory of stages to a great number of relationships.

A Theory of Relationship Dissolution

The study of **relationship disengagement** or dissolution (what in Knapp's model constitutes "coming apart") has been given a great deal of attention (Duck, 1982; Baxter, 1982, 1984). Several variables will determine how a relationship ends. According to Baxter's research, how a relationship breaks up depends on who wants to end it (both people? only one?), whether problems came on suddenly, whether the partners confront each other directly, whether their discussions are long or short, whether the two parties want to "save" the relationship, and whether their goal is to change the relationship or to end it.

One theory that deals specifically with relationship dissolution has been proposed by Duck (1982, 1992, 1999) on the basis of his own work and the findings of Baxter and others. Duck believes there are four distinct phases, as seen in Figure 8.3.

The intrapsychic phase: The first phase in the breakdown of a relationship is usually internal. Although nothing is made overt, a great deal of dissatisfaction and reflecting on the relationship is going on. Partners are not yet speaking to each other about their growing unhappiness, but each may be focusing on the other's inadequacies, imagining how a breakup would affect their lives, or even thinking about

Figure 8.3 *The Main Phases in Dissolving Personal Relationships*

BREAKDOWN: Dissatisfaction with relationship

Threshold: I can't stand this anymore

INTRAPSYCHIC PHASE
Personal focus on partner's behavior
Assess adequacy of partner's role performance
Depict and evaluate negative aspects of being in the relationship
Consider costs of withdrawal
Assess positive aspects of alternative relationships
Face 'express/repress dilemma'

Threshold: I'd be justified in withdrawing

DYADIC PHASE
Face 'confrontation/avoidance dilemma'
Confront partner
Negotiate in 'our relationship talks'
Attempt repair and reconciliation?
Assess joint costs of withdrawal or reduced intimacy

Threshold: I mean it

SOCIAL PHASE
Negotiate post-dissolution state with partner
Initiate gossip/discussion in social network
Create publicly negotiable face-saving/blame-placing stories and accounts
Consider and face up to implied social network effects, if any
Call in intervention teams?

Threshold: It's now inevitable

GRAVE DRESSING PHASE
'Getting over' activity
Retrospection; reformulative post-mortem attribution
Public distribution of own version of break-up story

Source: From *Personal Relationships 5: Repairing Personal Relationships* by Steve Duck, 1984. Reprinted by permission of Elsevier.

starting a relationship with someone else. Sometimes it is only one person who has reached the point of thinking, "I can't stand this anymore." "Just before exit from this phase," explains Duck, "people move up the scale of confidants so that they start to complain to their close friends" (1992, p. 95). (And for some people who are not in formal relationships, this may be where the breakup occurs.)

The dyadic phase: This phase is "the interpersonal mess"—the time when people actually confront each other. They may try talking out their differences, working out their difficulties, or ending the relationship and cutting their losses. Interestingly, Duck believes that people only talk about their relationships when things are not going well and that otherwise "the relationship" is usually a topic people avoid. This period is very stressful even for those who decide to stay in the relationship and attempt to repair it. They may resent the partner yet be unwilling to let go. It's a painful, chaotic time—often full of hostility, guilt, and conflict. If the couple agree to break up, they enter the next phase.

The social phase: In this phase people start seeking advice from others—usually friends or family—in their social network about their decision. "It is no good just leaving a relationship: we need other people to agree with our decision or to prop us up and support what we have done" (Duck, 1992, p. 95). People want to feel confirmed in their action and to be thought of as acting in a responsible and justified way. Although social networks may pressure a couple to stay together, once the breakup is imminent, they also spread the word that the couple is splitting up and help them recover after they do.

The grave dressing phase: To get over our distress we turn to others to justify ourselves. It seems we want to leave a relationship with some sort of narrative and, in effect, prepare a story that makes us seem acceptable for future relationships. Now the social network becomes even more important:

> They can side with our version of events and our version of the partner's and the relationship's faults. ("I always thought he/she was no good," "I could never understand how you two could get along—you never seemed right for each other.") . . . [O]nce the relationship is dead we have to bury it "good and proper"—with a tombstone saying how it was born, what it was like, and why it died. We have to create an account of the relationship's history. (pp. 95, 97)

Incidentally, several studies find that people tend to report that *they* were responsible for ending a previous relationship. "Apparently, individuals want to be the dumper rather than the dumpee" (Honeycutt and Cantrill, 2001, p. 152).

By emphasizing both the internal aspects of breakups—growing feelings of intense dissatisfaction and our misgivings about the relationship—and the role that people in social networks play when a couple is splitting up, Duck's theory broadens our understanding of how close relationships dissolve. His work also stresses that in ending a relationship both parties want to feel justified.

But are there truly set phases in interpersonal relationships? How do the theories you've been reading about correspond to your own experience? The concept of phases or stages enables us to categorize research findings about relational behaviors and to think of relationships in terms of movement and development. James Honeycutt (1993) and others argue that while the concept of phases in intimate relationships has been useful, it implies a final state—"bonding," for example, or "terminating"—although many actual relationships show continual fluctuations. Many relationships regress, become less intimate at times, but still endure. And even after divorce, formerly married couples may maintain some sort of relationship—and its quality may change many times. There are other difficulties with thinking in terms of stages. For example, how do we explain brief romances, one-night stands, and lifelong platonic friendships (p. 84)?

Honeycutt proposes a *memory structure approach* (Honeycutt and Cantrill, 2001). In this view, we all have expectations for relationship development. These are influenced not only by relationships we have actually had, but by what we have seen in the media, by observing our friends and family, and by what they tell us about their relationships. (If your best friend proposed to his wife three days after meeting her, "love at first sight" may be what you expect for yourself.) Our imagined interactions and fantasizing are also important.

In other words, we expect certain phases—each of which we associate with certain prototypes of behaviors—and these expectations affect how we interpret our relationships. Phases, Honeycutt believes, are constructed from our expectancies for relationships and exist in our memories, but the concept of stages may be helpful in looking at our perceptions and ideas about what should be happening over the span of a relationship (Honeycutt and Cantrill, 2001, p. 96).

MAINTAINING RELATIONSHIPS

Today there is high interest in the study of **relationship maintenance,** or, in simpler language, *how people—whether they are friends, romantic partners, or family members—can maintain close and satisfying relationships.* The question is how, once we establish it, we can sustain a relationship.

Two people may establish what they think will be a lifelong friendship or marriage yet soon discover the pleasure that they felt when the initial bond was made is slipping away. It can be puzzling, even painful, to learn that some kind of effort is needed to keep a relationship going. If a close friend is easily insulted, keeping up the friendship may seem just too difficult to you. If your parents never fought, fighting with your spouse may seem to you a sign that your marriage is in danger. Often we have the idea that if we have to "work at" a relationship, it wasn't meant to be. But as we saw in Chapter 6, conflict is not always destructive. When two people can resolve their conflicts about relationship roles, it tends to enhance their relationship.

Theorists and researchers have identified many important routine behaviors as well as more conscious strategies that people use in maintaining close relationships (Canary and Dainton, 2003; Dindia, 2000; Duck, 1999; Knapp and Vangelisti, 2000): for example, disclosures or openness, verbal and nonverbal expressions of commitment and intimacy, constructive conflict, and—most surprisingly—lying.

According to some communication scholars (Duck, 1994; Duck and Pittmann, 1994), the very core of relational maintenance is in ordinary life—much of it everyday talk. It allows people to share their experiences. Through talk, however trivial, two people create shared meanings and project the future of their relationship. And it is these meanings that sustain their relationship.

What is it that people are achieving by holding silly and insignificant conversations about trivial topics, telling one another jokes, discussing the clothing or demeanor of passersby, complaining about other people, speculating about other people's relationships, suggesting where to go for lunch, teasing one another, arguing and debating, or cajoling others? First, as *individuals,* they are giving off meaning . . . . Second, as *partners,* they are colluding with the other partner in the embodiment of the relationship. (Duck, 1994, pp. 53–54)

Interestingly, talk between lovers is not rated as high in quality as talk between best friends. But research has shown that even everyday talk confirms two people in their agreement on how they experience the world (p. 56).

Certainly, in a close long-term relationship we come to expect an atmosphere of openness and trust in which two people will share a significant amount of personal information—thoughts, feelings, even responses to the relationship itself. We mentioned in discussing information sharing that women tend to be more self-disclosing than men. For example, when husbands believe their marriage is "going well," they see no need to speak about their relationship (Acitele, 1987). These and other findings lend some support to Tannen's observation that women tend to favor "relationship talk" and that for most women talk plays an essential role in maintaining intimacy (1990, p. 86).

Though people tend to talk less about their commitment to each other after the intensifying stage of their relationship, threatened relationships often require assurances, both verbal and nonverbal, that reestablish commitment:

In troubled relationships, the "I love you" phrase may not be enough to convince one's partner he or she is loved. It has become an empty phrase because there have not been enough follow-up behaviors that specifically testify to the declaration of love . . . . *Intensity* has a lot to do with the perceived strength of the commitment talk. This may involve rapt attention and focus achieved through long mutual gazes and close proximity; voice volume ("He just kept yelling 'I love Linda' as we walked down the street. It was embarrassing, but it meant a lot to me"); or absolute statements ("I'll *always* love you," or "I'll *never* leave you"). (Knapp and Vangelisti, 2000, p. 298)

As we saw in Chapter 3, when two people are intimate, they often develop a private language. Intimacy can be conveyed through personal idioms—from pet names to private ways of talking about sex. In a study of intimate play, a less serious aspect of personal relationships, Baxter (1992) includes private verbal codes, physical play, role-playing, teasing, and gossiping games. "Private verbal code play (i.e., playful idiomatic expression) appears to be a particularly strong indicator of intimacy" (p. 359). In many studies, play is not only used as a measure of intimacy but is also thought to promote it. Considered a "low risk" or safe communication strategy, it enables people to moderate conflict and tensions.

Knapp notes how important it is that we initiate behaviors that maintain a relationship instead of simply receiving them. For example, a young woman we know once referred to her husband as "a guest in the marriage." Researchers have identified at least five maintenance strategies that have proved most successful in long-term romantic relationships:

Positivity: Being cooperative, cheerful, optimistic, not criticizing, being patient and forgiving, trying to build the other person's self-esteem (through compliments and other means).

Openness: Encouraging the other person's disclosure of thoughts and feelings, stating your feelings about the relationship, discussing the quality of the relationship as well as past relationship decisions, and what you need and want from it.

Assurances: Stressing commitment to the other person, implying the relationship has a future, showing love and faithfulness.

Networks: Spending time with common friends; showing willingness to be with the other person's friends or family, including them in activities.

Tasks: Sharing duties and tasks jointly including household chores and other responsibilities. ("Doing my fair share of the work we have to do.") (Canary and Stafford, 1992, adapted from pp. 262–263; 1994; Canary and Dainton, 2003)

Of these behaviors, sharing tasks is the most underrated and openness the most overrated (Dindia, 2000, p. 291). Other strategies mentioned are conflict management and giving advice.

In maintaining close friendships three kinds of behaviors seem especially important (Fehr, 2000):

Self-Disclosure: Openness between friends, sometimes used consciously to sustain and enhance the friendship. A good part of friendship includes self-disclosure. Often friendships break down when one person starts withholding information from the other. This is especially true of friendships between women. (Married women sometimes say that they disclose more to their friends than they do to husbands. In fact, a good part of friendship between women involves talking about personal problems together. Men tend to see friendships as based primarily on doing things together [Tannen, 2001, p. 32].)

Supportiveness: Friends seem to have an unwritten understanding that they will be there for each other—for example, listening and offering advice when a friend has a problem with a girlfriend, parents, or grades. And friends expect support through loyalty. Most young adults rely on peers for social support.

Spending Time Together: Though it seems obvious, friends keep their relationship going by doing things together—seeing movies, taking trips, shopping, celebrating holidays and birthdays. When they can't be together, they keep in touch through telephone calls, e-mail, letters, and cards (adapted from Fehr, 2000, pp. 77–78).

Psychologist John Gottman conducted a famous study of marital happiness. He devised what he calls the "Magic Ratio" to predict the marital success of 700 newly married couples. He predicted that couples who had a ratio of five positive interactions to every negative one would stay together. Ten years later, he conducted a follow-up study to see how many of the couples were still married. He found that 94 percent of the couples that he predicted would be divorced were no longer together (Shimoff and Kline, 2008, p. 255).

As you think about relationship maintenance, keep in mind that the concepts we speak of here are examined in many parts of this book. For example, we will look at other aspects of openness and commitment in Chapter 9. And remember that at times researchers define the same variable by somewhat different terminology and that there is no magic list of behaviors: You have to maintain and negotiate each relationship on its own terms.

FAMILY COMMUNICATION

A massive nationwide study of 645,000 students attempted to account for what caused students to do well in school. To everyone's shock, the Coleman Report found that the quality of schools explains almost nothing about differences in academic achievement. Measures such as the credentials of the teachers, the curriculum, the extensiveness and newness of physical facilities, money spent per student—none of the things people assumed were important in educational achievement were in fact important. *Family background was far and away the most important factor in determining student achievement* (Murray, 2008, p. 58, italics added for emphasis.)

Clearly, the relationships that matter most to us are those in our family: The family represents a very special constellation of relationships.

Currently, there is much debate about what constitutes a family. In their book on family theory (2006), Leslie Baxter and Dawn Braithwaite identify the five properties often used to define the concept of family:

Long-term commitment

Relations created through biology, law, or affection

Enmeshment in a kinship organization

Ongoing interdependence

Institutionalization (that is, legal or institutional recognition of the bond)

Baxter and Braithwaite give special emphasis to two qualities: commitment and interdependence. They define a family as "a social group of two or more persons, characterized by ongoing interdependence with long-term commitments that stem from blood, law, or affection" (Baxter and Braithwaite, 2006, p. 3).

Another broad and useful definition of **family** is "*networks of people who share their lives over long periods of time; who are bound by ties of marriage, blood, or commitment, legal or otherwise; who consider themselves as family; and who share future expectations of connected relationship*" (Galvin et al., 2003). So in addition to stepfamilies (also called remarried families) and single-parent families, such a definition includes heterosexual and same-sex couples who live together and who may or may not have children.

Table 8.3 *The First Ten Years of Marriage: Some Risk Factors*

Divorce rates can vary significantly. Here are the percentage-point increases in the probability of divorce or separation during the first ten years of marriage, depending on a variety of factors:

Annual income under $25,000 vs. over $50,000	+30%
Having a baby before marriage vs. seven months or more afterward	+24%
Marrying under 18 years of age vs. 25 or over	+24%
Own parents divorced vs. intact family of origin	+14%
No religious affiliation	+14%
High school dropout vs. some college	+13%
Central city vs. suburb dweller	+9%

Source: National Center for Health Statistics. Adapted from Sue Shellenbarger, "No Comfort in Numbers: Divorce Rate Varies Widely from Group to Group," *The Wall Street Journal*, April 22, 2004, D1 (with change in title of table). Copyright © 2004 Dow Jones and Co. Reprinted by permission of Dow Jones and Co. via Copyright Clearance Center.

According to one source on traditional marriage, "Half of all divorces occur within the first seven years of marriage." Several of the risk factors for divorce or separation during the first ten years of marriage appear in Table 8.3 (Shellenbarger, 2004).

Today people's family histories are growing more complex as each year "half of all the marriages that take place in the United States are remarriages for one or both partners" (Coleman et al., 2001). And by 2010, it's thought that remarried families will be the most common type in this country. The 2000 Census also reports a considerable rise in the number of gay and lesbian families, and an increasing number of them are raising children.

Stephanie Coontz, the author of a number of books on marriage and family life including *Marriage, a History: How Love Conquered Marriage* (2006a), sums up some interesting findings:

> For the first time in 150 years, [U.S.] households headed by single adults and unmarried couples now outnumber married-couple families. [This figure may be misleading, however. For example, there's been a slight decline in the divorce rate. And one reason for the greater number of unmarried households is that people now marry later—27 is now the median age for men, just about 26 for women. You're less likely to divorce if you marry later in life.]
>
> Thirty million unmarried men and women live alone, in their own household rather than with roommates or parents.
>
> The number of heterosexual couples who live together outside of marriage has soared from 500,000 in 1970 to more than five million today.
>
> Forty percent of cohabiting couples, compared to 45 percent of married couple households, have children in the home.
>
> Elders are the fastest growing segment of the cohabiting population. (Coontz, 2006b)

To read a variety of articles on marriage, go to *www.stephaniecoontz.com/articles*. Be sure to take the pop quiz on marriage. You may be quite surprised.

PRACTICAL TIPS   *Relationships—How to Listen to Your Children*

"The most valuable gift you can give your child is to listen to the little and big things in his life. Begin early so that the lines of communication will be open during the teenage years." The following are steps suggested on how to effectively listen to your children:

1. Stop what you are doing.
2. Look at your child.
3. Pay attention to your child's nonverbal language.

4. Be silent.
5. Use simple acknowledgement responses that show you are listening.
6. Use door-openers, phrases that encourage further talking.
7. Listen for and name the feelings you think you hear from what your child is telling you.
8. Use problem-solving phrases when needed.

(About.com, 2008)

Communication Rules

Today theorists emphasize the uniqueness of all families, happy or unhappy; they regard each as distinct, with its own history, values, and behavioral norms. Just as families have their own sets of values and expectations for their members, they have their own expectations about communication. There seem to be acceptable times to speak about certain topics, issues that are never raised, certain family members who should be approached or not approached, and so on. In other words, each family has a virtual handbook of understood communication rules.

Recent research shows that one of the most important predictors of successful family communication is simply having dinner together. Psychologist Bert Pitts says that "It can be a time of feeding in every way—physically, spiritually, and emotionally" (Seale, 2008, p. C3). Frequent dining together is also a predictor of lower rates of teen smoking, drinking, and drug use. Compared to teens who regularly have dinner with their family, teens who don't are 3.5 times more likely to abuse prescription drugs or illegal drugs other than marijuana. Also, according to research conducted at the University of Alabama, Birmingham, girls who have five or more meals a week with their families are 33 percent less likely to have eating disorders such as diet pill abuse and anorexia nervosa (Seale). All these findings are confirmed by additional studies conducted at Columbia University's National Center on Addiction and Substance Abuse (Powers, 2008, p. 3C).

Summary

This chapter was concerned with relationship processes, and its first focus of attention was the bases of human attraction. Other things being equal, we found the closer two people are geographically, the more likely they are to be attracted to each other. Although proximity is usually a precondition of attraction, people tend to attract and be attracted to those they perceive as similar to themselves. Conversely, they tend to dislike and be disliked by those perceived as different. Several variables qualify generalizations about the similarity thesis—including perceived reciprocity of liking, changes in self-esteem, anxiety, and isolation. We also looked at research on online dating and singles and their relationships.

We then turned to three defining characteristics of all relationships. We stressed the importance of social-psychological environment and spoke of what makes for confirming and supportive climates. Time and trust were also examined. Lying and deception as they affect close relationships were also discussed.

The next part of our chapter examined a theory about stages in the life cycle of a relationship and another about how people end their relationships. We also considered recent findings about the behaviors and strategies people use to maintain satisfying relationships. And in our final section, on family communication, we looked at gender development, divorce, the family as a system of communication rules, and the variables of cohesion and adaptability to change.

Key Terms

Communication climate
Confirmation
Context
Defensive climate
Defensiveness

Disconfirmation
Empathy
Family
Perceived reciprocity
  of liking

Proximity
Relationship
  disengagement
Relationship
  maintenance

Setting
Supportive climate

Review Questions

1. What are two ways in which proximity influences interpersonal relationships?

2. How is similarity related to attraction?

3. Describe four variables that qualify generalizations about attitude similarity.

4. Summarize some of the recent findings about online dating and singles and their relationships.

5. Explain the difference between communication climate and setting.

6. What are the major differences between confirming and disconfirming response styles? Give some examples.

7. How do supportive and defensive climates of communication differ?

8. In what ways can we define relationships in terms of time?

9. What is the relationship between trust, accuracy, and effectiveness in human relationships?

10. Discuss lying and deception, their frequency and effects, in close relationships.

11. Explain how the dominance/submission (control) dimension of a relationship functions. Give an example.

12. How does the love/hostility (affection) dimension of human relationships function?

13. Identify the building and declining stages of human relationships as defined by Knapp.

14. Describe Duck's four phases of relationship dissolution.

15. Explain the memory structure approach to human relationships.

16. Discuss at least three strategies that have proved most effective for maintaining romantic relationships.

17. Discuss the three most effective strategies for maintaining friendships.

18. Explain at least three defining characteristics of families and what makes family communication distinctive. Discuss gender development and the family.

19. Give three risk factors for divorce in the first ten years of marriage.

20. Discuss two major variables in family communication.

Exercises

1. Have some friends rate a number of topics on a scale such as the one shown here. Then create two paragraphs, one agreeing with the general attitude of the class on each issue—legalizing gay marriage, for example—and one disagreeing. Put a byline on each of the two paragraphs, using fictitious names. Then have your friends indicate the extent of their attraction to the authors. See whether they prefer the person whom they perceive as holding an attitude similar to their own. This would validate the theory that perceived attitude similarity yields attraction.

Strongly agree	Agree	Neither agree nor disagree	Disagree	Strongly disagree
5	4	3	2	1

2. Create a composite description of the kinds of people you are attracted to. What does this composite tell you about yourself?

3. Find ten people in your classes or among your friends who have met someone through the Internet, whether it was a dating service such as *match.com* or *www.personals.aol.com*, a chat room, or some other Web site. Describe how many of these relationships resulted in actual dating, how long they lasted, and how many of the relationships were satisfying. How many people represented themselves honestly when they were online? Do you think such relationships are different in any way from those that begin with face-to-face communication?

4. Describe a situation in which you entered into a relationship on the rebound. Analyze the positive and negative aspects of that relationship. If you were to encounter a similar situation, what, if anything, would you do differently?

5. The next time you observe a disagreement between two people, try to determine whether they are disagreeing on the content level, the relationship level, or both. Relate your observations to two other disagreements that you have experienced, and analyze those disagreements in the same way.

6. Write a paragraph describing someone you trust very much. Then write a description of someone you do not trust. Finally, elaborate on the behaviors that you want to develop and to avoid in building a trusting relationship with someone in the future.

7. Observe five communication events that illustrate five different outcomes of communication (see Chapter 1). Analyze the events in terms of the following questions:

   a. What were the relative frequencies of confirming and disconfirming response styles for each communication event? Does there appear to be any relationship between the type of communication outcome and the predominant response style? If so, why do you think this is the case, and what implications does this have for your own communication behavior?

   b. In which communication events was trust most apparent? Why do you think this was so?

Suggested Readings

Brooks, David. *The Social Animal*. New York: Random House, 2011.

This fascinating book explores human relationships from childhood through all of life's stages.

Coontz, Stephanie. *Marriage, a History: How Love Conquered Marriage*. New York: Viking Penguin, 2006.

An important and well-written history of marriage through the ages and how it has changed in the last 200 years—the shift, in the author's words, from obedience to intimacy.

Duck, Steve. *Relating to Others*, 2nd ed. Buckingham, UK: Open University Press, 1999.

A succinct, well-written discussion of interpersonal relationships by an authority on the subject.

Gladwell, Malcolm. *Blink: The Power of Thinking Without Thinking*. New York: Back Bay Books, 2007.

An informative and entertaining book about the way people make snap judgments. Several of the leading researchers on the subject are discussed. Be sure to read about John Gottman's work on married couples.

Hendrick, Clyde, and Susan S. Hendrick, eds. *Close Relationships: A Sourcebook*. Thousand Oaks, CA: Sage, 2000.

This is a comprehensive handbook on close relationships with contributions by many eminent researchers and theorists in the field. For the advanced student.

Hurley, Robert. *The Decision to Trust*. San Francisco: Jossey-Bass, 2012.

This is a good research-based analysis of how to build trust.

Karbo, Karen. "Friendship: The Laws of Attraction," *Psychology Today* 39 (November/December 2006), pp. 90–95.

A brief popular article on our choices of friends.

Knapp, Mark L., and Anita L. Vangelisti. *Interpersonal Communication and Human Relationships*, 5th ed. Newton, MA: Allyn & Bacon, 2004.

The authors analyze communication patterns in developing and declining relationships as well as the strategies and behaviors people use to maintain satisfying relationships.

My Big Fat Greek Wedding

A film about two young people of very different cultures who fall in love and decide to marry. The contrasts in family styles and expectations make for rich, good-natured comedy.

 # For Supplementary Information

Log onto the Online Learning Center at *www.mhhe.com/tubbshc13e*.

PART TWO

Contexts

9

Interpersonal Communication

Chapter Objectives

After reading this chapter, you should be able to:

1. Explain the concepts of norms, enacted roles, and role conflict and give examples of each. Discuss the effects of our expectations on close relationships.
2. Identify four ways to assess the quality of an interpersonal relationship.
3. Explain the concept of the Johari window. Give several reasons for self-disclosure and reluctance to disclose. Discuss self-disclosure and self-presentation in Internet dating. Explain when self-disclosure is appropriate.
4. Discuss the concepts of attachment styles in romantic relationships and unreciprocated love.
5. Discuss affiliation and commitment in interpersonal communication, marriage, and cohabitation and the theory about love styles.
6. State the relationship between needs for affiliation and dominance and explain how status affects interpersonal communication.
7. Discuss dominance, status, and power in interpersonal relationships and explain the four proposed bases of gendered power.
8. Explain the differences between assertive, nonassertive, and aggressive behaviors.

THE SOCIAL SETTING

Interpersonal communication most often occurs between two people. It is the most intense context of communication. It may also involve a certain closeness between the two parties. Stewart (2012) defines it this way: "The term interpersonal communication labels the kind of communication that happens when the people involved talk and listen in ways that maximize the presence of the personal" (p. 37). Interpersonal communication occurs along a continuum from extremely close between longtime lovers at one extreme, to casual friends and work colleagues in the middle, to exchanges with taxi drivers or sales clerks at the impersonal end of the continuum (DeVito, 2009, p. 5). No two people, no matter how intense their relationship, live totally untouched by the rules and expectations of society. As their relationship evolves, they also develop a kind of society in miniature, a two-person social system with some of its own rules and expectations, its own rewards and punishments.

The Marriage Killer

What do you think has the most toxic effect on marriages? Is it arguments over money, or sex, or the children? The answer turns out to be none of the above.

According to Dr. Howard Markman at the University of Denver, the answer is nagging, defined as "the interaction in which one person repeatedly makes a request, the other person repeatedly ignores it and both become increasingly annoyed." His conclusion is based on 30 years of research on married couples (Markman et al., 2010). Both parties can be a nag, but nags are more often women. They usually feel more responsible for managing the home and family, and they are usually more sensitive to early warning signs of a problem in the relationship. Men who are nagged often feel as if they are being scolded by their mother and retreat, rather than try to address this interpersonal communication problem. Couples eventually start arguing about the nagging rather than about the subjects that caused the problem in the first place. This eventually can lead to divorce. Five years into the marriage, couples who become unhappy had 20 percent more negative communication patterns such as nagging and a decrease of 12 percent of positive communication. Markman says, "Nagging is the enemy of love, if allowed to persist" (Bernstein, 2012, p. D2). Fortunately, if the couples develop new interpersonal communication skills, they can learn to stop the nagging.

Here are some recommendations for reducing nagging:

1. **Calm down.** Both parties need to admit they have a problem and focus on their communication through "Meta-communication," that is, communicating about their communication. Agree that both parties need to be responsible for keeping the relationship healthy.

2. **Discuss the reasons.** For example, he can say that he feels like he is being scolded by his mother. She can say that when he doesn't respond, it feels like he doesn't love her.

3. **Use "I messages."** Instead of saying, "You never pay the bills on time," you can say, "I am concerned about our finances, and if we pay our bills on time, we can avoid paying late fees, which is what we both want."

4. **Be patient.** Sometimes the light bulb doesn't have to be changed right that minute. Give him a reasonable amount of time to comply with your request.

5. **Set a time frame.** Let him tell you when he thinks it would be a good time to get it done. Also, he can take the initiative to look for things that need to be done and do them without being asked.

6. **Encourage.** Try to catch each other doing something you like and encourage it with a hug or kiss or going out for fun, or some other mutually enjoyable activity. (Bernstein, 2012, p. D2)

Improving interpersonal skills can go a long way toward building a long-lasting and happy marriage. Remember, it is not so much finding the right partner, as it is *being* the right partner.

Norms

The Office is a television show that documents the exploits of a paper supply company in Scranton, Pennsylvania. Head chief Michael Scott is a harmlessly deluded and ignorantly insensitive boss who cares about the welfare of his employees, but also tries to put his own spin on company policy by breaking current social norms. The following excerpt is from one such episode where social norms are irrelevant to Scott.

MICHAEL SCOTT: Go ahead, punch me.

JIM HALPERT: Can't. Just got a manicure.

MICHAEL SCOTT: Oh, queer!

[*remembers he's on camera*]

MICHAEL SCOTT: . . . eye. Queer Eye. That's a good show. Important show.

As suggested in Chapter 4, **norms** are *rules, whether implicit or explicit, about behavior,* rules from which we develop certain expectations about how people will act. We have norms for sex, eating, visiting, grading exams, tipping, childrearing— in fact, for every aspect of human life. Even two people meeting for the first time follow norms as to appropriate communication behaviors: "There are rules for taking and terminating a turn at talking; there are norms synchronizing the process of eyeing the speaker and being eyed by him; there is an etiquette for initiating an encounter and bringing it to an end" (Goffman, 1972).

When you and I first meet, each of us already has a great many expectations (however misguided) about how the other will behave. As we get to know one another, we may also establish some norms of our own. When dating, for example, a couple decides what are acceptable or unacceptable behaviors concerning a number of things, such as places to go, topics of conversation, sexual activity, and so on.

In general, certain relationships seem to establish more norms than others. One team of researchers reports that the frequency with which norms are established is linked to the *disruptive power* each person has over the other—that is, *the power one person has to keep the other from doing what he or she wants to do.* In some relationships, one person has much more disruptive power than the other. When both have high disruptive power, they tend to establish a greater number of normative agreements—perhaps because both know that overuse of their power can destroy the relationship. When disagreements between two people are common, normative agreements often reduce the level and frequency of conflict. If Matt always prefers watching football and basketball and Stephanie always wants to go to the movies, they can decide to alternate these activities. If Stephanie has greater disruptive power than Matt, they may end up going to the movies most of the time. Either arrangement is a normative agreement.

Norms are guidelines that limit and direct behavior. We accept them because they allow us to establish standard operating procedures—ground rules, if you will—that make the behavior of others more predictable and decrease the need for communicating about that behavior. If a married couple reaches an agreement about where to spend Christmas and Easter holidays each year or about who handles the finances, there is no need to renegotiate these decisions repeatedly.

Not all normative agreements are rewarding. Some are inappropriate. Some restrict communication in an unhealthy way. Others are too rigid. For example, if a normative agreement exists between father and son that the son will never question the father's judgments or decisions, the son may forfeit his own good judgment simply because it conflicts with his father's opinion. Norms can best serve us if we know that they exist and can periodically evaluate their appropriateness.

Roles

Child-parent, student-teacher, lover-lover, friend-friend, husband-wife, player-coach, patient-doctor, employee-supervisor, grandparent-grandchild. These are just a sampling of the many sets of roles possible within a two-person relationship. The term "role" is unsettling. Actors play roles, and you might be wondering what roles have to do with human communication—especially two-person communication—in which, ideally, communication is based on mutual trust, not game-playing. Roles relate to the norms we've just been talking about. In any given culture, some norms apply to all members and others apply to only some members. A **role** is simply *a set of norms that applies to a specific subclass within the society.* Each of us assumes multiple roles. Yet, in assuming them, we do not become automatons, nor do we necessarily sacrifice our individuality.

Expected versus Enacted Roles

A person's expected and enacted roles are often quite different. A parent is expected to minister to the needs of the child, to provide financial support, and so on. But the enacted role of parent may in fact be quite different. For example, one man might view the role of father as a stern disciplinarian, another as a completely permissive companion, another as a firm but loving teacher.

How would you respond to the following questions?

1. I prefer one-on-one conversations to group activities.
2. People tell me that I'm a good listener.
3. I'm not a big risk-taker.
4. I tend to think before I speak.
5. I often prefer to express myself in writing. (Cain, 2012, p. 13)

If you answered yes to these questions, you may be somewhat more of an introvert than an extrovert. Introverts and extroverts differ on the amount of stimulation that they need to function well. Introverts feel more comfortable with less stimulation, such as enjoying a quiet conversation with a good friend, solving a crossword puzzle, or reading a book. Extroverts prefer the extra "buzz" that comes from activities like meeting new people at parties, driving fast, and listening to loud music. Research has shown that extroverts get more stimulation of the "pleasure center" in the brain, called the amygdala, than introverts. The neurons in that part of the "primitive brain" send their signal through a neurotransmitter chemical called dopamine. Extroverts' dopamine pathways seem to be more active than those of introverts. Dopamine even stimulates the reward center of the brain *in anticipation of pleasures*, and it drives extroverts

"to go after rewards like sex, chocolate, money and status" (Cain, 2012, p. 160). Introverts have a more highly developed "modern brain" that tells us to slow down and think it through before acting. If you are either one of these types, it is very likely that you have had some challenges communicating interpersonally with a person of the other type. On the other hand, these two types complement each other quite nicely, since they each have some of what the other person lacks.

For example, in Montgomery, Alabama in December 1955, Rosa Parks refused to give up her seat to a white person on a bus simply because she was black. Her style was very quiet and introverted. However, when Dr. Martin Luther King spoke later on her behalf he said, "There comes a time that people get tired of being trampled over by the iron feet of oppression. There comes a time when people get tired of being pushed out of the glittering sunlight of life's July and left standing amidst the piercing chill of an Alpine November." When the introvert Rosa Parks joined the extrovert Dr. Martin Luther King, together they formed a partnership that launched a 381-day bus boycott that changed the course of American history (Cain, 2012, p. 2).

Based on: Susan Cain, *Quiet: The Power of Introverts in a World That Can't Stop Talking*. New York: Crown Publishers, 2012.

Granted, we "enact" roles. We shall not say, however, that we are actors in a completely theatrical sense: Some roles are more central to us than others. Thus the intensity with which a person takes on various roles differs: Some will be enacted casually, with little or no involvement, and others with great commitment. When we enact a role with any measure of intensity, we communicate from within that role—that is, we take a certain stance. We also internalize certain expectations about how we should respond and how other people should respond to us. ("How dare you talk to your mother that way?" asks the outraged mother.) Most communication takes place within the boundaries of these expectations (see Box 9.1).

Of course, we are more comfortable in some roles than in others. Usually the roles we don't enjoy playing are those that create conflict. Role conflict, and the misunderstandings to which it gives rise, illustrate the interdependence of role, self-concept, and communication. Let's look at two types of role conflict, both of which tend to create problems in communication.

Interrole Conflict

A person is likely to experience **interrole conflict** when *occupying two (or more) roles that entail contradictory expectations about a given behavior.* Suppose that while you are proctoring an exam, you see a friend cheating during the test. As a proctor, you are obliged to report the cheating. As a friend, you feel that loyalty demands overlooking what you've just seen. The options in this case seem clear. The demands of each role are known. They conflict, and one must be chosen over the other.

Intrarole Conflict

An **intrarole conflict** presents a different set of problems; it involves *contradictory expectations concerning a single role.* For example, Iyesha and Marie, two friends who are close and very supportive of each other, often discuss personal problems. Iyesha believes that Marie is making a big mistake by dropping out of school and moving in with an old boyfriend, that Marie is just compounding her problem, and that she very much needs counseling. As a friend, Iyesha sees herself primarily as a listener, someone who does not interfere but allows the other person to clarify her feelings. She also thinks that friends should be truthful, but she is afraid of being intrusive or meddling. She is not at all certain how she should respond. Questions such as these about appropriate behaviors and boundaries in given roles have to do with intrarole conflict.

ASSESSING THE QUALITY OF AN INTERPERSONAL RELATIONSHIP

Suppose you were to keep a journal for a week and record all your interactions with a romantic partner or same-sex friend. A recent study of close relationships (Emmers-Sommer, 2004) asked people to do just that. The researcher was interested in communication quality and quantity and how they were related to intimacy and satisfaction. She found that communication quality rather than quantity was more important for both satisfaction and intimacy in a relationship, though the number of exchanges between two people—their total time face-to-face—was also important for satisfaction. Although, as found in earlier research, the actual amount of time that two people spend together can be related to their satisfaction, intimacy in long-distance relationships does not seem to suffer as a result of less frequent contact.

Most, if not all, of our qualitatively high relationships involve only two people. In distinguishing interpersonal—that is, high-quality—from noninterpersonal—that is, low-quality—relationships, Miller and Steinberg (1975) were the first to introduce four important concepts:

In qualitatively high relationships, information about the other person is primarily psychological rather than cultural and sociological. Most cultural and sociological information is easy to come by. It includes the other person's sex, age, occupation, group memberships—in other words, information accessible to most people, even without knowing the other. But for me to have psychological information about you—to know what your likes and dislikes are, or your goals or perhaps your fears—the two of us must engage in a relationship.

Rules for that relationship are developed by the two people involved rather than being rules set by tradition. For example, our relationship may be such that although it's usually expected that a visitor calls before coming to someone's apartment, you may come to mine whenever you like—and without calling. You may open the refrigerator and help yourself. You may phone me even in the middle of the night. And you may always use my car. Remember, each interpersonal relationship establishes different rules, but they are individual rather than traditional rules.

The roles in a high-quality relationship are defined primarily by personal characteristics rather than by situation. For example, Ellen may always take care of bills, correspondence, and arranging for house repairs because Cliff, her husband, hates doing these things. In turn, he may do the weekly shopping and all the vacuuming because they agree that he is more efficient at both.

Emphasis in a qualitatively high relationship is on individual choices rather than on group choices. We shall see the importance of individual choices and psychological information—that is, knowledge of personal attitudes and beliefs, highly individualized behavior, and so on—as we discuss self-disclosure, one of several variables affecting relationship quality.

Remember that the concept of quality applies to all two-person relationships, not just intimate ones. Thus many of the variables to be examined here also have an impact on more casual relationships (power, for example, can be as much a factor in your work relationships as it is in your marriage). The first variable we shall consider is self-disclosure.

Self-Disclosure

One of the amazing things about the Internet is the degree to which people disclose themselves. On Facebook and MySpace, people reveal quite intimate details about themselves, apparently not realizing that there may be predators out there looking for potential victims. Some details revealed by young teens may even be read years later by potential employers screening candidates for a job. Computer mediated communication (CMC) is quite different from face-to-face communication between two parties. See for example Stewart (2012), Chapter 3. Self-disclosure is usually intended for the interpersonal communication context.

We disclose a great deal about ourselves through our facial expression, posture, clothing, tone of voice, and countless other nonverbal cues, though much of that behavior is unintentional. But **self-disclosure** as we use the term here is *intentionally* *making known information about oneself.* Not only is it an integral part of two-person communication, it occurs more often in this context than in any other kind of communication.

In one study that paired young men and women who were meeting for the first time (Clark et al., 2004) the more a person disclosed in the conversation, the more favorably he or she was rated in social attractiveness and positive qualities. What's especially interesting is that this was true for both men and women—and both men and women *thought* that they would be liked more if they disclosed more.

Self-disclosure is an attempt to let authenticity enter our social relationships, and it is often linked with both mental health and self-concept development:

Self-disclosure, depending on reactions of relationship partners, . . . plays an important role in validating self-worth and personal identity. (Greene et al., 2006, p. 409)

"I have known people," writes Jourard (1964), one of the foremost early researchers on self-disclosure, "who would rather die than become known . . . When I say that self-disclosure is a symptom of personality health, what I mean really is that a person who displays many of the other characteristics that betoken healthy personality . . . will also display the ability to make himself fully known to at least one other significant human being" (p. 24).

A variety of studies link self-disclosure with intimacy and marital satisfaction (Chelune et al., 1984). In fact, one analysis of disclosure studies (Dindia, 2002) confirms that self-disclosure causes liking, liking causes self-disclosure, and that self-disclosure is reciprocal.

The Johari Window

One of the most innovative models for conceptualizing levels of awareness and self-disclosure in human communication is the **Johari window** (Luft, 1969). ("Johari" derives from the first names of the two psychologists who developed it, Joseph Luft and Harry Ingram.) Essentially, the model offers a way of looking at the interdependence of intrapersonal and interpersonal affairs. The illustration in Figure 9.1 represents you as you relate to other human beings by four quadrants—in effect, four panes of a single window. The size of each quadrant or pane is determined by awareness, by yourself and by others, of your behavior, feelings, and motivations—and the degree to which this information is shared. Unlike most windowpanes, those of the Johari window sometimes change in size.

Each of you may be described by a Johari window. Quadrant 1, the *open quadrant,* will reflect your general openness to the world, your willingness to be known. It comprises *all aspects of yourself known to you and to others.* This quadrant is the basis for most two-person communication.

By contrast, quadrant 2, the *blind quadrant,* consists of *all the things about yourself that other people perceive but that are not accessible to you.* Perhaps you tend to monopolize conversation unwittingly, or you think of yourself as quite a wit but your friends find your humor heavy-handed. Then again you might feel quite confident and yet have several nervous mannerisms that others are aware of but you

Figure 9.1 *The Johari Window*

	KNOWN TO SELF	NOT KNOWN TO SELF
KNOWN TO OTHERS	Open 1	Blind 2
NOT KNOWN TO OTHERS	Hidden 3	Unknown 4

Source: From *Group Processes: An Introduction to Group Dynamics,* 3rd ed., by Joseph Luft, 1984. Reproduced with permission of The McGraw-Hill Companies.

are not. The blind quadrant could contain any of the unintentional communicative stimuli mentioned in Chapter 1.

In quadrant 3, the *hidden quadrant,* you are the one who exercises discretion. This quadrant is made up of *all the things you prefer not to disclose to someone else,* whether they concern you or other people: your salary, your parents' divorce, your feelings about your roommate's closest friends, your overdue bills, and so on. In short, this quadrant represents your attempts to limit input or information about yourself.

The last pane, quadrant 4, is the *unknown quadrant.* The blind quadrant, quadrant 2, is unknown to you though known to others. The hidden quadrant is unknown to others but known to you. Quadrant 4 is *completely unknown. It represents everything about yourself that has never been explored, either by you or by other people*—all your untapped resources, all your potential for personal growth. You can only infer that it exists or confirm its existence in retrospect.

Configurations of the Johari window depend upon one's interaction style. Thus Dan, who is unwilling to let business colleagues or even friends learn much about him, will have a very small open area (quadrant 1) and therefore a large hidden area (quadrant 3). His brother Kirk, who is very willing to disclose information but cannot receive feedback, will have a large open area (quadrant 1) and a large blind area (quadrant 2). Numerous configurations are possible.

The four quadrants of the Johari window are interdependent: a change in one quadrant will affect others. As you disclose something from the hidden quadrant, for example, you make it part of the open quadrant; you enlarge it and reduce the size of the hidden quadrant. Should friends tell you about your nervous mannerisms, this information becomes part of the open quadrant, with a corresponding shrinkage of the blind quadrant. Such change is not always desirable. Sometimes,

Figure 9.2   *An Improved Johari Window*

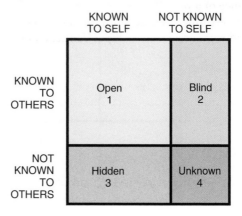

for example, telling a person that he or she seems nervous only makes him or her more ill at ease. Because inappropriate disclosure of a feeling or perception about another can be damaging, your friends will need to use some discretion in the feedback they give you about quadrant 2.

Basically, however, Luft proposes that it is rewarding and satisfying to enlarge the open quadrant—that is, not only to learn more about yourself and thus gain insight but also to reveal information about yourself so that others will know you better too. He also believes that greater knowledge of self in relation to others will result in greater self-esteem and self-acceptance. If you can learn more about yourself and others, you can change the shape of your own Johari window. An improved window might look something like the one in Figure 9.2.

Trust and Reciprocity

Authentic self-disclosure—whether between acquaintances, co-workers, friends, or lovers—is not one-sided: It tends to be reciprocal. It is an exchange process that can and often does prompt greater disclosure from the other person and often results in more positive feelings between the two. The classic work of Jourard (1979) and others confirms this sequence of behavior: *When one person discloses something about himself or herself to another, he or she tends to elicit a reciprocal level of openness in the second person.* Jourard calls the pattern the **dyadic effect.** Many studies support Jourard's principle: "One person's intimate disclosure encourages intimate disclosure by the listener, and superficial disclosure encourages superficial disclosure in return" (Derlega et al., 1987, p. 174).

Reciprocal self-disclosure tends to be gradual. And it seems to take place only after the two people have reached a basic level of trust (Dindia, 1996). Thus, we expect that early in a relationship disclosures will be less intimate and that as mutual trust is established, they will become more revealing. In the intensifying stage of a relationship, for example, there are often a great number of self-disclosures.

When relationships are going well, people continually match their cycles of openness. This evidence of a periodic ebb and flow "between openness and closedness, revelation and restraint" is true both for new acquaintanceships and for intact friendships and romantic relationships. VanLear's (1991) studies show that acquaintances "match the amplitude of their cycles to fit those of their partners," synchronizing the timing of cycles. In friendships and romantic relationships, partners actually perceive their own cycles of openness and those of the other person as being timed. This mutuality seems to be linked with satisfaction. If a relationship begins to deteriorate and satisfaction decreases, these cycles show increasing fluctuations.

From a dialectical perspective, self-disclosure is not a single event; "it is a dynamic, continuous, and circular process." And you can never fully reveal yourself. Self-disclosure is "a life-long/relationship-long process . . . [one] that changes as individuals and relationships change" (Dindia, 2000, pp. 147, 150).

To Reveal or Conceal

You choose to be open with another person for many different reasons. It may be because something very good has happened to you (a new job) or is troubling you (a financial problem or an imminent divorce). You may wish to clarify experiences for yourself (discussing a recent family argument might be almost therapeutic), or you may be trying to get the other person to reciprocate by also talking. At times, you use selective self-disclosure to create an impression of yourself that you would like the other person to have—for example, at a party Jake may let Nicole know that he's unhappily married because he finds himself attracted to her.

Indeed, self-disclosure can have many risks, and when we avoid disclosing, one of the primary reasons may be that we fear that information may be used against us. Some research on relationship dialectics (Dindia, 2000) has focused on the disclosure of information that is intimate, private, or risky—such as information about AIDS, sexual abuse, and homosexuality. For example, someone who is gay might reveal, then conceal, then reveal his homosexuality to others. Consider this comment:

> Coming out for me has basically moved from wanting to tell everybody, to not wanting to tell anybody, to kind of going in between those two.

Another participant said:

> I know that I've had to find a sense of equilibrium. I don't feel comfortable wearing a sign that says "I'm gay." . . . But I am becoming less tolerant as time goes on, with the "game playing" that I did in my head for a lot of years. (Dindia, 2000, p. 158)

Other reasons for not disclosing information include fear of projecting a negative image, losing control over the other person or the situation, not wanting to seem like an exhibitionist, and not wanting to commit oneself. Sometimes fear of rejection keeps us from disclosing essential aspects of ourselves, but this very with-holding makes it impossible to be known.

Self-Disclosure and Self-Presentation in Internet Dating

Given that self-disclosure is an important determinant of how people develop their relationships, how does it figure in online dating? While some theorists maintain that the more limited cues and information disclosed online tend to limit sharing and intimacy, other communication scholars believe that the Internet's anonymity actually intensifies the developing intimacy between people.

How would you respond to the following statements about Internet dating?

I am always honest in my self-disclosures to those I meet online.

The things I reveal about myself to those I meet online are always accurate reflections of who I really am.

I often disclose negative things about myself to those I meet online.

On the whole, my disclosures about myself to those I meet online are more positive than negative.

When I reveal my feelings about myself to those I meet online, I consciously intend to do so. (selected from Gibbs et al., 2006, p. 173; italics in original)

One study of self-disclosure and Internet dating using these and other test questions finds that when people who go online are interested in having a long-term relationship that they expect will become face-to-face, they disclose more and are more honest. Their disclosures tend to be intentional, offered consciously because it's anticipated that as the relationship develops it is better to be more candid. Interestingly, such disclosures aren't always more positive—and the effect of greater honesty is not always positive either (Gibbs et al., 2006, p. 169). In this study it was experience in dating online that turned out to be the most important predictor of how successful people thought themselves to be.

"What Makes You Click?" (Hitsch, Hortaçsu, and Ariely, 2005), another analysis of online dating, tracked the records of 23,000 users of an online dating service on which people posted their profiles. The authors of *Freakonomics* discuss some revealing aspects of this study—how people tend to present themselves online:

> More than 4 percent of the online daters claimed to earn more than $200,000 a year, whereas fewer than 1 percent of typical Internet users actually earn that much, suggesting that three of the four big earners were exaggerating. Male and female users typically reported that they are an inch taller than the national average. As for weight, the men were in line with the national average, but the women typically said they weighed about twenty pounds less than the national average.
>
> Most impressively, fully 72 percent of the women claimed "above average" looks, including 24 percent claiming "very good looks." The online men too were

gorgeous: 68 percent called themselves "above average," including 19 percent with "very good looks." This leaves only about 30 percent of the users with "average" looks, including a paltry 1 percent with "less than average" looks— which suggests the typical online dater is either a fabulist, narcissist, or simply resistant to the meaning of "average." (Levitt and Dubner, 2006, pp. 75–76).

A more recent study, with the clever title, "Liar, Liar, Hard Drive on Fire," found, as you might expect, that 70 percent of those surveyed said that they lied about their achievements and other attributes. But they were found to lie five times as much in instant messages and e-mails with same-sex friends than in face-to-face interactions (Zimbler and Feldman, 2011).

When Is Self-Disclosure Appropriate?

Self-disclosure is often an attempt to let authenticity enter our social relationships. At times it is an attempt to emphasize how we enact our roles rather than how others expect us to enact them. It may even be an attempt to step out of a role entirely. When does it work? When does it improve human relationships?

Fujishin (2000) offers the following guidelines for self-disclosure that is intended to create more effective and intimate communication:

1. Disclose only information you want to share. You have a choice in what you disclose to others.
2. Self-disclosure involves risk. Be careful in what you select to disclose.
3. Self-disclosure should be reciprocal. Unbalanced relationships occur when one person listens to the other's disclosures.
4. Self-disclosure should not be coerced. No relationship should be based on coercion or manipulation.
5. Self-disclosure always results in deeper understanding. Disclosure provides a deeper understanding of others.
6. Keep self-disclosure confidential. Nothing ends disclosure more quickly than breaking confidentiality.

Self-disclosure can be used to create greater intimacy, connection, and understanding in a relationship (pp. 42–43).

By applying these standards to any of your attempts at self-disclosure that didn't come off, you may be able to determine what went wrong.

Attachment Styles

Although a person's need for intimacy fluctuates in any close relationship, there are people who consistently fear it. Some researchers believe that our patterns and capacities for forming and maintaining intimate relationships are to some degree shaped by the quality of our first emotional bond (Feeney et al., 2000). Classic theory by John Bowlby (1973) focused on the early attachment bond between an infant and its mother or primary caretaker. Bowlby suggested that an infant learns to feel safe and secure enough to explore its environment when it makes a successful attachment to its mother. Thus, when the mother is nurturant, warm, and responsive, the infant learns to feel comfortable counting on other people, secure in the knowledge that its needs will be met. When the mother is cold, rejecting, or inconsistent, the infant learns not to rely on others for its support or comfort; instead, it tends to withdraw or to become exceptionally demanding. Studies of how an infant reacts when being separated from and then reunited with its mother (as opposed to a stranger) identified three different **attachment styles:** secure, avoidant, and anxious-ambivalent.

Studies of adults by Hazan and Shaver (1987, 1994) suggested that in later life attachment style also affects our romantic relationships. Some of their data were based on how subjects described themselves. Each of the three major attachment styles reflects our beliefs and expectancies about close relationships:

Secure: Secure people are comfortable with intimacy and dependence. They describe their close relationships as characterized by love, trust, and happiness. Secure people are easy to know and have few self-doubts. They describe their relationships with their parents as warm.

Avoidant: Closeness makes avoidant people uncomfortable. They fear the intimacy of close relationships and find it difficult to depend on others. They are not very accepting of romantic partners and don't view most of their love relationships as long-lasting, and the relationships they enter tend to decline in intensity. Avoidant people describe their mothers as cold and rejecting. Some researchers (Bartholomew, 1990) distinguish between fearful avoidance, trying to protect oneself from hurt or rejection, and dismissive avoidance, acting defensively by denying one's need for close relationships.

Anxious-Ambivalent: Although they yearn for extremely close relationships, anxious-ambivalent people have many fears about being abandoned and unloved. They are troubled by self-doubt and may feel misunderstood. Their great need for intimacy often drives others away. Preoccupied with their love relationships, they tend to be emotionally volatile. (Feeney et al., 2000, p. 185)

In one study of marital quality among newly married couples, similarity in attachment characteristics was most accurate in predicting marital satisfaction—stronger than a couple's similarity in personality or in attitude (Luo and Klohnen, 2005).

Attachment style also plays a significant role in nonverbal communication. For example, a person who has an anxious attachment style tends to have less fluent conversation and less composure when he or she is with a romantic partner (Guerrero and Floyd, 2006, p. 153). One communication scholar explains:

Overall, attachment security seems to act as a filter and affect both the encoding and the decoding of nonverbal behavior in close relationships. Highly anxious individuals, especially males, seem to have a general decoding deficit, to be less nonverbally expressive than other partners, and to engage in more avoidance. Thus, highly anxious individuals are likely to have difficulty in maintaining close relationships. (Noller, 2006, p. 414)

What of sexual passion and attachment style? Through an Internet survey of almost 2,000 people, researchers found that an avoidant attachment style is linked to "less overall passion and greater loss of passion over time," while sexual passion was greatest over time in those who had an anxiety-linked attachment style (Davis et al., 2004, p. 1,088). Sexual passion here does not necessarily mean that the relationship was functional.

What makes for love that is not reciprocated? We all know people who tend to fall in love with people who do not feel the same way about them. You might have a friend to whom this happens over and over. One recent study identified three variables that seem to predict how intense unrequited love will be. First, and most significant, is the "perceived desirability of the partner and the relationship." The second is especially interesting: how desirable does the person perceive "the state of being in love [to be], whether reciprocated or not." There are people who feel that being in love is all that matters, that if they are not in love they are not fully alive. Third in importance is "mistakenly believing at the outset that the other [person] would reciprocate the love" (Aron et al., 2006, p. 605).

Affiliation and Commitment

Another important variable of relationship quality and a significant predictor of how two people will interact is the strength of their affiliative needs. The *need for affiliation* may be seen as a continuum from highly affiliative to antisocial behavior. The high affiliater, who prefers being with others to being alone, enjoys and seeks out companionship. We describe such a person as friendly, gregarious, and generally sociable. The person who is low in the need for affiliation probably prefers being alone and has much less desire for companionship. Since this behavior is not very reinforcing to other people, the low affiliater is usually described as unfriendly or unsociable.

Most of us place ourselves somewhere between the two extremes on this continuum. Since interpersonal communication is potentially the most intimate, those of us with strong needs for affiliation seem to be the most willing to make the commitment it requires. **Commitment,** as we use the term here, is *the resolve to continue in a relationship indefinitely and to make the efforts necessary to ensure that it will continue.*

You may feel committed to someone and at the same time feel the need to be independent. Or you may express your commitment verbally and yet not act on it (Duck, 1999, p. 44). This pull between commitment and autonomy exists even in very close relationships, where it may not be acknowledged. Think of the last-minute jitters some people get right before their wedding.

Marriage and Cohabitation

For many the absolute commitment to another human being demanded by marriage is frightening or at best constraining. Today half the marriages in this country end in divorce, and it is still young people who are granted over half the divorces. More couples marry later though they have sex earlier; and more than half of all couples live together before they marry. Some men and women have lived with several partners. Current research shows that between 1960 and 2010, a major shift took place in American demographics and psychographics. Charles Murray (2012a) writes that among white college graduates, the marriage rate fell from 94 percent in 1960 to 83 percent in 2010. However, marriage rates of blue-collar whites with no degree higher than a high-school diploma and working in a low-skill service job fell from 84 percent to just 48 percent in 2010 (Murray, 2012a, p. C2; Murray, 2012b). The birth rate to unwed mothers has also changed during this time from 7 percent of American children in the 1960s to 40 percent by 2010. Among African Americans, that number has jumped to 70 percent of children born to unwed mothers (Romney, 2010, p. 266). In addition, "Compared with children living with married parents, children living with single mothers are ten times more likely to be physically abused, five times more likely to be poor, three times more likely to use cocaine, twice as likely to end up in jail, and twice as likely to be in the bottom of their class at school" (Romney, 2010, p. 266). These changes predict significantly greater interpersonal communication challenges for modern families.

In Chapter 2 we noted the connection between optimism and self-fulfilling prophecy. Among romantic partners, those with an optimistic outlook tended to be more satisfied in their romantic relationships. This was the case even during a conflict, with conflict partners feeling that after a week their conflicts were more successfully resolved. In a follow-up a year later the researchers found that the optimism of the male partner was a reliable predictor of the status of the relationship (Srivastava et al., 2006).

Satisfaction with relationships is also affected by self-esteem. One group of researchers recently found that people with low self-esteem, particularly women, "felt more accepted and loved by their partner on days when their professional lives were marked by success" (Murray et al., 2006, p. 866), much less so when they met with failure in their work lives. "In such ways, the successes and failures in low self-esteem people's outside lives may spill into their relationships" (p. 879).

The rapid increase in the number of unmarried couples who are living together has been well documented not only in the United States but in many other countries as well. For many couples, living together is a trial marriage of sorts, a way of getting to know each other well enough to find out whether a marriage would work. According to the 2000 Census, in the United States the number of unmarried couples living together increased tenfold between 1960 and 2000, and it increased by 72 percent from 1990 to 2000.

Yet some research shows a negative relationship between cohabitation and marital stability, with the divorce rate for couples who had lived together before marriage significantly higher than for couples who had not. Apparently this is not always the case. Researchers who compared cohabitation in 16 European countries found that stability varied significantly from one country to another. There was less stability, more risk of divorce only in countries where people who cohabited before marrying were a small minority or a large majority (Liefbroer and Dourleijn, 2006, p. 203).

But a look at the United States is instructive. For example, over a 10-year-period (1990–2000) in New York City, there was a 27 percent increase in the number of unmarried heterosexual couples who lived together. Perhaps because of the ease with which cohabiting couples can leave each other, half of such relationships tend to break up within a period of two years, and within five years only 10 percent of unmarried couples remain together (Fung, 2006, p. 27).

The lingering question is why this should be so, since living together would presumably allow people to learn more information about each other and more time to resolve possible conflicts.

According to Knapp's theory (see Chapter 8), if a relationship reaches the integrating stage, both people must intensify at least some aspects of their personalities and minimize others. If a relationship goes on to the bonding stage, that commitment is in some sense formalized. In a romantic relationship, the commitment might be the announcement that the couple is dating exclusively, it might be an engagement or a marriage, or it might mean that a couple decide to live together.

There are, of course, people who consistently fear and avoid commitment. One reason may be that previous commitments proved disappointing or constricting. In the television series *Sex and the City,* it was not only the men who feared commitment, it was the women as well. If we think of this tendency in terms of attachment styles, we might describe many as "avoidant." And there are people who have never made a complete commitment to another human being. One psychologist describes the fear of commitment as characterized by "the Dance-Away Lover":

> The Dance-Away's repeated romantic disillusionments are the consequences
> of his discomfort with the intimacy and commitment love entails. The Dance-
> Away Lover is preoccupied with the fear of being trapped. He clings to his
> independence lest, in her eagerness to possess him, someone succeed in sucking
> him into a web of obligations and responsibilities. (Goldstine et al., 1977, p. 27)

Even after making a partial commitment, he or she will later maneuver to avoid intimacy by becoming unavailable—forgetting appointments, working late, withdrawing emotionally, or even withholding sexually.

Matters of the heart are elusive. Throughout history philosophers, poets, and psychologists have theorized about love—and no doubt will continue to do so in the future. Aron and his colleagues discuss seven different theories of romantic love (2006). Here we look at two current theories about love relationships that take into account intimacy, commitment, and other variables we have been discussing.

Love Styles

When you say you love someone, how would you describe your love? Another theory about types of love is seen in the work on *love styles* by Clyde and Susan Hendrick (1986). A questionnaire appears in Table 9.1 (Hendrick et al., 1998). Before you read any further, stop and answer the questions. As you read on, you'll find out how to rate your responses.

Table 9.1   Love Attitudes Questionnaire

At the side of each of the following statements, indicate whether you agree or disagree.

	Agree	Disagree
1. My partner and I have the right physical "chemistry" between us.	___	___
2. I feel that my partner and I were meant for each other.	___	___
3. My partner and I really understand each other.	___	___
4. My partner fits my ideal standards of physical beauty/handsomeness.	___	___
5. I believe that what my partner doesn't know about me won't hurt him/her.	___	___
6. I have sometimes had to keep my partner from finding out about other lovers.	___	___
7. My partner would get upset if he/she knew of some of the things I've done with other people.	___	___
8. I enjoy playing the "game of love" with my partner and a number of other partners.	___	___
9. Our love is the best kind because it grew out of a long friendship.	___	___
10. Our friendship merged gradually into love over time.	___	___
11. Our love is really a deep friendship, not a mysterious, mystical emotion.	___	___
12. Our love relationship is the most satisfying because it developed from a good friendship.	___	___
13. A main consideration in choosing my partner was how he/she would reflect on my family.	___	___
14. An important factor in choosing my partner was whether or not he/she would be a good parent.	___	___
15. One consideration in choosing my partner was how he/she would reflect on my career.	___	___
16. Before getting very involved with my partner, I tried to figure out how compatible his/her hereditary background would be with mine in case we ever had children.	___	___
17. When my partner doesn't pay attention to me, I feel sick all over.	___	___
18. Since I've been in love with my partner, I've had trouble concentrating on anything else.	___	___
19. I cannot relax if I suspect that my partner is with someone else.	___	___
20. If my partner ignores me for a while, I sometimes do stupid things to try to get his/her attention back.	___	___
21. I would rather suffer myself than let my partner suffer.	___	___
22. I cannot be happy unless I place my partner's happiness before my own.	___	___
23. I am usually willing to sacrifice my own wishes to let my partner achieve his/hers.	___	___
24. I would endure all things for the sake of my partner.	___	___

Source: From Clyde Hendrick, Susan S. Hendrick, and Amy Dicke, *Journal of Social and Personal Relationships,* Vol. 15 (2). Reprinted by Permission of SAGE.

This questionnaire—it's actually called the Love Attitudes Scale—is keyed to a set of six love types, or styles, first identified by Lee (1973):

Eros: A passionate love style. This style is marked by intense emotion, a strong erotic component, and a strong commitment to the other person. Initial physical attraction—"love at first sight"—is very common.

Ludus: A game-playing love style. This kind of lover is often manipulative. Justifying deception of one's partner as "playing the field" while having a relationship with someone else are likely to be acceptable behaviors to a ludic lover. It's a type of love that often lacks emotional intensity and commitment.

Storge: A friendship-based love style. It tends to merge love and friendship. Storgic love is down-to-earth, though not passionate. It is committed and tends to be long-lasting.

Pragma: A practical love style. This type of lover makes choices based on rationality and in selecting a partner will focus on matching desired traits.

Mania: A possessive, dependent love style. This type of love often has elements of self-doubt and uncertainty about the other person. Because of their dependence, manic lovers can be very jealous and emotional.

Agape: A selfless, all-giving love. This style of love is altruistic and undemanding. It represents love without strings or qualifications.

Which love style do you think would best characterize your own? Which statements in Table 9.1 did you agree with? The questions you answered are linked to the six love styles described above. For example, agreeing with most or all of statements 1–4 would indicate someone rated high on Eros. Similarly, agreeing with statements about Ludus: 5–8; Storge: 9–12; Pragma: 13–16; Mania: 17–20; or Agape 21–24, would indicate a high rating on that attitude.

You might find that you can't be pinned down to one set of attitudes and that the way you think about love is far more complex. It's also possible that a person's love style will change over time. There's no doubt, though, that new theories about love will continue to emerge.

We spoke in the last chapter of control as a primary dimension of all relationships. It has two poles: dominance/submission. These elements are variables in all two-person relationships, as you will see in the discussion that follows.

Dominance, Status, and Power

Your mother and father have been married for 24 years. Who is the dominant partner? Who has the power? The first question is usually easy to answer. The second may be more difficult. Let's examine the issue of dominance first.

Dominance

Like the need for affiliation, the *need for dominance* can be imagined as a continuum: At one end is the person who always wants control over others; at the other end, the person with an extremely submissive style of communication. The vast majority of us fit somewhere in between.

We know some other things about people with a strong need for dominance. For example, they also tend to have a strong need for achievement. An association also seems to exist between dominance and self-concept: A person with an unfavorable self-concept tends to be submissive rather than dominant. In a dyad one person often defers to the other. This is true not only of friendships and romantic relationships but also of work and classroom situations. For example, the author assigned interpersonal projects to student pairs. One student, let's call him Paul, complained bitterly that Ahmed, his partner, made all the decisions and never let him participate in the planning. Yet each time the two were observed at work, Paul accepted all Ahmed's ideas and directives, making no attempt to express his own point of view. Paul's submissiveness is typical of the person with low self-esteem: unable or afraid to influence others yet resentful of always being the one who is dominated. Oddly enough, the hesitancy itself tends to intensify dominating behavior in others.

When we combine what we know about behaviors associated with the needs for affiliation and dominance (see Table 9.2), we see some of the communication patterns that are possible in an interpersonal relationship as well as in a larger group. Allowing for the uniqueness of each person, we can still make some predictions about how the two will interact if we know something about the strength of their individual needs for affiliation and dominance. Jennifer has a high need for dominance but a low need for affiliation, so we expect her to be analytic, to make

Table 9.2 *Some Behaviors Associated with Needs for Dominance and Affiliation*		
	High Dominance	**Low Dominance**
High Affiliation	Advises Coordinates Directs Initiates Leads	Acquiesces Agrees Assists Cooperates Obliges
Low Affiliation	Analyzes Criticizes Disapproves Judges Resists	Concedes Evades Relinquishes Retreats Withdraws

Source: From *Reaching Out: Interpersonal Effectiveness and Self-Actualization,* 8th ed., by David W. Johnson. Published by Allyn & Bacon, Boston, MA. Copyright © 2003 by Pearson Education. Reprinted by permission of the publisher.

many judgments, to be resistant, and so on; if Mark has a low need for dominance but a high need for affiliation, we expect him to acquiesce much of the time, to co-operate with Jennifer, and so on. But if, like Jennifer, Mark has a high need for dom-inance, there is likely to be conflict between them, or the two will have to work out some satisfactory agreements regulating their behavior—at least for a time. To put it in other terms, they themselves will have to develop rules for their relationship.

Dominance has been studied in research on relationship structure. Phillips and Wood (1983) define three relationship structures. *Complementary structures* are *based on differences between the partners;* one is dominant and the other submis-sive. *Symmetrical structures* are *based on similarities,* as when both partners are dominant or both are submissive. *Parallel structures,* on the other hand, *are based on some combination of complementary and symmetrical interactions;* suppose, for instance, that Javed is dominant and Shayla submissive with respect to finances, their roles reverse with respect to disciplining their two children, and both Javed and Shayla are dominant when it comes to deciding on family vacations.

Parallel structures are *the most flexible* and probably most common because they *enable us to adapt most easily to the demands of new situations.* Although the complementary relationship with the male dominant is seen as "typical," the number of such relationships seems to be declining with the rise of the dual-career marriage and the upswing in women's and minority-group rights. It's still the case, however, that the most rejected relationship is one in which the female is dominant. Some things haven't changed that much.

Status

Whether we like to acknowledge it or not, **status,** *the position of an individual in relation to another or others,* has at least some relationship to the issue of establish-ing control within an interpersonal relationship. "Status," write Knapp and Hall, "often connotes a socially valued quality that a person carries with her or him into different situations, whereas power and dominance are likely to be seen as a person-ality trait . . . in addition to a situational condition" (2002, p. 430). And as we saw in Chapter 4, status is often communicated nonverbally.

Status has marked effects on the form of all communication, no matter how unstructured, and it affects content as well as communication style. There is a good chance the person with higher status will control the topics of conversation as well as the length of the discussion. Higher status may even enable that person to avoid a discussion entirely. If a bank president and a teller are conversing, for example, and the teller asks a question that seems too personal, the bank president will probably respond in a way that makes the teller uncomfortable about pursuing the subject. On the other hand, subordinates sometimes "disclose personal problems to their supervisors, but the reverse does not usually happen. . . . Self-disclosures are most often employed between people of equal status" (Hargie et al., 1987, p. 192).

Perceptions of status are immediately reflected in greetings as well as in forms of address. "Hi" may be permissible for some encounters; "Hello" or

"Good morning" may be more appropriate for others. The higher-status person is often addressed by title and last name ("Good morning, Dr. Jones"), and the lower-status person by first name or even a briefer version of that name ("Hi, Judy"). One sociologist observes that greetings may also affirm a subordinate's willingness to maintain lower status (Goffman, 1972). American military practice, for instance, requires that the subordinate salute first and hold the salute until it is returned by the person of higher rank. Observe people of different status greeting one another and see whether these behavior patterns are borne out by your own experience.

Power

A book on a well-known auction house tells of how its chairman, then in his late fifties, first noticed a young woman who would later become its president and CEO:

> Dede Brooks first came to the attention of Albert Taubman when he walked into a meeting where she was the only woman and asked her for a cup of coffee. "With pleasure," she replied, handing him a sheaf of documents. "And could you please photocopy these for me?" (Lacey, 1998, p. 278)

One definition of **power** is *the capacity to influence the behavior of others and to resist their influence on oneself* (Pfeffer, 2010, p. 6). Identifying one person in a dyad as the more dominant doesn't always explain who wields the power. Power and dominance, as Wilmot (1995) reminds us, are not synonymous:

> One of the more exciting trends in the study of communication is viewing interpersonal power in relational terms. You do not have power—it is given to you by the others with whom you transact. (p. 105)

Wilmot is saying that power has to be granted by one person to the other. If I do not accept your authority, you cannot dominate me. In other words, power has much to do with how we perceive ourselves. Issues about power can occur in all kinds of interpersonal relationships from the most casual to the most intimate—those between landlord and tenant, co-workers, committee members, close friends, parent and child, siblings, and, of course, romantic partners. For a discussion about nonverbal cues of power and dominance, see page 103 in Chapter 4.

Gender and Power   "There is no society," write Pratto and Walker, "in which women have greater power than men." In their survey of research (2004), they propose four bases of gendered power: force, control of resources, control of ideology, and unequal, or asymmetric, obligations. Let's consider them one by one.

> *Force:* Men wield power not only through physical force and emotional violence but also in their social roles. For example, the number of women in military, government, and political life is negligible. As heads of state, lawyers and judges, and law enforcement officials, men far outnumber women.

Control of resources: Social roles that have hierarchic power, as do those just described, also bring greater financial resources and such resources are predominantly held by men. To illustrate the author points out that only 1 to 3 percent of top executives throughout the world and only 16 percent of corporate officers in this country are women. And women who do have high-status positions are paid less than men who hold the same positions. For example, "among U.S. physicians, 21 percent are women, and their median annual salary is $120,000, whereas that of male physicians is $175,000" (p. 248).

Control of ideology: It is, for the most part, men, not women, who through their roles control ideological content and how it is disseminated. This is true not only in religion and politics but also in the mass media where most of the decision makers are men who influence opinion leaders, as we will see in Chapter 15. An unusual moment occurs in the television series *The West Wing* when C. J. Cregg, the White House press secretary, is chosen over her peers, all men, to become the president's new chief of staff. She is clearly seen by the staff as an astonishing choice.

Unequal social obligations: According to gender stereotypes, women are warm and nurturant, suggesting that they are especially suited to caregiving roles. "The obligation to provide care may well constitute the center of the feminine gender role" (p. 25). Yet often it is the obligations to provide care that undercut women's power by taking up so much of their time and limiting both their freedom and financial resources.

Contemporary marriage, many experts agree, is still "an unequal partnership": Research finds that "even wives who earn as much or more than their husbands do not achieve relationship equality"(Steil, 2000, p. 129). Steil argues that equal power between men and women cannot exist because gender roles are still separate. When women commit themselves to working outside the home, there is often no parallel commitment from their husbands to increase the work they do in the house. In family life, two of the primary gendered roles are the roles of provider and nurturer. Even when she earns more money than her husband, a woman usually views the provider role as one that interferes with her role as nurturer. Taking care of the needs of others, especially children, and sometimes parents, comes first. After a couple has children, the power balance tends to shift back to traditional marital roles (McGoldrick, 1999).

Among married couples one of the major power struggles is about money—whose it is, how it will be spent, who decides. One marital therapist writes about discovering "the golden rule: whoever has the gold makes the rules" (Carter and Peters, 1996, p. 65). Sex, and the withholding of it, is another arena of power struggles between couples. And money, because it has great symbolic value, is often equated with caring.

In closing, we look briefly at some behaviors that can promote greater equality in our relationships and increase our sense of self-respect.

Equality and Assertiveness   Concerns about assertiveness surface in many interpersonal relationships, not just in marriage and romantic associations. Your doctor assures you that you do not need an expensive test, but you feel the test is necessary. Your landlord becomes very evasive about returning the security deposit when the lease on your apartment is up; you are getting ready to move and need the money. Your roommate constantly borrows your clothes without permission; you like your roommate but this really bothers you. Your parents are still telling you how to run your life.

When you think about behavior that is assertive, what are your first associations? For some, being called "assertive" has a negative connotation, perhaps because they equate assertiveness with aggression. Those who study assertiveness and conduct workshops on assertive training frame the concept differently. In a popular book on the subject, two psychologists write:

> Assertive behavior promotes equality in human relationships, enabling us to act in our own best interests, to stand up for ourselves without undue anxiety, to express feelings honestly and comfortably, to exercise personal rights without denying the rights of others. (Alberti and Emmons, 2001, p. 36)

Another well-known definition of assertiveness is "standing up for personal rights and expressing thoughts, feelings, and beliefs in direct, honest, and appropriate ways which do not violate another person's rights" (Lange and Jakubowski, cited in Yoshioka, 2000). Notice the word "violate." Assertive behavior is not aggressive. It acknowledges the rights of others and equality in interpersonal relationships.

Many other definitions proposed over the years seem to emphasize similar qualities: self-expression, honesty, directness, firmness. Self-expression as it is used here refers to both verbal and nonverbal communication. It's not only message content—what you say about your thoughts and feelings. It's your tone of voice and other vocal cues (do you whine or speak confidently? do you speak so that you can be heard?); your body positioning; your facial expression, and all the other nonverbal cues we discussed in Chapter 4. Think of how important these qualities would be in honest communication about sex.

Figure 9.3 highlights some of the differences between assertive, aggressive, and nonassertive behaviors—seen from the perspectives of both the sender and receiver. Nonassertive behavior (the sender on the left) is self-denying rather than self-expressive. By allowing other people to make choices for you, you often give up your own goals and desires. Behavior that is assertive (the sender on the right) allows you to be self-expressive, to make your own choices—or at least express those choices—and increase the possibility that you may achieve your own desires and goals. It also involves careful listening to how the other person responds.

Through aggressive behavior, on the other hand, you express your own thoughts and feelings and put forward your own choices—but at the other person's expense. Aggressive or forcing behaviors also include underhanded, passive actions in which you appear to be cooperative or seem to agree, but actually undercut the other person.

Figure 9.3 *What It Means to Be Assertive*

NONASSERTIVE BEHAVIOR	AGGRESSIVE BEHAVIOR	ASSERTIVE BEHAVIOR
Sender	**Sender**	**Sender**
Self-denying	Self-enhancing at expense of another	Self-enhancing
Inhibited		Expressive
Hurt, anxious	Expressive	Feels good about self
Allows others to choose	Chooses for others	Chooses for self
Does not achieve desired goal	Achieves desired goal by hurting others	May achieve desired goal
Receiver	**Receiver**	**Receiver**
Guilty or angry	Self-denying	Self-enhancing
Depreciates sender	Hurt, defensive, humiliated	Expressive
Achieves desired goal at sender's expense	Does not achieve desired goal	May achieve desired goal

Source: From *Your Perfect Right: Assertiveness and Equality in Your Life and Relationships,* 9th ed. Copyright © 2008 by Robert E. Alberti and Michael Emmons. Reproduced for Stewart Tubbs by permission of Impact Publishers, Inc., P.O. Box 6016, Atascadero, CA 93423, USA, www.impactpublishers.com. Further reproduction prohibited.

From the receiver's standpoint, nonassertive behavior elicits a number of responses from sympathy to contempt, impatience, or anger. Ideally, assertive behavior can lead to positive outcomes for both the sender and the receiver. As receivers of aggressive behavior we tend to feel hurt, abused, defensive, or humiliated. Anger, though sometimes suppressed, is often present—and it tends to build.

Despite the promises of assertiveness training and books on assertive behavior, assertive behavior is no guarantee that you will achieve all your goals, but it will make you feel that you are not being victimized.

Nor is assertive behavior appropriate for all situations. As one scholar suggests, the view that assertive behavior is always positive and functional in interpersonal communication may be "somewhat idealized" (Wilson, 1993, p. 56). Alberti and Emmons stress that assertive behavior is behavior "appropriate for the person and situation, not universal." In other words, it is specific to the situation and we must always "weigh the consequences" (Berko et al., 2001, p. 161). Clearly, people sometimes feel that the risks of being assertive in their closest relationships may be too great.

The effectiveness of assertive behavior will depend to a great degree on the relative strength of its rewards and how these stack up against the rewards for nonassertive behavior. Nonassertive behavior allows you to avoid conflict, anxiety, and disapproval. For example, it can be upsetting to stand up to your parents or to insist that you deserve a raise when you get a promotion. On the other hand, the increased feelings of self-respect and the satisfaction of individual needs that are often the result of a more assertive communication style are powerful rewards. As always, a reward has to be defined in terms of the individual.

In addition, a reward is also defined in terms of a given culture or co-culture. Members of various cultures and co-cultures interpret assertiveness very differently (what is assertive to you might be aggressive to me), and this is true for many interpersonal variables, as we will see in the following chapter.

Summary

Interpersonal communication is in many ways a microcosm of all larger groups and thus encompasses many kinds of relationships, from the most casual to the most intimate and long lasting. Our first major topic was the social setting within which interpersonal communication must be viewed. Members of a relationship are strongly influenced by the norms they have already adopted, and they also establish some normative agreements of their own as they interact. In addition, the roles they enact affect how they will respond to each other; we also looked at role expectations as they affect close relationships. We examined some consequences of conflicts within and between roles.

Because quality is so frequently an issue in assessing relationships, we suggested several measures of high quality. We first discussed the importance of self-disclosure, its relationship to trust, and the reasons people choose to self-disclose or to avoid disclosures. We also discussed self-disclosure and self-presentation in online dating, and also looked at a theory about attachment styles and unreciprocated love.

Affiliative need and willingness to make commitments were also seen as important variables—especially with respect to cohabitation and marriage. We considered two theories about love involving commitment and other variables that we had discussed. Dominance, status, and power were examined as other important variables. This included a discussion of the relationship between gender and power in relationships. In closing, we looked at assertiveness as a means of establishing equality and briefly at some of the differences between assertive, nonassertive, and aggressive behaviors.

Key Terms

Attachment style
Commitment
Dyadic effect

Interrole conflict
Intrarole conflict
Johari window

Norms
Power
Role

Self-disclosure
Status

Review Questions

1. How are disruptive power and norms related to interpersonal communication?

2. Explain the distinction between expected and enacted roles.

3. Discuss the effects of our expectations of marriage on other close relationships.

4. Distinguish between intrarole and interrole conflict and give an example of each.

5. What are four means by which we can assess the quality of an interpersonal relationship?

6. What are the four levels of awareness and disclosure exemplified by the Johari window?

7. State four reasons for self-disclosure and four for its avoidance.

8. What are some of the research findings on self-disclosure in Internet dating and on how people tend to present themselves in posting Internet profiles?

9. Identify five characteristics of appropriate self-disclosure.

10. Discuss at least three qualities that characterize intimacy in interpersonal communication.

11. Describe the concept of attachment styles as applied to romantic relationships.

12. Discuss three variables that seem to predict the intensity of unreciprocated love.

13. Explain how affiliation and commitment affect interpersonal relationships.

14. Discuss two theories about types of love relationships.

15. How are need for affiliation and need for dominance related?

16. Explain how complementary, symmetrical, and parallel relationship structures differ.

17. What are two ways in which status affects interpersonal communication?

18. What is the difference between dominance and power in an interpersonal relationship?

19. State four proposed bases for gendered power.

20. Explain the differences between nonassertive, assertive, and aggressive behavior. Give an example of each.

21. Discuss at least four qualities that characterize assertive behavior.

Exercises

1. Write a short paper in which you analyze some communication difficulties that might arise for a college student as a result of role conflicts.

2. In a small group—five people or so—have each person attempt to increase his or her awareness of self and others by telling each of the others one positive and one negative impression he or she has formed about that person. If there is

time, have a discussion in which group members go into greater depth, asking for and giving further impressions.

3. Go to *www.web-research-design.net/cgi-bin/crq/crq.pl* and take the Close Relationships Questionnaire. After you get your test results, you can read more about attachment theory and close relationships on the same site.

4. After observing a conversation between two people, try to determine what specific messages (nonverbal as well as verbal) reveal the dominance or submissiveness of each communicator. Make the same observations with respect to affiliative or antisocial behaviors. Do the characteristic roles shift from time to time?

5. Role-play the following exercises and try to use assertive (not aggressive) behaviors.

Scene 1

Bank Customer: You have been a customer of this bank for over 20 years. You request an installment loan on a new car and are refused.

Bank Employee: A long-time customer of the bank wants an installment loan to purchase a car. Current bank policy does not provide for installment loans on automobiles because the interest rates aren't profitable to the bank.

Scene 2

Bank Employee: A customer wants to cash a $10,000 check against uncollected funds (a check from another state). The bank policy requires a 10-day waiting period.

Bank Customer: You just came in from another state and you go to the bank to cash a $10,000 check drawn on an out-of-state bank. It is important that you have the cash on that day for the closing on the house you are purchasing. Because the check is drawn on an out-of-state bank, the teller refuses to give you the cash.

Suggested Readings

Alberti, Robert, and Michael Emmons. *Your Perfect Right,* 8th ed. Atascadero, CA: Impact Publishers, 2001.

This is a very popular guide to learning assertiveness skills and establishing greater equality in interpersonal relationships.

Cain, Susan. *Quiet: The Power of Introverts in a World That Can't Stop Talking.* New York: Crown, 2012.

This interesting new book explores two different methods for effective interpersonal communication (introvert and extrovert).

Devito, Joseph. *The Interpersonal Communication Book,* 12th ed. Boston: Pearson, 2009.

This classic is an outstanding, comprehensive overview of interpersonal communication.

Floyd, Kory. *Interpersonal Communication: The Whole Story.* New York: McGraw-Hill, 2009.

This book offers a comprehensive view of interpersonal communication. It has especially good chapters on intimate relationships and emotions.

In the Mood for Love

This is a haunting, subtle, and romantic movie about a man and a woman who live in the same building and slowly discover their spouses are having an affair.

Luft, Joseph. *Of Human Interaction.* Palo Alto, CA: National Press, 1969.

The author elaborates on the rationale behind the Johari window model as well as its application. He also explains more fully the value of self-disclosure. A classic and excellent treatment of the subject.

Neck, Christopher, and Charles Manz. *Mastering Self-Leadership: Empowering Yourself for Personal Excellence,* 6th ed. Boston: Pearson, 2013.

If you would like to work on self-improvement in any aspect of your communication competencies, this book offers some practical help.

Pfeffer, Jeffrey. *Power: Why Some People Have It and Others Don't.* New York: HarperCollins, 2010.

This interesting book digests a lot of research and makes the topic quite readable and useful.

Silver, Robert B., and Barbara Epstein, eds. *The Company They Kept.* New York: New York Review of Books, 2006.

Twenty-seven brief memoirs, each about a remarkable friend.

Sternberg, Robert J. *Cupid's Arrow: The Course of Love through Time.* New York: Cambridge University Press, 2000.

The author explains his own triangular theory of love, traces a brief history of cultural and literary conceptions of love, and goes on to examine the course of love during our lifetime.

Stewart, John. *Bridges Not Walls*, 11th ed. New York: McGraw-Hill, 2012.

This classic book examines virtually every aspect of interpersonal communication. Well worth the read.

Tannen, Deborah. *You're Wearing That? Understanding Mothers and Daughters in Conversation.* New York: Ballantine Books, 2006.

A book about mother-daughter communication by a well-known linguist with great sensitivity to dialogue.

Wood, Julia. *Interpersonal Communication—Everyday Encounters*, 6th ed. Boston: Wadsworth, 2010.

This book is a great overview of the context of interpersonal communication. It includes an especially interesting chapter on friendships.

 # For Supplementary Information

Log onto the Online Learning Center at *www.mhhe.com/tubbshc13e*.

Intercultural Communication

Chapter Objectives

After reading this chapter, you should be able to:

1. Define "intercultural communication" and discuss three major approaches to how it is studied.
2. Discuss the differences between individualist and collectivist cultures, high- and low-context cultures, and three other dimensions that measure cultural variation.
3. State three broad communication principles with important implications for intercultural communication.
4. Explain how verbal and nonverbal messages, including those that express emotion, can interfere with communication between cultures. Give three examples of each.
5. Describe how cultural roles and norms, including norms about conflict, affect intercultural communication.
6. Discuss the effects of differences in beliefs and values on people from different cultures, identify three ethical norms that appear in a great number of them, and give an example of adapting successfully to another culture.
7. Explain the concepts of ethnocentrism, stereotyping, and polarization as they affect interethnic and interracial conflict. Discuss the research findings on intergroup relations, and explain the principles of cosmopolitanism.
8. Describe some of the personal, political, and social effects of intercultural communication.

In August 1997, a Korean Air pilot with 8,900 hours of flying time and in excellent health crashed his Boeing 747 into a mountain in Guam while attempting to land, killing 228 of the 254 people aboard. After years of investigation, it was determined that the cause of the crash was the miscommunication between the pilot and the first officer (co-pilot) (Gladwell, 2008).

The Korean culture has formal linguistic rules about how people communicate, especially to an authority figure, such as the captain of an airline. There are five different ways that a person can communicate. The most explicit is called a *command* and the least explicit is called a *hint*. The co-pilot's duty is to navigate and tell the captain of impending problems. The cockpit flight recorder tapes revealed that the co-pilot consistently used the more respectful mode saying, "That turn . . . looks difficult" (hinting) rather than the more explicit mode saying, "Turn thirty degrees right" (command). As a result, the pilot did not realize that they were about to crash into the side of the mountain. In other words, the cultural norm to show respect for the authority figure got in the way of clear understanding between the two. Further investigations of plane crashes around the world revealed that this communication pattern was responsible for several crashes in countries that have similar cultures with strong norms showing respect for authority figures (Gladwell, 2008, pp. 177–223). As we shall see in this chapter, much of Asian culture is derived from Confucianism, based on the teachings of Confucius (Kong Fu-zi, 551–479 B.C.E.), who lived even before Aristotle, the founder of communication in the Western world (Kissinger, 2011, p. 13).

In this chapter we look at intercultural communication as it occurs in many contexts from interpersonal to mass communication. And whenever it occurs, the differences in our frames of reference make the task of communication more complex, difficult, and nuanced, for we cannot be aware of all aspects of other cultures. In fact, one reason intercultural communication has fascinated scholars is that it reveals so much about our own communication behavior that we might not have otherwise noticed as distinctive—for example, our attitudes toward time or our responses to conflict. As our involvement in intercultural communication increases—and it must—it becomes vital for each of us to understand some of its principles, problems, and implications.

A DEFINITION OF CULTURE

In Chapter 1, we defined *intercultural communication* as *communication between members of different cultures (whether defined in terms of racial, ethnic, or socioeconomic differences).* As this definition suggests, the divisions between cultural groups are not established or absolute; we may choose one or more of a variety of characteristics to identify a group of people as having a common culture. We may, for instance, speak of natives of California, Nebraska, and New Hampshire as being from different regional cultures (West Coast, Midwest, and New England); we may identify each of them as a member of an urban or rural culture, or as a member of a Jewish or Irish culture; we may speak of them all as members of a broader Western culture. Although scholars disagree as to which of these designations may properly be said to describe a cultural group, to a certain extent all of them do.

On November 3, 2010, President Obama stated, "We just learned that China now has the fastest supercomputer on Earth—that used to be us" (Friedman and Mandelbaum, 2011, p. 1). Our world has become a global competitive arena. Americans no longer just have to compete with each other, we must also compete with the best and brightest from all over the world. It also means that, more than ever, Americans from different cultural backgrounds will have to work together to successfully compete with teams from other countries.

Sociological studies have shown that even within the United States, seismic cultural shifts have been occurring. Murray (2012) reveals that there are growing difference between the college-educated and the blue-collar, non-college-educated people in America. His data show that the non-college groups have more illegitimate children, more marital discord, more divorces, more unemployment, and subsequently, more poverty and more crime. During the 2012 presidential campaign, Mitt Romney illustrated the cultural style of the college-educated group, while former senator Rick Santorum argued that someone who wants everyone to go to college is a snob. He is more typical of the type of candidate who would appeal to noncollege voters. College graduates represent about 25 percent and noncollege graduates the remaining 75 percent of the U.S.

population (Murray, 2012). The cultural and communication gaps between these two groups presents a growing American cultural challenge.

From a political perspective, Buchanan (2011) also demonstrates that America is becoming so ethnically diverse that the people of color (such as President Obama) will become the majority by 2041, and for those under age eighteen, whites will become the minority in 2019 (Buchanan, 2011, p. 125). To put it another way, American demographics have changed so much that if John McCain had run for president in 1976 instead of 2008, he would have won, because the fastest growing population segment is among Hispanics, who typically vote more Democratic than Republican (Buchanan, 2011, p. 338). The cultural changes from the historic demographic profile are quite dramatic.

Finally, Michael Lewis, author of *The Blind Side* and *Moneyball,* has also studied the financial aspects of various cultures. He argues that the United States will be facing more and more difficult financial choices in the not-too-distant future. And arguments over budget cuts will begin to strain the relations between younger and older Americans over such issues as Social Security, Medicare, and Medicaid. So, the cultural gaps between generations will be one more challenge that will have to be addressed (Lewis, 2011, p. 176).

Culture is *a way of life developed and shared by a group of people and passed down from generation to generation.* It is made up of many complex elements, including religious and political systems, customs, and language as well as tools, clothing, buildings, and works of art. The way you dress, your relationships with your parents and friends, what you expect of a marriage and of a job, the food you eat, the language you speak, are all profoundly affected by your culture. This does not mean that you think, believe, and act exactly as everyone else in your cultural group does. Not all members of a culture share all its elements. Moreover, a culture will change and evolve over time. Still, a common set of characteristics is shared by the group at large and can be traced, even through great changes, over many generations.

Culture as Learned

As we attempt to communicate with people from other cultures and reconcile our differences, it is important that we remember culture is learned. Because it is learned, not innate, an infant born in Vietnam of Vietnamese parents but brought to the United States and raised as an American will be culturally an American. Because culture is learned, it also changes as people come into contact with one another or as their experiences change their needs.

In a sense, it is the culture and its values that provide a coherent framework for organizing our activity and allowing us to predict the behavior of others. People from other cultures who enter our own may be threatening because they challenge our system of beliefs. In the same way, we ourselves may become threatening to others as we enter a foreign culture and challenge the cultural foundations of their beliefs (Griffin, 2009).

Distinctions among Cultures

Radical differences among cultures usually occur when there has been little exchange between them or, in some cases, with other cultures in general. What distinguishes one cultural group from another, however, is not always so evident. A New Yorker and a Californian will have cultural differences and similarities. Both may celebrate Thanksgiving and the Fourth of July with much the same sense of tradition associated with those holidays. On a day-to-day basis, however, they are likely to eat somewhat different foods, although probably with the same kind of utensils. They are likely to speak the same language but with different accents and a few different words or phrases. Both will speak more or less the same language as people who have always lived in England and Ontario, and they may even share many of the same values, but cultural differences are likely to become more evident as people from the United States, Canada, and England communicate with one another. Similarly, differences among cultures do not always occur abruptly at regional or national borders but gradually, over a range.

Three Approaches to Studying Culture

In the study of intercultural communication, three major approaches have emerged: social science, interpretive, and critical (Davis et al., 2000; Martin and Nakayama, 2007, pp. 52–69). Here we look briefly at each of them.

The Social Science Approach   This is the most traditional and is built on the methods and assumptions derived from psychology and sociology. It is assumed that behavior can be observed, measured, and predicted—that descriptive,

often quantitative methods, can be objective—and that we can discover universals about human behavior. Here communication is seen as influenced by culture, and the primary interest is in describing and comparing cultures. For example, researchers might conduct a cross-cultural study of proxemic norms or how conflict is expressed by people from the United States, Greece, Germany, Japan, and China.

The Interpretive Approach   This approach derives its methods from anthropology and linguistics. It emphasizes the subjective experience of the individual. Its research emphasis is qualitative rather than quantitative. It makes full use of field studies and personal observation. Researchers may get to know the people they study quite well, might collect personal narratives and stories that describe the lived experience of a given culture or co-culture. Usually, the goal is understanding rather than predicting behavior, taking a perspective from *within* the culture. Communication is seen as creating and maintaining culture. For example, one well-known interpretive study examined speech codes in Teamsterville, a working-class Chicago neighborhood.

The Critical Approach   Although some of its assumptions and methods overlap with an interpretive approach, the critical approach is primarily concerned with creating change by examining power relationships within cultures. It stresses the importance of social, political, economic, and historical contexts, and its focus is on social rather than individual relations. According to this view, power relationships characterize all intercultural transactions. Here the ultimate goal is not merely understanding behavior but also producing actual change. The critical approach involves analyses of "texts" or "cultural products," including those produced by the media (e.g., newspapers, movies, television, public relations material). For example, Rey Chow, a professor of cultural studies at Brown University, writes on Chinese cinema (2007). Some other critical studies have analyzed how minorities are represented in the movies in comparison with whites or how the language of news reports contributes to a new form of racism (van Dijk, 2000).

Nick Couldry, another cultural studies scholar, writes: "We cannot oversimplify the cultural experiences of others, without caricaturing our own. Cultural studies in this sense involves an ethic of reciprocity, a mutual practice of both speaking and listening, which is inextricably tied to taking seriously the complexity of cultures" (2006, p. 54).

Although much of the research we will be looking at grows out of the first of these approaches, one view does not exclude the contributions of the others. The study of intercultural communication is enriched by all three perspectives.

SOME DIMENSIONS OF CULTURAL DIFFERENCE

The last decades have seen a dramatic increase in intercultural communication, a social change that has been brought about in part through the technological innovations of both aviation and electronic communication networks. Once an experience for the privileged few, international air travel is now routine and accessible to millions. Satellite technology has brought the immediacy of political events into our homes, and the expansion of a vast electronic communications network now links peoples of the world many times over.

As a result, the experience of the immigrant population has also changed radically. For example, over one-third of New York City's population are immigrants—mainly from the Caribbean, Asia, and Latin America, and a variety of other nations (Foner, 2001). Many immigrants can afford to revisit their homeland regularly to see family and friends as well as conduct business. And the pervasive use of the Internet, e-mail, cell phone, and videophone, as well as other technological innovations, has brought together old and new cultures, making the understanding of cultural differences more vital than ever.

In 2002, the Census Bureau reported that the number of U.S. residents who were born outside the United States or are children of immigrants (i.e., first-generation Americans) was the highest it had ever been. About 70 percent have settled in California, Florida, Illinois, New Jersey, New York, or Texas, and over half live in large metropolitan areas (Scott, 2002).

It's not surprising, therefore, that in addition to identifying ourselves as part of a larger culture, many of us will identify ourselves as members of one or more co-cultures. It is likely, especially in a country as diverse as the United States, that groups within this culture, although they share many characteristics with members of the larger culture, will also be members of a **co-culture**—that is, *a culture within the larger culture*. That group or co-culture will often share "a specialized language system, shared values, a collective worldview, and common communication patterns" (Samovar and Porter, 2000, p. 115). Among such groups are Asian Americans, African Americans, gays, lesbians, women, and people with disabilities.

On the basis of his research findings on intercultural communication, Hofstede (1980, 1991) proposed several dimensions along which cultures vary. In the pages that follow we will look briefly at each of the major variables.

Individualism-Collectivism

Many theorists regard individualism-collectivism as the central dimension within which variations between cultures may be measured. By **individualism** scholars usually mean *the tendency of people in a given culture to value "individual identity over group identity, individual rights over group rights, and individual achievements over group concerns"* (Ting-Toomey and Chung, 1996, p. 239, emphasis added). At the other end of the continuum, **collectivism** has been defined as *the tendency of people in a given culture to value "group identity over the individual identity, group obligations over individual rights, and ingroup-oriented concerns over individual wants and desires"* (p. 240).

Members of an individualist culture tend to emphasize personal goals, to think of themselves as independent, and to be direct in communicating. In an individualist culture there are many in-groups (your family, your school, your church, your occupation), but their influence is specific and often limited.

10.2 PRACTICAL TIPS

What's Your Cultural Orientation?

For each of the items below, choose either a or b to indicate which is more like you.

1. I'd enjoy working most in groups
   a. in which there is little distinction between leaders and members.
   b. in which there is a clearly defined leader.

2. As a student (and if I feel well informed)
   a. I'd feel comfortable challenging a professor.
   b. I'd feel uncomfortable challenging a professor.

3. In choosing a life partner or even close friends, I'd feel more comfortable
   a. with just about anyone.
   b. with those from my own culture and class.

4. Of the following characteristics, the ones I feel more highly are
   a. aggressiveness, material success, and strength.
   b. modesty, tenderness, and quality of life.

5. In a conflict situation, I'd be more likely to
   a. confront conflicts and seek to win.
   b. confront conflicts with the aim of compromise.

6. If I were a manager of an organization I would stress
   a. competition and aggressiveness.
   b. worker satisfaction.

7. Generally, I'm
   a. comfortable with ambiguity and uncertainty.
   b. uncomfortable with ambiguity and uncertainty.

8. As a student, I'm more comfortable with assignments in which
   a. there is room for interpretation.
   b. there are clearly defined instructions.

9. Generally, when approaching an undertaking with which I've had no experience, I'd feel
   a. comfortable.
   b. uncomfortable.

10. Success, to my way of thinking, is best measured by
    a. the extent to which I surpass others.
    b. my contribution to the group effort.

11. My heroes are generally
    a. people who stand out from the crowd.
    b. team players.

12. The values I consider more important are
    a. achievement, stimulation, enjoyment.
    b. tradition, benevolence, conformity.

13. Generally, in my business transactions, I feel comfortable
    a. relying on oral agreements.
    b. relying on written agreements.

14. If I were a manager, I would likely
    a. reprimand a worker in public if the occasion warranted.
    b. always reprimand in private regardless of the situation.

15. In communicating, it's generally more important to be
    a. polite than accurate or direct.
    b. accurate and direct than polite.

SCORING

Items 1–3 refer to the power distance; a responses indicate a greater comfort with low power distance and b responses indicate a greater comfort with high power distance.

Items 4–6 refer to the masculine–feminine dimension; a responses indicate a masculine orientation and b responses indicate a feminine orientation.

Items 7–9 refer to the tolerance for ambiguity or uncertainty dimension; a responses indicate a high tolerance and b responses indicate a low tolerance.

Items 10–12 refer to the individualist-collectivist orientation; a responses indicate an individualist orientation and be responses indicate a collectivist orientation.

Items 13–15 refer to the high and low context characteristics; a responses indicate a high-context focus and b responses indicate a low-context focus.

Knowing your cultural orientation can help you understand others from other cultures and may help moderate communication difficulties when encountering those from other cultures.

Source: Adapted from Joseph DeVito, *The Interpersonal Communication Book*, 12th ed. Boston: Pearson, 2009.

For members of collectivist cultures, the emphasis is on the importance of fitting into the group. Because they are strongly connected with the group, they tend to regard the self as interdependent and to be aware of group goals and welfare rather than focusing on individual achievements and desires. And they tend to avoid direct conflict. Unlike individualist cultures, collectivist cultures have relatively few in-groups, but these exert considerable influence.

A dramatic example of how differently actions may be interpreted in collectivist and individualist cultures was seen after the release in spring of 2004 of three young Japanese civilians who had been taken hostage in Iraq: a woman who had created a nonprofit organization that helped Iraq street children, a freelance journalist, and a photographer. They were shown on television with their kidnappers, who held knives and were threatening to slit their throats.

Two weeks after they were seen on television, the three were freed by their captors and flown home. Instead of being welcomed, they were confronted by the resentment, anger, and criticism of many of the Japanese people because, it was said, to pursue their own goals the hostages had selfishly ignored the government's advisory against travel to Iraq. "Their sin . . . was to defy what people call here 'okami,' or, literally, 'what is higher'—in this case, the Foreign Ministry" (Onishi, 2004, A1). The level of hostility was so high that the three went into seclusion, virtual prisoners in their own homes.

The response in the United States, with its mainstream individualist culture, could not have been more different. The actions of the three hostages were seen as courageous rather than reckless, compassionate and generous rather than selfish. Former Secretary of State Colin Powell praised the three as "Japanese citizens [who] were ready to put themselves at risk, for a better purpose" (A11).

Following up on earlier studies, two researchers recently studied differences in how members of Western cultures and East Asian cultures perceive the consequences of four different events, including a car accident and the firing of employees by the CEO of the firm where they worked (Maddux and Yuki, 2006). They found a greater consciousness of the "ripple effects of events" and a sense of personal responsibility among people from East Asian cultures. Their greater sense of interdependence made them more aware of social ramifications:

> Japanese participants perceived social events as affecting a larger number of people than did Americans; they also perceived themselves as more responsible for the indirect distal consequences of explicitly social events, felt worse about these indirect consequences, and were more likely to apologize to indirectly affected targets. (p. 680)

This study helps explain the response in Japan to the kidnapping of the three Japanese civilians in Iraq.

Approximately two-thirds of the world's population are members of collectivist cultures. These include many Latino, Mediterranean, Middle Eastern, African, and Asian cultures. Despite this, researchers seem to have given more attention to individualist cultures such as the United States, Canada, Scandinavia, France, Great Britain,

Table 10.1 Individualistic and Collectivistic Cultures	
Individualistic	**Collectivistic**
Major Characteristics	
Emphasis on individual's goals	Emphasis on in-group's goals
Self-realization	Fitting into the in-group
Little difference between in-group and out-group communication	Large difference between in-group and out-group communication
Independent self-construal	Interdependent self-construal
"I" identity	"We" identity
Saying what you are thinking	Avoiding confrontations in in-group
Low-context communication: direct, precise, and absolute	High-context communication: indirect, imprecise, and probabilistic
*Example Cultures**	
Australia	Brazil
Belgium	China
Canada	Colombia
Denmark	Egypt
Finland	Greece
France	India
Germany	Japan
Great Britain	Kenya
Ireland	Korea
Israel	Mexico
Italy	Nigeria
Netherlands	Pakistan
New Zealand	Panama
Norway	Peru
South Africa	Saudi Arabia
Sweden	Thailand
Switzerland	Venezuela
United States	Vietnam

*The cultures are listed according to the *predominant* tendencies in the cultures.
Source: Adapted from *Communicating with Strangers*, 3rd ed., by William B. Gudykunst and Young Yun Kim, 1997.
Reproduced by permission of The McGraw-Hill Companies.

Germany, Switzerland, and Australia (Ting-Toomey and Chung, 1996, p. 239). (You can see a summary of differences along these dimensions in Table 10.1.)

High- and Low-Context Cultures

For students of communication, the distinction between high- and low-context cultures (Martin and Nakayama, 2008) is among the most fascinating. High- and low-context cultures have several important differences in the way information is coded. Members of **high-context cultures** are *more skilled in reading nonverbal behaviors,* *and they assume that other people will also be able to do so.* Thus, *they speak less* than members of low-context cultures *and they listen more;* in general, their communication tends to be indirect and less explicit. Members of **low-context cultures,** on the other hand, *stress direct and explicit communication. They emphasize verbal messages and the shared information they encode.* Many researchers link high-context communication style with collectivist cultures and low-context communication style with individualist cultures.

High- and low-context cultures range along a continuum, with such cultures as the Chinese and Japanese at the high end and the Scandinavian, German, and German-Swiss cultures at the low end. The United States would be within the low-context end of the spectrum, though not at the very bottom. (For a sampling of high- and low-context cultures see Figure 10.1.) In comparing people from the United States with Malays and Japanese, Althen offers a clear example of the high-context/low-context distinction:

> Americans focus on the words people use to convey their ideas, information, and feelings. They are generally quite unskilled in "reading" other people's nonverbal messages. "Oh, you Americans!" said an exasperated Japanese woman who was being pressed to express some details about an unpleasant situation, "You have to say everything!" (Althen, 1992, p. 416)

Figure 10.1   *High-Context versus Low-Context Rankings of Selected Countries and Groups*

■ Low-Context Cultures
(8 lowest countries, in order)

1. Germany	5. Norway
2. Switzerland	6. Finland
3. United States	7. Denmark
4. Sweden	8. Canada

■ High-Context Cultures
(8 highest countries, in order)

1. China	5. Native Americans
2. Japan	6. African Americans
3. South Korea	7. Mexican Americans
4. Taiwan	8. Latinos

Source: Reprinted by permission of Waveland Press, Inc. from Peter A. Andersen, *Nonverbal Communication: Forms and Functions,* 2nd ed. (Long Grove, IL: Waveland Press, Inc., 2008). All rights reserved.

As many have pointed out, "not all members of individualist cultures are individualists, and not all members of collectivistic cultures are collectivists" (Gudykunst and Kim, 1997, p. 69). Such qualifying statements could certainly be made about other dimensions such as high- and low-context cultures. Within any dimension there will be much variation within individuals and in how each culture interprets various concepts such as self (as just discussed), community, and conflict.

Power Distance

Power distance refers to *the degree to which people accept authority and hierarchical organization as a natural part of their culture.* They expect, then, that some members of the culture have higher status and are more powerful than others. Members of high power-distance cultures (France, India, and Mexico are examples) have a more authoritarian style of communication. Among low power-distance cultures (Israel, Ireland, and Australia are examples), people emphasize and assume equality. They tend to perceive the power others have as appropriate only as it is confined to a given role, whether it be that of teacher, doctor, or government official. And when necessary, they are accustomed to questioning people in power. Power distance is thought of as present to some degree in every culture.

Masculinity–Femininity

As its name makes clear, the masculinity–femininity dimension attempts to draw a parallel with gender. According to this view, so-called *masculine cultures value work, strength, competition, and assertiveness.* Sex roles are also seen as more strictly defined. In general, the emphasis is authoritarian. *Feminine cultures place more value on such traits as "affection, compassion, nurturing, and interpersonal relationships" and tend to be more fluid.* And they give considerable importance to nonverbal communication. In case you are wondering which countries have been described in this way, here is a summary by Dodd (1999):

> The highest masculinity index scores come from Japan, Australia, Venezuela, Switzerland, Mexico, Ireland, Great Britain, and Germany. The countries with the highest feminine scores are Sweden, Norway, the Netherlands, Denmark, Finland, Chile, Portugal, and Thailand. (p. 94)

To many, the masculinity–femininity metaphor seems out of date, and it remains to be seen how useful this distinction will turn out to be. Some researchers suggest that what is being described might be better termed "achievement-nurturance" (p. 94).

Uncertainty Avoidance

How much do you have to know about people to feel comfortable in their presence? Do you have to know anything at all to feel at ease in communicating with a stranger? **Uncertainty avoidance** is *a measure of the extent to which members of* *a given culture attempt to avoid uncertainty or ambiguity about others.* In cultures ranked as high in uncertainty avoidance (e.g., Belgium, Greece, and Spain), people are more comfortable in situations where there is little ambiguity and a great deal of information. They prefer more rules and predictable behavior and have less tolerance for diversity. Cultures that rank low in uncertainty avoidance (Canada, Jamaica, and the United States, to name a few) are more open to change and diversity. For cultures with low uncertainty avoidance, "what is different, is curious"; for cultures with high uncertainty avoidance, "what is different, is dangerous" (Hofstede, 1991, p. 119). Yet in a country such as the United States that brings together so many cultures, we are bound to see a wide range in the tolerance for uncertainty.

INTERCULTURAL COMMUNICATION: PRINCIPLES AND PROBLEMS

Although modern means of travel and communication have brought us into contact with virtually the whole world, the technical capacity to transmit and receive messages is not, in itself, enough to allow people of vastly different cultures to communicate. Dramatic improvements in the technological means of communication have in many instances outstripped our abilities to communicate effectively with people who have different languages, different beliefs and values, and different expectations of relationships. Repeatedly, interaction between people of different cultures has created far more misunderstanding than understanding.

Of the many principles used by theorists to describe the communication process, several clearly apply to intercultural exchanges. The first is *a shared code system,* which of course will have two aspects—verbal and nonverbal. Philipsen (2009) argues that without such a shared system, communication will be impossible. There will be degrees of difference, but the less a code system is shared, the less communication is possible.

Second, *different beliefs and behaviors between communicators establish the basis for different assumptions from which to respond.* In fact, our own beliefs and behaviors influence our perceptions of what other people do. Thus, two people of different cultures can easily attribute different meanings to the same behavior. If this happens, the two behave differently with neither being able to predict the other's response.

A third principle discussed by Sarbaugh with important implications for intercultural communication is *the level of knowing and accepting the beliefs and behaviors of others.* Notice that there are two components: knowledge and acceptance. It isn't so much the knowledge of such differences that creates a problem. It's also the level of your acceptance. For example, writing about a tribe of African hunters called the Ik, anthropologist Colin Turnbull tried to come to terms with his own feelings of repulsion. The Ik, he knew, were uprooted hunters and the violent way they now lived—killing, stealing each other's food, and so on—could be explained by the fact that their entire society had been uprooted. Turnbull knew a great deal about the beliefs and behaviors of the Ik, but he could not accept the people of that culture. As an anthropologist, however, he still brings to his perceptions a certain objectivity—simply in declaring his responses.

The degree to which we judge a culture by our own cultural values and refuse to consider other cultural norms will determine how likely it is that effective communication takes place. At one extreme, we have participants in a transaction who both know and accept the beliefs and behaviors of others; at the other, we have those who neither know nor accept. And in this instance, the probability of a breakdown in communication is extremely high.

Adopting a shared code system, acknowledging differences in beliefs and behaviors, and learning to be tolerant of the beliefs and behaviors of others all contribute to effective communication.

Verbal Messages

Peter Hessler is the Beijing correspondent for *The New Yorker.* An American, he once taught English in China and his students still write to him. When in a letter by one of his former students we read "*I have confidence in myself that one day I will be a VIP, not like toothbrush any more,*" we know that we have come upon a Chinese word whose meaning cannot be translated literally with any ease (2006, p. 49).

Language differences can go much deeper than simple translation ambiguities. Have you ever asked someone to translate a word from another language for you, only to have him say, "Well, it doesn't translate into English exactly, but it means something like . . . "? As we saw in our discussion of the Sapir-Whorf hypothesis in Chapter 3, languages differ more than strict word-for-word translations often indicate because the people who speak the languages have different needs.

In his first year at UCLA, Wen-Shu Lee, a graduate student from Taiwan, recalls adding a Chinese summary to his English notes at the end of class. A student looking over his shoulder remarked, "That's Greek to me!"

> I promptly corrected him: "No, it's Chinese." He was shocked for about one second and then burst into laughter. We spent 20 minutes or so clarifying that "Greek" did not mean "Greek," that "Greek" meant "foreign, difficult, and mysterious stuff," and I finally agreed that my Chinese was "Greek" to him. (Samovar and Porter, 2000, p. 217)

Even when we can manage to translate from one language to another with literal accuracy, the failure to understand idioms or slang creates many misunderstandings. And the deeper meanings of individual words—with their web of rich associations—are often lost because they are rooted in the culture of the language. The English word "love" is often used to describe intense and intimate personal relationships, but Koreans use the word "jung."

> *Jung* is a much broader concept than love. In addition to the affective aspect of love, *jung* comprises the forces of inertia of a relationship . . . *Jung* is unconscious and voluntary . . . [with] four properties: duration, togetherness, warmth, and solidarity. (Lim and Choi, 1996)

Literal translations from one language to another can also create misunderstandings because they do not account for culture-based linguistic styles. The elaborate style used in Arabic with its rhetoric of exaggeration, compliment, and multiple extended metaphors is puzzling to those unfamiliar with it:

> An Arab feels compelled to overassert in almost all types of communication because others expect him to. If an Arab says exactly what he means without the expected assertion, other Arabs may still think that he means the opposite. For example, a simple "No" by a guest to a host's request to eat or drink more will not suffice. To convey the meaning that he is actually full, the guest must keep repeating "No" several times coupling it with an oath such as "By God" or "I swear to God." (Cited in Gudykunst and Kim, 1997, p. 204)

You can also get an inkling from this of how an Arab might interpret a single succinct "No" from someone speaking in English.

We can see the importance of language style as well as differences in the values placed on spoken language by looking briefly at The Hispanic Leadership project. Based in Washington, D.C., it was intended to aid newly arrived Latino political leaders (Weigl and Reyes, 2001). But one of the stumbling blocks to forming political alliances and rapport between Anglos and Latinos was their contrasting views on the relationship between speech and politics:

> The Anglo political style demands constant talk: to clarify a viewpoint, to plan an action, to lobby for an interest, to resolve a dispute, to establish one's authoritative public profile. . . . Within Latino worlds what you *do* is far more important then what you say. . . . The constant flow of words, the frequent debate over ideology, the love of verbal analysis—basic features of local as well as national politics in Washington—seemed wasteful, foreign, and self-inflating to Latino leaders in their new U.S. home. (p. 252)

In another example, former President Eisenhower once wrote to his grandson saying, "Dear David, For many years I have been struck by the virtual impossibility of men of the Nordic strain to express, in a face-to-face meeting, their affection, even when of the same family and when ties of sentiment are strong. . . . I sometimes envy the Latins, who do not seem to fall prey to these particular inhibitions—but I would not go so far as to favor the habit of men kissing each other" (Eisenhower, 2010, p. 225).

This quote indicates just one example of differences between cultures.

Nonverbal Messages

A recent guidebook on Vietnam, Cambodia, and Laos gives prospective tourists this advice about customs and conduct:

> The head is considered pure and sacred in Buddhism; do not touch anyone, including children, on the head. The feet, which come into contact with dust on

the street, are lowly; do not point your feet at anyone, or at any Buddhist image. If sitting in a temple either squat or sit with the legs tucked to the side so the soles of the feet point backward. (Buckley, 2006, p. 645)

As for facial expressions,

An important cultural note: A smile on a Vietnamese face does not necessarily indicate amusement—it can also convey anger, fear, embarrassment, disagreement. Thus, as you pick up your mangled bicycle from a head-on collision with another cyclist, the other party may smile or even manage a nervous laugh. (Buckley, 2006, p. 645)

Nonverbal communication systems vary from culture to culture just as verbal systems do, but often we overlook the symbolic nature of nonverbal communication. Many American travelers abroad have been embarrassed when they discovered that the two-fingered gesture they use to mean "Give me two" is assigned a different, obscene meaning in many countries. They have also been mistaken when they assumed that a nod always means yes. In some countries, a nod means "no"; in others a nod, or yes, simply indicates that a person understood the question. In the United States, the gesture for "okay" is made by forming a circle with the thumb and forefinger while the other fingers are held up. But in France this gesture means "you're worthless," and in Greece it's a vulgar sexual invitation.

Greeting someone from another culture is an important part of intercultural competency. As we know, first impressions can be very powerful so understanding the different ways people greet each other is very important. Greetings can range anywhere from having physical contact with each other to having no physical contact at all. We are all aware of the American handshake with a good firm grip and looking the other right in the eye. Asian cultures all have different ways of greeting including nodding, handshakes, and most commonly, bowing. Just as a weak or limp handshake is considered distasteful by most Americans and many Europeans, an improper bow can send the wrong signals to the person you are greeting. Pressing your hands together above the eyes or bowing too low or too high can be disrespectful or rude. Another common way of greeting in some parts of the world is to kiss the other person's cheek. This is also different depending on where you are. In Mexico, it is proper to kiss only one cheek while in France it is proper to kiss both cheeks. Many Americans struggle to do this right and give too direct a kiss on the cheek. Generally, the right way to do it is to press the cheeks together and kiss the air (Neuliep, 2006, pp. 76–82).

Confusion in nonverbal indicators may be much more complex. In Chapter 4 we considered some of the different ways that cultures make use of time and space. As we discussed then, we rely on nonverbal cues to give us information about the meaning we are to assign to a verbal message. Because we often interpret these nonverbal cues unconsciously, the message received is often very different from the one the speaker intended.

Vocal cues can be particularly problematic when communication is between people from different countries. For example, in the Arab countries, men are expected to speak loudly to indicate strength and sincerity. A Saudi Arab may also lower his voice to indicate respect to a superior. In an exchange between an American and an Arab, the confusion of signals is likely to be disastrous.

The expression of emotion is also regulated by culture. For example, the French are often described by visitors as rude or cold, and one reason is that they usually smile at people only after they've known them rather well:

> . . . to smile at someone you do not know and say "hello" is frequently considered provocative, not friendly. On the other hand, to pass a friend on the street or bump into family acquaintances without offering conversation would be considered rude. (Gannon et al., 2001, p. 71)

One aspect of a shared code system that contributes to the smooth flow of conversation and ultimately to understanding is **synchrony,** *the sharing of rhythms* (Dodd, 1999; Douglis, 1987). Goleman sees synchrony as an aspect of social intelligence:

> Synchrony lets us glide gracefully through a nonverbal dance with another person. The foundation of social facility, it is the bedrock on which other aspects [of social intelligence] build. . . . Getting in synch demands that we both read nonverbal cues instantaneously and act on them smoothly—without having to think about them. (Goleman, 2006, p. 91)

When people speak, they develop a rhythm, a dancelike beat that emphasizes and organizes meaning during conversation—a phenomenon to be observed between family members, friends, and lovers—even business associates. It is during a beat or stress that a speaker will often reveal important information or introduce a new topic into the conversation. It seems that timing in conversation can be affected even by a few microseconds, and speakers who stay in sync not only have better understanding but also a better relationship.

This rhythmic pattern is also seen in the nonverbal behavior that accompanies conversation: Speaking patterns are accented by nonverbal gestures and movements that follow the beat. But when you are with someone from a different culture or linguistic background, even your expectations for speech rhythms and nonverbal behaviors may be vastly different. Consciousness about synchrony also seems to vary from culture to culture. Hall (1984) has found people from Northern Europe and North America less aware of such rhythms than people from Asia, Latin America, and Africa.

Relationships: Norms and Roles

Cultures also vary in the contexts in which verbal and nonverbal systems are used. When making friends with a foreign student or working with people abroad in business situations, it is important to remember that personal and working relationships are not the same and do not develop the same way in every culture. People in different cultures expect different behaviors from one another in a relationship. As we've seen, what you consider a friendly gesture might be considered aggressive or impertinent in another culture; your gesture of respect or deference might be interpreted as inappropriate reticence or as defiance, depending on the cultural context.

Norms

Norms, as we discussed in Chapter 9, are *established rules of what is accepted and appropriate behavior.* Although we often use these rules as if they are absolute or instinctive standards, they are actually culturally developed and transmitted. If you grew up in the United States, for instance, you may have been taught to "speak up" clearly and to look at a person who is speaking to you, and that mumbling and looking away when someone addresses you is disrespectful. But not all cultural groups interpret these behaviors as good manners. We have already seen that people in some cultures drop their voices as an indication of respect and deference. White American police officers patrolling Hispanic neighborhoods have often misinterpreted a similar gesture: Hispanic children are taught to lower their eyes, as a gesture of respect, when a person in authority addresses them. The police, who had been brought up with opposite norms, have interpreted the gesture as sullen and resentful, and reacted accordingly.

Understanding norms about conflict becomes particularly important when a disagreement seems to be brewing between two people from different cultures. One study (Ting-Toomey, 2009) looked at the conflict styles of acquaintances in each of four ethnic groups within the United States: African Americans, Asian Americans, Latino(a)s, and European Americans. It also studied ethnic identity (how strongly we identify with our own ethnic group) and cultural identity (in this case, how strongly members of a co-culture identified with the larger culture of the United States). Seven patterns or styles of managing conflict were seen: integrating (showing great concern for yourself and for the other person), compromising, dominating, avoiding, neglecting, emotional expression of conflict, and seeking third-party help. Here are some of the findings:

- Both Latino(a)s and Asian Americans use avoiding and seek third-party help more than African Americans do.
- Asian Americans use avoiding more than European Americans.
- African Americans tend to favor an emotionally expressive style.
- African Americans have a stronger ethnic identity and a weaker cultural identity than the other groups; European Americans have a weaker ethnic identity and a stronger cultural identity than the other groups.
- Individuals who have a strong cultural identity use a more integrating, compromising, and emotionally expressive style than those who have a weak ethnic identity (adapted from pp. 405–408).

At least two important variables distinguish how members of a given culture view interpersonal and family conflicts: (1) expressivity, and (2) privacy and individuality (Sillars and Weisberg, 1987). Even in the United States, there is considerable cultural variation in the amount of emphasis placed on expressive communication about conflict. For example, studies have shown that Jewish families frequently value discussion and analysis so highly that by mainstream standards they may seem argumentative and that Irish families in family therapy dealt with conflicts through allusion, sarcasm, and innuendo rather than engage in verbal confrontations. In each instance, we see a set of assumptions about what constitutes conflict and how it should be negotiated or resolved—or perhaps ignored.

One reason we cannot apply the expressive norms of mainstream culture to other groups is that so many cultures place far less value on individual self-disclosures. Talking about feelings and being open about one's dissatisfactions—even with a member of your family, for example—is not always considered appropriate behavior, and many of the suggestions for resolving conflict mentioned in Chapter 6 would be difficult to apply to intercultural contexts. In fact, in many cultures keeping problems to oneself is strongly favored, and a stoic attitude often develops. For example, in working-class families, problems are frequently regarded as "lying outside the family and within the realm of natural economic, social, and biological conditions that are futile for the family to address. Thus [family members] may adopt a passive problem-solving style that emphasizes family cohesion over active problem solving" (p. 159).

The direct expression of conflict is also considered inappropriate in high-context cultures, which deemphasize explicit verbal coding of information and pay more attention to subtle cues and indirect messages. In such cultures, discretion and indirectness are the norms for dealing with conflict, and they are upheld and understood by members. This is true of the Chinese and Japanese. So while members of low-context cultures might perceive the indirect treatment of conflict as cowardly, those from high-context cultures might perceive a more aggressive or combative response as lacking in taste (Gudykunst and Ting-Toomey, 1988, p. 160).

Cultural norms about privacy and individuality are equally variable. In the two-person and family relationships of mainstream America, a great deal of autonomy is expected—especially among the middle class. Thus during a conflict, you may consider advice from friends and others outside your immediate family an infringement on your privacy. You might not expect others to intervene. In extended families, however, there is a more public aspect of relationships: "Because extended networks promote communal and traditional norms, there are more definite guidelines for resolving conflicts" (Gudykunst and Ting-Toomey, 1988, p. 161). There are even times when conflicts are settled not through personal communication but through the intervention of a third party. In Japan this is sometimes the case.

Roles

Roles, as we discussed in Chapter 9, are *sets of norms that apply to specific groups of people in a society*. Roles, too, vary markedly among cultures. Differences in the respective roles of men and women may represent some of the most apparent cultural differences in human relationships: how unmarried couples should behave and whether they should be chaperoned, how men and women should behave toward each other in business situations, what a husband's and wife's responsibilities are to one another and to their respective families.

The widowed narrator in Gish Jen's short story "Who's Irish?" (1999) is a Chinese woman who long ago immigrated to the United States. She lives with her daughter, who is the vice president of a bank, her Irish-American husband, and their small feisty daughter Sophie, whom she tries to discipline in the old Chinese way. Daughter and granddaughter object repeatedly and when asked to be "supportive," the grandmother remarks that in China the daughter is supposed to take care of the mother and that here it works the other way: "Mother help daughter, mother ask 'Anything else I can do?' Otherwise daughter complain mother is not supportive. I tell my daughter, we do not have this word in Chinese, supportive" (p. 80). By the end of the story, the grandmother is asked to move (her presence is a source of conflict in her daughter's marriage) and ends up living with her son-in-law's Irish mother.

Beliefs and Values

Even if you've never traveled outside the United States, you have heard stories about how U.S. politicians and presidents have inadvertently insulted Polish or Latin American audiences when trying to speak to their audiences in unfamiliar languages. Movies and television programs provide a glimpse of many ways of life, including the roles and norms of Hawaiian American, Asian, Native American, and numerous other cultures. Although the portrayals are not always accurate, they help to give us a sense of some cultural differences.

It is much more difficult to comprehend and accept the values of another culture when they differ from our own. More than any other aspect of the culture taught us from birth, our values seem to us to be universal absolutes. Values determine what we think is right, good, important, beautiful; we find it difficult to accept that what is right or good is as relative to culture as the word for "book" or "stove," or as the way our food is prepared or our clothes are made. (See Box 10.3.) It may be difficult for a Westerner to adjust to the combinations or seasonings of unfamiliar Middle Eastern or Asian cuisine. It is even more difficult to accept that some cultures eat plants or animals that we do not classify as food or to understand why, in the face of mass starvation in India, cattle wander the streets unrestrained, protected by religious taboos. People of other cultures, meanwhile, may be appalled by the willingness of people in this country to eat meat, or at the casualness with which we often have meals "on the run," without ceremony.

Ethical Values

In Chapter 7 we discussed the work of two scholars who proposed that there is a single universal principle, or **protonorm,** that underpins all systematic ethics: *the sacredness of life* (Christians and Nordenstreng, 2004). They believe it relates to at least three basic ethical principles, or "master norms": respect for human dignity, truthtelling, and nonviolence. These **master norms,** sometimes called "core values," were identified in an earlier study of ethical norms in thirteen countries across five continents. Each norm takes different forms in different countries (Christians and Traber, 1997). We consider the three briefly here.

ISSUES IN COMMUNICATION

The Value of Beauty across Cultures

Physical beauty seems to be valued in all cultures, and within a given culture people tend to agree on those who are physically attractive. As we saw in Chapter 2, some researchers believe that there may even be certain universal standards for beauty (Guerrero and Floyd, 2006). In this country people who are perceived as physically attractive are also seen as socially desirable; and often the traits linked with attractive people are extraversion and dominance—both traits that our individualist culture values highly. On the other hand, research finds that in collectivist cultures—for example, Indonesia, China, and Japan—physical attractiveness is often linked with intelligence and integrity, two highly valued traits in societies that emphasize interdependence and cooperative rather than competitive behavior.

When it comes to ourselves, what qualities do we value? In one cross-cultural study, U.S. and Japanese university students were asked to identify three aspects of themselves that they would most like to change. Researchers found that more American than Japanese students opted for changes in their physical appearance, while more Japanese students were interested in changing "aspects of self pertaining to interpersonal harmony . . . American students . . . mentioned individualistic aspects of self as needing change (e.g., 'want to get more of what I deserve,' 'need to rely less on others for my happiness') more often than Japanese students" (Dion, 2002, p. 254).

Which traits do you most value and which do you link with physical attractiveness? What three aspects of yourself would you most like to change?

Respect for human dignity: This first master norm is closely linked with the acknowledgement that all life is sacred:

Native American discourse is steeped in reverence for life, an interconnectedness among all living forms. . . . In communalistic African societies, *likute* is loyalty to the community's reputation, to tribal honor. . . . In Islam, every person has the right to honor and a good reputation. (Christians and Nordenstreng, 2004, p. 21)

Truthtelling: Like the first, the second ethical principle is acknowledged in every culture:

The most fundamental norm of Arab-Islamic communication is truthfulness. Truth is one of the three highest values in . . . the Latin American experience of communication. In Hinduism, truth is the highest *dharma* [law] and the source of all other virtues. Among the Sushwap of Canada, truth as genuineness and authenticity is central to its indigenous culture. . . . Living with others is inconceivable if we cannot tacitly assume that people are speaking truthfully. (p. 22)

Nonviolence: This third principle might be expressed as compassion, willingness to forgive, and an appeal that no harm should be done to the innocent:

Gandhi and Martin Luther King Jr. developed this principle beyond a political strategy into a philosophy of life. . . . In communalistic and indigenous cultures,

Figure 10.2   *State of the World Forum Values*

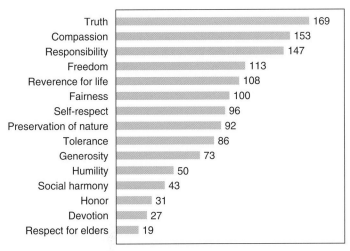

Source: From *Moral Courage*, by Rushworth M. Kidder, Figs. 2 (p. 51) and 7 (p. 73). Copyright © 2004 by Rushworth M. Kidder. Reprinted by permission of HarperCollins Publishers.

care for the weak and vulnerable (children, sick, and elderly) and sharing material resources are a matter of course. Along with *dharma, ahimsa* (nonviolence) forms the basis of the Hindu worldview. (p. 23)

In one survey of 55 possible ethical values, people from 40 countries and 50 different faith groups were asked to select the five values that were most important in their daily lives (Kidder, 2005). Their responses are summarized in Figure 10.2. Notice that truth heads the list. Which five ethical values are most important to you?

TOWARD GREATER INTERCULTURAL UNDERSTANDING AND TOLERANCE

There is probably no more eloquent essay on what it feels like to be seen as someone *other*—someone outside society—than "Stranger in the Village" (1985) by the American writer James Baldwin, who came to stay in a village in Switzerland during the 1950s where no one had ever seen a black person before. Today, despite great technological advances and more exposure to people of other cultures, divisions between people of different cultures at times seem to have only intensified. This is true not only for people from different countries but also sometimes for those who live within a single culturally diverse country such as the United States.

In the following pages we examine some of the processes that cloud our perceptions of others, making strangers out of human beings, and then consider efforts to further greater cultural understanding and tolerance.

PRACTICAL TIPS

When traveling to another country for an extended period of time whether it is for a work assignment or to live, be aware of culture shock. *Culture shock* (Neuliep, 2006) happens when the values, beliefs, customs, and behaviors of one's own culture clash with those of the new culture. Culture shock can be broken down into five stages.

Honeymoon Stage

Also known as the tourist phase, this is where the new culture is seen in a more romantic sense. The new scenery, buildings, foods, and people are fun and exciting. This stage is typical to those vacationing or traveling for brief business trips.

Culture Shock

This is where the excitement experienced from the honeymoon stage tends to turn into stress. The new environment is a cognitive overload and very mentally demanding and can cause frustration, fatigue, loneliness, and confusion. People experience a lack of familiarity and control as minor issues turn into major problems for day-to-day living.

Adjustment Stage

In this phase people tend to pull themselves together and actively seek out solutions to conflicts and problems. They begin to develop a positive attitude and appreciate the new culture as things start to make sense and they adapt to the environment. Although typically the longest stage, it is different for everyone depending on the degree of culture shock they experience.

Acculturation Stage

Also known as the adaptation stage, people have engaged with the culture and experience a cultural transformation. Individuals create an intercultural identity and reach a competent level of communication with the natives. Personal growth develops as things are now understood in a new light.

Re-entry Shock

Most people do not expect another culture shock when returning to their home country. After living and interacting with a different culture for an extended period of time, there are things you take away that are not present in the home culture. You have created an identity with another culture that makes you see your own culture through a new set of eyes (Neuliep, 2006, pp. 430–433).

Ethnocentrism

Culture is like a pair of sunglasses. It shields us from external harshness and offers us some measure of safety and comfort. It also blocks us from seeing clearly through our tinted lenses because of the same protectiveness. In brief, culture nurtures our ethnocentric attitudes and behaviors.

—Ting-Toomey (1999, p. 14)

Ethnocentrism is *the tendency to judge the values, customs, behaviors, or other aspects of another culture in terms of those that our own cultural group regards as desirable or ideal*. Literally, "ethnocentrism" refers to putting one's "nation" at the center—the word is Greek in origin and derives from *ethnos* ("nation") and *kentron* ("center"). We tend to be ethnocentric about our own country, our own region, or our own ethnic group, regarding it as the best and most important—whether it is about our music, food, art, or political system. The concept of ethnocentrism is not always negative. For example, when members of a group are being attacked or threatened ethnocentrism "forms the basis for patriotism and the willingness to sacrifice for one's central group" (Neuliep and McCroskey, 1997a).

In many of our interactions, our ethnocentric attitudes interfere with our perceptions of other cultural groups. A recent study of in-group favoritism (Hammond and Axelrod, 2006) finds that ethnocentric behaviors are extremely widespread and that we are predisposed to favor in-groups. Our membership in the group fosters higher levels of cooperation, even when that cooperation has negative consequences for us: "preferential cooperation within groups occurs even when it is individually costly" (p. 926). And our ethnocentrism can also foster anxiety about members of other cultures. For example, U.S. students who rated high in ethnocentrism tended to have a higher level of anxiety about other cultural groups when they were visiting foreign countries (Stephan and Stephan, 1992).

Ethnocentrism seems to be characteristic of every culture. Yet part of the recent Pew Global Attitudes Project (*www.people-press.org*) reports that although people worldwide take pride in their own culture

it is only in the West (North America and Western Europe) where that pride is markedly stronger among the older generations, while younger people tend to be less wedded to their cultural identities.

In the U.S., 68% of those ages 65 and older agree with the statement "our people are not perfect, but our culture is superior," while only 49% of those ages 18–29 agree.

This trend seems to be true of Western Europe, but Eastern European people of all ages are "more likely to say their culture is superior." In Asia, Africa, and Latin America ethnocentric feelings seem to be uniformly stronger, with little or no generation gap (except for Japan). Perhaps you've received the "compliment" that you are not like other Americans—ethnocentric attitudes can be deeply divisive and even impede negotiations between members of different cultures.

To illustrate how pervasive ethnocentrism is, one writer refers to the maps in schoolrooms around the world. For example, on the world map that appears in many classrooms throughout this country the center of its east-west axis is the United States, which means that the Eurasian landmass is split and distorted on either side. Classroom maps from other countries are equally revealing, placing their own culture at the world's center—with all the distortions that might require. "Maps become problematic," writes Blair, "when students (and adults) forget that they are maps and start believing in the worlds they represent. The same is true of cultures: One's own culture will likely seem universal until one finds a way of stepping outside its cloaking devices at least provisionally. As an old Chinese proverb has it: the fish does not discover water" (Blair, 2000, p. 25).

But is it possible to remove the "tinted lenses" of our own culture? Blair believes that to do this we must acknowledge two principles: (1) Ethnocentrism appears to be universal; and (2) "ethnocentrisms have, in principle, an equal claim on legitimacy" (p. 32). Although we may not find these "equally attractive or admirable" (p. 32), we have to find ways of going beyond them and becoming increasingly sophisticated in our awareness of other cultures—remembering perhaps that there are alternative maps of the world, many perceptions of the same experience.

> The most promising move we can make to counter the traps that cultures set for us lies not in seeking to get beyond culture altogether, but by changing our attitude toward whatever culture has been primary for us. Once we recognize that our own enculturation is neither universal nor authoritative for others, we can recognize it for what it is: OUR culture, one among OTHERS. [This] frees us to engage in cultural comparisons, in dialogue with OTHERS. (Blair, 2000, p. 32)

Because the Internet has become a source of increasing knowledge about the world some scholars suggest the possibility that "international news could cultivate a broad worldview, as reading international news in national and regional newspapers was found to be negatively related to ethnocentrism" (Kwak et al., 2006, pp. 192–193).

Stereotyping

As we saw in Chapter 2, we tend to impose stereotypes on groups of people, which limits our communication with those groups. It is almost impossible for us not to stereotype a group of people with whom we have no personal contact; furthermore, without personal contact, it is almost impossible for us to dispel the stereotypes we acquire about the group. We saw that stereotypes are inadequate because they are generalizations based on limited experience. Certainly, the sources of our information about people of different cultures are often inaccurate.

One recent series of studies explored how stereotypes guide **defensive projection**—that is, *seeing our own undesirable qualities in other people.* This is particularly the case when a person's self-concept is threatened in some way. In other words, our perceptions of self play a role in how much we stereotype others. Researchers also found that people who were stereotyped "are more likely to serve as targets of projection than are nonstereotyped individuals" (Govorun et al., 2006, p. 781).

Numerous cross-cultural studies identify the mass media, particularly television, as a major source of information about other cultures. Many scholars have called attention to how damaging stereotyped images can be. An example is the portrayal of Arabs, both in films and on television, as villains. This stereotyping predates 9/11, with such controversial films as *The Siege* and *Rules of Engagement*. One critic points out that since 9/11 there has been a "steady portrayal of the Arab as villain . . . CBS series, including *JAG, The District, The Agency* and *Family Law,* have represented Arabs as deceitful, brutish, lunatic terrorists and murderers. . . ." (Ross, 2003, p. 60). All minority cultures are greatly concerned over media representations and distortions and the stereotypes that such images create.

An implicit linguistic intergroup bias (LIB) in response to crime reporting is the subject of a recent study. Gorham (2006) looked at how people viewing a crime suspect on a television news program described him—that is, whether their choice of language was more abstract or concrete. When the suspect was African American, white adults were more likely to describe the suspect by using more abstract language; when describing a white suspect, they used more concrete descriptive terms. The data suggest that we use language that is more abstract than concrete in describing behaviors linked with stereotypes, especially if we are describing someone who is a member of an out-group (p. 289).

Gorham (2006) emphasizes that our choice of abstract or concrete language is not a conscious one. Rather, it sometimes stems from an underlying bias, "an implicit and unobtrusive way that language can reflect the dominant ideology of the race" (p. 305).

A study on racial stereotyping in comedy notes the increasing number of comedies—including *I Spy, Shanghai Knights,* and *Harold & Kumar Go to White Castle*—in which the leading men are Asian and/or African American (Park et al., 2006, p. 157). Subjects in the study watched the film *Rush Hour 2,* starring Jackie Chan and Chris Tucker as policemen in pursuit of Asian gang members involved in a counterfeiting scheme. The subjects in the study were Asian, African American, and white college students. Most were not offended by the many racial jokes—not even jokes about their own race. In the words of Justin, an 18-year-old Asian male:

> Chris Tucker and Jackie Chan complement each other. Obviously Jackie Chan is better in fighting and stuff. But Chris Tucker is better at talking and everything. So they kind of cancel each other out. They are a good combo. But I think with a White person and an Asian person, it always feels like the White person is better than the Asian person (p. 170).

The researchers note the film's sense of equality and friendship between Chan and Tucker's characters. They argue that the conventions of comedy "encourage the audience to naturalize racial difference rather than to challenge racial stereotypes"; "viewers' validation of racial stereotypes is the ideological effect of comedy that encourages them to perceive racial differences as essential and natural, not culturally constructed" (pp. 157, 174). Further research is needed to test whether the effects of racial stereotyping in comedy may be different from other kinds of programming.

ISSUES IN COMMUNICATION
Some Guidelines for Critical Viewers of Film and Television

In her study of stereotyping, *Latin Looks: Images of Latinas and Latinos in the U.S. Media*, Clara Rodriguez suggests some guidelines for critical viewers of film and television. Here are some questions to ask yourself when watching a film or television drama. Remember, these questions are relevant for all cultural groups:

1. Who is telling this story?

2. Given the perspective of the camera, which characters does the director want us to follow? With whom do you identify? Why?

3. Can you imagine the world of the film as seen by characters who are denied a point of view in this film? Can you develop an alternative scenario around the point(s) of view of characters who function as peripheral, almost invisible, reactors to the central characters, for example, butlers, maids, waitresses, bartenders, cab drivers, and anonymous victims?

4. Where else could the camera go?

5. Who else could tell us stories?

6. What stories have not been told yet?

7. Can you provide a socioeconomic profile of the typical hero in coming-of-age films? . . . Have you observed other types of people in other situations come of age in the United States? Have you seen their stories in movies?

8. How are the answers to these questions related to who the directors, writers, producers are? to the tenor of the times? to the audience with the most money to spend? (Rodriguez, 1997, p. 240)

Source: From *Latin Looks: Images of Latinas and Latinos in the U.S. Media* by Clara Rodriguez. Copyright © 1997 by Westview Press, a division of Perseus Books, L.L.C. Reprinted by permission of Westview Press, a member of Perseus Books Group.

How do members of different racial and ethnic groups react when they live with each other? In a study of intercultural contact between groups (Halualani et al., 2004), researchers chose a multicultural university in the western United States that had a commuter campus. The four groups studied were "Blacks/African Americans, Whites/European Americans, Asian Americans, and Latino/as." Despite the claims of the majority of students—70 percent of those studied said they appreciated the diversity on campus and that they participated in intercultural interactions—"student intercultural contact did not take place in community life or private homes" (p. 284). This study reflects the tendency toward insularity and ethnic enclaves in the United States.

Following the hijacking attacks of September 11, 2001, Arab Americans became the targets of bias crimes across the country. One source reported that between September 11 and October 2, 2001, there were over 700 reported bias crimes against Arab Americans and others including Hindus and Sikhs, who are neither Arab nor Muslim. Like the Japanese Americans in the film *Snow Falling on Cedars*, they have sometimes been seen as mysterious outsiders.

Many in the United States know little about Arab culture. Nor is there much understanding of the religion of Islam, which is not the religion of all Arabs. In some communities in the United States, fear and ignorance have turned anyone with darker skin into a focus of mistrust and anger. Sikhs have been singled out because they have beards and wear turbans (both mandated by their own religion). Several writers have pointed out that in the United States even before the events of 9/11, the turban had become a symbol for terrorism. Following 9/11, many Arab Americans lost their jobs. One Arab American who had lived in Dearborn, Michigan, all his life said:

> I don't want my kids to live the life I've had to lead, always apologizing for who I am. I can be either American or I can be an Arab, but I can't be both. You know what? I am both. (Wilgoren, 2001, p. B1)

Similarly, a young college student who had immigrated from Dar-es-Salaam, Tanzania, and described herself as a "hyphenated American" (American-Muslim) was harassed as she walked down a New York street:

> As I walked along Broadway, my headscarf was an open sign to anyone who wanted to let their frustrations out . . . by cursing, giving me dirty looks, and . . . walking into me. . . . I guess one couldn't tell that my scarf was not woven with hatred for this country and it doesn't represent a defunct interpretation of Islam as a militant, bloodthirsty religion that the media often portrays it to be. And finally, I guess one couldn't tell that I, and the majority of the world's Muslims, are not responsible. (Mambani, 2001, p. 14)

In an atmosphere shadowed by fear and suspicion, and often based on lack of knowledge about members of other cultural groups, it seems important to recall two ways in which we can improve person perception: awareness that our perceptions can be inaccurate and empathy, sensitivity, or responsiveness (see pp. 61–62). And in educating ourselves about other cultures, the Internet is sometimes a valuable resource. For example, the American-Arab Anti-Discrimination Committee has a Web site that offers information about Arab American culture (see *www.adc.org*). More broad-based Web sites such as *www.tolerance.org* explore the nature of prejudice and ways to foster tolerance.

Promoting Greater Tolerance and Harmony

The novel *Bel Canto* by Ann Patchett (2005) is set in an unnamed South American country. On an evening intended to celebrate the birthday of its vice president at his home, the guests, invited from all over the world, are mistakenly kidnapped by terrorists and held hostage over many days. Slowly these people, who did not know one another, come to forge a bond that goes far beyond national and linguistic boundaries. For all assembled it is an experience that changes their lives. This is a fable about what happens when people of many cultures are forced into sustained contact with one another.

Many studies have explored the effects of contact between members of different racial and ethnic groups. One important question is what, if anything, we gain from interacting with members of other cultures—does more interaction and increased communication contribute to greater rapport? *Intergroup contact theory,* proposed by Gordon Allport (1954) to explain racial and ethnic dynamics, holds that four conditions are needed for intergroup contact to be optimal—equal status between the groups, authority support, shared goals, and intergroup cooperation—so that contact between groups, if they were not competing with each other, would result in a decrease in prejudice.

The social psychologist Thomas Pettigrew later suggested that for ideal contact a fifth condition is necessary: friendship. He emphasizes the components of feeling and familiarity—that when we get to know individual people and more about their lives over a sustained period of time and when we are emotionally involved, prejudice declines and rapport increases. Pettigrew and Tropp (2006) recently examined over 500 different studies of the contact hypothesis. Their meta-analysis confirms that "intergroup contact typically reduces intergroup prejudice," and they believe that the findings can be extended to other large groups and contexts (p. 752).

Recent research on partisan social groups also finds that when we are partisan we have more misperceptions of disagreement and often overemphasize our differences of opinion with those of rival groups (out-groups) (Chambers et al., 2006; Chambers and Melnyk, 2006). And when we overemphasize disagreement with our own values, our perceptions alter how we evaluate out-group members; we tend to dislike them more, attribute negative stereotypes to them, and favor our own group more (pp. 1295, 1307). The stumbling block is our belief, sometimes unfounded, that our rivals are contesting the ideals and values we cherish most.

Several scholars are extending the study of intergroup relations. They are concerned not only with ways of reducing prejudice but also with identifying variables that promote social inclusion. Nagda and others (2006) are investigating communication processes as a new dimension of intergroup contact and education. They observe that "people often long to talk about race, but may not know how to do so" (p. 557). The greater the amount of intergroup dialogue—"speaking, listening, and asking questions"—the more engaged and positive participants become. The most important variables are (1) appreciating difference, (2) engaging the self, (3) critical self-reflection, and (4) alliance building (p. 553).

In the arts an unusual example of alliance building is seen in the West-Eastern Divan Orchestra, formed by the Israeli musician and conductor Daniel Barenboim. His orchestra brings together young Arab and Jewish musicians. They have performed in many countries throughout the world including Palestine, Spain, Germany, and the United States, and their ongoing project has been described as "a symbol of hope in troubled times."

Other efforts to promote understanding and tolerance include the study circles, held in many counties and cities, in which people can speak in depth about race relations and compare experiences. In small diverse groups, participants speak from personal experience about why racial and ethnic prejudice exist and how to change such attitudes. Most important, study circles often form action groups. Group initiatives include classroom forums and advocacy for greater media coverage of minority issues as well as greater legislative representation and media ownership by minorities.

Responding to an editorial by Harvard sociologist Orlando Patterson, letters to the editor of the *New York Times* recently took up the question of living with others in a diverse society. The headline above these letters was, "Is It Who We Are, or How We Act?" Patterson (2006) proposes that it's how we act toward others, not personal concern about authenticity, that matters most:

> I couldn't care less whether my neighbors and co-workers are authentically sexist, racist or ageist. What matters is that they behave with civility and tolerance, obey the rules of social interaction and are sincere about it. The criteria of sincerity are unambiguous: Will they keep their promises? Will they honor the meanings and understandings we tacitly negotiate? Are their gestures of cordiality offered in conscious good faith? (p. A35)

In *Cosmopolitanism: Ethics in a World of Strangers,* Kwame Anthony Appiah, a philosopher at Princeton, argues that cultural differences are overemphasized, their significance overstated. The term *cosmopolitan,* or "citizen of the world," links back to Greek philosophers in the fourth century B.C. **Cosmopolitanism,** the approach Appiah proposes, *has two interwoven strands: The first is our obligation to others, "the recognition of our responsibility for every human being." The second is our "recognition that human beings are different and that we can learn from each other's differences."* The ideals of his philosophy are "universal concern and respect for legitimate difference" (2006, pp. 4, 7–8).

Appiah, who grew up in Ghana and has lived on three continents, believes there are ways in which we can live in harmony with others while acknowledging that differences exist and that we may not and should not expect to always persuade others of our own beliefs and values. What we do need is ongoing conversation, both in the sense of simply living, associating with one another and of genuine exchange:

> Conversations across boundaries of identity—whether national, religious, or anything else—begin with the sort of imaginative engagement you get when you read a novel or watch a movie or attend to a work of art that speaks from some place other than your own. So I'm using the word "conversation" not only for literal talk but also as a metaphor for engagement with the experience and ideas of others. . . . Conversation doesn't have to lead to consensus about anything, especially not values; it's enough that it helps people get used to one another. (p. 85)

EFFECTS OF INTERCULTURAL COMMUNICATION

Effects on the Individual

Travel is easier and more affordable than it was for our parents and grandparents. Yet even within our own country we tend to stay within our own groups and subgroups. The needs and desires of many groups to affirm and preserve their cultures are reflected in demands for more bilingual education, multicultural programs and curriculums, and textbooks that better represent all cultural contributions to our literature and history. Among the swelling immigrant population in the largest cities of the United States we find ethnic groups clustering in their own neighborhoods. Take New York's "Little Bombay," for example, a densely packed area with rows of stores stocking Indian spices, saris, videos, newspapers—every imaginable evidence of this thriving culture.

For anyone who reads books and newspapers, who watches television, or gets news from the Internet and is concerned with international events, the world has grown larger. The mass media have brought us images of the war in Iraq, genocide in Darfur, bombings in London and Madrid, conflicts between Israelis and Palestinians, and the devastating tsunami in Southeast Asia as well as other natural disasters worldwide. We can no longer escape knowledge of terrorist acts or world hunger or turn away from the impact of international events.

Although it is often assumed that international understanding increases as a result of cultural and educational exchanges over an extended period of time, scholars believe that this hoped-for goal must be demonstrated empirically. Thus, there have been several studies of student exchange programs. For example, Rohrlich and Martin (1991) studied the adjustment of U.S. college students to studying abroad and found women to be more satisfied than men upon returning, perhaps because their lifestyle at home was more independent than when living with a host family. Carlson and Widaman (1988) compared students from the University of California who spent their junior year studying at a European university with students who remained on campus. At the end of the school year, the study-abroad group had higher levels of cross-cultural interest, international political concern, and cultural cosmopolitanism, as well as significantly more positive and more critical attitudes toward their own country (p. 14). So relatively long-term study abroad may contribute to more favorable attitudes and increased international understanding, but there is still much to be learned about how such attitudes develop.

Cultural Effects

Most people would not question the value of introducing sanitation methods that curb epidemics, or life-saving vaccines and medications, or agricultural methods that save thousands from starvation. But many, including a number of scholars of culture, question the value of other aspects of cultural exchange. They ask whether aboriginal communities that have been isolated for hundreds of years truly benefit from sudden contact with the outside world—whether, for example, exposure to war as well as sources of illness and pollution might outweigh what we consider the advances of civilization. The possibilities raise many ethical questions.

Some have argued that intercultural exchange leads to **cultural homogenization,** *the tendency for cultures in contact with one another to become increasingly similar to one another.* The belief the world is becoming more and more homogeneous implies that some aspects of one culture will dominate and eliminate the corresponding aspects of the other.

But to many scholars such a view of cultural influence seems simplistic. Even if we are familiar with foods from all over the world and blue jeans are as popular in Russia as in the United States, even if Shanghai has its Starbucks and McDonald's, each culture tends to modify and adapt what it receives from another. McDonald's in India serves Maharaja Macs and veggie burgers. "Local and regional ways of thinking and living do not disappear in the face of imported cultural influences," writes James Lull (2000, p. 234):

> What many contemporary observers conclude is that the global circulation of images, ideologies, and cultural styles—facilitated by the multinational culture and communications industries—actually fuels symbolic creativity, lessens homogeneity, and increases cultural diversity. (p. 232)

"The very concept of culture," Lull continues, "presumes difference" (p. 234).

Of course, awareness and understanding of difference can create greater cultural exchange. Carles Torner, a writer from Barcelona, pointed out that publishing in this country "runs the risk of helping to foster a culture in the U.S. with an increasingly narrow and insular view of other cultures. Only 3 percent of titles published in the United States are translations from other languages; in Europe it is between 20 to 40 percent" ("Mind the Gap," 2005, p. 116). Torner stressed the importance of equality in the dialogue between countries and how it can be enhanced by the availability of translations.

Summary

In this chapter, we discussed intercultural communication, which has become so pervasive within the last few decades. We defined "culture" as a way of life developed and shared by a people and passed down from generation to generation. Because cultures vary along a range, the differences between two cultures may be slight or very dramatic. Even when two cultural groups are very similar, however, the differences between them are likely to become more evident in intercultural communication. We looked at three major approaches to the study of intercultural communication. Several dimensions of cultural variability were then examined, including collectivism-individualism, high and low context, and power distance.

Intercultural communication has increased rapidly because of mass migrations and technological advances that have made long-distance communication more feasible and more available to the general public. Despite the advances in the means of sending and receiving messages, however, there are still many obstacles. Differences in cultural variables such as language, nonverbal communication systems, relational roles and norms (particularly conflict norms), and beliefs and values that are deeply rooted in the whole cultural system often lead to intercultural misunderstanding.

Because we are not aware of the aspects of our own cultures in ourselves, the barriers to intercultural communication are complex and formidable. Ethnocentrism and stereotyping both limit our ability to deal with people beyond our own communities. And the Internet, often used as a bridge to understanding and connection, can also be used to foster division and hostility—for example, through the proliferation of hate sites. We discussed intergroup contact theory and approaches to promoting greater tolerance and harmony. We also looked at the individual and social effects of our increasingly global culture and considered some principles for building community.

Key Terms

Co-culture
Collectivism
Cosmopolitanism
Cultural
  homogenization

Culture
Defensive projection
Ethnocentrism
High-context culture
Individualism

Low-context culture
Master norm
Power distance
Protonorm

Synchrony
Uncertainty avoidance

Review Questions

1. How do cultural groups differ from other groups that have shared characteristics?

2. Why is it important for effective intercultural communication to understand that culture is learned, rather than innate?

3. Describe the three major approaches to the study of intercultural communication and give an example of each.

4. What are the main reasons that intercultural communication has increased in the last decades?

5. How do such changes affect the new immigrant population in the United States?

6. Explain two major dimensions along which cultures are thought to vary. Give an example.

7. Discuss three other dimensions that measure cultural variation. Give an example of each.

8. State three broad communication principles with significant implications for intercultural communication.

9. Explain at least three ways in which language can be an obstacle to intercultural communication.

10. Describe at least three aspects of nonverbal communication that vary from culture to culture.

11. How can cultural roles and norms affect communication between cultures?

12. Discuss two variables that influence how members of a culture view conflict. Give an example of each.

13. Explain how differences in beliefs and values can become obstacles in intercultural communication.

14. Discuss three master norms that appear to function as core values in many different cultures. Propose one underlying principle for these.

15. Describe one culture's successful adaptation to living in a new country and explain how its beliefs and values contributed to that success.

16. What is ethnocentrism? Why does it interfere with intercultural communication? Give an example.

17. Give two reasons for the stereotyping of cultural groups and discuss its effects on interethnic and interracial conflict. Explain the concept of defensive projection.

18. Discuss some possible effects of the Internet on bigotry.

19. Explain the recent research findings on intergroup relations and discuss the principles of cosmopolitanism.

20. Identify several personal, political, and social effects of intercultural communication.

21. What is meant by "cultural homogenization"? How valid do you think this concept is? Support your answer with examples.

Exercises

1. Make a list of some of the cultural groups in your own region or state, including the group (or groups) that founded your community. To what extent have these groups been in contact with one another? To what extent have they remained distinct from one another? List some ways in which these cultural groups have affected your own culture, such as your traditions, religious beliefs, and language.

2. Find three current articles in print or on the Internet about a cultural group, such as a group in China, Mexico, or Israel, that has extended business, diplomatic contact, or cultural exchange with the United States. List at least five ways in which that culture, or that of the United States, has been affected by this contact.

3. Write a paragraph discussing whether you think you are prejudiced in any way. After this self-assessment, go to *www.tolerance.org* and select the heading "Dig Deeper": Take one or more of the hidden-bias tests. Compare your score with the paragraph you wrote. Discuss your agreement or disagreement with the rating.

4. List at least eight cultures, both inside and outside the United States, with which you communicate in some way (through personal contact, your work or business

communication, or mass media). With which of these groups is your communication personal? With which is it institutional? In at least one case in which your contact with the other culture is primarily institutional, describe some ways in which your understanding of the people in that group is limited by your communication with them.

5. Write down what you know about Arab Americans and Arab culture. Then go to *www.adc.org* and read about Arab Americans. Afterward revise anything you wrote that was incorrect and write a one-page summary of what you have learned.

6. Think of a group of people that you feel have specific shared cultural characteristics, for example, Californians, southerners, New Yorkers, African Americans, European Americans, Amish, Japanese, Russians, Chinese. Describe the people as a group and list the characteristics that you think distinguish that group from others. To what extent is your description a stereotype? What is the source of your information about the group? Can you think of some reasons your stereotype might be inaccurate? Can you think of some ways in which it might affect your communication with individual members of that group?

7. Find an essay or article in a book or magazine or on the Web that describes the experience of being a member of a culture other than your own. Write a brief essay comparing and contrasting it with your own experience.

Suggested Readings

Appiah, Kwame Anthony. *Cosmopolitanism: Ethics in a World of Strangers.* New York: Norton, 2006.

A philosopher from Princeton argues for both universal concern for the values of others and "respect for legitimate difference."

Buchanan, Patrick. *Suicide of a Superpower.* New York: Thomas Dunne Press, 2011.

This book is a conservative's view of the seismic changes in American culture.

Christians, Clifford, and Michael Traber, eds. *Communication Ethics and Universal Values.* Thousand Oaks, CA: Sage, 1997.

A collection of essays that looks at the value systems of individual cultures and also explores the possibility of creating a universal set of ethical norms. For the advanced reader.

Friedman, Thomas, and Michael Mandelbaum. *That Used to Be Us.* New York: Farrar, Straus and Giroux, 2011.

Two liberal writers' view of the changing American culture.

Hall, Edward T. *Beyond Culture.* Garden City, NY: Doubleday, 1976.

The author of this book, an anthropologist, is an important researcher in cultural differences and their effects on intercultural communication in business and diplomacy.

Hessler, Peter. *Oracle Bones: A Journey Between China's Past and Present.* New York: HarperCollins, 2006.

A fascinating book of enormous range about China's people and its culture—including its many minority peoples.

House of Sand and Fog

A compelling film about the painful collision of people from two very different cultures—members of an Iranian family and a young woman born in the United States. Based on a novel by Andre Dubus III, the film stars Ben Kingsley and Jennifer Connelly.

Lencioni, Patrick. *The Advantage.* San Francisco: Jossey-Bass, 2012.

This book looks at ways to improve organizations through improved intercultural communication.

Lester, Paul Martin, and Susan Dente Ross, eds. *Images That Injure,* 2nd ed. Westport, CT: Praeger, 2003.

Here is a collection of essays that looks at the effects of pictorial stereotypes that appear in the mass media, how they are created and how various groups of people are described and viewed by mainstream culture. There are sections on ethnic, gender, physical, sexual, and other stereotypes as well as a timely discussion of ethics and post–9/11 images.

Lewis, Michael. *Boomerang.* New York: W. W. Norton Company, 2011.

A shocking preview of America's future culture.

Martin, Judith N., and Thomas K. Nakayama. *Experiencing Intercultural Communication,* 3rd ed. New York: McGraw-Hill, 2008.

The authors introduce their subject from a dialectical perspective and integrate research from the social science, interpretive, and critical approaches, making use of many interesting examples.

Murray, Charles. *Coming Apart.* New York: Crown Forum, 2012.

A startling and well-researched profile of the enormous shifts in American culture.

Nueliep, James. *Intercultural Communication: A Contextual Approach.* Thousand Oaks, CA: Sage, 2011.

This is an outstanding current and comprehensive coverage of intercultural communication.

Schein, Edgar. *Organizational Culture and Leadership.* New York: John Wiley, 2010.

This book looks at culture and leadership effectiveness.

Stewart, Frank, and Brent Fujinaka. "Beyond Words: Asian Writers on Their Work," *Mānoa* 18, no. 1 (2006).

Manoa is an exceptional journal that brings together voices from all over Asia. In this issue writers from China, Tibet, Japan, Vietnam, Cambodia, the Philippines, Malaysia, and Indonesia discuss their writing, values, and beliefs.

Stewart, Rory. *The Places in Between.* Orlando, FL: Harcourt, 2006.

This is a beautifully written account, by turns harrowing and humorous, of a young Scotsman's trip on foot across Afghanistan. Unarmed and accompanied by a mastiff he names Babur, Stewart crosses five different tribal cultures, relying on the Afghan traditions of hospitality for his food and lodging.

 ## For Supplementary Information

Log onto the Online Learning Center at *www.mhhe.com/tubbshc13e.*

12

Small-Group Communication

Chapter Objectives

After reading this chapter, you should be able to:

1. Describe two theories that have been used to explain compliance with social pressure.
2. Describe the problem of "groupthink."
3. Describe the four phases of a typical group's development.
4. Describe the relationship between group size, member satisfaction, and group performance.
5. Distinguish between task and consideration functions in leadership.
6. Identify six common difficulties that small groups encounter in developing ideas and solving problems.
7. Describe four ways in which a group can arrive at a decision.

Suppose you were in one of the top leadership positions in the country and had to decide how best to deal with the war in Afghanistan. This was the challenge for the top officials of the Obama administration after having U.S. troops there for over ten years. The Pulitzer Prize–winning author Bob Woodward explains some of the dilemmas surrounding this war in his best-selling book *Obama's Wars* (Woodward, 2010).

On one hand, some in the administration felt that we should reduce troop strength as much and as soon as possible, since there didn't seem to be much progress in this, our nation's longest war. On the other extreme, the military generals lobbied for as many troops as possible, given that we have the world's strongest armed forces. After all, why not get the job done and get out of there? Others in the administration took positions somewhere in between these two extremes. Afghanistan was led by President Hamid Karzai, who seemed to be mentally unstable and was sometimes described as "being off his medications," and whose half-brother had worked with the CIA, but was known to be corrupt. He took large sums of money from the United States as rent for properties in Kandahar that he did not even own or control (p. 65). U.S. policy makers wondered openly whether we should even be associating with Karzai. In fact, the CIA had evidence that there was a staggering amount of corruption throughout the Afghan government (p. 66). At the same time, al Qaeda terrorists seemed to go out of Afghanistan across the border to Pakistan, where they were more likely to be safe. In fact, when Osama bin Laden was finally killed, he was in Pakistan in a compound within close proximity to Pakistani police. An unstable Afghanistan would lead to an unstable Pakistan. And since Pakistan had nuclear weapons, this was an extremely delicate situation.

If you were in this group of top government officials, what do you think you would do? Having attended countless business meetings, it never ceases to amaze me how few leaders know how to conduct one.

First, if you don't have anything important to say, don't schedule a meeting for the heck of it. When you *do* have something worthwhile to address, know what your message is—and just as important, know what you want people to get out of it. Otherwise, you're just wasting everyone's time—and people hate that.

The person who knows how to run a meeting will get twice as much out of his or her people, because when the meeting's over, they'll be ready to act on the message. That's what a meeting's *supposed* to accomplish! (Schembechler and Bacon, 2007, p. 65).

Consider the following facts:

- Eleven million meetings occur in the United States each and every day.
- Professionals attend a total of 61.8 meetings per month.
- Over 50 percent of this meeting time is wasted (Meetings in America, 1998).

James Surowiecki, an author and business columnist for *The New Yorker,* states that "under the right circumstances, groups are remarkably intelligent, and are often smarter than the smartest people in them" (Hannon, 2004, p. B8). Did you know that 17 international research labs harmonized their small-group efforts in order to unveil the SARS virus (Hannon)?

The power of group decisions over individual decisions has been dramatically demonstrated in the popular television show *Who Wants to Be a Millionaire?* As Surowiecki (2004) writes in his best-selling book *Wisdom of Crowds,* past incidents have shown that asking the crowd most of the time gave a higher chance of getting the correct answer than calling a friend through the "lifeline." This is but one of many such studies that show that groups of individuals consistently make better quality decisions than the same individuals trying to solve the same problems separately in the same amount of time (Tubbs, 2012).

Although group communication skills have been valued for many years, recently there has been a dramatic increase in the emphasis placed on this type of expertise. One professional association reported that Harvard, Syracuse, UCLA, the University of Illinois, the University of Michigan, BYU, SMU, and the University of Tennessee are just a few of the many universities that have increased their requirements for students to take group communication courses to improve their teamwork and communication skills (Walsh, 2011). One of the reasons is that more and more careers require teamwork and group committee work.

According to a national survey, the average number of meetings has jumped from 7 to 10 a week. Approximately 11 million meetings occur in the United States each day. Most professionals attend a total of 61.8 meetings per month, and research indicates that over 50 percent of this meeting time is wasted. Assuming each of these meetings is one hour long, professionals lose 31 hours per month in unproductive meetings, or approximately four work days. Those who attend meetings regularly admit to daydreaming (91 percent), missing meetings (96 percent), or missing parts of meetings (95 percent). A large percentage (73 percent) say they have brought other work to meetings, and 39 percent say they have dozed during meetings (www .effectivemeetings.com/meetingbasics/meetstate.asp, 2011). The following are a few tips on how to make meetings more useful:

- Have a reason for the meeting.
- Prepare ahead of time.
- Give participants at least one day's notice.
- Distribute an agenda ahead of time.
- Limit attendance and designate a leader.
- Encourage everyone to contribute.
- Keep a clock in the room and have a specific starting and ending time.
- Start and end on time. (Armour, 1997)

Most of us spend at least some of our time in problem-solving groups. A student council, a commission investigating the causes of prison riots, a fundraising committee for a political party, and a tenants' association organized to fight rent increases have much in common. Despite the diverse issues that concern them, each group consists of several human beings with different ideas, skills, and levels of interest. Each group has a problem to solve and must determine the best way to go about solving it—ideally by making use of the resources of all its members.

As you saw in the opening case study of the war in Afghanistan, this chapter is about the kind of communication that takes place in small groups, particularly in **problem-solving,** or *task-oriented,* **groups.** We shall focus first on the ways in which such groups typically function and second on the ways individual members can improve their effectiveness in them. In doing so, we begin to extend the communication model outlined in Chapter 1. The dyad is sometimes referred to as a "two-person group," and often two people will engage in problem solving. But in discussing the small group, particularly the problem-solving group, we shall follow the definition offered in Chapter 1—namely, that a small group is a collection of individuals who influence one another, derive some satisfaction from maintaining membership in the group, interact for some purpose, assume specialized roles, are dependent on one another, and communicate face to face (Tubbs, 2012). A small group will meet some but not necessarily all six criteria.

TYPES OF SMALL GROUPS

Small-group experience is by no means confined to problem solving. Each of us is simultaneously a member of many small groups. The first and most informal are primary groups, the basic social units to which we belong. Our first primary group is our family. Our childhood friends constitute another.

A social identity forms once a person realizes he or she belongs to a group. One of the major cognitive tools individuals use to define themselves vis-à-vis the world in which they live is social categorization, "the ordering of social environment in terms of groupings of persons in a manner which makes sense to the individual" (Gudykunst and Hammer, 1988, p. 571).

In the company of adult friends, neighbors, and others with whom we socialize— fraternity or sorority groups, classmates, teammates, even street gangs—we continue and *extend our primary-group relationships* to **casual** or **social groups.** While these relationships may be relatively short-lived, their influence on later thinking and behavior is often considerable. Newcomb (1963) found that the attitudes and values of college students were influenced significantly by the friends and acquaintances they made while at college. To a lesser degree, these changes were still present 30 years after graduation. Occasionally, members of primary or social groups solve problems together, but much of their communication is spontaneous and informal.

As members of **learning** or **education groups,** we come together in an attempt *to teach or learn something about a given subject*. Quarterback clubs meet to learn more about football. Film groups get together to share their interpretations of movies. Seminars and courses involving group interaction also constitute learning groups. Levine and Mooreland (2006) refer to such groups as "enlightenment groups," in which members may attempt to solve problems but have no authority to implement their decisions.

Sooner or later, most of us will belong to **work groups,** which *have specific goals to achieve,* often within the context of a job. Membership may be required by virtue of employment in an organization rather than because of individual interest in the group. Group members may have little in common other than that their jobs require them to interact. That they receive payment for their individual contributions adds a unique dimension to this type of group. And whereas a member of a social or a learning group might remain relatively inactive, the consequences of not participating in a work group can be more severe (reprimands, ostracism, or even loss of employment).

The most recent innovation in work groups is the **self-directed work team** (SDWT), defined by Kimball Fisher (1999) as "a group of employees who have day-to-day responsibility for managing themselves and the work they do with a minimum of direct supervision. Members . . . typically handle job assignments, plan and schedule work, make production and/or service related decisions, and take action on problems" (p. 15).

Increasingly, modern organizations are striving to use their employees more effectively. Huszczo (2004) identifies three reasons why SDWTs seem to work so well:

1. Those closest to the work know best how to perform and improve their jobs.
2. Most employees want to feel that they "own" their own jobs and are making meaningful contributions to the effectiveness of their organizations.
3. Teams provide possibilities for empowerment that are not available to individual employees. (p. 4)

Homans (1950, p. 1) has described membership in small groups as "the first and most immediate social experience of mankind." More specifically, he defines a group as "a number of persons who communicate with one another often over a span of time and who are few enough so that each person is able to communicate with all the others, not at secondhand, through other people, but face-to-face." As you read this chapter, you might give some thought to this definition.

GROUP DYNAMICS

We are all familiar with all the problems and pleasures associated with family roles, but in the business world we discover other aspects of group membership. One of the major complaints about committees and other problem-solving small groups is that they take up too much time and seldom accomplish as much as they should. To make better use of the time spent in small groups, we have to know something about how people ordinarily behave in them.

Remember when you first came to college? You encountered a lot of situations in which you didn't know exactly how you were supposed to act. In unfamiliar situations, we all look to others for cues on what is the appropriate thing to do. In these situations we are especially vulnerable to social influence. In the movie *Big*, Tom Hanks goes to a cocktail party in a light blue tuxedo, and everybody laughs at him for not dressing appropriately. All of us have been in situations like that.

Conformity Pressure

A person who challenges the norms of a group or of society is sometimes referred to as an iconoclast. The origin of the term comes from Leo III, the emperor of Constantinople (now Istanbul, Turkey) who destroyed the golden icon of Christ over his palace gates in 725 A.D. His act of defiance of the Christian church was to consolidate his power, and the word *iconoclast*, which means "destroyer of icons," stuck (Berns, 2008, p. 10). Most people are much more willing to follow prevailing norms both in society and in small groups.

A great deal of research has been done on conformity pressure and the effect it has on our behaviors. In one study, people had to estimate how much a point of light appeared to move in a dark room. Since the light did not move at all, the optical illusion regarding the amount of movement was highly sensitive to social influence. The researchers found that individual estimates of autokinetic movement vary a great deal. To one person it might seem that the light has moved 2 inches; to another the distance might seem to be 6 inches. Yet Sherif (1967) found that a person who first views this phenomenon when he or she is isolated from others and observes it several times under these conditions will develop a standard of his or her own so that all his or her subsequent estimates of distance fall within this range. On the other hand, when a person witnesses the autokinetic effect for the first time as a member of a group, the group establishes a norm; if that person is then exposed again to the autokinetic effect, he or she will make estimates in terms of the group norm. Moreover, a person who has made initial judgments in isolation and then overhears others estimate the distance will correct his or her own estimate so that it tends to converge with that of the others.

A more recent case of group conformity pressure was illustrated in the movie *A Few Good Men,* starring Jack Nicholson, Demi Moore, and Tom Cruise. In the film, the marines in a military unit would discipline a member of their unit who was out of line with the group's norms. This practice was referred to as a "Code Red" and usually consisted of some type of physical punishment. In this particular case it resulted in an accidental death. The entire movie illustrates several group dynamics concepts discussed in this chapter.

One of the criticisms of conformity research has been that subjects rarely get to argue their point of view against the majority opinion. Yet even in studies that allow dissenting members to present their arguments, considerable conformity behavior still occurs (Lovelace, Shapiro, and Weingart, 2001; Barr and Conlon, 1994). These studies distinguish between **private acceptance** of a judgment or opinion and **public compliance**—that is, *between whether people change their thinking as a result of hearing opinions different from their own or whether they say they agree with the group when in fact they disagree.*

Private acceptance is more likely to occur when (1) the individual greatly values membership in the group, (2) opinion is unanimously against him or her, (3) the issue in question is ambiguous to begin with, or (4) the group is under pressure to achieve an important goal (Tubbs, 2012). Public compliance usually stems from the desire to avoid the unpleasantness of conflict. After maintaining a dissenting opinion for a long time, a person may be made so uncomfortable by social pressures that as a peace-keeping gesture, he or she gives the impression of going along with the rest of the group. A number of studies have shown that the person who conforms readily tends to be (1) more submissive or dependent, (2) high in the need for social approval and low in the need to be outstanding, (3) more often female than male, and (4) lacking in self-confidence (Hare, 1962).

Social Influence

We have looked at conformity behavior in terms of the individual member. Now let us examine the behavior of the group. We know that the group tends to exert most pressure to conform on newcomers, who have not yet earned the right to deviate from group norms. Fraternities and sororities often deal out harsh criticism when rushees and pledges dress or act differently from other members of the group. Yet a great many of the same deviations are tolerated when they exist in fraternity members who are juniors or seniors. One may wonder if those involved in the abuse of the Abu Ghraib prisoners in Iraq would have participated in the abuse if acting out on their own. Or, were some conforming to the social influence of others at the prison?

Groups with a high level of cohesiveness tend to exert strong conformity pressures. It seems that the more closely knit the group, the more the members resist allowing anyone to become a member who does not share their values. Members with the greatest prestige tend to be "super representatives" of the attributes that are highly valued by the group. The typical football team captain is usually one of the best athletes on the team. Similarly, the gang leader is often one of the gang's toughest members. In each case, the person who best represents the qualities esteemed by the group has the most prestige.

How does the cohesive group behave when one of its members takes a stand quite different from that of the rest? Schachter (1951) found that initially the deviant gets most of the group's attention. Each member will probably say or do something to persuade the lone dissenter to come around to the position held by the rest of the group. These efforts may go on for some time. Eventually, the deviant either gives in—there is no way of knowing, of course, whether this is simply public compliance—or is ignored or rejected.

An explanation of what makes most of us yield to social pressure is offered by Festinger's **social comparison theory.** Festinger (1954) believes that *all human beings have a need to evaluate their own opinions and abilities and that when they cannot do so by objective nonsocial means, they compare them with those of other people.* How do you tell, for example, whether you are a good driver? Clearly, by comparing your performance with that of other drivers. Similarly, you find out whether you are liberal in your political views by comparing them with those of others. In other words, in the absence of objective criteria, you rely on the opinions of others to determine the validity of your own.

In the Schachter experiment, a discrepancy existed between the opinions of one group member and the rest of the group. Social comparison theory predicts that in such a situation group members will act to reduce the discrepancy and that the person with the discrepant opinion will tend to change his or her position so that it is closer to that of other group members. We saw this to be the case not only in the Schachter experiment but also in some of the studies of the autokinetic effect, where individual judgments tend to converge with group norms. However these phenomena are explained, the tendency to conform seems clear. In the following section, we shall examine conformity as it affects group decisions.

The Quality of Group Problem Solving

According to *Fast Company* magazine, in today's chaotic world, we all have become members of "Generation Flux." In other words, we have to be nimble, "adaptable in this world that is in a constant state of flux or change" (Safian, 2012, p. 60). The author argues, "No one in the rental car industry foresaw the popularity of auto-sharing Zipcar—and Zipcar didn't foresee the rise of outfits like Uber and Relay-Rides, which are already trying to steal its market. . . . Even the law business is under siege from companies like LegalZoom, an online DIY document service" (Safian, 2012, p. 65).

Given this dynamic backdrop, the study of group dynamics raises the question "How do groups compare with individuals in problem solving?" Will the number of people in the group affect the quality of the decision? Will people meeting together generate a greater number of novel ideas than they would working in isolation? In short, how does the presence of others influence the way we think?

Acceptance of Risk

It has been established that members of groups tend to conform. As yet, however, nothing has been said about the direction of that conformity. When we call someone a "conformist," we usually think of him or her as somewhat conservative. Conformists don't rock the boat. They don't create dissension. They go along with group norms. They probably go along with group decisions. It would seem that because they conform, they take few risks, and from this we might guess that the decisions of the group would also tend to be conservative or at least cautious.

Suppose you are on your way to a meeting in which your group will advise Gokhan, an electrical engineer, about the pros and cons of a certain career choice. Should he remain in the large electronics corporation for which he works, where he is assured a high level of security and moderate financial rewards, or should he accept an offer from a small, recently founded company that will offer him a higher starting salary and a share in the firm's ownership but whose future is highly uncertain? What odds will you give—1 in 10, 3 in 10, and so on—that the new company turns out to be financially sound and, thus, that Gokhan will do better joining it than remaining where he is? Whatever the odds you choose, chances are that if a group discussion follows, it will significantly increase your estimate of Gokhan's chances for success.

The **risky shift phenomenon** is the name given this *tendency of people to increase their willingness to take risks as a result of group discussions*. It is by no means confined to decisions about careers. Here, for example, are summaries of a few of the experimental problems that have demonstrated a shift toward risk after group communication:

> A man with a severe heart ailment must seriously curtail his customary way of life if he does not undergo a delicate medical operation which might cure him completely or might prove fatal.

A captain of a college football team, in the final seconds of a game with the college's traditional rival, may choose a play that is almost certain to produce a tie score, or a more risky play that would lead to sure victory if successful, sure defeat if not.

An engaged couple must decide, in the face of recent arguments suggesting some sharp differences of opinion, whether or not to get married. Discussions with a marriage counselor indicate that a happy marriage, while possible, would not be ensured. (Wallach et al., 1962, p. 77; see also Okhuysen, 2001)

Several explanations of the risky shift phenomenon have been proposed; we shall consider three of them in brief fashion. The first is that within a group no member feels totally responsible for the decision. This might explain the actions of lynch mobs: A person who might never dare commit a murder alone suddenly helps carry out a lynching. The second possibility is that those who argue in favor of risky positions are more persuasive than those who are conservative and that they therefore influence others in favor of riskier decisions. The first two hypotheses have little experimental support. A third and more likely possibility is that Western culture tends to value risk taking over conservative behavior.

As you find yourself participating in task-oriented groups, it is important to realize that the group decision is likely to be riskier than the average of the positions taken by individual group members before their interaction.

Groupthink

Suppose you work for Sears, and your company has been struggling lately. Your team has been asked to make a new product using your successful Craftsman line of tools. How might you do it? One way that Sears has answered this challenge is to market its work light as a stand-alone product, instead of bundling it as part of a toolkit (Bettencourt and Bettencourt, 2011). In order to come up with successful products like this, your group members have to be able to think independently from one another. Many groups are not able to do this and fall into a common group-related mistake called "groupthink."

In the small group, social influence is even more powerful than it is in the dyad. Moreover, as we know from the principles of balance theory, the judgments of other people affect our attitudes, beliefs, and values as well as our perceptions.

Norms need not be negative in their effect. Sometimes it's possible to establish constructive norms that will improve group functioning. Marv Patterson of Hewlett-Packard (HP) says that the norm for the company is to hire the "best of the best." This is how HP maintains a team environment that "crackles with creativity and intellectual spirit" (Kao, 1996, p. xvi). This constructive norm at HP is designed to avoid the "groupthink" problem that often occurs when subordinates in large organizations are afraid to disagree with the boss.

In general, groupthink refers to a problem-solving process in which ideas accepted by the group are not really examined, and opposing ideas are suppressed. The term "groupthink" was coined in 1972 by Irving Janis, a psychologist with Yale University. Janis defined groupthink as "a mode of thinking that people engage in when they are deeply involved in a cohesive in-group, when the members' strivings for unanimity override their motivation to realistically appraise alternative courses of action" (Schwartz & Wald, 2003, p. A15). This phenomenon has been investigated in very visible social and political arenas. For example, political critics assert that the 2003 false statements that Iraq was housing weapons of mass destruction were a result of political groupthink among the ultimate decision makers within the United States government (Lobe, 2004, p. 1). A groupthink problem has also been considered by some theorists in the February 1, 2003, failed *Columbia* space shuttle mission. Analysis of the incident raised questions about NASA regarding the decision made by Boeing engineers to allow *Columbia* to launch when there was a potential problem with a portion of the foam core detaching from the vessel. The critical group of engineers all seemed to be in agreement when the decision was made that the detached foam would not affect the mission, even though some engineers strongly disagreed at the onset of the decision-making process. The foam has now been identified as a key factor in the failure of the mission (Lobe, 2004, p. 1).

Kevin McManus (2007), writing in *Industrial Engineer* magazine, summarizes why the groupthink phenomenon is so powerful. First, most people are not aware of groupthink when it is occurring. Second, people are afraid to speak their minds because they don't want to appear to be an outsider or are insecure about taking a contrary position. The result is that groupthink often causes us to use limited organizational resources in suboptimal ways.

Janis (1982) lists eight main symptoms of groupthink: (1) Members share the illusion of invulnerability, providing the impetus to take extraordinary risks and failing to see early signs of danger; (2) warnings and other negative feedback are rationalized away; (3) members believe they are moral and thus can ignore the ethical implications of what they do; (4) leaders of other groups are considered evil and, therefore, not people with whom negotiations are reasonable; (5) members who stray from the group's beliefs are pressured to conform; (6) members avoid speaking out when not in favor of the group's actions, thus self-censure replaces group censure; (7) members share the illusion that agreement is unanimous; and (8) members screen the group, and especially the leader, from adverse information. With groupthink in operation, the group considers few alternatives, fails to scrutinize accepted ideas, fails to gather all the necessary information, fails to consider all the sides of an issue, and fails to consider alternative plans in the event the chosen plan is rejected by others or does not work.

Level of Creativity

IBM recently conducted a survey of 1,541 CEOs in 60 countries all over the world. They found that "CEOs cited creativity as the most important leadership quality over the next five years" (IBM, 2010, p. 24). Consider this problem. The Ideas and Images Advertising Agency has five writers on its staff. It is bidding for the Chevrolet account and must submit a sales presentation and advertising program to Chevrolet's marketing executives. Should all five writers work independently and submit their own programs to the advertising director, or should the five be brought together to tackle the problem? Which procedure will generate a greater number of original ideas?

In essence we are asking whether **brainstorming** is an effective problem-solving technique. This approach, first introduced in the advertising firm of Batten, Barton, Durstine & Osborn in 1939, was designed to offset tendencies of group members to be inhibited by pressures to conform. Brainstorming had several rules. There was to be no criticism of ideas. "Freewheeling" was encouraged: The more way-out the idea, the better. Quantity was desired: The greater the number of ideas, the better. Taking off on other people's ideas—either by improving one or by showing how two different ideas could be combined—is also encouraged (Tubbs, 2012). Raudsepp (1980) cites his own research at Princeton University, which indicates that by using this technique, individuals are able to increase their creative performance by 40 to 300 percent (p. 10). (See also Lipman-Blumen and Leavitt, 1999.)

Take the example of the popular TV show *Everybody Loves Raymond.* In 2004 the show was deciding whether to run another season. Creator Phil Rosenthal and star Ray Romano were reported to "have numerous brainstorming sessions with the writing staff to determine whether there's enough life left in *Raymond,* creatively speaking, to go another season" ("Raymond Mulls Future," 2004). Their brainstorming must have worked: The show decided to tape episodes for one final season.

Tubbs (2012) offers the following list of idea killers, which often serve to reduce group creativity as well as productivity:

- That's ridiculous.
- We tried that before.
- That will never work.
- That's crazy.
- It's too radical a change.
- We're too small for it.
- It's not practical.
- Let's get back to reality.
- You can't teach an old dog new tricks.
- We'll be the laughingstock.
- You're absolutely wrong.
- You don't know what you're talking about.
- It's impossible.
- There's no way it can be done. (pp. 75–76)

On the other hand, "igniter phrases" such as those listed below often promote creativity and group productivity by establishing a psychological climate in the group that encourages creative thinking:

- I agree.
- That's good!
- I made a mistake. I'm sorry.
- That's a great idea.
- I'm glad you brought that up.
- You're on the right track.

- I know it will work.
- We're going to try something different today.
- I never thought of that.
- We can do a lot with that idea.
- Real good, anyone else?
- I like that!
- That would be worth a try.
- Why don't we assume it would work and go from there.
(Tubbs, 2012, pp. 75–76)

For effective group creativity, a happy group yields the most positive results. Sutton (2002) recommends positive steps by the use of humor in small groups. He recommends waiting until the group has truly bonded to introduce difficult topics, teaching humor as an outlet for stress, telling stories of successful group conflict, and screening new group members to make sure that they are positive and energetic.

Additional research by Amabile (1998) found that individuals who were high producers of ideas perceived the brainstorming task as more attractive, were low in communication apprehension, and possessed higher ambiguity tolerance than those individuals low in idea productivity. The author concludes from her findings that the best brainstormers are those interested in the brainstorming topic who are not afraid to communicate their ideas. This indicates that although brainstorming may achieve its best effects by reducing the problems associated with criticism and the question of "quality," individual predispositions to communicate still play a major role in the outcome. (For an entire book on creativity games see Gray, Brown, and Macanufo, 2010.)

The Role of a Group Member

Nine psychotherapists have formed a group to help block the passage of mental health legislation that they consider repressive. Ostensibly, the group's members are equal in status. No leader has been appointed. In this context each of the therapists has the same role—that of group member. Because of your interest in small-group communication and your friendship with one of the therapists, you are allowed to attend the meetings as an observer.

After attending a few meetings, you begin to notice that Bob knows a lot about existing mental health laws. He also makes a number of suggestions for actions the group might take: contacting legislators, raising funds for a series of broadcasts on the issue, distributing handbills about the implications of the new law. Matt, another member of the group, has few ideas of his own and tends to go along with any concrete proposals for group action. "I'm for that. Why not try it?" he often says. Frank, on the other hand, has more ideas than he knows what to do with. He proposes solutions, one after another—some sound, others extreme. Initially, he is very enthusiastic, but he never seems to carry through on any of his suggestions. To the chagrin of most of the group, Kay usually punches holes in other people's arguments. "It will never work," she chides. "What do we use for money? People aren't going to contribute. They don't understand the issue."

Figure 12.1   *Categories for Interaction Process Analysis*

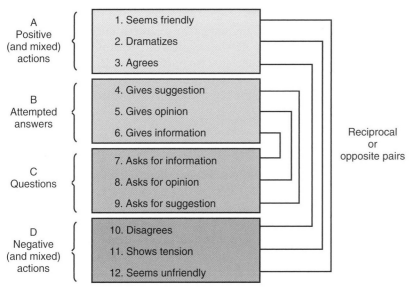

Source: From *Personality and Interpersonal Behavior* by Robert Freed Bales (New York: Holt, Rinehart and Winston, 1970). Reprinted with permission of the author.

Here are four people in the role of group member. Each interprets it somewhat differently. You think you see some individual patterns of interaction emerging, but to be accurate, you need a method of describing various behaviors.

One of the more important accomplishments of small-group research has been the development of several such systems. The most widely known is interaction process analysis (IPA), developed at Harvard University by Robert Bales (1970). The twelve categories of IPA are virtually self-explanatory (see Figure 12.1), and they offer a valuable framework from which to view the functions and patterns of communication. Each interaction is assigned to one of the categories, and when the scoring has been completed, certain behavior patterns become apparent.

In the group we have been discussing, Bob's statements would tend to fall in categories 4 (gives suggestion) and 6 (gives information), Matt's in 3 (agrees), Frank's in 4 (gives suggestion), and Kay's in 10 (disagrees). The responses of other members in the group may be more diversified so that no single category or set of categories predominates, but over an extended period we could probably identify the characteristic behaviors of each member. In any case, Bales's method of classifying human interaction gives us a systematic way to analyze group communication. By means of these categories, we can classify each communicative act regardless of its content.

As you look at the list in Figure 12.1, you might ask yourself which categories describe your own actions in small groups. There is a good chance that you will find yourself performing only a limited number of these behaviors. For example, one friend of mine summed up his participation in groups by saying, "I often like to play the devil's advocate and give people a bit of a hard time." If his statement is accurate, we would expect that most of his interactions (like those of Kay in the group we described) would fall in category 10 of the IPA. There are groups that need at least one critical member, someone willing to challenge others, but the last thing in the world some groups need is another devil's advocate. In general, it seems foolish to assume that any behavior or set of behaviors is appropriate in all situations; there is much to be said for developing some degree of role flexibility.

Tubbs (2012) has adapted the following classification of roles that originated with Benne and Sheats (1948).

Group Task Roles

These behaviors are directed toward accomplishing the group's objective through problem solving:

- *Initiating-contributing:* Proposing new ideas or a changed way of regarding the group goal. This may include a new goal or a new definition of the problem. It may involve suggesting a solution or some way of handling a difficulty the group has encountered. It may also include a new procedure for the group to better organize its efforts.
- *Information seeking:* Asking for clarification, for authoritative information and facts relevant to the problem under discussion.
- *Opinion seeking:* Seeking information related not so much to factual data as to the values underlying the suggestions being considered.
- *Information giving:* Offering facts or generalizations based on experience or authoritative sources.
- *Opinion giving:* Stating beliefs or opinions relevant to a suggestion made. The emphasis is on the proposal of what ought to become the group's values rather than on facts or information.
- *Elaborating:* Expanding on suggestions with examples or restatements, offering a rationale for previously made suggestions, and trying to determine the results if a suggestion were adopted by the group.
- *Coordinating:* Indicating the relationships among various ideas and suggestions, attempting to combine ideas and suggestions, or trying to coordinate the activities of group members.
- *Orienting:* Indicating the position of the group by summarizing progress made and deviations from agreed-upon directions or goals or by raising questions about the direction the group is taking.
- *Evaluating:* Comparing the group's accomplishments to some criterion or standard of group functioning. This may include questioning the practicality, logic, or procedure of a suggestion.
- *Energizing:* Stimulating the group to action or a decision, attempting to increase the level or quality of activity.
- *Assisting on procedure:* Helping or facilitating group movement by doing things for the group—for example, performing routine tasks such as distributing materials, rearranging the seating, or running a tape recorder.

- *Recording:* Writing down suggestions, recording group decisions, or recording the outcomes of the discussion. This provides tangible results of the group's effort.

Group-Building and Maintenance Roles

The roles in this category help the interpersonal functioning of the group. They help alter the way of working; they strengthen, regulate, and perpetuate the group. This is analogous to preventive maintenance done to keep a mechanical device such as a car in better working order:

- *Encouraging:* Praising, showing interest in, agreeing with, and accepting the contributions of others; showing warmth toward other group members, listening attentively and seriously to the ideas of others, showing tolerance for ideas different from one's own, conveying the feeling that one feels the contributions of others are important.
- *Harmonizing:* Mediating the differences among the other members, attempting to reconcile disagreements, relieving tension in moments of conflict through the use of humor.
- *Compromising:* Operating from within a conflict situation, one may offer a compromise by yielding status, by admitting a mistake, by disciplining oneself for the sake of group harmony, or by coming halfway toward another position.
- *Gatekeeping and expediting:* Attempting to keep communication channels open by encouraging the participation of some or by curbing the participation of others.
- *Setting standards or ideals:* Expressing standards for the group and/or evaluating the quality of group processes (as opposed to evaluating the content of discussion).
- *Observing:* Keeping a record of various aspects of group process and feeding this information, along with interpretations, into the group's evaluation of its procedures. This contribution is best received when the person has been requested by the group to perform this function. The observer should avoid expressing judgments of approval or disapproval in reporting observations.
- *Following:* Going along with the group, passively accepting the ideas of others, serving as an audience in group discussion.

Individual Roles

These behaviors are designed more to satisfy an individual's needs than to contribute to the needs of the group. These are sometimes referred to as self-centered roles:

- *Aggressing:* Deflating the status of others, disapproving of the ideas or values of others, attacking the group or the problem it is attempting to solve, joking maliciously, resenting the contributions of others and/or trying to take credit for them.

- *Blocking:* Resisting, disagreeing, and opposing beyond reason; bringing up dead issues after they have been rejected or bypassed by the group.
- *Recognition seeking:* Calling attention to oneself through boasting, reporting on personal achievements, acting in inappropriate ways, fighting to keep from being placed in an inferior position.
- *Self-confessing:* Using the group as an opportunity to express personal, non-group-related feelings, insights, ideologies.
- *Acting the jokester:* Showing a lack of involvement in the group's task. Displaying nonchalance, cynicism, horseplay, and other kinds of "goofing-off" behaviors.
- *Dominating:* Trying to assert authority or superiority by manipulating others in the group. This may take the form of flattery, asserting a superior status or right to attention, giving directions authoritatively, and/or interrupting others.
- *Help seeking:* Attempting to get sympathy from other group members through expressions of insecurity, personal inadequacy, or self-criticism beyond reason.
- *Special-interest pleading:* Speaking on behalf of some group such as "the oppressed," "labor," "business," usually cloaking one's own prejudices or biases in the stereotype that best fits one's momentary need.

Cohesiveness

Probably one of the most important by-products of group interaction is the emotional commitment that may evolve from having worked on a problem with others. For example, many organizations use self-managed work teams to solve internal problems. These are generally small groups in which cohesiveness is a necessity. A Kansas City Harley-Davidson plant study revealed that the group members' perceptions of fair treatment within the group and control over who was on the team led to higher levels of cohesion and performance (Chansler et al., 2003, p. 101).

A classic study conducted during World War II found that women who participated in group discussions on how best to cook unpopular cuts of meat (and thus leave favored cuts for the troops overseas) were much more likely to try out new recipes than were women who simply listened to a speech intended to persuade them to do so (Cartwright and Zander, 1968). Being in a cohesive group leads to greater effectiveness from individuals in the group.

This kind of emotional commitment seems to increase as attraction to the group increases. **Cohesiveness** has been defined as *"the total field of forces acting on members to remain in the group"* (Schachter, 1951, p. 191). It may also be considered in terms of the loyalty and high morale of group members. Think of groups you have either been in or observed that were closely knit. Two groups that are not necessarily problem-solving groups but that illustrate high levels of cohesion are the Kennedy clan and Michael Jackson's family. Cohesiveness, which connotes pride of membership, often intensifies as a group becomes more successful. We are all familiar with the popular chant of crowds at sporting events, "We're number 1. We're number 1."

In general, cohesive groups have interested and committed members who enjoy each other's company. The group is not always highly productive, but its members do tend to help each other with problems, to adapt well to crisis situations, and to ask questions openly. We referred earlier to the conformity demands made by a cohesive group on its members. It is true, however, that they may sometimes feel free to disagree more openly than members of less cohesive groups.

Any discussion of emotional reactions to groups must acknowledge that things do not always turn out so positively. Working with others can also be frustrating, boring, and unsettling. The point is that the socioemotional dimension of group interaction constitutes a very real and powerful part of group behavior. Many people think that feelings have no place in a problem-solving group. On the contrary, feelings are very much involved in group behavior and should be studied as vigorously as its logical and rational aspects.

Phases of Group Development

It has been said that, like a human being, each group has a life cycle: It has a birth, childhood, and maturity, and ultimately it ceases to exist. A number of theories have been proposed about what growth typically occurs in a group, and these are based on the study of either problem-solving or therapeutic groups (especially encounter groups). Understanding the phases of group development provides a framework upon which group growth may be measured, provides a basis for making predictions about the group's progress, and allows a leader to plan interventions aimed at affecting the group's growth. Understanding allows for the best predictions, and the best predictions allow for the best responses to the group. For example, avoiding group conflict is not a good response, since conflict is a normal part of group development.

Theorists seem to agree that growth and development in the group are the result of both the needs of the individual members and the social forces created within the group itself. Typically, these forces interact in a predictable way, with the group going through several stages or phases. Some theorists identify four phases, others three, and there are other differences in interpretation as well. For example, some theorists believe that the various phases occur even if a group meets only once (Tuckman, 1965; Fisher, 1970). Others hold that the phases occur over the life history of a group that meets repeatedly (Bennis and Shepard, 1956; Thelen and Dickerman, 1949). And still a third faction contends that all the group phases occur in each meeting and continue to recur throughout the group's life history (Schutz, 1958; Bales and Strodbeck, 1951; Blanchard, 2007). This third theory seems the most likely and the most valuable in providing insight into group development. Keeping these different viewpoints in mind, let us look at the four-phase model of group development as it is represented in the literature.

Phase 1: Forming really begins prior to the first meeting, when members begin the process of separating themselves from attachments that could interfere with the group and attempt to learn about the group and/or other members. Forming lasts anywhere from one day to several weeks, as members attempt to learn about the group members and the task that needs to be accomplished. Interaction is cautious, characterized by ambiguous language and a great deal of agreement (which is easy with ambiguous statements). Minimal work is accomplished, and the phase doesn't end until the norms are relatively clear. Questions uppermost in members' minds are "What is this group about?" "Do I fit in?" "Do I want to be in or out?"

Phase 1 is also a period in which group members break the ice and begin to establish a common base for functioning. This stage is sometimes referred to as a period of "orientation," "inclusion," or "group formation." Initially, people may ask questions about one another, tell where they are from, and generally make small talk. It seems that early in the life of a group, members are interested in building a working relationship that is psychologically comfortable. Even members of the most ambitious problem-solving groups usually spend some time socializing.

Phase 2: Storming is a normal and expected response to the orientation phase: Whereas the orientation or forming phase built group solidarity, storming or conflict is the assertion of individuality (often in response to feelings of being "swallowed up" by the group). The agreement and ambiguity of the first phase give way to clear, unambiguous, and direct language, and agreement now is on specific issues, albeit agreement is low. During this phase the group loses part of its group identity, confusion over goals may increase, and minimal work is accomplished (still!). Storming usually revolves around two issues (regardless of the specific content, these two issues are usually the bottom line, the real issues): How close/how far should we be from each other emotionally, and is the leader a fool or "all wise"? Control and affection are the issues (see Chapter 6).

This period of dissent and controversy is ripe for communication failures: The more emotionally charged the discussion, the more prone group members are to jump to conclusions, lose their tempers, or interpret the comments of others as threats or criticisms. One student description clearly tracks the movement from Phase 1 to Phase 2:

We talked about personal interests until some common ground was established, then we found we could talk about the assignment more freely. But after talking about non-subject things, it was hard to keep the line of talk on the problems at hand. Some wanted to get the assignment accomplished while two guys in the group continually swayed the conversation to things that were easier to talk about, but had nothing to do with the subject (Howard has a big thing for John Deere farm machinery). At first we were constantly trying not to hurt anyone's feelings, so we let the conversation drift. We didn't question or reject each other's ideas, and I feel we often settled for less than we should have. The longer we were in the group together, the more we got to know each other and the more times we voiced our real opinions. That's when the tempers started to flare!

Phase 3: Norming is marked by several levels of "balance" in response to the storming phase: Individuality and groupness balance, group goals and individual goals balance, closeness is balanced, and the role of the leader and the leader's authority are defined. Note that "balance" does not mean "resolved," since the balance is a delicate one easily upset.

In Phase 3, group cohesion begins to emerge, and the group starts functioning more smoothly as a unit. Here is B. Aubrey Fisher's (1970) description of Phase 3:

> Social conflict and dissent dissipate during the third phase. Members express fewer unfavorable opinions toward decision proposals. The coalition of individuals who had opposed those proposals which eventually achieve consensus also weakens in the third phase. (p. 142)

Phase 4: Performing is the *period of consensus and maximum productivity.* Dissent is very much out of place at this time so that few negative or unfavorable comments are expressed. Group spirit is high, and a great deal of mutual back patting takes place. Group members joke and laugh and reinforce each other for having contributed to the group's success.

In an early article, Thelen and Dickerman (1949) did a good job of summarizing the group phases:

> Beginning with individual needs for finding security and activity in a social environment, we proceed first to emotional involvement of the individuals with each other, and second to the development of a group as a rather limited universe of interaction among individuals and as the source of individual security. We then find that security of position in the group loses its significance except that as the group attempts to solve problems it structures its activities in such a way that each individual can play a role which may be described as successful or not in terms of whether the group successfully solved the problem it had set itself. (p. 316)

The tail end of Phase 4 is signaled by several member behaviors: Lateness increases, absence increases, daydreaming and other signs of withdrawal increase, and the overall level of involvement in the group decreases. There is a great deal of anxiety associated with ending the group, and members respond differently to this anxiety—all the way from those who refuse to admit the group is ending and run around collecting phone numbers and addresses and planning the party, to those who talk about how terrible the group experience was and are glad it's over. Just as the preorientation stage required potential group members to begin to invest themselves in the group, the final stage requires members to divest themselves of the group.

The four phases are different, but they are not mutually exclusive: Overlap in behaviors is apparent; however, predominant behaviors are recognizable and may be used to judge the phase the group is in. "Usual" problems associated with each phase are forcing the group to jump into the problem during forming, avoiding conflict (storming) during the second phase, norming or ignoring social aspects of group life during the third phase, not allowing members to respond as they feel (e.g., taking disparaging remarks seriously) or to talk out their feelings, and not providing methods for postgroup feedback during the last phase.

Most recently, Blanchard and his colleagues (2007) cite findings from a comprehensive review of over 200 studies on group development. Their conclusion is that these four phases have been confirmed along with one other, termination, for temporary groups that disband (pp. 185–186).

Of course, not every group will develop precisely along the lines described above. Nevertheless, an awareness of the recurring themes in group development should enable us to improve our perception and understanding of group dynamics.

The consequences of ignoring group dynamics was depicted on the show *The Apprentice*, hosted by Donald Trump. The teams on this show illustrate what happens when teams skip the development stages to attempt to reach the performing stage. In Episode 3 of Season 6, the team leader, Michelle, formed the team named Arrow and forced her team members to work all night. She was insistent that an all-nighter wouldn't hurt anyone. However, the team rebelled (storming). Team leaders who underestimate the team development stages as well as the importance of group cohesiveness are doomed to fail. Michelle ended up resigning, knowing that she was the candidate most likely to be fired.

GROUP STRUCTURE

The distinction between group structure and group dynamics is somewhat arbitrary, for the way a group is constituted has considerable influence on how it functions. In our discussion of structure, we shall be concerned with four communication variables: group size, networks, virtual groups and leadership.

Group Size

Think back to the groups you have belonged to that ranged in size from 3 to 15 members. As the group got larger, what did you notice about the quality of the communication? How did you feel about your part in the discussions? How satisfied were you with them? It has been known for a number of years that as group size increases, the satisfaction of each member decreases. In larger groups, a few people account for almost all the talking; the rest do very little. If you remember larger groups as boring and slow-moving, you probably were among the more silent members. We have seen a number of student groups fail to develop into effective decision-making bodies because a great many people spent most of their time listening to a few long, complicated speeches made by a handful of members.

Group size affects performance as well as satisfaction. For example, larger groups tend to take more time to reach decisions, particularly if unanimity is required. We also know that as group size increases, a number of subgroups may form, and that these factions tend to polarize and to distract members from the problems at hand.

You can get some idea of the subgroups that may develop by looking at the potential communication relationships within groups of various sizes. Bostrom (1970) showed that in a dyad, for example, only two relationships are possible—A to B or B to A; but in a triad, or three-person group, there are nine possibilities:

1. A to B	4. B to C	7. A to B and C
2. A to C	5. C to B	8. B to A and C
3. B to A	6. C to A	9. C to A and B

The following table shows how rapidly complexity increases as groups gain in size. Bostrom calculated all the communication relationships possible within groups of 3 to 8 people (pp. 257–258). Small wonder that to most people, belonging to a large group is less satisfying than belonging to a small one.

Number in Group	Interactions Possible
2	2
3	9
4	28
5	75
6	186
7	441
8	1,056

For our purposes, the most practical question we can ask is: What size group seems best for problem solving? In a tongue-in-cheek discussion of government cabinets, the world's most powerful committees, Parkinson (1964) reasons that ideally a cabinet should consist of 5 members. Nevertheless, membership usually increases to 7 or 9 and then from 10 toward 20. In addition to the obvious difficulty of assembling all these people at one time, writes Parkinson,

> there is a far greater chance of members proving to be elderly, tiresome, inaudible, or deaf. Relatively few were chosen from any idea that they are or could be or have been useful. A majority perhaps were brought in merely to conciliate some outside group. The tendency is therefore to report what happens to the group they represent. All secrecy is lost and, worst of all, members begin to prepare their speeches. They address the meeting and tell their friends afterward about what they imagine they have said. . . . Internal parties form and seek to gain strength by further recruitment. (p. 54)

As membership expands beyond 20, the whole quality of the committee changes so that "the 5 members who matter will have taken to meeting beforehand" (p. 55). While not to be taken literally, Parkinson's amusing description of the life cycle of the committee has essential validity. Although it is true that a greater variety of ideas tend to be expressed in large groups, such groups have several limitations we have already mentioned. Generally, the optimum size for a problem-solving group is 5 to 7 members. This figure seems to have the greatest number of advantages. After researching 750 companies, Blenko, Mankins, and Rogers (2010) created "The rule of seven. Every person added to the group over seven reduces decision effectiveness. If you take this rule to its logical conclusion, a group of seventeen or more rarely makes any decisions. Of course, a larger group may sometimes be necessary to ensure buy-in" (p. 88). So, if you have a large group, simply break it up into teams of about five people and have them report their findings. Then have each group send a representative to a secondary set of small groups until the decisions have been made by the original group representatives.

A recent study by Roberts and colleagues (2006) showed that both group size and social presence in groups affect individual instrumental voice, value-expressive voice, and the group interaction process. The results show that by increasing social presence through the use of collaborative software (software that allows individuals to work together, implicitly communicate about work, and see other group members' work through connectivity on the computer), it is possible to lessen the negative impact of increasing group size.

Communication Networks

Even before he became president, Barack Obama's meetings were praised for their streamlined group dynamics. Following are some of the reasons (Yang, 2008):

1. No drama Obama. He tries to maintain an emotional even keel and expects others to follow.
2. Make every person in the meeting participate. One participant wrote, "I can't tell you how many times he's looked at me when I haven't said a word, and he looks into my eyes and says, 'What are you thinking?'"
3. Establish a plan and stick to it.
4. Give feedback that is clear, direct, and immediate. One participant wrote, "If he's happy, you know it. If he prefers something different, you know it. . . . He's not shy about being clear."
5. Allow new ideas to come up from the bottom.
6. Genuinely listen to those who disagree with you. "He really questions his advisors aggressively," says Jeffrey Liebman, a Harvard professor and one of Obama's economic advisors. "He wants to see disagreements aired in front of him. Once he makes a decision, his staff knows to move on. . . . You don't sit and say, why didn't it go my way?" (Yang, p. 74).

In Figure 12.2 we see several frequently used communication networks: the Wheel, Chain, Y, Circle, and All-Channel networks. Note that in this illustration each is a five-person group. In the Wheel, one person—who usually becomes the leader—is the focus of comments from each member of the group. As the central person in the network, he or she is free to communicate with the other four, but they can communicate only with him or her. In the Chain network three people can communicate with those on either side of them, but the other two with only one other member of the group. The Y network resembles the Chain: Three of the five people can communicate with only one person. Unlike these systems, which are centralized and tend to have leaders, the Circle and All-Channel patterns are decentralized and sometimes leaderless. In the Circle each person may communicate with two others, those on either side of him. In the All-Channel network, sometimes called "Concom," all communication lines are open: Each member is able to communicate with all the other members.

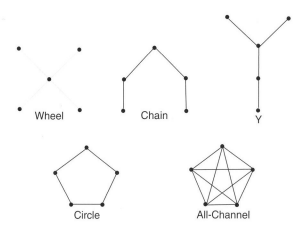

Figure 12.2
Five Types of
Communication
Networks

In studying small-group communications, we want to know how the type of network used affects group performance in problem solving and how given patterns affect interpersonal relationships within the group. Much of the research on networks is based on an experiment by Leavitt (1951) in which five subjects were each given different information essential to the solution of a problem in symbol identification. By using various networks (the Y, Wheel, Chain, and Circle), Leavitt manipulated the freedom with which information could be transmitted from one subject to another, and he then compared the results. The Wheel, the most centralized of the four networks, produced the best organized and fastest performance; the Circle group, the least centralized, was the most disorganized and unstable and proved slowest in solving the problem. The biggest drawback of the Circle network, as another researcher has observed, is that it tends to generate a large number of errors as members try to communicate information around it.

Numerous studies of networks have been patterned after the Leavitt experiment, but the results are not easy to summarize. It is sometimes argued, for example, that certain networks are inherently more effective because of their structure, but Guetzkow and Simon (1955) believe that there are other factors to be considered. A particular network may handicap a group not in its ability to solve a problem but in its ability to organize itself so that it can solve the problem. This is an interesting hypothesis, especially in the light of Leavitt's original finding that Y, Wheel, and Chain groups were able to organize themselves so that each eventually established one procedure it used over and over, whereas members of Circle networks did not. Guetzkow and Simon believe that, once a group has established a procedure for working together, it can perform efficiently regardless of its type of network.

The nature of the problem to be solved also affects performance. Groups with centralized networks are better at identifying colors, symbols, and numbers and solving other simple problems. Decentralized networks have the edge over centralized ones when dealing with problems that are more complex—arithmetic, word arrangement, sentence construction, and discussion problems (Shaw, 1981).

Because most of the communication we are concerned with relates not to symbol identification and the like but to more complex issues, decentralized networks will usually be most desirable. For example, the Wheel, though efficient in its use of time, tends to lower the cohesiveness of a group, reduce its inventiveness, and make it too dependent on its leader. Another advantage of decentralized networks is that they tend to provide the most satisfaction for individual members. The All-Channel network seems desirable for a number of reasons. Although initially it tends to be more inefficient and time-consuming, it maximizes the opportunities for corrective feedback, which ultimately should result in greater accuracy. Furthermore, freedom to speak to anyone else in the group creates high morale. These findings are important to keep in mind in the event that group discussions you participate in are characterized by inaccuracy or low morale.

Virtual Groups

Technology has taken groups of all sizes to a new level of efficiency. Software has allowed groups to have virtual meetings and use videoconferencing technologies that have united people across the globe instantaneously. Gerry Stahl in 2003 wrote a paper titled "Communication and Learning in Online Collaboration" to address the online communication medium and some of the benefits and shortcomings of the new technology. Groupware technologies have made instantaneous and affordable global groups possible and can create online records of all group communications for later reference. The shortcomings of the process include the inability of the group members to see the nonverbal communication of fellow group members, which makes group conflict situations much more difficult to resolve and interpret. Exchanged messages and individual technological challenges can slow interaction and conversation. Stahl recommends some of the following elements integral to successful online group communication to eliminate some of these shortcomings: The first is the necessity of constant availability of technical support. Second, there should be a way to know that other group members are logged on. Third, planned rules for decision making must be put in place proactively.

The successes of online group communication are numerous. First and foremost, online group communication technology eliminates physical boundaries and constraints. Everyone in the group can interact at different times of the day, forgoing personal timetables, to post messages for later discussion. Any visual physical bias is eliminated as group members cannot see one another (Stahl, 2003).

Videoconferencing is another form of group communication that allows real-time video discussions. This mode of communication requires set meeting times but can bring together global group members with ease. It has many benefits, including reduced cost and the ability to view the expressions and nonverbal communications of group members. The shortcomings, on the other hand, include technological problems, static movements of the group members as viewed through the screen, and limitations of this technology only to group members with the availability of videoconferencing technology. However, videoconference availability and utilization is increasing. In June 2004, two United States National Guard soldiers were married via a videoconference, with the groom in Colorado and the bride in Iraq. With this type of union occurring over videoconference, the possible uses of this medium for small groups of all kinds are limitless (Associated Press, 2004, p. A2).

Leadership

The single biggest way to impact an organization is to focus on leadership development. There is almost no limit to the potential of an organization that recruits good people, raises them up as leaders, and continually develops them.
—**John C. Maxwell**, *The 17 Indisputable Laws of Teamwork* (2001, p. 185)

For many years people believed that leaders are born, not made, and a search was conducted to determine the traits of the "born leader." The quest has been largely unsuccessful. We do know that usually a leader is more self-confident and more intelligent than other members of his or her group. Some studies suggest that the leader is better adjusted and more sensitive to the opinions of other group members. Nevertheless, these traits are by no means reliable predictors of leadership. No single set of traits seems important in all situations. The successful commander of an air force squadron is not necessarily effective in an administrative post at the Pentagon. The outstanding teacher is not always a worthwhile dean or department chair.

Recent studies have led us to view leadership not as a quality but as a series of functions that groups must have performed. The leader then becomes the person who successfully performs a number of these functions, and sometimes leadership will pass from one person to another or be divided among group members. Thus far, two major leadership activities have been identified: task functions and consideration functions. Neither set is in itself sufficient to satisfy all the group's needs.

Task functions are *activities that help the group achieve its goals.* In terms of the IPA categories in Figure 12.1 (on page 355), the activities might include giving and asking other members for suggestions, opinions, and information (categories 4 through 9). Other task functions might be orienting the group on how best to proceed, clarifying the remarks of others, and summarizing group process.

Consideration functions have to do with morale. They include *any activities that improve the emotional climate or increase the satisfaction of individual members:* showing agreement, support, or encouragement; gatekeeping (i.e., allowing members who might otherwise be ignored to speak); and so on.

It is often difficult for one person to perform task and consideration functions simultaneously (Tubbs, 2012). Suppose that an emergency meeting of a school board is called to prevent a walkout of the teachers and that two board members monopolize the discussion in an unconstructive way. Someone will have to steer the conversation back to the problem at hand, which requires immediate action, and in doing so he or she may bruise a few egos. It takes considerable skill for the person who has done the offending to also conciliate the offended. For this reason, the group often develops two or more leaders: a task leader, whose primary concern is that the job be done and the group perform well, and a social leader, whose first interest is in maintaining the group's high morale. Nevertheless, the most valuable leaders are those able to perform both task and consideration functions successfully.

Support for the concept that leaders are made, not born, comes from the study of communication networks. Whereas in decentralized networks there was found to be little agreement among members as to the identity of the group's leader, in centralized networks such as the Wheel, Chain, and Y, people who occupied central positions and were thus able to channel communication were considered leaders. (Leadership and popularity are by no means synonymous, however.)

Although we have stressed leadership functions rather than traits, specific behaviors are often characteristic of leaders. If we compare those who get weeded out with those who emerge as leaders, we see some clear-cut differences. The first tend to be quiet, uninformed or unskilled, inflexible, and bossy or dictatorial; they also spend a great deal of time socializing. In contrast, emergent leaders tend to speak up, to have good ideas and state them clearly, to care about the group, and to make sacrifices and build cohesiveness (Griffin, 2009). In sum, leadership functions include a number of behaviors that can be learned.

Recent leadership research has focused on the notion of emotional intelligence, or EQ, analogous to IQ (Goleman, 1998; Cherniss and Goleman, 2001). Emotionally intelligent people control their emotions and act more appropriately to the situation. One extreme example of the lack of emotional control is former President Bill Clinton and his relationship with Monica Lewinsky. Emotional intelligence comprises the five components shown in Table 12.1.

Table 12.1 *Five Components of Emotional Intelligence*

Component	Definition	Hallmarks
1. Self-awareness	The ability to recognize and understand your moods, emotions, and drives, as well as their effect on others; self-deprecating sense of humor	Self-confidence; realistic self-assessment
2. Self-regulation	The ability to control or redirect disruptive impulses and moods; the propensity to suspend judgment—to think before acting	Trustworthiness and integrity; comfort with ambiguity; openness to change
3. Motivation	A passion to work for reasons that go beyond money or status; a propensity to pursue goals with energy and persistence	Strong drive to achieve optimism, even in the face of failure; organizational commitment
4. Empathy	The ability to understand the emotional makeup of others; skill in treating people according to their emotional reactions	Expertise in building and retaining talent; cross-cultural sensitivity; service to others
5. Social skill	Proficiency in managing relationships and building networks; an ability to find common ground and build rapport	Effectiveness in leading change; persuasiveness; expertise in building and leading teams

Sources: Adapted from Goleman (1998) and Cherniss and Goleman (2001).

In conclusion, we remember the thoughts on leadership of E. M. Estes, former president of General Motors:

> Leadership is the courage to admit mistakes, the vision to welcome change, the enthusiasm to motivate others, and the confidence to stay out of step when everyone else is marching to the wrong tune.

CORRELATES OF EFFECTIVE GROUPS

Anyone who has participated in problem-solving group discussions knows that they can be time-consuming, boring, and sometimes infuriating. Furthermore, the decisions groups make may be of poor quality and may be ignored by those who must carry them out. Yet even totally ineffective committees are not that easily disbanded. There are countless situations in which we cannot make decisions on our own; we must work within a group.

James Surowiecki, in his book *The Wisdom of Crowds: Why the Many Are Smarter Than the Few and How Collective Wisdom Shapes Business, Economics, Societies, and Nations,* believes that a group, or "the crowd," often comes up with successful solutions. He believes that a group or crowd will make good decisions if it possesses four fundamental characteristics. First, the group must contain different kinds of people, which Surowiecki defines as "diversity." Second, there should not be an ultimate team leader, known as "decentralization." Third, the group members' thoughts should be combined into a unified answer. Lastly, each group member should be self-determining about the data the group has collected; in this case, Surowiecki references the group members as "independent people" (Hannon, 2004, p. B8).

Recent research by Whetten and Cameron (2011) summarized the research findings of the correlates of high-performing teams. They

1. Get results
2. Have a specific and shared purpose
3. Have mutual internal accountability
4. Have each member responsible for numerous roles and tasks
5. Exhibit high quality in their standards of performance
6. Continuously try to improve
7. Exhibit high credibility and trust
8. Focus on the task and avoid getting distracted by extraneous events (p. 476)

A recent example of a successful group effort occurred in Ann Arbor, Michigan. On December 22, 2005, Kelly Fuks was asked to stop breast-feeding her son in the YMCA (Young Men's Christian Association) pool area. When she refused, she was ejected from the pool area. Fuks was told that her breast-feeding was creating a distraction for the male lifeguards (Gershman, 2006). A few weeks later, a group of 50 women organized a "nurse-in" at which they all breast-fed their babies at the YMCA pool to protest its policy banning breast-feeding (Gantert and Tracy, 2006). On March 7, 2006, the Ann Arbor City Council voted 8–1 to allow women to breast-feed their children anywhere in places of "public accommodation" (Gershman, 2006). This is a vivid example of the power of effective groups to exert influence.

In this section, we shall be looking at some other correlates of small-group effectiveness.

It would be nice if we could automatically improve our communication behaviors by reading about what makes small groups successful. Unfortunately, improvement is not so easily attained. It does come, however, with participation. The adage "Practice makes perfect" seems to be fairly well substantiated by small-group research. The more training and experience group members have, the better they perform as individuals and as groups.

The process by which improvement takes place is probably that of social learning. Behaviors that are productive tend to be reinforced by other members of the group, and those that are unproductive tend to be extinguished because they go unrewarded. Granted that no amount of reading can replace the experience of being part of a group, there are still some lessons we can learn from reading about communication. We can learn what behaviors make for successful groups and then try to practice them when we do participate. In some situations, we may be able to do no more than improve our own performance within the group. In other cases, we may be able to design as well as engage in more effective group activities.

Idea Development and Problem Solving

For several years communication scholars have tried to identify ways of becoming a better small-group participant. For example, Gouran and his associates (1978) found three communication behaviors that were seen by members of small groups as particularly helpful or effective in solving problems. They were (1) introducing relevant issues or ideas, (2) amplifying or expanding on ideas, and (3) documenting assertions. For example, instead of saying all members of Sigma Phi Delta fraternity are goof-offs, it would be better to state that "according to the Office of the Dean of Students, Sigma Phi Delta fraternity has the lowest grade point average of all the fraternities on campus." Two helpful procedural behaviors were singled out: (1) maintaining a goal orientation rather than getting sidetracked and (2) pursuing issues systematically rather than in a disorganized fashion (p. 62). With these findings in mind, let's look at some of the communication behaviors to avoid in small groups.

If you were to interview members of several different kinds of small groups about the difficulties they encounter in developing ideas and solving problems, you would find at least six recurring complaints: (1) Group objectives are not clearly stated or agreed upon, (2) group members do not come up with enough ideas, (3) the group does not carry through discussion of each issue until it is resolved, (4) members rarely help one another, (5) conflict between members becomes so intense that it is counterproductive, and (6) conclusions are not reached or agreed upon.

Billionaire T. Boone Pickens offers this advice: "Be willing to make decisions. That's the most important quality in a leader. Don't fall victim to what I call the 'ready-aim-aim-aim-aim' syndrome. You must be willing to fire" (Pickens, 2008, p. 102).

Standard Agenda

By far, the most often used method for problem-solving is the so-called standard agenda. It is a standard way or method that can be applied to any problem. It has been adopted from a problem-solving sequence of questions developed several decades ago by John Dewey.

1. What are the limits and specific nature of the problem?
2. What are the causes and consequences of the problem?
3. What things must an acceptable solution to the problem accomplish?
4. What solutions are available to us?
5. What is the best solution?
6. What needs to be done to implement the solution?

Brainstorming

Another popular method for generating ideas is the process called "brainstorming" (Osborn, 1957). This technique can be used to generate ideas in any part of the standard agenda. It emphasizes right-brain activity.

RULES FOR BRAINSTORMING

1. *Put judgment and evaluation aside temporarily.*
   a. Acquire a "try anything" attitude.
   b. No faultfinding is allowed. It stifles ideas, halts association.
   c. Today's criticism may kill future ideas.
   d. All ideas are at least thought starters.
2. *Turn imagination loose and start offering the results.*
   a. The wilder the ideas are, the better.
   b. Ideas are easier to tame down than to think up.
   c. Freewheeling is encouraged; ideas can be brought down to earth later.
   d. A wild idea may be the only way to bring out another really good one.
3. *Think of as many ideas as you can.*
   a. Quantity breeds quality.
   b. The more ideas there are to choose from, the more chance there is of a good one.
   c. There is always more than one good solution to any problem.
   d. Try many different approaches.

4. *Seek combination and improvement.*

    a. Your ideas don't all have to be original.

    b. Improve on the ideas of others.

    c. Combine previously mentioned ideas.

    d. Brainstorming is a group activity. Take advantage of group association.

5. *Record all ideas in full view.*

6. *Evaluate at a later session.*

    a. Approach each idea with a positive attitude.

    b. Give each idea a fair trial.

    c. Apply judgment gradually.

Dave Gray and his colleagues (2010) offer additional tips to further stimulate the creation of ideas. After ideas are generated, think of adding, subtracting, multiplying, and dividing as ways of further modifying your existing ideas. For example, the Gillette Mach 3 razor, introduced in 1998, added a third blade. Cell phones and laptop computers have been made more portable by subtracting size and weight. McDonald's has added new products by doubling its list of menu items, and many manufacturing companies have increased their cost effectiveness by dividing up their suppliers to produce larger modules such as entire seating systems. Ford Motor Co. linked up with UPS to speed its delivery of new cars and trucks to owners. You can not only get your vehicle faster, but you can also track its progress online during shipment. This idea grew out of brainstorming sessions at Ford. Transit times have been reduced by 26 percent and savings have been over $1 billion in reduced inventory costs (Tubbs, 2012).

Keep in mind that after you have generated all these ideas, you still have to go back and evaluate their usefulness (see Box 12.1).

Nominal Group Technique

The use of discussion methods is one way to increase the effectiveness of a group. One method commonly used in business and industry is the nominal group technique (NGT).

The NGT method has six phases. First there is silent, independent generation of ideas, written down on paper. The second round is a round-robin listing of ideas on a large newsprint page so everyone can see. The third step is a discussion or clarification of points but without critique. In the fourth step, everyone individually rates the ideas. The fifth step is a clarification of the vote, and the sixth is a final ranking of ideas.

This method circumvents some of the problems of groupthink, such as the focus effect and the illusion of anonymity.

When compared with unstructured groups, NGT provided better decisions (Jarobe, 1988).

No matter which problem-solving technique is used, effective groups have some elements in common. In a fascinating study comparing effective with ineffective groups, Hirokawa (1983) found

12.1 **ISSUES IN COMMUNICATION**   *The Value of Work Teams*

One of the most dramatic innovations in the workplace in the past decade has been the increased use of teams, especially self-directed teams. Although the value of teamwork is certainly hard to dispute, implementing teams is not always as easy as it appears. What do you think about the two positions discussed below? How do you resolve them?

Anne Donnellon (1996) at Harvard has written the following observation: "The past 10 years of brouhaha over work teams have left managers and professionals in a quandary: We know we need teams (for at least certain organizational tasks), and we've learned a lot about them, but while the demands for high performance teams continue to increase, our ability to create and sustain them has plateaued.

Where there should be enhanced capability, greater confidence in the process, and satisfaction with outcomes, there is a growing sense of disappointment, frustration, and cynicism."

On the other hand, Noel M. Tichy (1997) at the University of Michigan writes, "Where single individuals may despair of accomplishing a monumental task, teams nurture, support and inspire each other. . . . For example, Focus: HOPE [a not-for-profit organization that transforms people's lives in the inner city of Detroit]. Although each student . . . is working to improve his or her own life, the common struggle serves to unite them as a team. They know that the program requires enormous effort from each student, and they draw strength from knowing that other people have chosen to make the commitment as well."

The "successful" groups make an attempt to analyze the problem before attempting to search for a viable solution to the problem, while the "unsuccessful" groups immediately begin working on a solution to the problem before attempting to analyze it and understand it. (p. 304)

This research supports the problem-solving sequence advocated in all three of the approaches discussed in this section.

Constructive Conflict

Neil Young once said, "If you agreed with me all the time, there wouldn't be any need for one of us. Guess which one?" (Sutton, 2002).

In 2002, Sutton described two types of conflict that can apply to small-group interaction: "destructive" and "constructive" conflict. Destructive conflict is linked to emotional and personal conflict; constructive conflict is seen as "intellectual." Effective small groups take part in intellectual conflict in which discussion occurs over decision making and ideas. This type of conflict does not attack individuals but challenges ideas. It allows the exploration of diverse solutions that would otherwise be ignored. The more ideas a small group can generate, the more effective they will be.

Additional research has revealed that groups that can laugh together are more effective in their use of constructive conflict. Humor lightens up tense moments of conflict and can help small groups address difficult topics with ease (Sutton, 2002).

Patterns of Decision Making

Decisions can be avoided, demanded, or agreed on. Assuming that decisions will actually be made, let us briefly examine four rather different ways of carrying out the process.

Consensus is the highest level of agreement in groups. It means unanimous agreement among all group members concerning a given decision. Juries in criminal cases must reach consensus, and those that cannot—hung juries—are ultimately dismissed.

Pace (1988) studies high- versus low-consensus groups. He has found the following differences in interaction:

HIGH CONSENSUS

1. Used more than one method of integrating or unifying diverging points of view into one decision
2. Changed integration methods from episode to episode
3. Generated a wide variety of possible solutions to the problem
4. Generated solutions to the problem in the early stages of discussion
5. Terminated episodes by voicing agreement for an idea or claim

LOW CONSENSUS

1. Rarely used more than one method of integration within a single episode
2. Repeated one type of integration method from episode to episode
3. Generated a limited number of possible solutions to the problem
4. Generated solutions to the problem in the later stages of discussion
5. Terminated episodes by changing topics or by introducing claims that went unacknowledged or undeveloped (p. 200)

Few groups are as concerned as they should be about trying to reach consensus on decisions. We tend to forget that the people who help make a decision are often those who are also expected to carry it out. And given a choice, most people who disagree will resist enacting it. Therefore, problem-solving groups should try to reach consensus to ensure maximum satisfaction and commitment to the decision by all members. On the other hand, consensus takes the longest to achieve, and a group may simply not have enough time to get everyone's agreement. In the case at the beginning of this chapter, President Obama took several months and many meetings of his top advisors in order to achieve a unanimous consensus on the troop strength in the Afghan war.

The **majority vote** represents *the wishes of at least 51 percent of a group's members*. Although it is not nearly as satisfying as consensus, it does allow some group harmony in decision making. After as much deliberation on the problem as time permits, there may still be a substantial split in opinion. The majority vote allows the group to proceed despite this. The major limitation of the majority vote is that the dissenting members may be numerous and may be bitterly opposed to the decision. If so, they may be expected to resist carrying it out. When feasible, the majority vote can be used to establish whether a group is near consensus. If a split still exists and time allows, deliberation should continue. If continued discussion does not prove fruitful, the majority vote may be used to reach the decision. Think about presidential elections. Often, the side of the losing candidate feels rather strongly against the winner. However, majority vote is the best way to get agreement and still get some agreement within a reasonable time limit.

A still less desirable method of arriving at a decision is **handclasping,** or **pairing.** This term applies when various *minority members within a group form a coalition to help each other achieve mutually advantageous goals.* Their decision may not represent common sentiment in the group, but they overpower the majority by dint of their collective numbers. This pattern seems characteristic of organizational politics. It is a common practice for individuals to vote for each other's proposals in order to compel support for their own. In the short run, coalitions may be quite successful, but ultimately they can have disastrous effects on group morale. Furthermore, members of coalitions sometimes forget that these bargains exact obligations.

Most groups have at some time been the victims of **railroading,** which occurs when *one or a few group members force their will on the group.* This technique is used most frequently by a leader or a particularly influential member, and, of course, it is the one most likely to produce resentment and resistance.

Testing the Group's Effectiveness

Most of us learn about what goes on in groups from our firsthand experience as members. Sometimes, however, this knowledge can be increased through special exercises. One frequently used technique is called the "fishbowl discussion." Two groups form concentric circles. The inner group carries on a discussion; the outer comments on what it has observed. The two groups then switch positions and repeat the procedure. Each member is allowed to leave the discussion long enough to observe the behavior of the others in the group. He or she may be aided by a list of pointers about what behaviors to be looking for.

Thomas Clay (2007), a consultant with 30 years of experience in the legal profession, explains how working with dozens of law firms and many practice groups allowed him to observe six elements that drive group effectiveness. If group leaders evaluate their groups against those six elements, they can determine whether they are, individually and collectively, serving their purpose and decide what needs to be done to improve group effectiveness. The six criteria are

- Clarifying roles of the participants
- Putting the right people in leadership positions

- Requiring plans
- Getting client feedback
- Investing in the groups
- Compensating the leaders appropriately

Summary

After touching on some characteristics of cohesive groups and on the phases of group development, we considered three aspects of the structure of a group that affect its functioning: size, communication network, virtual groups, and leadership. Limiting the size of the group to five to seven members seems to ensure maximum performance and satisfaction. Among communication networks, the All-Channel pattern offers the greatest opportunity for corrective feedback and high morale, though the centralized systems are more efficient. Two concepts of leadership were discussed, and analysis of leadership functions rather than traits was recommended.

The last question raised was practical: How can the small group be made more effective? First, the use of an agenda makes the most of time and resources. Second, an awareness of various attitudes toward conflict allows group members to resolve conflicts in a way that respects both task and human concerns. A third correlate of small-group effectiveness is an approach to decision making that ensures commitment to the decision by all members of the group.

Key Terms

Brainstorming	Handclasping or pairing	Private acceptance	Self-directed work team
Casual or social group	Learning or education	Problem-solving group	Social comparison
Cohesiveness	group	Public compliance	theory
Consensus	Majority vote	Railroading	Storming
Consideration function	Norming	Risky shift	Task function
Forming	Performing	phenomenon	Work group

Review Questions

1. Discuss two theories about compliance with social pressure. How does each explain this phenomenon?

2. How does groupthink encourage conformity?

3. Identify the four phases of group development and describe briefly the type of communication characteristic of each.

4. What is the relationship between group size, membership satisfaction, and group performance?

5. How do task and consideration functions in leadership differ?

6. What are six common difficulties that small groups encounter in developing ideas and solving problems?

7. What are four ways of arriving at a decision in a group? What are some relative advantages and disadvantages of each?

Exercises

1. Observe an actual problem-solving group. Listen carefully for statements that indicate the four phases of group development. Record any statements that represent any of these phases. Notice also whether the group does not seem to go through these four phases. Compare your observations with others who have observed different groups. Do most of the observations correspond to the research findings?

2. Conduct an in-depth study of a group of which you are a member. Keep a journal of the group's interaction pattern and activities and write a paper in which you analyze (a) the communication network(s) of the group, (b) the leadership functions, (c) the group's cohesiveness, (d) members' satisfaction, and (e) methods of conflict resolution.

3. Analyze the most successful group discussion that you have ever participated in. What specific factors were presented that accounted for its success?

Suggested Readings

Donnellon, Anne. *Team Talk: The Power of Language in Team Dynamics.* Cambridge, MA: Harvard Business School Press, 1996.

This unique and excellent book looks at the role of language in the work of teams. It offers a method for analyzing team discussion to determine the group's effectiveness.

Gray, Dave, Sunni Brown, and James Macanufo. *Gamestorming.* Sebastopol, CA: O'Reilly Media Inc., 2010.

This book focuses entirely on creativity techniques for problem-solving. A quick and delightful read.

Huszczo, Gregory. *Tools for Team Leadership.* Palo Alto, CA: Davies-Black, 2004.

This book is excellent for those interested in the leadership aspect of small groups. It includes numerous self-diagnostic instruments.

Kay, John. *Obliquity: Why Our Goals Are Best Achieved Indirectly.* New York: Penguin, 2011.

This book takes a totally fresh and very interesting view of problem-solving by taking an indirect instead of a head-on approach.

Levi, Daniel. *Group Dynamics for Teams*, 3rd ed. Thousand Oaks, CA: Sage Publishing, 2011.

For those who prefer a more theoretical treatment of teams.

Maxwell, John C. *The 17 Indisputable Laws of Teamwork.* Nashville, TN: Thomas Nelson Publishers, 2001.

This book offers a very readable and enjoyable insight into what makes teams successful. Very practical and user-friendly.

Rothwell, J. Dan. *In Mixed Company*, 7th ed. Boston: Wadsworth, 2010.

This book offers a communication emphasis of group dynamics.

Tubbs, Stewart L. *A Systems Approach to Small Group Interaction*, 11th ed. New York: McGraw-Hill, 2012.

A rather novel "systems approach" in the analysis of communication in the small group. Topics covered in the present chapter are dealt with in greater detail. Emphasis is on the complex interplay of 24 variables that relate to small-group processes.

 # For Supplementary Information

Log onto the Online Learning Center at *www.mhhe.com/tubbshc13e.*

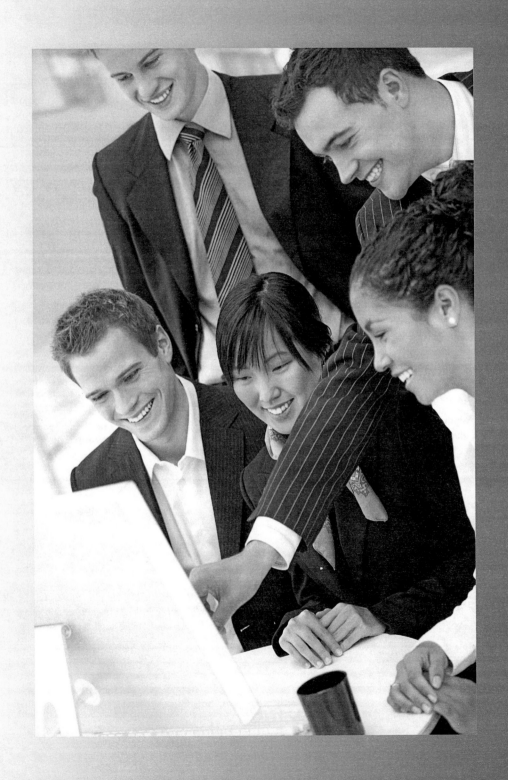

Organizational Communication

Chapter Objectives

After reading this chapter, you should be able to:

1. Explain three functions communication performs in organizations.
2. Define and illustrate supportive supervisory communication.
3. List five ways in which people adapt to information overload.
4. Explain the law of diminishing returns as it relates to downward communication.
5. Identify the five types of power.
6. List five functions of upward communication.
7. Describe the differentiation-integration problem in organizations as it relates to horizontal communication.
8. Explain the formula that expresses the important variables in the development of rumors.
9. Describe the three types of message distortion that occur during rumor transmission.

Did you know that Procter & Gamble has just launched hot chocolate in packages that you can eat and digest the packaging itself? Research by scientists has already produced edible packaging made from a combination of milk products and gum. Other products in the development pipeline include oatmeal, drink sticks that slide into water bottles, and spice strips that dissolve into the foods you are cooking (Mascai, 2012, p. 60). These products pave the way for a cleaner planet with many fewer landfills of discarded packaging.

In another example, Ford Motor Company is already making the hybrid Ford Focus that can get up to 100 miles per gallon of gasoline (Snavely, 2011).

And in another example, Disney has bought Babble Media, Inc., whose Web site carries news for parents and blogs written by moms and dads so that it can communicate better with parents via the blogosphere. Disney had previously purchased a company called Kaboose, Inc. in 2009 and iParenting Media in 2007 for the same purpose.

These are just a few of the innovations that have come from companies with excellent organizational communication practices.

To illustrate how dynamic the nature of organizational communication has become, the medical giant company Johnson & Johnson aired an advertisement on its Web site for Motrin pain reliever. The ad targeted new mothers and read as follows:

> Wearing your baby seems to be in fashion. I mean, in theory it's a great idea. There's the front baby carrier, sling, schwing, wrap, pouch. And who knows what else they've come up with. Wear your baby on your side, your front, go hands free. Supposedly, it's a real bonding experience. They say that babies carried close to the body tend to cry less than others. But what about me? Do moms that wear their babies cry more than those who don't? I sure do! These things put a ton of strain on your back, your neck, your shoulders. Did I mention your back? I mean, I'll put up with the pain because it's a good kind of pain; it's for my kid. Plus, it totally makes me look like an official mom. And so if I look tired and crazy, people will understand why.

Many mothers became outraged and micro-blogged their friends on Twitter.com criticizing the ad and calling for a boycott of Johnson & Johnson products. Within one day a 9-minute video appeared on YouTube ("Motrin ad makes moms mad") criticizing the company in very strong terms accompanied by the song "Danny Boy." There was such a firestorm of controversy that within 24 hours, Johnson & Johnson aired an apology from its vice president of marketing and pulled its advertisement. This example demonstrates the very rapidly changing type of organizational communication that occurs in today's social media environment. It also shows the close interplay between organizational communication and mass communication (Belkin, 2009).

Airbus, one of the world's leading commercial jet manufacturers, planned to launch its newest and biggest jet, the A380, in 2007. With the wings made in Britain, the horizontal tail stabilizer made in Spain, the nose section and center fuselage made in France, and the forward fuselage and vertical tail stabilizer made in Germany, this plane is the result of one of the most modern and advanced organizational communication marvels in the world. However, each plane contains over 348 miles of bundled electrical wiring. When the final assembly was attempted for the first time, they found out that the wires from front to back of the plane were too short to connect. It turns out that the engineers in Hamburg, Germany, were initially drawing on a two-dimensional computer program, while their counterparts in Toulouse, France, were working in 3-D. The delays caused Airbus enormous headaches and losses in the billions of euros—and even more in U.S. dollars (Burke, 2007).

Consider these other examples:

Ferrari, the automaker, sent a memo to its automobile dealers in the United States, instructing them to "monitor" cars that are privately imported into the United States to make sure the company was in compliance with U.S. laws, according to a report in *Auto Week*. Some dealers interpreted the memo to mean that they should intrusively inspect, and in some cases partially disassemble, certain Ferraris brought in for service to verify point-by-point compliance with a list of U.S. requirements. But by "monitor," the company meant only to inform its U.S. dealers that some privately imported Ferraris might not be in compliance and for the dealers to notify the company if they had noticed this problem.

The U.S. Army bought 461,000 helmets from the Gentex Corporation, then told the company that the helmets were unacceptable, according to a *Wall Street Journal* article. The helmets were to be manufactured with layers of Kevlar material. Apparently, the Army interpreted "layer" to be a solid sheet of material. The manufacturer interpreted "layer" to also include small scrap sheets of the material stitched together. As a result, the helmets were manufactured using layers of patchwork Kevlar material, and the Army declared the helmets to be defective (Catt et al., 2005).

By now you have probably figured out that all of these situations involve **organizational communication.** More correctly, they involve *human communication that occurs within the context of organizations*—for it is people who do the communicating, not organizations. These examples show the wide range of events that can be called "organizational communication." They also illustrate the overlap between organizational communication and the other communication contexts (interpersonal, small-group, public, and mass communication). Any and all of these four types of communication can be associated with organizations.

We spend a good part of our lives as members of organizations. Although we tend to think first of business organizations, this also includes schools and universities, hospitals, churches, military institutions, fraternities, sororities, and other social organizations. This chapter focuses on communicating in these organizations, especially communicating on the job.

The above examples are not unusual events where large companies are concerned. Carol Bobke of Mission Viejo, California, struggled for three months to resolve a problem with her health insurance company. After getting the runaround, she looked up the company's e-mail address and wrote to the president. By the next morning, the president's assistant had stepped in to fix the problem (Mulkern, 2001). If you are having a problem with a company, you can go to *www.Planetfeedback .com* to get some help. This is a firm that specializes in getting quick responses via the Internet.

ORGANIZATIONAL CULTURE

Apple, Google, Amazon, and Facebook are all tied as the most innovative companies in the world (as of 2012). Their cultures are all a bit different, but they do share one thing in common, and that is a corporate culture that encourages people to do what they do best through free and open communication within the company and with their customers (*Fast Company*, March 2012, pp. 70–80).

In an equally dramatic example of the power of organizational culture, Julie Roehm was fired as a marketing executive at Walmart after only 10 months. One of the reasons cited was that she was traveling so much that she routinely missed her immediate boss's staff meetings. In addition, her first day on the job, she brought in a painting crew and had her office painted chartreuse green with brown trim. This was within a corporate culture with plain white walls and no windows to symbolize its low-price customer image. Her flamboyant style finally caught up with her. After she was fired, one former colleague sarcastically said, "And take your paint crew with you" (Berner, 2007).

Similarly, Michael Ovitz was fired from the Disney Company after only 14 months. His colleague Michael Eisner wrote,

> He started to rub people the wrong way. We'd all take a bus (at the corporate retreat) and he had a limousine; a special driver. Everyone had a walkie talkie and you heard walkie talkies around the 30,000 acres saying, "Who was this guy and why was he demanding this?" The perception was that Michael Ovitz was a little elitist for the egalitarian Walt Disney World in Florida. It was a bad vibe. (Goffee and Jones, 2006, p. 110)

What comes to mind when you think of Southwest Airlines, Hewlett-Packard, Microsoft, or Disney? How do these images compare to your images of the U.S. Postal Service, or AT&T? The first four companies are each thought to have a culture that is highly innovative and responsive to changes in the environment. *Fortune* magazine notes that Hewlett-Packard's culture is focused on three tenets: "respect for others, a sense of community, and plain hard work." Southwest Airlines's CEO Herb Kelleher shares that the Southwest Airlines culture is based on "zealous" hiring, positive attitudes, dedicated personalities, and a sense of humor (Auxillium West, 2003). The second set of organizations is often associated with tradition and relative slowness to change. In part, each of their images is a reflection of their individual organizational cultures. The term "culture" originally comes from social anthropology. It refers to the totality of socially transmitted behavior patterns in an organization. In 2003, Auxillium West, a human resources software company, defined organizational, or corporate, culture as "the moral, social, and behavioral norms of an organization based on the beliefs, attitudes, and priorities of its members." It is important to note that most organizational cultures emerge passively over time, and cultural change is a long-term process. Many organizations consist of combinations of cultures that make it difficult to pin one down. For example, departments within companies can have varying cultures. An advertising department may be much more outgoing than an IT department, based on the combined personalities of its members (Auxillium West, 2003).

When you start your first day on a new job, you will notice that there are a lot of verbal and nonverbal cues that teach you how to fit into the organization's culture: the way people dress; how hard they work; the way space is used; the level of technological sophistication; who talks to whom and what type of language, terminology, and acronyms they use; and so on. One young worker who joined Ford said that his co-workers used so many three-letter acronyms they had them coming out his ears. He referred to them as having TLA–OYE (three letter acronyms–out your ears). The joke seemed to fit perfectly into their culture. Kouzes and Posner (2010) have written extensively on the numerous communication cues that make up organizational culture.

Deal and Kennedy (2000) have identified four predominant types of culture and the leadership styles that go with each.

Tough-Guy–Macho Culture   This type of organization is typical of high-risk organizations such as police departments, and among surgeons, since they deal with life and death. Other examples are the movie industry, management consulting, sports, construction, and venture capital firms where fortunes are made and lost.

Work-Hard–Play-Hard Culture   Organizations of this type focus on sales and on meeting customers' needs. Mary Kay Cosmetics, McDonald's, Xerox, Hewlett-Packard, IBM, and Frito-Lay are examples. Sales-type organizations also celebrate a lot to keep up their energy and motivation.

Bet-Your-Company Culture   Life in this culture requires that you endure high risks but slow feedback. For example, big oil companies invest millions in exploration before seeing their success or failure. Boeing spends billions to develop a new aircraft. The same is true with NASA. Mining companies, military organizations, and architectural firms are other examples.

Process Culture   This is a low-risk, slow-feedback type of culture. Most governmental organizations, utilities, and heavily regulated industries like pharmaceutical firms fall into this category. Employees in these cultures rarely see the results of their work. They focus on the processes of how things get done. Even the most trivial event can become the subject of a memo. And numerous memos are written just to "Cover Your A—" (CYA). This culture is also known for its long, rambling meetings. However, that does not always have to be the case. Note the leadership style of the president of one private university:

> I had an accreditor once who said to me that any [curriculum] change should take two years. My response was if it takes two years we don't need it. . . . We can take a program from idea to delivery in less than three months. And we do it all the time. In fact, the only time we can't do that is when accrediting agencies enter into the picture. (Hodgetts, 1998, p. 162)

Not only is the culture of many organizations changing, but the type of employees in those organizations is changing also. Lambert (1992) cites data from the Bureau of Labor Statistics that show these changes are dramatically influencing

Table 14.1	Net New Entrants to the Workforce by 2008					
	Population	Percent of Total	Median Age (years)	Mean Age (years)	Percent Male	Percent Female
All races	273,137	100	35.5	36.4	48.9%	51.1%
Caucasian	224,865	82.3	36.6	37.3	49.1	50.9
African American	34,948	12.8	30.1	32.1	47.5	52.5
American Indian	2,400	0.9	27.7	30.4	49.5	50.5
Eskimo, Aleut	10,924	4	31.7	32.6	47.9	52.1
Asian, Pacific Islander, and Hispanic	31,469	11.5	26.5	28.8	50.3	49.7

Source: Bureau of Labor Statistics, 2003.

organizational communication. Historically, organizations have been overwhelmingly male and white. Even as recently as 1985, white males composed 47 percent of the workforce and white females 36 percent. As indicated in Table 14.1, the Bureau of Labor Statistics found that women and minorities represented about 70 percent of net new entrants to the workforce by 2008.

Given such startling changes in demographics, it will become increasingly necessary to learn to communicate within a context of cultural diversity. And the study of human communication in organizations is more relevant today than ever before.

IMPORTANCE OF COMMUNICATION

Chester Barnard once wrote that "the first executive function is to develop and maintain a system of communication" (1938, p. 82). Barnard's statement has proved prophetic. Some years ago, a survey of the presidents of 100 of the largest corporations in the United States found that 96 percent believed there was a "definite relationship" between communication and employee productivity. Numerous studies have shown that when managers and other responsible businesspeople are asked how much of the workday they spend communicating, their replies range from about 85 to 99 percent. Most say above 90 percent. Most recently, work by Harvard researchers Cherniss and Goleman has shown that Emotional Intelligence (primarily comprising self-awareness and social awareness, i.e., communication competence) accounts for 85 to 90 percent of a leader's success (2001, p. xv).

Surveys conducted by the University of Michigan, Pennsylvania State University, and Wake Forest University have documented the importance of communication skills to organizational success. According to one recent *Wall Street Journal* survey of employers (Safon, 2007), the following were the most highly valued attributes that recruiters were seeking in people they wanted to hire:

1. Communication and interpersonal skills (89 percent)
2. Ability to work well in teams (87 percent)

3. Analytical and problem-solving skills (84 percent)

4. Leadership potential (73 percent)

All of these top attributes are discussed in this book.

After finishing college, young people who start new jobs often face a rude awakening. They feel that with their up-to-date knowledge and training, they should be making a major contribution. As they enter this new world of work, however, they find that developing interpersonal skills is of overriding importance. Their frustration is expressed in the following excerpts:

> All the problems I encounter boil down to communication and human relations. (Initiate in a consumer goods company)
> I thought I could sell people with logic and was amazed at the hidden agendas people have, irrational objections; really bright people will come up with stupid excuses. (Initiate in an aerospace company) (Schein, 1997, p. 18)

A study by Watson Wyatt Worldwide showed that companies with the most effective communication programs returned 57 percent more dividends to their shareholders than companies with the least effective communication programs. "The results of our study confirm that communication is a critical element in creating successful business results," says Kathryn Yates, global director of communication consulting (Watson Wyatt, 2006).

Based on his extensive research, Harvard organizational change guru John Kotter writes that the most important thing that leaders can do to bring about organizational change is to create a sense of urgency. If leaders fail to accomplish that, the change efforts fail over 70 percent of the time (Kotter, 2008, p. viii; Kotter and Whitehead, 2010).

If you are wondering just how to accomplish persuasion and influence in organizations, Kerry Patterson and his colleagues offer the following advice:

> As it turns out, it's the desire to be accepted, respected, and connected that really pulls at human heart strings. . . . Learn how to co-opt this awesome power, and you can change anything. (Patterson et al., 2008, p. 165)

Jennings (1971) conducted some classic studies of the common patterns of those who are promoted fastest and describes their communication style in the following way:

> Executives tend to use a feather-light touch with their subordinates and peers. The heavy hand of the lower positioned manager is frowned upon at high corporate levels. The terms "style" and "panache" are often used to mean the ability to say and do almost anything without antagonizing others. People tend to work better when they do not have to work at saving face. To be mobility-bright also means to present oneself in a manner becoming to the dignity and stature of the superiors above. It means to behave as though the executive were at a higher level than his present one. (p. 69)

One of the most wide-sweeping changes in organizational communication is the increase in teamwork. For example, Boeing announced that its new Boeing 777 jetliner was going to be built by teams. The company set up more than 200 "design-build" teams. These teams were composed of employees from engineering, quality control, finance, and manufacturing. Each one concentrates on a specific part of the aircraft. Even suppliers and potential customers are sometimes included in team meetings (Yukl, 2013).

Experts traditionally have identified three functions communication performs in organizations:

The Command Function   Communication allows members of the organization to "issue, receive, interpret, and act on commands" (Yukl, 2013, p. 31). The two types of communication that make up this function are directions and feedback, and the goal is the successful influence of other members of the organization. The outcome of the command function is coordination among the many interdependent members of the organization.

The Relational Function   Communication allows members of the organization "to create and maintain productive business and personal relationships with other members of the organization" (Yukl, 2013, p. 64). Relationships on the job affect job performance in many ways, for example, job satisfaction, the flow of communication both down and up the organizational hierarchy, and the degree to which commands are followed. The importance of good interpersonal skills is highlighted on the job when you consider that many of the necessary relationships are not chosen but forced by organizational circumstances, making the relationships less stable, more prone to conflict, less committed, and so on.

The Ambiguity-Management Function   Choices in an organizational setting are often made in highly ambiguous circumstances. For example, multiple motivations exist, given that choices affect co-workers, the organization, and oneself; the organization's objectives may not be clear; and the context within which the choice needs to be made may be unclear. Communication is the means for coping with and reducing the ambiguity inherent in the organization: Members talk with each other in an effort to structure the environment and make sense of new situations, which entails gaining and sharing information.

With the help of increased technology, the importance of communication is further demonstrated. The Internet "blog" trend has recently emerged as a way for businesses to improve communication. Blogs are "self-published chronicles of ideas, news, facts, opinions and inspirations that are frequently updated" (Aber, 2004). Businesses can use blogs in the following different ways:

- Communicate and collaborate among distributed colleagues, partners, suppliers, customers, and others.
- Use a unique, informal way to establish a company or individual's reputation or brand.

- Improve operations (as with project management or tech support knowledge-sharing).
- Demonstrate expertise.
- Establish competitive differentiation.
- Reach out to value chain members with organizational news, marketing promotions, new product announcements, and so forth.
- Share knowledge among professionals in the same industry, but not necessarily the same organization. (Aber, 2004)

In the next section, we see the critical role that the supervisor plays in the organization's success or failure.

Supervisory Communication

The Gallup Organization surveyed over one million people, including over 80,000 managers in over 400 countries, and found the single most important thing that people want to know in doing their jobs is this: Do I know what is expected of me at work? Supervisors who make this clear to workers are more likely to be successful (Rath, 2007; Rath and Conchie, 2008).

If we know that communication is important to organizational success, then it becomes important to know what types of communication are most important to the organization. A recent stream of research has focused on what is known as the Leader-Member Exchange (LMX) in organizations. According to this theory, the relationship between the employee and the leaders is influenced by both parties, and the leader develops a somewhat different relationship with each of his or her employees. Avolio and Luthans (2006) found that a positive LMX is associated with employees who practice organizational citizenship behaviors, defined as employees who help others with their work even when they are not required to do so. A number of research studies have shown that the leader is the one who starts this chain of events by setting a good example. The question is, What communication behaviors on the part of the leader tend to create this positive climate?

Supportive Communication Have you ever had a boss who seemed to be on your side? Or, on the other hand, one who seemed to be looking for ways to catch you in a mistake? This difference is the crux of supportive communication behaviors. Whetten and Cameron (2011) studied the effect of communication behaviors on employee creativity. They found that the following behaviors created a higher LMX score and were associated with higher employee creativity and productivity on the job. The supervisor

1. Helps employees solve problems.
2. Encourages employees to develop new skills.
3. Keeps informed about how employees think and feel about things.
4. Encourages employees to participate in important decisions.
5. Praises good work.

6. Encourages employees to speak up when they disagree with a decision.

7. Explains his or her actions.

8. Rewards employees for good performance.

These important guidelines will help improve your supportive communication behaviors as a leader.

Noncontrolling Communication

Noncontrolling Communication   Employees also respond well when they are not micromanaged or "snoopervised." Dean (2006) found that the following communication behaviors were associated with a high LMX score and with high employee creativity and productivity. The supervisor

1. Never seems to be checking on employees' work.

2. Never forces employees to do work his or her way.

3. Gives employees a chance to make important decisions on their own.

4. Leaves it up to employees to decide how to go about doing their jobs.

These are also important guidelines to show you how to improve your noncontrolling communication behaviors as a leader.

Trust   Trust is derived from the German word *trost,* which implies "a level of comfort with the other person" (Lennick and Kiel, 2005). It is based on our assessment of the other person's perceived competence at a certain task as well as his or her character.

Trust is often defined as "the degree of confidence you have that another party can be relied on to fulfill commitments, be fair, be transparent, and not take advantage of your vulnerability" (Hurley, 2012, p. 1). Researchers have found that there are two components of trust—one cognitive or rational, the other affective or emotional. They asked people to rate a supervisor's trust using the following statements to differentiate high from low:

COGNITIVE TRUST

1. This person approaches his or her job with professionalism and dedication.

2. Given this person's track record, I see no reason to doubt his or her competence.

3. I can rely on this person not to make my job more difficult by careless work.

AFFECTIVE TRUST

1. I have a sharing relationship with this person. We can both freely share our ideas, feelings, and hopes.

2. I can talk freely to this individual about difficulties I am having at work and know that he or she will want to listen.

3. If I shared my problems with this person, I know she or he would respond constructively and caringly (Lyman, 2012).

14.1 **PRACTICAL TIPS** | **How to Develop Trust***

14.1 **PRACTICAL TIPS** | **How to Develop Trust***

1. Practice what you preach—walk the talk.
2. Open lines of communication. Declare your intentions and be open to feedback.
3. Accept disagreements, differences of opinion—try no-fault problem solving.
4. Keep confidential information confidential—always.
5. Let others know what you stand for and what you value.
6. Create a supportive environment—let others know it is safe to open up to you.
7. Maintain a high level of honesty and integrity.
8. Know yourself. Build on your competencies and accept your limitations.
9. Build credibility by being consistent and reliable.
10. Avoid micromanaging. This conveys the message, "I don't trust you."

* Adapted from Suzanne de Janasz, Karen Dowd, and Beth Schneider. *Interpersonal Skills in Organizations* (3rd ed.). New York: McGraw-Hill, 2009, p. 36.

Many experts agree that the supervisor is the one who must initiate the trusting relationship. After all, the employee who comes into the organization learns very quickly what is acceptable and unacceptable behavior in that organization. The immediate supervisor is the person who most influences the employee's perception of the organization. Again, we see the importance of the Leader-Member Exchange.

In the remaining sections of this chapter, we shall examine four other factors for analyzing organization communication: (1) downward communication, (2) upward communication, (3) horizontal communication, and (4) informal communication.

Downward Communication

Jim Donald is president of Starbucks in Seattle. He states, "I'm fanatical about communication. . . . If anyone in our company e-mails me or leaves me a voice-mail, they get a response, quickly. We have to operate like a store. Nobody likes to wait. I get 200 to 250 e-mails a day, and I respond to 75 percent of them." Donald maximizes his efficiency by distributing his time as follows:

44 percent talking with direct reports

28 percent traveling to stores and roasting plants

17 percent meeting with employees

11 percent strategic thinking and employee evaluations

He also says, "When I'm traveling, I visit 10 Starbucks stores a day. I walk right back to the counter, put on an apron, and start talking to our partners. You can tell how a store is doing by smelling it, so I stick my nose in the pastry display. I check out the restrooms. . . . I learned this from Sam Walton, who hired me to run Wal-Mart's Supercenters six months before he died. Sam used to say, 'If you want to know what's wrong with the business, ask the people on the front line'" (Sellers, 2006, p. 51).

After supervisory communication, the second most important factor in determining communication climate in the organization is **downward communication.** Such communication *is initiated by the organization's upper management and then filters downward through the "chain of command."* In 2004, a *Wall Street Journal* article urged executives to take full responsibility for organizational communication. They must obtain buy-in from "superiors, subordinates, and peers," while sharing critical information. Superiors, peers, and subordinates need information and should be treated equally in its dissemination. Daly (2011) recommends that instead of making organizational decisions and drilling them down through the organization based on "what's right for the shareholders, or the executives, or the employees," executives should ask "what is right for the enterprise," or what is right for everyone, including employees at every level in the organization. To make organizations work, decisions must be made holistically and not in parts (Daly, 2011, p. 189).

Swift (1973) describes a problem in the downward communication that often faces managers:

> Let's suppose that everyone at X Corporation, from the janitor on up to the chairman of the board, is using the office copiers for personal matters; income tax forms, church programs, children's term papers, and God knows what else are being duplicated by the gross. This minor piracy costs the company a pretty penny, both directly and in employee time, and the general manager—let's call him Sam Edwards—decides the time has come to lower the boom. (p. 59)

If you were Sam Edwards, how would you communicate with your subordinates about this problem? First, you might consider some communication alternatives. Our model in Chapter 1 referred to these as "channels." Some typical channels of downward communication are

E-mail	Telephone calls
Department meetings	Speech to all employees
Face-to-face conversation with subordinates	Podcast
Company newspaper	Intraorganizational memos
Bulletin boards	Company Web site messages
Letters sent home	Instant messages
Posters	Facebook page
Fax	Twitter
Voice mail	

Any of these, alone or in combination, could be employed to get the message about photocopying to your employees.

A more recent study of 500 top executives conducted by the London School of Economics and Harvard Business School found that the average top executive spends one third of his or her time just in meetings (18 hours out of a 55-hour work week). This number is significantly higher than in previous studies (Silverman, 2012, p. B1). Social scientist Randy Gardner studied whether Post-it Notes made by 3M Corporation might have the power to enhance compliance with a written request made to another person. He sent surveys to people asking them to fill out the survey in one of three conditions: (1) the survey had a Post-it Note attached to the cover letter; (2) the survey had the same handwritten message written directly on the cover letter; and (3) the cover letter and survey were sent without a handwritten note. Which of the three conditions do you think worked the best? More than 75 percent responded with the Post-it Note, while 48 percent of the second group and only 36 percent of the third group filled out the survey. Garner suggests that people liked the extra effort of the Post-it Note and felt the need to reciprocate the extra effort (Goldstein, Martin, and Cialdini, 2008, pp. 50–51).

Sam Edwards of the X Corporation is an experienced manager, and he also knows that if he overloads his people with too much information, they will begin to make more errors. Given the costs and the potential benefits involved, Edwards decides to send an e-mail about the abuse of photocopying privileges. In doing so, he avoids bogging down his supervisors with more time-consuming forms of communication, such as meetings.

Scholars have identified seven ways in which people adapt to information overload. They are (1) *omission* (failing to handle all the information), (2) *error* (ignoring or failing to correct errors when made), (3) *queuing* (letting things pile up), (4) *filtering* (dealing with input in categories ranked according to a priority system), (5) *approximation* (lowering standards of precision), (6) *multiple channels* (delegation of information processing to others), and (7) *escape* (refusal to handle the input at all).

Effectiveness of Downward Communication

Research on the effectiveness of different forms of downward communication has shown that using a combination of channels tends to get the best results. Typically, channels were ranked in the following order of effectiveness (from most to least effective):

1. Combined oral and written
2. Oral only
3. Written only
4. Rumor

In other words, in terms of actually getting the information through to employees accurately, a combination of written and oral channels gets the best results.

Sending the same message through more than one channel creates *redundancy,* and redundancy seems to be helpful not only in getting messages through but in ensuring that they will be remembered. For example, a busy executive may get an e-mail message reminding her of an executive committee meeting that day at one o'clock. By lunch hour, however, her busy activity schedule has caused the meeting to slip her mind. At lunch, the chairperson of the executive committee says, "Don't forget the meeting at one this afternoon." The woman replies, "Thanks for reminding me. It almost slipped my mind. It's been one of those days."

One of the paradoxes of communicating in organizations is that busy people seem to require more reminders (i.e., more message redundancy) to act on the downward communication they receive. On the other hand, as the number of e-mails, texts, memos, meetings, phone calls, and so on increases, each person becomes that much busier, since it requires time to attend to each of these messages. Therefore, an important consideration in organization communication is the so-called **law of diminishing returns,** which states that *more is better, up to a point.* For example, a more open flow of communication is good up to a point, after which the receiver may become overloaded. A supervisor of my acquaintance believed very firmly in communicating fully with subordinates. The net result of her good intentions was that employees in the department had to check their e-mail about every hour to keep up with the continual barrage of memos. Naturally, this volume of communication kept employees from being as productive as they might otherwise have been. This relationship between communication frequency and desired effect is illustrated in Figure 14.1. To make matters worse, a national survey found that about 33 percent of the workers surveyed has a boss who sends e-mail messages on weekends and expects a reply. An additional 30 percent reported that they received e-mail messages "from time to time" from their boss on weekends (Fryer, 2011). It is now taken for granted that workers need to check their e-mails on weekends.

Another characteristic of downward communication is lack of accuracy; in other words, "people often don't get the message straight." This message distortion in downward communication is humorously illustrated in the following example:

> *Colonel communicates to Major:* At 9 o'clock tomorrow there will be an eclipse of the sun, something which does not occur every day. Get the men to fall out in the company street in their fatigues so that they will see this rare phenomenon, and I will then explain it to them. Now in the case of rain, we will not be able to see anything, of course, so then take the men to the gym.
>
> *Major passes message to Captain:* By order of the Colonel tomorrow at 9 o'clock there will be an eclipse of the sun. If it rains, you will not be able to see it from the company street, so, then, in fatigues, the eclipse of the sun will take place in the gym, something which does not occur every day.
>
> *The Captain then said to the Lieutenant:* By order of the Colonel in fatigues tomorrow, at 9 o'clock in the morning the inauguration of the eclipse of the sun will take place in the gym. The Colonel will give the order if it should rain, something which does occur every day.

Figure 14.1 *Communication and Probable Effectiveness*

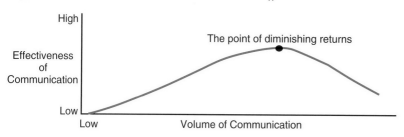

The Lieutenant then told the Sergeant: Tomorrow at 9, the Colonel in fatigues will eclipse the sun in the gym, as it occurs every day if it's a nice day. If it rains, then this occurs in the company street.

The Sergeant then instructed the Corporal: Tomorrow at 9, the eclipse of the colonel in fatigues will take place because of the sun. If it rains in the gym, something which does not take place every day, you will fall out in the company street.

Finally, one Private said to another Private: Tomorrow, if it rains, it looks as if the sun will eclipse the Colonel in the gym. It's a shame that this does not occur every day. (Zima, personal communication)

Because of this possible loss of accuracy in downward communication, message redundancy turns out to be both necessary and helpful. One study conducted by two professors at Northwestern University found that managers who sent out multiple messages with the very same content were 21 percent more effective than those who did not (Neeley and Leonardi, 2011). More will be said about message distortion in the section "Informal Communication." It seems obvious that as organizations increase in size, the frequency of these kinds of snafus* increases.

Upward Communication

The third most important factor in organizational communication is **upward communication**—*the process whereby the ideas, feelings, and perceptions of lower-level employees are communicated to those at higher levels in the organization.* The following example shows the dangers of inhibiting or not encouraging upward communication. In 2003 NASA was criticized for its lack of upward communication from frontline engineers during the time that led up to the *Columbia* shuttle crash. Large organizations like NASA have more levels of management and authority that can act as barriers to the flow of communication and that can lead to detrimental or, in this case, disastrous results (Wessel, 2003, p. C8).

Employees must be encouraged to communicate from the bottom up. When employees are not told why they must do things and are not shown the results of their efforts, they tend to become frustrated and disillusioned about their work.

---

*Situation normal, all fouled up.

ISSUES IN COMMUNICATION

According to an e-mail from the president of the author's university, in the first week of class in September 2004, there were 972,149 e-mail messages sent through the university computers! (Willis, 2004)

Have you ever felt as if all of those have come to you? E-mail use is a mixed blessing. So, let's take a look at some hints to manage your e-mail messages.

- Scan first, read second. Do just a quick scan to see if it is important.
- If you can't use it, nuke it. Avoid saving messages for later if you can. They just clutter your computer.
- Thin out. If you get many messages on the same topic, delete all but the most important

ones. These first three steps can reduce your in-box messages by 60 percent.

- Prioritize. Deal with the remaining e-mails in order of importance.
- Ask friends to stop sending unwanted e-mails.
- Don't be a cc rider. Ask to be removed from the cc lists you don't want to be on.
- Use your utilities. Use e-mail utilities to color code e-mails as they come into your in-box.
- Less is more. Respond only when needed.
- Avoid emotions. If you are tempted to send an angry e-mail, wait a day and read it again. Remember, "You can't unring a bell." (Cooper, 2004)

Several barriers prevent employees from freely communicating to their superiors, including fears of bureaucracy and of retaliation. Creating incentives is one way to encourage bottom-up communication (Conant and Norgaard, 2011). One worker told us that he had worked for company X for 30 years and for all he knew he had never done anything right because he got feedback only when he did something wrong.

Research has shown that upward communication can serve at least five important functions:

1. It provides management with needed information for decision making.
2. It helps employees relieve the pressures and frustrations of the work situation.
3. It enhances employees' sense of participation in the enterprise.
4. It serves as a measure of the effectiveness of downward communication.
5. As a bonus, it suggests more rewarding uses of downward communication for the future. (Goldhaber, 2003, pp. 156–159; see also Adler and Elmhorst, 2008)

Ironically, although its importance is obvious, upward communication is not always encouraged by management. One reason for this may be that the messages superiors hear from subordinates are not always pleasant or flattering. In one rather extreme case, a foundry manager was reportedly so unreceptive to bad news that his environmental engineers were afraid to tell him the extent to which their foundry was dumping pollutants into a neighboring river. Eventually, the foundry had legal problems with another factory located downstream. The problems could probably have been averted if the manager had been more responsive to the ideas and feelings of his subordinates.

The facetious employee performance appraisal form in Table 14.2 gives examples of the type of information subordinates might want to communicate to their bosses from time to time.

Some bosses might laugh with their employees, others might not think it funny at all. The employer who can see the good-natured humor in some of the entries may be said to have a higher degree of **upward receptivity** or *willingness to receive messages from subordinates*. Upward receptivity is most often associated with the so-called open-door policy in business. If a manager has his or her door open, this signals a willingness to communicate with employees. Unfortunately, an open door does not always signify an open mind. It has been pointed out that the best open-door policy is really one in which a superior opens the door of the subordinate's office to initiate communication. Such action indicates even greater willingness on the superior's part to meet employees halfway in opening the communication channels.

Indeed, initiative on the part of the employer would seem to be one of the best ways to "open the door" to communication within the organization. A number of studies have shown, for example, that most subordinates feel reluctant to communicate information to superiors. That reluctance can be increased (or decreased) by a number of circumstances. In conferences between college students and their professors, students rated professors as more receptive, more trustworthy, and better qualified if they did not sit with a desk between themselves and the students (Widgery and Stackpole, 1972). And, as might be expected, nervousness on the part of the students increased their sensitivity to such variables during the conference. So even such nonverbal factors as closed doors and imposing desks can serve as additional barriers to upward communication.

A special type of upward communication is **ingratiation.** This is defined by Liden and Mitchell (1988) as *"an attempt by individuals to increase their attractiveness in the eyes of others"* (p. 572). The authors identify three main forms of ingratiation. The first is flattery. Those who are attempting to "get in good" with others above them will often flatter or compliment the other person (often falsely). The second is self-disclosures and advice requests. Ingratiators may reveal personal information or may request the advice of a superior to gain favor. Third is attitude similarity and sincerity. The ingratiator will attempt to stress any similarities between himself or herself and the target person. However, research has shown that any of the ingratiating behaviors mentioned will be effective only if the target person perceives them as sincere (pp. 580–581). Cecily Cooper (2005) hypothesized the ways that humor might also work as an attempt to gain favor with the boss. Her theory contends that it will help to improve the boss-subordinate relationship.

Upward communication is less likely to occur if there are *psychological barriers* between superior and subordinate. The literature on this point suggests that three major psychological barriers affect upward communication:

1. If a subordinate believes that disclosure of his feelings, opinions, or difficulties may lead a superior to block or hinder the attainment of a personal goal (like getting a bonus or a promotion), he will conceal or distort them.

Table 14.2 Guide to Employee Performance Appraisal

	Performance Degrees				
Performance Factors	Far Exceeds Job Requirements	Exceeds Job Requirements	Meets Job Requirements	Needs Some Improvements	Does Not Meet Minimum Requirement
Quality	Leaps tall buildings with a single bound	Must take running start to leap over tall buildings	Can leap over only an average building with no spires	Crashes into buildings when attempting to jump over them	Cannot recognize buildings at all, much less jump them
Timeliness	Is faster than a speeding bullet	Is as fast as a speeding bullet	Not quite as fast as a speeding bullet	Would you believe a small bullet?	Wounds self with bullet when attempting to shoot
Initiative	Is stronger than a locomotive	Is stronger than a bull elephant	Is stronger than a bull	Shoots the bull	Smells like a bull
Adaptability	Walks on water consistently	Walks on water in emergencies	Washes with water	Drinks water	Passes water in emergencies
Communication	Talks with God	Talks with the angels	Talks to himself	Argues with himself	Loses those arguments

2. The more a superior rewards disclosure of feelings, opinions, and difficulties by subordinates, the more likely they will be to disclose them.

3. The more a superior discloses his own feelings, opinions, and difficulties to subordinates and his superior, the more likely subordinates will be to disclose theirs. (Rath and Conchie, 2008)

These findings seem to confirm what we have learned about downward communication—that is, that the supervisor who is seen as supportive is preferred. If we feel that we can be ourselves with a superior and that he or she will not use our mistakes against us, we are much more likely to communicate openly. And as a result, the superior is likely to have a better "feel" for the workings of his or her operation. In addition, Wiseman (2010) found that employees strongly valued the freedom to speak their minds to superiors. When employees' freedom of speech is reduced, their commitment to the organization is markedly reduced.

Even when upward communication is effective, however, bosses still have a hard time picturing the organizational realities at levels below them. The reasons for this difficulty are summarized by Yukl (2013):

Top executives know what they are told. In effect, they are "briefed" by others, and the briefing is both limiting and highly selective. The executive is far too busy to find out very much for himself; he [or she] must accept the information he gets, and this sets absolute limits to his horizons. Yet the briefing may be three steps removed from the facts, and thus be interpretation built upon interpretation—nearer fiction than fact by the time it reaches the man at the top. The person at the top turns out to be a broker, a decider between limited alternatives. (see also Daly, 2011).

As we have observed, organizational communication style differs according to the levels of the sender hierarchy. Rice (1987) writes:

Managers spend most of their time communicating (75–80 percent), about 60 percent of which is oral (phone, face-to-face, or in meetings). Higher-level managers spend more time communicating with subordinates than do lower-level managers; senior managers initiate more downward communication than upward communication; those at lower levels engage in more peer communication; only a small amount of managerial time is actually spent making decisions; managers communicate more in situations of greater innovation and uncertainty; and written communication is less likely to capture the attention of managers because of their fragmented, interrupted schedules. (p. 68)

Horizontal Communication

The survival of a modern organization often depends on the degree to which it specializes. Anyone who has visited a busy hospital, for example, will readily notice the high degree of specialization or differentiation that exists in such an organization. Medical services constitute only one part of the hospital organization. Other units that are vital to its operation include maintenance departments and administrative services such as accounting and personnel.

Coordination or integration of all these diverse units is required to keep the organization running efficiently. Many companies are trying new tactics to open up horizontal lines of communication by pushing employees out of their "comfort zones" through experiential training that will take employees with different department loyalties completely out of their element. These types of experiences (games and team challenges outside of the office and perhaps outside of departments) will open up the lines of communication and diminish obstructions to effective communication across equal levels of the organization (Ries, 2011). Consider the following example.

It is not unusual in a large university to find two or more departments teaching similar concepts and even using the same textbooks without knowing it because of a lack of coordination between units. This phenomenon is known as a "differentiation-integration problem" (Lawrence and Lorsch, 1969). It illustrates the intense need for effective **horizontal communication** in organizations—that is, *the exchanges between and among people on the same level of the organization.*

Horizontal communication frequently suffers in organizations because of employee loyalty to a given department. Groups within the organization compete for power and resources, and new employees are taught to be loyal to their department and not to trust or help those outside it. This situation is intensified in organizations that reward people and groups on a competitive basis. Naturally, if there are four promotions to be awarded among ten departments, rivalries will develop.

In such situations, each department may consider itself to be at the top of the organization. In a manufacturing plant, for example, production departments consider themselves to be the "stars" of the organization and regard accountants as "paper shufflers," engineers as "geeks," and human resources specialists as "the last to know and the first to go." Obviously, members of the other departments would hardly agree.

For example, Isaacson (2011) writes about the difference between Apple and Sony. Under Steve Jobs, Apple had seamless coordination between and among its various divisions such as design, engineering, and sales to develop such groundbreaking products as the iPod, iPhone, and iPad. However, Sony had divisions that competed against each other. "It had a consumer electronics division that developed sleek products and a music division with beloved artists. . . . But because each division tried to protect its own interests, the company as a whole never got its act together to produce end-to-end service [for downloading music] (Isaacson, 2011, p. 400). As a result of this and many other best practices, Apple is the most valuable company in the world, worth over $500 billion (Svensson, 2012, p. B1).

In summarizing the literature, Goldhaber (2003) identified four functions of horizontal communication in an organization:

1. *Task coordination:* The department heads may meet monthly to discuss how each department is contributing to the system's goals. Another example of coordination is the frequent use of team-teaching or team-writing found in university communities.
2. *Problem solving:* The members of a department may assemble to discuss how they will handle a threatened budget cut; they may employ brainstorming techniques.
3. *Information sharing:* The members of one department may meet with members of another department to give them some new data. One department at a university recently rewrote its entire curriculum. In order to inform other departments about these major revisions (which affected most segments of the university), the faculty held several meetings with representatives of the other departments to explain the new curriculum.
4. *Conflict resolution:* Members of one department may meet to discuss a conflict inherent in the department or between departments. (p. 124)

Innovative companies like Google, Ideo, and Starbucks have been cited for their best practices in horizontal communication. So, the question arises, how do they do it?

Reducing Barriers

Some steps can be taken to reduce the barriers to horizontal communication. Graban (2009) describes four procedures or guidelines that have proven successful in some cases:

1. Relatively greater emphasis given to *total organizational effectiveness* and the role of departments in contributing to it; departments measured and

rewarded on the basis of their *contribution* to the total effort rather than their individual effectiveness.

2. *High interaction and frequent communication* stimulated between groups to work on problems of intergroup coordination and help; organizational *rewards given partly on the basis of help* that groups give to each other. For example, at Starbucks stores employees sometimes cracked under the pressure. So, they instituted their "LATTE" communication method. This stands for Listen, Acknowledge, Take action, Thank the other person, and Explain why the problem occurred. Starbucks reported that both customer and employee satisfaction "skyrocketed" (Butta, 2012, p. 50).

3. Frequent *rotation of members* among groups or departments to stimulate high degrees of mutual understanding and empathy for one another's problems.

4. *Avoidance of any win–lose situation;* groups never put into the position of competing for some organizational reward; emphasis always placed on pooling resources to maximize organizational effectiveness; rewards shared equally with all the groups or departments.

A number of *organizational development (OD)* strategies include one form or another of team-building activities, which are designed to implement Graban's four guidelines. Keep in mind, however, that these are only guidelines and may not apply in every situation.

Communication and Organizational Change

Precision of communication is important, more important than ever, in our era of hair trigger balances, when a false or misunderstood word may create as much disaster as a sudden thoughtless act.

—**Thurber (***Leadership Now,* **2004)**

In the previous section you read about creating change within organizations from a bottom-up, or upward direction. Organizations must undergo frequent adaptation and change in order to survive in today's competitive business environment. We will now address the critical role of effective communication in the organizational change process.

As noted previously, one of the most challenging types of organizational change is *cultural* change. Chalice (2007) describes the aggregated results of a conglomeration of cultural change studies with a list of elements necessary for cultural change. Chalice references the necessity of common and consistent goals within an organization, role clarity and power among leaders, accountable employees, shared rewards, and encouragement of appropriate behaviors. Communication failures during cultural change can result in inconsistencies such as "split personality work environments." Lack of appropriate communication creates a churn within the organization, and portions of the organization split off, resulting in "split personalities" within the organization. The organization's "vision," for example, should be communicated to all levels of the organization and upheld through reinforcing behavior (Chalice, 2007).

There are three major tenets of the chaotic, or evolving, organization. First, organizations are webs of relationships that make up an evolving system. Second, times of perceived chaos within an organization are actually a means to an end of a greater order within the organization. Third, tiny nuances within the organization can result in significant effects, for better or for worse. Each employee within the organization has a high impact on the ability of an organization to create positive change (Kotter and Schlesinger, 2008).

These studies show that the development of information exchange systems within organizations is critical. The more that employees know, the more willing they will be to accept change and impending chaos as their organization adapts. First, there must be free flow of information at all times because lack of information leads to employee discomfort during times of change. Second, an organizational vision must be communicated across the organization. Third, buy-in must be achieved from all employees through effective communication channels. The more knowledge employees have, the less resistant they will be to change.

According to Margaret Wheatley, to adapt as an organization and survive organizational change, the whole organization must be engaged in the change effort, there should be openness and access to information, information should be reported quickly and without obstacles, and change must be accepted (Heath and Heath, 2010). The bottom line is that communication is essential to change. Communication arms employees with information to decrease their resistance and fear of change, allowing the organization to evolve, adapt, and reach a higher state of functioning. Kotter (2008) notes that "people deal far better with uncertainty and stress when they know what's going on."

Informal Communication

Last but not least, we shall examine the informal channels of communication used in organizations. Such channels are often labeled "rumor mills" and "the grapevine." The term "grapevine" is said to have originated during the Civil War. According to Smith, "In those days, intelligence telegraph lines were strung loosely from tree to tree in the manner of a grapevine, and the message was often garbled; thus, any rumor was said to be from the 'grapevine'" (Smith et al., 1972, p. 273).

Rosnow (1988) defines a rumor as "a proposition for belief . . . disseminated without official verification" (p. 14). Researchers theorize that rumors help relieve emotional tensions and generally arise under ambiguous circumstances.

It has long been known that ineffective or inadequate downward communication creates an information vacuum in an organization. This vacuum usually is filled by rumors, which are often educated guesses. For example, company X, an organization with over 10,000 employees in its home headquarters in the East, began construction of a new plant on the West Coast. Immediately, a rumor started circulating among the employees that the entire company was going to move its operation west in retaliation for severe union management problems that had recently developed. When management failed to communicate its intentions to stay in its present location in the East, great fear and unrest developed among the employees. In this case, the rumor was untrue; nevertheless, management felt that the employees' fears about their jobs might help "tame down" union activity. So they deliberately allowed the company's plans to remain ambiguous.

German and Rath (1987) stress the importance of the office "grapevine," writing that "many students tend to equate oral communication with formal public address. . . . But our research indicates that much, if not most, oral communication takes place in largely informal circumstances" (p. 340). They go on to say that one manager stated that when he really needed information, he had his greatest success around the water cooler (or the copying machine).

Sostek (2006) writes that gossip actually plays a part in helping employees bond. Erik Foster, a psychologist at Temple University, states, "Gossip greases the social wheels. We need to gossip to establish trust, to feel comfortable, to find out all kinds of things that allow us to operate effectively on an everyday basis." There are two kinds of gossip: self-serving and group-serving. Self-serving is when you spread rumors that hurt others. Group-serving is when you share information about how other units in the organization are doing better. This stimulates productivity and helps the organization (Sostek, 2006, p. D1).

Variables in Rumor Development

Rosnow (1988) further proposed that rumors are a function of the ambiguity of the situation multiplied by the importance of the issue. Obviously, the loss of over 10,000 jobs in a city of about 70,000 people is a matter of critical importance. However, rumor transmission is slowed down by a person's critical sense that the rumor might not seem valid. These three variables (importance, ambiguity, and critical sense) can be expressed in the following equation:

$$R = i \times a \times 1/c$$

According to this equation, rumor R is directly encouraged by importance i and ambiguity a but inversely related to one's critical sense c. In the case of company X, for example, many employees felt that it would probably be too costly to abandon all the company's facilities and technical equipment in the East and start operations all over again in the West; these people did not believe the rumor that was circulating among the other employees and thus did nothing to help spread it.

Types of Message Change

Rumors undergo three types of message change as they pass from one person to another. These changes are (1) leveling, (2) sharpening, and (3) assimilation. **Leveling** is *the process whereby some details are omitted.* Not all the details of a message are interesting to relate, so people tend to get to the point as soon as possible, leaving out what they consider the extraneous details. **Sharpening** is *the exaggeration of certain parts of the rumor.* Suppose, for example, Professor Smith was told to leave Dean Jones's office after a heated exchange of words. When the incident was described by Jones's secretary, Professor Smith had been "thrown out" of the dean's office. And by the third transmission there had been a "fight in the dean's office." As you can see, the story gets more interesting (and less accurate) with each telling. **Assimilation,** a more complicated change, refers to *the way people distort messages to accord with their own view of things.* In a classic study by Allport and Postman (1947), a picture was shown to subjects who were to describe the picture to a second person, who would then tell a third, and so on. The picture showed the interior of a subway car with a roughly dressed white man holding a razor in his hand and talking to a well-dressed black man. In the retelling of the story, the razor was moved from the white man's hand to that of the black man. Obviously, this detail fit in more closely with racial stereotypes held by the subjects in the experiment.

Speed and Accuracy

Using a method called *Episodic Communication Channels in Organizations* (ECCO) analysis in which subjects identify persons from whom they have heard a rumor and pinpoint when they heard it, Davis (1953) and others have described several additional characteristics of grapevine communication. The grapevine, they point out, is one of the fastest methods of communicating in an organization. The grapevine is also often quite accurate. (Davis [1972] found between 80 and 90 percent accuracy in the case of noncontroversial rumors.) And the grapevine may carry a lot of information. For example, think about the information you get from friends on which courses (and professors) to take and which to stay away from. Finally, the grapevine is not considered reliable by most people in an organization—mainly because of the three types of message distortions described in the previous section.

Hendrickson and Psarouthakis (1998) surveyed chief executive officers of small entrepreneurial companies and found they used the following methods for sharing company values with employees. You might think of these as alternatives to the grapevine.

Informal conversations (one on one) with employees	32%
Bringing up values as secondary agenda of meetings	26%
Social activities	17%
Companywide meetings	6%
Meetings with middle managers	6%
Others	13% (p. 116)

Results of an earlier study indicate that the grapevine ranked as the second most frequently used channel of organizational communication (the most used channel was the employee's immediate supervisor). As a source of information, however, the grapevine was ranked next to last on both reliability and desirability. So the grapevine is considered by employees to be an important, but not always preferred, channel of communication within an organization.

PRACTICAL TIPS   *Dealing with Office Politics*

Office politics is a major barrier to employee motivation. It can be defined as, "When the good of the sub-unit takes precedence over the good of the overall organization." So, how can individuals deal with office politics? Here are ten tips.

1. Realize that politics are inevitable. Accounts from the earliest recorded history in Egypt show people plotting against the pharaoh by those who wanted get his power.

2. Don't surprise your boss. Nobody likes surprises. Always keep your boss informed. Often, it is best to let her or him know in advance of your plans. They will appreciate the opportunity to offer advice before an event is announced.

3. Don't "shoot from the lip." One quick way to destroy trust is to tell tales out of school. Keep confidential information to yourself.

4. Don't go around your boss. If you don't get your boss's approval, avoid going over his or her head to their boss. Think of this as a corporate ladder and remember the old adage, "Skip a rung and your problems have just begun."

5. Don't turn idea opponents into personal opponents. Even worse, avoid alienating those who disagree with you about your ideas or proposals.

6. Take the initiative. The best way to win at politics is to be a star performer. People notice good work and soon ignore empty promises.

7. Bounce back. Perform especially well after a disappointment. You will impress people the most if you perform well after a setback such as the loss of a promotion. This is the most crucial time to show your strength of character.

8. Develop deviation power. One principle of organizations is that some people will be allowed to get away with things (deviate from the rules) that others are not. This results from showing outstanding performance.

9. Avoid being defensive. When people offer advice or even criticism, see it as a way of improving, rather than as a threat to your prestige. Don't argue with them.

10. Don't burn your bridges. You will be surprised how often you will run into former co-workers and former bosses. Leave graciously.

Source: Stewart L. Tubbs. *Keys to Leadership: 101 Tips for Success* (9th ed.). New York: McGraw-Hill, 2011. See also, Mauricio Goldstein and Phil P. Read. *Games at Work*. San Francisco: Jossey-Bass, 2009; and R. Don Steele. *Office Politics*. Whittier, CA: Steele Balls Press, 2011.

In a new application of informal communication, some professional organizations are organizing a speed-dating format for business to improve networking with other professionals. "You don't have time to make a business deal in eight minutes, but you'll gather a great list of people that might work with you in the future," says Tom Jaffee, founder of Match Events (*www.matchevents.com*), which organizes business meet-ups from its headquarters in Delray Beach, Florida. A few companies like Match Events and eXtreme Networking (*www.extremenetworking.biz*), which is based in Chicago, use software to help make good business matches (Bick, 2007).

Summary

In this chapter, we have discussed human communication that occurs in the context of organizations. We have seen that this context involves more people and is more complex than public communication.

We discussed the growing importance of communication in a postindustrial society. Evidence indicates that quality of communication in organizations relates to overall performance goals. This has been found to be true in such widely divergent organizations as engineering firms, hospitals, manufacturing plants, and universities.

In downward communication, a basic problem is how to communicate enough information to employees without "overloading them." In this respect, a combination of written (including electronic) and oral messages seems to be more effective than either written or oral messages alone. More message distortion seems to occur at lower levels in the organization, and superior-to-subordinate communication has been shown to be the single most important component in successful organizational communication. The most desired type of supervisory communication style is the supportive style.

Upward communication, or communication from subordinate to superior, has proved valuable to upper management in maintaining an accurate picture of day-to-day organizational operations. As we have seen, however, there are numerous nonverbal as well as psychological barriers to effective upward communication. Again, a supportive or receptive supervisory style is more likely to promote upward communication.

Horizontal communication was defined as the method that helps to coordinate all the diverse functions of an organization. We saw here the paradox between the need for specialization of functions on one hand and the need for coordination of these functions on the other.

In the last section, we examined the role of informal communication in organizations. Research has shown that transmission of rumors in an organization is influenced by the importance and ambiguity of the situation as well as by the critical sense of the people involved. Leveling, sharpening, and assimilation were shown as three forms of message distortion that commonly occur in the transmission of rumors. Finally, we found that grapevine communication is a frequently used but not necessarily preferred source of information in organizations.

Key Terms

Assimilation
Downward communication
Horizontal communication
Ingratiation
Law of diminishing returns
Leveling
Organizational communication
Sharpening
Upward communication
Upward receptivity

Review Questions

1. What are three functions communication performs in organizations?
2. What is the general research finding regarding the type of supervisory style that is preferred by employees?
3. What are five ways in which people adapt to information overload?
4. Explain the law of diminishing returns as it relates to downward communication.
5. Discuss and illustrate the five types of power.

6. What are five functions of upward communication?

7. What are two barriers to upward communication?

8. Explain the differentiation-integration problem in organizations.

9. How does this relate to horizontal communication?

10. Explain the formula $R = i \times a \times 1/c$ as it relates to rumors.

11. Identify the three types of message distortion that occur during rumor transmission.

Exercises

1. Have the class break up into groups of five or six and discuss the following. If you were Sam Edwards and were faced with the problem of employees using the photocopier for personal business, how would you try to solve it? Have each discussion group decide on a specific plan of attack for solving this problem. Then have the groups share their solutions with the entire class. What organizational communication issues are involved in this case problem? What other issues are indirectly related to this problem?

2. Divide the class into small groups and have each group discuss the following case problem. After each group has shared its reactions with the other groups, discuss the principles from this chapter that are illustrated by the case.

   In the men's sportswear department of Samson's Department Store, two men and four women are regularly employed as sales personnel. In addition to salary, they receive a bonus determined by how much their daily volume of sales exceeds a quota. Mr. Wilcox, the buyer, is head of the department, but during his frequent absences his assistant buyer, Ms. Jones, is in charge. In addition to six regulars, during the summer the department employs several extra salespeople. These are college students on vacation, who have been given some training by the store's personnel department. They are eager beavers and often outsell the regulars. They also work for a salary plus bonus.

   During Mr. Wilcox's absence on a buying trip, the regulars complained to Ms. Jones that the extras were making it difficult for them to make their quotas, that they mixed up the stock and generally were a nuisance. Ms. Jones, a close friend of one of the regulars, ordered the extras to take care of the stock and to sell only when customers were waiting. On his return, Mr. Wilcox countermanded this order; he told the extras to get in there and sell or look for other jobs. A competitive spirit, he said, was good for the department. The regulars are now more resentful than ever; customers are beginning to notice the bad feelings, and some of them have taken their trade elsewhere.

   Which one of the following comments on this situation seems to you most sound?

   a. Mr. Wilcox should return to the position taken earlier by his assistant—that is, instruct the extras to work on stock and handle customers only when no regular is free.

   b. In addition to telling the extras to sell at top capacity, Mr. Wilcox should call the regulars in, take a firm stand with them, and advise them to increase their sales or look elsewhere for work.

   c. Mr. Wilcox is right: A competitive spirit is good for the department. Beyond making this point clear, he should continue to maintain a hands-off policy and let the situation work itself out.

   d. Mr. Wilcox should pay the extras a straight hourly wage.

   e. Mr. Wilcox should investigate the activities of all employees and also check into the company's compensation plan.

3. Have five people leave the classroom. Then bring them back into the room one at a time. Start a rumor by giving the first person a short description of an event. Be sure the story has at least a few details such as time, location, names, number of people involved, and so on. Or show

a picture of an event and ask the person to describe what is going on in the picture. Then have each person in turn give his or her version of the story (or picture) to the next person who comes back into the room. Have the rest of the class try to keep track of the leveling, sharpening, and assimilation that occur as the story is told and retold.

4. Discuss the following case and determine answers to the three questions that follow:

A clinical psychologist at a university feels that his interviews with a client should be recorded and that the benefits to be derived from such recordings would be impaired if the client knew in advance that the recording was to be made. The psychologist sometimes uses these recordings in his classroom to illustrate his lectures, always without the knowledge of the client, though the client's name is not revealed to the class.

a. What should be the university's policy in this matter?

b. How should the policy be communicated?

c. What considerations are there in trying to communicate this policy?

5. Suppose you are a manager of an office and you hear that the head of your account department (who is married) is believed by many to be having an affair with a married woman in the personnel department. You (Mr. Wilson) call him (Mr. Townsend) into your office to discuss this matter. Have two people in the class role-play this conversation. How would you change the conversation if you were taking into account what we discussed about rumors in this chapter?

Suggested Readings

Argenti, Paul A. *Corporate Communication*, 2nd ed. New York: Irwin/McGraw-Hill, 1998.

This excellent book examines the subject of CorpComm. CorpComm is a term that refers to communication as one of the formal mechanisms in the organization. It covers such diverse topics as employee communication, investor relations, governmental affairs, and communication in a crisis.

Blanchard, Ken. *Leading at a Higher Level.* Upper Saddle River, NJ: Prentice-Hall, 2007.

This outstanding book synthesizes ways that leaders communicate in all aspects of the organization.

Daly, John. *Advocacy: Championing Ideas and Influencing Others.* New Haven, CT: Yale University Press, 2011.

Day, George. *Peripheral Vision.* Boston: Harvard Business School Press, 2006.

This excellent book explores ways to look outside the organization to see future trends for organization success or failure.

Goffee, Rob, and Gareth Jones. *Why Should Anyone Be Led by You?* Boston: Harvard Business School Press, 2006.

This book looks at all the ways that the reader can analyze himself or herself to improve communication and leadership skills.

Goldhaber, Gerald M. *Organizational Communication,* 8th ed. Dubuque, IA: Brown, 2003.

Certainly one of the best, if not the best, book available on this subject. It is comprehensive, accurate, and very well written. Must reading for anyone wanting to know more about this subject.

Hartman, Laura P., and Joe Desjardins. *Business Ethics.* New York: McGraw-Hill, 2008.

This outstanding book offers numerous practical tips on how to apply ethics in the business organization.

Michigan (University) Leading High Performance Teams—video. http://www.youtube.com/watch?v=fFKcEnAsAPE

Rath, Tom, and Barrie Conchie. *Strengths-Based Leadership.* New York: Gallup Press, 2008.

This best-selling book offers readers an assessment instrument to determine their top five interpersonal strengths. You will need to buy the book to log onto their Web site and take the test. To learn more about this, go to http://sf2.strengthsfinder.com/learnmore.

Tapscott, Don. *Growing Up Digital.* New York: McGraw-Hill, 1998.

Looks at the impact of the Internet Generation (N-Gen) on organizations and on the entire realm of electronic communication. Includes chapters on the N-Gen culture of interaction; the mind-set of typical members of this generation; and their impact on the workplace, family, and the N-Gen leaders of the future.

Welch, Jack. *Winning.* New York: Warner Books, 2005.

This book gives great insight into how a major corporate organization (General Electric) works. Welch offers many examples of the crucial role that communication plays in an organization's success or failure.

Yukl, Gary. Leadership In Organizations, 8th ed. New York: Pearson, 2013.

This excellent book focuses on the leadership aspects of organizational communication.

 # For Supplementary Information

Log onto the Online Learning Center at *www.mhhe.com/tubbshc13e.*

15

Mass Communication and the New Technologies

Chapter Objectives

After reading this chapter, you should be able to:

1. Explain how mass communication, because it is mediated, differs from personal encounters and identify four characteristics of mass communication.
2. Explain the concept of the gatekeeper.
3. State two theories concerning message flow from the mass media and explain the concept of the active audience.
4. Discuss the research findings on media uses and gratifications, including new research on the use of computer-mediated communication.
5. Discuss the extent to which the media disseminate information and influence attitudes. Explain the concepts of agenda setting and framing.
6. Discuss the new communication technologies, including their relationship to the mass media and the rise of new alternative media.
7. Describe the effects of the new technologies on interpersonal communication, their accessibility, and their implications for global communication.

In 2012 a new film entitled *Bully* created a controversy because of its R rating. Talk show host Ellen DeGeneres led the fight to change the rating to PG in order to make the film accessible to more audiences. To attend an R-rated film, those under 17 must be accompanied by a parent or guardian. The rating was imposed because of six "F-words" that are uttered during a bullying incident that was caught on film. Directed by Lee Hirsch and produced by the Weinstein Group, the film focuses on five young victims of bullying as a snapshot of the ordeals faced by more than 13 million American kids every year, according to U.S. Department of Education estimates. Harvey Weinstein, the producer of the film, called on celebrities like Lady Gaga to put pressure on the ratings association to reverse its decision.

Imagine a time when you had something humiliating happen to you. Then, imagine that the incident or the comments about you were posted on the Internet for anyone worldwide to see. This is just one of the many mass communication issues facing people today.

Since the Internet boom, people are depending on Web sites, blogs, and online news media for their information. Now, more than ever, Americans are getting their political knowledge through the World Wide Web. This made the 2008 presidential campaign much different from years past. Not only do the presidential candidates have to advertise on TV and print media, they also have to focus on online advertising. And according to comScore Ad Metrix, in the 2008 campaign BarackObama.com attracted nearly four times the average number of monthly visitors as JohnMcCain.com (2.2 million visits vs. 583,000 visits per month). Online advertising and Web site visitors seemed to be a large factor in determining the president of the United States (NPR Newswire, 2008).

Could YouTube founders Chad Hurley and Steve Chen become this generation's version of Bob Woodward and Carl Bernstein, the famed newspaper reporters who broke the Watergate scandal? According to a reporter at cnet.com, probably not, but their site has quickly become a competitor to investigative journalists everywhere. Now, instead of reading *The New York Times* or watching CNN, interested people can get their news direct from YouTube. "In the old world [traditional media] used to be the gatekeepers; the fact is those gates have been torn down" said Geneva Overholser, director of the School of Journalism at the University of Southern California and former ombudsman at *The Washington Post*. Now, we are getting unfiltered information direct from the source. Corruption, brutality, and injustice are now being exposed in situations where members of traditional media weren't around (Sandoval, 2008).

Mass communication as we know it—through the print media (newspapers, magazines, and books) and the electronic media (radio, film, recordings, television, and computer)—is undergoing a sustained transformation. For example, we are seeing the emergence of a new form of journalism that will include a complete spectrum of communication modalities (including 360-degree video); hyperlinks that place news in a far larger context; greater audience involvement; and news presentations that are customized for individuals (Pavlik and McIntosh, 2010). In this chapter we look at mass communication and the new technologies, the traditional media and the new media, exploring how such seemingly different experiences are related and the nature of their effects on human communication.

A FIRST DEFINITION

Mediated Encounters

As suggested in Chapter 1, every aspect of mass communication is *mediated*, and mediated encounters are different from personal encounters (Wimmer and Dominick, 2011). First, *the sensory input potential for receivers is more limited*. Second, *receivers* of a mediated message *have little or no control over its sources*—that is, feedback is extremely limited. And finally, the *sources* of mediated messages *are known either in a limited way or not known at all, only imagined*. Put more simply, mediated experience is not direct. When you read this book, for example, your experience is mediated. The book is the means, the medium, through which we communicate. If you wanted to ask me a question about it, you would have to write, e-mail, or telephone me.

As we amplify our definition of mass communication, keep in mind the point made by Wright (1986) that mass communication is not defined in terms of technological achievements: "Rather, it is a special kind of social communication involving distinctive characteristics of the audience, the communication experience, and the communicator" (p. 7). According to Wright, in *mass communication the audience is relatively large, heterogeneous, and anonymous to the source. The experience is public, rapid, and fleeting. The source works through a complex organization rather than in isolation, and the message may represent the efforts of many different people* (pp. 6–9).

Altering a woman's image is what a cosmetics company is supposed to do, right? Well, that depends on the alteration. The media is capable of making a pale person look like a seasoned Malibu surfer, making an overweight person appear thinner, or making a brunette look like Jessica Simpson. However, can they go too far when showing these people in their ads? In a recent ad for the L'Oreal hair coloring product Feria, Beyoncé was featured looking a little more white than she naturally is. People were upset, claiming that L'Oreal was subliminally saying light skin is the right skin. Although L'Oreal has denied touching up the color of Beyoncé's skin, the advertising damage may already be done (Kaufman, 2008).

The Audience

Consider again the first element in this definition: the audience. Perhaps most significant for our purpose is its size. Celebrations of the New Year as it is ushered in by country after country are seen by millions of viewers around the world. And in 2008, President Obama's inauguration was watched by millions on network television and CNN, who also followed the story through other media: radio, Internet, and newspapers. Although in person-to-group and organizational settings, face-to-face interaction is often possible, in mass communication the size of the audience makes it impossible for the mass communicator and audience members to interact face to face.

In addition to being a diversified group, the receivers in mass communication are, for the most part, unknown to the source. This is not to say that members of a mass communication audience are isolated from other human beings. It is possible—in fact, very likely—for us to experience mass communication as members of dyads, small groups, or organizations. You may be out with a friend seeing a movie. Half the dorm may be watching sporting events or *Modern Family* or reruns of *Seinfeld* on television. The day after a show opens, the entire cast of a theatrical production may be reading the newspaper reviews in the director's apartment. Or you may be online with a newsgroup, talking about politics or global warming.

The Communication Experience

As for the second element, the communication experience itself, it is intended for rapid consumption by great numbers of people. Moreover, it is characterized as public rather than private because the messages are not addressed to particular individuals. Think of a college president addressing a very large audience of parents in a public hall. Although she may not know any of them personally, she is aware of the audience as a group and is directing what is said to those people. If the same address were to be broadcast on C-Span, that message would be received by a highly diversified group of people who were, for the most part, unknown to the speaker. This is one of the important ways in which mass communication and the public, or person-to-group, communication described in Chapter 13 differ.

The Source of Communication

During the presidential campaign of 2008, a study of jokes by David Letterman and Jay Leno showed a seven-to-one ratio of negative jokes about Republicans compared to Democrats. The study was conducted by the Center for Media and Public Affairs, which has been tracking such data since 1988. From September 1 through October 24, 2008, there were 475 jokes making fun of the McCain-Palin ticket and 69 jokes making fun of the Obama-Biden ticket. In addition, Jon Stewart and Steven Colbert used the Republicans as the butt of their jokes 211 times while making fun of the Democrats 29 times. Dr. Robert Lichter, head of the center and professor at George Mason University said that, "In no other campaign in the last 20 years has one party's ticket been jabbed more than the other by even a 2-1 ratio." What conclusion would you draw from this study about bias in the media? (Bauder, 2008, p. C5).

The third element in this definition of mass communication, the source of the communication, is usually not working in isolation but rather from within a complex organization. The message itself often represents the efforts of many individuals, which we shall understand more clearly when we discuss the concept of the gatekeeper. These people may represent a complex organization that, in countries such as the United States, is usually concerned with making a profit.

Mass communication events sometimes require not only the efforts of hundreds of people but also often months of preparation and millions of dollars. Individual salaries can be spectacular. For example, David Letterman's annual salary

15.1

ISSUES IN COMMUNICATION

Media Consolidation and the News

Many media critics and scholars have voiced concerns about how the extreme concentration of media ownership might affect the content of the news (Chester, 2007; Kleinenberg, 2007; Bagdikian, 2004; Bennett, 2005, pp. 88–100). These concerns include:

- A focus on profits that results in less coverage of news and public affairs and more entertainment programming and "more infotainment and soft news— including news magazines, reality TV, and local TV news."
- Less competition, resulting in some independent media being forced out, and therefore less diversity and less representation of other points of view.
- News that is generic: "Innovation in packaging and branding disguises declining information diversity and content distinctiveness." (p. 89)
- Possible censorship and self-censorship motivated by self-interest.

Consider the last of these points. Media conglomerates have far-reaching interests, not only in a variety of mass media but in numerous other businesses. So what happens to news coverage in a media conglomerate when there is a breaking story about one of its many holdings? Is there self-censorship? And if not, can one division of a conglomerate report fairly and fully on another? Charles Lewis of the Center for Public Integrity says:

> *It means you're not going to be investigating certain subjects. It means you're not going to see NBC investigating General Electric. You're not going to have ABC doing a big investigation covering Disney. (cited in Foerstel, 2001, p. 20)*

Jeff Chester, the author of *Digital Destiny*, writes: "The CEOs of many media conglomerates have a clear political allegiance either to a candidate, a political party, or an ideology" (2007, p. 5).

Do you believe conflicts of interest are inevitable? And what do you think are the obligations of those who write and report the news?

is $31 million, and Katie Couric reportedly negotiated a five-year contract with CBS for $60 million. Now, contrast that type of mass communication with the lone blogger who has no editor, no fact checker, and can influence millions of people single-handedly with virtually no one to moderate his or her biases and errors (Kahneman, 2011).

We have said that in the United States the mass media are usually concerned with making a profit, and a good part of that profit depends on advertising. There are countries in which the mass media are independent of such concerns, but in the United States advertising dominates mass communication. And, certainly, awareness of the extent to which advertising maintains the mass media should affect the source credibility mass communicators have for their audiences. There are many ethical considerations as well. It is estimated that by age 16 the average viewer will have seen over 600,000 commercials, yet recent studies show that children have difficulty differentiating between programs and commercials. Conflicts of interest between profit-making functions and responsibilities to the public also affect the free flow of information.

Feedback

MSNBC "Morning Joe" host Joe Scarborough let the f-word slip at 8:13 EST Monday morning (November 10, 2008) at 8:13 a.m., talking about Rahm Emanuel's rumored dirty mouth. Unaware at first he had said "f**k" instead of "f-word," Scarborough was soon set straight.

When he realized he had slipped up, he grimaced thinking of his wife's reaction, and then apologized. He said, "Great apologies, did I say the word? . . . My wife is going to kill me when I get home. . . . I'm going to go get some soap. I'm so sorry" (Joe Scarborough's, November 10, 2008).

In this case, Scarborough got the feedback from his colleagues on the show. However, they routinely read e-mails from viewers who write in during the show with their feedback. This rapid form of feedback is relatively new to mass media.

Television viewers often fax, e-mail, write letters, or telephone a network concerning a given program and enough letters, calls, or responses to a rating survey will affect the future of that program. But usually those viewers will not be face to face with the television producer or, for that matter, with the executive in charge of programming, and the feedback will not usually be as immediate or complete as it would be on a face-to-face basis. And since mass communication usually involves a chain or network of individuals, the feedback intended for one person in the chain is likely to reach a different member of the chain.

Although feedback can be virtually immediate now, it is often impossible for the source in mass communication to respond to and make public all the feedback that is received. For example, large metropolitan papers such as *The Seattle Times, The Washington Post,* and *The New York Times* receive thousands of letters, faxes, and e-mails each year, of which they can print only a very small percentage. These "letters to the editor" may express praise or strong disagreement, offer observations from personal experience, comment on "shameless" editorials, or correct points of information. Today e-mails, "tweets," and faxes to the editor result in publication of much more rapid, indeed almost instantaneous, responses to opinion pieces. The editorial page of a metropolitan newspaper often runs several letters—pro and con—in response to an editorial that appeared only a day or two before.

So despite the striking differences that seem to set off mass communication from other kinds of human communication, there is also a degree of overlap between different modes. As we discuss the mass communication process, we shall also see some ways in which mass and face-to-face communication perform complementary functions.

THE PROCESS OF MASS COMMUNICATION

The Gatekeeper

Essential to an understanding of the workings of mass communication is the concept of the gatekeeper. A **gatekeeper** is *a person who, by selecting, changing, and/or rejecting messages, can influence the flow of information to a receiver or group of* *receivers.* Although the concept of the gatekeeper might be applied to other contexts of communication—think, for example, of our discussion in Chapter 14 about how rumors are created—it is particularly relevant to mass communication.

The Gatekeeper's Work

Imagine yourself for a moment as the wire editor of a metropolitan newspaper or, in many cases, the online version. You are looking at a computer screen. It is your job to go though all the news items provided by the various wire services to which your paper subscribes. On an average day there might be some 3,000 items, out of which only 200 will be selected. As you go over all this copy on the screen, you have to ask yourself questions: "Did we run anything in yesterday's paper that was like it?" "Will this copy be of broad enough interest for our readers?" "Are other papers covering it?" "Is there room for this story today?" "What are the chances that there will be more important stories later in the day?" "Will we make the deadline if we wait?"

These are some of the considerations that determine which items are discarded and which are selected and edited. Gatekeeping is a necessary aspect of mass communication, and gatekeepers exist in all the mass media. For example, a reader in a publishing house might select 5 out of 100 manuscripts for review by house editors. Or consider the film editor's work. For *Apocalypse Now,* a film about the Vietnam War by Francis Ford Coppola, Walter Murch had to edit 1.25 million feet of film; the final version ran 2 hours and 25 minutes. That film was released in 1979. In 2001, Coppola released *Apocalypse Now Redux.* It took Coppola and Murch six months to re-edit and remix this version of the original, adding some 53 minutes to the film and giving it the subdued, pacifist ending that Coppola had always wanted. You can get some inkling of what choices confront a film editor when you view the special features on the DVD of a current film. There you often find an interview with the director or film editor as well as scenes that were deleted from the final version.

In mass communication we find a network or *chain* of gatekeepers. The following is a simplified example of the gatekeeping process: The senior editor of a monthly travel magazine gets an article and discusses the idea with the editor-in-chief, who approves it. The senior editor then assigns it to a freelance writer and specifies the length of the article and the number of color transparencies needed for the illustrations. The writer decides which aspects of the story to include and adapts the coverage to the needs of the magazine, then selects appropriate color transparencies from several sources.

Once the article is written, it goes back to the senior editor, who reads it, suggests how much editing it needs, and then assigns the work to an assistant editor. (If it were a news article, it would—or should—be reviewed by a fact-checker.) The author of the article then reviews the changes and answers any editorial queries. The managing editor checks the color transparencies, selects half, and turns them over to the art director. The copy is set electronically, and the layout and photographs are handled by a member of the art department. Before the article appears in the magazine, it is reviewed and approved by the managing editor and the editor-in-chief. In 2012, the New York Knicks basketball sensation Jeremy Lin (a Harvard graduate) hit the nation by storm. However, after the Knicks lost a game, an ESPN writer, Anthony Federico, age 28, wrote a story with the title "Chink in the Armor." The story went out and caused the writer to be fired because the word "Chink" has been an offensive word applied to Asians in the past. In this case, the editing process was overlooked, and caused a very unpleasant controversy surrounding a really popular player.

Gatekeeping in mass communication involves a selection process that has analogies with the selection process going on in all other contexts of communication—from interpersonal to organizational.

The Gatekeeper's Choices

The gatekeeper's choices concerning what information to select and reject are influenced by many variables. Bittner (1985) identifies the following:

The first is *economics:* Most mass media in the United States are profit making, or concerned with how their money is raised and spent. Thus, advertisers, sponsors, and contributors may have a major impact on news selection and editorials. For example, some radio stations give listeners an opportunity to respond on the air to editorials with which they disagree.

Second, such *legal restrictions* as libel laws will affect media content and presentation. Federal Communications Commission regulations also have an impact, for example, on the issue of who will be allowed to own and operate a broadcasting facility. The Child Online Protection Act is a federal law designed to restrain commercial Web sites from making online pornography available to those under the age of 17.

Deadlines affect depth as well as the time available to determine the accuracy of news selected. And deadlines also affect what will be broadcast: When only a brief amount of time is available, the gatekeeper makes choices concerning relative importance. When the gatekeeper must choose between two stories of equal worth, the one that has a video story is usually selected (Bittner, p. 378).

The gatekeeper's *ethics,* both personal and professional, also influence the news that will be selected. It's an ethical judgment that determines how much back-bending will take place to be "fair" to a sponsor or a cause endorsed by that sponsor. Personal ethics—and the extent of the gatekeeper's awareness of his or her own beliefs—will influence whether the gatekeeper's likes and dislikes, attitudes, and interests play a part in news selection. For example, it's possible that a financial columnist could affect a company's stock with a story and allow friends to have inside information before the story is printed.

A fifth factor is *competition among media:* In a market with several available sources, it was hoped that competition would raise the overall level of professionalism, ensuring a more objective presentation of information. Often, though, the result has been an increasing amount of "infotainment," a blurring of the lines between information and entertainment in which news stories (e.g., *Dateline*) or interviews are often sensationalized in an effort to gain a wider audience: "The theory in the boardrooms is that consumers are attracted by entertainment, rather than information" (Nichols and McChesney, 2005, p. 7). In recent years competition between cable and network news has been intense, and network ratings have shown a significant decline and a definite increase in tabloid journalism.

Sixth, *news value, the intensity of an item in comparison with all others available,* and *news hole, the amount of space or time it takes to present the story,* need to be balanced. Besides balancing these two, gatekeepers must weigh the claims of local interest against those of national interest. For example, how much time should be given to a new statewide campaign to conserve water when the president has just made a major foreign policy announcement?

Another of the important variables affecting what gatekeepers select or reject is the *reaction to feedback,* although that feedback is delayed. If a political cartoon offends an ethnic group, for example, and that group has representatives who write irate letters or insist on a public apology, a magazine editor might deliberate a long time before including another cartoon of that kind. Here the gatekeeper must weigh media goals against public opinion.

Message Flow

Hypodermic Needle Model

Early studies of mass communication suggested that the flow of information from source to receiver was always direct and immediate. According to this view, often referred to as the **hypodermic needle model,** *each audience member receives messages directly from the source of a given medium.* The implication is that if the "injection" is powerful enough, it will influence the receiver in some way. A further implication of such a theory is that the mass media can have an almost magical, and sometimes a potentially dangerous, effect on audiences (especially if the media are used to mount massive propaganda campaigns).

Opinion Leaders and the Two-Step Flow Model

In 1948 a study changed the direction of thinking about message flow in mass communication. The researchers analyzed the general impact of mass media on voting behavior and especially on the people who changed their voting intention during the course of the 1940 presidential campaign. One important finding was that broad coverage of the campaign by the mass media simply reinforced the initial preferences of the voters. Even more significant, for people who did change their minds about how they would vote, the major source of influence was *personal influence— the influence of other people.* In other words, even in mass communication contexts, the receiver had to be viewed within a larger social setting (Lazarsfeld et al., 1968). The findings of Lazarsfeld and others take this a step further, suggesting that within the groups to which we belong, certain people have a particularly strong influence. Such a person has been called an **opinion leader**—*"someone who, through* *day-to-day personal contacts and communication, influences someone else's opinions and decisions . . . fairly regularly"* (Patterson, et al., 2008, p. 145). And the decisions concern all kinds of matters, not just voting—for example, what type of car to buy, the most fashionable way to dress, the best school to attend, and so on.

Opinion leaders can come from any social, economic, or occupational level. Within different levels of society, there are different opinion leaders. They all tend to be better informed. They read more newspapers and magazines; they watch the coverage of political and social issues by the broadcast media. And in addition to receiving greater exposure to mass media, they tend to be influenced by them. This influence, in turn, is passed on to others in face-to-face communication.

It was this discovery that generated a **two-step flow model** of mass communication. According to this theory, on many occasions *information is passed from the various mass media to certain opinion leaders and from these leaders to other people within the population.* Some studies suggest that it is often more accurate to think in terms of a *multiple,* or *n-step, flow model,* since opinion leaders may also be consulting with others whom they consider opinion leaders. "An opinion leader can best be thought of as a group member playing a key communications role" (Katz and Lazarsfeld, 1964). See Wimmer and Dominick (2011) for a reevaluation of this theory.

The Active Audience

Implicit in the hypodermic needle model is the concept of a passive audience, a group of rather compliant people who, given a potent enough message, receive and absorb whatever was intended by the mass media. Such an audience could be manipulated into buying whatever product was given the most advertising nationwide or voting for the candidate who had the most exposure on radio and television. It is an audience made up of people who do not interact with other human beings or accept group norms, people who are not, in fact, seen as living within a social context.

But today the receivers of mass communication are often conceptualized as an **active,** or obstinate audience (Webster, 1998). You have already seen some reference to this concept in Chapter 5, in our discussion of critical listening. Schramm and Roberts (1971) characterize this view of the mass communication audience well:

> . . . an intensely active audience, seeking what it wants, rejecting far more content than it accepts, interacting both with the members of the groups it belongs to and with the media content it receives, and often testing the mass media message by talking it over with other persons or comparing it with other media content. (p. 191)

Perhaps the most obvious way an audience is active is in its selection of the mass communication to which it will be exposed. You buy the newspaper of your choice. You choose the programs you watch on television, and if you find something you don't like, you turn it off. In many ways, we can control this aspect of communication more readily than we can control face-to-face communication. It is much

15.2 ISSUES IN COMMUNICATION   *Some Guidelines for Critical Viewers of Media Interviews*

When you watch or read an interview, is the person being interviewed answering the question? According to Bob Schieffer of *Face the Nation*, these days almost all the people interviewed by the press are "professional talkers." Very often we are watching politicians, public officials, and corporate executives who have been coached on how to speak with the press by "media trainers, who receive between $4,000 and $10,000 a day." The aim, writes the journalist Trudy Lieberman, is to control information in the interview (2004, p. 41). Among the techniques she identifies are these:

Taking control *with comments such as "Let's move on to other matters. I think we've covered this" or "What I'd like to talk about . . . ," or "I want to turn to . . . ,"—all without fully answering the question posed by the host/journalist/ interviewer. "One of the first rules of media training is to seize control of the interview, and skillful guests can do it from the very beginning" (pp. 40–41).*

Dodging the question *is another often used technique. "When guests don't want to answer, they use phrases such as: That's such a complex subject . . . Your question is not relevant . . . You bring up an interesting point, but before I discuss it, I want to talk about . . ." (p. 41)— after which the guest may go on to repeat the message he or she really wants to get across.*

Telling stories *through anecdotes, personal observations, or recollections of personal experience all take up time and tend to head off a follow-up question by the interviewer, often because of interview time constraints. People are coached not to return to the original question, to offer context in place of an answer—in short, not to allow the interviewer a second chance to ask the question differently.*

By **answering what's easy** *a guest can often navigate a two-part question, responding to the easier question at such length that the interviewer never gets around to follow-up on the second unanswered one. Thus the guest gets away with saying the question was answered.*

Journalists sometimes lose control of interviews when they can't pin down the guest or follow up sufficiently. We know from reading about interviewing that open questions facilitate talking—in public and mass communication they also empower people to say what they want to say. And of course open-ended questions can also be subverted by simple answers such as "Absolutely" or "Absolutely not."

Lieberman tells us that journalists also fear straining the guest's—and the audience's—tolerance of follow-up questions. There is a certain level of courtesy that interviewers wish to maintain so that important guests will be willing to return (Lieberman, 2004, pp. 40–43).

Set yourself the task of listening critically to radio, television, or cable interviews—and perhaps reading sections of them in the newspapers or online. Ask yourself how directly and completely the person being interviewed has answered the questions. How much information have you received? How skilled was the interviewer in posing the questions and following up on them?

easier, for example, to turn off the television set if we dislike a program or even to walk out of a theater in the middle of a bad film than it is to conclude face-to-face communication so abruptly. Widespread use of the DVD player, VCR, and streaming video have had an impact not only on family interaction but also on the mass media with a decline in movie-going and an increase in viewing movies at home. Today it offers a significant challenge to research in mass communication.

Selective Exposure

To put it another way, the person who watches a particular television program to the end or finishes reading a particular newspaper editorial tends to agree with the attitudes and opinions being presented. These are examples of **selective exposure,** *the tendency to choose communication that will confirm your own opinions, attitudes, or values.* This is a broad concept. In Chapter 8 we saw how it works on a one-to-one basis. We tend to like and seek out those whose beliefs, attitudes, and values are similar to our own, and to dislike and avoid people we perceive as different from us in these respects. Selective exposure is equally present in mass communication, where, for example, the vast majority of people who read *The Wall Street Journal* are conservatives, and most of the people who read *The New York Times* are liberals.

As our media communication technology expands, so does the opportunity for the networking channels to use some of these resources to their advantage. It has been said that "television executives decided viewers wanted screens crammed with banner headlines across the top, crawls along the bottom, talking heads in tiny boxes, moving graphics and unmoving logos. . . ." We can all relate to this phenomenon on some level. Sports and news broadcasts might be the biggest offenders; however, you will also see the entertainment channels trying to slide in an advertisement for their new season premier across the bottom of your favorite Monday night program: "*American Idol* begins tomorrow 8:00/9:00 central." You can't escape it.

This fog of advertisements, statistics, news flashes, and overall information overload has caused cognitive scientists to raise some interesting questions. "Can the human brain really make sense of so much [information]?" Kansas State University conducted a study to see what percentage of information was retained under different circumstances. They found that "viewers who watched TV broadcasts with a news crawl remembered 10 percent fewer facts than those who watched the same broadcast without the stream of headlines, sports scores and weather updates." Researchers concluded simply that "our brains are not as good at multitasking as we think." Ultimately, if viewers continue to provide positive feedback and enjoy seeing six camera angles of a single play, live stats, and a drawing of what the defensive team "should have done" during the football game, then they plan to continue. The standing joke was "just don't ask them who won" (Carr, 2011, p. 131).

Selective Attention

In addition to the selective nature of our exposure to the mass media, our perception itself is selective. In Chapter 2 we spoke about **selective attention,** in which *the* *receiver processes certain of the available stimuli while filtering out others.* This screening process takes place in mass communication just as it does in other contexts of human communication. It takes place whether we are watching a situation comedy, a political debate, or a sports event.

Selective attention is well illustrated by examples from the political arena. In the televised 2012 Republican debates, Romney supporters tended to see Romney as the winner, while Santorum supporters tended to see Santorum as the winner, and so on with Newt Gingrich and Ron Paul. As we assess the various outcomes of mass communication, we shall see other ways in which beliefs, attitudes, and values of the receiver influence his or her perceptions.

In discussing selective attention, we use the word "receiver" rather than "audience member" to emphasize the continuity between the receiving function in face-to-face communication and in mass communication. Message reception is an active process: It is behavior. Watching television is behavior, reading a best seller or a newspaper is behavior, and so is surfing the Net. When engaged in any of these activities, individual receivers are selecting and processing information.

At the other end of the communication cycle is a parallel selection process at work in the gatekeeping function. The flow of information from the mass communicator to the individual receiver sometimes involves opinion leaders and therefore face-to-face communication, so that at times there is a multiple-step flow rather than a direct flow of information. Similarly, the flow of feedback from the individual receiver to the mass communicator can also involve several steps. For example, parents concerned about violence in children's television programs may take group action through an organization such as Action for Children's Television, which in turn gives feedback not only to various television stations but also to governmental agencies that regulate the broadcast media.

Another way of looking at the selectivity of receivers of mass communication is to examine how and when they use particular mass media as well as the basis for their choices.

Media Uses and Gratifications

The relationship between personal and mediated communication—including the new media technologies—continues to be an important area of research (Turkle, 2011; Carr, 2011; Kahneman, 2012). For example, recent research finds that among college students the five most often used sources of news were "hometown newspapers, comedy news, cable news, Internet news, and broadcast news" and that habit turns out to be the best predictor of news consumption (Diddi and LaRose, 2006, p. 193). Those who study the interface between mass and interpersonal communication stress that the media to which we attend are an integral part of our interpersonal world. One earlier comparison of how various media and interpersonal communication sources are used finds that "media and interpersonal sources serve similar functions. . . . They are both used by people 'to connect (or sometimes disconnect) themselves . . . with different kinds of others (self, family, friends, nation, etc.)'" (Turkle, 2011, p. 157). Moreover, Rubin and Rubin (1985) argue that mass media use is goal directed—that is, people make choices about what media they will use for particular reasons.

The Internet has had a noticeable impact on the way media is mass communicated; for example, Internet-based activities such as wikis, blogs, and social networking. Twitter alone has had a huge impact worldwide with over 500 million active users. In 2012, Lady Gaga became the first person to have 20 million followers on Twitter, with Justin Bieber at 18,500 million close behind. Users can contribute their own pieces of information to form a huge social web. Trends show that daily circulation of printed newspapers has declined 3–4 percent annually since 2005. One out of every three Americans reads their news online. These older methods of mass communication are still necessary today because a digital divide exists, meaning there is a gap between those who can and cannot access the Internet and technology. This is closely tied into income levels and the cost of technology. As the cost of using technology keeps declining, we will see the digital divide come to more of a close in the years to come (Hanson et. al., 2008).

"When Michigan GOP Chairman Saul Anuzis decided to throw his hat in the ring to head the Republican Party, he announced his intentions on Twitter" (Mooney, 2008). A few years ago, making any major announcement over the Internet would have been absurd, but now making the announcement over a "tweet" on Twitter is commonplace. Even the 2012 presidential candidates found it acceptable to have a "live" debate via YouTube. Are blogs and vlogs (video blogs) the new open forum for the future? Will something else come along to take their place? It is uncertain, but for now, people and businesses alike are communicating in new ways. Otherwise "informed" people have to stay up to date with the latest avenues for communication in order to stay in the forefront of information.

At this point in our chapter, we turn to examine some of the effects and outcomes of mass communication. I hope first to illustrate more concretely the concepts we have been talking about and, second, to evaluate some of the various effects and outcomes of mass communication, particularly as they relate to less formal communication contexts.

SOME EFFECTS AND OUTCOMES

Most closely related to the concept of message flow is the study of how the mass media disseminate information.

The Diffusion of Information

Through the mass media we learn about innovations, discoveries, accidents, assassinations, revolutions, and natural disasters. How soon after these events we hear about them and what the sources of our information were are questions that preoccupy those interested in the **diffusion of information**—that is, *how quickly news or information travels and the communication channels through which it spreads to a community of receivers.*

Table 15.1   Mass Media and Internet Use Right After the Attacks of September 11, 2001

Even the most wired Americans were wedded to the television and the telephone after the attacks.

	All Americans	Heaviest Internet Users*
Main source of information		
Television	79%	80%
Radio	7	6
Newspaper	7	7
Internet	2	6
Talking with others	2	1
Communication activities: The phone was also used more by Internet users than by the general population.		
Phone family member about attack	63%	75%
E-mail family member		38
Phone friend about attack	55	70
E-mail friend		47

*The heaviest Internet users are those who have more than three years experience online and who log on from home every day. They make up about 20 percent of all Internet users and about 11 percent of the whole U.S. population.
Source: "How Americans Used the Internet After the Terror Attack," by Lee Rainie, September 15, 2001, Pew Internet & American Life Project, *www.pewinternet.org.*

Everett Rogers defines diffusion as "the process by which an innovation is communicated through certain channels over time among the members of a social system" (1995, p. 5). Although news events are ideas, their diffusion is similar to that of technological innovations (p. 75). "Diffusion" as we use it here refers to the spread of all kinds of information—not just news that generates shock or excitement. Thus, news of a flu immunization program or a citywide transportation strike is usually diffused to the public through several media.

After the attacks of September 11, 2001, the diffusion of information was virtually instantaneous. The collapse of the Twin Towers was seen by many who had already been watching the burning buildings on television. A study by the Pew Research Center finds that while 79 percent of all Americans got more of their news information from television, others turned to the radio (7 percent) and newspapers (7 percent), with less to the telephone (2 percent) and Internet (2 percent). In the days right after September 11, Internet use declined somewhat, but those who were online used it mainly to supplement other news sources and to e-mail family. Table 15.1 outlines the findings. For more on this report, go to *www.pewinternet.org/ppf/r/45/report-display.asp.*

There is some evidence that the way in which information will be disseminated depends on the importance of that information. Person-to-person communication will have a major role in disseminating information about lesser-known events.

For news events of intermediate levels of importance, however, the mass media will be the most pervasive first source of information.

It is important to think of the roles of face-to-face and mass communication as complementary rather than mutually exclusive. At times, meeting a friend who tells you about a recent news event prompts you to turn to one of the mass media such as Google or Bing on MSN for further information. Or something you learned from the mass media prompts a discussion with someone who then adds to your knowledge of the event by mentioning details that were not part of the magazine article you read or the televised news summary you heard. And then there are times when we experience mass communication in the company of others (e.g., family members, friends, co-workers), so that there is a constant interplay between what is being conveyed through the mass media and the awareness of personal responses to those communicative stimuli.

We have been speaking essentially about message flow and the spread of information through a community of receivers. But as you know from our discussion of persuasion in Chapter 13, some message senders have as their primary intention not information gain but attitude influence, and even messages intended primarily to inform often make persuasive appeals. Thus, once a message has been received, its persuasive impact must be evaluated.

Diffusion research also shows that any population usually follows a bell-shaped curve in the acceptance of new ideas. The first 2.5 percent are referred to as *innovators;* they are the very first to adopt new ideas. They are also referred to as progressives and experimentalists. The next 13.5 percent of the population is called *early adopters.* They also like to accept new ideas and perhaps fads. They would be some of the first to buy new electronic products such as iPhones. The third group is called the *early majority,* and they make up 34 percent of the population. The next to accept new ideas are called the *late majority,* and they also make up 34 percent of the population. Finally, those most resistant to adopting new ideas are the last 16 percent, who are referred to as *laggards.* They are extremely reluctant to adopt new ideas and may also be referred to as drones or diehards. These are the kinds of people who are still afraid to use the Internet or even e-mail (Berns, 2008, pp. 185–186).

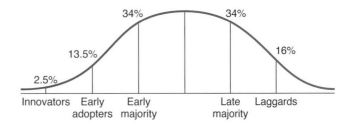

Attitude Influence

Because politicians believe that attitudes can be influenced through the media the sums spent on political advertising grow higher with each election. Oprah Winfrey has made a fortune appealing to women of all ages as a talk-show diva and actress. During the 2008 presidential elections, however, ratings for her show fell when she became publicly involved in politics for the first time. Winfrey, who endorsed Democratic presidential nominee Barack Obama, became widely criticized when news spread that she would not allow Republican vice-presidential nominee Sarah Palin to appear on her show. Winfrey commented, "At the beginning of the presidential campaign, when I decided that I was going to take my first public stance in support of a candidate, I made the decision not to use my show as a platform for any of the candidates." Many fans felt Winfrey was biased because of Obama's previous appearances on her show. They felt that Obama's timing and political aspirations when appearing on the show were "irrelevant and that Winfrey's decision to blacklist Palin from her show could very well backfire" (Friedman, 2008).

Early in 2007, hopefuls for the 2008 presidential election began using the Internet to announce their candidacy and to raise funds. The first was then Senator Barack Obama, who posted a video on his Web site, quickly followed by Senator Hillary Rodham Clinton and others. According to one study—*Election 2006 Online*—by the Pew Internet & American Life Project, "The number of Americans using the Internet as their main source of political news doubled since the last midterm election" (Rainie and Horrigan, p. 2):

THE AMERICAN NEWS MEDIASCAPE IS IN FLUX.

The news market has been fracturing for more than a decade and news audiences have become increasingly politicized as trust in the mainstream media has declined and public perceptions of the credibility of mainstream news sources has fallen. Over this period the Internet is playing an ever-more-important role in the news diet of Americans. A decade ago, just one-in-fifty Americans got the news with some regularity from what was then a brand new source—the Internet. Today, nearly one-in-three regularly gets news online. (pp. 3–4)

Table 15.2 summarizes the results of the Pew study.

Despite the growing influence of the Internet, however, the Pew study affirms the importance of television:

TELEVISION STILL WINS THE POLITICAL NEWS HORSERACE—BY A WIDE MARGIN.

As it has been said for generations, television remains ahead of other media in 2006 as a news source. . . . When it comes [to] the political news, television's lead is even more pronounced. Fully 69% of all Americans said they went to the television for most of their news about the campaign—twice the proportion of those who cited newspapers (34%), four times the proportion who singled out radio (17%) and the Internet (15%). (Rainie and Horrigan, 2006, p. 7)

However, the Internet and social media are rapidly overtaking television as the first source of news.

Table 15.2 *The Internet and Campaign 2006: Summary of Findings at a Glance*

- The number of Americans using the Internet as their main source of political news doubled since the last mid-term election.
- Thirty one percent of Americans used the Internet during the 2006 campaign to get political news and information and discuss the race through e-mail. We call them campaign Internet users.
- Relatively young broadband users say the Internet is a more important political news source than newspapers.
- A new online political elite is emerging as 23 percent of campaign Internet users became online political activists.
- While mainstream news sources still dominate the online news and information gathering by campaign Internet users, a majority of them now get political material from blogs, comedy sites, government Web sites, candidate sites, or alternative sites.
- While most campaign Internet users say convenience is a major reason they use the Internet, more than half cite the Internet's breadth of information and perspectives as a major reason for their online activity.
- Republicans and Democrats were equally likely to rely on the Internet—but there were partisan trends in usage of other political news sources.

Source: Adapted from Election 2006 Online, by Lee Rainie and John Horrigan. Washington, D.C.: Pew Internet & American Life Project and Pew Research Center for the People & the Press (January 17, 2007), p. vi. *www.pewinternet.org/pdfs/PIP_Politics_2006.pdf.*

One of the ways in which attitude influence has been studied is through the history of televised presidential debates. How presidential debates are presented on television has drawn much attention.

Roughly 70 million out of the 107 million adults in the United States either watched or listened to the first of four debates between John F. Kennedy and Richard Nixon in 1960. Moreover, many who did not see or hear the debates through the broadcast media soon read about them in the newspapers. But the consensus of opinion is that exposure to the Kennedy–Nixon debates through the mass media had little effect on changing initial voting intentions. As many studies have noted, when viewers were asked about who had "won," Kennedy supporters tended to see Kennedy as the winner of the debates, while Nixon supporters, for the most part, saw Nixon as the winner. We have seen more recent examples of this effect in the 2012 Republican debates, which destroyed Texas governor Rick Perry due to his consistently weak performances.

Other studies of presidential debates and elections (Wayne, 1992, 1996), attitude influence, and voting behavior suggest that, in addition to reinforcing previous attitudes, debates can sometimes influence attitudes when the voters are independent, less partisan, or undecided—and in some cases change perceptions. As a result of watching the debates, some people learn more about the issues, but they also form impressions of the candidates through the debaters' nonverbal cues. In the first presidential debate of the 2000 campaign, Al Gore's sighs and eye-rolling made him look arrogant and impatient. The second debate was in the format preferred by George W. Bush: The two men were seated at a table and Bush seemed more confident and at ease. In 1992 during the second

15.3

ISSUES IN COMMUNICATION

Political Satire, News, and Spin

When Ira Glass of National Public Radio was interviewed about his new television show *This American Life,* he was asked if he wrote or read fiction. "No. No. No, No," he joked. "I don't know how to read. I get all my news from Jon Stewart every day" (Solomon, 2007, p. 15). Jon Stewart's *Daily Show* has over 1.2 million viewers.

Communication and political science scholar Robert Entman (2006) cites a Pew survey: For 28 percent of those studied, late-night TV programs such as those of Jay Leno and David Letterman were a source of news about the 2004 presidential campaign. For those under age 30, late-night TV programs were twice as important as they were for older Americans. "Although this appears troubling," writes Entman, "it is worth noting that politically oriented comedians and satirists have been with us for centuries":

> *Mark Twain, Will Rogers, even Benjamin Franklin are some of the rather distinguished progenitors of today's Bill Maher and Jon Stewart. . . . in some cases, in part because such commentators are not bound by news conventions (timeliness, balance) that can turn journalists into tools of spin doctors and public relations operatives, they have the ability to speak truths that elude the front page or the network news. (Entman, 2006, pp. 57–58)*

Which media sources do you turn to for information about politics and news? Which do you feel are the most reliable?

presidential debate among Bill Clinton, George Bush, and Ross Perot, newspapers were quick to pick up on a moment when Bush looked at his watch while one of the other candidates was speaking. This was variously interpreted in the press; some read the gesture as discomfort, others as boredom. From facial expression, tone of voice, posture, hand movements, and other cues, viewers also tend to form stronger personality impressions of the candidates. But as is true in other communication contexts, increased understanding does not ensure persuasion or attitude influence.

It seems, then, that exposure to other points of view through the mass media often serves simply to strengthen or reinforce the receiver's initial attitudes and opinions. Many studies of voting behavior confirm this tendency. And although there are far more sophisticated formats and technologies possible for coverage of current presidential debates, since the election of 1964 the number of voters has decreased. Studies have shown that in the past people tended to seek political information from newspapers, but the declining number of newspaper readers may be the reason for declining voter turnout (see Box 15.3).

When do presidential debates matter; when do they influence attitudes? According to the Pew Research Center, from a historical standpoint, the debates have been most influential when the presidential race is close or when there are unresolved issues concerning the personal character of either or both of the candidates.

Often we listen and watch the debates through a filter—that of the press, which has the ability to frame what we see. Communication scholars Kathleen Hall Jamieson and Paul Waldman (2003) point out that:

- Opinion about debates is often shaped more by the postdebate interpretation than by the exchanges between the candidates.
- The power of the press's interpretation of debates takes on greater importance as audiences of debates decline.
- Debate coverage presents in miniature the press's approach to the campaign and candidates. (pp. 30–31)

During the presidential election of 2000, television analysts started calling the election prematurely in Gore's favor, which resulted in a night of confusion and a loss of credibility for the networks. According to a poll by CNN, 79 percent of Americans felt the networks had not acted in a responsible way—though that night there were the most viewers since the Nielsen ratings began in the 1960 Kennedy–Nixon race (Hickey, 2001b, p. 35).

One study (Cappella and Jamieson, 1997) suggests that the way the mass media cover political news and various issues has contributed, even activated, a "spiral of cynicism" among voters. The deciding factors are the emphasis on politics as a game and the coverage given to discussion of various political strategies. Cynicism, the authors suggest, is contagious, and they discuss ways to break this spiral. Another well-known study by Kathleen Hall Jamieson (1996) traces the media campaigns of many American presidents throughout history: her work reveals that political advertising—despite its sometimes questionable practices—plays an important role in "packaging" presidential candidates.

Issues of Importance and How We Think about Them

Agenda Setting

Look at the front page of your newspaper over several days or the lead stories on the television news night after night and you stand to learn a great deal about mass media agendas. There might be a string of stories about policy making and the Iraq war, or the firing of district attorneys by the Department of Justice, or a series of investigative articles about global warming or corporate corruption. An *agenda* in the mass media, explains communication scholar Maxwell McCombs, is "strictly a descriptive term for a prioritized list of items, the major topics found in newspapers, televisions news programs, and other mass media messages" (2005, p. 156).

More than 40 years ago McCombs and his colleague Donald Shaw (1972) developed a highly influential theory on the agenda-setting function of the press. According to **agenda-setting theory,** which has generated much research, *the press tells us what to think about by establishing the relative importance of certain issues.* And through framing, the press can also tell us *how* we should think about them.

Agenda setting works largely through "repetition of the major issues in the news day after day." If, for example, the press chooses to emphasize an ethical issue, the public is given more information on it and given that coverage more frequently. When the press ignores or avoids an issue, we, the public, receive little or no information about it. So the potential for influencing our attitudes is there just by raising the level of our consciousness.

How can you figure out what a newspaper's agenda is? In addition to identifying which issues the paper singles out, you can learn a lot from other cues. For example, ask yourself these questions:

- How long are the articles?
- How large are the headlines?
- What page numbers are the stories covered on? Is the story on the front page, in the middle of the paper, or at the end?
- Is the article at the top of the page or possibly at the very bottom? (Adapted from McCombs, 2005, p. 156)

McCombs points out that there are comparable cues and patterns in other mass media including television news. He also discusses the relative influence of newspapers versus television:

> For agenda-setting effects, a rough rule of thumb is that about half the time, there is no difference in the influence of newspapers and television. For the other half of the time, newspapers have greater influence about twice as often as television. There are ready explanations for this contradiction of the conventional wisdom about the power of television. First, television news is analogous to the opening pages of the newspapers, which means that newspaper readers frequently have a longer time to learn the emerging issue agenda. Second, citizens in many countries are aware that television is under a significant degree of influence from the government or a dominant political party. (McCombs, 2006, p. 160)

But who, it's often asked, sets the agenda for the agenda setters? We know that there is a public agenda, that the government has a policy agenda, and that other groups have agendas as well. For example, communication scholar Em Griffin observes:

> Current thinking on news selection focuses on the crucial role of public relations professionals working for government agencies, corporations, and interest groups. Even prestigious newspapers with large investigative staffs such as *The Washington Post* and *The New York Times* get over half of what they print straight from press releases and press conferences. (Griffin, 2009, p. 457)

Awareness of agenda-setting efforts can make you a more critical viewer of the mass media. And as we'll see, the concept of framing is closely linked with agenda setting.

Framing in the Media

What we perceive is colored, of course, by our own experience and biases—our own selective attention. But in mass communication our perceptions and attitudes are also influenced by how the information we receive—news stories are a good example—is ordered, framed by the media. Framing is also an aspect of politics. One definition of **framing** is *"choosing a broad organizing theme for selecting, emphasizing, and linking the elements of a story"* (Bennett, 2005, p. 37). Framing is also often called putting "spin" on a story to make it sound more like the way you would like audiences to perceive the story. In a classic analysis, communication scholar Robert Entman explains that frames function in four ways. They

- *Define problems*—determine what a causal agent is doing with what costs and benefits, usually measured in terms of common cultural values.
- *Diagnose causes*—identify the forces creating the problem.
- *Make moral judgments*—evaluate causal agents and their effects.
- *Suggest remedies*—offer and justify treatments for the problems and predict their likely effects. (1993, p. 52)

Above all, a frame is a narrative, a way of telling a story from a particular point of view. Like the frame of a picture, then, a frame of a story not only encloses but also leaves some things out:

> Frames select and call attention to particular aspects of the reality described, which logically means that frames simultaneously direct attention from other aspects. Most frames are defined by what they omit as well as include. (p. 55)

When reading a news story, or comparing two accounts, it's important to read critically, asking yourself what information might be missing, what might have been left out.

Choice of language also contributes significantly to framing. Political leaders and reporters frame their arguments and statements in many ways.

During the 2012 presidential campaign, Republicans argued that President Obama was making gasoline prices rise by telephoning senators to vote against the Keystone pipeline, which would bring abundant oil from Canada to reduce U.S. dependence on oil from Middle Eastern countries that are run by leaders who are not friendly to the United States. On the other hand, President Obama framed the argument by making fun of the Republicans as only wanting to "drill, baby, drill" their way out of the problem, instead of developing other sources of energy besides oil. Which framing of the argument do you think is more valid?

Language often frames debates in political campaigns. For example:

- Tax cuts or tax relief?
- Religious or faith-based?
- Death penalty or execution?
- Estate tax or death tax?
- Civilian deaths or collateral damage? (Jamieson and Waldman, 2003, p. xiv)

Attention to language is an essential part of critically viewing the media.

In their efforts to persuade us and to influence our attitudes and our actions, both advertising and public relations make use of mass communication. Yet the functions of these industries are different, although many of the largest public relations firms maintain a connection with advertising agencies.

Advertising has been defined as "any form of nonpersonal presentation and promotion of ideas, goods, and services usually paid for by an identified sponsor" (Dominick, 2009, p. 373).

Although there are thousands of advertising agencies throughout the country, the concentration of agencies is in large cities such as New York. These agencies plan ad campaigns; they do copywriting and create videos, along with graphics; and they also place their work with various media.

When we see advertising, we, the audience, know the source and can usually assume that what we're seeing has been paid for. And sometimes that knowledge helps us evaluate the credibility of the message—whether the advertising is about a new kind of Coca-Cola, a sports utility vehicle, a breakfast cereal, a mutual fund, or a political candidate. If we don't like what we see or hear, presumably we can also provide feedback to that source. For example, women's organizations such as NOW have objected to television spots and magazine ads that they found offensive to women; objections that Camel's cigarette advertising encouraged smoking among young people led to several advertising changes. On the other hand, it's far more difficult to police the presentation or claims of advertising appearing on the Web.

In some ways describing the functions of public relations is more complex—in part because instead of marketing or selling directly, public relations serves a management function. It is dealing, literally, with relations with the public—although sometimes that public may be a selected group of people who are opinion makers, leaders in a field, for a given industry

or organization. (And at times a public relations firm is engaged by an individual—e.g., a political candidate or a film star.)

Public relations firms plan strategies for disseminating information about a company (or an individual or organization) to a particular audience; they articulate an organization's goals; they increase an organization's visibility and highlight company expertise and accomplishments. One of their major concerns is public image.

Suppose a technology company came to a public relations firm. The firm may initiate surveys, create lists of influential media for their clients, write press releases and backgrounders (informational writing about a client's organization), and plan meetings and other events that will bring information to targeted segments of the public.

But unlike the ads we see, the source of work by public relations firms may be unknown to us. For example, we may read an article in a newspaper or magazine or see someone interviewed on television and not be aware that public relations may have led to the representation or discussion of what we see. In addition, the demand for 24-hour coverage has increased the reliance of the media on public relations press release as "news."

Another pivotal aspect of public relations is crisis management—suppose, for example, that your pharmaceutical company puts out a drug that has to be withdrawn from the market because of toxic side effects. Or suppose that the head of a public organization makes a speech that is offensive to members of an ethnic group. Whether it's setting the record straight or "damage control," the shaping and dissemination of this kind of information is often handled by a public relations firm.

The U.S. Department of Labor projects that jobs for advertising, marketing, and public relations managers will increase faster than the

Continued

average for all occupations through 2014 (2009, p. 34). The department expects keen competition for jobs as advertising, marketing, promotions, and public relations managers. Earnings can be high and the positions may involve considerable travel. "College graduates with related experience, a high level of creativity, and strong communication skills should have the best job opportunities. In particular, employers will seek those who have the computer skills to conduct advertising, marketing, promotions, public relations, and sales activities on the Internet" (p. 34).

You can learn more about careers in advertising at *www.aaaa.org* and *www.aaf.org*. For more information about careers in public relations, log onto *www.prsa.org*.

IMPLICATIONS OF THE NEW COMMUNICATION TECHNOLOGIES

We take for granted smart phones, personal computers, fax machines, e-mail, texting, and satellites. Electronic document interchange has revolutionized business communications by transferring information from one computer to another over telephone lines. And some experts believe that the "mediated home" will soon herald a new information age with the widespread use of interactive television. Through interactive television and other technologies, specialists hundreds of miles away can examine and diagnose patients in small hospitals or clinics in rural areas. At colleges and universities many courses are offered online, and the potential of cable and closed-circuit television is certainly being tapped.

In 2011 a new phenomenon called "flash mobs" began to occur. Group e-mail is used to have a crowd of people meet at a predetermined time and place, groups that are sometimes used to start riots. This has also turned to "flash robs" to steal from stores (Albom, 2011; Zimmerman and Bustillo, 2011). This is just one of many new and complex communication situations resulting from the new communication technologies.

One of the many changes made possible by the new technologies is the media trend toward narrowcasting as opposed to broadcasting. **Narrowcasting** refers to *programming designed to target a specific segment of the media audience*. Through sophisticated research techniques that take into account information about audience characteristics, lifestyles, needs, and preferences, the media often tailor their programs (and often their advertising) to various subgroups or selected audiences, for example, Spanish-speaking people, or teenagers, or people between the ages of 20 and 30. This means a media shift toward increasingly smaller audiences (Pavlik and McIntosh, 2010). The consequences of narrowcasting are not yet fully understood, though some critics feel that this trend toward greater and greater audience selectivity could result in a more fragmented society as audiences filter out what they do not wish to see.

The new technologies have increased the *speed* of communication at an exponential rate. International meetings are set up and documents exchanged at a previously unimagined pace. You can fax or e-mail your résumé to a prospective employer on the same day you see a job listing. And you most likely have found the listing on the Internet. Essential equipment for every office and many homes, fax machines allow people to send and receive messages almost instantaneously. We have also seen major changes in the *volume of information* transmitted, stored, and retrieved. For example, type is set electronically, and desktop publishing and online publishing have dramatically increased the number of books, blogs, online news, magazines, and newsletters available to us.

By means of the computer, scanner, camera phone, and fax, we can also transmit great numbers of images—visual materials such as graphs, maps, and photographs. The visual capabilities of the new technologies have had a powerful impact on how the media present news and other information. As a result of these and other changes, we have become an *increasingly visual society.* In fact, in a 2011 global survey of college students, 64 percent said that they would choose the Internet over having a car; 40 percent said that having a Web connection was more important to them than dating, having friends, or listening to music. The survey included responses from 1,400 students from 14 countries (Cisco, 2011).

In 2004, a technology called podcasts entered our lives. The word "podcast" comes from the combination of the Apple *iPod,* and *broadcast.* Podcasts are a series of audio or video digital media files that can be downloaded to your iPod, MP3 player, cell phone, or your computer. Podcasts have come a long way since 2004 and are used anywhere from listening to news clips to watching television series. Now, podcasts have also moved into the education realm. Libraries are using podcasts to promote their services and allow students to access their resources. Students can download and watch lectures right on their mobile device, further enhancing distance learning or supplementing an online class. The ability to replay a podcast over and over again can help international students who need to learn at their own pace, enabling them to understand the language better. Podcasts are a form of technology that is changing the way students learn higher education. Future advances will only continue to benefit students in the educational realm.

Many of the new technologies are linked with traditional levels of communication. We have been examining these links throughout this text not only in organizational communication but in interpersonal and intercultural contexts as well as in our study of person perception. In the pages that follow we will look at some of these connections more closely.

The Convergence of Computing, Telecommunications, and Media

Among the most striking results of technological advances is the trend toward **convergence,** *the merging or "coming together of computing, telecommunications, and media in a digital environment"*—for example, the future convergence of television and the PC (Pavlik and McIntosh, 2010, p. 547).

How will convergence affect our lives at home? Over a decade ago one vision of the future household included wireless fax and personal computer links; dial-up educational and television services; improved online banking and home shopping; integrated emergency alarm systems for fire, police, and medical assistance; customized electronic newspapers; as well as other services needed to work from one's home. Now much of this vision has become a reality—but only for the limited segment of the population who can afford it.

In the past, our views of mass communication assumed distinctions among the various media—print, film, broadcasting, and so on. What we are seeing now, in many aspects of our lives, is a blurring of distinctions among the media and an increasing overlap in functions. Writing of how the new media are transforming journalism, Pavlik (2001) argues that convergence is "neither inevitable nor necessarily good: Convergence merely holds the promise of a better, more efficient, more democratic medium for journalism and the public in the twenty-first century" (p. xiii).

Computer-Mediated Communication

Currently, it's estimated that there are 1.1 billion people online throughout the world. Asia has 418 million—the largest number of Internet users; Europe, 322 million; North America, 233 million; Latin America, 110 million; Africa, 34 million; the Middle East, 20 million; and Australia/Oceana, 19 million ("Internet Usage Statistics," 2007). Remember, of course, that the number of people online increases every day.

The Internet

In large part because of the Internet, *a global "network of computer networks,"* the computer is used not only for its word processing and graphic functions but also for an ever-expanding range of interactive activities (Dominick, 2009, p. 276, italics added). In the online world of computer networks—the term "cyberspace" was coined by William Gibson in his 1984 novel *Neuromancer*—you can participate in conferences, electronic brainstorming, newsgroups, support groups, and any number of online communities.

Through the Internet you can also keep in touch with friends halfway across the world, conduct research, or look for an apartment in another state. The 10 most popular Internet activities are sending e-mail, finding information through a search engine, searching for driving directions or maps, answering a specific question through an Internet search, researching services or product information, getting weather reports, searching for information about interests or hobbies, getting travel information, getting the news, and shopping ("Most Popular Internet Activities," 2007).

Many believe that the World Wide Web has changed the way we read and write. Online publishing now includes e-zines, out-of-print books, author home pages, and searchable classics libraries. During recent years several scholars have published full documentation of their new books online because the footnotes, filling hundreds of pages, were just too extensive to be printed within the book. The Google Cyberlibrary

Project in its initial stages will make vast numbers of books available online by scanning from the collections of the New York Public Library, and the libraries of Oxford, Stanford, and the University of Michigan. Harvard University, a more limited contributor, will make 40,000 books available for the project.

The Internet has become such a powerful tool in the business world today that airlines are implementing the use of in-flight Internet access via WiFi. In August 2008, American Airlines announced that it had launched its in-flight Internet service. "The service, called Gogo [offered by Aircell] . . . on nonstop flights between New York and San Francisco, New York and Los Angeles, and New York and Miami. The cost is $12.95 per flight. Passengers [can] sign up when they boot up their browsers." Many other airlines have indicated they will be using Aircell's Gogo service as well and planned to implement their service in 2009 (CNET News, 2008).

One of the newer waves in the Internet world is being made by a global Internet communications company named Skype. "Skype is the world's fastest-growing Internet communication offering, allowing unlimited free voice, video and instant messaging communication between users of Skype Software." In 2007, Skype released desktop Internet phones that "enable users to place and receive calls with Skype via broadband Internet connections without being connected to computers." Eric Lagier, director of business development for Skype said, "Communication today involves more than just free voice calls over the Internet. . . . Skype's goal is to set conversations free by making them possible in many forms and places. Skype-certified devices and accessories are a crucial part of this vision as their simplicity and power make Skype even more relevant to people's lives." During the wars in Iraq and Afghanistan, military personnel have raved about the benefits of Skype and the ability to keep in touch with their families from around the world (Businesswire.com, 2007.)

USC's Center for the Digital Future has issued a new report (2007) on American use of the Internet. Here are some highlights:

Americans on the Internet—more than three-quarters of Americans are Internet users; 77.6 percent of Americans age 12 or older go online.

The Internet at home—more than two-thirds of Americans (68.1 percent) use the Internet at home, a substantial increase from 46.9 percent . . . in 2000.

Hours online—the number of hours online continues to increase, rising to an average of 8.9 hours per week. . . . ("Online World . . . ," pp. 1–2, 4).

One of the most important long-term questions still to be answered is how Internet use will affect children.

E-Mail

Along with other research, a study from the Stanford Institute for the Quantitative Study of Society in 2005 finds that the most popular online activity is reading, sending, or answering *e-mail*, or electronic mail (46.6 percent of time is devoted to this),

ISSUES IN COMMUNICATION

According to MIT psychologist Sherry Turkle, we have become a "tethered society." Children get their first cell phone between ages 9 and 13 (Turkle, 2011, p. 173). Connecting from a distance has morphed from writing letters, to telephone calling, to texting, to tweeting. It has also become exhausting. Anxiety has become part of the new connectivity. If we do not stay constantly in touch, we feel that we are out of the loop and socially invisible. We feel that we must respond to every ping of the e-mail. A substantial amount of research has shown that this multitasking (doing everything we normally do, and also keeping in touch) degrades everything we try to do (Turkle, 2011, p. 242).

As of 2011, the average American teen received 3,300 texts a month, according to the *New York Times* best-selling author Nicholas Carr (2011, p. 228). This number keeps increasing each year. Young adults between the ages of twenty-five and thirty-four, who are among the most avid Net users, read printed works (on paper) a total of forty-nine minutes a week in 2008, down a whopping 29 percent from 2004, while all forms of electronic communication are up dramatically (Carr, 2011, pp. 87–88).

Additional research has shown that these new forms of mediated communication change our brains. The sound or light indicating a new message stimulates a release of dopamine in our brains. This is the same chemical released when we get other forms of reward like winning money or having sex. This results in changes within our brain circuitry called neuroplasticity (Carr, 2012, p. 116). Carr (2011) writes that this process "turns us into lab rats constantly pushing levers to get tiny pellets of social or intellectual nourishment" (p. 117). Duhigg (2012) writes that this biochemical mechanism is exactly how habits are acquired, and that they are often very difficult to break.

The Nobel Prize–winning Princeton professor Daniel Kahneman argues persuasively that mass media (including social media) warp our perception of the world. He confirms the old adage that says, "You take truth, and I will take repetition, and I will beat you nine times out of ten in persuading an audience." One study conducted at Kansas State University found that this message bombardment sometimes exceeds our attention capacity. The more we try to keep up with the multitasking, the less deliberate and the more shallow we become. The more we lose our deliberative and critical thinking skills, the shallower our brain functioning becomes. Carr (2011) refers to this as a form of "autoamputation" (p. 212). Our critical thinking skills are gradually being lost.

Sources: Nicholas Carr, *The Shallows: What the Internet Is Doing to Our Brains.* New York: W. W. Norton, 2011. Charles Duhigg, *The Power of Habit.* New York: Random House, 2012. Daniel Kahneman, *Thinking Fast and Slow.* New York: Farrar, Straus and Giroux, 2012. Sherry Turkle, *Alone Together.* New York: Basic Books, 2011.

followed by Internet browsing (33.7 percent) and instant messaging (6.8 percent). In all, the Stanford study reports, 57 percent of time spent on the Internet is devoted to communicating with others—a combination of e-mail, instant messaging, and chat rooms (*www.stanford.edu/group/siqss*).

For many, messages sent via e-mail and fax have replaced letters, not only in businesses but in personal life. For some, e-mail has basically replaced the telephone. Through e-mail you keep in touch with friends and family in a rapid and informal way. According to a 2004 survey by the Pew Internet & American Life Project, almost three-quarters of young people between ages 12 and 17 who are online use instant messaging to speak with friends—and over a third of them use it every day.

As we've seen in earlier chapters, e-mail is an essential part of organizational communication. But unlike letters, electronic mail is not necessarily private. The casual nature of e-mail messages within an organization became an issue in a 1998 lawsuit against Microsoft in which e-mail messages were used as evidence, prompting several large corporations to require that their employees periodically destroy "sensitive" e-mail messages. On a personal level, too, lack of privacy can become an issue. As mentioned in Chapter 7, there is growing surveillance of e-mail by employers. At one firm the intimate e-mail messages of an employee were posted on the company bulletin board (Wood and Smith, 2001). As with the use of other technologies, an etiquette for using e-mail seems to be needed.

Teleconferencing

With the growing popularity of **teleconferencing**—*holding a meeting with people who are in different, often distant locations*—have come many changes. If you have ever participated in a conference call, you know that the telephone technology is relatively simple. This is a form of *audioconferencing* used, for example, by many businesses and other organizations over the years as a substitute for face-to-face communication—one that drastically cuts down on business expenses and may result in greater and more rapid exchange of ideas and problem solving. For example, a cargo airline with international routes conducts daily morning briefings through audioconferencing.

Accomplished through the use of both video and audio links, videoconferencing is a form of conferencing we now take for granted as television viewers. For example, on news programs such as *Face the Nation* or *Meet the Press,* a moderator may interview a Washington correspondent and a senator in Idaho to discuss the implications of an upcoming election. The people being interviewed respond to questions, discuss their own views, listen to opposing views, and speak directly to each other. And you can see each person "live" and watch how he or she answers questions. All the nonverbal cues discussed in Chapter 4 also come into play as you watch.

Videoconferencing has many applications in the workplace, and its use is increasing not only by banks, law firms, and architectural offices, but also medical providers and universities. Even many small companies can now afford videoconferencing systems. They are being used for everything from sales presentations, creative meetings, brainstorming, to job interviews. The chances are that at some time you will be participating in them.

Cell Phones

With so many new communication technologies available, there are also new risks. One high school student in Pinckney, Michigan, found out the hard way. As a joke, she took explicit, fully nude pictures of herself on her cell phone and sent them to a few of her closest girlfriends (i.e., sexting). The pictures also showed her face.

Within a few weeks, those pictures were on the cell phones of over 200 of her high school classmates and even some of the students in neighboring schools. Someone anonymously left a printed copy of one of the photos on the school principal's desk. He called the police, which resulted in pornography charges being brought against the girl and those who distributed the pictures. When called by the newspaper, her mother sobbed into the phone saying that she had "no comment." It is safe to say that this girl's life may never be the same (Battaglia, 2008).

Similar incidents have been reported in New Jersey, New York, Alabama, Utah, Pennsylvania, Texas, Connecticut, and Ohio. If convicted, the young people will be registered as sex offenders, a designation that can stay with them for up to 25 years, according to Dr. Roger Kernsmith, a professor of criminology at Eastern Michigan University. In addition, sexual predators have recently been changing their targets from the Internet to cell phones. So, these girls may unwittingly become targets of sexual predators, putting them at a significantly increased risk. School Superintendent Dan Danosky said in a letter to the campus population that "The advent of the electronic age has brought with it conveniences and capabilities unimaginable even 10 years ago. [However], along with the benefits have also come some problems" (Mathis and Aisner, 2008).

The growing popularity of the cell phone, sometimes called "the communications Swiss Army knife," is confirmed in a joint study by Pew Research Center's Internet & American Life Project, the Associated Press, and AOL (Rainie and Keeler, 2006). People use cell phones not only to make and receive calls but also to send and receive text messages, take still pictures, access the Internet, trade instant messages, play music, and watch video and TV programs as well as engage in other activities.

As of 2006 there were 208 million cell phone users in the United States, a number that is sure to increase. Young adults are the largest population of users. Interestingly, 22 percent of people who own cell phones admit "they are not always truthful about exactly where they are when they are on the phone. Younger users are much more likely to say that they are not always honest about where they are: 39% of cell users ages 18–29 say that" (p. 3). The Pew study identifies several implications of their findings, among them:

> Cell phones enable real-time action and engagement.
> Cell phone use is encouraging people to reallocate portions of their time and their communications patterns.
> Cell phone use is changing expectations about when and how others are available to us. (p. 11)

A survey from the National Institute of Health produced some startling results in a new trend that shows more and more Americans leaving their landlines behind. The research shows that at the end of 2007 "almost one in six households are wireless only," meaning there was no landline telephone in the home. "This increasing trend towards owning nothing but wireless phones, or at least abandoning the use of landlines for most communication, has some major implications for the industry. . . . The move away from landlines is going to make life a bit more difficult for telemarketers already harried by the national Do Not Call Registry, as there's no centralized directory listing for cell phone numbers" (Chartier, 2008).

One additional problem with cell phones is the data that is left on them when they are lost. One study purposely left (or lost) cell phones to test the phone's security by seeing what the finders would do. The test was conducted by Symantec, a security company. False data were left on the phones along with monitoring software that allowed them to track the phones' whereabouts, and to track what information was accessed by the finders. A total of 50 phones were left in Silicon Valley, Washington, D.C. New York, and Los Angeles. Ninety percent of finders rifled through the phone's apps and files; 81 percent looked at the contact information left on the "lost" phones; 72 percent looked at private pictures; 64 percent looked at the social networking information; 47 percent looked at cloud-based documents; and 43 percent looked at online banking information left on the phones. In one case a finder looked up the Facebook information on the "lost" phone 21 times over a 45-minute period before turning the phone in 150 miles away from where it had been "lost" (Vance, 2012, pp. 37–38).

Telecommuting

In **telecommuting,** sometimes called *telework, people work at various locations outside the main office, often at home, and are usually connected to a main office by computer and a high-speed modem.* Newer technology and increasing use of broadband also offer people who telecommute an array of options that merge home and office including the fax, voice mail, cell phone, e-mail, and videoconferencing. For example, e-mail makes it possible to transmit and receive files almost instantaneously. All this can create far more flexible work arrangements.

Once considered experimental, telecommuting is becoming part of "mainstream practices" at some firms and will certainly have an impact on social, family, and professional relationships. For many, telecommuting is offered as an employee benefit, and over 50 percent of North American firms allow their employees to telecommute. Some people telecommute two or three days out of the workweek, and it is estimated that in addition to cutting costs, telecommuting can increase productivity by 5 to 20 percent.

Despite the convenience and benefits, however, not everyone wishes to work from home. A computer specialist we know was startled and somewhat disappointed when the firm she worked for decided that all employees would switch from working at home one or two days a week to working at home every day. The firm's potential savings in overhead were clear, but she regretted the lack of face-to-face contact with her colleagues.

The New Alternative Media

There have always been some alternatives to mainstream media from ham radio operators to independent publishers of political newsletters. But the growing dissatisfaction with traditional media along with advances in digital technologies that include greater interactive capability are enabling numerous efforts of individuals and groups to explore new media alternatives. *Columbia Journalism Review* refers to "a new age of alternative media." Some even believe that the new alternatives have the ability to "change some of the terms in the unwritten contract between the press and the people" ("The New Age," 2003, p. 20). Here we look briefly at two of these alternative media.

News-Related Blogs

In recent years there has been a proliferation of blogs of all kinds on the Internet. A **blog,** or *Weblog,* is *"a Web site where information is updated frequently and presented in reverse chronological order . . . [newest material coming first]. Typically, each post contains one and often several hyperlinks to other Web sites and stories, and usually . . . a standing list of links to the author's favorite bookmarks"* (Welch, 2003, p. 21).

As of 2006, a study by the Pew Internet & American Life Project reported that there were about 12 million bloggers in the United States (that number increases every year), and "thirty-four percent of them consider blogging to be a form of journalism" (cited in Lemann, 2006, p. 44). The technology for creating blogs is now so inexpensive that people can create their own for as little as $200 or far less. In the last few years, bloggers have influenced public opinion and events in many ways—for example, by criticizing political issues as well as politicians and media figures from Rush Limbaugh to Bill Maher for their extremely critical comments about women in 2012. And there are blogs that post eyewitness accounts of important events worldwide. In fact, writers of blogs are sometimes referred to as "amateur journalists" or "citizen journalists."

Much of the information on blogs as it relates to news is inaccurate and undocumented. And much of it is partisan—often it is a criticism of mainstream media. Yet one journalist writes that while 90 percent of news-related blogs may be mediocre, "the top 10 percent is among the most exciting new trends the profession has seen in a while" (Welch, 2003, p. 26). Nicholas Lemann, professor and dean of Columbia University's Graduate School of Journalism, disagrees. Of the work of so-called citizen journalists that appears on the Internet, including their press criticism, Lemann writes, "none of that yet rises to the level of a journalistic culture rich enough to compete in a serious way with the old media" (2006, p. 47).

The mainstream media also have an increasing number of Weblogs. *The Wall Street Journal* (*www.opinionjournal.com/best*), ABC News (*http://abcnews.go.com/Politics/TheNote*), and MSNBC (*www.msnbc.com/id/3032105*) are just a few.

Effects on Interpersonal Communication

How are the new technologies affecting interpersonal communication? For at least a segment of our population, a number of face-to-face transactions are now mediated by computers and other interactive technologies. This does not necessarily mean that there will be less interpersonal communication. For example, as discussed earlier, Skype is a "peer-to-peer" telephone network on the Internet that enables people to do voice and videoconferencing at no cost (*www.skype.com*). Through

Skype a friend of the author who lives in Connecticut is able to speak with and see her two children online every day: They work in Mauretania and India.

Applications of technological advances (e.g., customized television feeds) also intensify the *selectivity* of the mass communication audience. Conversely, technology has enabled the mass media to become far more selective. For example, in publishing, books can now be printed as needed, with specific sections added or dropped, according to the demands of a given readership.

As we've seen, certain technological innovations are well suited to enhancing rather than limiting communication. In organizational communication, for example, many companies use videoconferencing on a routine basis. The global nature of telecommunications has changed the structure of business today. As members of increasingly multinational businesses and institutions, we have opportunities to extend our relationships across local and national boundaries.

Several researchers view the Internet as a rapidly diffusing technology that extends social contact. But does using technology really affect our sense of well-being and connectedness? In particular, is the Internet isolating or does it extend social contact and enhance communication? These questions have been the subject of much ongoing research and debate. In Chapter 8 we saw that some people who meet online do go on to develop interpersonal relationships.

A study by Robert Kraut and colleagues at Carnegie Mellon University (1998) found that people who used the Internet at home (including the most social forms such as e-mail and chat rooms) showed higher levels of loneliness and depression than people who did not. Time people spent online seemed to correlate with less family interaction and a declining number of friends. In a later study (2002), Kraut and his colleagues changed their minds. "Internet Paradox Revisited," their follow-up study, finds that Internet use may not cause loneliness and depression, though it increases stress. Better outcomes for social well-being and connectedness are seen for extroverts than for introverts or others with less social support *(www.cmu.edu/cmnews)*.

New research on the use of social networks in the United States finds that 55 percent of online teenagers use social networking on such Web sites as Facebook, and 55 percent have posted an online personal profile (Lenhart and Madden, 2007, p. 2). The most popular site is Facebook, which "dominates the social networking world" (p. 4). Almost half of online teenagers access social networking sites daily, and two-thirds have limited the access to their profiles. Girls from ages 15 to 17 are even more likely to use them.

This survey examines five ways in which these sites are used: "The vast majority . . . say they use the sites to maintain their *current* friendships, while half report using the sites to make *new* friends":

To stay in touch with friends you see a lot: 91 percent

To stay in touch with friends you rarely see in person: 82 percent

Make plans with friends: 72 percent

Make new friends: 49 percent

Flirt with someone: 17 percent (adapted from Lenhart and Madden, 2007, pp. 2, 5)

Norman Nie, coauthor of Stanford University's "Internet and Society" survey (Nie and Erbring, 2002), is one exception; he disagrees with the more positive views of the Internet's social effects. He found that with the growing use of the Internet, people are spending more time at their jobs and less time with their families and friends (Nie, 2001). Their social isolation also increased steadily with the amount of time they spend online. Nie is also concerned that Internet use in telecommuting will undercut the social aspects of work. A later Stanford University study directed by Nie (Nie et al., 2005) seemed to add weight to his concerns. It reports that people spend one-third of online time at work; the other time they spend online takes away twice as much from time spent with family as from time spent watching television (*www.stanford.edu/group/siqss*). For Nie, no technology can replace the immediacy and warmth of face-to-face communication as it affects both individual well-being and our sense of connection with others.

Boase and Wellman believe that changes in social networks reflect changing social patterns that have been developing for over a century: "All in all, . . . the Internet is neither destroying nor radically enhancing society. Rather, the Internet is adding to the overall volume of communication, helping to maintain the kinds of relationships that have existed for decades" (2006 p. 721).

Our society and government have found many ways to use today's techno-logical advances and provide a public service to citizens. One way in which they have used technology is through the development of the AMBER Alert program. "The AMBER Alert Program, named for 9-year-old Amber Hagerman, is a volun-tary partnership between law-enforcement agencies, broadcasters, and transporta-tion agencies to activate an urgent bulletin in the most serious child-abduction cases. Broadcasters use the Emergency Alert System (EAS) to air a description of the ab-ducted child and the suspected abductor. The goal of an AMBER Alert is to instantly galvanize the entire community to assist in the search for and safe recovery of the child." Within hours, millions can be notified of a missing child by broadcasting an emergency response through television, radio, and Internet sources across the coun-try (National Center for Missing and Exploited Children, 2008).

Prospects for a Global Human Community

The hope that technological advances would contribute to a global human community—a world of "free-flowing information, borderless communities [and] increased democratization" (p. 356)—has been voiced by communication theorists for many years. One group of scholars (Kwak et al., 2006) writes of the potential to connect people from many nations and create what they characterize as "a psycho-logical sense of belonging to the international community":

> [T]he Internet matters for international engagement. . . . the Internet connects individuals to the international community by helping them increase their knowledge of the world, facilitating their sense of belonging in the greater world, and motivating them to participate in international events and foreign volunteer opportunities. (p. 207)

As we saw in Chapter 10, the new communication technologies have vastly increased the amount of intercultural communication. People of different cultures have more information about each other and are more accessible than ever before. They are also more interdependent. Thus the new media may have the potential for fostering extremism because they enable people to isolate themselves from opposing views and reinforce their own attitudes (Tolchin and Tolchin, 2006).

The new technologies have also been used to implement political or social change. People around the world have used electronic mail and the Internet to mount high-tech campaigns; for example, at times they have documented atrocities that they claim were not reported by the media, and they have organized protest rallies in many cities around the world. In general, online activism has become much more widespread. For example, there are Web sites on environmental concerns such as global warming. Web sites on human rights include *www.amnesty.org* (Amnesty International) and *www.aiusa.org* (the U.S. branch), which are concerned with human rights violations; and *www.oneworld.net*, a site with concerns about global issues, has established a portal promoting universal high-quality education. Numerous Web sites also deal with censorship issues and freedom of the press—for example, *www.dfn.org* (Digital Freedom Network).

Today we communicate across both real and electronic spaces. The long-term implications of the new technologies are still unfolding. Some communication scholars are especially concerned that within technologically rich societies an emphasis on the use and ongoing development of technology will overshadow human issues. Yet for the vast majority of the world's population, access to technology remains limited and a mediated home environment seems very far away.

The potential for creating a global community in the twenty-first century is in our hands, within our reach, but it will be determined not by the nature of the technology itself but the human uses to which technology is put. Ultimately, it may depend on our willingness to redefine our own self-interest so that it includes rather than excludes other groups of people. Communications scholar Nick Couldry writes:

> Since media are the principal means through which the world's realities are presented, media ethics is a necessity. . . . But media ethics, like all ethics, starts from where we find ourselves, not from where we would like to be. Ethics is a framework for building consensus, even where none seems available; without it . . . we shall not survive. (2006, p. 140)

Summary

In this chapter, we saw that mass communication, by its very nature, is mediated. We defined the audience in mass communication as relatively large, heterogeneous, and anonymous to the source. The experience itself was characterized as public, rapid, and fleeting, and the source was seen as often working through a complex organization. It was also pointed out that the feedback in mass communication was often limited and not as complete as it is in interpersonal communication.

We also discussed the mass communication process in terms of the gatekeeper concept and influences on gatekeeper choice. We gave special attention to gatekeeping and media conglomerates. We also looked at various theories about how messages flow from source to receiver, and at the concept of the active audience. We saw that the flow of information from the mass communicator to individual receivers sometimes involves opinion leaders, with mass and face-to-face communication playing complementary roles.

The next section of this chapter assessed some of the effects and outcomes of mass communication. Although the mass media are often extremely effective in disseminating information, information gain by no means ensures attitude influence. Often, exposure to several points of view through the mass media simply reinforces the receiver's initial attitudes, particularly with respect to voting intentions. We gave special attention to agenda setting

and framing in news reporting. We then looked at the functions of advertising and public relations.

In a final section of our chapter, we looked at several of the new communication technologies and explored some of their implications. Despite increases in the selectivity, speed, volume, and visual nature of communication, the new media were seen primarily as extensions of existing media. The convergence of computing, telecommunications, and media, as well as some effects on interpersonal communication were discussed. We also looked at the new alternative media and the problem of technological literacy. In closing, we tried to make clear that so-called revolutions in technology have historical precedents and that the possibility of a global human community will depend on the human application of technology rather than on technology itself.

Key Terms

Active audience
Agenda-setting theory
Blogs
Convergence
Diffusion of information

Framing
Gatekeeper
Hypodermic needle
   model

Narrowcasting
Opinion leaders
Selective attention
Selective exposure

Telecommuting
Teleconferencing
Two-step flow model

Review Questions

1. Identify three aspects of mass communication that are mediated.

2. What are four distinguishing characteristics of mass communication?

3. Discuss the concept of the gatekeeper. Give one example of how gatekeeping in mass communication differs from gatekeeping in face-to-face communication.

4. What are six variables that may influence the information a gatekeeper chooses to select or reject?

5. Identify three concerns about the concentration of media ownership and its possible effect on news content.

6. Identify some of the ways in which guests attempt to control media interviews and some of the problems interviewers have in getting them to answer questions.

7. Discuss two different theories about how messages flow from the mass media to individual receivers.

8. What is meant by the concept of the active audience?

9. What are some of the research findings on media uses and gratifications and the way the new technologies are used?

10. What is the general research finding concerning the relationship between a news event's importance and the channels through which it is disseminated?

11. How effective are the mass media in influencing the receiver's attitudes? Support your answer with an example.

12. Explain the concepts of agenda setting and framing in the media. How does the use of language contribute to framing? Give two examples.

13. What are the functions of advertising and public relations, how do they differ, and what is the relationship of both to mass communication?

14. Explain the relationship between the new technologies and the mass media as traditionally conceived.

15. What are two of the effects of the growing convergence of computing and telecommunications?

16. What are some of the ways in which the new technologies might affect interpersonal communication and media and what are the recent findings of a long-term study of Internet trends in this country?

17. Discuss the rise of the new alternative media and give two examples.

18. Discuss the new communication technologies and speculate upon their possible effects in bringing about a global human community.

Exercises

1. Follow a major news event as covered by a weekly magazine, a metropolitan newspaper, a local newspaper, and two Web-based news sites, both domestic and international—for example, *www.washingtonpost.com* and *www.bbc.co.uk*. Relate your findings to what you have read about the gatekeeping function of the media.

2. Identify a current issue related to fairness and accuracy in reporting by going to *www.fair .org* (this site has good Web links) or *www.ire .org* and compare the treatment of the subject with the coverage of a newspaper and television station. If there are differences, what are they? Did you use any of the Web links and, if so, what did they add to your understanding?

3. Watch a controversial television program (preferably a panel discussion or a talk show) in the company of at least five other people and observe the quality of their interaction and their comments about the program. Do the responses of the receivers reinforce each other? Is there an opinion leader in the group?

4. Compare the coverage of an event of moderate importance as presented by a newspaper, a television newscast, a radio program, and a news site on the Web. Which was the most comprehensive? Which seemed most objective and which most partisan? Give examples.

5. Do a content analysis of the news as presented by two different networks and two cable stations for the same evening. Discuss what each chose to emphasize and further discuss the worldview implied by each of the four choices. Compare these with an Internet newsgroup discussion and a news Web site from another country.

Suggested Readings

Bennett, W. Lance. *News: The Illusion of Politics*, 7th ed. New York: Pearson, 2007.
  A well-written and lively examination of the relation between the news media and politics *with interesting examples. The author looks at information biases in the news, freedom of the press issues, and the complex relationship between media and government.*

Bully.

A 2012 film about the effect of mass media humiliation on high school students.

Carr, Nicholas. *The Shallows: What the Internet Is Doing to Our Brains.* New York: W. W. Norton, 2011.

This fascinating book documents the physiological and psychological changes in our brains brought about by Internet usage.

Chester, Jeff. *Digital Destiny: New Media and the Future of Democracy.* New York: The New Press, 2007.

A book about current media policy, the special interests trying to shape it, and the future of digital technology in a democracy. Bill Moyers has called its author "the Paul Revere of the media revolution."

Dominick, Joseph. *The Dynamics of Mass Communication,* 10th ed. New York: McGraw-Hill, 2009.

This book is a classic comprehensive overview of the discipline.

Duhigg, Charles. *The Power of Habit.* New York: Random House, 2012.

This best-selling book discusses the ways that the public gets hooked through the media and how to break bad habits. It also shows how organizations use social media to invade our privacy.

Good Night, and Good Luck

An award-winning film about Edward R. Murrow, the legendary broadcaster at CBS, and his challenge, through television programming, to the intimidation and fear tactics of Senator Joseph McCarthy, who was head of the House Un-American Activities Committee during the 1950s.

Kahneman, Daniel. *Thinking Fast and Slow.* New York: Farrar, Straus and Giroux, 2011.

This Nobel Prize–winning author examines how our brains respond to stimulation such as that which we get from traditional media as well as social media.

Overholser, Geneva, and Kathleen Hall Jamieson, eds. *The Press, Institutions of American Democracy Series.* New York: Oxford University Press, 2005.

A comprehensive collection of essays by distinguished communication scholars on numerous aspects of the press including essays on the nature of the press, the First Amendment, the watchdog function of the press, minority concerns and Net neutrality, and the role of the press in a democracy.

Pavlik, John V., and McIntosh, Shawn. *Converging Media,* 2nd ed. Boston: Pearson, 2010.

This is a comprehensive text on communication and new media. John Pavlik is also the author of a book on journalism at the beginning of the twenty-first century.

Schneir, Bruce. *Liars & Outliers.* New York: John Wiley & Sons, 2012.

This book discusses the different influences the media have on the public trust.

Tapscott, Don. *Grown Up Digital.* New York: McGraw-Hill, 2009.

This book shows the ways in which the digital generation is changing our world.

Turkle, Sherry. *Alone Together.* New York: Basic Books, 2011.

This MIT scholar analyzes the effects of technology on relationships.

 # For Supplementary Information

Log onto the Online Learning Center at *www.mhhe.com/tubbshc13e.*

GLOSSARY

Active audience: The concept that receivers of mass communication seek out and select the media content that they want.

Advice giving: A judgmental method of counseling implying the other person can't find the solution.

Agenda setting: The theory that the press tells us what to think about by establishing the relative importance of certain issues.

Analogy: A form of supporting material comparing two things or ideas.

Anticlimax order: A method of presentation in which the speaker presents the strongest argument first.

Appeasement: Giving in to the other party in a conflict situation.

Arousal level: The level of mental alertness relating to one's readiness to listen.

Assimilation: A way people distort messages to agree with their own view of things.

Assimilation effect: An effect that occurs when a listener tends to accept a change in attitude urged by a speaker and perceives the speaker's position as closer to his or her preferred position than it really is.

Attachment style: A person's capacities and patterns of forming and maintaining intimate relationships, shaped in part by the quality of the first emotional bond with the mother or other primary caregiver.

Avoidance: Not dealing with a conflict between two or more parties.

Avoiding topics: Not bringing up topics that are sensitive in a conflict situation.

Backlash: When a person reacts in the opposite way intended by the speaker (same as boomerang effect).

Bandwagon appeal: A propaganda device using statistics to indicate that many people are doing something.

Blog: Web site where information is updated frequently and presented in reverse chronological order. Typically, each post contains one and often several hyperlinks to other Web sites and stories.

Body: The main part of a speech.

Boomerang effect: When the listener reacts opposite to that intended by the speaker (same as backlash).

Brainstorming: A group technique designed to create as many ideas as possible.

Casual or social group: A group intended for purely pleasurable purposes.

Categorical imperative: A command or obligation to act that is absolute and without exceptions or conditions.

Causal organization: A pattern of organization that tries to identify causes of problems.

Charisma: Personal magnetism that enables an individual to attract and influence people.

Chronemics: The study of how human beings communicate through their use of time.

Chronological organization: An organizational pattern that follows an idea through time.

Climax order: A way of ordering main points in a speech that builds from weaker arguments to the strongest.

Closed question: A form of question requiring a short answer such as a yes or no.

Co-culture: A group or culture within the larger culture that will often share a specialized language system, values, a collective worldview, and common communication patterns.

Coercive power: A type of power in which threat or coercion is used.

Cohesiveness: The total field of forces acting on members to remain in a group.

Collectivism: The tendency of people in a given culture to value group identity over individual identity, group objectives over individual rights, and group-oriented concerns over individual wants and desires.

Commitment: The resolve to continue in a relationship indefinitely and to make the efforts necessary to ensure that it will continue.

Communication: The process of creating a meaning between two or more people.

Communication climate: The social-psychological context of a relationship.

Communication context: The situation in which communication occurs (interpersonal, intercultural, interviewing, small group, public, organizational, and mass).

Competition: Where one party tries to use aggression or power to beat the other party in a conflict situation.

Concentration: A person's ability to focus his or her mental faculties.

Conclusion: The closing part of a speech.

Confirmation: Any behavior that causes another person to value herself or himself more.

Conflict: An expressed struggle between at least two interdependent parties each of whom perceives incompatible goals, scarce rewards, and interference from the other in attempts to achieve goals.

Connotation: The secondary associations a word has for one or more members of a linguistic community.

Consensus: Agreement among all members of a group concerning a given decision.

Consideration function: A role intended to build the rapport with other group members.

Context: The setting and social-psychological climate within which communication takes place.

Contrast effect: Trying to make a point by contrasting it with something very different.

Convergence: The merging or "coming together of computing, telecommunications, and media in a digital environment."

Cookies: Small files that Web sites place within the computers of visitors to track their preferences.

Cooptation: A way to get people to accept an idea by getting them involved.

Cosmopolitanism: The philosophy that our two governing principles should be universal concern for others and respect for legitimate differences.

Critical listening: Being able to detect flaws in a speaker's arguments.

Cross-examination: Using too many questions in a row resulting in the person feeling uncomfortable.

Cultural frame of reference: A person's point of view based on his or her cultural background.

Cultural homogenization: The view that there is a tendency for cultures in contact with one another to become increasingly similar.

Culture: A way of life developed and shared by a group of people and passed down from generation to generation.

Defensive climate: Evaluative or judgmental atmosphere established through communication that arouses behaviors used to protect ourselves from what we perceive to be a threat.

Defensive projection: Seeing our own undesirable qualities in other people.

Defensiveness: Behavior that results from perceiving or anticipating a threat by a person or group.

Denial: A negotiation tactic in which one party does not admit to an earlier agreement.

Denotation: The primary associations a word has for most members of a given linguistic community.

Diffusion of information: The dissemination of news or information through communication channels to a community of receivers.

Disconfirmation: Any behavior that causes another person to value herself or himself less, behavior rejecting both who the person is and what the person has to say.

Discriminative listening: Understanding and remembering a speaker's points.

Downward communication: Communication initiated by an organization's upper management, which then filters downward through the chain of command.

Dyadic effect: Eliciting a reciprocal level of openness from another person by disclosing something of oneself.

Empathic listening: Being able to demonstrate empathy for the speaker.

Empathy: Experiencing the other person's perception—that is, seeing and feeling things as the other person does.

Ethical protonorms: Underlying presuppositions that function as core values.

Ethics: The study of the general nature of morals and of the specific moral choices to be made by a person.

Ethnocentrism: The tendency to judge the values, customs, behaviors, or other aspects of another culture in terms of those that our own cultural group regards as desirable or ideal.

Example: A method of supporting material using a case or instance to illustrate a point.

Expert power: A type of power in which knowledge is used to influence someone.

Expressiveness: A dimension of nonverbal communication linked with animation, dynamism, expansiveness, and intensity.

Extemporaneous speaking: A mode of speech delivery in which minimal notes are used and that combines the advantages of careful speech outlining and planning with the spontaneity of impromptu speaking.

Extrinsic credibility: The credibility that a source is thought to have prior to the time when he or she delivers a message.

Family: Networks of people who share their lives over long periods of time; who are bound by ties of marriage, blood, or commitment, legal or otherwise; who consider themselves as family; and who share future expectations of connected relationship.

Feedback: The return of behavior you have generated.

Forming: The first stage of a group's development.

Forming of coalitions: Joining forces with others.

Framing: The use of a broad organizing theme to select, emphasize, and link the elements of a news story.

Funnel sequence: A method of interviewing in which an interviewer begins with broad questions and gradually proceeds to more specific questions.

Gatekeeper: A person who, by selecting, changing, and/or rejecting messages, can influence the flow of information to a receiver or group of receivers.

Gender: An aspect of self-concept shaped in part by culture and including one's "biological sex (male or female), psychological characteristics (femininity, masculinity, androgyny), attitudes about the sexes, and sexual orientation."

Golden mean: The Greek philosopher Aristotle's principle that morality is to be found in moderation and moral virtues are viewed as choices or modes of choice. Each virtue is seen as the middle path between the extremes of excess and deficiency.

Handclasping (pairing): A coalition between minority members of a group, formed for the purpose of helping one another to achieve mutually advantageous goals.

Haptics: The study of how we use touch to communicate.

Hasty generalization: Jumping to a conclusion on the basis of very limited information.

Hearing problems: Problems in the physiological process of receiving aural stimuli.

High-contact culture: A culture in which people touch each other more often, sit or stand closer to each other, make more eye contact, and speak louder than they do in low-contact cultures.

High-context culture: A culture whose members tend to be more skilled in reading nonverbal behaviors and to be more indirect and less explicit than members of low-context cultures.

Horizontal communication: Communication across the same level of an organization.

Humor: Using surprise with a funny ending to make a speech more interesting.

Hypodermic needle model: A view of communication in which each audience member receives messages directly from the source of a given medium.

Impromptu delivery: A mode of delivery requiring no advance planning.

Individualism: The tendency of people in a given culture to value individual identity over group identity, individual rights over group objectives, and personal needs and desires over those of the group.

Ineffective listening: When a receiver fails to understand or comprehend a speaker's message.

Ingratiation: A method of influencing others by complimenting them.

Inoculation theory: A theory that offers the listener a small exposure to an idea so that they will accept a stronger exposure later.

Input: All the stimuli, both past and present, that give us our information about the world.

Intensity: A measure of the power of words.

Interference: A general term used to describe anything that interferes with the communication process.

Intergroup conflict: Conflict between groups.

Intergroup contact theory: The theory that given certain conditions including equal status, shared goals, and group cooperation, sustained contact between noncompeting groups will result in decreased prejudice.

Interpersonal conflict: Conflict between individuals.

Interpersonal distance: Four distance zones within which different human interactions occur: intimate, personal, social, and public distance.

Interpersonal sensitivity: Success in decoding nonverbal communication.

Interpretation: Trying to guess the other person's reasons for how he or she feels.

Interrole conflict: Conflict that is likely to be experienced when a person occupies two (or more) roles that entail contradictory expectations about a given behavior.

Intragroup conflict: Conflict within a group.

Intrapersonal conflict: Conflict within an individual.

Intrarole conflict: Conflict experienced because of contradictory expectations concerning a single role.

Intrinsic credibility: A speaker's credibility or reputation as a direct result of his or her speech.

Introduction: The first part of a speech.

Johari window: A model for conceptualizing levels of awareness and self-disclosure in human communication: a way of looking at the interdependence of intrapersonal and interpersonal affairs.

Kinesic slips: Contradictory verbal and nonverbal messages.

Kinesics: The study of body movements (including the head and face) in communication.

Law of diminishing returns: The effectiveness of messages increases with the frequency up to a point and then diminishes.

Leading question: Suggesting the desired answer to the question.

Leak: A method of communicating information in which previously unknown information is made known to others, but its source remains anonymous to the general public.

Leakage: Signals of deception.

Learning or education group: A group primarily intended to be used as a vehicle to educate its members.

Legitimate power: A type of power based on a person's job position (i.e., the boss).

Leveling: The part of rumors in which details are left out.

Lie: An intentionally deceptive message that is stated.

Loaded question: Stacking the deck by implying the correct answer to the question.

Looking glass self: A sense of self that develops out of our relations and interactions with others; evaluating ourselves on the basis of how we think others perceive and evaluate us.

Low-contact culture: A culture in which people touch each other less often, maintain more interpersonal distance, make less eye contact, and speak in a lower, softer tone of voice.

Low-context culture: A culture whose members tend to emphasize verbal messages and stress direct and explicit communication.

Majority vote: A method of decision making in which the decision is determined by a simple majority of votes.

Master norm: One of a group of core ethical values; each norm takes different forms in different countries.

Materials of support: Methods of developing a point that make the point more interesting, understandable, and/or persuasive.

Memorized speech: A mode of delivery in which the speaker commits the entire speech to memory.

Memory structure approach: The view that our expectations are influenced by past experiences, what we have seen in the media, observations of others, and what we imagine and fantasize.

Message variables: Factors that a speaker can change to make a speech more effective.

Messages: Any type of verbal or nonverbal, conscious or unconscious communication.

Metacommunication: Communication about communication.

Metaphor: A comparison between two or more things or ideas.

Mindset: A set of beliefs and attitudes that influence an individual's behavior. For example, a person with a positive mindset tends to work hard and that tends to lead to success. But, a person with a negative mindset will often not give their best effort, which tends to lead to failure.

Mode of delivery: One of four methods for delivering a speech (impromptu, reading from manuscript, memorized, and extemporaneous).

Monochronic culture: A culture in which time is compartmentalized, viewed as segmented and linear. Emphasis is on tasks and agendas—doing one thing at a time.

Moral courage: The courage to be moral, involving three interrelated elements: commitment to one's moral principles, awareness of danger in supporting them, and willingness to endure the danger.

Narrowcasting: Programming designed to target a specific segment of the media audience.

Neutral question: Asking a question that does not suggest the desired answer.

Noise: A general term used to describe anything that interferes with the communication process.

Nonverbal message: All the messages we convey, whether intentionally or unintentionally, without words or over and above the words we use.

Norming: The third phase in a group's development.

Norms: Rules, whether explicit or implicit, about behavior.

Objectics: The study of how we select and make use of physical objects in our nonverbal communication.

Oculesics: The study of the role of eye behaviors, including eye contact, eye movements, and pupil dilation in communicating.

Open question: Resembles an essay question on a test. It places no restrictions on the length of the answer.

Opinion leaders: People who have a particularly strong influence on others in forming opinions and making decisions.

Organizational communication: All communication that is associated with an organizations such as, but not limited to, businesses, health care facilities, universities, churches, government, and the military.

Orientation: The angle of your body as you interact with another person.

Overload: Having to attend to too many stimuli.

Paralinguistics: The study of vocal phenomena beyond or in addition to language itself: voice qualities (such as pitch and resonance) and vocalizations (noises without linguistic structure such as sighs and groans).

Paraphrasing: Using your own words to express or restate someone else's words or ideas. Also an interview technique that restates the content as well as the emotions of the other person's answer.

Perceived reciprocity of liking: Feeling that people you like, like you.

Perceptual filters: Physiological limitations that are built into human beings and cannot be reversed.

Performing: The fourth phase in a group's development.

Personal space: A person's portable territory, which each individual carries along wherever he or she may go.

Persuasibility: A person's level of receptivity toward being persuaded.

Plagiarism: Using or presenting as your own the ideas, images, or words of another source—for example, from books or online information—without acknowledgment or permission.

Plain folks: A propaganda technique of using testimony to falsely appear like the listener.

Pleasurable listening: Listening for social enjoyment.

Polychronic: A culture in which time is seen as flexible and many things are done simultaneously. There is more emphasis on commitment to human relationships than on keeping to schedules.

Postponement: Putting off an agreement in a negotiation.

Power: The capacity to influence the behavior of others and to resist their influence on oneself.

Power distance: The degree to which people accept authority and hierarchical organizations as a natural part of their culture.

Presumptive attribution: Making statements that attribute to another person's feelings, thoughts, or motives that he or she does not acknowledge.

Primacy effect: In impression formation, the belief that the first information we receive about a person is the most decisive in forming our impression.

Primary question: Questions that introduce a new topic in an interview.

Principled negotiation: An approach to negotiation in which an issue is decided on the basis of its merits rather than by taking positions and trying to get the other parties to change their positions; developed by Roger Fisher and his colleagues at Harvard University.

Private acceptance: A true measure of a person's level of commitment to an idea.

Private theory of personality: How we select and organize information about others on the basis of what behaviors we think go together.

Probe: A type of secondary question intended to follow up on earlier questions.

Problem-solving group: A group that is primarily intended to solve problems and make decisions.

Problem solution: An organizational pattern of a speech, going from the problem to the proposed solution.

Protonorm: A single universal principle that underpins all systematic ethics.

Proxemics: The study of how human beings use space to communicate nonverbally.

Proximity: Geographic closeness.

Psychological sets: Expectancies or predispositions to respond that have a profound effect on one's perception of objects.

Public compliance: Forcing a person to go along with the group. This may be quite different from his or her private acceptance.

Purpose-oriented audience analysis: A method for analyzing an audience that examines the information the audience most needs to know.

Qualification: A collaborative tactic to help resolve conflict, which involves disclosing one's own thoughts and feelings and soliciting disclosures from the other person.

Railroading: A style of group decision making in which one person may force the rest of the group to go along.

Rapid thought: Our brains can process words many times faster than the normal rate of speaking.

Reading from manuscript: A mode of delivery in which the speaker first prepares a word-for-word copy of the speech.

Reassurance: Attempting to make the other party feel comfortable.

Recency effect: An effect in which the most recent arguments are the strongest in influencing the listener's attitude.

Referent power: A type of personal power that has the ability to influence someone because of his or her desire to identify with the power source.

Relationship disengagement: The dissolution of a relationship.

Relationship maintenance: Behaviors by which people sustain close and satisfying relationships—whether routinely or strategically.

Remembering: Retaining points a speaker has made.

Reward power: A type of power in which rewards or incentives are used to gain cooperation.

Risky shift phenomenon: The tendency of people to increase their willingness to take risks as a result of group discussions.

Role: A set of norms that applies to a specific subclass within the society.

Sapir-Whorf hypothesis: A hypothesis that the world is perceived differently by members of different linguistic communities and that this perception is transmitted and sustained by language.

Secondary question: A follow-up to a primary question, intended to elicit elaboration from the interviewee.

Selective attention: The receiver processes certain of the available stimuli while filtering out others.

Selective exposure: The tendency to choose communication that will confirm your own opinions, attitudes, or values.

Selective use of objective criteria: When objective criteria are used only some of the time.

Self-concept: Your relatively stable impressions about yourself.

Self-directed work team: A form of work group that does not have a boss.

Self-disclosure: Intentionally making known information about oneself.

Self-esteem: Your feelings of self-worth.

Self-fulfilling prophecy: Expectation about another's behavior influences unwittingly leads to the predicted behavior.

Semantic focus: An attempt to avoid a conflict in which a person focuses on what is being said and then makes statements about what the words mean or how to characterize the ongoing conflict.

Semantic interference: Interference that occurs when a receiver does not attribute the same meaning to a signal that the sender does.

Setting: Physical environment.

Sexist language: Language reflecting a negative bias toward one gender.

Shadow page: A page established anonymously on a Web site to destroy the reputation of a person, group, or organization, or another Web site.

Shared meaning: Some correspondence between the message as perceived by the sender and the receiver.

Sharpening: A part of rumors in which details are exaggerated or distorted.

Shifting: Changing your requirements within the course of a negotiation.

Signal-to-noise ratio: A measure of interference that looks at the relationship between essential and extraneous information contained in a message.

Sleeper effect: An effect in which the source of a message is forgotten over time.

Social comparison theory: A theory based on the idea that each person decides what is true in relation to other people.

Spatial organization: An organizational pattern that is based on locations.

Standardized interview: A set of prepared questions from which an interviewer is not allowed to deviate.

Statistics: Numerical methods of describing events or ideas.

Status: The position of an individual in relation to another or others.

Stereotype: A generalization, based on limited experience, about a class of people, objects, or events that is widely held by members of a given culture.

Storming: The second phase of group development.

Supportive climate: Nonjudgmental atmosphere established through communication that conveys empathy and equality.

Synchrony: The sharing of rhythms between speakers, which helps to emphasize and organize meaning during conversation.

Task function: A role designed to help a group accomplish work.

Technical interference: Factors that cause a receiver to perceive distortion in the intended information or stimuli.

Telecommuting: Working at various locations outside the main office, often at home; telecommuters are usually connected to a main office by computer and high-speed modem.

Teleconferencing: Using audio and/or video links to hold a meeting with people who are in different, often distant, locations.

Testimony or quotations: A method of supporting materials in which the speaker quotes other sources.

Topical organization: A method of arranging a presentation in which a speaker moves from one topic to the next in a way that clearly demonstrates how the topics are related.

Touch avoidance: A negative attitude toward touch that also affects spatial distances between individuals and other types of nonverbal communication.

Transition: A verbal bridge connecting two parts of a speech.

Two-step flow model: A theory that information is passed from the various mass media to certain opinion leaders and from these leaders to other people within the population.

Uncertainty avoidance: A measure of the extent to which members of a culture attempt to avoid uncertainty or ambiguity about others.

Underresponsiveness: When the other party is not responding to your communication efforts.

Unstandardized interview: An interview that allows the interviewer as well as the respondent considerable latitude.

Upward communication: Communicating to those higher in the organization.

Upward receptivity: The willingness to receive messages from subordinates.

Utilitarianism: A doctrine that places primary value on the outcomes or consequences of our actions rather than our moral intentions.

Veil of ignorance: A principle of justice or fairness that insures protection of those whose position is weakest; according to this view, proposed by contemporary American philosopher John Rawls, what is moral is what is fair for all.

Verbal message: Any type of spoken communication that uses one or more words.

Whistleblowing: A member of a group makes a charge about the violation of ethical standards or norms within that group itself.

Work group: A type of group designed to accomplish a specific task.

REFERENCES

Chapter 1   The Process of Human Communication

Albom, Mitch. *Tuesdays with Morrie* (New York: Doubleday, 1997).

Barbaro, Michael. "Wal-Mart Enlists Bloggers in P.R. Campaign," *New York Times* (March 7, 2006).

Batista, E. "She's Gotta Have It: Cell Phone." *Wired News, 11.05* (May 16, 2003). Retrieved from *www.wired.com/news/culture/0,1284,58861,00.html.*

Begley, Sharon, and Fiona Gleizes. "My Granddad, Neanderthal?" *Newsweek* (October 16, 1989), 70–71.

Bishop, Todd. "Microsoft Files Patent for 'Immortal Computing,'" *Ann Arbor News* (January 23, 2007), D3.

Braud, Gerard. "What Does That Mean?" *Communication World* 24, no. 1 (January/February 2007).

Byrne, Zinta S., and Elaine LeMay. "Different Media for Organizational Communication: Perceptions of Quality and Satisfaction," *Journal of Business and Psychology* 21, no. 2 (Winter 2006).

Camp, Richaurd, Mary Vielhaber, and Jack L. Simonetti. *Strategic Interviewing: How to Hire Good People* (San Francisco: Jossey Bass, 2001).

Carr, Nicholas. "Lessons in Corporate Blogging," *BusinessWeek Online* (July 18, 2006).

Carr, Nicholas. *The Shallows: What the Internet Is Doing to Our Brains.* (New York: W. W. Norton, 2011).

Carville, James, and Paul Begala. *Buck Up, Suck Up . . . and Come Back When You Foul Up* (New York: Simon & Schuster, 2002).

Chin, Chen-Oi, John Gu, and Stewart L. Tubbs. "Developing Global Leadership Competencies," *The Journal of Leadership Studies* (Winter/Spring, 2001), 20–31.

Correia, A. C., and E. L. Menezes De Faria. "An Intranet Success Story," *Computers & Auditing* 61, no. 3 (2004), 32–34.

Dominick, Joseph. *The Dynamics of Mass Communication* (New York: McGraw-Hill, 2009).

Dvorak, Phred. "MBA Programs Hone 'Soft Skills,'" *The Wall Street Journal* (February 12, 2007), B3.

Finney, 2006.

Freud, Sigmund. *The Psychopathology of Everyday Life,* in A. A. Brill, ed. and trans., *The Basic Writings of Sigmund Freud* (New York: Modern Library, 1938).

Garrett, Wilbur E., ed. *National Geographic* 176 (October 1989), 560.

Glassman, Audrey. *Can I Fax a Thank-You Note?* (New York: Berkley Books, 1998).

Goldberg, Bernard. *Bias: A CBS Insider Exposes How the Media Distort the News.* (Washington, DC: Regnery Publishing, 2002).

Goulston, Mark. *Just Listen.* (New York: AMACOM, 2010).

Gudykunst, William B., and Young Yun Kim. *Communicating with Strangers,* 3rd ed. (New York: McGraw-Hill, 2002).

Haney, William V. *Communication and Interpersonal Relations,* 6th ed. (Homewood, IL: Irwin, 1992).

Harmon, Amy. "Internet Use Increases Depression, Loneliness," *Ann Arbor News* (August 30, 1998), A4.

Harris, Thomas, and Mark D. Nelson. *Applied Organizational Communication,* 3rd ed. (New York: Lawrence Erlbaum Associates, 2008).

Hotz, Robert Lee. "Decoding Our Chatter," *The Wall Street Journal* (October 1–2, 2011), C1–C2.

Huszczo, Gregory. *Making a Difference* (Mountain View, CA: Black-Davis, 2009). *Internet Movie Database,* 2008. Retrieved December 15, 2008, from *http://www.imdb.com/title/tt0386676/quotes.*

Imamoglu, Salih Zeki. "An Empirical Analysis Concerning the User Acceptance of E-Learning," *Journal of American Academy of Business* (Cambridge) 11, no. 1 (March 2007).

Kanaley, Reid. "Cell Phones Raise Privacy Concerns," *Detroit Free Press* (May 14, 2001), 8F.

Kaweevisultrakul, Tanin, and Peng Chan. "Impact of Cultural Barriers on Knowledge Management Implementation: Evidence from Thailand," *Journal of American Academy of Business* (Cambridge) 11, no. 1 (March 2007).

Kelley, Robert E. *How to Be a Star at Work* (New York: Times Books, 1998).

Knapp, Mark L., and Judith A. Hall. *Nonverbal Communication in Human Interaction,* 7th ed. (New York: Harcourt Brace, 2011).

Korn, Melissa. "As the World Turns, Wharton Adapts," *The Wall Street Journal* (February 3, 2011), B9.

LeDuc, Doug. "Teens Become Big Cell Phone Market," *Detroit Free Press* (May 14, 2001), 3F.

"Lessons from a Blackout," *New York Times* (April 12, 2004), A18.

Liker, Jeffrey, and James Franz. *The Toyota Way to Continuous Improvement.* (New York: McGraw-Hill, 2011).

Lorek, 1998.

Lucas, Stephen. *The Art of Public Speaking,* 10th ed. (New York: McGraw-Hill, 2008).

Middleton, Diana, and Joe Light. "Harvard Changes Course," *The Wall Street Journal* (February 3, 2011), B8.

Rath, Tom, and Jim Harter. *Wellbeing: The Five Essential Elements* (New York: Gallup Press, 2010).

Reynolds, Garr. *Presentation Zen* (Berkeley, CA: New Riders, 2008).

Rosenberg, Morris. *Conceiving the Self* (New York: Basic Books, 1979).

Schein, Edgar H. *Career Dynamics: Matching Individual and Organizational Needs* (Reading, MA: Addison-Wesley, 1978).

Schellenberger, Sue. "Dealing with the Dead Zone: Spouses Too Tired to Talk," *Wall Street Journal* (February 22, 2007), D1.

Sisoda, Raj, Jag Sheth and David Wolfe. *Firms of Endearment*. Upper Saddle River, NJ: Wharton School Publishing, 2007.

"Staffer of New Orleans Mayor Responds to Error in Press Release Regarding Carnival 2004," *New Orleans City Business* (Metairie, LA) (March 1, 2004), 1.

Stewart, John. *Bridges Not Walls,* 11th ed. (New York: McGraw-Hill, 2012).

Sultan, F., et al. "A Meta-Analysis of Applications of Diffusion Models," *Journal of Marketing Research* 27 (February 1990), 70–77.

Tubbs, Stewart L. *A Systems Approach to Small Group Interaction,* 11th ed. (New York: McGraw-Hill, 2012).

Turkle, Sherry. *Alone Together* (New York: Basic Books, 2011).

Valentis, J. "How 'Heart' Smart," *Lancaster (PA) Intelligencer Journal* (April 20, 2004), 1.

Vandermeer, Jim. "Seven Habits of Highly Successful Enterprise E-mail Managers," *EDPACS* (Reston) 34, no. 2 (August 2006).

"Wall Street Journal Examines New Hospital Communications Standards Examined to Prevent Medical Errors," *Medical News Today* (June 30, 2006). Retrieved from *http://wwwmedicalnewstoday.com/medicalnews.php?newsid=46175.*

Whetten, David A., and Kim S. Cameron. *Developing Management Skills,* 8th ed. (Upper Saddle River, NJ: Prentice-Hall, 2010).

Chapter 2   Person Perception

Achor, Shawn. *The Happiness Advantage: The Seven Principles of Positive Psychology That Fuel Success and Performance at Work* (New York: Crown Business, 2010).

Adelmann, Pamela. "Possibly Yours," *Psychology Today* 22 (April 1988), 8, 10.

Asch, S. E. "Forming Impressions of Personality," *Journal of Abnormal and Social Psychology* 41 (1946), 258–290.

Asch, Solomon E., and M. Zukier. "Thinking about Persons," *Journal of Personality and Social Psychology* 46 (1984), 1230–1240.

Baron-Cohen, Simon. *The Essential Difference* (New York: Basic Books, 2003).

Beall, Anne E., Alice H. Eagly, and Robert J. Sternberg. "Introduction," in Alice H. Eagly, Anne E. Beall, and Robert J. Sternberg, eds., *The Psychology of Gender,* 2nd ed. (New York: Guilford Press, 2004), 1–8.

Berscheid, Ellen, and Harry T. Reis. "Attraction and Close Relationships," in Daniel Gilbert, Susan Fiske, and Gardner Lindzey, eds., *Handbook of Social Psychology,* 4th ed., vol. 2 (New York: McGraw-Hill, 1998), 193–281.

Best, Deborah L., and Jennifer J. Thomas. "Cultural Diversity and Cross-Cultural Perspectives," in Alice H. Eagly, Anne E. Beall, and Robert J. Sternberg, eds., *The Psychology of Gender,* 2nd ed. (New York: Guilford Press, 2004), 296–327.

Boone, R. Thomas, and Ross Buck. "Emotional Expressivity and Trustworthiness: The Role of Nonverbal Behavior in the Evolution of Cooperation," *Journal of Nonverbal Behavior* 27 (Fall 2003), 163–182.

Brooks, David. *The Social Animal: The Hidden Sources of Love, Character and Achievement* (New York: Random House, 2011).

Bruner, Jerome. *Actual Minds, Possible Worlds* (Cambridge, MA: Harvard University Press, 1986).

Bussey, Kay, and Albert Bandura. "Social Cognitive Theory of Gender Development and Functioning," in Alice H. Eagly, Anne E. Beall, and Robert J. Sternberg, eds., *The Psychology of Gender,* 2nd ed. (New York: Guilford Press, 2004), 92–199.

Cherlin, Andrew J. "By the Numbers," *New York Times Magazine* (April 5, 1998), 391.

Christiansen, Neil D., Shaina Wolcott-Burnam, Jay E. Janovics, Gary N. Burns, and Stuart W. Quirk. "The Good Judge Revisited," *Human Performance* 18, no. 2 (2005), 123–149.

Davis, Mark H., and Linda A. Kraus. "Personality and Empathic Accuracy," in William Ickes, ed., *Empathic Accuracy* (New York: Guilford Press, 1997), 144–168.

Deaux, Kay, and Marianne LaFrance. "Gender," in Daniel Gilbert, Susan Fiske, and Gardner Lindzey, eds., *Handbook of Social Psychology,* 4th ed., vol. 1 (New York: McGraw-Hill, 1998), 788–827.

DePaulo, Bella M., and Howard Friedman. "Nonverbal Communication," in Daniel Gilbert, Susan Fiske, and Gardner Lindzey, eds., *Handbook of Social Psychology,* 4th ed., vol. 2 (New York: McGraw-Hill, 1998), 3–40.

Dion, Karen. "Cultural Perspectives on Facial Attractiveness," in Gillian Rhodes and Leslie A. Zebrowitz, eds., *Facial Attractiveness: Evolutionary, Cognitive, and Social Perspectives* (Westport, CT: Ablex, 2002), 239–260.

Eagleman, David. *Incognito: The Secret Lives of the Brain* (New York: Pantheon Books, 2011).

Fletcher, Garth J. O., Jacqueline M. Tither, Claire O'Loughlin, Myron Friesen, and Nickola Overall. "Warm and Homely or Cold and Beautiful? Sex Differences in Trading Off Traits in Mate Selection," *Personality and Social Psychology Bulletin* 30 (June 2004), 659–672.

Gardner, Wendi L., and Shira Gabriel. "Gender Differences in Relational and Collective Interdependence," in Alice H. Eagly, Anne E. Beall, and Robert J. Sternberg, eds., *The Psychology of Gender,* 2nd ed. (New York: Guilford Press, 2004), 169–191.

Graham, Tiffany, and William Ickes. "When Women's Intuition Isn't Greater Than Men's," in William Ickes, ed., *Empathic Accuracy* (New York: Guilford Press, 1997), 117–143.

Guerrero, Laura, and Kory Floyd. *Nonverbal Communication in Close Relationships* (Mahwah, NJ: Erlbaum, 2006).

Gustafson, Robert, Mark Popovich, and Steven Thomsen, "Subtle Ad Images Threaten Girls More," *Marketing News,* 35 (June 4, 2001), 12–13.

Hall, Judith A. "Women's and Men's Nonverbal Communication," in Anita Vangelisti and Daniel Perlman, eds., *Cambridge Handbook of Personal Relationships* (New York: Cambridge University Press, 2006), 201–218.

Hall, Judith A., Nora Murphy, and Marianne Mast. "Recall of Nonverbal Cues: Exploring a Definition of Interpersonal Sensitivity," *Journal of Nonverbal Behavior* 30 (Winter 2006), 141–155.

Harper, Marcel, and Wilhelm J. Schoeman. "Influences of Gender as a Basic-Level Category in Person Perception on the Gender Belief System," *Sex Roles* 49, no. 9/10 (2003), 517–526.

Hiller, D., and W. Philliber. "Predicting Marital and Career Success among Dual-Working Couples," *Journal of Marriage and Family* 44 (1982), 53–62.

Hinde, Robert A., Catrin Finkenauer, and Ann Elisabeth Auhagen. "Relationships and the Self-Concept," *Personal Relationships* 8 (2001), 187–204.

Honeycutt, James M., and James G. Cantrill. *Cognition, Communication, and Romantic Relationships* (Mahwah, NJ: Lawrence Erlbaum, 2001).

Hopkins, Christopher. *Staging Your Comeback: A Complete Beauty Revival for Women Over 45* (Deerfield Beach, FL: Health Communications Inc., 2008).

Ivy, Diana K., and Phil Backlund. *Genderspeak: Personal Effectiveness in Gender Communication,* 3rd ed. (New York: McGraw-Hill, 2004).

Jacobson, 1999.

James, William. *Principles of Psychology,* vol. I (New York: Dover, 1950).

Jones, Melinda. "Stereotyping Hispanics and Whites: Perceived Differences in Social Roles as a Determinant of Ethnic Stereotypes," *Journal of Social Psychology* 131 (1991), 469–475.

Joshi, Mohit. "Feeling of Prejudice May Be Part of a Self-fulfilling Prophecy," *www.newslocale.org* (June 10, 2008).

Kanagawa, Chie, Susan E. Cross, and Hazel Rose Markus. "Who Am I? The Cultural Psychology of the Conceptual Self," *Personality and Social Psychology Bulletin* 27 (2001), 90–103.

Keating, Caroline F. "Charismatic Faces: Social Status Cues Put Face Appeal in Context," in Gillian Rhodes and Leslie A. Zebrowitz, eds., *Facial Attractiveness: Evolutionary, Cognitive, and Social Perspectives* (Westport, CT: Ablex, 2002), 153–192.

LaFrance, M., and C. Mayo. "A Review of Nonverbal Behaviors of Women and Men," *Western Journal of Speech Communication* 43 (1979), 76–95.

Lombarde, Michael. "Conservatives, Liberals Come to Defense of Michele Bachmann's *Newsweek* Cover," e-Tidbits (August, 2011).

Luchins, A. S. "Primacy-Recency in Impression Formation," in Carl I. Hovland et al., eds., *The Order of Presentation in Persuasion,* vol. I (New Haven, CT: Yale University Press, 1957), 33–61.

Madon, Stephanie, Jennifer Willard, Max Guyll, Linda Trudeau, and Richard Spoth. "Self-Fulfilling Prophecy Effects of Mothers' Beliefs on Children's Alcohol Use," *Journal of Personality and Social Psychology* 90 (June 2006), 911–926.

Maner, Jon K., Douglas T. Kenrick, D. Vaughn Becker, Andrew W. Delton, et al. "Sexually Selective Cognition: Beauty Captures the Mind of the Beholder," *Journal of Personality and Social Psychology* 85 (December 2003), 1107–1120.

Mast, Marianne Schmid, and Judith A. Hall. "Women's Advantage at Remembering Others' Appearance," *Personality and Social Psychology Bulletin* 32 (March 2006), 353–364.

McCroskey, J. C., and V. P. Richmond. "Power in the Classroom I: Teacher and Student Perceptions," *Communication Education* 32 (1983), 175–184.

Noller, Patricia. "Nonverbal Communication in Close Relationships," in Anita Vangelisti and Daniel Perlman, eds., *Cambridge Handbook of Personal Relationships* (New York: Cambridge University Press, 2006), 403–420.

Pearson, 1995.

Random House Webster's College Dictionary (New York: Random House, 2000), 223.

Reed, James, and Paul G. Stoltz. *Put Your Mindset to Work* (New York: Portfolio/Penguin, 2011).

Rimm, Sylvia. *See Jane Win: The Rimm Report on How 1,000 Girls Became Successful Women* (New York: Crown, 1999).

Riniolo, Todd C., Katherine C. Johnson, Tracy R. Sherman, and Julie A. Misso. "Hot or Not: Do Professors Perceived as Physically Attractive Receive Higher Student Evaluations?" *Journal of General Psychology* 133 (January 2006), 19–35.

Rosenthal, Robert, and B. M. DePaulo. "Expectancies, Discrepancies, and Courtesies in Nonverbal Communication," *Western Journal of Speech Communication* 43 (1979), 76–95.

Rosenthal, Robert, and Leonore Jacobson. *Pygmalion in the Classroom,* newly expanded ed. (New York: Irvington, 1992).

Sargent, Michael J., and Amy L. Bradfield. "Race and Information Processing in Criminal Trials," *Personality and Social Psychology Bulletin* 30 (August 2004), 995–1008.

Seligman, Martin. *Flourish: A Visionary New Understanding of Happiness and Well-Being* (New York: Free Press, 2011).

Shorter Oxford English Dictionary on Historical Principles, 5th ed., vol. 1 (Oxford, UK: Oxford University Press, 2002), 382.

Srivastava, Sanjay, Kelly M. McGonagal, Jane M. Richards, Emily A. Butler, and James J. Gross. "Optimism in Close Relationships," *Journal of Personality and Social Psychology* 91 (July 2006), 143–153.

Sternberg, Robert J., and John Kolligian, Jr., eds. *Competence Considered* (New Haven, CT: Yale University Press, 1990).

Sunnafrank, Michael, and Artemio Ramirez Jr. "At First Sight: Persistent Relational Effects of Get-Acquainted Conversations," *Journal of Social and Personal Relationships* 21, no. 3 (2004), 361–379.

Surawski, Melissa K., and Elizabeth P. Ossoff. "The Effects of Physical and Vocal Attractiveness on Impression Formation of Politicians," *Current Psychology* 25 (Spring 2006), 15–27.

Ting-Toomey, Stella. *Communicating Across Cultures* (New York: Guilford Press, 1999).

Todorov, Alexander, Anesu N. Mandisodza, Amir Goren, and Crystal C. Hall. "Inferences of Competence from Faces Predict Election Outcomes," *Science* 308 (2005), 1623–1626.

Trenholm, S., and T. Rose. "The Complaint Communicator: Teacher Perceptions of Appropriate Classroom Behavior," *Western Journal of Speech Communication* 45 (1981), 13–26.

Veenendall, Tom, and Rita Braito. "Androgeny in Spouse Interaction," in Lea P. Stewart and Stella Ting-Toomey, eds., *Communication, Gender, and Sex Roles in Diverse Interaction Contexts* (Norwood, NJ: Ablex, 1987), 31–48.

Willis, Janine, and Alexander Todorov. "First Impressions: Making Up Your Mind After a 100-Ms Exposure to a Face," *Psychological Science* 17 (July 2006), 592–598.

Zebrowitz, 1997.

Zebrowitz, Leslie A., and Gillian Rhodes. "Nature Let a Hundred Flowers Bloom," in Gillian Rhodes and Leslie A. Zebrowitz, eds., *Facial Attractiveness* (Westport, CT: Ablex, 2002), 261–293.

Zimbardo, P. "Psychological Power and Pathology of Imprisonment," unpublished manuscript, Stanford University, Palo Alto, CA, 1971.

———. *Shyness* (Reading, MA: Addison-Wesley, 1990).

Chapter 3   The Verbal Message

Adams, Scott. *Dilbert.* Retrieved January 16, 2007, from *www.unitedmedia.com/comics/dilbert/.*

Applebome, Peter. "The Birth of a Novel: Up North, Down South," *New York Times* (May 19, 1998), E1.

Becker, Carl. "Reasons for the Lack of Argumentation and Debate in the Far East," in Larry A. Samovar and Richard Porter, eds., *Intercultural Communication: A Reader,* 6th ed. (Belmont, CA: Wadsworth, 1991), 234–243.

Bell, Robert A., Nancy L. Buerkel-Rothfuss, and Kevin E. Gore. "Did You Bring the Yarmulke for the Cabbage Patch Kid?" *Human Communication Research* 14 (1987), 47–67.

Berryman, C. L., and L. R. Wilcox. "Attitudes toward Male and Female Speech: Experiments on the Effects of Sex-Typed Language," *Western Journal of Speech Communication* 44 (1980), 50–59.

Bradac, J. J., M. R. Hemphill, and C. H. Tardy. "Language Style on Trial: The Effects of 'Powerful' and 'Powerless' Speech upon Judgments of Victims and Villains," *Western Journal of Speech Communication* 45 (1981), 327–341.

Bradac, J. J., and A. Mulac. "A Molecular View of Powerful and Powerless Speech Styles," *Communication Monographs* 51 (1984), 307–319.

Brown, Roger, and Eric Lenneberg. "A Study in Language and Cognition," *Journal of Abnormal and Social Psychology* 49 (1954), 454–462.

Burgoon, M., J. P. Dillard, and N. E. Doran. "Friendly or Unfriendly Persuasion: The Effects of Violations of Expectations by Males and Females," *Human Communication Research* 10 (1983), 283–294.

Cameron, Deborah, ed. *The Feminist Critique of Language* (London: Routledge, 1990).

Candlish, S. "Private Language," *The Stanford Encyclopedia of Philosophy,* 2004.

Carlic, Steve. "You Can Book It: Webster's Adds 100 Words," Central New York News, Syracuse.com (July 7, 2008). Retrieved December 15, 2008, from *http://www.syracuse.com/news/index.ssf/2008/07/.*

Chandler, T. "The Laureate's Choice—Re-seeing and Re-thinking the Familiar," *Providence Journal* (February 24, 2002), p. I9.

Condor, Bob. "Prunes Get an Image Makeover," *Detroit Free Press* (February 6, 2001).

Crane, Loren, Richard Dieker, and Charles Brown. "The Physiological Response to the Communication Modes: Reading, Listening, Writing, Speaking, and Evaluating," *Journal of Communication* 20 (1970), 231–240.

Daly, John. *Advocacy: Championing Ideas and Influencing Others* (New Haven, CT: Yale University Press, 2011).

Davis, Hayley. "What Makes Bad Language Bad?" *Language and Communication* 9, no. 23 (1989), 1–9.

Friedlander, John. "Abstract, Concrete, General and Specific Terms." Retrieved January 20, 2007, from *http://faculty.southwest.tn.edu/jfriedlander/abstract_and_concrete.htm.*

Galvin, Kathleen M., and Bernard J. Brommel. *Family Communication: Cohesion and Change* (New York: HarperCollins, 1991).

Gordon, Peter. "Numerical Cognition Without Words: Evidence from Amazonia," *Science* 306, no. 5695 (October 15, 2004), 496–499.

Griffin, Em. *A First Look at Communication Theory,* 7th ed. (New York: McGraw-Hill, 2009).

Hamilton, William L. "Low Down, Repulsed, Yet Watching All the Same," *New York Times* [Electronic version] (December 6, 2006), section 4, 5.

Haney, William V. *Communication and Organizational Behavior* (Homewood, IL: Irwin, 1992).

Haslett, B. J. *Communication: Strategic Action in Context* (Hillsdale, NJ: Erlbaum, 1987).

Hayakawa, S. I. *Language in Thought and Action,* 4th ed. (Orlando, FL: Harcourt Brace Jovanovich, 1978).

Heilbrun, A. B. "Measurement of Masculine and Feminine Sex-Role Identities as Independent Dimensions," *Journal of Consulting and Clinical Pathology* 44 (1976), 183–190.

Hood, James. "AT&T Plans to Kill Cingular Name," *ConsumerAffairs.com* (May 4, 2006).

Kirkwood, William G. "Truthfulness as a Standard for Speech in Ancient India," *Southern Communication Journal* 54 (1989), 213–234.

Lavoie, Denise. "Case Seeks Redefinition of 'Mother.'" *Ann Arbor News* (August 31, 2001), A7.

Legum, Colin. "The End of Cloud-Cuckoo-Land," *New York Times Magazine* (March 28, 1976), 63–64.

Lei, Xiaolan. "Sexism in Language," *Journal of Language and Linguistics* 5, no. 1 (2006).

Lewis, Michael. *Boomerang: Travels in the New Third World* (New York: W. W. Norton, 2011).

Liska, J., E. W. Mechling, and S. Stathas. "Differences in Subjects' Perceptions and Believability between Users of Deferential and Nondeferential Language," *Communication Quarterly* 29 (1981), 40–48.

Luntz, Frank. *Win* (New York: Hyperion, 2011).

Luntz, Frank. *Words That Work* (New York: Hyperion, 2007).

Martin, Judith, and Thomas Nakayama. *Experiencing Intercultural Communication,* 3rd ed. (New York: McGraw-Hill, 2008).

McGready, Lynne. "Call Me Fisher or Postie," *The Star* Online. (August 14, 2008). Retrieved December 15, 2008, from *http://thestar.com.my/english/story.asp?file=/2008/8/14/lifefocus/1634232&sec=lifefocus.*

Ministry of Education. "Exploring Language Online," *Learning Media Limited* (1996). Ministry of Education, Wellington, NZ.

Motluk, Alison. "You Are What You Speak," *New Scientist* 176, no. 2371 (2002), 34.

NetLingo. *http://www.netlingo.com,* accessed July 2007.

Osgood, Charles, George Suci, and Percy Tannenbaum. *The Measurement of Meaning* (Urbana, IL: University of Illinois Press, 1957), chaps. 1–4.

Pearson, Judy Cornelia, Lynn H. Turner, and William Todd-Mancillas. *Gender and Communication,* 2nd ed. (Dubuque, IA: William C. Brown, 1991).

Pennebaker, James. *The Secret Life of Pronouns* (New York: Bloomsbury Press, 2011).

Quina, Kathryn, Joseph A. Wingard, and Henry G. Bates. "Language Style and Gender Stereotypes in Person Perception," *Psychology of Women Quarterly* 11 (1987), 111–122.

Reuters News Agency "Gossip," *Detroit Free Press* (September 4, 2001), 5A.

Ruben, 2007.

Salant, Jonathon D. "FCC: Don't Use the F-word," *Ann Arbor News* (March 19, 2004), C1.

"Sapir-Whorf-Hypothesis Redux." *ETC: A Review of General Semantics* (Concord) 59 (Winter 2002/2003), 456–457.

Sapolsky, Barry S., and Barbara K. Kaye. "The Use of Offensive Language by Men and Women in Prime Time Television Entertainment," *Atlantic Journal of Communication* (February 2008), vol. 13, issue 4, 292–303.

Sillars, Alan L., and Judith Weisberg. "Conflict as a Social Skill," in Michael E. Roloff and Gerald R. Miller, eds., *Interpersonal Processes: New Directions in Communication Research* (Newbury Park, CA: Sage, 1987), 140–171.

Stewart, John. *Bridges Not Walls,* 11th ed. (New York: McGraw-Hill, 2012).

Tan, Amy. "Mother Tongue," in Joyce Carol Oates, ed., *The Best American Essays 1991* (New York: Ticknor and Fields, 1991).

Tannen, Deborah. *You Just Don't Understand: Women and Men in Conversation* (New York: Ballantine Books, 1990).

Tubbs, Stewart L. *A Systems Approach to Small Group Interaction,* 9th ed. (New York: McGraw-Hill, 2012).

Urban Dictionary. *http://www.urbandictionary.com,* accessed July 2007.

Wain, M. "African Wildlife Photography: Communication Components." Retrieved on May 19, 2004, from M. Wain Web site: *www.mcdcwain.freeserve.co.uk/behaviour7.htm.*

Wikipedia, 2011.

Whorf, Benjamin Lee. *Language, Thought, and Reality,* ed. John B. Carroll (Cambridge, MA: MIT Press, 1956).

"Words Can Heal." Retrieved May 21, 2004, from *Words Can Heal* Web site: *www.wordscanheal.com/aboutus/whosinvolved.htm#Advisors.*

www.generalsemantics.org, 2009.

Chapter 4   The Nonverbal Message

Alvarez, Julia. *In the Time of the Butterflies* (Chapel Hill, NC: Algonquin Books, 1994).

Andersen, Peter. *Nonverbal Communication: Forms and Functions* (Mountain View, CA: Mayfield, 1999).

Andersen, Peter, and Laura Guerrero, eds. *Handbook of Communication and Emotion* (San Diego, CA: Academic Press, 1998).

Anderson, P. A., and K. K. Sull. "Out of Touch, Out of Reach: Tactile Predispositions as Predictors of Interpersonal Distance," *Western Journal of Speech Communication* 49 (1985), 57–72.

Argyle, Michael. *The Psychology of Interpersonal Behavior*, rev. ed. (Baltimore: MD, Penguin, 1985).

Barnlund, Dean C. *Interpersonal Communication: Survey and Studies* (Boston, MA: Houghton Mifflin, 1968).

Baron-Cohen, Simon. *The Essential Difference: The Truth About the Male and Female Brain* (New York: Basic Books, 2003).

Bates, Brian, with John Cleese. *The Human Face* (London: BBC, 2001).

Birdwhistell, Ray L. *Introduction to Kinesics* (Louisville, KY: University of Louisville Press, 1952).

———. *Kinesics in Context* (Philadelphia, PA: University of Pennsylvania Press, 1970).

Bodenhausen, Galen V., and C. Neil Macrae. "Putting a Face on Person Perception," *Social Cognition* 24, no. 5 (2006), 511–515.

Burgoon, Judee K., David B. Buller, and W. Gill Woodall. *Nonverbal Communication: The Unspoken Dialogue* (New York: McGraw-Hill, 1996).

Caso, Letizia, Fridanna Marricciolo, Marino Bonaiuto, Aldert Vrij, and Samantha Mann. "The Impact of Deception and Suspicion on Different Hand Movements," *Journal of Nonverbal Behavior* 30 (March 2006), 1–19.

Chang, Eileen. "Red Rose, White Rose," in Eileen Chang, *Love in a Fallen City*, Karen S. Kingsbury, trans. (New York: New York Review of Books, 2007).

Dibiase, Rosemarie, and Jaime Gunnoe. "Gender and Culture Differences in Touching Behavior," *Journal of Social Psychology* 144, no. 1 (2004), 49–62.

Doherty, R. William. "The Emotional Contagion Scale: A Measure of Individual Differences," *Journal of Nonverbal Behavior* 21 (Summer 1997), 131–154.

Ekman, Paul, and Wallace V. Friesen. "Constants across Cultures in the Face and Emotion," *Journal of Personality and Social Psychology* 17 (1971), 124–129.

———. *Unmasking the Face: A Guide to Recognizing Emotions from Facial Cues*, 2nd ed. (Palo Alto, CA: Consulting Psychologists Press, 1984).

Ekman, Paul, and Maureen Sullivan. "Who Can Catch a Liar?" *American Psychologist* 46 (1991), 913–920.

Elfenbein, Hillary Anger. "Learning in Emotion Judgments Training and the Cross-Cultural Understanding of Facial Expressions," *Journal of Nonverbal Behavior* 30 (Spring 2006), 21–36.

Forgas, Joseph P. "The Role of Physical Attractiveness in the Interpretation of Facial Cues," *Personality and Social Psychology Bulletin* 13 (1987), 478–489.

Frank, Mark G., and Paul Ekman. "Appearing Truthful Generalizes Across Different Deception Situations," *Journal of Personality and Social Psychology* 86, no. 3 (2004), 486–495.

Gladwell, Malcolm. *What the Dog Saw* (New York: Little, Brown, 2009).

Goldin-Meadow, Susan. *Hearing Gesture* (Cambridge, MA: Belknap Press, 2003).

Greene, J. O., H. D. O'Hair, M. J. Cody, and C. Yen. "Planning and Control of Behavior during Deception," *Human Communication Research* 11 (1985), 335–364.

Guerrero, Laura, and Kory Floyd. *Nonverbal Communication in Close Relationships* (Mahwah, NJ: Lawrence Erlbaum, 2006).

Hall, Edward T. *The Silent Language* (New York: Fawcett, 1959).

———. "Monochronic and Polychronic Time," in Laura K. Guerrero et al., eds., *The Nonverbal Reader: Classic and Contemporary Readings*, 2nd ed. (Prospect Heights, IL: Waveland Press, 1999), 237–240.

Hall, Judith A. "Women's and Men's Nonverbal Communication," in Anita Vangelisti and Daniel Perlman, eds., *Cambridge Handbook of Personal Relationships* (New York: Cambridge University Press, 2006), 201–218.

Hall, Judith A., Nora Murphy, and Marianne Mast. "Recall of Nonverbal Cues: Exploring a Definition of Interpersonal Sensitivity," *Journal of Nonverbal Behavior* 30 (Winter 2006), 141–155.

Hanzal, Alesia, Chris Segrin, and Sybilla M. Dorros. "The Role of Marital Status and Age on Men's and Women's Reactions to Touch from a Relational Partner," *Journal of Nonverbal Behavior* 32 (March 2008), 21–35.

Hargie, Owen, Christine Saunders, and David Dickson. *Social Skills in Interpersonal Communication* (Cambridge, MA: Brookline Books, 1987).

Hargrave, Jan. "Do You Speak Body Language? Mastering the Art of Nonverbal Communication Key in Interrogations," *The Forensic Examiner* (Fall 2008), 17–18.

Heingartner, Douglas. "It's the Way You Say It, Truth Be Told," *New York Times* (August 1, 2004), G1, 7.

Heslin, R., and T. Alper. "Touch: The Bonding Gesture," in M. Wiemann and R. P. Harrison, eds., *Nonverbal Interaction* (Beverly Hills, CA: Sage, 1983).

Jacobson, David. "Impression Formation in Cyberspace," *JCMC* 5 (September 1999).

James, Caryn. "After All That Goodness, A Sudden Fall from Grace," *New York Times* (January 22, 2007), E7.

Jones, Stanley E. "Communicating with Touch," in Laura Guerrero et al., eds., *The Nonverbal Communication Reader: Classic and Contemporary Readings*, 2nd ed. (Prospect Heights, IL: Waveland Press, 1999), 192–201.

Jones, S. E., and E. Yarbrough. "A Naturalistic Study of the Meanings of Touch," *Communication Monographs* 52 (1985), 19–56.

Kawamura, Satoru, and Keiko Kageyama. "Smiling Faces Rated More Feminine than Serious Faces in Japan," *Perception & Motor Skills* 103 (August 2006), 210–214.

Kinzel, August. "Towards an Understanding of Violence," *Attitude* 1 (1969).

Kleinke, Chris L. *Meeting and Understanding People* (New York: Freeman, 1986).

Knapp, Mark L., and Judy A. Hall. *Nonverbal Communication in Human Interaction,* 7th ed. (Belmont, CA: Wadsworth, 2008).

Konner, Melvin J. *Becoming a Doctor: A Journey of Initiation in Medical School.* (New York: Viking, 1987).

Lakin, Jessica L., Valerie E. Jefferis, Clara Michelle Cheng, and Tanya L. Chartrand. "The Chameleon Effect as Social Glue," *Journal of Nonverbal Behavior* 27 (Fall 2003), 145–162.

Levine, Robert. *A Geography of Time* (New York: Basic Books, 1997).

Lohr, Steve. "Slow Down, Brave Multitasker; And Don't Read This in Public," *New York Times* (March 25, 2007), 1, 27.

Martin, Judith, and Thomas Nakayama. *Experiencing Intercultural Communication,* 3rd ed. (New York: McGraw-Hill, 2008).

Mast, Marianne Schmid, and Judith A. Hall. "Women's Advantage at Remembering Others' Appearance," *Personality and Social Psychology Bulletin* 32 (March 2006), 353–364.

Matsumoto, David. "Culture and Nonverbal Behavior," in Valerie Manusov and Miles Patterson, eds., *The SAGE Handbook of Nonverbal Communication* (Beverly Hills, CA: Sage, 2006), 219–235.

McDaniel, Ed, and Peter A. Andersen. "International Patterns of Interpersonal Tactile Communication," *Journal of Nonverbal Behavior* 22, no. 1 (Spring 1998), 58–72.

Mehrabian, Albert. "Orientation Behaviors and Nonverbal Attitude Communication," *Journal of Communication* 17 (1967), 324–332.

———. "Communication without Words," *Psychology Today* 2 (1968), 53–56.

Meyer, Pamela. *Liespotting* (New York: St. Martin's Griffin, 2010).

Morris, Desmond, Peter Collett, Peter Marsh, and Marie O'Shaughnessy. *Gestures* (New York: Stein and Day, 1979).

Mottet, Timothy P., Steven A. Beebe, Paul C. Raffeld, and Michelle L. Paulsel. "The Effects of Student Verbal and Nonverbal Teachers' Liking of Students and Willingness to Comply with Student Requests," *Communication Quarterly* 52, no. 1 (Winter 2004), 27–38.

Moynihan, Colin. "City of a Thousand Handshakes," *New York Times* (May 22, 2004), B1, 4.

Nelson, Audrey, with Susan Golant. *You Don't Say: Navigating Nonverbal Communication between the Sexes* (New York: Prentice Hall, 2004).

Noller, Patricia. "Nonverbal Communication in Close Relationships," in Anita Vangelisti and Daniel Perlman, eds., *Cambridge Handbook of Personal Relationships* (New York: Cambridge University Press, 2006), 403–420.

Parnes, Amie. "Dress-Down Is Down If Not Quite Out," *New York Times* (June 13, 2001), G1.

Pease, Alan, and Barbara Pease. *The Definitive Book of Body Language* (New York: Bantam Books, 2006).

Penton-Voak, Ian S., Nicholas Pound, Anthony C. Little, and David I. Perrett. "Personality Judgments from Natural and Composite Facial Images: More Evidence for a 'Kernel of Truth' in Social Perception," *Social Cognition* 24 (October 2006), 607–640.

"Phones Are the New Cars." In "Technology Quarterly," in *The Economist* (December 2, 2006), 16–18.

Prager, Karen. "Intimacy in Personal Relationships," in Clyde Hendrick and Susan S. Hendrick, eds., *Close Relationships: A Sourcebook* (Thousand Oaks, CA: Sage, 2000), 229–242.

Robinson, Jeffrey D. "Nonverbal Communication and Physician-Patient Interaction Review and New Directions," in Valerie Manusov and Miles Patterson, eds., *The SAGE Handbook of Nonverbal Communication* (Beverly Hills, CA: Sage, 2006), 437–459.

Rodgers, Joan Ellison. "Flirting Fascination," *Psychology Today* (January/February 1999), 37–70.

Rosenfeld, Howard M. "Effect of Approval-Seeking Induction in Interpersonal Proximity," *Psychological Reports* 17 (1965), 120–122.

Scheflen, Albert E. "Quasi-Courtship Behavior in Psychotherapy," *Psychiatry* 28 (1965), 245–257.

Schmitt, Ben, "Pull 'em Up or Pay Up!" *Detroit Free Press* (July 9, 2008), 1A, 9A.

Semic, Beth. "Vocal Attractiveness," in Laura Guerrero et al., eds., *The Nonverbal Communication Reader: Classic and Contemporary Readings,* 2nd ed. (Prospect Heights, IL: Waveland Press, 1999), 149–155.

Simpson, Jeffry A., Steven W. Gangestad, and Michael Biek. "Personality and Nonverbal Social Behavior: An Ethological Perspective of Relationship Initiation," *Journal of Experimental Social Psychology* 29 (1993), 434–461.

Smith, Jack. "To Say Luxury in Chinese, Start by Sitting in the Back," *New York Times* (October 27, 2004), G14.

Sommer, Robert. *Personal Space: The Behavioral Basis of Design* (Englewood Cliffs, NJ: Prentice-Hall, 1969).

Stewart, J., and G. D'Angelo. *Together: Communicating Interpersonally,* 2nd ed. (New York: Random House, 1980).

Ting-Toomey, Stella. *Communicating Across Cultures* (New York: Guilford Press, 1999).

Trager, George L. "Paralanguage: A First Approximation," *Studies in Linguistics* 13 (1958), 1–12.

Tusing, Kyle James, and James Price Dillard. "The Sounds of Dominance: Vocal Precursors of Perceived Dominance During Interpersonal Influence," *Human Communication Research* 26, no. 1 (2000), 148–157.

Vrij, Aldert. "Nonverbal Communication and Deception," in Valerie Manusov and Miles Patterson, eds., *The SAGE Handbook of Nonverbal Communication* (Beverly Hills, CA: Sage, 2006), 341–359.

Vrij, Aldert, Lucy Akehurst, Stavroula Soukara, and Ray Bull. "Detecting Deceit via Analyses of Verbal and Nonverbal Behavior in Children and Adults," *Human Communication Research* 30, no. 1 (2004), 8–41.

Walther, Joseph B. "Nonverbal Dynamics in Computer-Mediated Communication," in Valerie Manusov and Miles Patterson, eds. *The SAGE Handbook of Nonverbal Communication* (Beverly Hills, CA: Sage, 2006), 461–479.

Watts, Geoff. "You Need Hands," *The Lancet* 367 (April 29–May 5, 2006), 1383–1384.

Weinstein, Harvey. "Hard Choices," *Bloomberg Business Week* (January 30–February 5, 2012), 84.

Willis, F. N., and H. K. Hamm. "The Use of Interpersonal Touch in Securing Compliances," *Journal of Nonverbal Behavior* 5 (1980), 49–55.

Zebrowitz, Leslie A. "Finally, Faces Find Favor," *Social Cognition* 24, no. 5 (2006), 657–701.

Chapter 5   Listening

Acuff, Frank L. *How to Negotiate Anything with Anyone Anywhere Around the World,* 2nd ed. (New York: AMACOM, 1997).

Adler, Ron, and Jeanne Elmhorst. *Communicating at Work,* 9th ed. (New York: McGraw-Hill, 2008).

Armstrong, A. "Critical Listening," *About, Inc.* Retrieved June 1, 2004, from About, Inc. Web site: *http://stereos.about.com/cs/trainingyourear/a/listening.htm.*

Athos, Anthony G., and John J. Gabarro. *Interpersonal Behavior: Communication and Understanding in Relationships* (Englewood Cliffs, NJ: Prentice-Hall, 1978).

Barker, Larry. *Listening Behavior* (Englewood Cliffs, NJ: Prentice-Hall, 1971).

Barker, L., R. Edwards, C. Gaines, K. Gladney, and F. Holley. "An Investigation of Proportional Time Spent in Various Communication Activities by College Students," *Journal of Applied Communication Research* 8 (1981), 101–109.

Beagrie, Scott. "How to Listen Meaningfully," *Personnel Today* (April 26, 2005), 23.

Bernstein, Elizabeth. "Putting the Honey Back in 'Honey, I'm Home,'" *The Wall Street Journal* (October 4, 2011, D4).

Blanchard, G. "Is Listening Through a Stethoscope a Dying Art?" *Boston Globe* (May 25, 2004), C1.

Bostrom, Robert. "Patterns of Communicative Interaction in Small Groups," *Speech Monographs* 3 (1970), 257–263.

Bostrom, Robert N., and Enid S. Waldhart. "Memory Models and the Measurement of Listening," *Communication Education* 37 (1988), 1–13.

Broadbent, Donald. *Perception and Communication* (Elmsford, NY: Pergamon, 1958).

Brooks, Bill. "The Power of Active Listening," *The American Salesman* 51, no. 6 (June 2006), 12.

Brooks, David. *The Social Animal* (New York: Random House, 2011).

Brooks, William D. *Speech Communication,* 4th ed. (Dubuque, IA: Brown, 1981).

Brownell, Judi. "The Skills of Listening-Centered Communication," in Andrew Wolvin (ed.), *Listening and Human Communication* (West Sussex, UK: Wiley-Blackwell, 2010), 141–157.

Carr, Nicholas. *The Shallows: What the Internet Is Doing to Our Brains* (New York: W.W. Norton, 2011).

Cohen, L. "Few of Us Are Really Good at Listening," *Boston Globe* (February 27, 2003), H5.

Covey, Stephen. *The 7 Habits of Highly Effective People* (New York: Simon & Schuster, 1990).

Crane, Loren, Richard Dicker, and Charles Brown. "The Physiological Response to the Communication Modes: Reading, Listening, Writing, Speaking, and Evaluating," *Journal of Communication* 20 (1970), 231–240.

Dulye, Linda. "Get Out of Your Office," *HR Magazine* 51, no. 7 (July 2006), 99–101.

Eagleman, David. *Incognito: The Secret Lives of the Brain* (New York: Pantheon Books, 2011).

Foer, Joshua. *Moonwalking with Einstein: The Art and Science of Remembering Everything* (New York: Penguin Press, 2011).

Fox News Channel. "Statement from Cubs Fan Steve Bartman" (October 15, 2003), from *www.foxnews.com/story/0,2933,100218,00.html.*

Frymier, Ann, and Marjorie Nadler. *Persuasion: Integrating Theory, Research, and Practice,* 2nd ed. (Dubuque, IA: Kendall Hunt, 2010).

Fuimano, Julie. "Sharp Listening Skills Point Staff in Right Direction," *Nursing Management* 35 (May 2004), 12.

Goss, Blain. *Processing Information* (Belmont, CA: Wadsworth, 1982).

Goulston, Mark. *Just Listen* (New York: AMACOM, 2010).

Griffin, Michael. "Open Door Policy, Closed Lip Reality," *Harvard Business Review Daily Briefings,* September 20, 2011.

Guttman, Howard M. "Power Listening," *Leadership Excellence* (Provo) 22, no. 2 (February 2005), 18.

Hargie, Owen, Christine Saunders, and David Dickson. *Social Skills in Interpersonal Communication* (Cambridge, MA: Brookline Books, 1987).

Imhoff, Margarete. "What Is Going On in the Mind of a Listener? The Cognitive Psychology of Listening," in Andrew Wolvin (ed.), *Listening and Human Communication* (West Sussex, UK: Wiley-Blackwell, 2010), 97–126.

Kotter, John. *A Sense of Urgency* (Boston: Harvard Business School Press, 2008).

Kouzes, James, and Barry Posner. *The Truth about Leadership* (San Francisco: Jossey-Bass, 2010).

Malone, Patrick. "A Prelude to Profit: The Finest Listening Skills in the World," in Melanie Bullock, Charla Friday, Kathy Belcher, Bonnie Bisset, Simon Hurley, Casey Foote, and Diem Thai, *1998 International Conference on Work Teams Proceeding* (Dallas, TX, 1998).

Moore, Kenny. "Become a Better Communicator by Keeping Your Mouth Shut," *The Journal for Quality and Participation* 28, no. 2 (2005), 8–10.

Moray, Neville. *Listening and Attention* (Baltimore, MD: Penguin, 1969).

Munoz, Gisela M. "The Five R's of Listening," *Practical Lawyer* 52, no. 2 (April 2006), 11–18.

Nadig, L. *Tips on Effective Listening.* (April 7, 2004). Retrieved May 24, 2004, from Larry Alan Nadig, Ph.D., Clinical Psychology, Marriage and Family Therapist Web site: *www.drnadig.com/listening.htm*.

Nadler, Scott, and Roy L. Simerly. "The Effect of Listening on the Formation of Students' Trust and Commitment in Academic Advising: A Study at a United States University," *International Journal of Management* 23, no. 2 (2006), 215–221.

Price, Jill. *The Woman Who Can't Forget: A Memoir* (New York: The Free Press, 2008).

Rankin, Paul. "The Measurement of the Ability to Understand Spoken Language," unpublished Ph.D. dissertation, University of Michigan, 1926, 43.

Reik, Theodore. *Listening with the Third Ear* (New York: Grove Press, 1948).

Rogers, Carl. *On Becoming a Person* (Boston, MA: Houghton Mifflin, 1961).

Rowh, Mark. "Listen Up!" *Career World* 34, no. 6 (April/May 2006), 22–24.

Schmid, John. "Driven to Distraction: Put that BlackBerry Down and Listen Up, Author Advises," *Milwaukee Journal Sentinel* (January 8, 2007).

Seligman, Martin. *Flourish* (New York: Free Press, 2011).

Tannen, Deborah. *You Just Don't Understand: Women and Men in Conversation* (New York: Ballantine Books, 1990).

Tubbs, Stewart L. A Systems Approach to Small Group Interaction (10th ed). New York: McGraw-Hill, 2012.

Turkle, Sherry. *Alone Together* (New York: Basic Books, 2011).

Walters, Jamie. "Fostering a Culture of Deep Inquiry and Listening," *The Journal for Quality and Participation* (Cincinnati) 28, no. 2 (Summer 2005), 4–7.

Wiseman, Liz. *Multipliers* (New York: HarperBusiness, 2010).

Wolvin, Andrew. *Listening and Human Communication in the 21st Century.* New York: Blackwell Publishing, 2010.

Chapter 6 Conflict and Negotiation

Akin, J. "Escalation Limiting Language," *Beyond Intractability.org.* (2003). Retrieved July 7, 2004, from Beyond Intractability Web site: *www.beyondintractability.org/m/escalation-limiting_language.jsp*.

Babitsky, Steven, and James Mangravati. *Never Lose Again* (New York: Thomas Dunne Books, 2011).

Baumeister, Roy, and John Tierney. *Willpower: Rediscovering the Greatest Human Strength* (New York: Penguin Group, 2011).

Bester, Helmut, and Karl Warneryd. "Conflict and the Social Contract," *Scand. J of Economics* 108, no. 2 (2006), 231–249.

Boles, Terry, and Lon Moeller. *The Road to Success: Learning How to Become an Effective Negotiator* (Dubuque, IA: Kendall Hunt, 2012).

Brahm, E. "Conflict Stages" *Beyond Intractability.org* (2003). Retrieved July 7, 2004, from Beyond Intractability Web site: *www.beyondintractability.org/m/conflict_stages.jsp*.

"Canton Township Paints Over Big Boy Statue Controversy," *America's Newspapers* (July 13, 2004), 10A. Retrieved from *www.infoweb.newsbank.com/iwsearch/we/InfoWeb?p_action=doc&p_docid=103D53F0168BBDCF&p_docnum=11&NBID=G5EB50WIMTA5MDQzMDY2IC41Mjg3MTM6MTo2OjE2NC43Ng*.

Cheung, Sai On, Tak Wing Yiu Yiu, and Sau Fung Yeung. "A Study of Styles and Outcomes in Construction Dispute Negotiation," *Journal of Construction Engineering and Management* (August 2006).

Cloke, Kenneth, and Joan Goldsmith. *Resolving Conflicts at Work*, 2nd ed. (San Francisco, CA: Jossey-Bass, 2005).

Cohen, Herb. *You Can Negotiate Anything* (Secaucus, NJ: Lyle Stuart, 1996).

Cohen, Herb. *Negotiate This!* (New York: Warner Books, 2003).

Covey, Stephen. *The 7 Habits of Highly Effective People* (New York: A Fireside Book, 1990).

Donaldson, Michael. *Fearless Negotiating* (New York: McGraw-Hill, 2007).

Dzwonkowski, Ron, "Let's Have a Heart-to-Heart Every Day," *Detroit Free Press* (July 5, 1998), 2H.

Fisher, Roger, William Ury, and Bruce Patton. *Getting to Yes*, 2nd ed. (New York: Penguin Books, 1991).

Friedman, Thomas, and Michael Mandelbaum. *That Used to Be Us* (New York: Farrar, Straus and Giroux, 2011).

Goleman, Daniel. *Leadership: The Power of Emotional Intelligence.* Northampton, Mass: More Than Sound, LLC, 2011.

———. "Emotional Intelligence: Issues in Paradigm Building," in G. Cherniss and D. Goleman, eds., *The Emotionally Intelligent Workplace* (San Francisco, CA: Jossey-Bass, 2001), 13–26.

Goleman, D., R. Boyatzis, and A. McKee. *The New Leaders: Transforming the Art of Leadership into the Science of Results* (London: Little Brown, 2002), 182.

———. *Primal Leadership: Learning to Lead with Emotional Intelligence* (Boston: Harvard Business School Press, 2004).

Goudakov, Vladimir. "Gumilev and Huntington: Approaches and Terminologies," *Diogenes* 210 (2006), 82–90.

Hames, David. *Negotiation* (Thousand Oaks, CA: Sage, 2012).

Hede, Andrew. "The Shadow Group: Towards an Explanation of Interpersonal Conflict in Work Groups," *Journal of Managerial Psychology* 22, no. 1 (2007), 25–39.

Hoffmann, Michael H. G. "Logical Argument Mapping: A Method for Overcoming Cognitive Problems," *International Journal of Conflict Management* 16, no. 4 (2005), 305–335.

Horn, S. *Tongue Fu: How to Deflect, Disarm, and Defuse any Verbal Conflict.* (New York: St. Martin's Press, 1996).

———. "Ten Tongue Fu!® Tips," *Samhorn.com.* (2004). From *www.samhorn.com/article_10_Tongue_Fu_Tips.html.*

J. D. Power and Associates. "The Saturn Way" (September 1992). Los Angeles: J. D. Power and Associates. Retrieved from *http://home.business.utah.edu/mgths/pdf/CMR11.PDF.*

Jannetta, Candy. "Handling Gatecrashers: Conflict Management and Resolution," *Legal Information Management* 6 (2006), 28–30.

Kilmann, R., and K. W. Thomas. "Interpersonal Conflict–Handling Behavior as Reflections of Jungian Personality," *Psychological Reports* 37 (1975), 971–980.

Lage, L. "Dumars: Pistons in 'Same Neighborhood' with Rasheed Wallace," (July 16, 2004). Retrieved from *www.mlive.com/sportsflash/michigan/index.ssf?/base/sports-8/1089969540293320.xml.*

Lewicki, Roy, Bruce Barry, and David Saunders. *Essentials of Negotiation,* 5th ed. (New York: McGraw-Hill, 2010).

Lewis, Michael. *Boomerang: Travels in the New Third World* (New York: W. W. Norton, 2011).

Lim, John, and Yin Ping Yang. "Enhancing Negotiators' Performance with Computer Support for Pre-Negotiation Preparation and Negotiation: An Experimental Investigation in an East Asian Context," *Journal of Global Information Management* 15, no. 1 (January-March 2007), 1–2.

Molm, Linda D., Jessica L. Collett, and David R. Schaefer. "Conflict and Fairness in Social Exchange," *Social Forces* 84, no. 4 (June 2006), 2331–2352.

Reed, James, and Paul Stoltz. *Put Your Mindset to Work* (New York: Portfolio/Penguin, 2011).

Sillars, A. L. "Procedures for Coding Interpersonal Conflict," Department of Communication Studies, University of Montana, 1986.

Walker, Michael A., and George L. Harris. *Negotiations: Six Steps to Success* (Upper Saddle River, NJ: Prentice-Hall, 1995).

Wilmot, William, and Joyce Hocker. *Interpersonal Conflict,* 7th ed. (New York: McGraw-Hill, 2005).

Wiseman, Liz. *Multipliers: How the Best Leaders Make Everyone Smarter* (New York: HarperBusiness, 2010).

Chapter 7   Ethics and Communication

Abelson, Raziel. "History of Ethics," in Paul Edwards, ed., *The Encyclopedia of Philosophy,* vol. 3 (New York: Macmillan and Free Press, 1967), 81–117.

Albergotti, Reed, and Rachel Bachman, "Two Views on Administrator," *The Wall Street Journal,* November 23, 2011, A3.

American Heritage Dictionary of the English Language. (Boston, MA: Houghton Mifflin, 2004).

Aristotle. *Introduction to Aristotle,* Richard McKeon, ed. (New York: Random House, Modern Library, 1947).

Augustine. *Enchiridion,* Henry Paolucci, ed. (Chicago, IL: Regnery, 1961).

Barnes, Christopher, John Schaubroeck, Megan Huth, and Sonia Ghumman, "Lack of sleep and unethical conduct," *Organizational Behavior and Human Decision Processes,* 115, no. 2 (July 2011), 169–180.

Barry, Dan, David Barstow, Jonathan D. Glater, Adam Liptak, and Jacques Steinberg. "Times Reporter Who Resigned Leaves Long Trail of Deception," *New York Times* (May 11, 2003), A1.

Bavelas, Janet Beavin, Alex Black, Nicole Chovil, and Jennifer Mullett. *Equivocal Communication* (Newbury Park, CA: Sage, 1990).

Beauchamp, Tom, Norman Bowie, and Denis Arnold. *Ethical Theory and Business,* 8th ed. (Upper Saddle River, N.J.: Prentice-Hall, 2009).

Bennis, Goleman, O'Toole, and Biederman, 2008, pp.14–17 p. 212.

Bok, Sissela. *Secrets: On the Ethics of Concealment and Revelation* (New York: Vintage, 1989).

Carr, David. "Skipping Merrily Along as Others Take the Heat," *New York Times* (February 5, 2007), C1–C7.

Christians, Clifford G., Mark Fackler, Kim B. Rotzoll, and Kathy Brittain. *Media Ethics: Cases and Moral Reasoning,* 5th ed. (Reading, MA: Addison-Wesley, 1998).

Christians, Clifford, and Kaarle Nordenstreng. "Social Responsibility Worldwide," *Journal of Mass Media Ethics* 19, no. 1 (2004), 3–28.

Christians, Clifford, and Michael Traber, eds. *Communication Ethics and Universal Values* (Thousand Oaks, CA: Sage, 1997).

Colvin, Geoffrey. "Wonder Women of Whistleblowing," *Fortune* 146, no. 3 (2002), 56.

Couldry, Nick. *Listening Beyond the Echoes: Media, Ethics, and Agency in an Uncertain World* (Boulder, CO: Paradigm Publishers, 2006).

Ekman, Paul. *Telling Lies* (New York: Norton, 1985).

Farhi, Paul. "U.S. Media Settle with Wen Ho Lee," *Washington Post* (June 3, 2006), A1.

Fox, Richard Wightman. "A Heartbreaking Problem of Staggering Proportions," *Journal of American History* 90 (March 2004), 1341–1346.

Franklin, Nancy. "Show and Tell: When Did Privacy Go Public?" *New Yorker* (August 24–31, 1998), 11–12.

Freedman, Samuel G. "The Predictable Scandal," *Columbia Journalism Review* 44 (March/April 2006), 50–53.

Gay, Jason. "No Easy Cleanup at Penn State," *The Wall Street Journal*, November 23, 2011, D6.

Glazer, Sarah, "Combating Scientific Misconduct: The Issues," *CQ* (January 10, 1997), 3–23.

Griffin, Em. *A First Look at Communication Theory,* 6th ed. (New York: McGraw-Hill, 2006).

Hafner, Katie. "Lessons in the School of Cut and Paste," *New York Times* (June 28, 2001), G1, 6.

Hassan, Adeel. "Blair's Victims: That Helpless Feeling," *Columbia Journalism Review* 42 (July/August 2003), 19–22.

Hauser, Marc D. *Moral Minds: How Nature Designed Our Universal Sense of Right and Wrong* (New York: HarperCollins, 2006).

Interlandi, Janeen. "An Unwelcome Discovery," *New York Times Magazine* (October 22, 2006), 98–103.

Jensen, J. Vernon. *Ethical Issues in the Communication Process* (Mahwah, NJ: Erlbaum, 1997).

Johnson, Craig. *Meeting the Ethical Challenges of Leadership*, 4th ed. Los Angeles: Sage, 2012.

Kant, Immanuel. *Foundations of the Metaphysics of Morals*, Lewis White Beck, trans. (Indianapolis: Bobbs-Merrill, Library of Liberal Arts, 1959).

Kidder, Rushworth M. *Moral Courage* (New York: HarperCollins, 2005).

Kleinfield, N. R. "Mideast Tensions Are Getting Personal on Campus at Columbia," *New York Times* (January 18, 2005), B1.

Knapp, Mark L. "Lying and Deception in Close Relationships," in Anita Vangelisti and Daniel Perlman, eds., *Cambridge Handbook of Personal Relationships* (New York: Cambridge University Press, 2006), 517–532.

Knapp, Mark L., and Anita L. Vangelisti. *Interpersonal Communication and Human Interaction,* 4th ed. (Boston, MA: Allyn & Bacon, 2000).

Lacayo, Richard, and Amanda Ripley. "Persons of the Year 2002: Cynthia Cooper, Coleen Rowley and Sherron Watkins." *www.time.com/time/personoftheyear/2002/poyintro.html.*

Lea, Martin, and Russell Spears. "Love at First Byte? Building Personal Relationships over Computer Networks," in Julia T. Wood and Steve Duck, eds., *Under-Studied Relationships: Off the Beaten Track* (Thousand Oaks, CA: Sage, 1995), 197–233.

Levitt, Steven D., and Stephen J. Dubner. *Freakonomics: A Rogue Economist Explores the Hidden Side of Everything,* revised and expanded ed. (New York: HarperCollins, 2006).

Lewin, Tamar. "Dean at M.I.T. Resigns, Ending a 28-Year-Lie," *New York Times* (April 27, 2007).

Liptak, Adam. "Reporters Face Scrutiny in C.I.A. Leak Inquiry," *New York Times* (September 28, 2004), A18.

Matthews, Chris. *Jack Kennedy: Elusive Hero* (New York: Simon & Schuster, 2011).

"Media Advisory: FAIR Calls for Revealing Sources in Plame, Lee Cases" (September 5, 2004). From *www.fair.org/press-releases/plame-lee.html.*

Mieth, Dietmar. "The Basic Norm of Truthfulness," in Clifford Christians and Michael Traber, eds., *Communication Ethics and Universal Values* (Thousand Oaks, CA: Sage, 1997), 87–103.

Mill, John Stuart. *Selected Writings of John Stuart Mill,* Maurice Cowling, ed. (New York: New American Library, 1968).

Miller, John. "Sandusky Hearing Delayed, Judges Are Recused," *The Wall Street Journal*, November 23, 2011, A3.

New York Times, 2008.

Neale, Larry, and Sam Fullerton. "The International Search for Ethics Norms," *Journal of Services Marketing,* 24 (2010), 476–486.

NPR, 2008.

"NSA Whistleblower Tells House Subcommittee Domestic Spying Could Effect [*sic*] 'Millions of Americans,'" Federal News Service (Washington, DC: February 14, 2006).

Posner, Richard A. *The Little Book of Plagiarism* (New York: Pantheon, 2007).

Rainie, Lee, Susannah Fox, and Mary Madden. "One Year Later: September 11 and the Internet." (September 11, 2004). From *www.pewinternet.org/PPF/r/69/report)display.asp.*

Rawls, John. *A Theory of Justice* (Cambridge, MA: Harvard University Press, 1971).

Rost, Peter. *The Whistleblower: Confessions of a Healthcare Hitman* (New York: Soft Scull Press, 2006).

Rowley, Coleen. "Coleen Rowley's Memo to FBI Director Robert Mueller," *Time* (May 21, 2002). From *www.time.com/time/covers/110120603/memo.html.*

Schrader, Steve. "JoePa in Charge, Ex-Official Says," *The Detroit Free Press*, November 23, 2011, 3B.

Schuller, Robert H. *Life's Not Fair but God Is Good* (Nashville, TN: Thomas Nelson, 1991).

Schwartz, John. "As Big Brother Watches, Users Encounter Frustration," *New York Times* (September 5, 2001), A1.

"See Evil, Hear Evil, Speak Evil," *New York Times* (March 19, 2001), 7.

Shad, Joe. http://espn.go.com/college-football/story/_/ id/7214380/joe-paterno-president-graham-spanier-penn-state.

Simpson, Kevin. "To ID or Not to ID: Debate Renewed on Rape Victims," *Denver Post* (October 17, 2004), C1.

Smith, Richard Norton. "'The President Is Fine' and Other Historical Lies," *Columbia Journalism Review* (September/October 2001), 30–32.

"Whistleblowing Workers: Becoming an Endangered Species?" *HR Focus* 83, no. 6 (2006), 9.

Widener, Chris. *The Art of Influence* (New York: Doubleday, 2008).

Wiener, Jon. *Historians in Trouble* (New York: New Press, 2007).

Williams, Patricia J. "Shrieking Violets," *Nation*, (February 14, 2005), 9.

Wood, Andrew F., and Matthew J. Smith. *Online Communication* (Mahwah, NJ: Lawrence Erlbaum, 2001).

Zakaria, Fareed. *The Post-American World* (New York: W.W. Norton, 2008).

Chapter 8   Relationships in Process

Ablow, Keith. "Finding New Passion After the Pain of Infidelity," *New York Times* (June 20, 2006), F5.

Acitele, L. K. "When Spouses Talk to Each Other about Their Relationship," *Journal of Social and Personal Relationships* 5 (1987), 185–199.

Aron, Arthur, Helen E. Fisher, and Greg Strong. "Romantic Love," in Anita Vangelisti and Daniel Perlman, eds., *Cambridge Handbook of Personal Relationships* (New York: Cambridge University Press, 2006), 595–614.

Barry, Ellen, with Nicholas Kulish and Michal Piotrowski. "Polish President Dies in Jet Crash in Russia," *New York Times* e-version, April 10, 2010.

Baxter, Leslie. "Strategies for Ending Relationships: Two Studies," *Western Journal of Speech Communication* 46 (1982), 223–241.

———. "Trajectories of Relationship Disengagement," *Journal of Social and Personal Relationships* 1 (1984), 223–241.

———. "Forms and Functions of Intimate Play in Interpersonal Relationships," *Human Communication Research* 18 (1992), 336–363.

Baxter, Leslie A., and Dawn O. Braithwaite. "Introduction: Meta-Theory and Theory in Family Communication Research," in Dawn O. Braithwaite and Leslie A. Baxter, eds., *Engaging Theories in Family Communication: Multiple Perspectives* (Thousand Oaks, CA: Sage, 2006).

Berscheid, Ellen, and Harry T. Reis. "Attraction and Close Relationships," in Daniel Gilbert, Susan Fiske, and Gardner Lindzey, eds., *Handbook of Social Psychology*, 4th ed., vol. 2 (New York: McGraw-Hill, 1998), 193–281.

Brooks, David. *The Social Animal* (New York: Random House, 2011).

Buber, Martin. "Distance and Relation," *Psychiatry* 20 (1957).

Bury, Martine. "You and Me Against the World," in Edwidge Danticat, ed., *The Butterfly's Way* (New York: Soho Press, 2001), 101–108.

Buss, David. M., Todd K. Shackelford, Lee A. Kirkpatrick, and Randy J. Larsen. "Human Mate Selection," *American Scientist* 73 (January–February, 1985), 47–51.

Canary, Daniel J., and Marianne Dainton, eds. *Maintaining Relationships through Communication: Relational, Contextual, and Cultural Variations* (Mahwah, NJ: Erlbaum, 2003).

Canary, Daniel J., and Laura Stafford. "Relational Maintenance Strategies and Equity in Marriage," *Communication Monographs* 59 (1992), 243–267.

———, eds. *Communication and Relational Maintenance* (San Diego, CA: Academic Press, 1994).

Chelune, G. J., J. T. Robison, and M. J. Kommor. "A Cognitive Interaction Model of Intimate Relationships," in V. J. Derlega, ed., *Communication, Intimacy, and Close Relationships* (Orlando, FL: Academic Press, 1984).

Coleman, Marilyn, Mark A. Fine, Lawrence H. Ganong, Kimberly J. M. Downs, and Nicole Pauk. "When You're Not the Brady Bunch: Identifying Perceived Conflicts and Resolution Strategies in Step Families," *Personal Relationships* 8 (2001), 55–73.

Coontz, Stephanie. *Marriage, a History* (New York: Viking Penguin, 2006a).

——— "Marriage as Social Contract/The Decline in Married Couple Households," *Philadelphia Inquirer* (October 20, 2006b). Retrieved July 19, 2007, from *www .stephaniecoontz.com/articles/article31*.

deJong, Bart, and Tom Elfring. "How Does Trust Affect the Performance of Ongoing Teams?" *The Academy of Management Journal* (June 2010), 535–549.

Dhillon, Anand. "Building High Self-Esteem," AnandDhillon. com (July 14, 2008). Retrieved November 25, 2008, from *http://www.ananddhillon.com/blog/2008/07/building-high-self-esteem/*.

Dindia, Kathryn. "Relational Maintenance," in Clyde Hendrick and Susan S. Hendrick, eds., *Close Relationships: A Sourcebook* (Thousand Oaks, CA: Sage, 2000), 287–298.

Duck, Steve. "A Topography of Relationship Disengagement and Dissolution," in Steve Duck, ed., *Personal Relationships 4: Dissolving Personal Relationships* (London: Academic Press, 1982).

———. *Human Relationships,* 2nd ed. (London: Sage, 1992).

———. "Steady as (S)he Goes," in Daniel J. Canary and Laura Stafford, eds., *Communication and Relational Maintenance* (San Diego, CA: Academic Press, 1994), 45–60.

———. *Relating to Others* (Buckingham, UK: Open University Press, 1999).

Duck, Steve, and Garth Pittmann. "Social and Personal Relationships," in Mark L. Knapp and Gerald R. Miller, eds., *Handbook of Interpersonal Communication*, 2nd ed. (Thousand Oaks, CA: Sage, 1994), 676–695.

Fehr, Beverly. "The Life Cycle of Friendship," in Clyde Hendrick and Susan S. Hendrick, eds., *Close Relationships: A Sourcebook* (Thousand Oaks, CA: Sage, 2000), 71–84.

Galvin, Kathleen M., Carma L. Bylund, and Bernard J. Brommel. *Family Communication: Cohesion and Change,* 6th ed. (Boston, MA: Allyn & Bacon, 2003).

Gibb, Jack R. "Defensive Communication," *Journal of Communication* 11:3 (1961), 141–148.

Gladwell, Malcolm. *Blink: The Power of Thinking Without Thinking* (New York: Little, Brown, 2005).

Guerrero, Laura, and Kory Floyd. *Nonverbal Communication in Close Relationships* (Mahwah, NJ: Erlbaum, 2006).

Hawken, Leila, Robert L. Duran, and Lynne Kelly. "The Relationship of Interpersonal Communication Variables to Academic Success and Persistence in College," *Communication Quarterly* 39 (1991), 297–308.

Heider, Fritz. *The Psychology of Interpersonal Relations* (Hillsdale, NJ: Lawrence Erlbaum, 1983).

Hendrick, Clyde, and Susan S. Hendrick, eds. *Close Relationships: A Sourcebook* (Thousand Oaks, CA: Sage, 2000).

Honeycutt, James M. "Memory Structures for the Rise and Fall of Personal Relationships," in Steve Duck, ed., *Individuals in Relationships* (Thousand Oaks, CA: Sage, 1993), 60–86.

Honeycutt, James M., and James G. Cantrill. *Cognition, Communication, and Romantic Relationships* (Mahwah, NJ: Lawrence Erlbaum, 2001).

Hurley, 2012. p. 233.

Kaplan, Daniel L., and Christopher B. Keys. "Sex and Relationship Variables as Predictors of Sexual Attraction in Cross-Sex Platonic Friendships between Young Heterosexual Adults," *Journal of Social and Personal Relationships* 14 (1997), 191–206.

Knapp, Mark L., *Interpersonal Communication and Human Relationships* (Boston, MA: Allyn & Bacon, 1984).

Knapp, Mark L., and Gerald R. Miller, eds. *Handbook of Interpersonal Communication*, 2nd ed. (Thousand Oaks, CA: Sage, 1994).

Knapp, Mark L., and Anita L. Vangelisti. *Interpersonal Communication and Human Relationships*, 4th ed. (Newton, MA: Allyn & Bacon, 2000).

Lehr, Andrew T., and Glen Geher. "Differential Effects of Reciprocity and Attitude Similarity Across Long-Versus Short-Term Mating Contexts," *Journal of Social Psychology* 146, no. 4 (2006), 423–439.

Lippard, Paula V. "'Ask Me No Questions, I'll Tell You No Lies': Situational Exigencies for Interpersonal Communication," *Western Journal of Speech Communication* 52 (Winter 1988), 91–103.

———. "Lying and Deception in Close Relationships," in Anita Vangelisti and Daniel Perlman, eds., *Cambridge Handbook of Personal Relationships* (New York: Cambridge University Press, 2006), 517–532.

Madden, Mary, and Amanda Lenhart. "Online Dating," *Pew Internet & American Life Project* (March 5, 2006). Retrieved July 16, 2007, from *www.pewinternet.org.* PIP_Online_Dating.pdf.

Markman, H. J., Rhoades, G. K., Stanley, S. M., Ragan, E., & Whitton, S. "The Premarital Communication Roots of Marital Distress: The First Five Years of Marriage." *Journal of Family Psychology* 24 (2010), 289–298.

Murray, Charles. *Real Education* (New York: Crown Forum, 2008).

Newcomb, Theodore M. *The Acquaintance Process* (New York: Holt, Rinehart and Winston, 1961).

Pearce, L., and S. Newton. *The Conditions of Human Growth* (New York: Citadel, 1963).

Pfeffer, Jeffrey. *Power: Why Some ZPeople Have It and Others Don't* (New York: HarperCollins, 2010).

Powers, Nancy. "Eat Dinner with the Family Tonight," *Detroit Free Press* (September 22, 2008), 3C.

Previti, Denise, and Paul R. Amato. "Is Infidelity a Cause or a Consequence of Poor Marital Quality?" *Journal of Social and Personal Relationships* 21, no. 2 (2004), 217–230.

Roker, Al. *Don't Make Me Stop This Car!* (New York: Scribner, 2000).

Ruesch, Jurgen, and Gregory Bateson. *Communication: The Social Matrix of Psychiatry* (New York: Norton, 1968).

Schachter, Stanley. *The Psychology of Affiliation* (Palo Alto, CA: Stanford University Press, 1959).

Schimel, Jeff, Tom Pyszcynski, Jamie Arndt, and Jeff Greenberg. "Being Accepted for Who We Are," *Journal of Personality and Social Psychology* 80 (2001), 35–52.

Seale, Kathy, "Dining Together Instills Sense of Belonging, Well-Being," *Ann Arbor News* (September 25, 2008), C3.

Shellenbarger, Sue. "No Comfort in Numbers: Divorce Rate Varies Widely from Group to Group," *Wall Street Journal* (April 22, 2004), D1.

Shimoff, Marci, and Carole Kline. *Happy For No Reason* (New York: The Free Press, 2008).

Sieburg, Evelyn, and Carl Larson. "Dimensions of Interpersonal Response," paper delivered at the annual conference of the International Communication Association, Phoenix, April 1971.

Sobczyk, Marcin. "Polish Crash Probe Focuses on General," *The Wall Street Journal*, May 27, 2010, A10.

Stafford, Laura, Susan L. Kline, and Caroline T. Ranking. "Married Individuals, Cohabiters, and Cohabiters Who Marry: A Longitudinal Study of Relational Well-Being," *Journal of Social and Personal Relationships* 21, no. 2 (2004), 231–248.

Tannen, Deborah. *You Just Don't Understand: Women and Men in Conversation* (New York: Ballantine Books, 1990).

Lyman, 2012.

———. *I Only Say This Because I Love You* (New York: Random House, 2001).

Tubbs, Stewart L. "Two-Person Game Behavior, Conformity-Inducing Messages, and Interpersonal Trust," *Journal of Communication*, December 1971, 326–341.

Walsh, Tom. "Detroit 3 Chiefs, UAW Can Try Trust," *Detroit Free Press*, June 13, 2010, A1.

Watzlawick, Paul, Janet Helmick Beavin, and Don D. Jackson. *Pragmatics of Human Communication* (New York: Norton, 1967).

Zajonc, Robert B. "Attitudinal Effects of Mere Exposure," *Journal of Personality and Social Psychology* 9 (1968), 1–29.

Chapter 9   Interpersonal Communication

Alberti, Robert, and Michael Emmons. *Your Perfect Right* (Atascadero, CA: Impact Publishers, 2001).

Aron, Arthur, Helen E. Fisher, and Greg Strong. "Romantic Love," in Anita Vangelisti and Daniel Perlman, eds., *Cambridge Handbook of Personal Relationships* (New York: Cambridge University Press, 2006), 595–614.

Bartholomew, K. "Avoidance of Intimacy: An Attachment Perspective," *Journal of Social and Personal Relationships* 7 (1990), 147–148.

Berko, R. M., A. D. Wolvin, and D. R. Wolvin. *Communicating: A Social and Career Focus*, 8th ed. (Boston, MA: Houghton Mifflin, 2001).

Bernstein, 2012.

Bowlby, John. *Attachment and Loss: vol. 2, Separation: Anxiety and Anger* (New York: Basic Books, 1973).

Cain, 2012.

Carter, Betty, and Joan K. Peters. *Love, Honor and Negotiate* (New York: Pocket Books, 1996).

Chelune, G. J., J. T. Robison, and M. J. Kommor. In V. J. Derlega, ed., *Communication, Intimacy, and Close Relationships* (Orlando, FL: Academic Press, 1984).

Clark, Ruth Anne, Michael Dockum, Heidi Hazeu, Meikuan Huang et al. "Initial Encounters of Young Men and Women: Impressions and Disclosure Estimates," *Sex Roles* 50 (2004), 699–709.

Davis, Deborah, Philip R. Shaver, and Michael L. Vernon. "Attachment Style and Subjective Motivations for Sex," *Personality and Social Psychology Bulletin* 30 (August 2004), 1076–1090.

Derlega, Valerian J., Barbara A. Winstead, Paul T. P. Wong, and Michael Greenspan. "Self-Disclosure and Relationship Development: An Attributional Analysis," in Michael E. Roloff and Gerald R. Miller, eds., *Interpersonal Processes: New Directions in Communications Research* (Beverly Hills, CA: Sage, 1987), 172–187.

DeVito, Joseph. *The Interpersonal Communication Book*, 12th ed. (Boston, MA: Pearson Education, 2009).

Dindia, Kathryn. "Self-Disclosure, Self-Identity, and Relationship Development: A Transactional/Dialectical Perspective," in Steve Duck, ed., *Handbook of Personal Relationships*, 2nd ed. (New York: Wiley, 1996), 411–426.

Dindia, Kathryn. "Relational Maintenance," in Clyde Hendrick and Susan S. Hendrick, eds., *Close Relationships: A Sourcebook* (Thousand Oaks, CA: Sage, 2000), 287–298.

———. "Self-Disclosure Research: Knowledge through Meta-Analysis," in Mike Allen, Raymond W. Preiss, Barbara Mae Gayle, and Nancy A. Burrell, eds., *Interpersonal Communication: Advances through Meta-Analysis* (Mahwah, NJ: Erlbaum, 2002), 169–186.

Duck, Steve. *Relating to Others* (Buckingham, UK: Open University Press, 1999).

Emmers-Sommer, Tara M. "The Effect of Communication Quality and Quantity Indicators on Intimacy and Relational Satisfaction," *Journal of Social and Personal Relationships* 21 (2004), 399–411.

Feeney, Judith A., Patricia Noller, and Nigel Roberts. "Attachment and Close Relationships," in Clyde Hendrick and Susan S. Hendrick, eds., *Close Relationships: A Sourcebook* (Thousand Oaks, CA: Sage, 2000), 185–201.

Fujishin, R. *Creating Communication: Exploring and Expanding Your Fundamental Communication Skills*, 2nd ed. (New York: Rowman & Littlefield, 2000), 42–43.

Fung, Amanda. "Love and No Marriage," *Crain's New York Business* (February 13, 2006), 27–28.

Gibbs, Jennifer, Nicole B. Ellison, and Rebecca D. Heino. "Self-Presentation in Online Personals," *Communication Research* 33 (April 2006), 152–177.

Goffman, Erving. *Relations in Public: Microstudies of the Public Order* (New York: Harper and Row, 1972).

Goldstine, Daniel, et al. *The Dance-Away Lover and Other Roles We Play in Love, Sex, and Marriage* (New York: Morrow, 1977).

Greene, Kathryn, Valerian J. Derlega, and Alicia Mathews. "Self-Disclosure in Personal Relationships," in Anita Vangelisti and Daniel Perlman, eds., *Cambridge Handbook of Personal Relationships* (New York: Cambridge University Press, 2006), 409–427.

Guerrero, Laura, and Kory Floyd. *Nonverbal Communication in Close Relationships* (Mahwah, NJ: Erlbaum, 2006).

Hargie, Owen, Christine Saunders, and David Dickson. *Social Skills in Interpersonal Communication* (Cambridge, MA: Brookline Books, 1987), 187–208.

Hazen & Shaker, 1994

Hazan, Cindy, and Phillip Shaver. "Romantic Love Conceptualized as an Attachment Process," *Journal of Personality and Social Psychology* 52 (1987), 511–524.

Hendrick, Clyde, and Susan Hendrick. "A Theory and Method of Love," *Journal of Personality and Social Psychology* 50 (1986), 392–402.

Hendrick, Clyde, Susan Hendrick, and Amy Dicke. "The Love Attitudes Scale: Short Form," *Journal of Social and Personal Relationships* 15, no. 2 (1998), 147–159.

Hitsch, Hortaçsu, and Ariely, 2005. p. 264.

Hitsch, Gunter J., Ali Hortaçsu, and Dan Ariely. "What Makes You Click? An Empirical Analysis of Online Dating," *www.aeaweb.org/annual_mtg_papers/2006/0106_0800_0502.pdf*.

Jourard, Sidney M. *The Transparent Self, Self-Disclosure and Well Being* (Princeton, NJ: Van Nostrand, 1964).

———. *Self-Disclosure: An Experimental Analysis of the Transparent Self* (Melbourne, FL: Kreiger, 1979).

Knapp, Mark L., and Judy Hall. *Nonverbal Communication in Human Interaction,* 5th ed. (New York: Harcourt Brace Jovanovich, 2002).

Lacey, Robert. *Sotheby's—Bidding for Class* (Boston, MA: Little, Brown, 1998).

Lee, J. A. *The Colors of Love* (Don Mills, Ontario: New Press, 1973).

Levitt, Steven D., and Stephen J. Dubner. *Freakonomics,* rev. ed. (New York: HarperCollins, 2006).

Liefbroer, Aart C., and Edith Dourleijn. "Unmarried Cohabitation and Union Stability," *Demography* 43 (May 2006), 203–221.

Luft, Joseph. *Of Human Interaction* (Palo Alto, CA: National Press, 1969).

Luo, Shanhong, and Eva C. Klohnen. "Assortative Mating and Marital Quality in Newlyweds," *Journal of Personality and Social Psychology* 88 (2005), 304–326.

Markman, H. J., Rhoades, G. K., Stanley, S. M., Ragan, E., and Whitton, S. (2010). "The Premarital Communication Roots of Marital Distress: The First Five Years of Marriage," *Journal of Family Psychology, 24,* 289–298.

McGoldrick, Monica. "Becoming a Couple," in Betty Carter and Monica McGoldrick, eds., *The Expanded Family Cycle,* 3rd ed. (Boston, MA: Allyn & Bacon, 1999), 231–248.

Miller, G. R., and M. Steinberg. *Between People* (Chicago: Science Research Association, 1975).

Murray, Charles. *Coming Apart: The State of White America.* New York: Crown Forum, 2012.

Murray, Charles. "The New American Divide," *The Wall Street Journal,* January 21, 2012, C1–C2.

Murray, Sandra L., Dale W. Griffin, Paul Rose, and Gina Bellavia. "For Better or Worse? Self-Esteem and the Contingencies of Acceptance in Marriage," *Personality and Social Psychology Bulletin* 32 (July 2006), 866–880.

Noller, Patricia. "Nonverbal Communication in Close Relationships," in Anita Vangelisti and Daniel Perlman, eds., *Cambridge Handbook of Personal Relationships* (New York: Cambridge University Press, 2006), 403–420.

Pfeffer, Jeffrey. *Power: Why Some People Have It and Others Don't.* New York: HarperCollins, 2010.

Phillips, G. M., and J. T. Wood. *Communication and Human Relationships* (New York: Macmillan, 1983).

Pratto, Felicia, and Angela Walker. "The Bases of Gendered Power," in Alice H. Eagly, Anne E. Beall, and Robert J. Sternberg, eds., *The Psychology of Gender,* 2nd ed. (New York: Guilford Press, 2004), 242–268.

Romney, Mitt. *No Apology: The Case for American Greatness* (New York: St. Martin's Press, 2010).

Rosenfeld, L. B., and W. L. Kendrick. "Choosing to Be Open: Subjective Reasons for Self-Disclosing," *Western Journal of Speech Communication* 48 (1984), 326–343.

Srivastava, Sanjay, Kelly M. McGonagal, Jane M. Richards, Emily A. Butler, and James J. Gross. "Optimism in Close Relationships," *Journal of Personality and Social Psychology* 91 (July 2006), 143–153.

Steil, Janice M. "Contemporary Marriage: Still an Unequal Partnership," in Clyde Hendrick and Susan S. Hendrick, eds., *Close Relationships: A Sourcebook* (Thousand Oaks, CA: Sage, 2000), 125–136.

Stewart, John. *Bridges Not Walls,* 10th ed. (New York: McGraw-Hill, 2012).

VanLear, C. Arthur, Jr. "The Formation of Social Relationships: A Longitudinal Study of Social Penetration," *Human Communication Research* 13 (1987), 299–322.

———. "Testing a Cyclical Model of Communicative Openness in Relationship Development: Two Longitudinal Studies," *Communication Monographs* 58 (1991), 337–361.

Wilmot, William. *Relational Communication,* 4th ed. (New York: McGraw-Hill, 1995).

Wilson, Keithia. *Assertiveness and Its Social Context* (New York: Pergamon Press, 1993).

Yoshioka, Mariane. "Substantive Differences in the Assertiveness of Low-Income African American, Hispanic and Caucasian Women,"*Journal of Psychology* 134, no. 3 (2000).

Zimbler, Mattyityahu and Robert Feldman, "Liar, Liar, Hard Drive on Fire: How Media Context Affects Lying Behavior," *Journal of Applied Psychology,* October, 2011.

Chapter 10   Intercultural Communication

Allport, Gordon W. *The Nature of Prejudice* (Cambridge, MA: Addison-Wesley, 1954).

Althen, Gary. "The Americans Have to Say Everything," *Communication Quarterly* 40 (1992), 413–421.

Appiah, Kwame Anthony. *Cosmopolitanism: Ethics in a World of Strangers* (New York: Norton, 2006).

Baldwin, James. "Stranger in the Village," in James Baldwin, *The Price of the Ticket: Collected Nonfiction 1948–1985* (New York: St. Martin's, 1985), 79–90.

Blair, John G. "Thinking Through Binaries: Conceptual Strategies for Interdependence," *American Studies International* 38, no. 2 (2000), 23–38.

Buchanan, Patrick. *Suicide of a Superpower* (New York: St. Martin's Press, 2011).

Buckley, Michael. *Moon Handbook: Vietnam, Cambodia & Laos,* 4th ed. (Emeryville, CA: Avalon Travel Publishing, 2006).

Carlson, Jerry S., and Keith F. Widaman. "The Effects of Study Abroad during College on Attitudes toward Other Cultures," *International Journal of Intercultural Relations* 12 (1988), 1–17.

Chambers, John R., Robert S. Baron, and Mary L. Imman. "Misperceptions in Intergroup Conflict," *Psychological Science* 17, no. 1 (2006), 38–45.

Chambers, John R., and Darya Melnyk. "Why Do I Hate Thee? Conflict Misperceptions and Intergroup Mistrust," *Personality and Social Psychology Bulletin* 32 (October 2006), 1295–1311.

Chow, Rey. *Sentimental Fabulations, Contemporary Chinese Films* (New York: Columbia University Press, 2007).

Christians, Clifford, and Kaarle Nordenstreng. "Social Responsibility Worldwide," *Journal of Mass Media Ethics* 19, no. 1 (2004), 3–28.

Christians, Clifford, and Michael Traber, eds. *Communication Ethics and Universal Values* (Thousand Oaks, CA: Sage, 1997).

Couldry, Nick. *Listening Beyond the Echoes: Media, Ethics, and Agency in an Uncertain World* (Boulder, CO: Paradigm Publishers, 2006).

Davis, Olga I., Thomas K. Nakayama, and Judith N. Martin. "Current and Future Directions in Ethnicity and Methodology," *International Journal of Intercultural Relations* 24 (2000), 525–539.

Dion, Karen. "Cultural Perspectives on Facial Attractiveness," in Gillian Rhodes and Leslie A. Zebrowitz, eds., *Facial Attractiveness: Evolutionary, Cognitive, and Social Perspectives* (Westport, CT: Ablex, 2002), 239–260.

Dodd, Carley H. *Dynamics of Intercultural Communication,* 5th ed. (New York: McGraw-Hill, 1999).

Douglis, Carole. "The Beat Goes On," *Psychology Today* 21 (November 1987), 36–42.

Eisenhower, David. *Going Home to Glory* (New York: Simon & Schuster, 2010).

Foner, Nancy. *New Immigrants in New York* (New York: Columbia University Press, 2001).

Friedman, Thomas, and Michael Mandelbaum. *That Used to Be Us* (New York: Farrar, Straus and Giroux, 2011).

Gannon, Martin J., Peter Brown, and Sharon Ribas. "French Wine: An Illustration of a Cultural Metaphor," in Martin J. Gannon, ed., *Cultural Metaphors* (Thousand Oaks, CA: Sage, 2001), 59–78.

Gladwell, Malcolm. *Outliers* (New York: Little, Brown and Company, 2008).

Goleman, Daniel. *Social Intelligence* (New York: Bantam Books, 2006).

Gorham, Bradley W. "News Media's Relationship with Stereotyping: The Linguistic Intergroup Bias in Response to Crime News," *Journal of Communication* 56, no. 2 (2006), 289–308.

Govorun, Olesya, Kathleen Fuegen, and B. Keith Payne. "Stereotypes Focus Defensive Projection," *Personality and Social Psychology Bulletin* 32 (June 2006), 781–793.

Griffin, Em. *A First Look at Communication Theory,* 7th ed. (New York: McGraw-Hill, 2009).

Gudykunst and Kim, 1997.

Gudykunst, William B., and Young Yuri Kim. *Communicating with Strangers: An Approach to Intercultural Communication,* 3rd ed. (New York: McGraw-Hill, 1997).

Gudykunst, William B., and Stella Ting-Toomey. *Culture and Interpersonal Communication* (Newbury Park, CA: Sage, 1988).

Guerrero, Laura, and Kory Floyd. *Nonverbal Communication in Close Relationships* (Mahwah, NJ: Erlbaum, 2006).

Hall, Edward T. *The Silent Language* (New York: Doubleday, 1959).

———*The Dance of Life: The Other Dimension of Time* (New York: Anchor Books, 1984).

Halualani, Rona Tamiko, Anu S. Chitgopekar, Jennifer Huynh Thi Ahn Morrison, and Patrick Shaou Whea Dodge. "Diverse in Name Only? Intercultural Interaction at a Multicultural University," *Journal of Communication* 54, no. 2 (2004), 270–286.

Hammond, Ross A., and Robert Axelrod. "The Evolution of Ethnocentrism," *Journal of Conflict Resolution* 50, no. 6 (2006), 926–936.

Hessler, Peter. *Oracle Bones: A Journey Between China's Past and Present.* (New York: HarperCollins, 2006).

Hofstede, Geert. *Culture's Consequences* (Newbury Park, CA: Sage, 1980).

———. *Culture and Organizations* (New York: McGraw-Hill, 1991).

Jen, Gish. *Who's Irish?* (New York: Knopf, 1999).

Kidder, Rushworth M. *Moral Courage* (New York: HarperCollins, 2005).

Kissinger, Henry. *On China* (New York: The Penguin Press, 2011).

Kong Fu-zi, 551–479 B.C.E., p. 284.

Kwak, Nojin, Nathaniel Poor, and Marko M. Skoric. "Honey, I Shrunk the World! The Relation Between Internet Use and International Engagement," *Mass Communication & Society* 9, no. 2 (2006), 189–213.

Lewis, Michael. *Boomerang: Travels in The New Third World* (New York: W. W. Norton & Company, 2011).

Lim, Tae-seop, and Soo Hyang Choi. "Interpersonal Relationships in Korea," in William B. Gudykunst, Stella Ting-Toomey, and Tsukasa Nishida, eds., *Communication in Personal Relationships across Cultures* (Thousand Oaks, CA: Sage, 1996).

Lull, James. *Media Communication, Culture: A Global Approach* (New York: Columbia University Press, 2000).

Maddux, William W., and Masaki Yuki. "The 'Ripple Effect': Cultural Differences in Perceptions of the Consequences of Events," *Personality and Social Psychology Bulletin* 32 (May 2006), 669–683.

Mambani, Zehra. "When a Hyphen Barely Holds Up," *Barnard: Special Section: The Aftermath of September 11* (Fall 2001), 14.

Martin, Judith N., and Thomas K. Nakayama. *Intercultural Communication in Contexts*, 4th ed. (New York: McGraw-Hill, 2007).

Martin, Judith, and Thomas Nakayama. *Experiencing Intercultural Communication*, 3rd ed. (New York: McGraw-Hill, 2008).

"Mind the Gap," *PEN America: A Journal for Writers and Readers* 3, no. 6 (2005), 114–120.

Murray, Charles. *Coming Apart* (New York: Crown Forum, 2012).

Nagda, Biren (Ratnesh) A. "Breaking Barriers, Crossing Borders, Building Bridges: Communication Processes in Intergroup Dialogues," *Journal of Social Issues* 62 (September 2006), 553–576.

Neuliep, James. *Intercultural Communication: A Contextual Approach*, 3rd ed. (New York: Sage Publications, 2006).

Neuliep, James, and James C. McCroskey. "The Development of a U.S. and Generalized Ethnocentrism Scale," *Communication Research Reports* 14 (1997a), 385–398.

———. "The Development of Intercultural and Interethnic Communication Apprehension Scales," *Communication Research Reports* 14 (1997b), 145–156.

Onishi, Norimitsu. "Freed from Captivity in Iraq; Japanese Return to More Pain," *New York Times* (April 23, 2004), A1, A11.

Park, Ji Hoon, Nadine G. Gabbadon, and Ariel R. Chernin. "Naturalizing Racial Differences through Comedy," *Journal of Communication* 56 (2006), 157–177.

Patchett, Ann. *Bel Canto* (New York: HarperCollins, 2005).

Patterson, Orlando. "Our Overrated Inner Self," *New York Times* (December 26, 2006), A35.

Pettigrew, Thomas F., and Linda R. Tropp. "A Meta-Analytic Test of Intergroup Contact Theory," *Journal of Personality and Social Psychology* 90 (May 2006), 751–783.

Pew Global Attitudes Project. Retrieved November 9, 2004 from *www.people-press.org/commentary/display.php3?AnalysisID=86*.

Philipsen, Gerry. "Speech Codes Theory," in Em Griffin, *A First Look at Communication Theory*, 7th ed. (New York; McGraw-Hill, 2009), 414–425.

Rodriguez, Clara E. "Promoting Analytical and Critical Viewing," in Clara E. Rodriguez, ed., *Latin Looks: Images of Latinas and Latinos in the U.S. Media* (New York: Westview Books, HarperCollins, 1997).

Rohrlich, Beulah, and Judith N. Martin. "Host Country and Reentry Adjustment of Student Sojourners," *International Journal of Intercultural Relations* 15 (1991), 163–182.

Ross, Susan Dente. "Unequal Combatants on an Uneven Media Battlefield: Palestine and Israel," in Paul Martin Lester and Susan Dente Ross, eds., *Images that Injure: Pictorial Stereotypes in the Media* (Westport, CT: Praeger, 2003), 58–63.

Samovar, Larry A., and Richard Porter, eds. *Intercultural Communication: A Reader*, 9th ed. (Belmont, CA: Wadsworth, 2000).

Scott, Janny. "Foreign Born in U.S. at Record High," *New York Times* (February 7, 2002), A26.

Sillars, Alan L., and Judith Weisberg. "Conflict as a Social Skill," in Michael E. Roloff and Gerald R. Miller, eds., *Interpersonal Processes: New Directions in Communication Research* (Newbury Park, CA: Sage, 1987), 140–171.

Stephan, Cookie White, and Walter G. Stephan. "Reducing Intercultural Anxiety through Intercultural Contact," *International Journal of Intercultural Relations* 16 (1992), 89–106.

Ting-Toomey, Stella. *Communicating Across Cultures* (New York: Guilford Press, 1999).

Ting-Toomey, Stella, "Face-Negotiation Theory," in Em Griffin, *A First Look at Communication Theory*, 7th ed. (New York: McGraw-Hill, 2009), 400–413.

Ting-Toomey, Stella, and Leeva Chung. "Cross-Cultural Interpersonal Communication: Theoretical Trends and Research Directions," in William B. Gudykunst, Stella Ting-Toomey, and Tsukasa Nishida, eds., *Communication in Personal Relationships across Cultures* (Thousand Oaks, CA: Sage, 1996), 237–261.

Ting-Toomey, Stella, Kimberlie K. Yee-Jung, Robin B. Shapiro et al. "Ethnic/cultural Identity Salience and Conflict Styles in Four U.S. Groups," *International Journal of Intercultural Relations* 24 (2000), 47–81.

van Dijk, Teun A. "New(s) Racism: A Discourse Analytical Approach," in Simon Cottle, ed., *Ethnic Minorities and the Media* (Buckingham, UK: Open University Press, 2000), 33–49.

Weigl, Robert C., and Jesus M. Reyes. "Latino and Anglo Political Portraits: Lessons from Intercultural Field Research," *International Journal of Intercultural Relations* 25 (2001), 235–259.

Wilgoren, Jodi. "A Nation Challenged: Arab American: Struggling to Be Both Arab and American," *New York Times* (November 4, 2001), B1.

Chapter 11   Interviewing

Banville, Thomas G. *How to Listen—How to Be Heard* (Chicago, IL: Nelson-Hall, 1978).

Byham, William C. and Debra Pickett. *Landing the Job You Want*, 2nd ed. (Pittsburgh, PA: Three Rivers Press, 1999).

Camp, Richaurd, Mary Vielhaber, and Jack Simonetti. *Strategic Interviewing: How to Hire the Best People* (San Francisco, CA: Jossey-Bass, 2001).

Coopman, Stephanie. "Conducting the Information Interview," (2004). From Web site: *www.roguecom.com/interview/module5.html*.

Crowley, E. "Making CEO Selection Work," *Directorship* 30, no. 2 (February 2004), 13–16.

Deep, Sam, and Lyle Sussman. *Yes, You Can* (Reading, MA: Addison-Wesley, 1998).

Deluca, Matthew J. *Best Answers to the 201 Most Frequently Asked Interview Questions* (New York: McGraw-Hill, 1997).

Groysberg, Boris, and Robin Abrahams. "Five Ways to Bungle a Job Change," *Harvard Business Review*, January–February, 2010, 137–140.

Kahn, Robert L., and Charles F. Cannell. *The Dynamics of Interviewing: Theory, Technique and Cases*, 2nd ed. (New York: Wiley, 1968).

Kennedy, J. "Killer Interview Tactic Can Help Candidate Score," *Milwaukee Journal Sentinel* (April 2003), 22.

Korn, Melissa, "B-Schools Send Rejections to Unlikely Group: Alumni," The Wall Street Journal, January 5, 2012, B1.

Margolis, Joshua, and Paul Stoltz. "How to Bounce Back from Adversity," *Harvard Business Review*, January–February, 2010, 87–92.

McCabe, C. "Interview Is about Boss, Too, Not Just Job Hunter," *Boston Globe* (June 2004), G15.

Murnighan, J. Keith. *Bargaining Games* (New York: William Morrow, 1992).

"On the Job; Interview Tips," *Augusta (GA) Chronicle* (January 2003), F1.

Raudsepp, E. "Body-Language Tactics That Sway Interviewers," *Career Journal* (2004). Retrieved July 13, 2004, from *Career Journal* Web site: *www.careerjournal.com/jobhunting/interviewing/20021205-raudsepp.html*.

Reed, James, and Paul Stoltz. *Put Your Mindset to Work*. New York: Portfolio/Penguin, 2011.

Scott, T. "Foti's New Applications Ask for Age, Race; Forms Not Illegal but May Expose Agency to Lawsuits," *New Orleans Times-Picayune* (April 2004), 1.

Shalett, K. "Steps to Success; Appearance Opens Doors," *New Orleans Times-Picayune,* (May 2004), 1.

Sheridan, M. "The Ten-Minute Manager's Guide to Interviewing New Hires," *Restaurants & Institutions* 114, no. 1 (January 2004), 26.

Stewart, Charles J., and William B. Cash. *Interviewing: Principles and Practices,* (New York: McGraw-Hill, 2007).

"Turning the Tables on the Job Interview," *PR Newswire* (New York, May 2004), 1.

University of Alabama at Birmingham. Illegal Interview Questions, *UAB Career Services* (2004) from UAB Career Services Web site: *www.careercenter.uab.edu/gethired/interview/illegalquest.htm*.

Whetten, David, and Kim Cameron. *Developing Management Skills*, 6th ed. (Upper Saddle River, NJ: Prentice-Hall, 2005).

Wilson, Gerald L., and H. Lloyd Goodall, Jr. *Interviewing in Context* (New York: McGraw-Hill, 1991).

Chapter 12   Small-Group Communication

Amabile, Teresa. "How to Kill Creativity," *Harvard Business Review* (September–October, 1998), 77–87.

Armour, Stephanie. "Team Efforts, Technology Add New Reasons to Meet," *USA Today* (December 9, 1997), 1A.

Associated Press, "Soldiers Marry by Videoconference," *Dubuque (IA) Telegraph-Herald* (June 10, 2004), A2.

Bales, Robert. *Personality and Interpersonal Behavior* (New York: Holt, Rinehart and Winston, 1970).

Bales, Robert, and Fred Strodbeck. "Phases in Group Problem Solving," *Journal of Abnormal and Social Psychology* 46 (1951), 485–495.

Barr, Steve H., and Edward J. Conlon. "Effects of Distribution of Feedback in Work Groups," *Academy of Management Journal* (June 1994), 641–655.

Benne, Kenneth D., and Paul Sheats. "Functional Roles of Group Members," *Journal of Social Issues* (1948), 41–49.

Bennis, Warren G., and Herbert A. Shepard. "A Theory of Group Development," *Human Relations* 9 (1956), 415–457.

Berns, Gregory. *Iconoclast* (Boston: Harvard Business School Press, 2008).

Bettencourt, Lance, and Scott Bettencourt. "Innovating on the Cheap," *Harvard Business Review,* June 2011, 88–94.

Blanchard, Ken. *Leading at a Higher Level* (Upper Saddle River, NJ: Prentice Hall, 2007).

Blenko, Marcia, Michael Mankins, and Paul Rogers. *Decide & Deliver*. Boston: Harvard Business Review Press, 2010.

Bostrom, Robert. "Patterns of Communicative Interaction in Small Groups," *Speech Monographs* 37 (1970), 257–263.

Cartwright, Dorwin, and Alvin Zander. *Group Dynamics,* 3rd ed. (New York: Harper and Row, 1968), 139–151.

Chansler, P., P. Swamidass, and C. Cammann. "Self-managing Work Teams: An Empirical Study of Group Cohesiveness in 'Natural Work Groups' at a Harley-Davidson Motor Company Plant," *Small Group Research* 343, no. 1 (February 2003), 101–120.

Cherniss, Cary, and Daniel Goleman, eds. *The Emotionally Intelligent Workplace* (San Francisco, CA: Jossey-Bass, 2001).

Clay, Thomas. *A Litmus Test for Practice Group Effectiveness* (Newtown Square, PA: Altman Weil Publications, 2007).

Donnellon, Anne. *Team Talk: The Power of Language in Team Dynamics* (Cambridge, MA: Harvard Business School Press, 1996).

Festinger, Leon. "A Theory of Social Comparison Processes," *Human Relations* 7 (1954), 117–140.

Fisher, B. Aubrey. "Decision Emergence: Phases in Group Decision Making," *Speech Monographs* 37 (1970), 53–66.

Fisher, Kimball. *Leading Self-Directed Work Teams: A Guide to Developing New Team Leadership Skills,* 2nd ed. (New York: McGraw-Hill, 1999).

Gantert and Tracy, 2006.

Gershman, 2006.

Goleman, Daniel. "What Makes a Leader?" *Harvard Business Review* (November–December 1998), 93–102.

Gouran, Dennis S., Candace Brown, and David R. Henry. "Behavioral Correlates of Quality in Decision-Making Discussions," *Communication Monographs* 45 (1978), 51–63.

Gray, Dave, Sunni Brown, and James Macanufo. *Gamestorming* (Sebastopol, CA: O'Reilly Media, Inc., 2010).

Griffin, Em. *A First Look at Communication Theory,* 7th ed. (New York: McGraw-Hill, 2009)

Gudykunst, William, and Mitchell R. Hammer. "The Influence of Social Identity and Intimacy of Interethnic Relationships on Uncertainty Reduction Processes," *Human Communication Research* 14 (1988), 569–607.

Guetzkow, Harold, and Herbert A. Simon. "The Impact of Certain Communication Nets upon Organization and Performance in Task-Oriented Groups," *Management Science* 1 (1955), 233–250.

Hannon, K. "Group Wisdom Is More Widespread Than We Know," *USA Today* (June 2004), B8.

Hare, A. Paul. *Handbook of Small Group Research* (New York: Free Press, 1962).

Hirokawa, Randy Y. "Group Communication and Problem-Solving Effectiveness: An Investigation of Group Phases," *Human Communication Research* 9 (1983), 291–305.

Homans, George C. *The Human Group* (San Diego, CA: Harcourt Brace Jovanovich, 1950).

Huszczo, Gregory. *Tools for Team Leadership* (Palo Alto, CA: Davies-Black, 2004).

IBM. *Capitalizing on Complexity*. Somers, NY: IBM Global Business Services, 2010.

Janis, Irving L. *Group Think,* 2nd ed. (Boston, MA: Houghton Mifflin, 1982).

Jarobe, Susan P. "A Comparison of Input-Output, Process-Output, and Input-Process-Output Models of Small Group Problem-Solving Effectiveness," *Communication Monographs* 55 (1988), 121–142.

Kao, John. *Jamming* (New York: Harper Business, 1996).

Leavitt, Harold J. "Some Effects of Certain Communication Patterns on Group Performance," *Journal of Abnormal and Social Psychology* 46 (1951), 38–50.

Levine & Mooreland, 2006.

Lipman-Blumen, Jean, and Harold J. Leavitt. *Hot Groups* (New York: Oxford University Press, 1999).

Lobe, J. "Iraq: A Certified Case of 'Chickenhawk Groupthink,'" *Global Information Network* (May 12, 2004), 1.

Lovelace, Kay, Dera L. Shapiro, and Laurie R. Weingart, "Maximizing Cross-Functional New Product Teams' Innovativeness and Constraint Adherence: A Conflict Communications Perspective," *Academy of Management Journal,* 44 (2001), 779–793.

Maxwell, John C. *The 17 Indisputable Laws of Teamwork* (Nashville, TN: Thomas Nelson Publishers, 2001).

McManus, Kevin. "Have You Been to Abilene?" *Industrial Engineer* (March 2007), 20.

Meetings in America: A Study of Trends, Costs and Attitudes toward Business Travel, Teleconferencing, and Their Impact on Productivity. MCI Networking white paper (Greenwich, CT: INFOCOMM, 1998), 3.

Newcomb, Theodore M. "Persistence and Regression of Changed Attitudes: Long-Range Studies," *Journal of Social Issues* 19 (1963), 3–14.

Newvine, Colleen. "Meeting Mania," *Ann Arbor News* (June 7, 1998), E1.

Okhuysen, Gerardo Andres. "Structuring Change: Familiarity and Formal Interventions in Problem-Solving Groups," *Academy of Management Journal,* 44 (2001), 794–808.

Osborn, Alex F. *Applied Imagination* (New York: Scribner, 1957).

Pace, Roger C. "Communication Patterns in High and Low Consensus Discussion: A Descriptive Analysis," *Southern Speech Communication Journal* 53 (1988), 184–202.

Parkinson, Cyril Northcote. *Parkinson's Law* (New York: Ballantine, 1964).

Picken, 2008.

Raudsepp, Eugene. *More Creative Growth Games* (New York: Perigee, 1980).

"Raymond Mulls Future," *CNN.com* (February 11, 2004). From *www.cnn.com/2004/SHOWBIZ/02/11/showbuzz/index.html.*

Roberts, 2006.

Safian, Robert. "Generation Flux," *Fast Company*, February, 2012, 60–71.

Schachter, Stanley. "Deviation, Rejection and Communication," *Journal of Abnormal and Social Psychology* 46 (1951), 190–208.

Schembechler, Bo, and John Bacon. *Bo's Lasting Lessons* (New York: Business Plus, 2007).

Schutz, William. *FIRO: A Three-Dimensional Theory of Interpersonal Behavior* (New York: Holt, Rinehart and Winston, 1958).

Schwartz, J., and M. Wald. "Is 'Groupthink' Part of Problem with NASA Again?" *Grand Rapids Press* (March 23, 2003), A15.

Shaw, Marvin E. *Group Dynamics: The Psychology of Small Group Behavior*, 3rd ed. (New York: McGraw-Hill, 1981).

Sherif, Muzafer. *Social Interaction: Process and Products* (Chicago, IL: Aldine, 1967).

Stahl, Gerry "Communication and Learning in Online Collaboration." College of Information Science and Technology, Drexel University (2003). From Web site: *www.cis.drexel.edu/faculty/gerry/publications/conferences/2003/group/group03.doc.*

Surowiecki, James. *The Wisdom of Crowds: Why the Many Are Smarter Than the Few and How Collective Wisdom Shapes Business, Economies, Societies and Nations* (London: Little Brown, 2004).

Sutton, R. "Why Innovation Happens When Happy People Fight," *Ivey Business Journal* 67, no. 1 (November/December 2002).

Thelen, Herbert, and Watson Dickerman. "Stereotypes and the Growth of Groups," *Educational Leadership* 6 (1949), 309–316.

Tichy, Noel M., with Eli Cohen. *The Leadership Engine* (New York: Harper Business, 1997).

Tubbs, Stewart L. *A Systems Approach to Small Group Interaction*, 11th ed. (New York: McGraw-Hill, 2012).

Tuckman, Bruce. "Developmental Sequence in Small Groups," *Psychological Bulletin* 63 (1965), 384–399.

Wallach, Michael A., Nathan Kogan, and Daryl J. Bem. "Group Influence on Individual Risk-Taking," *Journal of Abnormal and Social Psychology* 65 (1962), 75–86.

Walsh, Tom. "Action-Based Education," *The Detroit Free Press*, August, 14, 2011, B1.

Whetten, David, and Kim Cameron. *Developing Management Skills,* 7th ed. (Upper Saddle River, NJ: Prentice-Hall, 2011).

Woodward, Bob. *Obama's Wars*. New York: Simon & Schuster, 2010.

Yang, Jia Lynn, "How Obama Manages," *Fortune* (July 7, 2008), 74.

Chapter 13   Public Communication

Alexander, Benjamin. "Reflections on Education and Our Society," *Vital Speeches of the Day* 55 (1989), 563–565.

Baumeister, Roy, and John Tierney. *Willpower: Rediscover the Greatest Human Strength* (New York: Penguin Press, 2011).

Beaver, Dennis. "Warning: Humor Can Be Hazardous," *ABA Banking Journal* 98, no. 10 (October 2006), 72.

Berns, Gregory. *Iconoclast: A Neuroscientist Reveals How To Think Differently*. Boston: Harvard Business Press, 2008.

Bess, A. "Convention Helps Public Speakers Find Their Voice—and Funny Bone," *St. Louis Post-Dispatch* (February 29, 2004), C3.

Bohner, 2003.

Boorstin, Daniel J. "Dissent, Dissension, and the News," in Wil A. Linkugel, R. R. Allen, and Richard L. Johannesen, eds., *Contemporary American Speeches,* 2nd ed. (Belmont, CA: Wadsworth, 1969), 203–211.

Bowers, John Waite. "Language Intensity, Social Introversion, and Attitude Change," *Speech Monographs* 30 (1963), 345–352.

Brunel, F., and M. Nelson. "Message Order Effects and Gender Differences in Advertising Persuasion," *Journal of Advertising Research* 43, no. 3 (September 2003), 330.

Cain, Susan. *Quiet: The Power of Introverts in a World That Can't Stop Talking* (New York: Crown Publishers, 2012).

Carter, Jimmy. "Address Accepting Democratic Nomination for Presidency," *New York Times* (July 16, 1976), A10.

Chekhov, Anton. *Letter to A. P. Chekhov* (April 11, 1889).

Clevenger, Theodore, Jr. *Audience Analysis* (Indianapolis, IN: Bobbs-Merrill, 1966).

Cole, J., and J. McCroskey. "The Association of Perceived Communication Apprehension, Shyness, and Verbal Aggression with Perceptions of Source Credibility and Affect in Organizational and Interpersonal Contexts," *Communication Quarterly* 51, no. 1 (Winter 2004), 101.

Collins, Rebecca, et al. "The Vividness Effect: Elusive or Illusory?" *Journal of Experimental Social Psychology* 24 (1988), 1–18.

Conger, Jay A. *Winning 'Em Over* (New York: Simon & Schuster, 1998).

"The Credibility Question," *PC World* (San Francisco) 22, no. 4 (April 2004), 86.

Dabbs, J. M., Jr., and H. Leventhal. "Effects of Varying the Recommendations of a Fear-Arousing Communication," *Journal of Personality and Social Psychology* 4 (1966), 525–531.

Daly, John. *Advocacy: Championing Ideas and Influencing Others* (New Haven, CT: Yale University Press, 2011).

Das, E., J. de Wit, and W. Stroebe. "Fear Appeals Motivate Acceptance of Action Recommendations: Evidence for a Positive Bias in the Processing of Persuasive Messages," *Personality and Social Psychology Bulletin* 29, no. 5 (May 2003), 650.

Dean, Howard. "I Have a Scream Speech: The Making of A Media Event." From Rachet Up Digiteyes Web site: *ratchetup.typepad.com/eyes/2004/03/howard_deans_i_.html.*

Detweiler, Michael. "Para-Verbal Avoidance During Public Speaking: The Relationship Between Self-Disclosure and Social Anxiety" (Ph.D. dissertation, West Virginia University, 2005).

Detz, J. "10 Tips for Better Speeches," (2004). From Joan Detz Web site: *www.joandetz.com/tips.html.*

Deutsch, Babette. *Poetry Handbook: A Dictionary of Terms* (New York: Funk and Wagnalls, 1957).

Downing, Joe, and Cecile Garmon. "Teaching Students in the Basic Course How to Use Presentation Software," *Communication Education* 50 (2001), 218–229.

Foer, Joshua. *Moonwalking with Einstein* (New York: The Penguin Press, 2011).

Friedman, Thomas. *Hot, Flat and Crowded* (New York: Farrar, Straus and Giroux, 2008).

Frymier, Ann, and Marjorie Nadler. *Persuasion: Integrating Theory, Research, and Practice,* 2nd ed. (Dubuque, IA: Kendall Hunt, 2010).

Gallo, Carmine. "Terminate Your Public Speaking Fears," *Business Week Online* (May 22, 2006a).

———. "How to PowerPoint Like a Pro," *Business Week Online* (June 2, 2006b).

———. "How to Be an Ace Speaker," *Business Week Online* (June 15, 2006c).

Gergen, David. *Eyewitness to Power* (New York: Simon & Schuster, 2000).

Germano, W. "The Scholarly Lecture: How to Stand and Deliver," *Chronicle of Higher Education* 50, no. 14 (November 28, 2003), B15.

Goldstein, Noah, Steve Martin, and Robert B. Cialdini. *Yes! 50 Scientifically Proven Ways to Be Persuasive* (New York: The Free Press, 2008).

Gruner, C. R. "The Effect of Humor in Dull and Interesting Informative Speeches," *Central States Speech Journal* 21 (1970), 160–166.

———. "Advice to the Beginning Speaker on Using Humor— What Research Tells Us," *Communication Education* 34 (1985), 142–147.

Halperin, Mark and John Heilemann. *Game Change.* New York: HarperCollins, 2010.

Hovland, Carl, Irving Janis, and Harold Kelley. *Communication Persuasion* (New Haven, CT: Yale University Press, 1953).

Iacocca, Lee. "The Will to Take Leadership," *Vital Speeches of the Day 55* (1989), 454–458.

Ivry, B. "Can a Movie Halt Making of 'Bush II'?; Political Camps Debate Impact of 'Fahrenheit 9/11,'" *Bergen County (NJ) Record* (July 2, 2004), A1.

James-Enger, K. "Talk It Up," *The Writer* (Boston) 117, no. 5 (May 2004), 41–42.

Janis, Irving, and Peter Field. "Sex Differences and Personality Factors Related to Persuasibility," in Carl Hovland and Irving Janis, eds., *Personality and Persuasibility* (New Haven, CT: Yale University Press, 1959), 55–68.

Jesse, David. "U-M's Reputation Improves Worldwide," *Detroit Free Press*, March 15, 2012, 4A.

Kahneman, Daniel. *Thinking Fast and Slow.* New York: Farrar, Strauss and Giroux, 2011.

Karlins, M., and H. Abelson. *Persuasion: How Opinions and Attitudes Are Changed,* 2nd ed. (New York: Springer, 1970).

King, Martin Luther, Jr. "I Have a Dream," in Wil Linkugel, R. R. Allen, and Richard L. Johannesen, eds., *Contemporary American Speeches,* 2nd ed. (Belmont, CA: Wadsworth, 1969), 290–294.

Knapp, Mark L., and Judith A. Hall. *Nonverbal Communication in Human Interaction,* 7th ed. (Boston, MA: Wadsworth/Cengage Learning, 2009).

Kouzes, James M., and Barry Z. Posner. *The Truth about Leadership* (San Francisco, CA: Jossey-Bass, 2010).

Lightman, David. "Bush's Legacy Already Written," *Detroit Free Press* (January 4, 2009), 4A.

Lublin, 2007.

Luntz, Frank. *Win: The Key Principles to Take Your Business From Ordinary to Extraordinary.* New York: Hyperion, 2011.

Maxwell, John C. *The 17 Indisputable Laws of Teamwork* (Nashville, TN: Thomas Nelson Publishers, 2001).

McCroskey, James C. *An Introduction to Rhetorical Communication,* 6th ed. (Upper Saddle River, NJ: Prentice Hall, 1993).

McEwen, William J., and B. S. Greenberg. "The Effects of Message Intensity on Receiver Evaluations of Source, Message, and Topic," *Journal of Communication* 20 (1970), 340–350.

McGinn, Daniel. "Happy Birthday Harvard B-School," *Newsweek* (November 3, 2008), E22.

McGuire, William J. "Personality and Susceptibility to Social Influence," in E. F. Borgatta and W. W. Lambert, eds., *Handbook of Personality Theory and Research* (Chicago: Rand McNally, 1968), 1130–1187.

———. "The Nature of Attitude Change," in Gardner Lindzey and Elliot Aronson, eds., *The Handbook of Social Psychology,* 2nd ed., vol. III, *The Individual in a Social Context* (Reading, MA: Addison-Wesley, 1969), 136–314.

————. "Attitudes and Attitude Changes," in Gardner Lindzey and Elliot Aronson, eds., *The Handbook of Social Psychology*, 3rd ed., vol. II (New York: Random House, 1985), 233–346.

Miller, Merle. *Plain Speaking: An Oral Biography of Harry S. Truman* (New York: Berkley Publishing, 1973).

Miller, N., and C. T. Campbell. "Recency and Primacy in Persuasion as a Function of the Timing of Speeches and Measurements," *Journal of Abnormal and Social Psychology* 59 (1959), 1–9.

Noonan, Peggy. *What I Saw at the Revolution: A Political Life in the Reagan Era* (New York: Random House, 1990).

Pausch, Randy. *The Last Lecture* (New York: Hyperion, 2008).

Pawlak, J. "Add Some Show Biz to Seminars," *Arlington Heights (IL) Daily Herald* (January 9, 2004), 2.

Petrie, C. "Informative Speaking: A Summary and Bibliography of Related Research," *Speech Monograph* 20 (1963), 79–91.

Pratkanis, Anthony R., et al. "In Search of Reliable Persuasion Effects: The Sleeper Effect Is Dead, Long Live the Sleeper Effect," *Journal of Personality and Social Psychology* 54 (1988), 203–218.

Reagan Foundation. "Tear Down This Wall," *www.reaganfoundation.org/reagan/speeches/wall.asp*, retrieved July 8, 2007.

Reagan, Maureen. *First Father, First Daughter: A Memoir* (Boston, MA: Little, Brown, 1989).

Reagan, Ronald. "We the People," *Vital Speeches of the Day* 55 (1989), 10–13.

Safire, William. *Lend Me Your Ears: Great Speeches in History* (New York: W. W. Norton, 1992).

Samovar, Larry, and Edwin McDaniel. *Public Speaking in a Multicultural Society* (Los Angeles: Roxbury Publishing, 2007).

Shell, Richard and Mario Mousa. *The Art of WOO.* New York: Portfolio, 2007.

Sedlack, Robert, Barbara Shwon, and Karl Keller. *Graphics and Visual Communication for Managers* (Mason, OH: Thomson South-Western, 2008).

"Speaking of Fears . . . " *Springfield (IL) State Journal Register* (April 27, 2004), 9.

Sprague, Jo, and Douglas Stuart. *The Speaker's Handbook*, 4th ed. (New York: Harcourt Brace, 1996).

Thistlethwaite, D. L., H. De Haan, and J. Kamenetzky. "The Effect of 'Directive' and 'Non-Directive' Communication Procedures on Attitudes," *Journal of Abnormal and Social Psychology* 51 (1955), 107–118.

Thomas, Martha W. "Business Communication in the Modern Age," *Business and Economic Review* (July–September 1998), 20–23.

Tieger, Paul D., and Barbara Barron-Tieger. *The Art of Speed Reading People* (Boston, MA: Little, Brown, 1998).

Tubbs, Stewart. "Explicit versus Implicit Conclusions and Audience Commitment," *Speech Monographs* 35 (1968), 14–19.

Werts, C. E. "Before-and-After Magic," *Information Outlook* 8, no. 3 (March 2004), 21–24.

Whalen, Joel. *The Professional Communications Toolkit* (Thousand Oaks, CA: Sage Publications, 2007).

Whetten, David A., and Kim S. Cameron. *Developing Management Skills*, 6th ed. (Upper Saddle River, NJ: Prentice-Hall, 2005).

Chapter 14   Organizational Communication

Aber, R. "The Bottom Line in Business Blogs," *Entrepreneur.com.* August 1, 2004.

Adler, Ron, and Jeanne Elmhorst. *Communicating at Work*, 9th ed. (New York: McGraw-Hill, 2008).

Allport, Gordon, and Leo Postman. *The Psychology of Rumor* (New York: Holt, 1947).

Auxillium West. "Corporate Culture." (2003). From Auxillium West: Human Resources Software Web site: *www.aulillium.com/culture.shtml*.

Avolio, Bruce, and Fred Luthans. *The High Impact Leader* (New York: McGraw-Hill, 2006).

Barnard, Chester I. *The Functions of the Executive* (Cambridge, MA: Harvard University Press, 1938).

Belkin, Lisa. "Moms and Motrin," *NewYorkTimes.com* (January 3, 2009).

Berner, Robert. "My Year at Wal-Mart," *Business Week* (February 12, 2007), 70–74.

Bick, Julie. "Speed-dating Format Adapted for Business," *Ann Arbor News* (January 3, 2007), C3.

Burke, Doris. "Anatomy of an A380: Missed Connections," *Fortune* (March 5, 2007), 101–108.

Butta, Philip. "Habitual Learning," *Fast Company*, March 2012, p. 50.

Catt, Stephen E., Donald S. Miller, and Nitham M. Hindi. "Don't Misconstrue Communication Cues: Understanding Miscues Can Help Reduce Widespread and Expensive Miscommunication," *Strategic Finance* (June 2005), 51.

Chalice, Robert. *Improving Healthcare Using Toyota Lean Production Methods,* 2nd ed. (Milwaukee, WI: ASQ Quality Press, 2007).

Cherniss, Cary, and Daniel Goleman, eds. *The Emotionally Intelligent Workplace* (San Francisco, CA: Jossey-Bass, 2001).

Conant, Douglas, and Mette Norgaard. *TouchPoints* (San Francisco, CA: Jossey-Bass, 2011).

Cooper, Cecily. "Just Joking Around? Employer Humor Expression as an Ingratiatory Behavior," *Academy of Management Review* 30, no. 4 (2005), 765–776.

Cooper, Cord. "Ease Your E-mail Angst," *Investor's Business Daily* (January 15, 2004), A3.

Daly, John. Advocacy: Championing Ideas and Influencing Others. New Haven, CT: Yale University Press, 2011.

Davis, Keith. "A Method of Studying Communication Patterns in Organizations," *Personnel Psychology* 6 (1953), 301–312.

———. *Human Behavior at Work* (New York: McGraw-Hill, 1972).

Deal, Terrence E., and Allan A. Kennedy. *Corporate Cultures,* 2nd ed. (Reading, MA: Addison-Wesley, 2000).

Dean, Peter. *Leadership Is for Everyone* (New York: McGraw-Hill, 2006).

Fast Company, "The 50 Most Innovative Companies," March 2012, pp. 70–80.

Fryer, Shari. "One in Three Workers Get Weekend Emails from Boss," Right Management Press Release, June 21, 2011.

German, Carol J., and William R. Rath. "Making Technical Communication a Real-World Experience," *Journal of Technical Writing and Communication* 14 (1987), 335–346.

Goffee, Rob, and Gareth Jones. *Why Should Anyone Be Led by You?* (Boston: Harvard Business School Press, 2006).

Goldhaber, Gerald. 2003.

Goldhaber, Gerald M. *Organizational Communication,* 6th ed. (Dubuque, IA: Brown, 1993).

Goldstein, Noah, Steve Martin, and Robert B. Cialdini. *Yes! 50 Scientifically Proven Ways to Be Persuasive* (New York: The Free Press, 2008).

Graban, Mark. *Lean Hospitals* (New York: Productivity Press, 2009).

Heath, Chip and Dan Heath. *Switch: How to Change Things When Change is Hard.* New York: Broadway Books, 2010.

Hendrickson, Lorraine, and John Psarouthakis. *Dynamic Management of Growing Firms,* 2nd ed. (Ann Arbor, MA: University of Michigan Press, 1998).

Hodgetts, Richard M. "An Interview with Ed Kurtz," *Journal of Leadership Studies* 5 (Winter 1998), 156–162.

Isaacson, Walter. Steve Jobs. (New York: Simon & Schuster, 2011).

Hurley, Robert. *The Decision to Trust.* San Francisco, CA: Jossey-Bass, 2012.

Jennings, Eugene E. *Routes to the Executive Suite* (New York: McGraw-Hill, 1971).

Kotter, John. *A Sense of Urgency* (Boston, MA: Harvard Business School Press, 2008).

Kotter and Schlesinger, 2008.

Kotter, John, and Lorne Whitehead. *Buy*In: Saving Your Idea from Getting Shot Down* (Boston, MA: Harvard Business Review Press, 2010).

Kouzes, James M., and Barry Posner. *The Truth about Leadership* (San Francisco, CA: Jossey-Bass, 2010).

Lambert, Jack. *The Work Force Challenges of the 21st Century* (Washington, DC: National Association of Manufacturers, 1992).

Lawrence, Paul R., and Jay W. Lorsch. *Developing Organizations: Diagnosis and Action* (Reading, MA: Addison-Wesley, 1969).

Lennick, Doug, and Fred Kiel. *Moral Intelligence* (Upper Saddle River, NJ: Wharton School Publishing, 2005).

Liden, Robert C., and Terence R. Mitchell. "In Behaviors in Organization Settings," *Journal of Management Review* 13 (1988), 572–578.

Lyman, Amy. *The Trustworthy Leader* (San Francisco, CA: Jossey-Bass, 2012).

Mascai, Dan. "Can I Pour You a Pouch?" *Fast Company,* March 2012, 60.

Mulkern, Anne. "More Consumers Are Calling The Shots," *Detroit Free Press* (July 2, 2001), 6F.

Neeley, Tsedal, and Paul Leonardi. "Defend Your Research: Effective Managers Say the Same Thing Twice (or More)," *Harvard Business Review,* May, 2011.

Patterson, Kerry, Joseph Grenny, David Maxfield, Ron McMillan, and Al Switzler. *Influencer: The Power to Change Anything* (New York: McGraw-Hill, 2008).

Pennsylvania State University survey, personal correspondence, April 6, 1992.

Rath, Tom. *Strengths Finder 2.0* (New York: Gallup Press, 2007).

Rath, Tom, and Barry Conchie. *Strengths-Based Leadership* (New York: Gallup Press, 2008).

Rice, Ronald E. "Computer Mediated Communication and Organizational Innovations," *Journal of Communication* 37 (1987), 64–94.

Ries, Eric. *The Lean Startup* (New York: Crown Business, 2011).

Rosnow, Ralph. "Rumor as Communication: A Contextualist Approach," *Journal of Communication* 38 (1988), 12–28.

Safon, Vicente. "Factors That Influence Recruiters' Choice of B-Schools and Their MBA Graduates: Evidence and Implications for B-Schools." *The Academy of Management Learning and Education* 6 (June 2007), 217–233.

Schein, Edgar. *Organizational Culture and Leadership,* 2nd ed. (San Francisco, CA: Jossey-Bass, 1997).

Sellers, Patricia. "A Double Shot of Productivity," *Fortune* (October 16, 2006), 51.

Silverman, Rachel. "Trapped in a Meeting," *The Wall Street Journal,* Februart 14, 2012, B1.

Smith, Ronald L., Gary A Richetto, and Joseph P. Zima. "Organizational Behavior: An Approach to Human Communication," in Richard W. Budd and Brent D. Ruben, eds., *Approaches to Human Communication* (New York: Spartan Books, 1972).

Snavely, Brent. "2012 Ford Model May Get Equivalent of 100 m.p.g.," *Detroit Free Press,* December 15, 2011, B1.

Sostek, Anya. "Studies Shows a Bit of Office Talk Can Boost Productivity," *Pittsburgh Post-Gazette* (May 2006).

Svensson, Peter. "Apple Market Capitalization Exceeds $500 Billion Mark," *Detroit Free Press,* March 1, 2012, B1.

Swift, Marvin H. "Clear Writing Means Clear Thinking Means . . .," *Harvard Business Review* (January–February 1973), 59–62.

Watson Wyatt Worldwide, Inc. *Press Release* (July 16, 2006). *www.watsonwyatt.com.*

Wessel, H. "Talking It Up: Business Works Best When Lower-level Workers Have a Say," *San Diego Union-Tribune* (March 17, 2003), C8.

Whetten, David A., and Kim S. Cameron. *Developing Management Skills,* 7th ed. (Upper Saddle River, NJ: Prentice-Hall, 2011).

Widgery, Robin, and Cecil Stackpole, "Desk Position, Interviewee Anxiety, and Interviewer Credibility: An Example of Cognitive Balance in a Dyad," *Journal of Counseling Psychology* 19, no. 3 (May 1972), 173–177.

Willis, Craig. "Remarks to the Board of Regents," Eastern Michigan University (September 21, 2004).

Wiseman, Liz. *Multipliers: How the Best Leaders Make Everyone Smart* (New York: HarperBusiness, 2010).

Yukl, Gary. *Leadership In Organizations,* 8th ed. Upper Saddle River, NJ: Pearson, 2013.

Chapter 15   Mass Communication and the New Technologies

Albom, Mitch. "Flash Mobs: Quick to Start, Hard to Stop," *Detroit Free Press,* August 14, 2011, 21A.

Bagdikian, 2004.

Battaglia, Tammy Stables. "Girl's Joke May Turn into Porn Charges," *Detroit Free Press* (October 16, 2008), 1A, 11A.

Bauder, David. "Heard the One about McCain?" *The Ann Arbor News* (October 30, 2008), C5.

Bennett, W. Lance. *News: The Politics of Illusion,* 7th ed. (New York: Pearson, 2005).

Bennett, W. Lance, Regina G. Lawrence, and Steen Livingston. "None Dare Call It Torture: Indexing and the Limits of Press Independence in the Abu Ghraib Scandal," *Journal of Communication* 56 (September 2006), 467–485.

Berns, Gregory. *Iconoclast* (Boston, MA: Harvard Business School Press, 2008).

Bittner, John R., *Fundamentals of Communication* (Englewood Cliffs, NJ: Prentice-Hall, 1985).

Boase, Jeffrey, and Barry Wellman. "Personal Relationships: On and Off the Internet," in Anita Vangelisti and Daniel Perlman, eds., *Cambridge Handbook of Personal Relationships* (New York: Cambridge University Press, 2006), 709–723.

Businesswire.com, 2007.

Cappella, Joseph N., and Kathleen Hall Jamieson. *Spiral of Cynicism: The Press and the Public Good* (New York: Oxford University Press, 1997).

Carr, Nicholas. *The Shallows: What the Internet Is Doing to Our Brains* (New York: W. W. Norton, 2011).

Chartier, David. "More Americans Snipping Landlines in Favor of Cell Phones," *ARS Technica: The Art of Technology* (May 2008). Retrieved December 15, 2008, from *http://arstechnica.com/news.ars/post/20080514-more-americans-snipping-landlines-in-favor-of-cell-phones .html.*

Chester, Jeff. *Digital Destiny: New Media and the Future of Democracy* (New York: The New Press, 2007).

Cisco Technology Report, 2011. http://www.cisco.com/en/US/netsol/ns1120/index.html

CNET News, 2008.

Couldry, Nick. *Listening beyond the Echoes: Media, Ethics, and Agency in an Uncertain World* (Boulder, CO: Paradigm Publishers, 2006).

Diddi, Arvind, and Robert LaRose. "Getting Hooked on News," *Journal of Broadcasting & Electronic Media* 50 (June 2006), 193–210.

Dominick, Joseph. *The Dynamics of Mass Communication* (New York: McGraw-Hill, 2009).

Duhigg, 2012.

Entman, Robert M. "Framing: Toward Clarification of a Fractured Paradigm," *Journal of Communication* 43, no. 4 (1993), 51–58.

———. "The Nature and Sources of News," in Geneva Overholser and Kathleen Hall Jamieson, eds., *The Press, Institutions of American Democracy Series* (New York: Oxford University Press, 2006), 48–65.

Fallows, Deborah. "The Internet and Daily Life," *Pew Internet & American Life Project* (August 11, 2004). Retrieved September 11, 2004, from *www.pewinternet .org/PPF/r/131/report-display-asp.*

Foerstel, Herbert N. *From Watergate to Monicagate: Ten Controversies in Modern Journalism and Media* (Westport, CT: Greenwood Press, 2001).

Friedman, Emily. "Is Oprah Biased? Won't Interview Palin," *ABC News* (September 5, 2008). Retrieved December 15, 2008, from URL *http://abcnews.go.com/entertainment/ Story?id=5736716&page=1.*

Griffin, Em. *A First Look at Communication Theory,* 7th ed. (New York: McGraw-Hill, 2009).

Hanson, Carl, Rosemary Thackeray, Michael Barnes, Brad Neiger, and Emily McIntyre. "Integrating Web 2.0 in Health Education Preparation and Practice," *American Journal of Health Education* 9.3 (May–June 2008): 157(10). Academic OneFile. Retrieved December 15, 2008.

Hickey, Neil. "Election Night: The Big Mistake," *Columbia Journalism Review* (January/February 2001), 32–35.

"Internet Usage Statistics: The Big Picture." *Internet World Stats.* Retrieved July 22, 2007, from *internetworldstats. com/stats.htm.*

Jamieson, Kathleen Hall. *Packaging the Presidency: A History and Criticism of Presidential Campaign Advertising* (New York: Oxford University Press, 1996).

Jamieson, Kathleen Hall, and Paul Waldman. *The Press Effect: Politicians, Journalists, and the Stories That Shape the Political World* (New York: Oxford University Press, 2003).

"Joe Scarborough's F**k Up: Swears On Air," *Huffington Post* (November 10, 2008), 6. Retrieved December 15, 2008, from *http://www.huffingtonpost.com/2008/11/10/joe-scarboroughs-f**k-up_n_142598.html?page=6*.

Kahneman, Daniel. *Thinking Fast and Slow* (New York: Farrar, Straus and Giroux, 2011).

Katz, Elihu, and Paul Lazarsfeld. *Personal Influence: The Part Played by People in the Flow of Mass Communications* (Glencoe, IL: Free Press, 1964).

Kaufman, Gil. "L'Oreal Denies Altering Beyonce's Skin Color In Ad," www.mtv.com. (August 8, 2008). Retrieved December 15, 2008, from *http://www.mtv.com/news/articles/1592434/20080808/knowles_beyonce.jhtml*.

Kelliher, Laurie. "Low Power, High Intensity," *Columbia Journalism Review* (September/October 2003), 31–33.

———. "Fox Watch," *Columbia Journalism Review* (March/April 2004), 8.

Kleinenberg, Eric. *Fighting for Air: The Battle to Control America's Media* (New York: Metropolitan Books, 2007).

Kovach, Bill, and Tom Rosenstiel. *The Elements of Journalism* (New York: Crown, 2001).

Kraut, Robert, Sara Kiesler, Bonka Boneva, et al. "Internet Paradox Revisited," *Journal of Social Issues* 58, no. 1 (2002).

Kraut, R., M. Patterson, V. Lundmark, S. Kiesler, T. Mukhopadhyay, and W. Scherlis. "Internet Paradox: A Social Technology that Reduces Social Involvement and Psychological Well-Being?" *American Psychologist* 53, no. 9 (1998), 1017–1031.

Kwak, Nojin, Nathaniel Poor, and Marko M. Skoric. "Honey, I Shrunk the World! The Relation Between Internet Use and International Engagement," *Mass Communication & Society* 9, no. 2 (2006), 189–213.

Lazarsfeld, Paul, Bernard Berelson, and H. Gaudet. *The People's Choice* (New York: Columbia University Press, 1968).

Lemann, Nicholas. "Amateur Hour," *The New Yorker* (August 7 & 14, 2006), 44–47.

Lenhart, Amanda, and Mary Madden. "Pew Internet Project Data Memo: Social Networking Websites and Teens: An Overview," *Pew Internet & American Life Project* (January 7, 2007) *www.pewinternet.org*.

Lieberman, Trudy. "Answer the &%$#* Question!" *Columbia Journalism Review* (January/February 2004), 40–43.

Mathis, Jo, and Art Aisner, "Teen's Photo Considered Child Porn," *Ann Arbor News* (October 16, 2008), A1, A12.

McCombs, Maxwell. "The Agenda-Setting Function of the Press," in Geneva Overholser and Kathleen Hall Jamieson, eds., *The Press*, Institutions of American Democracy Series (New York: Oxford University Press, 2005), 156–168.

McCombs, Maxwell, and Donald Shaw. "The Agenda-Setting Function of Mass Media," *Public Opinion Quarterly* 36, no. 2 (1972), 176–185.

Mooney, Alexander. "GOP Warned to Embrace Technology or Face 'Suicide.'" Retrieved from *www.cnn.com* (December 12, 2008). Retrieved December 15, 2008, from *http://www.cnn.com/2008/POLITICS/12/12/gop.technology/index.html*.

"Most Popular Internet Activities." *Infoplease.com*. Retrieved July 22, 2007, from *www.infoplease.com/ipa/A0921862.html*.

National Center for Missing and Exploited Children, the AMBER Alert Program (Updated October 6, 2008). Retrieved October 10, 2008, from *www.missingkids.com*.

"The New Age of Alternative Media." *Columbia Journalism Review* (September/October 2003), 20.

Nichols, John, and Robert McChesney. *Tragedy and Farce: How the American Media Sell Wars, Spin Elections, and Destroy Democracy* (New York: The New Press, 2005).

Nie, Norman H. "Sociability, Interpersonal Relations, and the Internet: Reconciling Conflicting Findings," *American Behavioral Scientist* 45 (2001), 420–435.

Nie, Norman H., and Lutz Erbring. "Internet and Society: A Preliminary Report," *IT & Society 1*, no. 1 (2002), 275–283.

Nie, Norman H., Irena Stepanikova, Heili Pals, Lu Zheng, and Xiaobin He. "Ten Years after the Birth of the Internet: How Do Americans Use the Internet in Their Daily Lives?" *Stanford Institute for the Quantitative Study of Society 2005 Report*. Retrieved July 23, 2007, from *www.stanford.edu/group/siqss/researchtimes_study_files/ProjectReport2005.pdf*.

NPR Newswire. 2008. "Obama Expands Lead on McCain in Online Advertising Battle in June, According to comScore Ad Metrix." Market Watch PR Newswire (September 4, 2008).

"Online World as Important to Internet Users as Real World?" *2007 Digital Future Report*. Retrieved July 22, 2007, from *www.digitalcenter.org/pdf/2007-Digital-Future-Report-Press-Release-112906.pdf*.

Orden, Erica."Disney Buys Mom Blogs, Plans to Integrate Content," *The Wall Street Journal*, November 15, 2011, B1.

Patterson, Kerry, Joseph Grenny, David Maxfield, Ron McMillan, and Al Switzler. *Influencer: The Power to Change Anything* (New York: McGraw-Hill, 2008).

Pavlik, John V. *Journalism and New Media* (New York: Columbia University Press, 2001).

Pavlik, John V., and Shawn McIntosh. *Converging Media* (Boston, MA: Pearson, 2010).

Rainie, Lee, and John Horrigan. "Election 2006 Online," *Pew Internet & American Life Project, www.pewinternet.org*.

Rainie, Lee, and Scott Keeler. "Pew Internet Project Data Memo" (April 2006). Retrieved July 22, 2007, from *www.pewinternet.org/pdfs/PIP_Cell_phone_study.pdf*.

Rogers, Everett M. *Diffusion of Innovations*, 4th ed. (New York: Free Press, 1995).

Rubin, Alan M., and Rebecca B. Rubin. "Interface of Personal and Mediated Communication: A Research Agenda," *Critical Studies in Mass Communication* 2 (1985), 36–53.

Rubin, Rebecca B., Elizabeth M. Perse, and Carole A. Barbato. "Conceptualization and Measurement of Interpersonal Communication Motives," *Human Communication Research* 14 (1988), 602–628.

Sandoval, Greg, "Video Site Scooped the Journalism Star," CNET, (July 30, 2008). Retrieved December 15, 2008, from *http://news.cnet.com/8301-1023_3-10002238-93.html.*

Schramm, Wilbur, and Donald F. Roberts, eds. *The Process and Effect of Mass Communications,* rev. ed. (Urbana: University of Illinois Press, 1971).

Solomon, Deborah. "This American TV Show," *New York Times Magazine* (March 4, 2007), 15.

Tolchin, Martin, and Susan Tolchin. *A World Ignited* (Lanham, MD: Rowan & Littlefield, 2006).

Turkle, Sherry. *Alone Together* (New York: Basic Books, 2011).

U.S. Department of Labor and Bureau of Labor Statistics. *Occupational Outlook Handbook 2006–2007 Edition* (Indianapolis, IN: JIST Works, 2006).

Vance, Ashley. "Have You Seen This Android," *Bloomberg BusinessWeek,* March 12–March 18, 2012, pp. 37–38.

"The View from Inside the Military," *Nieman Reports* (Summer 2003), 88–89.

Wade, Nigel. "The Story We Didn't Print on Page 1," *New York Times* Op-Ed (May 23, 1998), A15.

Wayne, Stephen J. *The Road to the White House 1992: The Politics of Presidential Elections* (New York: St. Martin's, 1992).

———. *The Road to the White House 1996: The Politics of Presidential Elections* (New York: St. Martin's, 1996).

Webster, James G. "The Audience," *Journal of Broadcasting and Electronic Media* 42 (Spring 1998), 190–207.

Welch, Matt. "Blogworld and Its Gravity," *Columbia Journalism Review* (September/October 2003), 21–26.

Wimmer, Roger, and Joseph Dominick. *Mass Media Research: An Introduction,* 9th ed. (Boston, MA: Wadsworth/Cengage Learning, 2011).

Wood, Andrew F., and Matthew J. Smith. *Online Communication* (Mahwah, NJ: Lawrence Erlbaum, 2001).

Wright, Charles R. Mass *Communication—A Sociological Perspective,* 3rd ed. (New York: Random House, 1986).

Zimmerman, Ann, and Miguel Bustillo. "Retailers Brace for 'Flash Robs' This Shoplifting Season," *The Wall Street Journal,* October 21, 2011, B1.

CREDITS

Chapter 3

Table 3.1: Judy Cornelia Pearson, Gender and Communication, 1985. Reprinted by permission.
Figure 3.2: From Hayakawa. Language in Thought and Action, 4E. © 1978 Heinle/Arts & Sciences, a part of Cengage Learning, Inc. Reproduced by permission. *www.cengage.com/permissions*
Figure 3.3: Blake and Moutron, "The Fifth Achievement," Journal of Applied Behavioral Science, December 1970, vol 6, no 4. Reprinted by permission of the publisher.
Figure 3.4: DILBERT: © Scott Adams/Dist. By United Feature Syndicate, Inc.

Chapter 4

Table 4.1: From Edward T. Hall and Mildred R. Hall, Understanding Cultural Differences, 1990. Used by permission.
Table 4.2: Nonverbal communication in close relationships by Guerrero, Laura K. Copyright 2006 Reproduced with permission of Taylor & Francis Group LLC—BOOKS in the format Textbook via Copyright Clearance Center.
Figure 4.1: Simon Baron-Cohen, "The 'Reading the Mind in the Eyes' Test," The Essential Difference: The Truth About the Male and Female Brain. Reprinted by permission of the publisher.
Figure 4.2: From Edward T. Hall, The Silent Language, 1959, 1982. Reprinted by permission of the publisher.
Figure 4.3: Reprinted by permission of Waveland Press, Inc. from Peter A. Anderson, Nonverbal Communications: Forms and Functions, 2nd ed. (Long Grove, IL: Waveland Press, Inc., 2008). All rights reserved.
Figure 4.4: Adapted from Hargie, et al, Social Skills in Interpersonal Communication, Taylor & Francis, 1987, 2nd ed, 9780415045070. Reprinted by permission of the publisher (Taylor & Francis Ltd, *http://www.tandf.co.uk/journals*).
Figure 4.5: From Knapp. Nonverbal Communication in Human Interaction, 5E. © 2002 Wadsworth, a part of Cengage Learning, Inc. Reproduced by permission. *www.cengage.com/permissions.*
Figure 4.6: From Desmond Morris, P. Collette, P. Marsh and M. O'Shaughnessy, Gestures, 1979. Reprinted by permission of the publisher.

Chapter 5

Figure 5.1: Larry Barker, "An Investigation of Proportional Time Spent in Various Communication Activities by College Students," Journal of Applied Communication Research, 8(2), 1980. Reprinted by permission of the publisher (Taylor & Francis Ltd, *http://www.tandf.co.uk/journals)*.

Chapter 6

Figure 6.1: From "Conflict and Negotiation Process in Organizations" by K. Thomas, 1992. In M.D. Dunnette and L.M. Hough (Eds.), Handbook of Industrial and Organizational Psychology (2nd ed., vol. 3, p. 660). Palo Alto, CA: Consulting Psychologists Press. Copyright 1992 by L.M. Hough. Adapted by permission.

Chapter 7

Figure 7.1: Copyright © 2011 Gallup, Inc. All rights reserved. The content is used with permission; however, Gallup retains all rights of republication.
Figure 7.2: Rushworth M. Kidder, Moral Courage, 2004, figs 2 (p.51) and 7 (p.73). Reprinted by permission of HarperCollins.

Chapter 8

Table 8.1: Pew Internet & American Life Project On-line Dating Survey, September-December 2005. Used by permission.
Figure 8.2: Knapp, Mark L.; Vangelisti, Anita L., Interpersonal Communication and Human Relationships, 4th Edition, © 2000. Reprinted by permission of Pearson Education, Inc., Upper Saddle River, NJ.
Figure 8.3: Steve Duck, Personal Relationships vol 5: Repairing Personal Relationships, Elsevier, 1984. Reprinted by permission of the author.
Table 8.2: Jack R. Gibb, "Defensive Communication," Journal of Communication, 11 (3), 1961. Reprinted by permission of the publisher.

Chapter 9

Figure 9.1: Joseph Luft, Group Processes: An Introduction to Group Dynamics, 3rd ed., 1984. Used by permission of McGraw-Hill.

NAME INDEX

Note: Page numbers in **BOLD** indicate key terms and definitions. Page numbers followed by *fig* or *t* indicate a figure or table.

SUBJECT INDEX

Note: Page numbers in **BOLD** indicate key terms and definitions. Page numbers followed by *fig* or *t* indicate a figure or table.